Lecture Notes in Computer Science 4590

Commenced Publication in 1973
Founding and Former Series Editors:
Gerhard Goos, Juris Hartmanis, and Jan van Leeuwen

Werner Damm   Holger Hermanns (Eds.)

Computer Aided Verification

19th International Conference, CAV 2007
Berlin, Germany, July 3-7, 2007
Proceedings

 Springer

Volume Editors

Werner Damm
Carl von Ossietzky University Oldenburg
Department of Computer Science
26121 Oldenburg, Germany
E-mail: damm@offis.de

Holger Hermanns
Saarland University
Department of Computer Science
66123 Saarbrücken, Germany
E-mail: hermanns@cs.uni-sb.de

Library of Congress Control Number: 2007929320

CR Subject Classification (1998): F.3, D.2.4, D.2.2, F.4.1, I.2.3, B.7.2, C.3

LNCS Sublibrary: SL 1 – Theoretical Computer Science and General Issues

ISSN   0302-9743
ISBN-10   3-540-73367-1 Springer Berlin Heidelberg New York
ISBN-13   978-3-540-73367-6 Springer Berlin Heidelberg New York

Springer is a part of Springer Science+Business Media

springer.com

© Springer-Verlag Berlin Heidelberg 2007

Typesetting: Camera-ready by author, data conversion by Scientific Publishing Services, Chennai, India
Printed on acid-free paper   SPIN: 12084203   06/3180   5 4 3 2 1 0

Preface

This volume contains the proceedings of the International Conference on Computer Aided Verification (CAV), held in Berlin, Germany, July 3–7, 2007. CAV 2007 was the 19th in a series of conferences dedicated to the advancement of the theory and practice of computer-assisted formal analysis methods for software and hardware systems. The conference covers the spectrum from theoretical results to concrete applications, with an emphasis on practical verification tools and the algorithms and techniques that are needed for their implementation.

We received 134 regular paper submissions and 39 tool paper submissions. Of these, the Program Committee selected 33 regular papers and 14 tool papers. Each submission was reviewed by at least three members of the Program Committee. The reviewing process included a PC review meeting, and – for the first time in the history of CAV – an author feedback period. About 50 additional reviews were provided by experts external to the Program Committee to assure a high quality selection.

The CAV 2007 program included three invited talks from industry:

- Byron Cook (Microsoft Research) on *Automatically Proving Program Termination,*
- David Russinoff (AMD) on *A Mathematical Approach to RTL Verification,* and
- Thomas Kropf (Bosch) on *Software Bugs Seen from an Industrial Perspective.*

The conference featured four tutorials:

- Tom Henzinger (EPFL) on *Modeling, Verification, and Synthesis of Component Interfaces,*
- Natarajan Shankar (SRI) on *A Tutorial on Satisfiability Modulo Theories,*
- Gary T. Leavens (Iowa State University) on *A JML Tutorial: Modular Specification and Verification of Functional Behavior for Java,* and
- Martin Fränzle (Carl von Ossietzky Universität Oldenburg) on *Verification of Hybrid Systems.*

CAV 2007 had seven affiliated workshops:

- AHA 2007: International Symposium on Automatic Heap Analysis
- ARTIST2 Workshop on Tool Platforms for Modelling, Analysis and Validation of Embedded Systems
- FMICS 2007: 12th Int. Workshop on Formal Methods for Industrial Critical Systems
- GVD 2007: 3rd German Verification Day

- PDMC 2007: 6th Int. Workshop on Parallel and Distributed Methods in verifiCation
- SMT 2007: 5th International Workshop on Satisfiability Modulo Theories
- SPIN 2007: 14th International SPIN Workshop on Model Checking of Software

In addition to these events, two tool competitions were held. The third "Satisfiability Modulo Theories Competition" and the first "Hardware Model Checking Competition" reported about their results within the scientific program of CAV 2007.

We gratefully acknowledge financial support for CAV 2007 from the Artist2 Network of Excellence, Cadence Design Systems, the German Science Foundation, IBM, Informatik Saarland, Intel Corporation, Microsoft Research, NEC and Synopsys.

We thank the Program Committee members, the external experts, and the sub-referees for their work in evaluating the submissions and assuring a high quality program. We also thank the Steering Committee and the Chairs of CAV 2006 for their help and advice. The organization of CAV was supported by AVACS, and we thank Jürgen Niehaus and his team for their excellent support. Special thanks also to the organizing committee (Christoph Scholl, Universität Freiburg, workshops; Henning Dierks, OFFIS, tool exhibition; Holger Schlingloff, Humboldt Universität Berlin, local organization). Finally, we thank Andrei Voronkov for creating and supporting the outstanding EasyChair conference management system.

July 2007   Werner Damm
                                                          Holger Hermanns

Conference Organization

Program Chairs

Werner Damm (Carl von Ossietzky Universität Oldenburg)
Holger Hermanns (Universität des Saarlandes)

Program Committee

Parosh Aziz Abdulla (Uppsala University, Sweden)
Rajeev Alur (University of Pennsylvania, USA)
Sergey Berezin (Synopsys, USA)
Armin Biere (Johannes Keppler Universität Linz, Austria)
Roderick Bloem (TU Graz, Austria)
Ahmed Bouajjani (University Paris 7, France)
Alessandro Cimatti (IRST Trento, Italy)
Edmund M. Clarke (Carnegie Mellon University, USA)
Limor Fix (Intel Corporation, USA)
Patrice Godefroid (Microsoft Research, USA)
Ganesh Gopalakrishnan (University of Utah, USA)
Susanne Graf (Verimag, France)
Orna Grumberg (Technion, Israel)
Robert Jones (Intel Corporation, USA)
Orna Kupferman (Hebrew University, Israel)
Robert P. Kurshan (Cadence, USA)
John Lygeros (ETH Zürich, Switzerland)
Ken McMillan (Cadence, USA)
Tom Melham (Oxford University, UK)
Jakob Rehof (Universität Dortmund, Germany)
Koushik Sen (University of California at Berkeley, USA)
Fabio Somenzi (University of Colorado at Boulder, USA)
Ashish Tiwari (SRI International, USA)
Frits Vaandrager (University of Nijmegen, The Netherlands)
Yaron Wolfstal (IBM Haifa, Israel)

Steering Committee

Edmund M. Clarke (Carnegie Mellon University, USA)
Mike Gordon (University of Cambridge, UK)
Robert P. Kurshan (Cadence, USA)
Amir Pnueli (New York University, USA)

Sponsors

Artist2 Network of Excellence
Cadence Design Systems
German Science Foundation
IBM
Informatik Saarland
Intel Corporation
Microsoft Research
NEC
Synopsys

Referees

Sara Adams
Nina Amla
Tamarah Arons
Eugene Asarin
Didier Aucal
Gadi Auerbach
Omer Barilan
Sharon Barner
Bernd Becker
Bernhard Beckert
Noomene Ben Henda
Massimo Benerecetti
Mikhail Bernadsky
Jesse Bingham
Per Bjesse
Magnus Björk
Bernard Boigelot
Patricia Boyer
Marius Bozga
Marco Bozzano
Aaron Bradley
Ingo Brückner
Robert Brummayer
Roberto Bruttomesso
Annette Bunker
Jan van den Bussche
Doron Bustan
Thierry Cachat
Didier Caucal
Pavol Cerny
Rohit Chadha

Supratik Chakraborty
Krishnendu Chatterjee
Swarat Chaudhuri
Xiaofang Chen
Yu-Fang Chen
Hana Chockler
Ching-Tsun Chou
Eugenio Cinquemani
Koen Claessen
Byron Cook
Eva Cruck
Badis Djeridane
Giorgio Delzanno
Henning Dierks
Dino Distefano
Xiaoqun Du
Stefan Edelkamp
Cindy Eisner
Michael Emmi
Kai Engelhardt
Lars-Henrik Ericsson
Javier Esparza
Johannes Faber
Azadeh Farzan
Ansgar Fehnker
Bernd Finkbeiner
Alon Flaisher
Anders Franzen
Carsten Fritz
Martin Fränzle
Severine Fratani

Oded Fuhrmann
Ziv Glazberg
Benny Godlin
Amit Goel
Laure Gonnord
Denis Gopan
Mike Gordon
Andreas Griesmayer
Alberto Griggio
Marcus Groesser
Roland Groz
Jim Grundy
Sumit Gulwani
Dilian Gurov
Peter Habermehl
Hyojung Han
Tamir Heyman
Gerard Holzmann
Hardi Hungar
Kim Hyondeuk
Catalin Ionescu
Radu Iosif
Himanshu Jain
David N. Jansen
Bertrand Jeannet
Sumit Jha
Barbara Jobstmann
Bengt Jonsson
Bernhard Josko
Marcin Jurdzinski
Toni Jussila

Table of Contents

Session IV: Infinitive State Verification

Session V: Tool Environment

Session VI: Shapes

Session VII: Concurrent Program Verification

Session VIII: Reactive Designs

Session IX: Parallelisation

Session X: Constraints and Decisions

Session XI: Probabilistic Verification

Session XII: Abstraction

Session XIII: Assume-Guarantee Reasoning

Session XIV: Hybrid Systems

Session XV: Program Analysis

Session XVI: SAT and Decision Procedures

Automatically Proving Program Termination
(Invited Talk)

Byron Cook

Microsoft Research

In this talk I will describe new tools that allow us to automatically prove termination and other liveness properties of software systems. In particular I will discuss the TERMINATOR program termination prover and its application to the problem of showing that Windows device driver event-handling routines always eventually stop responding to events.

W. Damm and H. Hermanns (Eds.): CAV 2007, LNCS 4590, p. 1, 2007.

A Mathematical Approach to RTL Verification
(Invited Talk)

David M. Russinoff

Advanced Micro Devices, Inc.
david.russinoff@amd.com

The formal hardware verification effort at Advanced Micro Devices, Inc. has emphasized theorem proving using ACL2, and has focused on the elementary floating-point operations. Floating-point modules, along with the rest of our microprocessor designs, are specified at the register-transfer level in a small synthesizable subset of Verilog. This language is simple enough to admit a clear semantic definition, providing a basis for formal analysis and verification. Thus, we have developed a scheme for automatically translating RTL code into the ACL2 logic, thereby reducing the potential for error in the development of formal hardware models.

Formal statements of correctness (IEEE compliance) of arithmetic operations are encoded in the same language and translated into ACL2 along with the RTL. Their proofs are developed interactively and mechanically checked with the ACL2 prover.

Much of the effort involved in this project has been in the development and formalization of a general theory of floating-point arithmetic and its bit-level implementation, resulting in an ACL2 library of lemmas pertaining to bit vectors, logical operations, floating-point representations, and rounding. The library is publicly available as a part of the standard ACL2 release.

In this talk, I will describe my experience over the past decade in the development and application of this methodology. I will describe lessons learned through the process, especially regarding the relevance of the established principles and methodologies of both software verification and traditional mathematics to the hardware problem. Finally, I will discuss prospects for extending these methods to functional areas beyond the floating-point unit and the ultimate objective of a fully verified microprocessor design.

W. Damm and H. Hermanns (Eds.): CAV 2007, LNCS 4590, p. 2, 2007.
© Springer-Verlag Berlin Heidelberg 2007

Software Bugs Seen from an Industrial Perspective
or
Can Formal Methods Help on Automotive Software Development?
(Invited Talk)

Thomas Kropf

Robert Bosch GmbH

Developing software for automotive applications is a challenging task. To stay competitive conflicting goals must be met: complex and innovative algorithms with many versions for different car line variants have to be implemented within the tight resource boundaries of embedded systems; high reliability especially for safety critical applications like airbag or braking applications has to be ensured under immense cost pressure. Despite these demanding constraints in recent years automotive software development has made significant progress in terms of productivity and quality. All this has been achieved without direct usage of formal methods.

However, software is still a good part away from being bug-free. If looking closer it becomes apparent that often unclear specifications or an incomplete understanding of the application domain is the root cause of erroneous software. In such cases any validation approach for a given piece of software would not succeed. Still there are many cases where the software implementation indeed violates a given specification.

Consequently, the second part of the talk gives a set of application areas where current development and validation techniques still lead to unsatisfactory results, i.e., where software bugs are still hard to detect. In these cases, formal methods may help to improve the current situation. Some examples are given where and how those approaches are already used or where an introduction into real-life design flows is imminent. The talk ends with some challenging problems where basic research is still needed.

W. Damm and H. Hermanns (Eds.): CAV 2007, LNCS 4590, p. 3, 2007.
© Springer-Verlag Berlin Heidelberg 2007

Algorithms for Interface Synthesis*
(Invited Tutorial)

Dirk Beyer[1], Thomas A. Henzinger[2], and Vasu Singh[2]

[1] Simon Fraser University, B.C., Canada
[2] EPFL, Switzerland

Abstract. A temporal interface for a software component is a finite automaton that specifies the legal sequences of calls to functions that are provided by the component. We compare and evaluate three different algorithms for automatically extracting temporal interfaces from program code: (1) a *game* algorithm that computes the interface as a representation of the most general environment strategy to avoid a safety violation; (2) a *learning* algorithm that repeatedly queries the program to construct the minimal interface automaton; and (3) a *CEGAR* algorithm that iteratively refines an abstract interface hypothesis by adding relevant program variables. For comparison purposes, we present and implement the three algorithms in a unifying formal setting. While the three algorithms compute the same output and have similar worst-case complexities, their actual running times may differ considerably for a given input program. On the theoretical side, we provide for each of the three algorithms a family of input programs on which that algorithm outperforms the two alternatives. On the practical side, we evaluate the three algorithms experimentally on a variety of Java libraries.

1 Introduction

Large software systems are built using components and libraries, which are often developed by different teams, or even different companies. Quality component interfaces facilitate the integration and validation process for such systems. This explains the recent interest in rich interfaces for existing code, such as software libraries. We consider *temporal interfaces* [4], which specify the legal sequences of function calls to a library, i.e., those sequences that do not cause the library to enter an error state. Consider, for example, the library shown in Fig. 1, which supports read and write accesses to files. The safe use of the library requires that a file be opened for read or for read-write access before being read, and be opened for read-write access before being written. The library interface can be represented by the regular expression $((\texttt{ropen} \cdot \texttt{read}^* \cdot \texttt{close}) \cup (\texttt{rwopen} \cdot (\texttt{read} \cup \texttt{write})^* \cdot \texttt{close}))^*$. This interface is both *safe*, in that it accepts no sequence of function calls that leads to an error in the library, and *permissive*, in that it accepts all other sequences.

* This research was supported in part by the grant SFU/PRG 06-3, and by the Swiss National Science Foundation.

W. Damm and H. Hermanns (Eds.): CAV 2007, LNCS 4590, pp. 4–19, 2007.

```
void ropen(File f) {
  if (!f.rdflag)
    f.rdflag = true;
  else
    f.error = true; }
```

```
void close(File f) {
  if (f.rdflag) {
    f.rdflag = false;
    f.wrflag = false; }
  else
    f.error = true; }
```

```
void rwopen(File f) {
  if (!f.rdflag) {
    f.rdflag = true;
    f.wrflag = true; }
  else
    f.error = true; }
```

```
void read(File f) {
  if (!f.rdflag)
    f.error = true; }
```

```
void write(File f) {
  if (!f.wrflag)
    f.error = true; }
```

Fig. 1. Example of a library that supports read and write accesses to files

Several algorithms have been proposed for automatically extracting safe and permissive temporal interfaces (in the form of finite automata) from library code. Like many questions of sequential synthesis, interface extraction is fundamentally a *game* problem, namely, the problem to compute the most general environment strategy for calling library functions without causing a safety violation. We call the algorithm that solves the safety game on the library code the 'direct' algorithm. As the complexity of this algorithm grows with the number of library states, two very different improvements have been suggested. The first is based on techniques for *learning* a finite automaton by repeatedly querying a teacher [1]. The learning algorithm guarantees the construction of a deterministic interface automaton with a minimal number of states, and thus performs well if the number of states required in the interface is small. The second improvement is based on *counterexample-guided abstraction refinement* [3]. The CEGAR algorithm computes a library abstraction, then extracts an interface automaton for the abstract library, then checks if the extracted interface is both safe and permissive for the concrete library (using two reachability tests), and if not, iteratively refines the library abstraction [5]. This algorithm performs well if there exists a small abstraction of the library from which a safe and permissive interface can be constructed.

Our aim is to compare and analyze the three approaches (direct; learning; and CEGAR) both theoretically and experimentally. Even though they address the same problem, the three algorithms proceed very differently. Moreover, the learning algorithm was published and previously implemented in the context of Java libraries without guaranteeing interface permissiveness [1], and the CEGAR algorithm was published and previously implemented in the context of C programs without ensuring interface minimality [5]. For a fair comparison, we formalize and reimplement all three algorithms in a uniform setting. In order to disregard orthogonal issues as much as possible, we remove all effects of the programming language by choosing, as input to the three algorithms, the transition graph of a library. We assume the transition graphs to be finite-state, so that all three algorithms are guaranteed to terminate (on infinite-state systems, none of the algorithms is guaranteed to terminate, although different algorithms may terminate on different inputs). In order to further level the playing field, we add a permissiveness check to the learning algorithm of [1], and we add a minimization step to the direct and the CEGAR algorithm. We also make some improvements to the published algorithms. For example, we simplify the CEGAR algorithm by combining the safety and permissiveness checks into a single reachability test (rather than using two separate tests on different automata, as suggested in [5]).

On the theoretical side, we construct parametric families of input programs that amplify the differences in the performance of the three algorithms. In experiments, we find that these input families do not represent uninteresting corner cases, but commonly occur in applications such as Java libraries. As expected, abstraction refinement performs best if only few program variables[1] are needed to prove an interface both safe and permissive. If this is the case, then the resulting interface automaton has few states. Learning also requires the interface automaton to be small, and performs better than CEGAR if the interface states reflect the values of many different program variables. The direct (game) algorithm outperforms both other approaches if the interface is not small, but the size of the state space is not too large to be explored and minimized (this is because the direct algorithm does not involve any of the overhead necessary for either learning or automatic abstraction refinement).

2   Open Programs and Interfaces

We investigate sequences of calls to a software library. We formalize the library code as an open program. In order to remove language effects, we describe an open program as a labeled transition graph over a finite set of boolean variables. The labels are function calls; one of the variables marks the error states. Certain sequences of function calls may lead the open program to an error state. At the concrete level, an open program is deterministic, and thus each sequence of function calls either causes or does not cause an error (this will not be true in general for abstractions of open programs). The set of all sequences of function calls that do not cause an error is called the *safe and permissive interface* of the open program. We strive to construct a minimal deterministic finite-state representation of that interface, called an *interface automaton*.

Finite automata. Consider a finite automaton $A = (Q, \Sigma, q_0, \delta)$ with the set Q of states, the input alphabet Σ, the initial state $q_0 \in Q$, and the transition relation $\delta \subseteq Q \times \Sigma \times Q$ (there are no accepting states). The automaton A is *serial* if for all states $q \in Q$, there exists an input symbol $f \in \Sigma$ and a state $q' \in Q$ such that $(q, f, q') \in \delta$. The automaton A is *input-enabled* if for all states $q \in Q$ and all input symbols $f \in \Sigma$, there exists a state $q' \in Q$ such that $(q, f, q') \in \delta$. The automaton A is *deterministic* if for all states $q, q', q'' \in Q$ and all input symbols $f \in \Sigma$, if $(q, f, q') \in \delta$ and $(q, f, q'') \in \delta$, then $q' = q''$. The transitive closure $\xrightarrow{w}_\delta$ of the transition relation is defined as usual: let $q \xrightarrow{\epsilon}_\delta q'$ if $q = q'$, and let $q \xrightarrow{f \cdot w}_\delta q'$ if there exists a state q'' such that $(q, f, q'') \in \delta$ and $q'' \xrightarrow{w}_\delta q'$. The *reachable region* of the automaton is $Reach(A) = \{q \in Q \mid \exists w : q_0 \xrightarrow{w}_\delta q\}$. A *trace* α of A is a finite or infinite sequence $\langle p_0, f_0, p_1, f_1, \ldots \rangle$ such that $p_0 = q_0$,

---

[1] We perform abstraction by hiding variables. Similar criteria can be obtained for predicate abstraction.

and $p_j \xrightarrow{f_j}_\delta p_{j+1}$ for all $j \geq 0$. The *word* induced by the trace α is the sequence $f_0 \cdot f_1 \cdot f_2 \cdots$ of input symbols. The *language* $L(A)$ is the set of finite and infinite words $w \in \Sigma^* \cup \Sigma^\omega$ such that there exists a trace of A that induces w. The ω-*language* $L^\omega(A)$ is the set of infinite words in $L(A)$; that is, $L^\omega(A) = L(A) \cap \Sigma^\omega$.

Open programs. An *open program* $P = (X, \Sigma, s_0, \varphi, x_e)$ consists of a finite set X of boolean variables, whose truth-value assignments $[\![X]\!]$ represent the states of the program; a finite alphabet Σ of exported function names; an initial state $s_0 \in [\![X]\!]$; a set φ containing a transition predicate φ_f over $X \cup X'$ for every function $f \in \Sigma$, where the set X' contains a primed variable x' for each variable $x \in X$; and an error variable $x_e \in X$. The semantics of the open program P is given by a finite automaton $A_P = ([\![X]\!], \Sigma, s_0, \delta_P)$ and a set E_P of error states. The transition relation δ_P is defined by $(s, f, t) \in \delta_P$ iff $s \cup t'$ satisfies the transition predicate φ_f, where the state $t' \in [\![X']\!]$ is obtained by giving each primed variable $x' \in X'$ the value $t(x)$. We require of every open program P that the automaton A_P be input-enabled. The open program P is *concrete* if A_P is deterministic. For a concrete open program, in every state, every function call leads to a unique successor state. We will also consider open programs that result from abstraction; in general these do not have deterministic transition relations. The set E_P of *error states* is the set of states s with $s(x_e) = \text{T}$. Without loss of generality we assume that for all states $s \in E_P$, if $(s, f, s') \in \delta_P$, then $s' \in E_P$.

Interfaces. An *interface* for an open program P is a closed[2] (in the Cantor topology) set of infinite words over the alphabet Σ of function names. A finite or infinite word $w \in \Sigma^* \cup \Sigma^\omega$ is *safe* for P if for all finite prefixes w' of w, if $s_0 \xrightarrow{w'}_{\delta_P} s$, then $s \notin E_P$. A language $L \subseteq \Sigma^* \cup \Sigma^\omega$ is *safe* for P if every word in L is safe for P. A language $L \subseteq \Sigma^* \cup \Sigma^\omega$ is *permissive* for P if L contains every word that is safe for P. The *safe and permissive interface* for P is the set $I(P) \subseteq \Sigma^\omega$ of infinite words that are safe for P. Interfaces for P can be specified by serial automata over the input alphabet Σ. We look for deterministic interface specifications, which can be used to monitor the legality of a sequence of function calls. Such serial and deterministic automata can be minimized. Thus, the interface synthesis problem is defined as follows:

> *Given a concrete open program P, we wish to find the (unique) minimal serial and deterministic finite automaton B such that the ω-language $L^\omega(B)$ is the safe and permissive interface for P; that is, $L^\omega(B) = I(P)$.*

Checking interface automata for safety. Let $P = (X, \Sigma, s_0, \varphi, x_e)$ be an open program, and let $B = (Q, \Sigma, q_0, \lambda)$ be a finite automaton. The *product* of P and B is the finite automaton $A_P \times B = (Q^\times, \Sigma, q_0^\times, \lambda^\times)$ with $Q^\times = [\![X]\!] \times Q$, $q_0^\times = (s_0, q_0)$, and $\lambda^\times = \{((s, q), f, (s', q')) \mid (s, f, s') \in \delta_P \text{ and } (q, f, q') \in \lambda\}$. The language $L(B)$ is safe for P iff $s \notin E_P$ for all states $(s, q) \in Reach(A_P \times B)$. Based on this characterization of safety, we use a procedure $checkSafe(P, B)$ to check if $L(B)$ is safe for P. If $L(B)$ is safe for P, then $checkSafe(P, B)$ returns

---

[2] A set L of infinite words is *closed* if for every infinite word w, if every finite prefix of w is a prefix of some word in L, then $w \in L$.

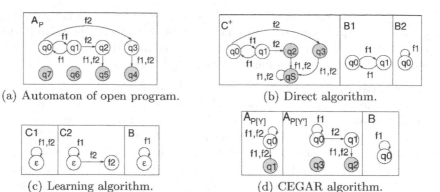

(a) Automaton of open program.   (b) Direct algorithm.

(c) Learning algorithm.   (d) CEGAR algorithm.

Fig. 2. Example concrete open program and the output of the three algorithms

YES; otherwise it returns a finite trace $\langle(s_0, q_0), f_0, (s_1, q_1), f_1, \ldots, (s_n, q_n)\rangle$ of the product $A_P \times B$ such that $s_n \in E_P$.

Checking interface automata for permissiveness. Given an open program $P = (X, \Sigma, s_0, \varphi, x_e)$, the *errorless automaton* $A_P^- = (\llbracket X \rrbracket, \Sigma, s_0, \delta_P^-)$ has the transition relation $\delta_P^- = \{(s, f, s') \in \delta_P \mid s' \notin E_P\}$. Given a finite automaton $B = (Q, \Sigma, q_0, \lambda)$, the *serialized automaton* $B^+ = (Q \cup \{q_{sink}\}, \Sigma, q_0, \lambda^+)$ has the sink state q_{sink} and the transition relation $\lambda^+ = \lambda \cup \{(q, f, q_{sink}) \mid q \in Q$ and $f \in \Sigma$, and $(q, f, q') \notin \lambda$ for all $q' \in Q\} \cup \{(q_{sink}, f, q_{sink}) \mid f \in \Sigma\}$. We have the following sufficient condition on permissiveness [5]: the language $L(B)$ is permissive for P if $Reach(A_P^- \times B^+)$ contains no state of the form (s, q_{sink}). For deterministic B, the other direction also holds: if $L(B)$ is permissive for P, then $Reach(A_P^- \times B^+)$ contains no state of the form (s, q_{sink}). Based on this characterization of permissiveness, we use, for deterministic B, a procedure $checkPermissive(P, B)$ to check if $L(B)$ is permissive for P. If $L(B)$ is permissive for P, then $checkPermissive(P, B)$ returns YES; otherwise it returns a finite trace $\langle(s_0, q_0), f_0, (s_1, q_1), f_1, \ldots, (s_n, q_n)\rangle$ of the product $A_P^- \times B^+$ such that $q_n = q_{sink}$. The procedures $checkSafe(P, B)$ and $checkPermissive(P, B)$ are implemented as reachability analyses.

3   Three Algorithms for Interface Synthesis

We discuss three different algorithms for synthesizing interface automata. Figure 2(a) shows the automaton of a concrete open program, which we use as an example. The grey circles denote the error states.

3.1   Direct Algorithm

Given a concrete open program P, the algorithm *Direct* first constructs the errorless automaton A_P^-, and then calls the procedure *Prune*, which prunes the serialized automaton $(A_P^-)^+$ backwards, starting from q_{sink}, to eliminate all states

Algorithm 1. *Direct(P)*

Input: a concrete open program $P = (X, \Sigma, s_0, \varphi, x_e)$
Output: the minimal serial deterministic automaton B such that $L^\omega(B) = I(P)$
   return *Minimize(Prune(A_P^-))*

---

all of whose successors lead to q_{sink}. The pruning removes all unrecoverable
states of P, from which all infinite input sequences cause an error. Formally,
a state $q \in Q$ of a deterministic automaton $C = (Q, \Sigma, q_0, \lambda)$ is *recoverable*
if there exists an infinite trace $\langle p_0, f_0, p_1, f_1, \ldots \rangle$ of C such that $p_0 = q$, and
$p_i \neq q_{sink}$ for all $i \geq 0$. This yields a (still deterministic) automaton D, which
we refer as the intermediate automaton obtained in the direct algorithm. Then
the procedure *Minimize* produces from D a minimal automaton B, using the
DFA minimization algorithm [6]. (More precisely, we serialize D to obtain D^+,
and consider the sink state of D^+ as rejecting, and all other states as accepting.
We then minimize the automaton and remove the introduced sink state.) The
result B is the minimal serial and deterministic automaton such that $L^\omega(B)$ is
the safe and permissive interface for P.

Example. Figure 2(b) shows the serialized errorless automaton (C^+), its pruned
version (B1), and its minimized version (B2), for the automaton A_P from Fig. 2(a)
The grey circles represent the set Err in the procedure *Prune*. The error states
from E_P are unreachable and not shown. The state qS is the sink state q_{sink}.

Time complexity. For an open program with k variables, pruning requires
worst-case time $O(|\Sigma| \cdot 2^k)$. If the pruned automaton D has n states, then sub-
sequent minimization needs $O(|\Sigma| \cdot n \cdot \log n)$ time. The worst case occurs if
$n = O(2^k)$, giving a running time of $O(|\Sigma| \cdot k \cdot 2^k)$ for the direct algorithm.

Theorem 1. *Given a concrete open program P with variables X and exported
function names Σ, the direct algorithm (Alg. 1) produces the minimal serial and
deterministic finite automaton B such that $L^\omega(B)$ is the safe and permissive
interface for P, in time linear in $|\Sigma|$ and exponential in $|X|$.*

Note that if A_P is not deterministic, then the pruning performed by the direct
algorithm does not guarantee to result in a safe interface. To work on abstract
open programs, the direct algorithm would have to be preceded by an exponential determinization step, i.e., subset construction. However, even for concrete
open programs P, where no determinization is necessary, the direct algorithm
needs to explore the entire state space of P and minimize an intermediate automaton D of possible size $O(2^k)$, where k is the number of variables of P. In
software libraries, we expect many recoverable states —i.e., states from which
some sequences of function calls are allowed— and this gives rise to large intermediate automata. Hence the direct algorithm is often too expensive. Therefore
the following two alternative algorithms have been proposed. While no better
in worst-case complexity, in many cases the two alternatives outperform the direct algorithm. They do so by employing very different strategies: the learning

---

Algorithm 2. *Prune(C)*

Input: a deterministic automaton $C = (Q, \Sigma, q_0, \lambda)$
Output: a serial deterministic automaton B such that $L^\omega(B) = L^\omega(C)$
Variables: a serial automaton C^+, a state $q_{sink} \notin Q$, and
               three state sets $Err, Wait, Pre \subseteq (Q \cup \{q_{sink}\})$
$C^+ :=$ serialized automaton $(Q \cup \{q_{sink}\}, \Sigma, q_0, \lambda^+)$ for C
$Err := \{q_{sink}\};$ $Wait := Err$
while $Wait \neq \emptyset$ **do**
   choose $s \in Wait;$ $Wait := Wait \setminus \{s\}$
   $Pre := \{r \in Q \mid (r, f, s) \in \lambda^+ \text{ for some } f \in \Sigma\}$
   for each state $r \in Pre$ **do**
     if $r \notin Err$ **and** $(\forall f \in \Sigma : r \xrightarrow{f}_{\lambda^+} s' \text{ and } s' \in Err)$ **then**
       $Err := Err \cup \{r\};$ $Wait := Wait \cup \{r\}$
   return $(Q \setminus Err, \Sigma, q_0, \{(q, f, q') \in \lambda \mid q' \notin Err\})$

---

algorithm queries the concrete open program; the CEGAR algorithm automatically constructs and refines an abstract open program.

3.2 Learning Algorithm

An approach based on learning the interface was proposed by Alur et al. [1]. The learning algorithm learns the interface language by asking membership and equivalence questions to the teacher, i.e., the given concrete open program P. In a membership question, the algorithm asks whether a particular word is safe for P or not. In an equivalence question, the algorithm asks if the language of the conjectured automaton $C = (Q, \Sigma, q_0, \lambda)$ is safe and permissive for P. To construct the conjectured automaton, the learning algorithm maintains information about a finite collection of words over Σ in an observation table (R, E, G), where R and E are finite sets of words over Σ, and G is a function from $(R \cup (R \cdot \Sigma)) \times E$ to $\mathbb{B}$. The set R is a set of representative words. For each word $r \in R$ that is safe for P, there exists a state q_r in the automaton C such that $q_\epsilon \xrightarrow{r}_\lambda q_r$. The set E is a set of suffix words that distinguish the states. For all representative words $r_1, r_2 \in R$, there exists a word $e \in E$ such that only one of $r_1 \cdot e$ and $r_2 \cdot e$ is safe for P. The function G stores the results of the membership questions, i.e., it maps a pair of two words $r \in R \cup (R \cdot \Sigma)$ and $e \in E$ to T if $r \cdot e$ is safe for P, and to F otherwise. For a detailed description of the learning algorithm we refer to Alur et al. [1] (cf. also [2] and [7]). For a fair comparison between the algorithms, the learning algorithm described here learns the interface from the concrete open program rather than from a manual abstraction of the same, as proposed by Alur et al. [1]. Since a concrete open program is deterministic, the learning algorithm produces an interface that is not only safe, but also permissive.

Algorithm. The learning algorithm starts with R and E set to $\{\epsilon\}$, and G is initialized for every combination of two words from $R \cup (R \cdot \Sigma)$ and E using membership questions (procedure *memb*). Then, the algorithm checks whether the table (R, E, G) is closed (procedure *checkClosure*). If not, the algorithm adds

Algorithm 3. *Learning*(P)

Input: a concrete open program $P = (X, \Sigma, s_0, \varphi, x_e)$
Output: the minimal serial deterministic automaton B such that $L^\omega(B) = I(P)$
Variables: two sets of words R and E over Σ, two words r_{new} and e_{new} over Σ
            an array G that maps $(R \cup (R \cdot \Sigma)) \times E$ to $\mathbb{B}$,
            an automaton $C = (Q, \Sigma, q_0, \lambda)$, and
            a finite trace $\alpha^\times$ of a product automaton
  $R := \{\epsilon\};$ $E := \{\epsilon\};$ $G[\epsilon, \epsilon] := memb(P, \epsilon \cdot \epsilon);$
  for each $f \in \Sigma$ **do**
    $G[\epsilon \cdot f, \epsilon] := memb(P, \epsilon \cdot f \cdot \epsilon)$
  while true do
    $r_{new} := checkClosure(R, E, G)$
    while $r_{new} \neq$ YES **do**
      $R := R \cup \{r_{new}\}$
      for each $f \in \Sigma, e \in E$ **do**
        $G[r_{new} \cdot f, e] := memb(P, r_{new} \cdot f \cdot e)$
      $r_{new} := checkClosure(R, E, G)$
    $C := makeConjecture(R, E, G)$
    $\alpha^\times := checkSafe(P, C)$
    if $\alpha^\times =$ YES **then**
      $\alpha^\times := checkPermissive(P, C)$
      if $\alpha^\times =$ YES **then**
        return $Prune(C)$
    $w :=$ the word induced by the trace $\alpha^\times$
    $e_{new} := findSuffix(P, R, w);$ $E := E \cup \{e_{new}\}$
    for each $r \in R$ and $f \in \Sigma$ **do**
      $G[r, e_{new}] := memb(P, r \cdot e_{new})$
      $G[r \cdot f, e_{new}] := memb(P, r \cdot f \cdot e_{new})$

---

new representative words and rechecks for closure. Once (R, E, G) is closed, an automaton C is conjectured (procedure *makeConjecture*). Then, the algorithm checks if $L(C)$ is safe and permissive for P (this check represents an equivalence question). If not, a counterexample trace is returned. The longest suffix of the counterexample (found by the procedure *findSuffix*) is added to E, and the algorithm rechecks for closure. The learning algorithm constructs a deterministic automaton C whose states correspond to the trace-equivalence classes of $Reach(A_P)$. Two states $s, t \in [\![X]\!]$ are *trace-equivalent* if there are no word $w \in \Sigma^*$ and no states $s', t' \in [\![X]\!]$ such that $s \xrightarrow{w}_{\delta_P} s'$ and $t \xrightarrow{w}_{\delta_P} t'$ and $s'(x_e) \neq t'(x_e)$. Then, the algorithm calls the procedure *Prune* to produce the minimal serial and deterministic finite automaton B such that $L^\omega(B)$ is the safe and permissive interface for P.

Example. Figure 2(c) shows in the first two boxes the two conjectured automata. Automaton C2 is the final conjecture, which is used to produce the serial deterministic finite automaton B.

Procedures used in the learning algorithm

- $memb(P, w)$ returns T if w is safe for P. Otherwise it returns F.
- $checkClosure(R, E, G)$ returns YES if for every $r \in R$ and $f \in \Sigma$, there exists an $r' \in R$ such that $G[r \cdot f, e] = G[r', e]$ for every $e \in E$. Otherwise it returns the word $r \cdot f$ such that there is no r' satisfying the above condition.
- $makeConjecture(R, E, G)$ returns a deterministic automaton $C = (Q, \Sigma, q_0, \lambda)$, where $Q = R \setminus \{r \in R \mid G[r, \epsilon] = F\}$, and $q_0 = \epsilon$, and for every $r \in Q$ and every $f \in \Sigma$, if $G[r \cdot f, \epsilon] = T$, then $(r, f, r') \in \lambda$, where r' is the word such that $G[r \cdot f, e] = G[r', e]$ for every $e \in E$.
- $findSuffix(P, R, w)$ finds the longest suffix w' of w such that for some $r \in R$ and $f \in \Sigma$, $memb(P, r \cdot f \cdot w') \neq memb(P, r' \cdot w')$, where $r \xrightarrow{f}_\lambda r'$.

Time complexity. For an open program with k variables and m trace-equivalence classes, the generation of a conjectured automaton has the time complexity $O(2^k \cdot (m^2 \cdot |\Sigma| + m \cdot \log c))$, where c is the length of the longest counterexample trace $\alpha^\times$ seen by the algorithm. At the end, a call to the procedure *Prune* takes $O(m \cdot |\Sigma|)$ time. Thus the learning algorithm has the worst-case time complexity $O(|\Sigma| \cdot 2^{3k})$ when the number of trace-equivalence classes is $O(2^k)$. However, when the number m of trace-equivalence classes (which determines the size of the output automaton) is small compared to the number 2^k of concrete program states, then the learning algorithm may perform better than the direct algorithm. This is because learning produces the minimal interface automaton, whereas the direct algorithm needs to explicitly minimize an intermediate automaton of potential size $O(2^k)$.

Theorem 2. *Given a concrete open program P with variables X and exported function names Σ, and m trace-equivalence classes in $Reach(A_P)$, the learning algorithm (Alg. 3) produces the minimal serial and deterministic finite automaton B (with $O(m)$ states) such that $L^\omega(B)$ is the safe and permissive interface for P, in time linear in $|\Sigma|$, quadratic in m, and exponential in $|X|$.*

3.3   CEGAR Algorithm

A different approach based on automatic abstraction refinement was proposed by Henzinger et al. [5].

Abstraction. An *abstraction* for an open program $P = (X, \Sigma, s_0, \varphi, x_e)$ is a set $Y \subseteq X$ of variables, where $x_e \in Y$. The abstraction hides the variables in $X \setminus Y$. Given a state $s \in [\![X]\!]$, the state $s[Y]$ is the valuation in $[\![Y]\!]$ such that $s(x) = s[Y](x)$ for all $x \in Y$. An open program P and an abstraction Y for P yield the *(abstract) open program* $P[Y] = (Y, \Sigma, s_0[Y], \varphi[Y], x_e)$, where for each $f \in \Sigma$, the transition predicate $\varphi_f[Y]$ is the projection $\exists (X \cup X') \setminus (Y \cup Y') : \varphi_f$ of φ_f to the variables in $Y \cup Y'$ (existential abstraction). The semantics of $P[Y]$ is given by the abstract automaton $A_{P[Y]}$ and the set $E_{P[Y]}$ of abstract error states. Note that $(s, f, s') \in \delta_{P[Y]}$ iff $(t, f, t') \in \delta_P$ for some concrete states $t, t' \in [\![X]\!]$ with $s = t[Y]$ and $s' = t'[Y]$. The original CEGAR algorithm for interface synthesis [5] uses two abstractions: one for checking safety and a possibly different one for

---

Algorithm 4. $CEGAR(P)$

Input: a concrete open program $P = (X, \Sigma, s_0, \varphi, x_e)$
Output: the minimal serial deterministic automaton B such that $L^\omega(B) = I(P)$
Variables: an abstraction Y for P, the open program $P[Y]$, an automaton C

$\quad Y := \{x_e\}$
$\quad$ **while** $Y \neq X$ **do**
$\quad\quad C := A^-_{P[Y]}$
$\quad\quad \alpha^\times := checkSafe(P[Y], C)$
$\quad\quad$ **if** $\alpha^\times = $ YES **then**
$\quad\quad\quad$ **return** $Minimize(Prune(Determinize(C)))$
$\quad\quad$ **else**
$\quad\quad\quad \alpha := findSpuriousTrace(P, \alpha^\times); \quad Y := getNewVars(P, \alpha, Y)$
$\quad$ **return** $Minimize(Prune(Determinize(A^-_P)))$

---

checking permissiveness. We use a single abstraction, based on the following observations. An open program P with initial state s_0 and error variable x_e is *visibly deterministic* [5] if there is no word $w \in \Sigma^*$ and no states $s, t \in [\![X]\!]$ such that $s_0 \xrightarrow{w}_{\delta_P} s$ and $s_0 \xrightarrow{w}_{\delta_P} t$ and $s(x_e) \neq t(x_e)$.

Lemma 1. *Given the errorless automaton $A^-_P = (Q, \Sigma, q_0, \lambda)$ of an open program P, if the language $L(A^-_P)$ is safe for P, then $L(A^-_P)$ is permissive for P and P is visibly deterministic.*

Proof. (i) We know that the safety and permissiveness conditions are reachability questions on $A_P \times A^-_P$ and $A^-_P \times A^{-+}_P$, respectively. As A_P is input-enabled, we know that if $(q, f, q_{sink}) \in \lambda^+$, then $(q, f, q') \in \delta_P$ with $q' \in E_P$. Thus, if there exists no state $(t, q) \in Reach_{A_P \times A^-_P}$ such that $t \in E_P$, then there exists no state $(t, q_{sink}) \in Reach_{A^-_P \times A^{-+}_P}$. Hence, $L(A^-_P)$ is a permissive interface for P.

(ii) The fact that $L(A^-_P)$ is safe for P guarantees that there exists no word w such that w is not safe for P and $q_0 \xrightarrow{w}_\lambda q$ for some state $q \in Q$. Also, we know that the automaton A^-_P is the errorless automaton for P, and $L(A^-_P)$ is permissive for P. Therefore, there exists no word w such that there exist two states u and v with $s_0 \xrightarrow{w}_{\delta_P} u$ and $s_0 \xrightarrow{w}_{\delta_P} v$ and $u(x_e) \neq v(x_e)$. Hence, P is visibly deterministic. $\quad\square$

Lemma 2. *Let Y be an abstraction for a concrete open program P such that $P[Y]$ is visibly deterministic. If a language L is safe and permissive for $P[Y]$, then L is safe and permissive for P.*

Proof. Let a word $w \in L$ be a counterexample for safety of P. By construction of $A_{P[Y]}$, we know that the word w is also unsafe for the abstract open program $P[Y]$, which is a contradiction to our assumption that L is safe for $P[Y]$. Similarly, permissiveness of L for $P[Y]$ guarantees that L is permissive for P. $\square$

Algorithm 5. *getNewVars*(P, α, Y)

Input: a concrete open program $P = (X, \Sigma, s_0, \varphi, x_e)$, an abstraction Y for P, and
    a finite trace $\alpha = \langle t_0, f_0, \ldots, t_n \rangle$ of the automaton $A_{P[Y]}$
Output: a new abstraction Y' for P such that $Y \subset Y'$ and α is not a trace of $A_{P[Y']}$
Variables: states $s, s' \in [\![X]\!]$ and $t, t_s, t' \in [\![Y]\!]$, a set $R \subseteq [\![X]\!]$ of states, and $f \in \Sigma$
    $s := s_0; \quad t := s_0[Y]$
    for $i := 1$ **to** n **do**
        $t_s := t_i; \quad f := f_{i-1}$
        let $s' \in [\![X]\!]$ be such that $s \xrightarrow{f}_{\delta_P} s'$;   let $t' \in [\![Y]\!]$ be such that $t' = s'[Y]$
        if $t' \neq t_s$ **then**
            $R := \{ r \in Reach(A_P) \mid t = r[Y]$ and there exists $u \in [\![X]\!]$ such that $t_s = u[Y]$
                and $r \xrightarrow{f}_{\delta_P} u \}$
            return *splitState*(s, R, Y)
        $s := s'; \quad t := t'$

Algorithm. We start with an abstraction that contains only the error variable; that is, $Y = \{x_e\}$. We construct the abstract open program $P[Y]$ and its errorless automaton $C = A^-_{P[Y]}$. Then, we check whether $L(C)$ is safe for $P[Y]$. If so, then we know that $L(C)$ is also permissive and that $P[Y]$ is visibly deterministic (by Lemmas 1 and 2). Otherwise, we obtain a counterexample trace $\alpha^\times = \langle (s_0[Y], q_0), f_0, \ldots, (s_n[Y], q_n) \rangle$ of the product automaton $A_{P[Y]} \times C$. Now we use the procedure *findSpuriousTrace*$(P, \alpha^\times)$ to check if the word w induced by the trace $\alpha^\times$ is safe for the concrete open program P. If w is safe (resp. unsafe) for P, then the procedure declares the projection α of $\alpha^\times$ that is followed by the component automaton $A_{P[Y]}$ (resp. C) as spurious. Formally, the finite trace $\alpha = \langle t_0, f_0, \ldots, t_n \rangle$ of the abstract automaton $A_{P[Y]}$ (resp. $C = A^-_{P[Y]}$) is *spurious* if there exists no trace $\langle s_0, f_0, \ldots, s_n \rangle$ of the concrete automaton A_P such that $t_i = s_i[Y]$ for all $0 \leq i \leq n$. Next, we add more variables from X to the abstraction Y such that the spurious trace α is eliminated from $A_{P[Y]}$ (resp. C). This is done by the procedure *getNewVars*, which constructs a trace $\beta = \langle s_0, f_0, \ldots, s_n \rangle$ of A_P, and its corresponding abstract trace $\beta[Y]$, such that β induces the same word as α. The procedure locates the first position i where the spurious abstract trace α differs from the genuine abstract trace β. Then it finds a set R of states in A_P that cause the spurious abstract trace, and a set $Y' \subseteq X$ of variables such that $Y \subset Y'$ and if $t = s_{i-1}[Y']$, then there does not exist a state $r \in R$ with $t = r[Y']$. This concludes one refinement step.

In the next refinement iteration, we construct the refined abstract open program $P[Y']$, and check if it is safe (and therefore visibly deterministic using Lemma 1). We say that an abstraction Y *suffices to prove the safety* of P if $P[Y]$ is visibly deterministic. Once the CEGAR algorithm finds a visibly deterministic abstract open program $P[Y]$, we call the procedure *Determinize* followed by *Prune* and *Minimize*, to obtain the minimal serial and deterministic finite automaton B such that $L^\omega(B)$ is the safe and permissive interface for P. This is because before minimization, the abstract automaton $A_{P[Y]}$ found by the CEGAR algorithm may not be minimal. Note that given a concrete open program P, finding an abstraction Y for P with a minimal number of variables such that the abstract open program $P[Y]$ is visibly deterministic, is NP-hard [3].

Example. Figure 2(d) shows in the first box automaton $A_{P[Y]}$ with the abstraction $Y = \{x_e\}$. Adding one more variable yields the automaton $A_{P[Y']}$, whose open program is found to be visibly deterministic. The result B is computed by first determinizing, then pruning and minimizing.

Procedures used in the CEGAR algorithm

- $splitState(s, R, Y)$ for $s \in [\![X]\!]$, $R \subseteq [\![X]\!]$, and Y being the current abstraction, finds a set $Y' \subseteq X$ of variables such that $Y \subset Y'$ and there is no state $r \in R$ such that $t = r[Y']$, where $t \in [\![Y']\!]$ with $t = s[Y']$. It returns Y'.
- $findSpuriousTrace(P, \alpha^\times)$ first checks whether the word w induced by the finite trace $\alpha^\times$ of the product automaton is safe for P. If so, then returns the trace $\langle s_0[Y], f_0, \ldots, s_n[Y] \rangle$ of $A_{P[Y]}$ in $\alpha^\times$. Otherwise, it returns the trace $\langle q_0, f_0, \ldots, q_n \rangle$ of $C = A^-_{P[Y]}$ in $\alpha^\times$.
- $Determinize(A)$ determinizes the serial automaton $A = (Q, \Sigma, q_0, \delta)$. We note that since A is the automaton for a visibly deterministic open program, the automaton A is 'almost' deterministic, and it is straightforward to determinize A. Determinization does not change the set of states, the alphabet, and the initial state, only the transition relation: for every state $q \in Q$ and every function $f \in F$, if there exist more than one transitions from q on f, then we choose arbitrarily one of the transitions $(q, f, q') \in \delta$ to be in the new transition relation of the resulting deterministic automaton.

Time complexity. Let X and abstraction Y be sets of k and c variables, respectively. One iteration of the algorithm requires $O(|\Sigma| \cdot 2^{\max\{k, 2c\}})$ time. At the end of the refinement procedure, the call to procedure $Determinize$ runs in time $O(|\Sigma| \cdot 2^l)$, where l is the number of variables in the abstraction that suffices to prove the safety of P. The procedure $Prune$ requires time $O(|\Sigma| \cdot 2^l)$ followed by the procedure $Minimize$, which takes time $O(|\Sigma| \cdot l \cdot 2^l)$. Thus, the worst-case time complexity of the CEGAR algorithm is $O(|\Sigma| \cdot 2^{2k})$, which is encountered if the abstraction refinement introduces all k program variables. However, when the number l of variables that suffice to prove the safety of P (which determines the size of the output automaton) is small compared to the number k of all program variables, then the CEGAR algorithm may perform better than the direct algorithm, because the exponential time dependency on k is due only to the cost of constructing the abstract program. To be precise, to check whether there is an abstract transition $(s, f, s') \in \delta_{P[Y]}$ between two given abstract states $s, s' \in [\![Y]\!]$ requires time $O(2^k)$ but only space $O(k)$. Such a check can often benefit from symbolic methods.

Theorem 3. *Given an open program P with variables X and exported function names Σ, the CEGAR algorithm (Alg. 4) produces the minimal serial and deterministic finite automaton B (with $O(2^l)$ states) such that $L^\omega(B)$ is the safe and permissive interface for P, in time linear in $|\Sigma|$ and exponential in $|X| + l$, where l is the size of an abstraction that suffices to prove the safety of P.*

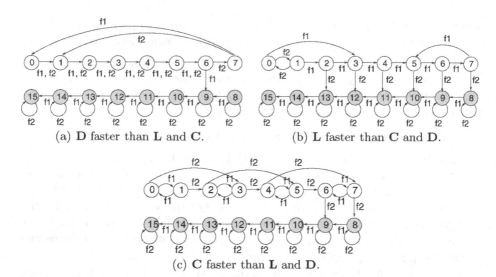

Fig. 3. Examples of concrete open programs where one algorithm performs better than others. The grey circles denote the error states.

4   Theoretical Separation of the Algorithms

We describe three theoretical classes of examples that amplify the differences between the three algorithms presented in the previous section. These examples suggest that the three algorithms are important in their own right, and it is worthwhile to understand them properly for efficient usage.

We consider concrete open programs with k variables and a fixed alphabet $\Sigma = \{f_1, f_2\}$. We denote the set of states by $\{s_0, s_1, ...s_{2^k-1}\}$. The boolean value of the variables is encoded in the index of the state; for example, at s_1, the first $k-1$ variables are 0, and the last variable is 1. Also, the first variable is the error variable. Thus, the first half of the states are non-error states, and the second half are error states. We consider all pairs of the direct (**D**), learning (**L**), and CEGAR (**C**) algorithm. We evaluate the pairs on the metric of time complexity. We show graphical examples with $k = 4$ in Fig. 3, which can be scaled to arbitrary k. We assume that the CEGAR algorithm finds the minimal sufficient abstraction in each case.

- **D** *faster than* **L** *and* **C**. For the open program in Fig. 3(a), the interface automaton has size $O(2^k)$; that is, the interface is no smaller than the library. The direct algorithm requires $O(2^k \cdot k)$ time, whereas the learning algorithm requires $O(2^{3k})$ time and the CEGAR algorithm requires $O(2^{2k})$ time. The direct algorithm is the fastest, because it avoids the overhead of learning and abstraction refinement.
- **L** *faster than* **C** *and* **D**. The interface automaton for the open program in Fig. 3(b) has two states (for all k). Hence, the learning algorithm requires $O(2^k)$ time. On the other hand, the CEGAR algorithm has to continue

Table 1. Run time for different algorithms, measured on a 3.0 GHz Pentium IV machine with 1 GB memory. The parameter k is described for each class in the text.

k	Interface automaton size	Learning time	CEGAR time
\multicolumn{4}{c}{List Iterator}			
5	2	0.19 s	0.91 s
6	2	0.43 s	1.53 s
7	2	1.10 s	4.31 s
8	2	2.31 s	12.12 s
\multicolumn{4}{c}{Piped Output Stream}			
12	2	2.12 s	0.89 s
13	2	5.30 s	1.83 s
14	2	12.32 s	3.76 s
15	2	27.82 s	7.68 s

refinement until adding $k - 1$ variables to the abstract program, and thus produces an intermediate automaton with $O(2^k)$ states. Hence, including minimization, CEGAR requires $O(2^{2k})$ time. The direct algorithm prunes the concrete program. This yields an intermediate automaton with $O(2^k)$ states, which is then minimized to obtain the interface automaton with two states. Thus, the direct algorithm requires $O(2^k \cdot k)$ time.

- **C** *faster than* **L** *and* **D**. For the open program in Fig. 3(c), the number of trace-equivalence classes is exponential in the number l of variables that suffice to prove the safety of the program, and l is logarithmic in the number of all variables; that is, $l = O(\log k)$. Thus the CEGAR algorithm requires $O(2^k \cdot \log k)$ time. On the other hand, the learning algorithm requires $O(2^k \cdot k^2)$ time, because it depends quadratically on the size of the interface automaton. The direct algorithm again has to minimize $O(2^k)$ recoverable states, to produce the interface automaton with $O(2^l)$ states. Thus, the direct algorithm runs in $O(2^k \cdot k)$ time.

5   Practical Evaluation of the Algorithms

We implemented the three algorithms in C++. We experimented with a variety of Java libraries [1], all of which have a finite number of states. For comparison purposes, we wanted the direct algorithm to succeed on the concrete open programs; thus we first simplified the Java classes. We retained all fields in a class, but reduced their sizes, and hence the state spaces. The Java libraries were manually translated into such simplified, but still concrete, open programs. The input to the tool is the transition relation of a concrete open program. Table 1 reports some results of our experiments.

Direct works fastest. The following example is similar to Fig. 3(a), where the direct algorithm performs better than the other algorithms.

- *java.util.Stack:* We consider the class with $k+1$ boolean variables. The first variable encodes error, and the remaining k variables encode the current size of the stack (thus, the maximal size of the stack is 2^k). We create an interface for the methods *push()*, *pop()*, and *peek()*. The algorithms produce the interface automaton with $O(2^k)$ states. The direct algorithm is fastest.

In general, the direct algorithm performs best if either the number of recoverable library states is small, or as in the example above, the number of trace-equivalence classes of the library is of the order of the number of library states. Neither is the case for the following three examples.

Learning works fastest. The following example is similar to Fig. 3(b).

- *java.util.ListIterator:* We compute the interface for four methods: *next()*, *prev()*, *remove()*, *add()*. The list iterator is encoded by $2k+1$ boolean variables, one for error, k to encode the previous returned iterator location l_p, and another k to encode the current iterator location l_c. The methods *next()* and *prev()* store l_c in l_p, and update l_c. The method *remove()* checks if l_p is valid; if so, then *remove()* removes the entry in location l_p. Both *add()* and *remove()* invalidate l_p. The CEGAR algorithm finds that only the last k variables are redundant, and thus produces an automaton of size $O(2^k)$. This automaton is then minimized to obtain the interface automaton with two states, which is shown in Fig. 4(a). On the other hand, the learning algorithm learns that only one value of l_p (reached on calling *add()* or *remove()*) marks the previous iterator location as invalid, and that all other values are equivalent. Hence, the learning algorithm finishes after distinguishing two states of the interface.

CEGAR works fastest. The following programs are similar to Fig. 3(c).

- *com.sun.se.impl.activation.ServerTableEntry:* We encode the class using $k+3$ boolean variables. The first variable encodes error, the next two encode the state of the system, and the remaining k encode the current server ID. The interface is built for six methods, as shown in Fig. 4(b). The CEGAR algorithm finds that the two variables that encode the state of the system suffice to prove the safety of the class; after minimization it produces the interface automaton with three states, which is shown in Fig. 4(b). The learning algorithm learns the three distinguishable states of the interface, but takes a longer time to do so.
- *java.io.PipedOutputStream:* The class is represented by $k+2$ boolean variables. The first variable encodes error, the second encodes the connect flag, and the remaining k variables encode the buffer. We build an interface for the following methods: *connect()*, *write()*, *flush()*, and *close()*. We model invocations of *connect()* returning different values (0 or 1) as different methods. The CEGAR algorithm discovers that the variable that encodes the connect flag suffices to prove the safety of the class. The output is an interface automaton with two states, which is shown in Fig. 4(c). Again, the learning algorithm needs more time to find the two distinguishable states.

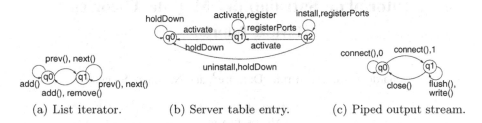

(a) List iterator.   (b) Server table entry.   (c) Piped output stream.

Fig. 4. Interface automata for list iterator, server table entry, and piped output stream

6   Conclusion

We formalized and implemented three different algorithms for interface synthesis in a uniform framework. For each of the three algorithms, we identified classes of open programs for which the algorithm is better suited for interface synthesis than the two alternatives. The direct algorithm has the advantage in scenarios where the interface automaton of the library is large, or the program has few recoverable states, i.e., states from which some sequences of function calls are legal. The CEGAR algorithm is the most efficient solution when many variables of the input program can be hidden in the interface automaton. The learning algorithm performs best if the interface automaton is much smaller than the set of recoverable program states, but does not correspond to an abstraction of the input program over a small set of program variables.

References

1. Alur, R., Cerny, P., Gupta, G., Madhusudan, P.: Synthesis of interface specifications for Java classes. In: Proc. POPL, pp. 98–109. ACM Press, New York (2005)
2. Angluin, D.: Learning regular sets from queries and counterexamples. Information and Computation 75, 87–106 (1987)
3. Clarke, E.M., Grumberg, O., Jha, S., Lu, Y., Veith, H.: Counterexample-guided abstraction refinement. In: Emerson, E.A., Sistla, A.P. (eds.) Proc. CAV 2000. LNCS, vol. 1855, pp. 154–169. Springer, Heidelberg (2000)
4. de Alfaro, L., Henzinger, T.A.: Interface automata. In: Proc. FSE, pp. 109–120. ACM Press, New York (2001)
5. Henzinger, T.A., Jhala, R., Majumdar, R.: Permissive interfaces. In: Proc. FSE, pp. 31–40. ACM Press, New York (2005)
6. Hopcroft, J.E.: An $n \cdot \log n$ algorithm for minimizing states in a finite automaton. In: Proc. Theory of Machines and Computations, pp. 189–196. Acad. Press, San Diego (1971)
7. Rivest, R.L., Schapire, R.E.: Inference of finite automata using homing sequences. Information and Computation 103, 299–347 (1993)

A Tutorial on Satisfiability Modulo Theories*
(Invited Tutorial)

Leonardo de Moura[1], Bruno Dutertre[2], and Natarajan Shankar[2]

[1] Microsoft Research
1 Microsoft Way,
Redmond WA 98052 USA
leonardo@microsoft.com
http://research.microsoft.com/leonardo/
[2] Computer Science Laboratory
SRI International
Menlo Park CA 94025 USA
{bruno,shankar}@csl.sri.com
http://www.csl.sri.com/~{bruno,shankar}/

Abstract. Solvers for satisfiability modulo theories (SMT) check the satisfiability of first-order formulas containing operations from various theories such as the Booleans, bit-vectors, arithmetic, arrays, and recursive datatypes. SMT solvers are extensions of Boolean satisfiability solvers (SAT solvers) that check the satisfiability of formulas built from Boolean variables and operations. SMT solvers have a wide range of applications in hardware and software verification, extended static checking, constraint solving, planning, scheduling, test case generation, and computer security. We briefly survey the theory of SAT and SMT solving, and present some of the key algorithms in the form of pseudocode. This tutorial presentation is primarily directed at those who wish to build satisfiability solvers or to use existing solvers more effectively.

1   Introduction

Satisfiability is the basic and ubiquitous problem of determining if a formula expressing a constraint has a model or a solution. A large number of problems can be described in terms of satisfiability, including graph problems, puzzles such as Sudoku, planning, scheduling, software and hardware verification, extended static checking, optimization, test case generation, among others. Many of these problems can be encoded by Boolean formulas and solved using Boolean satisfiability (SAT) solvers. Other problems require the added expressiveness of equality, uninterpreted function symbols, arithmetic, arrays, datatype operations, and quantifiers. Such problems can be handled by solvers for theory satisfiability or satisfiability modulo theories (SMT). In recent years, satisfiability procedures have undergone dramatic improvements in efficiency and expressiveness. SAT solvers like WalkSAT [SKC96], SATO [Zha97],

---

* This research was supported NSF Grants CCR-ITR-0326540 and CCR-ITR-0325808. We thank Sam Owre and Ashish Tiwari for their comments and corrections.

W. Damm and H. Hermanns (Eds.): CAV 2007, LNCS 4590, pp. 20–36, 2007.

GRASP [MSS99], Chaff [MMZ⁺01], zChaff [ZM02,Zha03], Siege [Rya04], and Min-iSAT [ES03] have introduced several enhancements to the efficiency of SAT solving. Though SMT technology has been in development since the late 1970s with the work of Shostak [Sho79] and Nelson and Oppen [NO79,Nel81], the incorporation of SAT-based search has yielded very significant efficiencies. Satisfiability is an active and growing area of research with a number of exciting applications and connections to artificial intelligence, operations research, and computational biology. The present tutorial is mostly based on the Yices SMT solver [DdM06b]. It is directed at non-experts and aims to explain some of the basic principles of SAT and SMT solving.

Section 2 covers the basic background on logic and satisfiability. In Section 3, we explain the basic DPLL search procedures for satisfiability. Procedures for solving constraints in individual theories are discussed in Section 4. Theory combinations are discussed in Section 5, and the DPLL-based search procedure for satisfiability modulo theories is presented in Section 6. E-graph matching [Nel81,DNS03] described in Section 7 is an important technique for introducing relevant instantiations of quantified formulas within a search procedure.

2 Preliminaries

We explain the basic syntactic and semantic background needed to follow the rest of the tutorial.

2.1 Propositional Logic

A propositional formula ϕ can be a propositional variable p or a negation $\neg\phi_0$, a conjunction $\phi_0 \wedge \phi_1$, a disjunction $\phi_0 \vee \phi_1$, or an implication $\phi_0 \Rightarrow \phi_1$ of smaller formulas ϕ_0, ϕ_1. A truth assignment M for a formula ϕ maps the propositional variables in ϕ to $\{\top, \bot\}$. A given formula ϕ is *satisfiable* if there is a truth assignment M such that $M \models \phi$ under the usual truth table interpretation of the connectives. If $M \models \phi$ for every truth assignment M, then ϕ is valid. A propositional formula is either valid or its negation is satisfiable.

A literal is either a propositional variable p or its negation $\neg p$. The negation of a literal p is $\neg p$, and the negation of $\neg p$ is just p. A formula is a clause if it is the iterated disjunction of literals of the form $l_1 \vee \ldots \vee l_n$ for literals l_i, where $1 \leq i \leq n$. A formula is in conjunctive normal form (CNF) if it is the iterated conjunction of clauses $\Gamma_1 \wedge \ldots \wedge \Gamma_m$ for clauses Γ_i, where $1 \leq i \leq m$.

2.2 First-Order Logic

In defining a first-order signature, we assume countable sets of variables X, function symbols $\mathcal{F}$, and predicates $\mathcal{P}$. A first-order logic signature Σ is a partial map from $\mathcal{F} \cup \mathcal{P}$ to the natural numbers corresponding to the *arity* of the symbol. A Σ-*term* τ has the form

$$\tau := x \mid f(\tau_1, \ldots, \tau_n),$$

where $f \in \mathcal{F}$ and $\Sigma(f) = n$. For example, if $\Sigma(f) = 2$ and $\Sigma(g) = 1$, then $f(x, g(x))$ is a Σ-term. A Σ-*formula* has the form

$$\psi := p(\tau_1, \ldots, \tau_n) \mid \tau_0 = \tau_1 \mid \neg\psi_0 \mid \psi_0 \vee \psi_1 \mid \psi_0 \wedge \psi_1 \mid (\exists x : \psi_0) \mid (\forall x : \psi_0),$$

where $p \in \mathcal{P}$ and $\Sigma(p) = n$, and each τ_i, $1 \leq i \leq n$ is a Σ-term. For example, if $\Sigma(<) = 2$ for a predicate symbol $<$, then $(\forall x : (\exists y : x < y))$ is a Σ-formula. The set of free variables in a formula ψ is represented as $vars(\psi)$. A *sentence* is a formula with no free variables.

A Σ-structure M consists of a nonempty domain $|M|$ where for each $f \in F$ such that $\Sigma(f) = n$, $M(f)$ is an n-ary map on $|M|$, for each $p \in \mathcal{P}$ such that $\Sigma(p) = n$, $M(p)$ is a subset of $|M|^n$, and for each $x \in X$, $M(x) \in |M|$. The interpretation of a term a in M is given by $M[\![x]\!] = M(x)$ and $M[\![f(a_1, \ldots, a_n)]\!] = M(f)(M[\![a_1]\!], \ldots, M[\![a_n]\!])$. For a Σ-formula ψ and a Σ-structure M, satisfaction $M \models \psi$ can be defined as

$$M \models a = b \iff M[\![a]\!] = M[\![b]\!]$$
$$M \models p(a_1, \ldots, a_n) \iff (M[\![a_1]\!], \ldots, M[\![a_n]\!]) \in M(p)$$
$$M \models \neg\psi \iff M \not\models \psi$$
$$M \models \psi_0 \vee \psi_1 \iff M \models \psi_0 \text{ or } M \models \psi_1$$
$$M \models \psi_0 \wedge \psi_1 \iff M \models \psi_0 \text{ and } M \models \psi_1$$
$$M \models (\forall x : \psi) \iff M\{x \mapsto \mathbf{a}\} \models \psi, \text{ for all } \mathbf{a} \in |M|$$
$$M \models (\exists x : \psi) \iff M\{x \mapsto \mathbf{a}\} \models \psi, \text{ for some } \mathbf{a} \in |M|$$

A first-order Σ-formula ψ is satisfiable if there is a Σ-structure M such that $M \models \psi$, and it is valid if in all Σ-structures M, $M \models \psi$. A Σ-sentence is either satisfiable or its negation is valid. We focus on the satisfiability problem for quantifier-free first-order formulas.

3   SAT Solving

The principles of modern SAT solving have their origin in the 1960 procedure of Davis and Putnam [DP60], as simplified in 1962 by Davis, Logemann, and Loveland [DLL62]. The first step in the Davis–Putnam–Logemann–Loveland (DPLL) procedure is to convert the formula to conjunctive normal form (CNF) by introducing new variables to label the subformulas. A formula can be converted to clausal form by introducing fresh variables for each compound subformula and adding suitable clauses, e.g., in converting $\neg p \vee (\neg q \wedge r)$, we label $\neg q \wedge r$ as b and $\neg p \vee b$ as a to obtain the clauses $a, a \vee p, a \vee \neg b, \neg a \vee \neg p \vee b, b \vee q \vee \neg r, \neg b \vee \neg q, \neg b \vee r$.

The input to the satisfiability procedure is given as a set of clauses K representing the CNF formula $\bigwedge K$. The DPLL procedure builds a *partial truth assignment* for the variables in K by successively guessing an assignment for an unassigned literal, propagating the consequences of the partial assignment with respect to the clauses, and backtracking on the partial assignment when a conflict is detected in the form of a falsified clause. The procedure terminates either with a truth assignment satisfying each of

$$dpll(K) := dpllr(0, \emptyset, K, \emptyset) \qquad\qquad (init)$$
$$dpllr(0, M, K, C) := \bot, \text{ if} \qquad\qquad (contrad)$$
$$propagate(M, K, C) = \bot[\Gamma]$$
$$dpllr(h + 1, M, K, C) := dpllr(h', M_{h'}, K, C'), \text{ where} \qquad (backjump)$$
$$propagate(M, K, C) = \bot[\Gamma],$$
$$analyze(h + 1, M, \Gamma) = \Gamma',$$
$$C' = C \cup \{\Gamma'\},$$
$$h' = L2(\Gamma')$$
$$dpllr(h, M, K, C) := dpllr(h + 1, M'', K, C), \text{ where} \qquad (split)$$
$$M' = propagate(M, K, C) \neq \bot,$$
$$l = select(M', K) \neq \bot,$$
$$M'' = M'; l$$
$$dpllr(h, M, K, C) := M', \text{ where} \qquad\qquad (sat)$$
$$M' = propagate(M, K, C) \neq \bot,$$
$$select(M', K) = \bot$$

Fig. 1. The DPLL Boolean Satisfiability Procedure

the clauses, or with a demonstration that no such assignment can be constructed. The state of the search procedure is a 4-tuple $\langle h, M, K, C \rangle$ consisting of the *decision level* h, the partial assignment M, the input clause set K, and a set C of *conflict clauses* derived from K that are constructed during the search.

At a decision level h, the partial assignment consists of a sequence $M_0; \ldots; M_h$. Each M_i at decision level i is of the form $d; \langle l_1[\Gamma_1], \ldots, l_k[\Gamma_k] \rangle$ for some k, where d is the *decision literal* at level i, and each l_i is an *implied literal* and the clause Γ_i occurs in $K \cup C$. The assignment M_0 contains no decision literal. A decision literal or implied literal in M is said to be an assigned literal in M. No assigned literal in M occurs twice in M, nor does it occur negated in M. The assignment corresponding to M maps a variable p to $\top$ (respectively, $\bot$) if p (respectively, $\neg p$) is an assigned literal in M. If neither p nor $\neg p$ occurs in M, then the assignment is undefined. Given an assigned literal l occurring in M at level i, the assignment preceding l, written as $M_{<l}$, consists of $M_0; \ldots; M_{i-1}; M_i^{<l}$, where $M_i^{<l}$ consists of the part of the assignment of M_i preceding the occurrence of l. For each entry $l[\Gamma]$ in M, the clause Γ occurs in $K \cup C$ and is of the form $l \vee \Gamma'$, where $M_{<l} \models \neg\Gamma'$. The notation $M_{\overline{h}}$ represents the sequence $M_0; \ldots; M_h$.

The DPLL search algorithm shown in Figure 1 works by constructing the partial assignment M through the use of *propagation, analysis/backjumping,* and decision literal *selection,* until it has constructed an assignment satisfying the input clauses K or it can be shown that there is no such assignment. For decision level $h > 0$, the propagation operation $propagate(h, M, K, C)$ shown in Figure 2 works by adding $l[\Gamma]$ to M_h, where $\Gamma \in K \cup C$ is of the form $l \vee \Gamma'$, where $M \models \neg\Gamma'$. When $h = 0$, each unit clause l in $K \cup C$ is placed in M_0 as $l[l]$. Propagation can also detect a conflict where there is a clause of the form Γ such that $M \models \neg\Gamma$. If a conflict is detected at decision level 0, then the $dpll$ algorithm reports unsatisfiability. If no conflict is detected, then a literal that is unassigned in M is selected using the $select(M, K)$ operation and added to the partial assignment. The procedure is then invoked at level $h + 1$.

$$propagate(M, K, C) := propagate(\langle M, l[\Gamma]\rangle, K, C), \text{ where} \qquad (unit)$$
$$\Gamma \in K \cup C,$$
$$\Gamma \equiv l \vee l_1 \vee \ldots \vee l_n,$$
$$M \not\models l,$$
$$M \models \neg l_i \wedge \ldots \wedge \neg l_n$$
$$propagate(M, K, C) := \bot[\Gamma], \text{ where} \qquad (conflict)$$
$$\text{if } \Gamma \in K \cup C : M \models \neg\Gamma$$
$$propagate(M, K, C) := M, \text{ where} \qquad (terminate)$$
$$\text{for each } \Gamma \in K \cup C,$$
$$M \models \Gamma \text{ or}$$
$$\Gamma \equiv l \vee l' \vee \Gamma', \text{ and } l, l' \notin dom(M)$$

Fig. 2. DPLL Propagation

Otherwise, if clause Γ in $K \cup C$ is the source of the conflict, it can be analyzed by the $analyze(h, M, \Gamma)$ operation to construct a conflict clause that is added to C. Here, Γ is of the form $l_1 \vee \ldots \vee l_n$ where M contains $\neg l_i [\neg l_i \vee \Gamma_i]$, for $1 \leq i \leq n$. The analysis phase successively replaces Γ with the result of resolving Γ with each clause $\neg l_i \vee \Gamma_i$ for l_i occurring at level h until Γ contains a unique literal l at level h. Note that $M \models \neg\Gamma$ for each such clause Γ generated through analysis. Furthermore, the clause Γ contains at least one literal l such that $\neg l$ is assigned at level h since the conflict is detected at level h. The analysis process is iterated until there is a unique such literal l such that $M_h \models \neg l$. The clause $\Gamma' = analyze(h, M, \Gamma)$ constructed by the analysis phase is added as a conflict clause to C to obtain the new conflict clause set C'. Let $h' = L2(\Gamma')$ be the highest level below h such that there is a literal l' in Γ' with $M_{h'} \models \neg l'$. The unique literal l at level h in Γ' is implied by the partial assignment $M_{\overline{h'}}$ and Γ'.

The search is resumed with the state $\langle h', M_{\overline{h'}}, K, C'\rangle$. Though the partial assignment has shrunk, it now contains more implied literals at level h'. On the other hand, if no conflict is detected at level h, then an unassigned literal d is *selected* as the decision literal at level $h+1$, and the search is resumed with the state $\langle h+1, \langle M; d\rangle, K, C\rangle$. If no unassigned literals remain, then the algorithm terminates with a satisfying assignment M for K. Termination [NOT06,Sha05] follows since each step of propagation, backjumping (with propagation), or selection increases the quantity $\sum_{i=0}^{h} |M_i| * N^{(N-h)}$ towards the bound $N^{(N+1)}$ for $N = |vars(K)|$.

We have assumed that the propagation phase is complete, but the procedure works even when the propagation step is incomplete so that M_h need not contain all the literals that are implied by $M_0; \ldots; M_h$. Thus it is possible that M_j contains literals that are actually implied at some level i, with $i < j$. In this case, a conflict can still be traced to some level $\hat{h}$ below the current level h, and the $analyze$ operation can be modified to construct a conflict clause Γ that contains a unique literal at level $\hat{h}$.

The algorithm can either terminate with an assignment M satisfying the input clause set K, or with an unsatisfiability when a conflict is reported at the decision level 0. The SAT procedure can also generate a proof of unsatisfiability since a conflict at level 0 implies that some clause Γ in K when resolved with other clauses from $K \cup C$ yields a contradiction. The clauses in C are themselves derived by resolution.

step	h	M	K	C	Γ
select s	1	; s	K	$\emptyset$	-
select r	2	; s; r	K	$\emptyset$	-
propagate	2	; s; r, $\neg q[\neg q \vee \neg r]$	K	$\emptyset$	-
propagate	2	; s; r, $\neg q$, $p[p \vee q]$	K	$\emptyset$	-
conflict	2	; s; r, $\neg q$, p	K	$\emptyset$	$\neg p \vee q$
analyse	0	$\emptyset$	K	q	-
propagate	0	$q[q]$	K	q	-
propagate	0	q, $p[p \vee \neg q]$	K	q	-
propagate	0	q, p, $r[\neg p \vee r]$	K	q	-
conflict	0	q, p, r	K	q	$\neg q \vee \neg r$

Fig. 3. Example of the DPLL Satisfiability Procedure

Example 1. An example computation of the DPLL algorithm for demonstrating the unsatisfiability of the input K given by $\{p \vee q, \neg p \vee q, p \vee \neg q, s \vee \neg p \vee q, \neg s \vee p \vee \neg q, \neg p \vee r, \neg q \vee \neg r\}$. is shown in Figure 1. In this example, there are no unit input clauses. The partial assignment M_0 is therefore empty. The literal s is selected as the decision literal at level 1. Propagation does not yield any new implied literals at level 1. Then, literal r is selected as the decision literal at level 2. Now propagation adds the literals $\neg q$ and p, but then detects the conflict with clause $\neg p \vee q$. Analyzing this conflict, we obtain the conflict clause q which is added to C while backjumping to level 0. Now there is a unit clause q, and propagation adds the literals p and r to M_0 before detecting the conflict on the clause $\neg q \vee \neg r$. Since this conflict is at level 0, the input clause is judged to be unsatisfiable.

The proof of unsatisfiability for the example in Figure 1 can be constructed by resolution. The conflict clause q is proved by resolving $\neg p \vee q$ with $p \vee q$. The proof of unsatisfiability is constructed by resolving $\neg q \vee \neg r$ with $\neg p \vee r$ to obtain $\neg p \vee \neg q$ which is in turn resolved with $p \vee \neg q$ to obtain $\neg q$ which is resolved with the conflict clause q to derive $\bot$.

Given two clause sets K_1 and K_2 such that $K_1 \cup K_2$ is unsatisfiable, a *Craig interpolant* [Cra57] is a formula ϕ whose propositional variables appear in both K_1 and K_2 such that $K_1 \implies \phi$ and ϕ, K_2 is unsatisfiable. Interpolants are useful for a number of applications and can be extracted from proofs of unsatisfiability [McM05]. The DPLL procedure can also be used for computing the disjunctive normal form (DNF) or Binary Decision Diagram (BDD) representation corresponding to all satisfying assignments for a formula. The DPLL procedure can also be used to construct a minimal unsatisfiable core of clauses from the input and a maximal subset of the input clauses that is satisfiable. Pseudo-Boolean constraints are of the form $\sum_{i=1}^{n} c_i * p_i \geq N$, where for $1 \leq i \leq n$, c_i is an integer constant, N is an integer constant, and $c_i * p_i$ equals c_i if p_i, and 0, otherwise. The conjunction of a clause set K together with pseudo-Boolean constraints can also be solved.

SAT solving can be used to solve constraints over finite domains involving planning and scheduling, and in the verification of finite-state hardware and software systems. Key ideas in the development of efficient SAT solvers originate from SATO [Zha97],

GRASP [MSS99], and Chaff [MMZ$^+$01]. Efficient implementations of SAT algorithms include ZChaff [ZM02,Zha03], Berkmin [GN02], Siege [Rya04], and MiniSAT [ES03].

4   Theory Constraint Solving

We now examine satisfiability in first-order theories. These theories can be presented axiomatically or as a class of first-order structures. We define a theory over a signature Σ as a class of first-order structures closed under isomorphism and variable reassignment. The current section will examine the clausal validity problem (CVP) of determining if a clause $l_1 \vee \ldots \vee l_n$ is valid, or equivalently, if the conjunction $\neg l_1 \wedge \ldots \wedge \neg l_n$ is satisfiable. For SMT applications, it is important that these procedures support the incremental assertion of literals, efficient backtracking, and the production of explanations in the form of the subset of input literals needed for unsatisfiability.

4.1   Equivalence

CVP for an equivalence relation given by axioms for reflexivity, symmetry, and transitivity can be solved using the union-find algorithm. The input literals are equalities and disequalities between variables. The algorithm maintains two data structures: a mapping F on the variables in the input and a set of input disequalities D. The *find structure* F must be acyclic so that for any $n > 0$ and variable x, either $F(x) = x$ or $F^n(x) \neq x$. The operation $F^*(x)$ can be defined to return the *canonical* representative of the equivalence class containing x. The operation $union(F)(x, y)$ is used to construct the find structure in which the equivalence classes of x and y are merged. It assumes a total ordering $\prec$ on the variables.

$$union(F)(x, y) = \begin{cases} F[x' := y'], y' \prec x' \\ F[y' := x'], otherwise \end{cases}$$
$$\text{where } x' \equiv F^*(x) \not\equiv F^*(y) \equiv y'$$

The *addeqlit* procedure shown in Figure 4 takes as input a literal l (an equality or disequality), the find structure F, and the disequality set D. Initially $F(x) = x$ for each variable x, and D is empty. The operation $addeqlit(l, F, D)$ updates the *state* $\langle F, D \rangle$ with the constraint given by the literal l.

There are many variations on this basic theme that involve path compression and tree-weight directed union which together yield the near-linear $O((m + n) * \alpha(n))$ complexity for m union/find operations over n variables [GF64,Tar75]. The algorithm can also be augmented to maintain proofs in the form of transitivity chains and to support efficient retraction [dMRS04,NO05]. The algorithm can be applied to equivalence relations other than equality.

4.2   Congruence Closure

The free theory $\Phi(\Sigma)$ over a signature Σ is the first-order theory with an empty set of non-logical axioms. Equality is treated as a logical symbol with the axioms of reflexivity, symmetry, transitivity, and congruence. Note that the equivalence theory above is

$$addeqlit(x = y, F, D) := \langle F, D \rangle, \text{ if} \qquad (skip)$$
$$F^*(x) \equiv F^*(y)$$

$$addeqlit(x = y, F, D) := \begin{cases} \bot, \text{ if } F'^*(u) \equiv F'^*(v) \text{ for some } u \neq v \in D \\ \langle F', D \rangle, \text{ otherwise} \end{cases} \qquad (union)$$
where
$$x' = F^*(x) \not\equiv F^*(y) = y',$$
$$F' = union(F)(x, y),$$
$$addeqlit(x \neq y, F, D) := \bot, \text{ if } F^*(x) \equiv F^*(y) \qquad (contrad)$$
$$addeqlit(x \neq y, F, D) := \langle F, D \rangle, \text{ if } F^*(x) \equiv F^*(x'), F^*(y) \equiv F^*(y'), \quad (skipdiseq)$$
$$\text{for } x' \neq y' \in D$$
$$addeqlit(x \neq y, F, D) := \langle F, \{x \neq y\} \cup D \rangle, \text{ otherwise.} \qquad (adddiseq)$$

Fig. 4. Adding an Equality to a Union-Find Structure

just the free theory $\Phi(\emptyset)$ over an empty signature. CVP for $\Phi(\Sigma)$ requires the extension of the union–find procedure to the computation of the congruence closure [Koz77,Sho78]. Bachmair, Tiwari, and Vigneron [BTV03] give an elegant presentation of congruence closure in the form of inference rules. Our presentation is closer to a typical implementation.

A congruence relation extends equivalence with the rule that for each n-ary function f, $f(s_1, \ldots, s_n) = f(t_1, \ldots, t_n)$ if $s_i = t_i$ for each $1 \leq i \leq n$. The operation $congruent(F, s, t)$ checks if $s \equiv f(s_1, \ldots, s_n)$, $t \equiv f(t_1, \ldots, t_n)$ such that $F^*(s_i) \equiv F^*(t_i)$ for $1 \leq i \leq n$. The term universe T which includes every term in the CVP is assumed to be given. Any subterm of a term in T is also a member of T. For any term t in T, $\pi(t)$ returns the set of terms t' in T of the form $f(t_1, \ldots, t_n)$ such that for some i, $1 \leq i \leq n$, $t \equiv t_i$. The congruence closure operation for closing a find structure under congruence is shown in Figure 5.

$$close(F, D, Q, \pi) := close(F', D, Q', \pi), \qquad (congruence)$$
$$\text{when } s, t : s = t \in Q, F^*(s) \not\equiv F^*(t),$$
$$congruent(F, s, t)$$
$$\langle F', D, \pi' \rangle = addeqlit(s = t, F, D, Q, \pi),$$
$$Q' = Q \cup \{s' = t' \mid \begin{matrix} s' \in \pi(s), t' \in \pi(t), \\ congruent(F', s', t') \end{matrix}\}$$
$$close(F, D, Q, \pi) := \langle F, D, \pi \rangle, \text{ otherwise.} \qquad (terminate)$$

Fig. 5. Congruence Closure

The $addeqlit$ operation can be modified to make use of $close$, and the only relevant case of this definition is shown below.

$$addeqlit(s = t, F, D, \pi) := \begin{cases} \bot, \text{ if } F'(u) \equiv F'(v) \text{ for some } u \neq v \in D \\ close(F', D, \emptyset, \pi), \text{ otherwise} \end{cases}$$
where
$$s' = F^*(s), t' = F^*(t), s' \not\equiv t',$$
$$s' \prec t', F' = F[t' := s'], \pi' = \pi[s' := \pi(s') \cup \pi(t')]$$

The *Ackermann reduction* is a simple alternative to congruence closure. It works by reducing congruence to equivalence by successively replacing each term $f(\overline{x})$ in the given formula ψ with a fresh variable $x_{f(\overline{x})}$ to obtain ψ'. The satisfiability of ψ is equivalent to that of $\psi' \wedge \bigwedge \{x_1 \neq y_1 \vee \ldots \vee x_n \neq y_n \vee x_{f(\overline{x})} = x_{f(\overline{y})} \mid x_{f(\overline{x})}, y_{f(\overline{x})} \in vars(\psi')\}$, and the latter formula is in $\Phi(\emptyset)$.

4.3 Difference Arithmetic

Difference arithmetic (DA) deals with arithmetic constraints of the form $x - y \leq c$, where c is an integer constant. Equality constraints $x = y$ can be expressed as $x - y \leq 0 \wedge y - x \leq 0$. Strict inequalities can also be captured so that $x - y < c$ is just $x - y \leq c - 1$, and the negation of $x - y \leq c$ is just $y - x \leq -c - 1$. By introducing a special variable x_0 representing 0, we can also express unary constraints of the form $x \leq c$ as $x - x_0 \leq c$ and $x \geq c$ as $x_0 - x \leq -c$.

A conjunction of such constraints is satisfiable if there is an assignment ρ of integers to the variables such that for each inequality $x - y \leq c$, the integer difference $\rho(x) - \rho(y)$ evaluates to a value that is at most c.

Difference constraints can be modeled by means of a weighted directed graph with the variables as vertices with an edge of weight c from y to c corresponding to each constraint $x - y \leq c$. The Bellman–Ford algorithm can be employed in an incremental form to find an integer assignment, when one exists, for the variables satisfying the constraints. If there is a negative-weight cycle of edges such that $x - x_1 \leq c_1, x_1 - x_2 \leq c_2, \ldots x_n - x \leq c_n$, where $\sum_{i=1}^{n} c_n < 0$, then the constraints are unsatisfiable since there is no assignment to x or the other variables in the cycle that would satisfy the chaining of these inequalities.

The procedure maintains a variable assignment ρ so that it satisfies the inequality constraints processed, and an edge map E such that for each vertex y, $E(y)$ is a set of pairs $\langle x, c \rangle$ such that $x - y \leq c$ is a constraint that has been processed. Initially, the assignment ρ can be arbitrary, and the edge map E is empty. The $addineq(x, y, c, \rho, E)$ operation adds a constraint $x - y \leq c$ to $\langle \rho, E \rangle$.

$$addineq(x, y, c, \rho, E) := \langle \rho, E[y := E(y) \cup \{\langle x, c \rangle\}] \rangle, \text{ if}$$
$$\rho(x) - \rho(y) \leq c$$
$$addineq(x, y, c, \rho, E) := \begin{cases} \bot, \text{ if } \rho'' = \bot \\ \langle \rho'', E' \rangle, \text{ otherwise} \end{cases}$$
$$\text{where } \rho(x) - \rho(y) > c$$
$$\rho' = \rho[x := \rho(y) + c]$$
$$E' = E[y := E(y) \cup \{\langle x, c \rangle\}],$$
$$\rho'' = relaxv(y, \rho', E', \{x\})$$

The operation $relaxv(y, \rho, E, Q)$ is defined to *relax* each edge $\langle x, z \rangle$ by ensuring that $\rho(z) - \rho(x) \leq c$ for $\langle z, c \rangle \in E(x)$. If the vertex y itself appears in the queue of vertices to be processed, then a negative weight cycle is signaled.

$relaxv(y, \rho, E, \emptyset) := \rho$

$relaxv(y, \rho, E, Q) := \bot$, if $y \in Q$

$relaxv(y, \rho, E, Q) := relaxv(y, \rho', E, Q')$, where

$$\langle \rho', Q' \rangle = relax(x, \rho, Q), \text{ for } x \in Q$$

$relax(x, \rho, Q) := \langle \rho', Q' \rangle$, where

$$Q' = (Q - \{x\}) \cup \{z \mid \langle z, c \rangle \in E(x), \rho(z) - \rho(x) > c\}$$
$$\rho' = \rho \circ [z \mapsto \rho(x) + c \mid \langle z, c \rangle \in E(x), \rho(z) - \rho(x) > c]$$

The above incremental procedure is based on the incremental Bellman–Ford algorithm of Wang, Ivančić, Ganai, and Gupta [WIGG05]. Cherkassky and Goldberg [CG96] give a survey of negative-weight cycle detection algorithms.

4.4 Linear Arithmetic

Linear arithmetic (LA) constraints have the form $c_0 + \sum_{i=1}^{n} c_i * x_i \leq 0$, where each c_i, for $0 \leq i \leq n$ is a rational constant, and the variables x_i range over the reals. The LA solver described below is based on the method of de Moura and Dutertre [DdM06a]. This method is often faster than the Bellman–Ford procedure on difference arithmetic constraints, and supports an efficient but incomplete check for unsatisfiability that is useful in an SMT solver.

The input to the procedure is

- A set of n real-valued variables $x_1, \ldots, x_n$
- A set of m linear equalities (where $m \leq n$)

$$a_{11}x_1 + \ldots + a_{1n}x_n = 0$$
$$\vdots$$
$$a_{m1}x_1 + \ldots + a_{mn}x_n = 0$$

  written in matrix form, $Ax = 0$.
- Bounds on all variables: $l_i \leq x_i \leq u_i$ where l_i is either $-\infty$ or a rational number, and u_i is either $+\infty$ or a rational number.

The goal is to determine whether there is x such that $Ax = 0$ and $l_i \leq x_i \leq u_i$ for $i = 1, \ldots, n$ (i.e., whether the constraints are satisfiable).

The solver maintains a *tableau* and an *assignment*.

- The tableau is defined by dividing the variables into a set B of m basic variables and a set N of $n - m$ non-basic variables, then rewriting the constraints $Ax = 0$ as follows:

$$x_{i_1} = \sum_{x_j \in N} b_{1j}x_j$$
$$\vdots$$
$$x_{i_m} = \sum_{x_j \in N} b_{mj}x_j$$

where $x_{i_1}, \ldots, x_{i_m}$ are the basic variables.

- The assignment β assigns a rational value $\beta(x_i)$ to every variable x_i, such that
  - For all non-basic variable x_j, we have $l_j \leq \beta(x_j) \leq u_j$.
  - For all basic variable x_{i_k}, we have

$$\beta(x_{i_k}) = \sum_{x_j \in N} b_{kj}\beta(x_j).$$

If β also satisfies the bounds on basic variables, namely,

$$l_{i_k} \leq \beta(x_{i_k}) \leq u_{i_k}$$

for $k = 1, \ldots, n$ then the constraints are satisfiable and $\beta(x_1)...\beta(x_n)$ is a feasible solution. Otherwise, if there is a basic variable x_{i_k} with $\beta(x_{i_k}) < l_{i_k}$, then a pivoting step is used to swap it with a non-basic variable x_j such that $b_{kj} > 0$ and $x_j < u_j$ or $b_{kj} < 0$ and $x_j > l_j$, and symmetrically when $\beta(x_{i_k}) > u_{i_k}$.

$A_0 = \begin{cases} s_1 = -x + y \\ s_2 = x + y \end{cases}$			$\beta_0 = (x \mapsto 0, y \mapsto 0, s_1 \mapsto 0, s_2 \mapsto 0)$
$A_1 = A_0$		$x \quad \leq -4$	$\beta_1 = (x \mapsto -4, y \mapsto 0, s_1 \mapsto 4, s_2 \mapsto -4)$
$A_2 = A_1$	$-8 \leq$	$x \quad \leq -4$	$\beta_2 = \beta_1$
$A_3 = \begin{cases} y = x + s_1 \\ s_2 = 2x + s_1 \end{cases}$	$-8 \leq$	$x \quad \leq -4$ $s_1 \quad \leq 1$	$\beta_3 = (x \mapsto -4, y \mapsto -3, s_1 \mapsto 1, s_2 \mapsto -7)$

Fig. 6. Example

Figure 6 illustrates the algorithm on a small example. Each row represents a state. The columns contain the tableaux, bounds, and assignments. The first row contains the initial state. Suppose $x \leq -4$ is asserted. Then the value of x must be adjusted, since $\beta_0(x) > -4$. Since s_1 and s_2 depend on x, their values are also modified. No pivoting is required since the basic variables do not have bounds, so $A_1 = A_0$. Next, $x \geq -8$ is asserted. Since $\beta_1(x)$ satisfies this bound, nothing changes: $A_2 = A_1$ and $\beta_2 = \beta_1$. Next, $s_1 \leq 1$ is asserted. The current value of s_1 does not satisfy this bound, so s_1 is pivoted with y to decrease s_1. The resulting state S_3 is shown in the last row; all constraints are satisfied.

If $s_2 \geq -3$ is asserted in S_3 then an inconsistency is detected: Tableau A_2 does not allow s_2 to increase since both x and s_1 are at their upper bound. Therefore, $s_2 \geq -3$ is inconsistent with state S_3.

5   Combining Theories

We have shown solutions to the CVP problem for individual theories such as linear arithmetic and the theory of equality over uninterpreted terms. Many natural constraint solving problems contain symbols from multiple theories. Given two theories T_1 and T_2

over signatures Σ_1 and Σ_2, the union theory $T_1 + T_2$ is the class of Σ-structures, with $\Sigma = \Sigma_1 \cup \Sigma_2$ whose projection to Σ_i is a T_i-model, for $i = 1, 2$. The easiest case to consider is when Σ_1 and Σ_2 are disjoint. The Nelson–Oppen procedure [NO79] gives a method for composing CVP-solvers for T_1 and T_2 into one for $T_1 + T_2$. For example, T_1 the free theory $\Phi(\Sigma_1)$ over a signature Σ and T_2 is the difference arithmetic theory DA.

A quantifier-free Σ-formula ψ can be *purified* so that each literal in the formula is a Σ_i-literal for $i = 1, 2$. Let $\psi[t := s]$ be the result of replacing each occurrence of t in ψ by s. A *pure* Σ_i-term, for $i = 1, 2$, is a Σ_i-term that is not a variable.

$$purify(\psi, R) := purify(\psi[t := x], R \cup \{x = t\}),$$

$$\text{for fresh } x,$$

$$\text{pure } \Sigma_i\text{-term } t \text{ in } \psi, i = 1, 2$$

$$purify(\psi, R) := (\bigwedge R) \wedge \psi, \text{ otherwise.}$$

The main point of purification is that if $purify(\psi, \emptyset) = \psi'$, then ψ and ψ' are equi-satisfiable and each literal in ψ' is a Σ_1-literal or a Σ_2-literal.

A *partition* Π on a set of variables γ is a disjoint collection subsets $\gamma_1, \ldots, \gamma_n$ such that $\bigcup_{i=1}^n \gamma_i = \gamma$. Given a partition Π of the form $\gamma_1, \ldots, \gamma_n$, an arrangement A_Π is a union of the set of equalities $\{x = y \mid \text{ for some } i : x, y \in \gamma_i\}$ and the set of disequalities $\{x \neq y \mid \text{ for some } i, j : i \neq j, x \in \gamma_i, y \in \gamma_j\}$.

A Boolean implicant P for a quantifier-free Σ-formula ψ containing the set of literals L is a subset of literals in L such that $\bigwedge P \implies \psi$ in propositional logic. The formula ψ is T-satisfiable if there is an Boolean implicant P of ψ that is T-satisfiable. If $T = T_1 \cup T_2$ for Σ_1-theory T_1 and Σ_2-theory T_2, with $\Sigma_1 \cap \Sigma_2 = \emptyset$, and $P = P_1 \cup P_2$, where each P_i consists of Σ_i-literals and $\gamma = vars(P_1) \cap vars(P_2)$, then P is T-satisfiable if there is an arrangement A_Π of γ such that each $P_i \cup A_\Pi$ is T_i-satisfiable. For this joint satisfiability result to hold, the theories T_1 and T_2 must be stably infinite [Opp80], i.e., if a formula is T_i-satisfiable, it must be satisfiable in a countable model.

We now show how the T-satisfiability of a quantifier-free Σ-formula can be solved by an extension of the *dpll* procedure.

6   Satisfiability Modulo Theories

The extension of the *dpll* satisfiability procedure to T-satisfiability of quantifier-free Σ-formulas employs an oracle for T-satisfiability of implicants. This procedure adds a context S for the incrementally updated state of the theory solver. We assume that there is a procedure $assert(l[\Gamma], S)$ that adds a literal implied by S and the clause $\Gamma \in K \cup C$ to the state S. When the added literal l is a decision literal, we indicate the absence of an implying clause by $l[]$. This procedure need not be complete with respect to detecting unsatisfiability, so we have a complete procedure $check(S)$ which checks if the state S is satisfiable. We also have a third procedure $ask(l, S)$ which is an incomplete test for determining if the result of adding l to state S is unsatisfiable. We assume that all three procedures when they return $\bot$ also return an explanation clause Γ' of the form $l_1 \vee \ldots \vee l_n$ such that $\neg l_i$ is an input literal. We assume that the state S is check-pointed

$$tdpll(K) := tdpllr(0, \emptyset, \emptyset, K, \emptyset) \qquad\qquad (tinit)$$
$$tdpllr(0, M, S, K, C) := \bot, \text{ where} \qquad\qquad (tcontrad)$$
$$\qquad scanprop(M, S, K, C) = \bot[\Gamma]$$
$$tdpllr(h + 1, M, S, K, C) := tdpllr(h', M, S_{\overline{h'}}, K, C'), \text{ where} \qquad (tbackjump)$$
$$\qquad scanprop(M, S, K, C) = \bot[\Gamma],$$
$$\qquad tanalyze(h + 1, M, \Gamma) = \Gamma',$$
$$\qquad C' = C \cup \{\Gamma'\},$$
$$\qquad h' = L2(\Gamma')$$
$$tdpllr(h, M, S, K, C) := tdpllr(h + 1, M', S'', K, C), \text{ where} \qquad (tsplit)$$
$$\qquad \langle M', S' \rangle = scanprop(M, S, K, C) \neq \bot,$$
$$\qquad l = tselect(M, S, K) \neq \bot,$$
$$\qquad S'' = assert(l[], S')$$
$$tdpllr(h, M, S, K, C) := \begin{cases} S', \text{ if } check(S') \neq \bot \\ tdpllr(h', M, S_{h'}, K, C'), \text{ where} \\ \quad check(S') = \bot[\Gamma], \\ \quad h' = L2(\Gamma), \ C' = C \cup \{\Gamma\} \end{cases} \qquad (tcheck)$$
$$\qquad \text{with } S' = scanprop(M, S, K, C) \neq \bot,$$
$$\qquad tselect(M, S', K) = \bot$$

Fig. 7. DPLL Search for Satisfiability Modulo Theories

at each level so that S_i represents the state at level i including all the input assertions up to that point.

With these, we can modify the *dpll* procedure from Section 3 as shown in Figure 7. The main difference from *dpll* is that the selected literal is asserted to the context S and the complete *check* procedure is used to check for $\mathcal{T}$-satisfiability of the context S when there are no splitting literals left. The procedure of literal selection *tselect* can be identical to *select*. The theory propagation procedure *scanprop* is defined below. It first identifies some of the literals l such that l or $\neg l$ appears in K that are entailed by the context S.

$$scanprop(M, S, K, C) := tpropagate(M', S, K, C'), \text{ where}$$
$$\qquad\qquad \langle M', C' \rangle = scanlits(M, S, K, C)$$
$$scanlits(M, S, K, C) := \langle M', C' \rangle, \text{ where}$$
$$\qquad\qquad M' = M \circ \langle l \in lits(K) - lits(M) \mid ask(\neg l, S) = \bot[\Gamma] \rangle,$$
$$\qquad\qquad C' = C \cup \{\Gamma \mid \exists l \in lits(K) - lits(M) : ask(\neg l, S) = \bot[\Gamma]\}$$

The *tpropagate* procedure is adapted from the *propagate* procedure from Section 3 and shown in Figure 8. The literals that are added to M are also asserted to the context S.

Methods combining DPLL SAT solving with theory constraint solving were introduced in CVC [BDS02], ICS [dMRS02], and Verifun [FJOS03], and Nieuwenhuis, Oliveras, and Tinelli [NOT06] give a rigorous and abstract presentation of this combination.

$$tpropagate(M, S, K, C) := \begin{cases} \bot[\Gamma], \text{ if } S' = \bot[\Gamma] \\ tpropagate(\langle M, l[\Gamma]\rangle, S', K, C), \text{ otherwise} \end{cases} \quad (tunit)$$

$$\begin{aligned} &\text{where} \\ &\quad \Gamma \in K \cup C, \\ &\quad \Gamma \equiv l \vee l_1 \vee \ldots \vee l_n, \\ &\quad M \not\models l, \\ &\quad M \models \neg l_i \wedge \ldots \wedge \neg l_n \\ &\quad S' = assert(l, S) \end{aligned}$$

$$tpropagate(M, S, K, C) := \bot[\Gamma], \text{ where} \quad\quad (tconflict)$$
$$\text{if } \Gamma \in K \cup C : M \models \neg\Gamma$$

$$tpropagate(M, S, K, C) := \langle M, S\rangle, \text{ where} \quad\quad (tterminate)$$
$$\begin{aligned} &\text{for each } \Gamma \in K \cup C, \\ &M \models \Gamma \text{ or} \\ &\Gamma \equiv l \vee l' \vee \Gamma', \text{ and } l, l' \notin dom(M) \end{aligned}$$

Fig. 8. Theory Propagation

7   E-Graph Matching

Most SMT solvers incorporate quantifier reasoning using *matching* over E-graphs (i.e., *E-matching*) [Nel81,DNS03]. An E-graph data-structure is the find structure F maintained in Section 4.2. Each equivalence class containing a term t has a canonical representative $F^*(t)$. Let $class(t)$ denotes the equivalence class that contains t, i.e., $\{s \mid F^*(s) = F^*(t)\}$.

Semantically, the formula $\forall x_1, \ldots, x_n.\psi$ is equivalent to the infinite conjunction $\bigwedge_\beta \beta(F)$ where β ranges over all substitutions over the $\bar{x}$. In practice, solvers use heuristics to select from this infinite conjunction those instances that are "relevant" to the conjecture. The key idea is to treat an instance $\beta(\psi)$ as relevant whenever it contains enough terms that are represented in the current E-graph. That is, non-ground terms t_p from ψ are selected as *patterns*, and $\beta(\psi)$ is considered relevant whenever $\beta(t_p)$ is in the E-graph.

An abstract version of the *E-matching* algorithm is shown in Fig. 9. The set of relevant substitutions for a pattern p can be obtained by taking $\bigcup_{t \in E} match(t_p, t, \emptyset)$. The abstract matching procedure returns all substitutions that E-match a pattern t_p with term t. That is, if $\beta \in match(t_p, t, \emptyset)$ then $U \cup \beta \models t_p = t$, and conversely, if $U \cup \beta \models t_p = t$, then there is a β' congruent to β such that $\beta' \in match(t_p, t, \emptyset)$.

$$\begin{aligned} match(x, t, \mathcal{S}) &:= \{\beta \cup \{x \mapsto t\} \mid \beta \in \mathcal{S}, x \notin dom(\beta)\} \cup \\ &\quad\quad \{\beta \mid \beta \in \mathcal{S}, F^*(\beta(x)) = F^*(t)\} \\ match(c, t, \mathcal{S}) &:= \mathcal{S} \text{ if } c \in class(t) \\ match(c, t, \mathcal{S}) &:= \emptyset \text{ if } c \notin class(t) \\ match(f(p_1, \ldots, p_n), t, \mathcal{S}) &= \bigcup_{f(t_1, \ldots, t_n) \in class(t)} match(p_n, t_n, \ldots, match(p_1, t_1, \mathcal{S})) \end{aligned}$$

Fig. 9. E-matching (abstract) algorithm

8   Conclusions

Satisfiability is the process of finding an assignment of values to variables given some constraints on these variables, or explaining why the constraints have no solution. Many computational problems are instances of satisfiability. For this reason, it is important to have efficient solvers for Boolean constraints, constraints over finite domains, constraints in specific theories, and constraints in combinations of theories. SMT solving is an active and exciting area of research with many practical applications. We have presented some of the basic algorithms, but a real implementation requires careful attention to a large number of implementation details and heuristics that we have not covered.

SAT and SMT solving technologies are already making a profound impact on a number of application areas. The theoretical challenges include better representations and algorithms, efficient methods for combining theories and for quantifier reasoning, and various extensions to the basic search method. A lot of experimental work also remains to be done on the careful evaluation of different algorithms and heuristics. In the next few years, satisfiability is likely to become the core engine underlying a wide range of powerful technologies.

References

BDS02.   Barrett, C.W., Dill, D.L., Stump, A.: Checking satisfiability of first-order formulas by incremental translation to SAT. In: Brinksma, E., Larsen, K.G. (eds.) CAV 2002. LNCS, vol. 2404, Springer, Heidelberg (2002)

BTV03.   Bachmair, L., Tiwari, A., Vigneron, L.: Abstract congruence closure. Journal of Automated Reasoning 31(2), 129–168 (2003)

CG96.   Cherkassky, B.V., Goldberg, A.V.: Negative-cycle detection algorithms. In: European Symposium on Algorithms, pp. 349–363 (1996)

Cra57.   Craig, W.: Three uses of the Herbrand-Gentzen theorem in relating model theory and proof theory. Journal of Symbolic Logic 22(3), 269–285 (1957)

DdM06a.   Dutertre, B., de Moura, L.: A fast linear-arithmetic solver for dpll(t). In: Ball, T., Jones, R.B. (eds.) CAV 2006. LNCS, vol. 4144, pp. 81–94. Springer, Heidelberg (2006)

DdM06b.   Dutertre, B., de. Moura, L.: The Yices SMT solver (2006)

DLL62.   Davis, M., Logemann, G., Loveland, D.: A machine program for theorem proving. Communications of the ACM 5(7), 394–397 (1962) Reprinted in Siekmann and WrightsonSiekmannWrightson83, pp. 267–270, (1983)

dMRS02.   de Moura, L., Rue, H., Sorea, M.: Lazy theorem proving for bounded model checking over infinite domains. In: Voronkov, A. (ed.) Automated Deduction - CADE-18. LNCS (LNAI), vol. 2392, pp. 438–455. Springer, Heidelberg (2002)

dMRS04.   de Moura, L., Rue\ss, H., Shankar, N.: Justifying equality. In: Proceedings of PDPAR '04 (2004)

DNS03.   Detlefs, D., Nelson, G., Saxe, J.B.: Simplify: A theorem prover for program checking. In: Technical Report HPL-2003-148, Hewlett-Packard Systems Research Center (2003)

DP60.   Davis, M., Putnam, H.: A computing procedure for quantification theory. JACM 7(3), 201–215 (1960)

ES03.   Eén, N., Sörensson, N.: An extensible SAT-solver. In: SAT 2003 (2003)

FJOS03.   Flanagan, C., Joshi, R., Ou, X., Saxe, J.B.: Theorem proving using lazy proof explication. In: Hunt Jr., W.A., Somenzi, F. (eds.) CAV 2003. LNCS, vol. 2725, pp. 355–367. Springer, Heidelberg (2003)

GF64.   Galler, B.A., Fisher, M.J.: An improved equivalence algorithm. Commun. ACM 7(5), 301–303 (1964)

GN02.   Goldberg, E., Novikov, Y.: Berkmin: A fast and robust sat solver (2002)

Koz77.   Kozen, D.: Complexity of finitely presented algebras. In: Conference Record of the Ninth Annual ACM Symposium on Theory of Computing, pp. 164–177, Boulder, Colorado (May 2–4 ,1977)

McM05.   McMillan, K.L.: An interpolating theorem prover. Theor. Comput. Sci. 345(1), 101–121 (2005)

MMZ⁺01.   Matthew, W., Moskewicz, C.F., Zhao, Y., Zhang, L., Malik, S.: Chaff: Engineering an Efficient SAT Solver. In: Proceedings of the 38th Design Automation Conference (DAC'01) (June 2001)

MSS99.   Marques-Silva, J., Sakallah, K.: GRASP: A search algorithm for propositional satisfiability. IEEE Transactions on Computers 48(5), 506–521 (1999)

Nel81.   Nelson, G.: Techniques for program verification. Technical Report CSL-81-10, Xerox Palo Alto Research Center, Palo Alto, Ca (1981)

NO79.   Nelson, G., Oppen, D.C.: Simplification by cooperating decision procedures. ACM Transactions on Programming Languages and Systems 1(2), 245–257 (1979)

NO05.   Nieuwenhuis, R., Oliveras, A.: Robert Nieuwenhuis and Albert Oliveras. In: Giesl, J. (ed.) RTA 2005. LNCS, vol. 3467, pp. 453–468. Springer, Heidelberg (2005)

NOT06.   Nieuwenhuis, R., Oliveras, A., Tinelli, C.: Solving SAT and SAT Modulo Theories: From an abstract Davis–Putnam–Logemann–Loveland procedure to DPLL(T). J. ACM 53(6), 937–977 (2006)

Opp80.   Derek, C.: Complexity, convexity and combinations of theories. Theoretical Computer Science 12, 291–302 (1980)

Rya04.   Ryan, L.: Efficient algorithms for clause-learning SAT solvers. Master's thesis, Simon Fraser University, M.Sc. Thesis (2004)

Sha05.   Shankar, N.: Inference systems for logical algorithms. In: Ramanujam, R., Sen, S. (eds.) FSTTCS 2005. LNCS, vol. 3821, pp. 60–78. Springer, Heidelberg (2005)

Sho78.   Shostak, R.: An algorithm for reasoning about equality. Comm. ACM 21, 583–585 (1978)

Sho79.   Shostak, R.: A practical decision procedure for arithmetic with function symbols. JACM 26(2), 351–360 (1979)

SKC96.   Selman, B., Kautz, H., Cohen, B.: Local search strategies for satisfiability testing. In: Johnson, D.S., Trick, M.A. (eds.) Cliques, Coloring, and Satisfiability: Second DIMACS Implementation Challenge, vol. 26 of DIMACS Series in Discrete Mathematics and Theoretical Computer Science. AMS (1996)

SW83.   Siekmann, J., Wrightson, G. (eds.): Automation of Reasoning: Classical Papers on Computational Logic, vol. 1 & 2. Springer, Heidelberg (1983)

Tar75.   Tarjan, R.E.: Efficiency of a good but not linear set union algorithm. J. ACM 22(2), 215–225 (1975)

WIGG05.   Wang, C., Ivančić, F., Ganai, M., Gupta, A.: Deciding separation logic formulae by SAT and incremental negative cycle elimination. In: Sutcliffe, G., Voronkov, A. (eds.) LPAR 2005. LNCS (LNAI), vol. 3835, pp. 322–336. Springer, Heidelberg (2005)

Zha97.   Zhang, H.: SATO: An efficient propositional prover. In: Conference on Automated Deduction, pp. 272–275 (1997)

Zha03.   Zhang, L.: Searching for Truth: Techniques for Satisfiability of Boolean Formulas. PhD thesis, Princeton University (2003)

ZM02.   Zhang, L., Malik, S.: The quest for efficient boolean satisfiability solvers. In: Voronkov, A. (ed.) Proceedings of CADE-19, Berlin, Germany, Springer, Heidelberg (2002)

A JML Tutorial:
Modular Specification and Verification of Functional Behavior for Java
(Invited Tutorial)

Gary T. Leavens[1], Joseph R. Kiniry[2], and Erik Poll[3]

[1] Dept. of Computer Science, Iowa State University, Ames, IA 50011 USA
leavens@cs.iastate.edu
[2] School of Computer Science and Informatics, University College Dublin,
Belfield, Dublin 4, Ireland
kiniry@acm.org
[3] Computing Science Department, Radboud University Nijmegen,
Toernooiveld 1, 6525 ED Nijmegen, The Netherlands
erikpoll@cs.ru.nl

JML, the Java Modeling Language, is the *lingua franca* of researchers working on specification and verification techniques and tools for Java. There are over 23 research groups worldwide working on various aspects of the JML project. These groups have built a large suite of tools for automated checking and verification (see http://jmlspecs.org).

This tutorial will present JML features useful for specifying the functional behavior of sequential Java classes and interfaces. Participants will get hands-on experience writing JML specifications for data types, including pre- and post-conditions, frames, invariants, history constraints, ghost and model fields, and specfication inheritance. They will also see how to verify object-oriented code using supertype abstraction for modular Hoare-style reasoning. Finally there will be an exchange of ideas on improving existing JML tools, open research problems, and future directions for research related to JML, including ways to connect JML to various theorem provers.

Acknowledgments. Thanks to all involved in JML. Leavens was funded in part by the US National Science Foundation under grant CCF-0429567. Kiniry and Poll were funded in part by the Information Society Technologies programme of the European Commission, Future and Emerging Technologies under the IST-2005-015905 MOBIUS project.

References

1. Leavens, G.T., Baker, A.L., Ruby, C.: Preliminary design of JML: A behavioral interface specification language for Java. ACM SIGSOFT Software Engineering Notes 31(3), 1–38 (2006)
2. Burdy, L., Cheon, Y., Cok, D.R., Ernst, M.D., Kiniry, J.R., Leavens, G.T., Leino, K.R.M., Poll, E.: An overview of JML tools and applications. International Journal on Software Tools for Technology Transfer 7(3), 212–232 (2005)

Verification of Hybrid Systems
(Invited Tutorial)

Martin Fränzle

Department Informatik
Carl von Ossietzky Universität Oldenburg
D-26111 Oldenburg, Germany
fraenzle@informatik.uni-oldenburg.de

Embedded digital systems have become ubiquitous in everyday life. Many such systems, including many of the safety-critical ones, operate within or comprise tightly coupled networks of both discrete-state and continuous-state components. The behavior of such *hybrid discrete-continuous systems* cannot be fully understood without explicitly modeling and analyzing the tight interaction of their discrete switching behavior and their continuous dynamics, as mutual feedback confines fully separate analysis to limited cases. Tools for building such integrated models and for simulating their approximate dynamics are commercially available, e.g. Simulink with the Stateflow extension[1]. Simulation is, however, inherently incomplete and has to be complemented by *verification*, which amounts to showing that the coupled dynamics of the embedded system and its environment is well-behaved, regardless of the actual disturbance and the influences of the application context, as entering through the open inputs of the system under investigation. Basic notions of being well-behaved demand that the system under investigation may never reach an undesirable state (*safety*), that it will converge to a certain set of states (*stabilization*), or that it can be guaranteed to eventually reach a desirable state (*progress*).

Within this tutorial, we concentrate on automatic verification and analysis of hybrid systems, with a focus on fully symbolic methods manipulating both the discrete and the continuous state components symbolically. We provide an introduction to hybrid discrete-continuous systems, demonstrate the use of predicative encodings for compactly encoding operational high-level models, and continue to a number of methods for automatically analyzing safety, stability, and progress. These methods entail semi-decision and approximation methods for dealing with the general undecidability and for improving scalability, corresponding data structures and decision diagrams, the use of advanced arithmetic constraint solvers for manipulating large and complex-structured Boolean combinations of undecidable arithmetic constraints, and the automatic generation of Lyapunov-like witness functions for stability and progress.

The tutorial in particular provides an overview over recent results of the Transregional Collaborative Research Center "Automatic Verification and Analysis of Complex Systems" (AVACS)[2] pertaining to hybrid systems.

---

[1] http://www.mathworks.com/products
[2] Supported by the German Research Foundation (DFG) under contract SFB/TR 14 AVACS, see www.avacs.org

W. Damm and H. Hermanns (Eds.): CAV 2007, LNCS 4590, p. 38, 2007.

SAT-Based Compositional Verification Using Lazy Learning*

Nishant Sinha and Edmund Clarke

Carnegie Mellon University, USA
{nishants,emc}@cs.cmu.edu

Abstract. A recent approach to automated assume-guarantee reasoning (AGR) for concurrent systems relies on computing environment assumptions for components using the L^* algorithm for learning regular languages. While this approach has been investigated extensively for message passing systems, it still remains a challenge to scale the technique to large shared memory systems, mainly because the assumptions have an exponential communication alphabet size. In this paper, we propose a SAT-based methodology that employs both induction and interpolation to implement automated AGR for shared memory systems. The method is based on a new *lazy* approach to assumption learning, which avoids an explicit enumeration of the exponential alphabet set during learning by using symbolic alphabet clustering and iterative counterexample-driven localized partitioning. Preliminary experimental results on benchmarks in Verilog and SMV are encouraging and show that the approach scales well in practice.

1 Introduction

Verification approaches based on compositional reasoning allow us to prove properties (or discover bugs) for large concurrent systems in a divide-and-conquer fashion. Assume-guarantee reasoning (AGR) [21, 18, 24] is a particular form of compositional verification, where we first generate environment assumptions for a component and discharge them on its environment (i.e., the other components). The primary bottleneck is that these approaches require us to manually provide appropriate environment assumptions. Recently, an approach [12] has been proposed to automatically generate these assumptions using learning algorithms for regular languages assisted by a model checker. Consider an AGR rule, called **NC**. This rule states that given finite state systems M_1, M_2 and P, the parallel composition $M_1 \parallel M_2$ satisfies P (written as $M_1 \parallel M_2 \vDash P$) iff there exists an *environment assumption* A for M_1 such that the composition of

* This research was sponsored by the National Science Foundation under grant nos. CNS-0411152, CCF-0429120, CCR-0121547, and CCR-0098072, the US Army Research Office under grant no. DAAD19-01-1-0485, the Office of Naval Research under grant no. N00014-01-1-0796, the Defense Advanced Research Projects Agency under subcontract no. SA423679952, the General Motors Corporation, and the Semiconductor Research Corporation grant no. TJ-1366.

W. Damm and H. Hermanns (Eds.): CAV 2007, LNCS 4590, pp. 39–54, 2007.

M_1 and A satisfies P ($M_1 \parallel A \vDash P$) and M_2 satisfies A ($M_2 \vDash A$). It is known that if M_1 and P are finite-state (their languages are regular), then a finite state assumption A exists. Therefore, the task of computing A is cast as a machine learning problem, where an algorithm for learning regular languages L^* [6, 26] is used to automatically compute A. The L^* *learner* computes a deterministic finite automaton (DFA) corresponding to an unknown regular language by asking queries to a *teacher* entity, which is capable of answering membership (whether a trace belongs to the desired assumption) and candidate (whether the current assumption hypothesis is correct) queries about the unknown language. Using these queries, the learner improves its hypothesis DFA using iterative state-partitioning (similar to the DFA minimization algorithms [17]) until the teacher replies that a given hypothesis is correct. In our context, a model checker plays the role of the teacher. It answers the queries by essentially checking the two premises of the rule **NC** with respect to the a given hypothesis A. While this approach is effective for small systems, there are a number of problems in making it scalable:

- *Efficient Teacher Implementation:* The teacher, i.e., the model checker, must be able to answer membership and candidate queries efficiently. More precisely, each query may itself involve exploration of a large state space making explicit-state model checking infeasible.
- *Alphabet explosion:* If M_1 and M_2 interact using a set X of global shared communication variables (referred to as a *shared memory system* subsequently), the alphabet of the assumption A consists of all the valuations of X and is exponential in size of X. The learning algorithm explicitly enumerates the alphabet set at each iteration and performs membership queries for enumeration step. Therefore, it is prohibitively expensive to apply L^* directly to shared memory systems with a large number of shared communication variables. Indeed, it is sometimes impossible to enumerate the full alphabet set, let alone learning an assumption hypothesis. We refer to this problem as the *alphabet explosion* problem.
- *System decomposition:* The natural decompositions of a system according to its modular syntactic description may not be suitable for compositional reasoning. Therefore, techniques for obtaining good decompositions automatically are required.

In this work we address the first two problems. More precisely, we propose (i) to efficiently implement the teacher using SAT-based model checking; and (ii) a *lazy* learning approach for mitigating the alphabet explosion problem. For an approach dealing with the third problem, see, for instance, the work in [22].

SAT-based Teacher. In order to allow the teacher to scale to larger models, we propose to implement it using a SAT-based symbolic model checker. In particular, we use SAT-based bounded model checking (BMC) [9] to process both membership and candidate queries. BMC is effective in processing membership queries, since they involve unrolling the system transition relation to a finite depth (corresponding to the given trace t) and require only a Boolean answer.

The candidate queries, instead, require performing unbounded model checking to show that there is no counterexample for any depth. Therefore, we employ complete variants of BMC to answer the candidate queries. In particular, we have implemented two different variants based on k-induction [27] and interpolation [20] respectively. Moreover, we use a SMT solver as the main decision procedure [29, 3].

Lazy Learning. The main contribution of our work is a *lazy* learning algorithm l^* which tries to ameliorate the alphabet explosion problem. The lazy approach avoids an expensive eager alphabet enumeration by *clustering* alphabet symbols and exploring transitions on these clusters symbolically. In other words, while the states of the assumption are explicit, each transition corresponds to a set of alphabet symbols, and is explored symbolically. The procedure for learning from a counterexample ce obtained from the teacher is different: besides partitioning the states of the previous hypothesis as in the L^* algorithm, the lazy algorithm may also partition an alphabet cluster (termed as *cluster-partitioning*) based on the analysis of the counterexample. Note that since our teacher uses a SAT-based symbolic model checker, it is easily able to answer queries for traces where each transition corresponds to a set of alphabet symbols. Moreover, this approach is able to avoid the quantifier elimination step (expensive with SAT) that is used to compute the transitions in earlier BDD-based approach to AGR [4]. We have developed several optimizations to l^*, including a SAT-based counterexample generalization technique that enables coarser cluster partitions.

Our hope, however, is that in real-life systems where compositional verification is useful, we will require only a few state and cluster partitions until we converge to an appropriate assumption hypothesis. Indeed if the final assumption has a small number of states and its alphabet set is large, then there must be a large number of transitions between each pair of states in the assumption which differ only on the alphabet label. Therefore, a small number of cluster partitions should be sufficient to distinguish the different outgoing clusters from each state. Experiments based on the earlier BDD-based approach to AGR [4, 22] as well as our approach have confirmed this expectation.

We have implemented our SAT-based compositional approach in a tool called SYMODA (stands for SYmbolic MODular Analyzer). The tool implements SAT-based model checking algorithms based on k-induction and interpolation together with the lazy learning algorithms presented in this paper. Preliminary experiments on Verilog and SMV examples show that our approach is effective as an alternative to the BDD-based approach in combating alphabet explosion and is able to outperform the latter on some examples.

Related Work. Compositional verification based on learning was proposed by Cobleigh et al. [12] in the context of rendezvous-based message passing systems and safety properties using explicit-state model checking. It has been extended to to shared memory systems using symbolic algorithms in [4, 22]. The problem of whether it is possible to obtain good decompositions of systems for this approach has been studied in [11]. An overview of other related work can be found in

[16, 22, 28]. SAT-based bounded model checking for LTL properties was proposed by Biere et al. [9] and several improvements, including techniques for making it complete have been proposed [25, 5]. All the previous approaches are non-compositional, i.e., they build the transition relation for the whole system. To the best of our knowledge, our work in the first to address automated compositional verification in the setting of SAT-based model checking.

The symbolic BDD-based AGR approach [4] for shared memory systems using automated system decomposition [22] is closely related to ours. The technique uses a BDD-based model checker and avoids alphabet explosion by using eager state-partitioning to introduce all possible new states in the next assumption, and by computing the transition relation (edges) using BDD-based quantifier elimination. In contrast, we use a SAT-based model checker and our lazy learning approach does not require a quantifier elimination step, which is expensive with SAT. Moreover, due to its eager state-partitioning, the BDD-based approach may introduce unnecessary states in the assumptions. Two other approaches to improve learning based on alphabet set underapproximation and iterative enlargement have been proposed [10, 16]. Our lazy approach is complementary and can learn assumptions effectively in cases where a small alphabet set is not sufficient. Further, it is possible to combine the previous approach with ours by removing variables from assumption alphabets and adding them back iteratively. Finally, a learning algorithm for parameterized systems (where the alphabet consists of a small set of basis symbols, each of which is parameterized by a set of boolean variables) was proposed in [8]. Our lazy algorithm, in contrast, performs queries over a set of traces using a SAT-based model checker and performs more efficient counterexample analysis.

2   Notation and Preliminaries

We define the notions of symbolic transition systems, automata, and composition which we will use in the rest of the paper. Our formalism borrows notation from [23, 19]. Let $X = \{x_1, \ldots, x_n\}$ be a finite set of typed variables defined over a non-empty finite domain of values $\mathcal{D}$. We define a *label* a as a total map from X to $\mathcal{D}$ which maps each variable x_i to value d_i. An X-*trace* ρ is a finite sequence of labels on X. The next-time label is $a' = a\langle X/X'\rangle$ is obtained from a by replacing each $x_i \in dom(a)$ by x_i'. Given variables X and the corresponding next-time variables X', let us denote the (finite) set of all predicates on $X \cup X'$ by Φ_X (TRUE and FALSE denote the boolean constants). Given labels a and b on X, we say that a label pair (a, b') satisfies a predicate $\phi \in \Phi_X$, denoted $\phi(a, b')$, if ϕ evaluates to TRUE under the variable assignment given by a and b'.

CFA. A *communicating finite automata* (CFA) C on a set of variables X (called the support set) is a tuple $\langle X, Q, q0, \delta, F\rangle$; Q denotes a finite set of states, $q0$ is the initial state, $\delta \subseteq Q \times \Phi_X \times Q$ is the transition relation and F is the set of final states. For states $q, q' \in Q$ and $\phi \in \Phi_X$, if $\delta(q, \phi, q')$ holds, then we say that ϕ is a transition predicate between q and q'. For each state q, we define its follow set $fol(q)$ to be the set of outgoing transition predicates, i.e.,

$fol(q) = \{\phi | \exists q' \in Q. \ \delta(q, \phi, q')\}$. We say that $fol(q)$ is complete iff $\bigvee\{\phi \in fol(q)\}$ = TRUE and disjoint iff for all $\phi_i, \phi_j \in fol(q)$, $\phi_i \wedge \phi_j =$ FALSE. Also, we say that δ is complete (deterministic) iff for each $q \in Q$, $fol(q)$ is complete (disjoint). The alphabet Σ of C is defined to be the set of label pairs (a, a') on variables X and X'. The above definition of transitions (on current and next-time variables) allows compact representation of CFAs and direct composition with STSs below.

A *run* of C is defined to be a sequence $(q_0, \ldots, q_n)$ of states in Q such that $q_0 = q0$. A run is said to be accepting if $q_n \in F$. Given a W-trace $(X \subseteq W)$, $\rho = a_0, \ldots, a_n$, is said to be a trace of C if there exists an accepting run $(q_0, \ldots, q_n)$ of C, such that for all $j < n$, there exists a predicate ϕ, such that $\delta(q_j, \phi, q_{j+1})$ and $\phi(a_j, a'_{j+1})$ holds. In other words, the labels a_j and a_{j+1} must satisfy some transition predicate between q_j and q_{j+1}. The W-trace language $\mathbb{L}_W(C)$ is the set of all W-traces of C. Note that this definition of W-trace allows a sequence of labels on X to be *extended* by all possible valuations of variables in $W \setminus X$ and eases the definition of the composition operation below. In general, we assume W is the universal set of variables and write $\mathbb{L}(C)$ to denote the language of C.

A CFA can be viewed as an ordinary finite automaton with alphabet Σ which accepts a regular language over Σ. While the states are represented explicitly, the *follow* function allows clustering a set of alphabet symbols into one transition symbolically. The common automata-theoretic operations, viz., union, intersection, complementation and determinization via subset-construction can be directly extended to CFAs. The complement of C is denoted by $\overline{C}$, where $\mathbb{L}(\overline{C})$ = $\overline{\mathbb{L}(C)}$. An illustration of a CFA is given in the extended version [28].

Symbolic Transition System. A *symbolic transition system* (STS) M is a tuple $\langle X, S, I, R, F \rangle$, defined over a set of variables X called its *support*, where S consists of all labels over X, $I(X)$ is the initial state predicate, $R(X, X')$ is the transition predicate and $F(X)$ is the final state predicate. Given a variable set W $(X \subseteq W)$, a W-trace $\rho = a_0, \ldots, a_n$ is said to be a trace of M if $I(a_0)$ and $F(a_n)$ hold and for all $j < n$, $R(a_j, a'_{j+1})$ holds. The trace language $\mathbb{L}(M)$ of M is the set of all traces of M.[1]

CFA as an STS. Given a CFA $C = \langle X_C, Q_C, q0_C, \delta_C, F_C \rangle$, there exists an STS $M = \langle X, S, I, R, F \rangle$ such that $\mathbb{L}(C) = \mathbb{L}(M)$. We construct M as follows: (i) $X = X_C \cup \{q\}$ where q is a fresh variable which ranges over Q_C, (ii) $I(X) = (q = q0)$, (iii) $F(X) = \exists q_i \in F_C.(q = q_i)$, and (iv) $R(X, X') =$
$(\exists q_1, q_2 \in Q_C, \phi \in \Phi. \ (q = q_1 \wedge q' = q_2 \wedge \delta_C(q_1, \phi, q_2) \wedge \phi(X_C, X'_C))$

Synchronous Composition of STSs. Suppose we are given two STSs $M_1 = \langle X_1, S_1, I_1, R_1, F_1 \rangle$ and $M_2 = \langle X_2, S_2, I_2, R_2, F_2 \rangle$. We define the composition $M_1 \parallel M_2$ to be a STS $M = \langle X, S, I, R, F \rangle$ where: (i) $X = X_1 \cup X_2$, (ii) S consists of all labels over X, (iii) $I = I_1 \wedge I_2$, (iv) $R = R_1 \wedge R_2$, and (v) $F = F_1 \wedge F_2$.

Lemma 1. *Given two STSs M_1 and M_2, $\mathbb{L}(M_1 \parallel M_2) = \mathbb{L}(M_1) \cap \mathbb{L}(M_2)$.*

---

[1] We overload the symbol $\mathbb{L}()$ to describe the trace language of both CFAs and STSs.

We use STSs to represent system components and CFA on shared variables to represent automata computed in the various AGR sub-tasks. We assume that all STSs have total transition predicates. We define the composition of an STS M with a CFA C, denoted by $M \parallel C$, to be $M \parallel M_C$, where M_C is the STS obtained from C. Although we use a synchronous notion of composition in this paper, our work can be directly extended to asynchronous composition also.

Definition 1 (Model Checking STSs). *Given an STS M and a property CFA P, the model checking question is to determine if $M \vDash P$ where $\vDash$ denotes a conformance relation. Using the trace semantics for STSs and CFAs and set containment as the conformance relation, the problem can be reduced to checking if $\mathbb{L}(M) \subseteq \mathbb{L}(P)$.*

Since CFAs are closed under negation and there is a language-equivalent STS for each CFA, we can further reduce the model checking question to checking if $\mathbb{L}(M \parallel M_{\overline{P}})$ is empty, where the STS $M_{\overline{P}}$ is obtained by complementing P to form $\overline{P}$ and then converting it into an STS. Let STS $\mathcal{M} = M \parallel M_{\overline{P}}$. In other words, we are interested in checking if there is an *accepting* trace in $\mathcal{M}$, i.e., a trace that ends in a state that satisfies $F_{\mathcal{M}}$.

2.1   SAT-Based Model Checking

It is possible to check for existence of an accepting trace in an STS $\mathcal{M}$ using satisfiability checking. A particular instance of this problem is bounded model checking [9] where we check for existence of an accepting trace of length k using a SAT solver.

Bounded Model Checking(BMC). Given an integer bound k, the BMC problem can be formulated in terms of checking satisfiability of the following formula [9]:

$$BMC(\mathcal{M}, k) := I_{\mathcal{M}}(s_0) \wedge \bigwedge_{0 \leq j \leq k-1} R_{\mathcal{M}}(s_j, s_{j+1}) \wedge \bigvee_{0 \leq j \leq k} F_{\mathcal{M}}(s_j) \qquad (1)$$

Here s_j ($0 \leq j \leq k$) represents the set of variables $X_{\mathcal{M}}$ at depth j. The transition relation of $\mathcal{M}$ is unfolded up to k steps, conjuncted with the initial and the final state predicates at the first and the last steps respectively, and finally encoded as a propositional formula that can be solved by a SAT solver. If the formula is SAT then the satisfying assignment corresponds to an accepting trace of length k (a counterexample to $M \vDash P$). Otherwise, no accepting trace exists of length k or less. It is possible to check for accepting traces of longer lengths by increasing k and checking iteratively.

Unbounded Model Checking(UMC). The unbounded model checking problem involves checking for an accepting trace of any length. Several SAT-based approaches have been proposed to solve this problem [25]. In this paper, we consider two approaches, one based on k-induction [27, 14, 15] and the other based on interpolation [20].

The k-induction technique [27] tries to show that there are no accepting traces of any length with the help of two SAT checks corresponding to the base and induction cases of the UMC problem. In the base case, it shows that no accepting trace of length k or less exists. This exactly corresponds to the BMC formula (Eq. 1) being UNSAT. In the induction step, it shows that if no accepting trace of length k or less exists, then there cannot be an accepting trace of length $k+1$ in $\mathcal{M}$, and is represented by the following formula:

$$Step(\mathcal{M}, k) := \bigwedge_{0 \leq j \leq k} R_{\mathcal{M}}(s_j, s_{j+1}) \wedge \bigwedge_{0 \leq j \leq k} \neg F_{\mathcal{M}}(s_j) \wedge F_{\mathcal{M}}(s_{k+1}) \wedge \bigwedge_{0 \leq i \leq j \leq k} s_i \neq s_{j+1}$$

$$(2)$$

The induction step succeeds if $Step(\mathcal{M}, k)$ is UNSAT. Otherwise, the depth k is increased iteratively until it succeeds or the base step is SAT (a counterexample is found). The set of constraints of form $s_i \neq s_{j+1}$ in (Eq. 2) (also known as simple path or uniqueness constraints) are necessary for completeness of the method and impose the condition that all states in the accepting trace must be unique. The method can be implemented efficiently using an incremental SAT solver [14], which allows reuse of recorded conflict clauses in the SAT solver across iterations of increasing depths. The k-induction technique has the drawback that it may require as many iterations as the length of the longest simple path between any two states in $\mathcal{M}$ (also known as recurrence diameter [9]), which may be exponentially larger than the longest of all the shortest paths (or the diameter) between any two states. Translating the above formulas to propositional logic may involve loss of structural information; we avoid it by using a SMT solver [29, 3, 28] as our main decision procedure.

Another approach to SAT-based UMC is based on using interpolants [20]. The method computes an over-approximation $\mathcal{I}$ of the reachable set of states in $\mathcal{M}$, which is also an inductive invariant for $\mathcal{M}$, by using the UNSAT proof of the BMC instance (Eq. 1). If $\mathcal{I}$ does not overlap with the set of final states, then it follows that there exists no accepting trace in $\mathcal{M}$. An important feature of this approach is that it does not require unfolding the transition relation beyond the diameter of the state space of $\mathcal{M}$, and, in practice, often succeeds with shorter unfoldings. We do not present the details of this approach here; they can be found in [20, 5].

3   Assume-Guarantee Reasoning Using Learning

Assume-Guarantee reasoning allows dividing the verification task of a system with multiple components into subtasks each involving a small number of components. AGR rules may be syntactically circular or non-circular in form. In this paper, we will be concerned mainly with the following non-circular AGR rule:

Definition 2. Non-circular AGR (NC) *Given STSs M_1, M_2 and CFA P, show that $M_1 \parallel M_2 \vDash P$, by picking an assumption CFA A, such that both* **(n1)** *$M_1 \parallel A \vDash P$ and* **(n2)** *$M_2 \vDash A$ hold.*

The **NC** rule is sound and complete [23, 4, 28] and can be extended to a system of n STSs $M_1 \ldots M_n$ by picking a set of assumptions $\langle A_1 \ldots A_{n-1} \rangle$ [12]. The proof of completeness of **NC** relies on the notion of weakest assumptions [2].

Lemma 2. (Weakest Assumptions) *Given a finite STS M with support set X_M and a CFA P with support set X_P, there exists a unique weakest assumption CFA, WA, such that (i) $M \parallel WA \vDash P$ holds, and (ii) for all CFA A where $M \parallel A \vDash P$, $\mathbb{L}(A) \subseteq \mathbb{L}(WA)$ holds. Moreover, $\mathbb{L}(WA)$ is regular and the support variable set of WA is $X_M \cup X_P$.*

As mentioned earlier (cf. Section 1), a learning algorithm for regular languages, L^*, assisted by a model checker based teacher, can be used to automatically generate the assumptions [12, 7]. However, there are problems in scaling this approach to large shared memory systems. Firstly, the teacher must be able to discharge the queries efficiently even if it involves exploring a large state space. Secondly, the alphabet Σ of an assumption A is exponential in its support set of variables. Since L^* explicitly enumerates Σ during learning, we need a technique to curb this alphabet explosion. We address these problems by proposing a SAT-based implementation of the teacher and a lazy algorithm based on alphabet clustering and iterative partitioning (Section 4).

3.1   SAT-Based Assume-Guarantee Reasoning

We now show how the teacher can be implemented using SAT-based model checking. The teacher needs to answer membership and candidate queries.

Membership Query. Given a trace t, we need to check if $t \in \mathbb{L}(WA)$ which corresponds to checking if $M_1 \parallel \{t\} \vDash P$ holds. To this end, we first convert t into a language-equivalent STS M_t, obtain $M = M_1 \parallel M_t$ and perform a single BMC check $BMC(M, k)$ (cf. Section 2.1) where k is the length of trace t. Note that since M_t accepts only at the depth k, we can remove the final state constraints at all depths except k. The teacher replies with a TRUE answer if the above formula instance is UNSAT; otherwise a FALSE answer is returned.

Candidate Query. Given a deterministic CFA A, the candidate query involves checking the two premises of **NC**, i.e., whether both $M_1 \parallel A \vDash P$ and $M_2 \vDash A$ hold. The latter check maps to SAT-based UMC (cf. Section 2.1) in a straightforward way. Note that since A is deterministic, complementation does not involve a blowup. For the previous check, we first obtain an STS $M = M_1 \parallel M_A$ where the STS M_A is language-equivalent to A (cf. Section 2) and then use SAT-based UMC for checking $M \vDash P$.

In our implementation, we employ both induction and interpolation for SAT-based UMC. Although the interpolation approach requires a small number of iterations, computing interpolants, in many cases, takes more time in our implementation. The induction-based approach, in contrast, is faster if it converges

---

[2] Although we focus our presentation on **NC** rule, our results can be applied to a circular rule **C** presented in literature [7, 22] in a straightforward way. We implement and experiment with both the rules (cf. Section 5).

within small number of iterations. Using the above SAT-based query implementations, automated AGR is carried out in the standard way [12, 22, 28]. Note that the support variable set for the assumption A is initialized to that of the weakest assumption WA, i.e., $X_{M_1} \cup X_P$. Also, in practice, the AGR procedure terminates with an assumption A with significantly fewer states than WA.

4   Lazy Learning

This section presents our new lazy learning approach to address the alphabet explosion problem (cf. Section 1); in contrast to the eager BDD-based learning algorithm [4], the lazy approach (i) avoids use of quantifier elimination to compute the set of edges and (ii) introduces new states and transitions lazily only when necessitated by a counterexample. We first propose a generalization of the L^* [26] algorithm and then present the lazy l^* algorithm based on it. Due to lack of space, we omit the full details of our generalization here. The details can be found in the technical report [28].

Notation. We represent the empty trace by ϵ. For a trace $u \in \Sigma^*$ and symbol $a \in \Sigma$, we say that $u \cdot a$ is an extension of u. The membership function $[\![\cdot]\!]$ is defined as follows: if $u \in \mathbb{L}_U$, $[\![u]\!] = 1$, otherwise $[\![u]\!] = 0$. We define a *follow* function $follow : \Sigma^* \to 2^\Sigma$, where $follow(u)$ consists of the set of alphabet symbols $a \in \Sigma$ that u is extended by, in order to form $u \cdot a$. A counterexample trace ce is positive if $[\![ce]\!] = 1$, otherwise, it is said to be negative.

Generalized L^*. Given an unknown language $\mathbb{L}_U$ defined over alphabet Σ, L^* maintains an observation table $\mathcal{T} = (U, UA, V, T)$ consisting of trace *samples* from $\mathbb{L}_U$, where $U \subseteq \Sigma^*$ is a prefix-closed set, $V \subseteq \Sigma^*$ is a set of suffixes, UA contains extensions of elements in U and T is a map so that $T(u, v) = [\![u \cdot v]\!]$ for some $u \in U \cup UA$ and $v \in V$. In contrast to L^*, which extends each $u \in U$ by the full alphabet Σ to obtain UA, the generalized algorithm only allows each u to be extended by the elements in the corresponding *follow set*, $follow(u)$. The follow sets may vary for different $u \in U$. We assume that a procedure Close_Table makes $\mathcal{T}$ closed by introducing new elements u into U and adding extensions of u on elements in $follow(u)$ to UA. Note that with $follow(u) = \Sigma$, the generalized algorithm is able to compute a deterministic and complete hypothesis CFA C from a closed table $\mathcal{T}$. Given any $t \in \Sigma^*$, we define its representative trace $[t]^r$ to be the unique $u \in U$ corresponding to the final state q of a run on t in C. Also, the procedure Learn_CE analyzes a counterexample ce obtained from the teacher, obtains a split $ce = u_i \cdot v_i$ with distinguishing suffix v_i using the classification function $\alpha_i = [\![[u_i]^r \cdot v_i]\!]$, and adds v_i to V [26, 28]. An illustration of the algorithm can be found in the extended version.

Lazy l^* Algorithm. The main bottleneck in generalized L^* algorithm is due to alphabet explosion, i.e., it enumerates and asks membership queries on all extensions of an element $u \in U$ on the (exponential-sized) Σ explicitly. The lazy approach avoids this as follows. Initially, the follow set for each u contains a singleton element, the alphabet cluster TRUE, which requires only a single enumeration step. This cluster may then be partitioned into smaller clusters in the later learning iterations, if necessitated by a counterexample. In essence, the lazy algorithm not only determines the states of the unknown CFA, but also computes the set of distinct alphabet clusters outgoing from each state lazily.

More formally, l^* performs queries on trace sets, wherein each transition corresponds to an alphabet cluster. We therefore augment our learning setup to handle sets of traces. Let $\hat{\Sigma}$ denote the set 2^Σ and concatenation operator $\cdot$ be extended to sets of traces S_1 and S_2 by concatenating each pair of elements from S_1 and S_2 respectively. The follow function is redefined as $follow : \hat{\Sigma}^* \rightarrow 2^{\hat{\Sigma}}$ whose range now consists of alphabet cluster elements (or alphabet predicates). The observation table $\mathcal{T}$ is a tuple (U, UA, V, T) where $U \subseteq \hat{\Sigma}^*$ is prefix-closed, $V \subseteq \hat{\Sigma}^*$ and UA contains all extensions of elements in U on elements in their follow sets. $T(u, v)$ is defined on a sets of traces u and v, so that $T(u, v) = [\![u \cdot v]\!]$ where the membership function $[\![\cdot]\!]$ is extended to a set of traces as follows: given a trace set S, $[\![S]\!] = 1$ iff $\forall t \in S. [\![t]\!] = 1$. In other words, a $[\![S]\!] = 1$ iff $S \subseteq \mathbb{L}_U$. This definition is advantageous in two ways. Firstly, the SAT-based teacher (cf. Section 3.1) can answer membership queries in the same way as before by converting a single trace set into the corresponding SAT formula instance. Secondly, in contrast to a more discriminating 3-valued interpretation of $[\![S]\!]$ in terms of 0, 1 and *undefined* values, this definition enables l^* to be more lazy with respect to state partitioning.

Figure 1 shows the pseudocode for the procedure Learn_CE, which learns from a counterexample ce and improves the current hypothesis CFA C. Note that for each u, $follow(u)$ is set to TRUE initially. The procedure Learn_CE calls the Learn_CE_0 and Learn_CE_1 procedures to handle negative and positive counterexamples respectively. Learn_CE_0 is the same as Learn_CE in generalized L^*: it finds a split of ce at position i (say, $ce = u_i \cdot v_i = u_i \cdot o_i \cdot v_{i+1}$), so that $\alpha_i \neq \alpha_{i+1}$ and adds a new distinguishing suffix v_{i+1} (which must exist by Lemma 3 below) to V to partition the state corresponding to $[u_i \cdot o_i]$. The procedure Learn_CE_1, in contrast, may either partition a state or partition an alphabet cluster. The case when v_{i+1} is not in V is handled as above and leads to a state partition. Otherwise, if v_{i+1} is already in V, Learn_CE_1 first identifies states in the current hypothesis CFA C corresponding to $[u_i]$ and $[u_i \cdot o_i]$, say, q and q' respectively, and the transition predicate ϕ corresponding to the transtion on symbol o_i from q to q'. Let $u_r = [u_i]^r$. Note that ϕ is also an alphabet cluster in $follow(u_r)$ and if $o_i = (a_i, b_i')$, then $\phi(a_i, b_i')$ holds (cf. Section 2).

The procedure Partition_Table partition ϕ using o_i (into ϕ_1 and ϕ_2) and updates the follow set of u_r. Also, it modifies the sets U and UA so that U remains prefix-closed and UA only contains extensions of U on the new follow set [28]. Note that since all the follow sets are disjoint and complete at each iteration, the hypothesis CFA obtained from a closed table $\mathcal{T}$ is always deterministic and complete (cf. Section 2).

Example. Figure 2 illustrates the l^* algorithm for the unknown language $\mathbb{L}_U$ $= (a|b|c|d) \cdot (a|b)^*$. Recall that the labels a, b, c and d are, in fact, predicates over program variables. The upper and lower parts of the table represent U and

Init: $\forall u \in \Sigma^*$, set $follow(u) = \text{TRUE}$

Learn_CE(ce)
  if ($[\![ce]\!] = 0$)
    Learn_CE_0(ce)
  else Learn_CE_1(ce)

Learn_CE_1(ce)
  Find i so that $\alpha_i = 1$ and $\alpha_{i+1} = 0$
  if $v_{i+1} \notin V$
    $V := V \cup \{v_{i+1}\}$
    For all $u \in U \cup UA$: Fill(u, v_{i+1})
  else
    Let $ce = u_i \cdot o_i \cdot v_{i+1}$
    Let $q = [u_i]$ and $q' = [u_i \cdot o_i]$
    Suppose $R_C(q, \phi, q')$ and $o_i \in \phi$
    Partition_Table($[u_i]^r$, ϕ, o_i)

Learn_CE_0(ce)
  Find i so that $\alpha_i = 0$ and $\alpha_{i+1} = 1$
  $V := V \cup \{v_{i+1}\}$
  For all $u \in U \cup UA$: Fill(u, v_{i+1})

Partition_Table(u_r, ϕ, a)
  $\phi_1 := \phi \wedge a$, $\phi_2 := \phi \wedge \neg a$
  $follow(u_r) := follow(u_r) \cup \{\phi_1, \phi_2\} \setminus \{\phi\}$
  Let $Uext = \{u \in U \mid \exists v \in \hat{\Sigma}^*. \ u = u_r \cdot \phi \cdot v\}$
  Let $UAext = \{u \cdot \phi_f \mid u \in Uext \wedge \phi_f \in follow(u)\}$
  $U := U \setminus Uext$
  $UA := UA \setminus UAext$
  For $u \in \{u_r \cdot \phi_1, u_r \cdot \phi_2\}$
    $UA := UA \cup \{u\}$
  For all $v \in V$: Fill(u, v)

Fig. 1. Pseudocode for the lazy l^* algorithm (mainly the procedure Learn_CE)

UA respectively, while the columns contain elements from V. The Boolean table entries correspond to the membership query $[\![u \cdot v]\!]$ where u and v are the row and column entries respectively. The algorithm initializes both U and V with element ϵ and fills the corresponding table entry by asking a membership query. Then, it asks query for a single extension of ϵ on cluster T (the L^* algorithm will instead asks queries on each alphabet element explicitly). Since $\epsilon \not\equiv T$, in order to make the table closed, the algorithm further needs to query on the trace $T \cdot T$. Now, it constructs the first hypothesis (Figure 2(i)) and asks a candidate query with it. The teacher replies with a counterexample $a \cdot a$, which is then used to partition the follow set of T into elements a and $\bar{a}$. The table is updated and the algorithm continues iteratively. The algorithm converges to the final CFA using four candidate queries; the figure shows the hypotheses CFAs for first, third and last queries. The first three queries are unsuccessful and return counterexamples $a \cdot a$ (positive), $a \cdot b$ (positive), $a \cdot d \cdot c$ (negative). The first two counterexamples lead to cluster partitioning (by a and b respectively) and the third one leads to state partitioning. Note that the algorithm avoids explicitly enumerating the alphabet set for computing extensions of elements in Σ. Also, note that the algorithm is insensitive to the size of alphabet set to some extent: if $\mathbb{L}_U$ is of the form $\Sigma \cdot (a|b)^*$, the algorithm always converges in the same number of iterations since only two cluster partitions from state q_1 need to be made.

The drawback of this lazy approach is that it may require more candidate queries as compared to the generalized L^* in order to converge. This is because the algorithm is lazy in obtaining information on the extensions of elements in U and therefore builds candidates using less information, e.g., it needs two candidate queries to be able to partition the cluster T on both a and b (note that the corresponding counterexamples $a \cdot a$ and $a \cdot b$ differ only in the last transition). We have developed a SAT-based method [28] that accelerates learning in such cases by generalizing a counterexample ce to include a set of similar counterexamples (ce') and then using ce' to perform a *coarser* cluster partition.

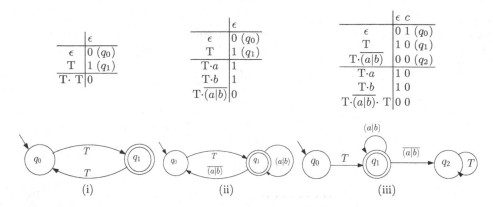

Fig. 2. Illustration of the l^* algorithm for $\mathbb{L}_U = (a|b|c|d)(a|b)^*$. Rows and column represent elements of $U \cup UA$ and V respectively. Alphabets are represented symbolically: $\mathrm{T} = (a|b|c|d)$, $\overline{(a|b)} = (c|d)$.

Lemma 3. *The procedure* Learn_CE_0 *must lead to addition of at least one new state in the next hypothesis CFA.*

Lemma 4. *The procedure* Learn_CE_1 *either leads to addition of at least one new state or one transition in the next hypothesis CFA.*

Theorem 1. l^* *terminates in $O(k{\cdot}2^n)$ iterations where k is the alphabet size and n is the number of states in the minimum deterministic CFA C_m corresponding to $\mathbb{L}_U$.*

Optimizing l^*. Although the theoretical complexity of l^* is high (mainly due to the reason that l^* may introduce a state corresponding to each subset of states reachable at a given depth in C_m), our experimental results show that the algorithm is effective in computing small size assumptions on real-life examples. Moreover, in the context of AGR, we seldom need to learn C_m completely; often, an approximation obtained at an intermediate learning step is sufficient.

5   Implementation and Experiments

We have implemented our SAT-based AGR approach based on **NC** and **C** rules in a tool called SYMODA, written in C++. The l^* algorithm is implemented together with related optimizations. SMV and Verilog benchmarks are translated into an intermediate input language of the tool using automated scripts [28]. We use the incremental SMT solver YICES [3, 13] as the main decision procedure. Interpolants are obtained using the library interface to the FOCI tool [1]. We represent states of a CFA explicitly while BDDs are used to represent transitions compactly and avoid redundancy.

Experiments. All experiments were performed on a 1.4GHz AMD machine with 3GB of memory running Linux. Table 1 compares three algorithms for

Table 1. Comparison of BDD-based and Lazy AGR schemes. P-AGR uses a learning algorithm for parameterized systems [8] while Lazy-AGR uses l^*. TV and GV represent the number of total and global boolean variables respectively. The Mono column shows the time taken with SAT-based UMC. All times are in seconds. TO denotes a timeout of 3600 seconds.#A denotes states of the largest assumption. '-' denotes that data could not be obtained due to the lack of tool support (The tool does not support the **NC** rule or Verilog programs as input). The superscript ^{i} denotes that interpolant-based UMC was used.

Example	TV	GV	Mono	BDD-AGR				P-AGR				Lazy-AGR			
				NC		C		NC		C		NC		C	
				#A	Time	#A	Time	#A	Time	#A	Time	#A	Time	#A	Time
s1a	86	5	0.54	2	754	2	223	3	3	3	3	3	3.5	3	1.3
s1b	94	5	0.58	2	TO	2	1527	3	3.3	3	3.3	3	3.9	3	2
guidance	122	22	129	2	196	2	6.6	1	31.5^i	5	146^i	1	40^i	3	55^i
msi(3)	57	22	1.2	2	2.1	2	0.3	1	8	*	TO	1	8	3	17
msi(5)	70	25	2.2	2	1183	2	32	1	16	*	TO	1	15	3	43
syncarb	21	15	3.16	-	-	67	30	*	TO^i	*	TO^i	*	TO^i	*	TO^i
peterson	13	7	0.54	-	-	34	2	6	53^i	8	210^i	6	13	6	88^i
CC(2a)	78	30	3.9	-	-	-	-	1	8	*	TO	1	8	4	26
CC(3a)	115	44	3.7	-	-	-	-	1	8	*	TO	1	7	4	20
$CC(2b)^i$	78	30	337	-	-	-	-	*	TO	*	TO	10	1878	5	87
$CC(3b)^i$	115	44	526	-	-	-	-	*	TO	*	TO	6	2037	11	2143

automated AGR: a BDD-based approach [4, 22] (BDD-AGR), our SAT-based approach using l^* (Lazy-AGR) and (P-AGR), which uses a learning algorithm for parameterized systems [8]. The last algorithm was not presented in context of AGR earlier; we have implemented it using a SAT-based teacher and other optimizations for comparison purposes. The BDD-AGR approach automatically partitions the given model before learning assumptions while we manually assign each top-level module to a different partition. Benchmarks *s1a*, *s1b*, *guidance*, *msi* and *syncarb* are derived from the NuSMV tool set and used in the previous BDD-based approach [22] while *peterson* and *CC* are obtained from the VIS and Texas97 benchmark sets [2]. All examples except *guidance* and *CC* can be proved using monolithic SAT-based UMC in small amount of time. Note that in some of these benchmarks, the size of the assumption alphabet is too large to be even enumerated in a short amount of time.

The SAT-based Lazy-AGR approach performs better than the BDD-based approach on *s1a* and *s2a* (cf. Table 1); although they are difficult for BDD-based model checking [4], SAT-based UMC quickly verifies them. On the *msi* example, the Lazy-AGR approach scales more uniformly compared to BDD-AGR. BDD-AGR is able to compute an assumption with 67 states on the *syncarb* benchmark while our SAT-based approaches with interpolation timeout with assumption sizes of around 30. The bottleneck is SAT-based UMC in the candidate query checks; the k-induction approach keeps unfolding transition relations to increasing depths while the interpolants are either large or take too much time to compute. On the *peterson* benchmark, BDD-AGR finishes earlier but with larger assumptions of size up to 34 (for two partitions) and 13 (for four partitions). In contrast, Lazy-AGR computes assumptions of size up to 6 while P-AGR computes assumptions of size up to 8. This shows that it is possible to generate much smaller assumptions using the lazy approach as compared to the eager BDD-based approach. Both the *guidance* and *syncarb* examples require interpolation-based UMC and timeout inside a candidate query with the k-induction based approach. P-AGR timeouts in many cases where Lazy-AGR finishes since the former performs state partitions more eagerly and introduces unnecessary states in the assumptions. We also compare the impact of various optimizations in the extended version [28].

6   Conclusions

We have presented a new SAT-based approach to automated AGR for shared memory systems based on lazy learning of assumptions; alphabet explosion during learning is avoided by representing alphabet clusters symbolically and performing on-demand cluster partitioning during learning. Experimental results demonstrate the effectiveness of our approach on hardware benchmarks. Since we employ off-the-shelf SMT solvers, we can directly leverage future improvements in SAT/SMT technology. Our techniques can be applied to software and other infinite state systems provided the weakest assumption has a finite bisimulation quotient. Future work includes investigating techniques to exploit incremental SAT solving for discharging each AGR premise, faster counterexample detection and obtaining good system decompositions for AGR.

Acknowledgements. We would like to thank Flavio Lerda for help wth the translator from SMV to SIL and the C interface to FOCI and also for numerous helpful discussions. We would like to thank Constantinos Bartzis and Tamir Heyman for several informative discussions. We also thank Dilsun Kaynar for carefully reading through a draft of this paper and providing useful comments.

References

[1] Foci: An interpolating prover, http://www.kenmcmil.com/foci.html
[2] http://vlsi.coloradu.edu/~vis/
[3] Yices: An smt solver, http://yices.csl.sri.com/
[4] Alur, R., Madhusudan, P., Nam, W.: Symbolic compositional verification by learning assumptions. In: Etessami, K., Rajamani, S.K. (eds.) CAV 2005. LNCS, vol. 3576, Springer, Heidelberg (2005)
[5] Amla, N.: An analysis of sat-based model checking techniques in an industrial environment. In: Borrione, D., Paul, W. (eds.) CHARME 2005. LNCS, vol. 3725, pp. 254–268. Springer, Heidelberg (2005)
[6] Angluin, D.: Learning regular sets from queries and counterexamples. In: Information and Computation, vol. 75(2), pp. 87–106 (1987)

[7] Barringer, H., Giannakopoulou, D., Pasareanu, C.S.: Proof rules for auto-mated compositional verification. In: SAVCBS (2003)

[8] Berg, T., Jonsson, B., Raffelt, H.: Regular inference for state machines with parameters. In: Baresi, L., Heckel, R. (eds.) FASE 2006 and ETAPS 2006. LNCS, vol. 3922, pp. 107–121. Springer, Heidelberg (2006)

[9] Biere, A., Cimatti, A., Clarke, E.M., Strichman, O., Zue, Y.: Bounded Model Checking. In: Zelkowitz, M. (ed.) Advances in computers, vol. 58 (2003)

[10] Sagar Chaki and Ofer Strichman. Optimized L* for assume-guarantee rea-soning. In: TACAS, To Appear

[11] Cobleigh, J., Avrunin, G., Clarke, L.: Breaking up is hard to do: an inves-tigation of decomposition for assume-guarantee reasoning. In: ISSTA, pp. 97–108 (2006)

[12] Cobleigh, J.M., Giannakopoulou, D., Pasareanu, C.S.: Learning assump-tions for compositional verification. In: Garavel, H., Hatcliff, J. (eds.) ETAPS 2003 and TACAS 2003. LNCS, vol. 2619, Springer, Heidelberg (2003)

[13] Dutertre, B., de Moura, L.: A fast linear-arithmetic solver for DPLL(T). In: Ball, T., Jones, R.B. (eds.) CAV 2006. LNCS, vol. 4144, pp. 81–94. Springer, Heidelberg (2006)

[14] Eén, N., Sörensson, N.: Temporal induction by incremental sat solving. Electr. Notes Theor. Comput. Sci. 89(4) (2003)

[15] Armoni, R. et al.: Sat-based induction for temporal safety properties. Electr. Notes Theor. Comput. Sci. 119(2), 3–16 (2005)

[16] Gheorghiu, M., Giannakopoulou, D., Pasareanu, C.S.: Refining interface alphabets for compositional verification. In: TACAS (To Appear)

[17] Hopcroft, J.E., Ullman, J.D.: Introduction to Automata Theory, Languages, and Computation. Addison-Wesley, Reading, Massachusetts (1979)

[18] Jones, C.B.: Tentative steps toward a development method for interfering programs. ACM Trans. Program. Lang. Syst. 5(4), 596–619 (1983)

[19] Maier, P.: A set-theoretic framework for assume-guarantee reasoning. In: Orejas, F., Spirakis, P.G., van Leeuwen, J. (eds.) ICALP 2001. LNCS, vol. 2076, pp. 821–834. Springer, Heidelberg (2001)

[20] McMillan, K.L.: Interpolation and sat-based model checking. In: Hunt Jr., W.A., Somenzi, F. (eds.) CAV 2003. LNCS, vol. 2725, pp. 1–13. Springer, Heidelberg (2003)

[21] Misra, J., Chandy, K.M.: Proofs of networks of processes. IEEE Trans. Software Eng. 7(4), 417–426 (1981)

[22] Nam, W., Alur, R.: Learning-based symbolic assume-guarantee reasoning with automatic decomposition. In: Graf, S., Zhang, W. (eds.) ATVA 2006. LNCS, vol. 4218, pp. 170–185. Springer, Heidelberg (2006)

[23] Namjoshi, K.S., Trefler, R.J.: On the completeness of compositional reason-ing. In: Emerson, E.A., Sistla, A.P. (eds.) CAV 2000. LNCS, vol. 1855, pp. 139–153. Springer, Heidelberg (2000)

[24] Pnueli, A.: In transition from global to modular temporal reasoning about programs. In: Logics and models of concurrent systems, Springer, Heidelberg (1985)

[25] Prasad, M.R., Biere, A., Gupta, A.: A survey of recent advances in sat-based formal verification. STTT 7(2), 156–173 (2005)
[26] Rivest, R.L., Schapire, R.E.: Inference of finite automata using homing sequences. In: Inf. Comp. vol. 103(2), pp. 299–347 (1993)
[27] Sheeran, M., Singh, S., Stalmarck, G.: Checking safety properties using induction and a sat-solver. In: Johnson, S.D., Hunt Jr., W.A. (eds.) FMCAD 2000. LNCS, vol. 1954, pp. 108–125. Springer, Heidelberg (2000)
[28] Sinha, N., Clarke, E.: SAT-based compositional verification using lazy learning. In: Technical report CMU-CS-07-109, Carnegie Mellon University, Pittsburgh, Pennsylvania, USA (February 2007)
[29] Tinelli, C., Ranise, S.: SMT-LIB: The Satisfiability Modulo Theories Library (2005), http://goedel.cs.uiowa.edu/smtlib/

Local Proofs for Global Safety Properties

Ariel Cohen[1] and Kedar S. Namjoshi[2]

[1] New York University
arielc@cs.nyu.edu
[2] Bell Labs
kedar@research.bell-labs.com

Abstract. This paper explores the concept of locality in proofs of global safety properties of asynchronously composed, multi-process programs. Model checking on the full state space is often infeasible due to state explosion. A local proof, in contrast, is a collection of per-process invariants, which together imply the global safety property. Local proofs can be compact: but a central problem is that local reasoning is incomplete. In this paper, we present a "completion" algorithm, which gradually exposes facts about the internal state of components, until either a local proof or a real error is discovered. Experiments show that local reasoning can have significantly better performance over a reachability computation. Moreover, for some parameterized protocols, a local proof can be used to show correctness for *all* instances.

1 Introduction

The success achieved by model checking [5,24] in various settings has always been tempered by the problem of state explosion [3]. Strategies based on abstraction and compositional analysis help to ameliorate the adverse effects of state explosion. This paper explores a particular combination of the two, which may be called "local reasoning". The context is the analysis of invariance properties of shared-variable, multi-process programs. Many protocols for cache coherence and mutual exclusion, and multi-threaded programs, fit this program model. Other, more complex, safety properties can be reduced to invariance by standard methods.

Model checking tools typically prove an invariance property through a reachability computation, computing an inductive assertion (the reachable states) that is defined over the full state vector. In contrast, a *local proof* of invariance for an asynchronous composition, $P_1//P_2//\ldots//P_n$, is given by a vector of assertions, $\{\theta_i\}$, one for each process, such that their conjunction is inductive, and implies the desired invariance property. Locality is ensured by *syntactically* limiting each assertion θ_i to the shared variables, X, and the local variables, L_i, of process P_i. The vector θ is called a *split invariant*.

In recent work [20], it is shown that the *strongest* split invariant exists, and can be computed as a least fixpoint. Moreover, the split invariance formulation is nearly identical to the deductive proof method of Owicki and Gries [21] for compositional verification.

W. Damm and H. Hermanns (Eds.): CAV 2007, LNCS 4590, pp. 55–67, 2007.

Intuitively, a local proof computation has advantages over a reachability computation. For one, each component of a split invariant can be expected to have a small BDD representation, as it is defined over the variables of a single process. Moreover, as the local assertions are loosely coupled—their only interaction is through the shared variables—BDD ordering constraints are less stringent.

On the other hand, a central problem with local reasoning is that it is incomplete: i.e., some valid properties do not have local proofs. This is because a split invariant generally over-approximates the set of reachable states, which may cause some unreachable error states to be included in the invariant. The over-approximation is due to the loose coupling between local states, as a joint constraint on L_i and L_j can be enforced only via X, by $\theta_i(X, L_i) \wedge \theta_j(X, L_j)$. Owicki and Gries showed that completeness can be achieved by adding auxiliary history variables to the shared state. Independently, Lamport showed in [18] that sharing all local state also ensures completeness. For finite-state processes, Lamport's construction has an advantage, as the completed program retains its finite-state nature, but it is also rather drastic: ideally, a completion should expose only the information necessary for a proof.

The main contribution of the paper is a fully automatic, gradual, *completion procedure* for finite-state programs. This differs from Lamport's construction in exposing *predicates* defined over local variables, which can be more efficient than exposing variables. The starting point is the computation of the strongest split invariant. If this does not suffice to prove the property, *local* predicates are extracted from an analysis of error states contained in the current invariant, added to the program as *shared* variables, and the split invariance calculation is repeated. Unreachable error states are eliminated in successive rounds, while reachable error states are retained, and eventually detected.

The procedure is not optimal, in that it does not always produce a minimal completion. However, it works well on a number of protocols, often showing a significant speedup over forward reachability. It is also useful in another setting, that of parameterized verification. In [20], it is shown that split invariance proofs for small instances of a parameterized protocol can be generalized (assuming a small model property) to inductive invariants which show correctness of *all* instances. Completion helps in the creation of such proofs.

In summary, the main contributions of this paper are (i) a completion procedure for split invariance, and (ii) the experimental demonstration that, in many cases, the fixpoint calculation of split invariance, augmented with the completion method, works significantly better than forward reachability. Parameterized verification, while not the primary goal, is a welcome extra!

An extended version of the paper, with complete proofs, and full experimental results, is available from http://www.cs.bell-labs.com/who/kedar/local.html .

2   Background

This section defines split invariance and gives the fixpoint formulation of the strongest split invariant. A more detailed exposition may be found in [20]. In the following, we assume that the reader is familiar with the concept of a state transition system.

Definition 1. *A component program is given by a tuple (V, I, T), where V is a set of (typed) variables, $I(V)$ is an initial condition, and $T(V, V')$ is a transition condition, where V' is a fresh set of variables in 1-1 correspondence with V.*

The semantics of a program is given by a transition system (S, S_0, R) where S is the state domain defined by the Cartesian product of the domains of variables in V, $S_0 = \{s : I(s)\}$, and $R = \{(s, t) : T(s, t)\}$. We assume that T is left-total, i.e., every state has a successor. A *state predicate* is a Boolean expression over the program variables. The truth value of a predicate at a state is defined in the usual way by induction on formula structure.

Inductiveness and Invariance. A state predicate φ is an *invariant* of program M if it holds at all reachable states of M. A state assertion ξ is an *inductive invariant* for M if it is initial (1) and inductive (2) (i.e., preserved by every program transition). Here, *wlp* is the weakest liberal precondition transformer introduced by Dijkstra; the notation $[\psi]$, from Dijkstra and Scholten [8], indicates that ψ is valid.

$$[I_M \Rightarrow \xi] \tag{1}$$

$$[\xi \Rightarrow wlp(M, \xi)] \tag{2}$$

An inductive assertion is *adequate* to show the invariance of a state predicate φ if it implies φ (condition (3)).

$$[\xi \Rightarrow \varphi] \tag{3}$$

From the Galois connection between *wlp* and the strongest post-condition operator *sp* (also known as *post*), condition (2) is equivalent to

$$[sp(M, \xi) \Rightarrow \xi] \tag{4}$$

The conjunction of (1) and (4) is equivalent to $[(I_M \lor sp(M, \xi)) \Rightarrow \xi]$. As function $f(\xi) = I_M \lor sp(M, \xi)$ is monotonic, by the Knaster-Tarski theorem (below), it has a least fixpoint, which is the set of reachable states of M.

Theorem 1. *(Knaster-Tarski) A monotonic function f on a complete lattice has a least fixpoint, which is the strongest solution to $Z : [f(Z) \Rightarrow Z]$. Over finite-height lattices, it is the limit of the sequence $Z_0 = \bot; Z_{i+1} = f(Z_i)$.*

Program Composition. The *asynchronous composition* of programs $\{P_i\}$, written as $(//i : P_i)$ is the program $P = (V, I, T)$, where the components are defined as follows. Let $V = (\cup i : V_i)$, and $I = (\wedge i : I_i)$. The *shared variables*, denoted X, are those that belong to $V_i \cap V_j$, for a distinct pair (i, j). The *local variables* of process P_i, denoted L_i, are the variables in V_i that are not shared (i.e., $L_i = V_i \setminus X$). The set of local variables is $L = (\cup i : L_i)$. The transition condition T_i of program P_i is constrained so that it leaves local variables of other processes unchanged. I.e., T_i is extended to $T_i(V_i, V_i') \wedge (\forall j : j \neq i : L_j' = L_j)$. Then T can be defined simply as $(\vee i : T_i)$, and $wlp(P, \varphi)$ is equivalent to $(\wedge i : wlp(P_i, \varphi))$.

2.1 Split Invariance

For simplicity, we consider a two-process composition $P = P_1//P_2$; the results generalize to multiple processes. The desired invariance property φ is defined over the full product state of P. A *local* assertion for P_i is an assertion that is based only on V_i (equivalently, on X and L_i). A pair of local assertions $\theta = (\theta_1, \theta_2)$ is called a *split assertion*. Split assertion θ is a *split invariant* if the conjunction $\theta_1 \wedge \theta_2$ is an inductive invariant for P.

Split Invariance as a Fixpoint. The conditions for inductiveness of $\theta_1 \wedge \theta_2$ can be rewritten to the simultaneous pre-fixpoint form below, based on the (sp, wlp) Galois connection and locality. In particular, the existential quantification over local variables encodes locality, as θ_i is independent of L_j, for $j \neq i$.

$$[(\exists L_2 : I \vee sp(P_1, \theta_1 \wedge \theta_2) \vee sp(P_2, \theta_1 \wedge \theta_2)) \Rightarrow \theta_1] \tag{5}$$

$$[(\exists L_1 : I \vee sp(P_1, \theta_1 \wedge \theta_2) \vee sp(P_2, \theta_1 \wedge \theta_2)) \Rightarrow \theta_2] \tag{6}$$

Let $\mathcal{F}_i(\theta)$ refer to the left-hand side of the implication for θ_i. By monotonicity of $\mathcal{F}_i$ in terms of (θ_1, θ_2) and the Knaster-Tarski theorem, there is a strongest solution, θ^*, which is also a simultaneous least fixpoint: $[\theta_i^* \equiv \mathcal{F}_i(\theta^*)]$. For finite-state programs, $\mathcal{F}_i(\theta)$ can be evaluated using standard BDD operations.

Theorem 2. *A split invariance proof of the invariance of φ exists if, and only if, $[(\theta_1^* \wedge \theta_2^*) \Rightarrow \varphi]$.*

Early Quantification. For a program with more than two processes, the general form of $\mathcal{F}_1(\theta)$ is $(\exists L \setminus L_1 : I \vee (\vee j : sp(P_j, (\wedge m : \theta_m))))$. This expression may be optimized with early quantification, as follows. Distributing $\exists$ over $\vee$ and over sp, and using the fact that the θ_i's are local assertions, $\mathcal{F}_1(\theta)$ may be rewritten to $(\exists L \setminus L_1 : I) \vee (\vee j : lsp_1(P_j, \theta))$, which quantifies out variables as early as possible. In this expression, $lsp_1(P_j, \theta)$ is defined as follows: for $j \neq 1$, it is $(\exists L_j : sp(P_j, \theta_1 \wedge \theta_j \wedge (\wedge k : k \notin \{1, j\} : (\exists L_k : \theta_k))))$, and for $j = 1$, it is $sp(P_1, \theta_1 \wedge (\wedge k : k \neq 1 : (\exists L_k : \theta_k)))$.

3 The Completion Procedure

The completeness problem, and its solution, is nicely illustrated by the mutual exclusion protocol in Figure 1(a). For a 2-process instance, the strongest split invariant is $(true, true)$. This includes (unreachable) states that violate mutual exclusion, making it impossible to prove the property. On the other hand, modifying the program by adding the auxiliary variable *last*, which records the last process to enter the critical section (Figure 1(b)), results in the strongest split invariant given by $\theta_i = ((C_i \vee E_i) \equiv ((\neg x) \wedge last = i))$. This suffices to prove mutual exclusion. The completion algorithm, COMPLETION, defined below, automatically discovers auxiliary variables such as this one.

A second route to completion, which we refer to as COMPLETION-PAIRWISE, is to widen the scope of local assertions to pairs of processes. A split invariant is now

$$
\begin{array}{l}
\text{x: boolean initially x = 1}\\[4pt]
\text{loop forever do}\\
\displaystyle\mathop{\|}_{i=1}^{N} P[i] ::
\left[
\begin{array}{l}
I:\ \textit{Non-Critical}\\
T:\ \textbf{request } x\\
\\
C:\ \textit{Critical}\\
E:\ \textbf{release } x
\end{array}
\right]
\end{array}
$$

(a) protocol MUX-SEM

$$
\begin{array}{l}
\text{x: boolean initially x = 1}\\
\text{last: } 0..N \text{ initially last} = 0\\
\text{loop forever do}\\
\displaystyle\mathop{\|}_{i=1}^{N} P[i] ::
\left[
\begin{array}{l}
I:\ \textit{Non-Critical}\\
T:\ \textbf{request } x\\
\ \ \ \ \text{last} := i;\\
C:\ \textit{Critical}\\
E:\ \textbf{release } x
\end{array}
\right]
\end{array}
$$

(b) protocol MUX-SEM-LAST

Fig. 1. Illustration of the (In)Completeness of Local Reasoning

a matrix of entries of the form $\theta_{ij}(X, L_i, L_j)$. The 1-index fixpoint algorithm is extended to compute 2-index θ's as follows. Instead of n simultaneous equations, there are $O(n^2)$ equations, one for each pair (i,j) such that $i \neq j$. The operator, $\mathcal{F}_{ij}$, is defined as $(\exists L \setminus (L_i \cup L_j) : I \vee (\vee k : sp(P_k, \hat{\theta})))$, where $\hat{\theta}$ is $(\wedge m, n : m \neq n : \theta_{mn})$. For the original program from Figure 1(a), COMPLETION-PAIRWISE produces the solution $\theta_{ij}(X, L_i, L_j) = ((x \Rightarrow ((I_i \vee T_i) \wedge \neg C_j)) \wedge ((\neg x \wedge C_i) \Rightarrow \neg C_j))$, which suffices to prove mutual exclusion. It is interesting that, in some of our experiments, pairwise split invariance outperformed both single-index split invariance (with completion) and reachability.

3.1 The Completion Algorithm

We first provide a description of the main steps of the algorithm COMPLETION. The input is a concurrent program, P, with n processes, $\{P_i\}$, and a global property φ. We use θ^i to represent the i'th approximation $\theta_1^i \wedge \theta_2^i \wedge \ldots \wedge \theta_n^i$. The *refinement phase* (steps 3 and 4) can be optimized without violating the correctness argument; this is discussed in the extended version of the paper.

1. If the initial condition violates φ, halt with "Error".
2. Compute the split invariant using the fixed point algorithm. If, at the i'th stage, θ^i violates φ, go to step 3. If a fixpoint is reached, halt with "Verified" and provide the split invariant as proof.
3. Let $viol = \theta^i \wedge \neg\varphi$. For each state in $viol$, find new *essential predicates* and add auxiliary variables for these to the program. If new predicates are found, return to step 1, which starts a new split invariance calculation; otherwise, continue to step 4.
4. Add the immediate predecessors of $viol$ to the error condition—i.e., modify φ to $\varphi \wedge \neg\mathsf{EX}(viol)$—and return to step 3.

3.2 The Refinement Phase

As $\theta_1 \wedge \theta_2 \wedge \ldots \wedge \theta_n$ is always an over-approximation of the reachable states, COMPLETION may detect states that violate φ but are not actually reachable. Those states should be identified and left out of the split invariant. To do so, once a violating state is detected, COMPLETION computes essential predicates using a greedy strategy. For each *local* variable (from some process), the algorithm tests whether it is relevant to the error for that state; this is considered to be the case if an alternative value for the variable results in a non-error state. (Sometimes, a group of variables may need to be considered together.) For example, mutual exclusion is violated for a global state if two processes are at the critical location, but the locations of other processes are not relevant, since they could be set to arbitrary values while retaining the error condition.

For each relevant variable v in an error state s, a predicate of the form $v = v(s)$ is added to the program. This is a local predicate, as v is a local variable for some process. To add a predicate $f(L_i)$, a corresponding Boolean variable b is added to the shared state, and initialized to the value of $f(L_i)$ at the initial state. It is updated as follows: for process P_i, the update is given by $b' \equiv f(L_i')$, and for process P_j, $j \neq i$, the update is given by $b' \equiv b$. This augmentation clearly does not affect the underlying transitions of the program: the new Boolean variables are purely auxiliary, and the transitions enforce the invariant ($b \equiv f(L_i)$).

Each component θ_i is now defined over X, L_i, and the auxiliary Boolean variables. The auxiliary variables act as additional constraints between θ_i and θ_j, sharpening the split invariant. A rough idea of how the sharpening works is as follows. (A precise formulation is in Section 3.4.) Consider a state s to be "fixed" by the values of the auxiliary variables $b_1, \ldots, b_n$ (one for each process) if the local state components in s form the only satisfying assignment for ($\wedge i : b_i(s) \equiv f_i(L_i)$). The correctness proof shows (cf. Lemmas 2 and 3) that an unreachable error state with no predecessors is eliminated from the split invariance once it is fixed. However, a fixed, but unreachable, error state may be detected for the second time, if it has predecessors (which must be unreachable). In this case, the predecessors need to be eliminated, so they are considered as error states by modifying φ, and predicates are extracted from them.

Adding predecessors continues until (i) at least one new predicate is exposed, and a new computation is initialized, or (ii) the modified φ violates the initial condition – an indication that a state violating the original φ is reachable.

3.3   Illustration

We illustrate some of the key features of this algorithm on the MUX-SEM example from Figure 1(a). For simplicity we have only two processes; thus, the safety property is $\varphi \equiv \neg(C_1 \wedge C_2)$.

Iteration 0

Step 1. The initial condition is $x = 1 \wedge I_1 \wedge I_2$. φ does not violate it.

Step 2. COMPLETION computes the split invariant until $\theta_1 \wedge \theta_2$ violates φ. At this stage,

$$\theta_1 \wedge \theta_2 \equiv \quad x = 1 \wedge ((I_1 \vee T_1) \wedge (I_2 \vee T_2))$$
$$\vee \, x = 0 \wedge ((I_1 \vee T_1 \vee C_1) \wedge (I_2 \vee T_2 \vee C_2))$$

Step 3. Let *viol* be the set of states that satisfy $\theta_1 \wedge \theta_2 \wedge \neg\varphi$. The only state in *viol* is the one which satisfies $x = 0 \wedge C_1 \wedge C_2$. The global predicate variables b_1 and

b_2, which are associated with the essential predicates C_1 and C_2, respectively, are added to the program, as described previously.

Iteration 1

Step 2. A new computation of the split invariant sets off. Once again it is computed until $\theta_1 \wedge \theta_2$ violates φ. The description of $\theta_1 \wedge \theta_2$ is long, and is omitted, but the important point is that $x = 0 \wedge C_1 \wedge C_2 \wedge b_1 \wedge b_2$ satisfies it.

Step 3. Since $(x = 0, C_1, C_2)$ was already detected, the negations of its predecessors that satisfy $\theta_1 \wedge \theta_2$ are added to φ, i.e. φ is augmented by $\neg(x = 1 \wedge C_1 \wedge T_2)$ and $\neg(x = 1 \wedge T_1 \wedge C_2)$ and the corresponding states are analyzed as well. Since both predecessors satisfy $\theta_1 \wedge \theta_2$, violate φ, and are detected for the first time, new global predicate variables b_3 and b_4, which are associated with the essential predicates T_2 and T_1, respectively, are added to the program.

Iteration 2

Again, the split invariance calculation does not succeed. This time, the error states $(x = 1, C_1, T_2, b_1, \neg b_2, b_3, \neg b_4)$ and $(x = 1, T_1, C_2, \neg b_1, b_2, \neg b_3, b_4)$ are part of the split invariant.

Step 3. Since both of these states were already detected, the negations of their predecessors that belong to $\theta_1 \wedge \theta_2$ are added to φ, i.e. φ is augmented by $\neg(x = 1 \wedge C_1 \wedge I_2)$ and $\neg(x = 1 \wedge I_1 \wedge C_2)$, and they are analyzed as well. Since both predecessors belong to $\theta_1 \wedge \theta_2$, violate φ, and are detected for the first time, new global predicate variables b_5 and b_6, which are associated with the essential predicates I_2 and I_1, respectively, are added to the program.

Iteration 3

The split invariance calculation succeeds, establishing mutual exclusion.

3.4   Correctness

The correctness argument has to show that the procedure will eventually terminate, and detect correctly whether the property holds. The theorems are proved for the 2-process case, the proof for the general case is similar. Lemmas 1, 2, and 3 make precise the effect that adding auxiliary boolean variables has on subsequent split invariance calculations. Lemma 4 shows that a split invariant is always an over-approximation to the reachable states.

To represent the state of a 2-process instance, we use variables X, b_1, b_2, L_1, L_2, where X represents the shared variables, L_1, L_2 are the local variables of processes P_1, P_2 respectively, and b_1, b_2 are auxiliary Boolean variables added for predicates $f_1(L_1)$ and $f_2(L_2)$, respectively. For a variable w, and a state s, let $w(s)$ denote the value of w in s.

Define states s and t to be *equivalent*, denoted $s \sim t$, if they agree on the values for X, b_1, and b_2. A set of states S is closed under $\sim$ if, for each state in S, its equivalence class is included in S. A set of states is *pre-closed* if all predecessors of states in S are included in S.

Lemma 1. *(Invariance Lemma) The assertion* $(b_1 \equiv f_1) \wedge (b_2 \equiv f_2)$ *holds for all states in* $\theta_1^i \wedge \theta_2^i$, *for all approximation steps* i.

Lemma 2. *If state* s *is in the* $(i+1)$*'st approximation to the split invariant, there is an equivalent state* t *that is also in the* $(i+1)$*'st approximation, and either* t *is initial, or it has a predecessor in the* i*'th approximation.*

Lemma 3. *(Exclusion Lemma) Let* S *be a set of states that is pre-closed, closed under* $\sim$, *and unreachable. Then* S *is excluded from the split invariant.*

Lemma 4. *(Reachability Lemma) The split invariant fixpoint is always an over-approximation of the set of reachable states.*

Theorem 3. *(Soundness) (a) If* φ *is declared to be proved, it is an invariant. (b) If* φ *is declared to fail, there is a reachable state where* φ *is false.*

Proof
Part (a): If the split invariant implies φ, by Lemma 4, φ is true of all reachable states, and is therefore invariant.

Part (b): This follows as the error states, which are initially a subset of $\neg\varphi$, are enlarged by adding predecessors. Thus, if an initial state is considered to be an error, there is a path to a state falsifying φ.

Theorem 4. *(Completeness I) If the property* φ *is an invariant for* $P_1//P_2$, *it is eventually proved.*

Proof. If φ is an invariant, any states in the first split invariant that do not satisfy φ are unreachable. Call this set *error*. The procedure used to add predicates (steps 3 and 4), in the limit, extracts predicates from all states in $\mathsf{EF}(error)$, as it adds predecessors to the error set. The set $\mathsf{EF}(error)$ is pre-closed, and unreachable. If this set is not $\sim$-closed, there are states s and t such that $s \sim t$, but s is an error state, while t is not—this triggers the addition of a new predicate in Step 3 of the algorithm. As there are only finitely many predicates, eventually, enough predicates are added so that the set is $\sim$-closed. By Lemma 3, once $\sim$-closure is obtained, the set is excluded from the split invariant. At this stage, the split invariant has no error states, and the property is declared proved. $\qquad\square$

Theorem 5. *(Completeness II) If* φ *is not an invariant of* $P_1//P_2$, *this is eventually detected.*

Proof. If the property is not invariant, there is a reachable state on which it fails. By the Reachability Lemma, the split invariant always includes these states. The completion procedure, at each step, will enlarge the error set, effectively computing $\mathsf{EF}(error)$. At some stage (defined by the length of the shortest path to an error state) this has a non-empty intersection with the initial states, at which point the error is detected. $\qquad\square$

Theorems 4 and 5 also show termination of the procedure.

4   Experiments and Results

We implemented COMPLETION using TLV [23], a BDD-based model checker, and tested it on protocols taken from the literature. The tests were conducted on a 2.8GHz Intel Xeon with 1GB RAM.

The primary aim of the experiments is to compare split invariance with the two forms of completion against a forward reachability calculation on the full state space. The split invariance calculation is uniformly faster (sometimes significantly so) than forward reachability. We also compared it against model checking using inverse reachability (i.e., AG). In three examples (PETERSON'S, BAKERY, and an incorrect mutual exclusion protocol), split invariance performs significantly better than the AG calculation; in other examples, the AG calculation is somewhat faster.

For many of these protocols, including BAKERY and MUX-SEM, the split invariance calculation also results in an inductive invariant that shows correctness for *all* instances, using the results in [20]. Split invariance (as opposed to reachability) is essential for obtaining this result.

As previously explained, COMPLETION consists of a loop with three main phases: computing the split invariant, refining the system by exposing predicates over local variables, and analyzing the predecessors of violating states. It is important to point out that not all examples require the use of all three phases.

For two examples: PETERSON'S mutual exclusion protocol and algorithm BAKERY, COMPLETION terminated much faster than traditional forward or backward model checking. It appears that these examples contain sufficient global information for computing the split invariant, without having to employ any refinements. Table 1 compares COMPLETION, forward reachability and inverse reachability for PETERSON'S mutual exclusion protocol. The run times achieved by COMPLETION are significantly better for larger instances.

Table 1. Test results for PETERSON'S mutual exclusion protocol

Method	Processes	BDDs	Bytes	Time(s)	Refinements	New Variables
Forward Reachability	2	2k	524k	0	-	-
Backward Reachability	2	1.7k	524k	0	-	-
COMPLETION	2	2k	524k	0	0	0
Forward Reachability	5	23k	917k	0.05	-	-
Backward Reachability	5	42k	1.2M	0.29	-	-
COMPLETION	5	20k	852k	0.04	0	0
Forward Reachability	10	194k	3.7M	0.94	-	-
Backward Reachability	10	13M	211M	680	-	-
COMPLETION	10	173k	3.4M	0.26	0	0
Forward Reachability	20	1.8M	30M	127	-	-
Backward Reachability	20	-	-	>2hrs	-	-
COMPLETION	20	1.7M	29M	9.9	0	0

Another tested example was protocol MUX-SEM, provided in Figure 1. When running COMPLETION in its basic form, the obtained run times and the number of BDDs were not as good as those of traditional forward model checking, due to the overhead of the multiple split invariance runs. However, when we use a pairwise split invariant computation, as explained in the introduction of Section 3, the results turn over, and the run times are in COMPLETION's favor. Backward reachability obtained the best results for this protocol.

All examples provided before were of correct protocols, i.e they all satisfied their safety properties. The next and last example is of an incorrect mutual exclusion protocol, MUX-SEM-TRY, and it illustrates the ability of COMPLETION to cope with systems that violate their own safety property and its ability to identify real violations. In this case, when performing the computation all three phases had to be employed, together with several refinements in which multiple new variables where added and the predecessors of violating states had to be analyzed.

Table 2 compares forward and backward reachability to COMPLETION for MUX-SEM-TRY. Both the number of BDDs and the run times achieved by COMPLETION are significantly better. When performing tests on 20 processes, what requires more than 2 hours when using model checking is completed in 52 seconds when using COMPLETION, and we can only assume that as the number of processes increases - the difference increases as well.

Table 2. Test results for protocol MUX-SEM-TRY

Method	Processes	BDDs	Bytes	Time(s)	Refinements	New Variables
Forward Reachability	2	877	524k	0	-	-
Backward Reachability	2	1.1k	524k	0	-	-
COMPLETION	2	4.8k	589k	0.01	5	8
Forward Reachability	5	11k	720k	0.12	-	-
Backward Reachability	5	10k	655k	0.26	-	-
COMPLETION	5	10k	720k	0.16	7	14
Forward Reachability	10	337k	6M	27.7	-	-
Backward Reachability	10	450k	7.8M	25.8	-	-
COMPLETION	10	70k	1.7M	1.3	7	24
Forward Reachability	20	-	-	>2hrs	-	-
Backward Reachability	20	-	-	>2hrs	-	-
COMPLETION	20	1M	18M	35	7	44

5   Related Work

Early work on compositional reasoning is primarily on deductive proof methods [7]. The pioneering methods of Owicki and Gries [21] and Lamport [18] are extended to assume-guarantee reasoning by Chandy and Misra [2] and Jones [17]. The split invariance calculation can be viewed as mechanizing the Owicki-Gries proof rule, while the completion algorithm is inspired by Lamport's method.

Recent work on compositional reasoning is more algorithmic. Tools like Cadence SMV provide support for compositional proofs [19,16]. "Thread-modular" reasoning [9,10,14] computes a per-process transition relation abstraction in a modular way. In [13], this abstraction is made more precise by including some aspects of the local states of other processes, and extended to parameterized verification.

Split invariance is based on a simpler, state-based representation. A key new aspect of this paper is that it addresses the central incompleteness problem. While a transition relation abstraction is more precise than one based on states, it is incomplete nonetheless [10].

The "invisible invariants" method [22] heuristically generates quantified invariants for parameterized protocols. This can prove correctness for many of the protocols considered here, but it requires the user-guided addition of auxiliary variables in several cases. One of the contributions of this paper is to automate the addition of such auxiliaries.

The completion procedure is in the spirit of failure-based refinement methods, such as counter-example guided refinement [4]. Given a composition $P = P_1 // \ldots // P_n$, earlier refinement algorithms may be viewed as either (1) abstracting P to a single process, which is successively refined; or (2) applying compositional analysis to individual abstractions of each P_i. However, method (2) is incomplete, though compositional; while method (1) is non-compositional, though complete. The procedure given here achieves both compositionality and completeness.

A different type of assume-guarantee reasoning applies machine learning to determine the weakest interface of a process as an automaton [12,25,11,1]. This is complete, but the algorithms are complex, and may be expensive [6].

Hu and Dill propose in [15] to dynamically partition the BDD's arising in a reachability computation. The partitioning is not necessarily local. A fixed local partitioning allows a simpler fixpoint procedure, and especially a simpler termination condition. Unlike split invariance, the Hu-Dill method computes the exact set of reachable states. As the experiments show, however, over-approximation is not necessarily a disadvantage.

6   Conclusions and Future Work

This paper provides an algorithm—the first, to the best of our knowledge—which address the incompleteness problem for local reasoning. The local reasoning strategy itself computes a split state invariant, which is a simpler object than the transition relations or automata considered in other work.

Conceptually, local reasoning is an attractive alternative to model checking on the full state space. Our experiments show that this is justified in practice as well: split invariance, augmented with the completion procedure, can be a valuable model checking tool. In many cases, a split invariance proof can be used to show correctness of all instances of a parameterized protocol.

The completion procedure is defined for finite-state components. Extending this method to unbounded state components (e.g., C programs) would require a procedure that interleaves internal, per-process abstraction with split invariance and completion. Other interesting questions include the design of a split invariance procedure for synchronous composition, and the investigation of local reasoning for liveness properties.

Acknowledgement. This research was supported, in part, by NSF grant CCR-0341658.

References

1. Chaki, S., Clarke, E.M., Sinha, N., Thati, P.: Automated assume-guarantee reasoning for simulation conformance. In: Etessami, K., Rajamani, S.K. (eds.) CAV 2005. LNCS, vol. 3576, pp. 534–547. Springer, Heidelberg (2005)
2. Chandy, K.M., Misra, J.: Proofs of networks of processes. IEEE Transactions on Software Engineering 7 (1981)
3. Clarke, E.M., Grumberg, O.: Avoiding the state explosion problem in temporal logic model checking. In: PODC, pp. 294–303 (1987)
4. Clarke, E.M., Grumberg, O., Jha, S., Lu, Y., Veith, H.: Counterexample-guided abstraction refinement for symbolic model checking. J. ACM 50(5), 752–794 (2003)
5. Clarke, E.M., Emerson, E.A.: Design and synthesis of synchronization skeletons using branching time temporal logic. In: Kozen, D. (ed.) Logics of Programs. LNCS, vol. 131, Springer, Heidelberg (1982)
6. Cobleigh, J.M., Avrunin, G.S., Clarke, L.A.: Breaking up is hard to do: an investigation of decomposition for assume-guarantee reasoning. In: ISSTA, pp. 97–108 (2006)
7. Roever, W-P.d., Boer, F.d., Hannemann, U., Hooman, J., Lakhnech, Y., Poel, M., Zwiers, J.: Concurrency Verification: Introduction to Compositional and Noncompositional Proof Methods. Cambridge University Press, Cambridge (2001)
8. Dijkstra, E.W., Scholten, C.S.: Predicate Calculus and Program Semantics. Springer, Heidelberg (1990)
9. Flanagan, C., Freund, S.N., Qadeer, S., Seshia, S.A.: Modular verification of multithreaded programs. Theor. Comput. Sci. 338(1-3), 153–183 (2005)
10. Flanagan, C., Qadeer, S.: Thread-modular model checking. In: Ball, T., Rajamani, S.K. (eds.) Model Checking Software. LNCS, vol. 2648, pp. 213–224. Springer, Heidelberg (2003)
11. Giannakopoulou, D., Pasareanu, C.S.: Learning-based assume-guarantee verification (tool paper). In: Godefroid, P. (ed.) Model Checking Software. LNCS, vol. 3639, pp. 282–287. Springer, Heidelberg (2005)
12. Giannakopoulou, D., Pasareanu, C.S., Barringer, H.: Assumption generation for software component verification. In: ASE, pp. 3–12 (2002)
13. Henzinger, T.A., Jhala, R., Majumdar, R.: Race checking by context inference. In: PLDI, pp. 1–13 (2004)
14. Henzinger, T.A., Jhala, R., Majumdar, R., Qadeer, S.: Thread-modular abstraction refinement. In: Hunt Jr., W.A., Somenzi, F. (eds.) CAV 2003. LNCS, vol. 2725, pp. 262–274. Springer, Heidelberg (2003)
15. Hu, A.J., Dill, D.L.: Efficient verification with BDDs using implicitly conjoined invariants. In: Courcoubetis, C. (ed.) CAV 1993. LNCS, vol. 697, pp. 3–14. Springer, Heidelberg (1993)
16. Jhala, R., McMillan, K.L.: Microarchitecture verification by compositional model checking. In: Berry, G., Comon, H., Finkel, A. (eds.) CAV 2001. LNCS, vol. 2102, pp. 396–410. Springer, Heidelberg (2001)
17. Jones, C.B.: Development methods for computer programs including a notion of interference. PhD thesis, Oxford University (1981)

18. Lamport, L.: Proving the correctness of multiprocess programs. IEEE Trans. Software Eng. 3(2) (1977)
19. McMillan, K.L.: A compositional rule for hardware design refinement. In: Suciu, D., Vossen, G. (eds.) WebDB 2000. LNCS, vol. 1997, Springer, Heidelberg (2001)
20. Namjoshi, K.S.: Symmetry and completeness in the analysis of parameterized systems. In: Roddick, J.F., Hornsby, K. (eds.) TSDM 2000. LNCS (LNAI), vol. 2007, Springer, Heidelberg (2001)
21. Owicki, S.S., Gries, D.: Verifying properties of parallel programs: An axiomatic approach. Commun. ACM 19(5), 279–285 (1976)
22. Pnueli, A., Ruah, S., Zuck, L.D.: Automatic deductive verification with invisible invariants. In: Margaria, T., Yi, W. (eds.) ETAPS 2001 and TACAS 2001. LNCS, vol. 2031, pp. 82–97. Springer, Heidelberg (2001)
23. Pnueli, A., Shahar, E.: A platform for combining deductive with algorithmic verification (web: www.cs.nyu.edu/acsys/tlv). In: Alur, R., Henzinger, T.A. (eds.) CAV 1996. LNCS, vol. 1102, pp. 184–195. Springer, Heidelberg (1996)
24. Queille, J.P., Sifakis, J.: Specification and verification of concurrent systems in CESAR. In: Dezani-Ciancaglini, M., Montanari, U. (eds.) International Symposium on Programming. LNCS, vol. 137, Springer, Heidelberg (1982)
25. Tkachuk, O., Dwyer, M.B., Pasareanu, C.S.: Automated environment generation for software model checking. In: ASE, pp. 116–129 (2003)

Low-Level Library Analysis and Summarization[*]

Denis Gopan[1] and Thomas Reps[1,2]

[1] University of Wisconsin
[2] GrammaTech, Inc.
{gopan,reps}@cs.wisc.edu

Abstract. Programs typically make extensive use of libraries, including dynamically linked libraries, which are often not available in source-code form, and hence not analyzable by tools that work at source level (i.e., that analyze intermediate representations created from source code). A common approach is to write *library models* by hand. A library model is a collection of function stubs and variable declarations that capture some aspect of the library code's behavior. Because these are hand-crafted, they are likely to contain errors, which may cause an analysis to return incorrect results.

This paper presents a method to construct summary information for a library function automatically by analyzing its low-level implementation (i.e., the library's binary).

1 Introduction

Static program analysis works best when it operates on an entire program. In practice, however, this is rarely possible. For the sake of maintainability and quicker development times, software is kept modular with large parts of the program hidden in libraries. Often, commercial off-the-shelf (COTS) modules are used. The source code for COTS components and libraries (such as the Windows dynamically linked libraries) is not usually available.

In practice, the following techniques are used to deal with library functions:

- **stop at library calls:** this approach reduces analysis coverage and leads to incomplete error detection;
- **treat library calls as identity transformers:** this approach is generally unsound; furthermore, this approach is imprecise because the analysis models a semantics that is different from that of the program;
- **define transformers for selected library calls:** this approach is not extensible: new transformers must be hardcoded into the analyzer to handle additional calls;
- **use hand-written source-code stubs that emulate some aspects of library code:** while this approach is both sound and extensible, the process of crafting stubs is usually time-consuming and error-prone.

In this paper, we describe a static-analysis tool that automatically constructs summaries for library functions by analyzing their low-level implementation (i.e., binary

---

[*] Supported by ONR under grant N00014-01-1-0796 and by NSF under grants CCF-0540955 and CCF-0524051.

W. Damm and H. Hermanns (Eds.): CAV 2007, LNCS 4590, pp. 68–81, 2007.

code). A library function's summary consists of a set of *error triggers* and a set of *summary transformers*. Error triggers are assertions over the program state that, if satisfied at the call site of the function, indicate a possibility of program failure during the function's invocation. Summary transformers specify how the program state is affected by the function call: they are expressed as *transfer relations*, i.e., the relations that hold among the values of global variables and function parameters *before* and *after* the call.

To use the function summaries, a client analysis must approximate the set of program states that reach the call site of a library function. The analysis should report an error if the approximation contains states that satisfy an assertion that corresponds to some error trigger. Summary transformers are applied as follows: the "before" values of global variables and function parameters are restricted to those that reach the call site; the restricted transfer relation is projected onto the "after" values to yield an approximation for the set of program states at the function's return point.

Our work makes the following contributions:

– It provides a way to create library summaries automatically, which frees tool developers from having to create models for standard libraries by hand.
– The library summaries obtained have applications in both verification tools and bug-finding/security-vulnerability-detection tools, and thus help in both kinds of code-quality endeavors.
– The library summaries obtained by our tool could be used in client analysis tools that work on either source code or low-level code (i.e., assembly code, object code, or binary executable code). In particular, they satisfy the needs of many source-code bug-finding analyses, which propagate symbolic information through the program, including the amount of memory allocated for a buffer, the offset of a pointer into a corresponding buffer, the length of a string, etc. [25,10].
– In some cases, the tool might allow static analysis to be carried out more efficiently. That is, the application/library division provides a natural modularity border that could be exploited for program-analysis purposes: typically, many applications link against the same library; summarizing the functions in that library obviates the need to reanalyze the library code for each application, which could improve analysis efficiency. (See §5 for a discussion of other work that has had the same motivation.)

During development, application code is changed more frequently than library code. Because an application can be analyzed repeatedly against the same set of library summaries, it is possible to recoup the cost of applying more sophisticated analyses, such as polyhedral analysis [8], for library summarization.

Some may argue against our choice of analyzing the low-level implementation of library functions: programs link against any possible implementation of the library, possibly across different platforms. Thus, it would be desirable to verify programs against more abstract function summaries derived, for instance, from library specifications. Below, we list some of the reasons why we believe that constructing library functions from low-level implementations deserves attention.

– Formal library specifications are hard to get hold of, while a low-level implementation for each supported platform is readily available.

- Even if formal specification is available, there is no easy way to verify that a particular library implementation conforms to the specification.
- The analysis of an actual library implementation may uncover bugs and undesirable features in the library itself. For instance, while summarizing memory-management functions, we discovered that the *libc* implementation that came with Microsoft Developer Studio 6 assumes that the direction flag, the x86 flag that specifies the direction for string operations, is set to *false* on entry to the library. This can be a security vulnerability if an adversary could control the value of the direction flag prior to a subsequent call to memcpy.

The remainder of the paper is organized as follows: §2 provides an overview of our goals, methods, and results obtained. §3 discusses the individual steps used to generate summary information for a library function. §4 summarizes two case studies. §5 discusses related work.

2   Overview

We use the function memset as the running example for this paper. The function is declared as follows:

```
void * memset ( void * ptr, int value, size_t num );
```

Its invocation sets the first *num* bytes of the block of memory pointed to by *ptr* to the specified value (interpreted as an unsigned char). The value of *ptr* is returned.

In this paper, we address two types of memory-safety errors: buffer overruns and buffer underruns. Typically, analyses that target these types of errors propagate allocation bounds for each pointer. There are many ways in which this can be done. We use the following model. Two auxiliary integer variables are associated with each pointer variable: $alloc_f$ is the number of bytes that can be safely accessed "ahead" of the address stored in the pointer variable, $alloc_b$ is the number of bytes that can be safely accessed "behind" the address stored in the pointer variable. We believe that this scheme can be easily interfaced with other choices for representing allocation bounds. We use dot notation to refer to allocation bounds of a pointer variable, e.g., $ptr.alloc_f$.

Analysis goals. The function summary specifies how to transform the program state at the call site of the function to the program state at its return site. Also, it specifies conditions that, if satisfied at the call site, indicate that a run-time error is possible during the function call. Intuitively, we expect the summary transformer for the memset function to look like this (for the moment, we defer dealing with memory locations overwritten by *memset* to §3.2):

$$ret = ptr \wedge ret.alloc_f = ptr.alloc_f \wedge ret.alloc_b = ptr.alloc_b, \qquad (1)$$

where ret denotes the value that is returned by the function. We expect the sufficient condition for the buffer overflow to look like this:

$$num \geq 1 \wedge ptr.alloc_f \leq num - 1. \qquad (2)$$

The goal of our analysis is to construct such summaries automatically.

00401070	mov	edx, dword ptr [esp + 12]	$edx \leftarrow count$
00401074	mov	ecx, dword ptr [esp + 4]	$ecx \leftarrow ptr$
00401078	test	edx, edx	
0040107A	jz	004010C3	**if**$(edx = 0)$ **goto** 004010C3
0040107C	xor	eax, eax	$eax \leftarrow 0$
0040107E	mov	al, byte ptr [esp + 8]	$al \leftarrow (char)value$
00401082	push	edi	
00401083	mov	edi, ecx	$edi \leftarrow ecx$
00401085	cmp	edx, 4	
00401088	jb	004010B7	**if**$(edx < 4)$ **goto** 004010B7
0040108A	neg	ecx	$ecx \leftarrow -ecx$
0040108C	and	ecx, 3	$ecx \leftarrow ecx\ \&\ 3$
0040108F	jz	00401099	**if**$(ecx = 0)$ **goto** 00401099
00401091	sub	edx, ecx	$edx \leftarrow edx - ecx$
00401093	mov	byte ptr [edi], al	$*edi \leftarrow al$
00401095	inc	edi	$edi \leftarrow edi + 1$
00401096	dec	ecx	$ecx \leftarrow ecx - 1$
00401097	jnz	00401093	**if**$(ecx \neq 0)$ **goto** 00401093
00401099	mov	ecx, eax	$ecx \leftarrow eax$
0040109B	shl	eax, 8	$eax \leftarrow eax << 8$
0040109E	add	eax, ecx	$eax \leftarrow eax + ecx$
004010A0	mov	ecx, eax	$ecx \leftarrow eax$
004010A2	shl	eax, 10h	$eax \leftarrow eax << 16$
004010A5	add	eax, ecx	$eax \leftarrow eax + ecx$
004010A7	mov	ecx, edx	$ecx \leftarrow edx$
004010A9	and	edx, 3	$edx \leftarrow edx\ \&\ 3$
004010AC	shr	ecx, 2	$ecx \leftarrow ecx >> 2$
004010AF	jz	004010B7	**if**$(ecx = 0)$ **goto** 004010B7
004010B1	rep stosd		**while**$(ecx \neq 0)$ { $*edi \leftarrow eax;\ edi++;\ ecx--;$ }
004010B3	test	edx, edx	
004010B5	jz	004010BD	**if**$(edx = 0)$ **goto** 004010BD
004010B7	mov	byte ptr [edi], al	$*edi \leftarrow al$
004010B9	inc	edi	$edi \leftarrow edi + 1$
004010BA	dec	edx	$edx \leftarrow edx - 1$
004010BB	jnz	004010B7	**if**$(edx \neq 0)$ **goto** 004010B7
004010BD	mov	eax, dword ptr [esp + 8]	$eax \leftarrow ptr$
004010C1	pop	edi	
004010C2	retn		**return**
004010C3	mov	eax, dword ptr [esp + 4]	$eax \leftarrow ptr$
004010C7	retn		**return**

Fig. 1. The disassembly of memset. The rightmost column shows the semantics of each instruction using a C-like notation.

Analysis overview. Fig. 1 shows the disassembly of memset from the C library that is bundled with Visual C++.[1] Observe that there are no explicit variables in the code; instead, offsets from the stack register (**esp**) are used to access parameter values. Also, there is no type information, and thus it is not obvious which registers hold memory addresses and which do not. Logical instructions and shifts, which are hard to model numerically, are used extensively. Rather than addressing all these challenges at once, the analysis constructs the summary of a function in several phases.

Intermediate Representation (IR) recovery. First, *value-set analysis (VSA)* [1,2] is performed on the disassembled code to discover low-level information: variables that are accessed by each instruction, parameter-passing details, and, for each program point,

---

[1] We used Microsoft Visual Studio 6.0, Professional Edition, *Release* build.

an overapproximation of the values held in the registers, flags, and memory locations at that point. Also, VSA resolves the targets of indirect control transfers.

In x86 executables, parameters are typically passed via the stack. The register **esp** points to the top of the stack and is implicitly updated by the **push** and the **pop** instructions. VSA identifies numeric properties of the values stored in **esp** and maps offsets from **esp** to the corresponding parameters. To see that this process is not trivial, observe that different offsets map to the same parameter at addresses *0x4010BD* and *0x4010C3*: at *0x4010BD* an extra 4 bytes are used to account for the push of **edi** at *0x401082*.

Numeric Program Generation. VSA results are used to generate a numeric program that captures the behavior of the library function. The primary challenge that is addressed in this phase is to translate non-numeric instructions, such as bitwise operations and shifts, into a program that numeric analysis is able to analyze. Bitwise operations are used extensively in practice to perform certain computations because they are typically more efficient in terms of CPU cycles than corresponding numeric instructions. The ubiquitous example is the use of **xor** instruction to initialize a register to zero. In Fig. 1, the **xor** at *0x40107C* is used in this way.

The generation phase also introduces the auxiliary variables that store allocation bounds for pointer variables. A simple type analysis is performed to identify variables and registers that may hold addresses. For each instruction that performs address arithmetic, additional statements that update corresponding allocation bounds are generated. Also, for each instruction that dereferences an address, a set of numeric assertions are generated to ensure that memory safety is not violated by the operation. The assertions divert program control to a set of *error program points*.

Numeric Analysis and Summary Construction. The generated numeric program is fed into an off-the-shelf numeric analyzer. We use a numeric analysis that, instead of approximating sets of reachable program states, approximates program transfer functions. That is, for each program point, the analysis computes a function that maps an approximation for the set of initial states at the entry of the program to an approximation for the set of states that arise at that program point. The numeric-analysis results are used to generate a set of error triggers and a set of summary transformers for the library function. The transfer functions computed for program points corresponding to the return instructions form a set of summary transformers for the function. Error triggers are constructed by projecting transfer functions computed for the set of error program points onto their domains.

The summary obtained for memset. Memset uses two loops and a "**rep stosd**" instruction, which invokes a hardware-supported loop. The "**rep stosd**" instruction at *0x4010B1* is the workhorse; it performs the bulk of the work by copying the value in eax (which is initialized in lines *0x40107C–0x40107E* and *0x401099–0x4010A5* to contain four copies of the low byte of memset's *value* parameter) into successive 4-byte-aligned memory locations. The loops at *0x401093–0x401097* and *0x4010B7–0x4010BB* handle any non-4-byte-aligned prefix and suffix. If the total number of bytes to be initialized is less than 4, control is transfered directly to the loop at *0x4010B7*.

$memset(ptr, value, num)$

00401070		$edx \leftarrow count;$
00401074		$ecx \leftarrow ptr; ecx.alloc_f \leftarrow ptr.alloc_f; ecx.alloc_b \leftarrow ptr.alloc_b;$
00401078-7A		$\textbf{if}(edx = 0) \textbf{ goto } L5;$
0040107C-82		...
00401083		$edi \leftarrow ecx; edi.alloc_f \leftarrow ecx.alloc_f; edi.alloc_b \leftarrow ecx.alloc_b;$
00401088		$\textbf{if}(edx < 4) \textbf{ goto } L3;$
0040108A		$ecx \leftarrow -ecx;$
0040108C		$ecx \leftarrow ?; \textbf{assume}(0 \leq ecx \leq 3);$
0040108F		$\textbf{if}(ecx = 0) \textbf{ goto } L2;$
00401091		$edx \leftarrow edx - ecx;$
00401093	L1:	$\textbf{assert}(edi.alloc_f >= 1); \textbf{ assert}(edi.alloc_b >= 0);$
00401095		$edi \leftarrow edi + 1; edi.alloc_f \leftarrow edi.alloc_f - 1; edi.alloc_b \leftarrow edi.alloc_b + 1;$
00401096		$ecx \leftarrow ecx - 1;$
00401097		$\textbf{if}(ecx \neq 0) \textbf{ goto } L1;$
00401099-A5	L2:	...
004010A7		$edx.rem_4 = ?; edx.quot_4 = ?;$
		$\textbf{assume}(0 \leq edx.rem_4 \leq 3); \textbf{ assume}(edx = 4 \times edx.quot_4 + edx.rem_4);$
		$ecx \leftarrow edx; ecx.quot_4 \leftarrow edx.quot_4; ecx.rem_4 = edx.rem_4;$
004010A9		$edx \leftarrow edx.rem_4;$
004010AC		$ecx \leftarrow ecx.quot_4;$
004010AF		$\textbf{if}(ecx = 0) \textbf{ goto } L3;$
004010B1		$\textbf{assert}(edi.alloc_f >= 4 \times ecx); \textbf{ assert}(edi.alloc_b >= 0);$
		$edi \leftarrow edi + 4 \times ecx;$
		$edi.alloc_f \leftarrow edi.alloc_f - 4 \times ecx; edi.alloc_b \leftarrow edi.alloc_b + 4 \times ecx;$
004010B3-B5		$\textbf{if}(edx = 0) \textbf{ goto } L4;$
004010B7	L3:	$\textbf{assert}(edi.alloc_f >= 1); \textbf{ assert}(edi.alloc_b >= 0);$
004010B9		$edi \leftarrow edi + 1; edi.alloc_f \leftarrow edi.alloc_f - 1; edi.alloc_b \leftarrow edi.alloc_b + 1;$
004010BA		$edx \leftarrow edx - 1$
004010BB		$\textbf{if}(edx \neq 0) \textbf{ goto } L3;$
004010BD	L4:	$eax \leftarrow ptr; eax.alloc_f = ptr.alloc_f; eax.alloc_b \leftarrow ptr.alloc_b;$
004010C2		$\textbf{return } eax, eax.alloc_f, eax.alloc_b;$
004010C3	L5:	$eax \leftarrow ptr; eax.alloc_f = ptr.alloc_f; eax.alloc_b \leftarrow ptr.alloc_b;$
004010C7		$\textbf{return } eax, eax.alloc_f, eax.alloc_b;$

Fig. 2. The numeric program generated for the code in Fig. 1; parts of the program that are not relevant for the summary construction are omitted

The application of our technique to the code in Fig. 1 yields exactly the summary transformer we conjectured in Eqn. (1). The situation with error triggers is slightly more complicated. First, observe that there are three places in the code where the buffer is accessed: at addresses $0x401093$, $0x4010B1$, and $0x4010B7$. Each access produces a separate error trigger:

$$0x401093: \quad num \geq 4 \wedge ptr.alloc_f \leq 2$$
$$0x4010B1: \quad num \geq 4 \wedge ptr.alloc_f \leq num - 1$$
$$0x4010B7: \quad num \geq 1 \wedge ptr.alloc_f \leq num - 1$$

Note that the first trigger is stronger than the one conjectured in Eqn. (2): it gives a constant bound on $alloc_f$; furthermore, the bound is less than 3, which is the smallest bound implied by the conjectured trigger. The issue is that the instruction at $0x401093$

accesses at most three bytes. In case $ptr.alloc_f$ is equal to 3, memset will generate a buffer overrun at one of the other memory accesses. The other two triggers are similar to the trigger conjectured in Eqn. (2) and differ only in the value of num.

3   Library Code Analysis

3.1   Intermediate Representation Recovery

The IR-recovery phase recovers intermediate representations from the library's binary that are similar to those that would be available had one started from source code. For this phase, we use the CodeSurfer/x86 analyzer that was developed jointly by Wisconsin and GrammaTech, Inc. This tool recovers IRs that represent: control-flow graphs (CFGs), with indirect jumps resolved; a call graph, with indirect calls resolved; information about the program's variables; possible values of pointer variables; sets of used, killed, and possibly-killed variables for each CFG node; and data dependences. The techniques employed by CodeSurfer/x86 do not rely on debugging information being present, but can use available debugging information (e.g., Windows .pdb files) if directed to do so.

The analyses used in CodeSurfer/x86 (see [1,2]) are a great deal more ambitious than even relatively sophisticated disassemblers, such as IDAPro [15]. At the technical level, they address the following problem: *Given a (possibly stripped) executable E (i.e., with all debugging information removed), identify the procedures, data objects, types, and libraries that it uses, and, for each instruction I in E and its libraries, for each interprocedural calling context of I, and for each machine register and variable V, statically compute an accurate over-approximation to the set of values that V may contain when I executes.*

Variable and Type Discovery. One of the major stumbling blocks in analyzing executables is the difficulty of recovering information about variables and types, especially for aggregates (i.e., structures and arrays).

When debugging information is absent, an executable's data objects are not easily identifiable. Consider, for instance, a data dependence from statement a to statement b that is transmitted by write/read accesses on some variable x. When performing source-code analysis, the programmer-defined variables provide us with convenient compartments for tracking such data manipulations. A dependence analyzer must show that a defines x, b uses x, and there is an x-def-free path from a to b. However, in executables, memory is accessed either directly—by specifying an absolute address—or indirectly—through an address expression of the form "[*base* + *index* × *scale* + *offset*]", where *base* and *index* are registers and *scale* and *offset* are integer constants. It is not clear from such expressions what the natural compartments are that should be used for analysis. Because, executables do not have *intrinsic* entities that can be used for analysis (analogous to source-level variables), a crucial step in IR recovery is to identify variable-like entities.

The variable and type-discovery phase of CodeSurfer/x86 [2], recovers information about variables that are allocated globally, locally (i.e., on the run-time stack), and dynamically (i.e., from the heap). An iterative strategy is used; with each round of the analysis—consisting of aggregate structure identification (ASI) [19,2] and value-set analysis (VSA) [1,2]—the notion of the program's variables and types is refined. The net result is that CodeSurfer/x86 recovers a set of proxies for variables, called *a-locs* (for "abstract locations"). The a-locs are the basic variables used in the method described below.

3.2 Key Concepts of Numeric Program Generation

The generation of a numeric program is the central piece of our work. We strive as much as possible to generate a sound representation of the binary code.[2] The target language is very simple: it supports assignments, assumes, asserts, if-statements, and gotos. The expression "?" selects a value non-deterministically. The condition "*" transfers control non-deterministically.

Translating x86 instructions. Due to space constraints, we only describe several translation issues that are particularly challenging. The numeric instructions, such as **mov**, **add**, **sub**, **lea**, etc., are directly translated into the corresponding numeric statements: e.g., the instruction "**sub** edx, ecx" at *0x401091* in Fig. 1 is translated into numeric statement $edx \leftarrow edx - ecx$.

The bitwise operations and shifts typically cannot be precisely converted into a single numeric statement, and thus pose a greater challenge. Several numeric statements, including ifs and assumes, may be required to translate each of these instructions. At first we were tempted to design universal translations that would work equally well for all possible contexts in which the instruction occurs. In the end, however, we noticed that these instructions, when used for numeric computations, are only used in a few very specific ways. For instance, bitwise-and is often used to compute the remainder from dividing a variable by a power of two. The instruction "**and** ecx, 3" at *0x40108C* in Fig. 1 is used to compute ecx **mod** 4. The translation treats these special cases with precision; other cases are treated imprecisely, but soundly. The instruction "**and** op_1, op_2" is translated into "$op_1 \leftarrow$?; **assume**$(0 \leq op_1 \leq op_2)$;" if op_2 is an immediate operand that has a positive value; otherwise, it is translated into "$op_1 \leftarrow$?;".

Recovering conditions from the branch instructions. An important part of numeric program generation is the recovery of conditional expressions. In the x86 architecture, several instructions must be executed in sequence to perform a conditional control transfer. The execution of most x86 instructions affects the set of flags maintained by the processor. The flags include the *zero flag*, which is set if the result of the currently executing instruction is zero, the *sign flag*, which is set if the result is negative, and many others. Also, the x86 architecture provides a number of control-transfer instructions each of which performs a jump if the flags are set in a specific way. Technically, the flag-setting instruction and the corresponding jump instructions do not have to be adjacent and can, in fact, be separated by a set of instructions that do not affect the flags (such as **mov** instruction.

We symbolically propagate the expressions that affect flags to the jump instructions that use them. Consider the following sequences of instructions and their translation:

---

[2] Currently, we assume that numeric values are not bounded. In the future, we hope to add support for bounded arithmetic.

```
cmp eax,ebx
mov ecx,edx                    ecx ← edx;
jz label                       if(eax − ebx = 0) goto label;
```

We derive a flag-setting expression $eax - ebx$ from the **cmp** instruction; the **mov** instruction does not affect any flags; the **jz** instruction transfers control to label if the zero flag is set, which can only happen if the expression $eax - ebx$ is equal to zero. Note, however, that if the intervening move affects one of the operands in the flag-setting expression, that expression is no longer available at the jump instruction. This can be circumvented with the use of a temporary variable:

```
cmp eax,ebx
mov eax,edx                    temp ← eax − ebx; eax ← edx;
jz label                       if(temp = 0) goto label;
```

Allocation bounds. As we mentioned above, each variable var that may contain a memory address is associated with two auxiliary variables that specify allocation bounds for that address. The auxiliary variable $var.alloc_f$ specifies the number of bytes following the address that can be safely accessed; the auxiliary variable $var.alloc_b$ specifies the number of bytes preceding the address that can be safely accessed. These auxiliary variables are central to our technique: the purpose of numeric analysis is to find constraints on the auxiliary variables that are associated with the function's parameters and return value. These constraints form the bulk of the function summaries.

The updates for the auxiliary variables are generated in a straightforward way. That is, the translation of the **mov** instruction contains assignments for the corresponding allocation bounds. The instructions **add**, **sub**, **inc**, **dec**, and **lea**, as well as the x86 string-manipulation instructions, are translated into affine transformations on variables and their associated allocation bounds.

The auxiliary variables are used to generate memory-safety checks: checks for buffer overflows and checks for buffer underflows. We generate these checks for each indirect memory access that does not access the current stack frame. As mentioned in §3.1, general indirect memory accesses in x86 instructions have the form "[$base + index \times scale + offset$]", whose base and index are registers and scale and offsets are constants. Let $size$ denote the number of bytes to be read or written. The following checks are generated:

- Buffer-overflow check: **assert**($base.alloc_f \geq index * scale + offset + size$)
- Buffer-underflow check: **assert**($base.alloc_b + index * scale + offset \geq 0$)

The checks generated for the x86 string-manipulation instructions, such as **stos** and **movs** are only slightly more complicated and are omitted for brevity.

Type Analysis. Maintaining allocation bounds for all variables is unnecessarily expensive. For this reason, we only associate allocation bounds with variables that can hold memory addresses. To identify this set of variables, we construct an *affine-dependence graph (ADG)*: a graph in which the nodes correspond to program variables and the edges indicate that the value of the destination variable is computed as an affine transformation of the value of the source variable. The construction of the ADG is straight-forward: e.g., instruction "**mov** foo, bar" generates an edge from the node that corresponds to variable bar to the node that corresponds to foo, etc. To determine the set of pointer variables, we start with nodes that correspond to variables that are used as *base pointers* in memory-safety checks and mark as pointers all the variables whose corresponding nodes are reached by a backward traversal through the graph.

Note that the precision of the ADG does not affect the soundness of the overall analysis: if some dependences are not present in the graph, then some allocation bounds will not be tracked and the overall analysis will be less precise. If some non-existing dependences are present in the graph, then some useless allocation bounds will be tracked and the analysis will be slowed down.

In contrast to variables, which keep the same type throughout their lifetime, registers are reused in different contexts, and can have a different type in each context. Limiting each register to a single node in the ADG generates many "spurious" dependences because all of the contexts in which the register is used are collapsed together. Thus, when constructing the ADG, we create a separate node for each register's live-range.

Handling integer division and remainders. Memory functions, such as memset, rely heavily on integer division and remainder computations to improve the efficiency of memory operations. In low-level code, the quotient and remainder from dividing by a power of two are typically computed with a shift-right (**shr**) instruction and a bitwise-and (**and**) instruction, respectively. In Fig. 1, the two consecutive instructions at *0x4010A9* establish the property: $edx_0 = 4 \times ecx + edx$, where edx_0 denotes the value contained in edx before the instructions are executed. This property is essential for inferring precise error triggers for memory accesses at *0x4010B1* and *0x4010B7*. However, polyhedral analysis is not able to handle integer division with sufficient precision.

We overcome this problem by introducing additional auxiliary variables: each variable var that may hold a value for which both a quotient and remainder from division by k are computed is associated with two auxiliary variables $var.quot_k$ and $var.rem_k$, which denote the quotient and the remainder, respectively. To identify such variables, we use the ADG: we look for the nodes that are reachable by backward traversals from both the quotient and remainder computations. The auxiliary variables are associated with all of the nodes that are visited by the traversals up to the first shared node. For the above example, the starting point for the "quotient" traversal is the use of **ecx** at *0x4010AC*, and the staring point for the "remainder" traversal is the use of **edx** at *0x4010A9*: at these points, we generate assignments that directly use the corresponding auxiliary variables. The first shared node is the use of **edx** at *0x4010A7*: at that point, we generate numeric instructions that impose semantic constraints on the values of auxiliary variables (see Fig. 2). The intermediate updates for the auxiliary variables are generated in a straightforward way. Polyhedral analysis of the resulting program yields precise error triggers for both memory accesses.

Modeling the environment. The goal of our technique is to synthesize the summary of a library function by looking at its code in isolation. However, library functions operate in a larger context: they may access memory of the client program that was specified via their parameters, or they may access global structures that are internal to the library. The IR-recovery phase has no knowledge of either the contents or the structure of that memory: they are specific to the client application. As an example, from the IR-recovery perspective, memset parameter *ptr* may contain any memory address. Thus, from the point of view of numeric-program generation, a write into $*ptr$ may potentially overwrite any memory location: local and global variables, a return address on the stack, or even the code of the function. As the result, the generated numeric program, as well as the function summary derived from it, will be overly conservative (causing the client analysis to lose precision).

We attempt to generate more meaningful function summaries by using *symbolic constants* to model memory that cannot be confined to a specific a-loc by the IR-recovery phase. A unique symbolic constant is created for each unresolved memory access. From numeric-analysis perspective, a symbolic constant is simply a global variable that has a special auxiliary variable *addr* associated with it. This auxiliary variable represents the address of a memory location that the symbolic constant models. If the memory location may hold an address, the corresponding symbolic constant has allocation bounds associated with it. We illustrate this technique in §4.

3.3   Numeric Analysis and Summary Generation

Our numeric analyzer is based on the Parma Polyhedral Library (PPL) and the WPDS++ library for weighted pushdown systems (WPDSs) and supports programs with multiple procedures, recursion, global and local variables, and parameter passing. The analysis of a WPDS yields, for each program point, a *weight*, or abstract state transformer, that describes how the program state is transformed on all the paths from the entry of the program to that program point. Linear-relation analysis [8] is encoded using weights that maintain two sets of variables: the *domain* describes the program state at the entry point; the *range* describes the program state at the destination point. The relationships between the variables are captured with linear inequalities. Given a weight computed for some program point, its projection onto the range variables approximates the set of states that are reachable at that program point. Similarly, its projection onto the set of domain variables approximates the precondition for reaching that program state.

Function summaries are generated from the numeric-analysis results. Summary transformers are constructed from the weights computed for the program points corresponding to procedure returns. Error triggers are constructed by back-projecting weights computed for the set of error program points.

4   Case Studies

We used our technique to generate summaries for library functions memset and _lseek. The IR-recovery and numeric-program generation was done on 1.83GHz Intel Core Duo T2400 with 1.5Gb of memory. The numeric analysis was done on 2.4GHz Intel Pentium 4 with 4Gb of memory.

The summary obtained for memset. The detailed description of memset, as well as the analysis results, were given in §2 and §3. It took 70 seconds to both execute the IR-recovery phase and generate a numeric program for memset. The resulting numeric

```
mov    eax,  dword ptr [4×ecx + 0424DE0h]
              assume(mc₁.addr = 0x424DE0 + 4 * ecx);
              eax ← mc₁; eax.allocf = mc₁.allocf; eax.allocb = mc₁.allocb;
movsx  ecx,  byte ptr [eax + 8×edx + 4]
              assert(eax.allocf ≤ 8 * edx + 5); assert(eax.allocb + 8 * edx + 4 ≥ 0);
              assume(mc₂.addr = eax.allocb + 8 * edx + 4 ≥ 0); ecx ← mc₂;
```

Fig. 3. Symbolic memory modeling: the symbolic constants mc_1 and mc_2 model the memory location accessed by **mov** and **movsx** instructions, repsectively

program has one procedure with 8 global variables and 11 local variables. The numeric analysis took 1 second.

The summary obtained for _lseek. the function _lseek moves a file pointer to a specified position within the file. It is declared as follows:

```
off_t _lseek(int fd, off_t offset, int origin);
```

fd is a file descriptor; *offset* specifies the new position of the pointer relative to either its current position, the beginning of the file, or the end of the file, based on *origin*.

A recurring memory-access pattern in _lseek is to read a pointer from a global table and then dereference it. Fig. 3 shows a portion of _lseek that contains a pair of such memory accesses: the first **mov** instruction reads the table entry, the second dereferences it. The registers **ecx** and **edx** hold the values $fd/32$ and $fd \bmod 32$, respectively. The global variable *uNumber* gives the upper bound for the possible values of *fd*. Symbolic constants mc_1 and mc_2 model the memory locations accessed by the first and second **mov** instructions, respectively. Our technique synthesizes the following buffer-overrun trigger for the second **mov** instruction:

$$\text{0x424DE0} \leq mc_1.addr \leq \text{0x424DE0} + (uNumber - 1)/8 \wedge mc_1.allocf <= 251$$

The above trigger can be interpreted as follows: *if any of the addresses stored in the table at 0x424DE0 point to a buffer of length that is less than 252 bytes, there is a possibility of a buffer-overrun error.* The error trigger is sufficient for a client analysis to implement sound error reporting: if the client analysis does not know the allocation bounds for pointers in the table at *0x424DE0*, it should emit an error report for this trigger at the call site to _lseek. However, we hope that the summary generated by our technique for the library-initialization code will capture the proper allocation bounds for the pointers in the table at *0x424DE0*. Thus, the analysis will not emit spurious error reports. The error triggers for other memory accesses look similar to this one.

The analysis took about 70 seconds to recover intermediate representation and generate a numeric program. The generated program has 41 global variables (22 of which are used for symbolic memory modeling) and contains three procedures with 21, 8, and 2 local variables, respectively. The numeric analysis of the program took 117 seconds.

5   Related Work

Summary functions have a long history, which goes back to the seminal work by Cousot and Halbwachs on linear-relation analysis [8] and the papers on interprocedural analysis of Cousot and Cousot [7] and Sharir and Pnueli [24]. Other work on analyses based on summary functions includes [16,20,3], as well as methods for pushdown systems [11,4,5,21], where summary functions arise as one by-product of an analysis.

A substantial amount of work has been done to create summary functions for alias analysis or points-to analysis [18,26,14,6,22], or for other simple analyses, such as lock state [27]. Those algorithms are specialized for particular problems; more comprehensive approaches include the work on analysis of program fragments [23], componential set-based analysis [12], and use of SAT procedures [27].

Some of the work cited above explicitly mentions separately compiled libraries as one of the motivations for the work. Although the techniques described in the aforementioned papers are language-independent, all of the implementations described are for source-code analysis.

Guo et al. [13] developed a system for performing pointer analysis on a low-level intermediate representation. The algorithm is only partially flow-sensitive: it tracks registers in a flow-sensitive manner, but treats memory locations in a flow-insensitive manner. The algorithm uses partial transfer functions [26] to achieve context-sensitivity, where the transfer functions are parameterized by "unknown initial values".

Kruegel et al. [17] developed a system for automating mimicry attacks. Their tool uses symbolic-execution techniques on x86 binaries to discover attacks that can give up and regain execution control by modifying the contents of the data, heap, or stack so that the application is forced to return control to injected attack code at some point after a system call has been performed. Cova et al. [9] used this platform to apply static analysis to the problem of detecting security vulnerabilities in x86 executables. In both of these systems, alias information is not available.

In our work, we make use of a-locs (variable proxies), alias information, and other IRs that have been recovered by the algorithms used in CodeSurfer/x86 [1,2]. The recovered IRs are used as a platform on which we implemented a relational analysis that synthesizes summary functions for procedures.

Acknowledgements. We thank D. Vitek for sharing with us his insights on the problem of creating function summaries.

References

1. Balakrishnan, G., Reps, T.: Analyzing memory accesses in x86 executables. In: Duesterwald, E. (ed.) CC 2004. LNCS, vol. 2985, Springer, Heidelberg (2004)
2. Balakrishnan, G., Reps, T.: DIVINE: DIscovering Variables IN Executables. In: Cook, B., Podelski, A. (eds.) VMCAI 2007. LNCS, vol. 4349, Springer, Heidelberg (2007)
3. Ball, T., Rajamani, S.K.: Bebop: A path-sensitive interprocedural dataflow engine. In: PASTE (2001)
4. Bouajjani, A., Esparza, J., Maler, O.: Reachability analysis of pushdown automata: Application to model checking. In: Mazurkiewicz, A., Winkowski, J. (eds.) CONCUR 1997. LNCS, vol. 1243, Springer, Heidelberg (1997)
5. Bouajjani, A., Esparza, J., Touili, T.: A generic approach to the static analysis of concurrent programs with procedures. In: POPL (2003)
6. Chatterjee, R., Ryder, B.G., Landi, W.: Relevant context inference. In: POPL (1999)

7. Cousot, P., Cousot, R.: Static determination of dynamic properties of recursive procedures. In: Formal Descriptions of Programming Concepts, North-Holland, Amsterdam (1978)

8. Cousot, P., Halbwachs, N.: Automatic discovery of linear constraints among variables of a program. In: POPL (1978)

9. Cova, M., Felmetsger, V., Banks, G., Vigna, G.: Static detection of vulnerabilities in x86 executables. In: Jesshope, C., Egan, C. (eds.) ACSAC 2006. LNCS, vol. 4186, Springer, Heidelberg (2006)

10. Dor, N., Rodeh, M., Sagiv, M.: CSSV: Towards a realistic tool for statically detecting all buffer overflows in C. In: PLDI (2003)

11. Finkel, A., Willems, B., Wolper, P.: A direct symbolic approach to model checking pushdown systems. Elec. Notes in Theor. Comp. Sci. 9 (1997)

12. Flanagan, C., Felleisen, M.: Componential set-based analysis. In: PLDI (1997)

13. Guo, B., Bridges, M.J., Triantafyllis, S., Ottoni, G., Raman, E., August, D.I.: Practical and accurate low-level pointer analysis. In: 3nd Int. Symp. on Code Gen. and Opt. (2005)

14. Harrold, M.J., Rothermel, G.: Separate computation of alias information for reuse. TSE 22(7) (1996)

15. IDAPro disassembler, http://www.datarescue.com/idabase/

16. Knoop, J., Steffen, B.: The interprocedural coincidence theorem. In: Pfahler, P., Kastens, U. (eds.) CC 1992. LNCS, vol. 641, Springer, Heidelberg (1992)

17. Kruegel, C., Kirda, E., Mutz, D., Robertson, W., Vigna, G.: Automating mimicry attacks using static binary analysis. In: USENIX Sec. Symp. (2005)

18. Landi, W., Ryder, B.G.: A safe approximate algorithm for interprocedural pointer aliasing. In: PLDI (1992)

19. Ramalingam, G., Field, J., Tip, F.: Aggregate structure identification and its application to program analysis. In: POPL (1999)

20. Reps, T., Horwitz, S., Sagiv, M.: Precise interprocedural dataflow analysis via graph reachability. In: POPL (1995)

21. Reps, T., Schwoon, S., Jha, S., Melski, D.: Weighted pushdown systems and their application to interprocedural dataflow analysis. Sci. of Comp. Prog. 58(1–2) (2005)

22. Rountev, A., Ryder, B.G.: Points-to and side-effect analyses for programs built with precompiled libraries. In: Wilhelm, R. (ed.) CC 2001 and ETAPS 2001. LNCS, vol. 2027, Springer, Heidelberg (2001)

23. Rountev, A., Ryder, B.G., Landi, W.: Data-flow analysis of program fragments. In: Knudsen, L.R. (ed.) FSE 1999. LNCS, vol. 1636, Springer, Heidelberg (1999)

24. Sharir, M., Pnueli, A.: Two approaches to interprocedural data flow analysis. In: Program Flow Analysis: Theory and Applications, Prentice-Hall, Englewood Cliffs (1981)

25. Wagner, D., Foster, J., Brewer, E., Aiken, A.: A first step towards automated detection of buffer overrun vulnerabilities. In: NDSS (2000)

26. Wilson, R.P., Lam, M.S.: Efficient context-sensitive pointer analysis for C programs. In: PLDI (1995)

27. Xie, Y., Aiken, A.: Scalable error detection using Boolean satisfiability. In: POPL (2005)

Verification Across Intellectual Property Boundaries*

Sagar Chaki[1], Christian Schallhart[2], and Helmut Veith[2]

[1] Software Engineering Institute, Carnegie Mellon University, USA
chaki@sei.cmu.edu
[2] Institut für Informatik, Technische Universität München, Germany
schallha@in.tum.de, veith@in.tum.de

Abstract. In many industries, the share of software components provided by third-party suppliers is steadily increasing. As the suppliers seek to secure their intellectual property (IP) rights, the customer usually has no direct access to the suppliers' source code, and is able to enforce the use of verification tools only by legal requirements. In turn, the supplier has no means to convince the customer about successful verification without revealing the source code. This paper presents a new approach to resolve the conflict between the IP interests of the supplier and the quality interests of the customer. We introduce a protocol in which a dedicated server (called the "amanat") is controlled by both parties: the customer controls the verification task performed by the amanat, while the supplier controls the communication channels of the amanat to ensure that the amanat does not leak information about the source code. We argue that the protocol is both practically useful and mathematically sound. As the protocol is based on well-known (and relatively lightweight) cryptographic primitives, it allows a straightforward implementation on top of existing verification tool chains. To substantiate our security claims, we establish the correctness of the protocol by cryptographic reduction proofs.

1 Introduction

In the classical verification scenario, the software author and the verification engineer share a common interest to verify a piece of software; the author provides the source code to be analyzed, whereon the verification engineer communicates the verification verdict. Both parties are mutually trusted, i.e., the verification engineer trusts that he has verified production code, and the author trusts that the verification engineer will not use the source code for unintended purposes.

Industrial production of software-intensive technology however often employs supply chains which render this simple scenario obsolete. Complex products are being increasingly assembled from multiple components whose development is outsourced to supplying companies. Typical examples of outsourced software components comprise embedded controller software in automobiles and consumer electronics [1,2] as well as Windows device drivers [3]. Although the suppliers may well use verification

---

* Supported by the European FP6 project ECRYPT, the DFG grant FORTAS, and the Predictable Assembly from Certifiable Components (PACC) initiative at the Software Engineering Institute, Pittsburgh, USA.

W. Damm and H. Hermanns (Eds.): CAV 2007, LNCS 4590, pp. 82–94, 2007.

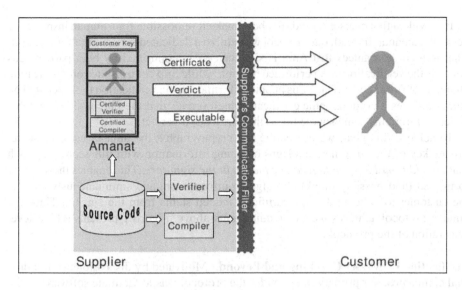

Fig. 1. A High-Level View of the Amanat Protocol

techniques for internal use, they are usually not willing to reveal their source code, as the intellectual property (IP) contained in the source code is a major asset for their company.

This setting constitutes a principal conflict between the *supplier* Sup who owns the source code, and the *customer* Cus who purchases o n l y the executable. While both parties share a basic interest in producing high quality software, it is in the customer's interest to have the source code inspected, and in the supplier's interest to protect the source code. More formally, this amounts to the following basic requirements:

(a) **Conformance.** The customer must be able to validate that the purchased executable was compiled from successfully verified source code.
(b) **Secrecy.** The supplier must be able to validate that no information about the source code other than the verification result is revealed to the customer.

The main technical contribution of this paper is a new cryptographic verification protocol tailored for IP-aware verification. Our protocol is based on standard cryptographic primitives, and provably satisfies both the above requirements with little overhead in the system configuration. Notably, the proposed scheme applies not only to automated verification in a model checking style, but also encompasses a wide range of validation techniques, both automated and semi-manual.

Our solution centers around the notion of an *amanat*. This terminology is derived from the historic judicial notion of amanats, i.e., noble prisoners who were kept hostage as part of a contract. Intuitively, our protocol applies a similar principle: The amanat is a trusted expert of the customer who settles down in the production plant of the supplier and executes whatever verification job the customer has entrusted on him. The supplier accepts this procedure because (i) all of the amanat's communications are subject to the censorship of the supplier, and, (ii) the amanat will never return to the customer again.

It is evident that clauses (i) and (ii) above make it impossible for a human inspector to act as the amanat; instead, our protocol will utilize a dedicated server Ama for this task. The protocol guarantees that Ama is simultaneously controlled by both parties: Cus controls the verification task performed by Ama, while Sup controls the communication channels of Ama. To convince Cus about conformance, the verification tool executed on Ama produces a cryptographic certificate which proves that the purchased executable is derived from the same source file as the verification verdict.

To achieve this goal, we use public key cryptography; the amanat uses the secret private key of the customer, and signs outgoing information with this secret key such that *no additional information can be hidden in the signature.* This enables the supplier to inspect (and possibly block) all outgoing information, and simultaneously enables the customer to validate that the certificate indeed stems from the amanat. Thus, the amanat protocol achieves the two requirements above. Figure 1 presents a high-level illustration of the protocol.

Verification by Model Checking and Beyond. Motivated by discussions with industrial companies, our primary intention for the protocol was to facilitate software model checking across IP boundaries in a B2B setting where the supplier and the customer are businesses. Our guiding examples for this B2B setting have been Windows device drivers and automotive controller software, for which our protocols are practically feasible with state-of-the-art technology.

Software model checking is now able to verify important properties of simply structured code [4,5,6]. Most notably, SLAM/SDV is a fully automatic tool for a narrow application area, and we expect to see more such tools. Note that SDV has built-in specifications because the device drivers access and implement a clearly defined API. Other tools such as Terminator [7] and Slayer [8] do not require specifications as they are built to verify specific critical properties – termination and memory-safety, respectively. Automotive software is similar to device drivers in that it also accesses standardized APIs.

For less standardized software and more specific properties, it may be necessary for the customer and the supplier to negotiate about the formulation of the specification without revealing the source code. In the course of this negotiation, the supplier can decide to reveal a blueprint of the software, and the amanat can certify the accuracy of the blueprint by a mutually agreed algorithm.

The example of blueprints shows that the amanat protocol is *not restricted* to model checking, because the amanat can run any verification/validation tool whose output does not compromise the secrecy of the source code. For example, in future work and applications, Ama can:

1. apply static analysis tools such as ASTREE [9] and TVLA [10].
2. check the correctness of a manual proof provided by Sup, e.g., in PVS, ISABELLE, Coq or another prover [11].
3. evaluate worst case execution times experimentally [12] or statically [13].
4. generate white box test cases, and execute them.
5. validate that the source code comes with a set of test cases which satisfies previously agreed coverage criteria.
6. check that the source code is syntactically safe, e.g. using LINT.

7. compute numerical quality and quantity measures which are agreed between Sup and Cus, e.g. nesting depth, LOC, etc.
8. compare two versions of the source code, and quantify the difference between them; this is important in situations where Sup claims charges for a reimplementation.
9. check if third party IP is included in the source code, e.g. libraries etc.
10. ensure that certain algorithms are (not) used.
11. check that the source is well documented.
12. ensure a certain senior programmer has put his name on the source code.
13. validate the development steps by analyzing the CVS or SVN tree.
14. ensure compatibility of the source code with language standards.

We note that in all scenarios the code supplier *bears the burden of proof*: either the supplier has to write the source code in such a way that it is accepted by Ama as is, or the supplier has to provide auxiliary information (*e.g.* proofs, command line options, abstraction functions, test cases, etc.) which help the amanat in the verification without affecting correctness.

Security of the Amanat Protocol. In Section 4, we present a cryptographic proof for the *secrecy* and *conformance* of the amanat verification protocol. Stronger than term-based proofs in the Dolev-Yao model, these proofs assure that under standard cryptographic assumptions, randomized polynomial time attacks against the protocol (which may involve e.g. guessing the private keys) can succeed only with negligible probability [14]. The practical security of the protocol is also ensured by the simplicity of our protocol: As the protocol is based on well-known cryptographic encryption and signing schemes, it can be readily implemented.

The IP boundary between the supplier and the customer makes is inevitable that the amanat owns a *secret* unknown to the supplier, namely the private key of the customer; this secret enables the amanat to prove its identity to the customer and to compute the certificate. Consequently, the cryptographic proofs need to assume a system configuration where Ama can neither be reverse-engineered, nor closely monitored by the supplier. Thus, from the point of view of the supplier, Ama is a black box with input and output channels. For secrecy, the supplier requires ownership of Ama to make sure it will not return to the customer after verification. There are two natural scenarios to realize this hardware configuration:

A Ama is physically located at the site of a trusted third party. All communication channels of Ama are hardwired to go through a second server, the communication filter of the supplier, cf. Figure 1.

While scenario A involves a trusted third party, its role is limited to providing physical security for the servers. Thus, the third party does not need any expertise beyond server hosting. For the supplier, scenario A has the disadvantage that the encrypted source code has to be sent to the third party, and thus, to leave the supplier site.

B Ama is physically located at the site of the supplier, but in a sealed location or box whose integrity is assured through (i) regular checks by the customer, (ii) a third party, (iii) a traditional alarm system, or (iv) the use of sealed hardware. All communication channels of Ama are hardwired to the communication filter of the supplier.

In scenarios B(ii) and B(iii), the third party again plays a very limited role in that it only ensures physical integrity of the amanat. We believe that in our B2B settings, scenario B is realistic. We do not require custom-made hardware, but just a sealed location at the supplier's site, e.g. a locked room. Off-the-shelf hardware ensures that neither party can evade the protocol by radio transmission etc. In the B2B setting, it is realistic that before final deployment of a new controller software (but after the verification), the integrity of the seal is checked. Thus, there is no business incentive for the supplier to break the seal.

The supplier has total control over the information leaving the production site. Thus, it can also prevent attempts by the amanat to leak information by sending messages at specific time points. Because the supplier can read all outgoing messages, there is also a convincing argument for the supplier's non-technical management that no sensitive information is leaking. In our opinion, this simplicity of the amanat protocol is a major advantage for practical application.

Organization of the Paper. In Section 2, we survey related work and discuss alternative approaches to the amanat protocol. The protocol is described in detail in Section 3, and the correctness is addressed in Section 4. The paper is concluded in Section 5.

2   Related Work and Alternative Solutions

The last years have seen renewed activity in the analysis of executables from the verification and programming languages community. Despite remarkable advances (see e.g. [15,16,17,18]), the computer-aided analysis of executables remains a hard problem; natural applications are reverse engineering, automatic detection of low level errors such as memory violations, as well as malicious code detection [19,20]. The technical difficulties in the direct analysis of executables are often exacerbated by code obfuscation to prevent reverse engineering, or, in the case of malware, recognition of the malicious code. Although dynamic analysis [21] and black box testing [22,23] are relatively immune to obfuscation, they only give a limited assurance of system correctness.

The current paper is orthogonal to executable analysis. We consider a scenario where the software author is willing to assert the quality of the source code by formal methods, but not willing or able to make the source code available to the customer. It is evident that the visibility of the source code to the amanat and the cooperation of the software author/supplier significantly increase the leverage of formal methods.

Proof-Carrying Code [24] is able to generate certificates directly from binaries, but only for a restricted class of safety policies. It is evident that a proof for a non-trivial system property will for all practical purposes explain the internal logic of the binary. Thus, publishing this proof is tantamount to losing intellectual property.

The current paper takes an engineer's view on computer security. The results of the paper are quite specific to verification, as it exploits the conceptual difference between the source code and the executable. While we are aware of advanced methods such as secure multiparty computation [25] and zero-knowledge proofs [26], we believe that they are not practicable for our problem. To implement secure multiparty computation, it would be necessary to convert significant parts of the model checking tool chain into a Boolean circuit which is not a realistic option. To apply zero-knowledge proofs, one would require the verification tools to produce highly structured and detailed formal proofs. Except for the provers in item 2 of the list in Section 1, it is impractical to obtain such proofs by state of the art technology. More generally, we believe that any advanced method for which secrecy is not intuitively clear to the supplier will be hard to establish in practice. Thus, we are convinced that the conceptual simplicity of our protocol is an asset for practical applicability.

3   The Amanat Protocol

The amanat protocol aims to resolve the conflict between the code customer Cus who wants to verify the source code, and the code supplier Sup who needs to protect its IP. To this end, the amanat Ama computes a certificate which contains enough information to assure the correctness of the program. On the other hand, to secure the IP of Sup, the certificate must not reveal any information beyond the intentionally communicated correctness properties.

3.1   Requirements and Tool Landscape

To make the protocol requirements more precise, we fix some notation and assumptions about the tool landscape. Note that all tools are available to all involved parties.

The *compiler* Compiler takes an input source and computes an executable exec = Compiler(source). Note that Compiler does not take any other input. In practice, this means that source can be thought of as a directory tree containing a make file, and Compiler stands for the tool chain composed of the make command, the compiler, the linker etc.

The *verification tool* Verifier also takes the input source and computes two verification verdicts, $\log_{Sup}$ and $\log_{Cus}$. Here, $\log_{Sup}$ is the "internal" verdict for the supplier which may contain, for example, detailed IP-critical information such as counterexamples or witnesses for certain properties. The second output $\log_{Cus}$ in contrast contains only uncritical verification verdicts about which Sup and Cus have agreed beforehand. Similar as for the compiler, we assume that Verifier does not take any other input parameters. In particular, this means that the specifications are part of source, i.e., they are agreed between the parties and output into $\log_{Cus}$ together with the verification result. Moreover, all auxiliary information necessary for a successful run of Verifier– command line parameters, code annotations, abstraction functions *etc.* – are provided by Sup as part of source.

Before we formally describe the cryptographic primitives for signing and verifying messages, we note that the underlying algorithms are not deterministic but randomized. This randomization is a countermeasure to attacks against naive implementations of RSA and other schemes which exploit algebraically related messages, see for example [27]. In most applications, the randomization is not important for the protocol, as each participant can locally generate random values. In our protocol however, we have to make sure that the signatures generated by Ama do not contain hidden information for Cus. The way for Ama to leak information to Cus would be to replace the random bits by specifically chosen bits which describe (part of) the source code, similar to steganography [28]. Then, Cus could try to reconstruct the bits from the received message. To exclude this possibility, our protocol will enforce Ama to commit its random bits *before* it sees the source code. Thus, in our description of the cryptographic primitives, we have to treat the random values explicitly.

We also note that in our discussions of randomized algorithms, we usually describe the behavior of the algorithm as it occurs in all but a negligible fraction of the executions of the algorithm [29].

- All parties employ the same *asymmetric encryption and signing scheme* [30] which is based upon RSA [31] and SHA [32]. Given a key pair $\langle K_{pri}, K_{pub} \rangle$ and a message m, we write $c = K_{pub}(m)$ for the encryption of m with key K_{pub} yielding the cipher text c. Similarly, $m = K_{pri}(c)$ denotes the decryption of the cipher text c with key K_{pri} resulting again in the original message m. Furthermore, we write $s = \mathsf{csign}(K_{pri}, m, R)$ for the signature s of a message m signed with key K_{pri} and generated with random seed R. If a signature s is valid and has been generated with seed R, then $\mathsf{cverify}(K_{pub}, m, s, R)$ will succeed and fail otherwise. In situations where the random seed is of no concern, we can also use $\mathsf{cverify}(K_{pub}, m, s)$ which succeeds if s is a valid signature. [1] The algorithms for encryption, decryption, signature generation and signature verification are assumed to require polynomial time with respect to the length of their inputs.
- *Communication Channels.* We assume that the channels between Sup, Cus and Ama are secure, i.e., the protocol is not concerned with eavesdropping on these channels. Moreover, all ingoing and outgoing information for Ama is controlled by Sup, i.e., Sup can manipulate all data exchanged between Ama and Cus.

Having fixed the environment and the notation, we can paraphrase the requirements in a more precise manner:

1. *Conformance* enables Cus to validate that exec and $\log_{\mathsf{Cus}}$ have been produced from the same source.
2. *Secrecy* prevents Cus from extracting, by any tractable process, any IP of Sup except exec and $\log_{\mathsf{Cus}}$.

We note that some of the possible verification tasks discussed in Section 1 – in particular 7, 10, 11, 12 – are concerned with non-functional properties of the source code which do not affect the executable produced by the compiler. The conformance property proves to the customer that at the time of compilation, a source with the required properties did exist. Thus, in the case of a legal conflict, a court can require the supplier to provide a source code which (i) compiles into the purchased executable, and (ii) produces the same verification output $\log_{\mathsf{Cus}}$. There is no mathematical guarantee however, that the revealed code will be *identical* to the original code. This stronger property can be achieved by requiring Verifier to compute a hash of source, and output it into $\log_{\mathsf{Cus}}$.

---

[1] The existence of the 4-parameter variant of cverify is specific to the chosen scheme [30].

3.2   Summary Description of the Protocol

Our protocol is based on the principle that Cus trusts Ama, and thus, Cus will believe that a verification verdict $\log_{\text{Cus}}$ originating from Ama is conformant with a corresponding binary exec. Therefore, Cus and Sup install Ama at Sup's site such that Sup can use Ama to generate trusted verification verdicts subsequently. On the other hand, Sup controls all the communication to and from Ama and consequently Sup is able to prohibit the communication of any piece of information beyond the verification verdict, i.e., Sup can enforce the *secrecy* of its IP. To ensure that Sup does not alter the verdict of Ama, Ama signs the verdicts with a key which is only known to Ama and Cus but not to Sup. Also, to ensure that the tools Compiler and Verifier given to Ama are untampered, Sup must provide certificates which guarantee that these tools have been approved by Cus.

A protocol based on this simple idea does indeed ensure the conformance property, but a naive implementation with common cryptographic primitives may fail to guarantee the secrecy property: As argued above, the certificates generated by Ama involve random seeds, and Sup *cannot check* that these random seeds do not carry hidden information. In our protocol, to prohibit such hidden transmission of information, Ama is not allowed to generate the required random seeds after it has accessed source. Instead, Ama generates a large supply of random seeds *before* it has access to source, and sends them to Sup. In this way, Ama commits to the random seeds, because later, Sup will check that Ama actually uses the random values which it has sent before. Thus, Ama is not able to encode any information about source into these seeds.

The only remaining problem is that Sup is *not allowed to know the random seeds in advance*, since it could use this knowledge to compromise the cryptographic security of the certificates computed by Ama. Thus, Ama encrypts the random seeds before transmitting them to Sup. Each random seed is encrypted with a specific key, and each time a random seed is used by Ama, the corresponding key is revealed to Sup.

3.3   Detailed Protocol Description

Our protocol consists of three phases, namely the *installation,* the *session initialization,* and the *certification.*

Installation Phase. Cus initializes Ama with a master key pair $\langle K_{\text{Cus}}^m, K_{\text{Pub}}^m \rangle$ which will be used later to exchange a session key pair. Then, Ama is transported to and installed at Sup's site. All further communication between Ama and Cus will be controlled by Sup.

I1 *Master Key Generation*   [Cus]
   Cus generates the master keys $\langle K_{\text{Cus}}^m, K_{\text{Pub}}^m \rangle$ and initializes Ama with $\langle K_{\text{Cus}}^m, K_{\text{Pub}}^m \rangle$.
I2 *Installation of the Amanat*   [Sup, Cus]
   Ama is installed at Sup's site and Sup receives K_{Pub}^m.

Session Initialization Phase. After installation, Sup and Cus must agree on a specific Verifier and Compiler. Once Verifier and Compiler have been fixed, the session initialization phase starts: First, Cus generates a new pair of session keys $\langle K_{\text{Cus}}, K_{\text{Pub}} \rangle$ and sends them to Ama via Sup. Then, the new session keys are used to produce certificates cert$_{\text{Verifier}}$ and cert$_{\text{Compiler}}$ for Verifier and Compiler, respectively. Sup checks the contents of the certificates and uses them, if they are indeed valid certificates for Verifier and Compiler, to setup Ama with Verifier and Compiler. Ama in turn accepts Verifier and Compiler if their certificates are valid.

In the last step of the initialization, Ama generates a supply of random seeds $R_1, \ldots, R_t$ for t subsequent executions of the certification phase. It also generates a sequence of key pairs $\langle KR^1_{\text{Cus}}, KR^1_{\text{Pub}} \rangle, \ldots, \langle KR^t_{\text{Cus}}, KR^t_{\text{Pub}} \rangle$ for each random seed R_i. Ama finally encrypts each random seed to obtain and send $KR^i_{\text{Pub}}(R_i)$ to Sup. Ama and Sup both keep a variable round which is initialized to 0 and will be incremented by 1 for each execution of the certification phase.

S1 *Session Key Generation*   [Cus, Sup]
Cus generates the session keys $\langle K_{\text{Cus}}, K_{\text{Pub}} \rangle$ and sends $K^m_{\text{Pub}}(K_{\text{Cus}})$ and K_{Pub} to Sup. Sup forwards $K^m_{\text{Pub}}(K_{\text{Cus}})$ and K_{Pub} unchanged to Ama.

S2 *Generation of the Tool Certificates*   [Cus]
Cus computes the certificates
 – cert$_{\text{Verifier}} = $ csign$(K_{\text{Cus}}, $ Verifier$)$ and
 – cert$_{\text{Compiler}} = $ csign$(K_{\text{Cus}}, $ Compiler$)$.
Cus sends both certificates to Sup.

S3 *Supplier Validation of the Tool Certificates*   [Sup]
Sup checks the contents of the certificates, i.e., Sup checks that
 – cverify$(K_{\text{Pub}}, $ Verifier, cert$_{\text{Verifier}})$ and
 – cverify$(K_{\text{Pub}}, $ Compiler, cert$_{\text{Compiler}})$ succeed.
If one of the checks fails, Sup aborts the protocol.

S4 *Amanat Tool Transmission*   [Sup]
Sup sends to Ama both Verifier and Compiler as well as the certificates cert$_{\text{Verifier}}$ and cert$_{\text{Compiler}}$.

S5 *Amanat Validation of the Tool Certificates*   [Ama]
Ama checks whether Verifier and Compiler are properly certified, i.e., it checks whether
 – cverify$(K_{\text{Pub}}, $ Verifier, cert$_{\text{Verifier}})$ and
 – cverify$(K_{\text{Pub}}, $ Compiler, cert$_{\text{Compiler}})$ succeed.
If this is not the case, then Ama refuses to process any further input.

S6 *Amanat Random Seed Generation*   [Ama]
Ama generates
 – a series of random seeds $R_1, \ldots, R_t$ together with a series of corresponding key pairs $\langle KR^1_{\text{Cus}}, KR^1_{\text{Pub}} \rangle, \ldots, \langle KR^t_{\text{Cus}}, KR^t_{\text{Pub}} \rangle$,
 – encrypts the random seeds with the corresponding keys $KR^i_{\text{Pub}}(R_i)$ for $i = 1, \ldots, t$, and
 – initializes round counter round $= 0$.
Ama then sends all $KR^i_{\text{Pub}}(R_i)$ and KR^i_{Pub} for $i = 1, \ldots, t$ to Sup.

Certification Phase. Ama is now ready for the certification phase, i.e., it will accept source and produce a certified verdict on source which can be forwarded to Cus and whose trustworthy origin can be checked by Cus.

During certification, Ama runs Verifier and Compiler on source, generates a certificate cert for the output log$_{\text{Cus}}$ dedicated to Cus. The certificate is based upon the random seed R_{round} which Ama committed to use in this round of the certification protocol during the session initialization phase. Ama sends the certificate cert, the outputs log_{Sup} and log_{Cus}, and the key KR^{round}_{Cus} to Sup.

To validate secrecy, Sup computes the random seed $R_{round} = KR^{round}_{Cus}(KR_{Pub}(R_{round}))$ which Ama supposedly used for the generation of cert. Then Sup checks that the certificate cert is indeed a valid certificate and is based upon the random seed R_{round}. If this is the case, i.e., the certificate is valid and is generated based on the predetermined random seed, then Ama cannot hide any unintended information in the certificates. If the checks fails, Sup aborts the protocol. Depending on the output of the Verifier, Sup decides whether to forward the results to Cus or whether to abort the certification phase. Finally, Cus checks conformance of output log_{Cus} using cert.

C1 Source Code Transmission   [Sup]
Sup sends source to Ama.

C2 Source Code Verification by the Amanat   [Ama]
Ama computes
- the verdict $\langle log_{Sup}, log_{Cus}\rangle = $ Verifier(source) of Verifier on source,
- the binary exec = Compiler(source),
- increments the round counter round, and
- computes cert = csign($K_{Cus}, \langle exec, log_{Cus}\rangle, R_{round}$).

Ama sends exec, log_{Sup}, log_{Cus}, cert, and KR^{round}_{Cus} to Sup.

C3 Secrecy Validation   [Sup]
Upon receiving exec, log_{Sup}, log_{Cus}, cert, and KR^{round}_{Cus}, Sup
- decrypts the random seed $R_{round} = KR^{round}_{Cus}(KR^{round}_{Pub}(R_{round}))$, and
- verifies that cverify($K_{Pub}, \langle exec, log_{Cus}\rangle, cert, R_{round}$) succeeds.

If the checks fails, Sup **concludes that the secrecy requirement was violated**, and refuses to further work with Ama.

Otherwise, Sup evaluates log_{Cus} and log_{Sup} and decides whether to deliver the binary exec, log_{Cus}, and cert to Cus in step **C4** or whether to abort the protocol.

C4 Conformance Validation   [Cus]
Upon receiving exec, log_{Cus}, and cert, Cus verifies that cverify($K_{Pub}, \langle exec, log_{Cus}\rangle, cert$) succeeds.

If the checks fails, Cus **concludes that the conformance requirement was violated**, and refuses to further work with Sup.

Otherwise Cus evaluates the contents of log_{Cus} and decides whether the verification verdict supports the purchase of the product exec.

4   Protocol Correctness

In this section, we prove conformance and secrecy of our protocol using standard cryptographic assumptions. Following [14], we assume that the public-key encryption is *semantically secure* and that the used signature scheme is *secure against adaptive chosen message attacks*, such as the RSA-based scheme proposed in [30]. We briefly introduce these security properties:

Semantic security means that whatever can be learnt from the ciphertext within probabilistic polynomial time, can be computed, again within probabilistic polynomial time, from the length of the plaintext alone. Formally, semantic security means that each probabilistic polynomial time algorithm which takes as arguments a security parameter, a public key, a number of messages encrypted with this key, the respective messages lengths, and any further partial information on the messages, can be replaced by another probabilistic polynomial time algorithm which only receives the security parameter, the message lengths, and the partial information on the messages [14]. In other words, no probabilistic polynomial time algorithm can extract any information from a set of encrypted messages.

An *adaptive chosen message attack* is an attack against a signature scheme, where the attacker has access to an oracle which can sign arbitrary messages, and uses this ability to sign some new message *without consulting the oracle*. More formally, a *signing oracle* $S[K_{Cus}]$ with private key K_{Cus} is a function which takes a message m and returns a signature $s = \mathrm{csign}(K_{Cus}, m, R)$ for a uniformly and randomly chosen random seed R. An attack is a forging algorithm F which (i) knows the public key K_{Pub} and (ii) has access to the signing oracle $S[K_{Cus}]$, where K_{Cus} is the private key corresponding to K_{Pub}. The algorithm F is allowed to query $S[K_{Cus}]$ for an arbitrary number of signatures. F can adaptively choose the messages to be signed, i.e., each newly chosen message can depend on the outcome of the previous queries. At the end of the computation, a successful attack F must output a message m and a signature s such that $\mathrm{cverify}(K_{Pub}, m, s)$ succeeds, although m has never been sent to $S[K_{Cus}]$. A signature scheme is secure against adaptive chosen message attacks, if there is no probabilistic polynomial time algorithm F which has a non-negligible success probability.

We can now precisely state the main theorems.

Theorem 1 (Conformance). *If the protocol terminates (in Step **C4** of the certification phase) with the customer* Cus *accepting the binary* exec *and the output file* $\log_{Cus}$, *then* exec *and* $\log_{Cus}$ *must be produced from the same* source *in all but a negligible fraction of the protocol executions (under standard cryptographic assumptions).*

Proof Sketch. Towards a contradiction, we assume that with non-negligible probability, Sup can forge a certificate which is accepted by Cus in step **C4**. Thus, Sup computes a certificate cert for a pair ⟨exec, $\log_{Cus}$⟩ which has not been signed by Ama but is accepted by Cus. Using semantic security, we show that such a malicious instance MSup of Sup gives rise to a forging algorithm F which implements a successful adaptive chosen message attack. This implies that the underlying signature scheme is not secure against adaptive chosen message attacks—which is a contradiction.   □

We present a more extensive proof of Theorem 1 in [33]. We now turn to secrecy, which, not surprisingly, is quite straight forward to prove.

Theorem 2 (Secrecy). *By the execution of the protocol,* Cus *cannot extract any piece of information on the source* source *which is not contained in* exec *and* $\log_{Cus}$.

Proof. During the execution of the protocol, Cus receives the binary exec, the output file $\log_{Cus}$, and the certificate cert. The certificate cert = $\mathrm{csign}(K_{Cus}, \langle exec, \log_{Cus}\rangle, R_i)$ can be generated from exec, $\log_{Cus}$, the key K_{Cus}, and the underlying random seed R_i. Cus generates K_{Cus} itself and obtains access to exec and to $\log_{Cus}$. Thus the only additional information communicated from Ama to Sup is the underlying random seed

R_i. But this random seed R_i has been fixed by Ama before having access to source, and consequently Ama cannot encode any information on the source source which is not contained in exec and $\log_{Cus}$ into the certificate.   □

5 Conclusion

We have introduced the amanat protocol which facilitates software verification without violating IP rights on the source code. The intended scenario for our protocol is a B2B setting with a small numbers of customers, e.g. controller software and device drivers.

We also envision wider applications of our protocol in a B2C setting, i.e., for commercial-off-the-shelf software. In this case, the customer party of the amanat protocol will not be enacted by an end customer, but by a certification agency which provides commercial verification services. A detailed exploration of this scenario will be part of future work.

Acknowledgments. We are thankful to Josh Berdine and Byron Cook for discussions on the device driver scenario and to Andreas Holzer and Stefan Kugele for comments on early draft of the paper.

References

1. Heinecke, H.: Automotive Open System Architecture-An Industry-Wide Initiative to Manage the Complexity of Emerging Automotive E/E Architectures. In: Society of Automotive Engineers World Congress (2004)
2. Broy, M.: Challenges in automotive software engineering. In: ICSE '06., pp. 33–42 (2006)
3. Ball, T., Cook, B., Levin, V., Rajamani, S.: SLAM and Static Driver Verifier: Technology Transfer of Formal Methods inside Microsoft. In: Boiten, E.A., Derrick, J., Smith, G.P. (eds.) IFM 2004. LNCS, vol. 2999, Springer, Heidelberg (2004)
4. Ball, T., Rajamani, S.K.: Automatically Validating Temporal Safety Properties of Interfaces. In: Dwyer, M.B. (ed.) Model Checking Software. LNCS, vol. 2057, Springer, Heidelberg (2001)
5. Henzinger, T.A., Jhala, R., Majumdar, R., Sutre, G.: Lazy Abstraction. In: Proc. 29th POPL, Association for Computing Machinery, pp. 58–70 (2002)
6. Chaki, S., Clarke, E., Groce, A., Jha, S., Veith, H.: Modular verification of software components in C. In: Proc. ICSE '03, pp. 385–395 (2003)
7. Cook, B., Podelski, A., Rybalchenko, A.: Terminator: Beyond safety. In: Ball, T., Jones, R.B. (eds.) CAV 2006. LNCS, vol. 4144, pp. 415–418. Springer, Heidelberg (2006)
8. Gotsman, A., Berdine, J., Cook, B.: Interprocedural shape analysis with separated heap abstractions. In: Yi, K. (ed.) SAS 2006. LNCS, vol. 4134, pp. 240–260. Springer, Heidelberg (2006)
9. Cousot, P., Cousot, R., Feret, J., Mauborgne, L., Miné, A., Monniaux, D., Rival, X., Miné, A., Monniaux, D., Rival, X.: The astrée analyser. In: Sagiv, M. (ed.) ESOP 2005. LNCS, vol. 3444, pp. 21–30. Springer, Heidelberg (2005)
10. Sagiv, S., Reps, T.W., Wilhelm, R.: Parametric shape analysis via 3-valued logic. ACM Trans. Program. Lang. Syst. 24(3), 217–298 (2002)
11. Wiedijk, F. (ed.): The Seventeen Provers of the World. LNCS (LNAI), vol. 3600. Springer, Heidelberg (2006)

12. Wenzel, I., Kirner, R., Rieder, B., Puschner, P.P.: Measurement-based worst-case execution time analysis. In: SEUS 2005, pp. 7–10 (2005)
13. Ferdinand, C., Heckmann, R., Wilhelm, R.: Analyzing the worst-case execution time by abstract interpretation of executable code. In: Broy, M., Krüger, I.H., Meisinger, M. (eds.) ASWSD 2004. LNCS, vol. 4147, pp. 1–14. Springer, Heidelberg (2006)
14. Goldreich, O.: Foundations of Cryptography. In: Basic Applications, vol. II, Cambridge University Press, Cambridge (2004)
15. Balakrishnan, G., Reps, T.: DIVINE: DIscovering Variables IN Executables. In: Cook, B., Podelski, A. (eds.) VMCAI 2007. LNCS, vol. 4349, pp. 1–28. Springer, Heidelberg (2007)
16. Debray, S.K., Muth, R., Weippert, M.: Alias analysis of executable code. In: Proc. 26th POPL. (1999)
17. Reps, T.W., Balakrishnan, G., Lim, J., Teitelbaum, T.: A next-generation platform for analyzing executables. In: Yi, K. (ed.) APLAS 2005. LNCS, vol. 3780, pp. 212–229. Springer, Heidelberg (2005)
18. Cifuentes, C., Fraboulet, A.: Intraprocedural static slicing of binary executables. In: ICSM, pp. 188–195 (1997)
19. Christodorescu, M., Jha, S., Seshia, S.A., Song, D.X., Bryant, R.E.: Semantics-aware malware detection. In: IEEE Symposium on Security and Privacy, pp. 32–46. IEEE Computer Society Press, Los Alamitos (2005)
20. Kinder, J., Katzenbeisser, S., Schallhart, C., Veith, H.: Detecting malicious code by model checking. In: Julisch, K., Krügel, C. (eds.) DIMVA 2005. LNCS, vol. 3548, pp. 174–187. Springer, Heidelberg (2005)
21. Colin, S., Mariani, L.: Run-Time Verification. In: Broy, M., Jonsson, B., Katoen, J.-P., Leucker, M., Pretschner, A. (eds.) Model-Based Testing of Reactive Systems. LNCS, vol. 3472, Springer, Heidelberg (2005)
22. Lee, D., Yannakakis, M.: Testing finite-state machines: State identification and verification. IEEE Transactions on Computers 43(3), 306–320 (1994)
23. Lee, D., Yannakakis, M.: Principles and methods of testing finite state machines – a survey. In: Proceedings of the IEEE, vol. 84(8), pp. 1090–1126 (1996)
24. Necula, G.C.: Proof-Carrying Code. In: Proc. 24th POPL, Paris, France, January 15–17, 1997, pp. 106–119. Association for Computing Machinery, York, NY (1997)
25. Goldreich, O.: Secure multi-party computation. Final Draft, Version 1.4 (2002)
26. Ben-Or, M., Goldreich, O., Goldwasser, S., Hastad, J., Kilian, J., Micali, S., Rogaway, P.: Everything Provable is Provable in Zero-Knowledge. In: CRYPTO '88, pp. 37–56 (1988)
27. Dolev, D., Dwork, C., Naor, M.: Non-Malleable Cryptography. Siam Journal on Computing 30(2), 391–437 (2000)
28. Petitcolas, F., Katzenbeisser, S. (eds.): Information Hiding Techniques for Steganography and Digital Watermarking. Artech House (2000)
29. Menezes, A.J., van Oorschot, P.C., Vanstone, S.A.: Handbook of Applied Cryptography. CRC Press (1997)
30. Cramer, R., Shoup, V.: Signature Schemes Based on the String RSA Assumption. ACM Transactions on Information and System Security 3(3), 161–185 (2000)
31. Rivest, R.L., Shamir, A., Adleman, L.M.: A Method for Obtaining Digital Signatures and Public-Key Cryptosystems. Communications of the ACM 21(2), 120–126 (1978)
32. NIST: NIST FIPS PUB 180-1, Secure Hash Standard (1995)
33. Chaki, S., Schallhart, C., Veith, H.: Verification Across Intellectual Property Boundaries (2007), http://arxiv.org/abs/cs.OH/0701187

On Synthesizing Controllers
from Bounded-Response Properties

Oded Maler[1], Dejan Nickovic[1], and Amir Pnueli[2,3]

[1] Verimag, 2 Av. de Vignate, 38610 Gières, France
{Dejan.Nickovic,Oded.Maler}@imag.fr
[2] Weizmann Institute of Science, Rehovot 76100, Israel
[3] New York University, 251 Mercer St. New York, NY 10012, USA
Amir.Pnueli@cs.nyu.edu

Abstract. In this paper we propose a complete chain for synthesizing controllers from high-level specifications. From real-time properties expressed in the logic MTL we generate, under bounded-variability assumptions, *deterministic* timed automata to which we apply safety synthesis algorithms to derive a controller that satisfies the properties by construction. Some preliminary experimental results are reported.

1 Introduction

The problem of synthesizing controllers automatically from high-level specifications has been posed by Church [Chu63] and solved theoretically by Büchi and Landweber [BL69, TB73]. Although the topic has been subject to further, more modern, investigations, synthesis has not enjoyed the passage from theory to practice as did the similar and simpler problem of verification, mostly due to the practical complexity of the proposed algorithms. Recently some improvements have been made for untimed [PPS06, PP06] and timed [CDF+05] systems, that led to the synthesis of some non trivial controllers. This work is a further step in this direction which attempts to give a general feasible solution for the following problem:

Given a bounded-response temporal property φ defined over two distinct action alphabets A and B (encoded using mutually-disjoint sets of propositional variables), build a finite-state transducer (controller) from A^ω to B^ω such that all of its behaviors satisfy φ at all positions.

The controller in question is realized by an automaton that observes what the environment does (some $a \in A$), changes its state accordingly and outputs some $b \in B$. The whole situation can be viewed as a two-player zero-sum game between the controller and its environment where one seeks a winning strategy for the controller (see [M07] for a unified game-theoretic model). Unlike other approaches, for example those used in the control of discrete event systems [RW89] or our previous work [MPS95, AMP95], we do not start with a given "plant" or "arena" in a form of a transition system and an acceptance/winning condition expressed in terms of its states. Our starting point, like in [PR89], is a temporal logic formula which specifies constraints on the behaviors of the players as well as desired properties of their interaction. Hence the first step in the

W. Damm and H. Hermanns (Eds.): CAV 2007, LNCS 4590, pp. 95–107, 2007.
© Springer-Verlag Berlin Heidelberg 2007

synthesis procedure is to derive the automaton *from the formula* and then apply synthesis algorithms to this automaton.

A major difficulty in such a procedure stems for the fact that synthesis algorithms are more naturally defined over *input-deterministic* automata, or, to be more precise, over automata where each non-deterministic choice can be *unambiguously* attributed to one of the two players. In such automata each joint choice of the two players induces only one transition from every state.[1] In contrast, the commonly-used procedures for translating temporal logic formulae go through non-deterministic automata whose determinization leads to automata of prohibitively-large size. Another obstacle toward the efficient realization of synthesis algorithms is the fact that the acceptance conditions in the generated automata require a complicated fixed-point computation in order to find the winning states and strategies.

In this work we avoid some of these problems by restricting our attention to *bounded-response* properties which are known to be equivalent to safety properties. These properties represent a large part of what users are interested in (especially in hard real-time systems) and lead to automata with simpler acceptance conditions (just avoid bad states) and hence to a simpler synthesis procedure. Concerning the limited scope of bounded-response properties compared to more general *liveness* properties, we can make the following comments. Liveness properties typically specify something that should "eventually" happen without specifying an upper bound on the time to elapse between now and that eventuality. Obviously, liveness properties can be viewed as an abstraction of the real specification which requires not only that some response is eventually forthcoming (which is often useless by itself), but also provides an *upper bound* on the maximal delay on the arrival of the response. In some cases, the use of such abstractions may be justified on various grounds. However, we hope to convince the reader that, in many other cases, the synthesis from bounded-response properties is very relevant and preferable and can be carried out efficiently for non-trivial problems. For such cases, why settle for an abstraction when you can work directly with the precise specification?

The main contribution of this paper is an efficient machinery that allows one to synthesize controllers automatically from specifications expressed using the real-time temporal logic MTL [Koy90], often interpreted of the time domain $\mathbb{R}_+$. Our first contribution is a transformation of such formulae, under *bounded variability assumptions* to *deterministic* timed automata. This detrminization is of particular interest as it is based on transforming the formula into a *past* formula and then applying the ideas presented in [MNP05]. The obtained automaton is then interpreted as a timed game automaton [MPS95, AMP95] to which we apply a synthesis algorithm to derive the controller.

The rest of the paper is organized as follows: Section 2 presents the syntax and semantics of the bounded-response fragment of MTL. Section 3 shows how to translate future bounded MTL formulae into past formulae and deterministic timed automata. Section 4 reports some preliminary experiments in synthesizing an arbiter from its specifications, while Section 5 mentions ongoing and future efforts to improve the performance.

---

[1] A notable exception is the case where the controller has limited observability and thus, after observing a sequence of adversary actions it may find itself in one of several states and its chosen action should be good with respect to *all* these states. In this case, the nondeterminism plays in favor of the adversary.

2 Signals and Their Bounded Temporal Logic

Timed behaviors can be described using either *time-event sequences* consisting of instantaneous events separated by time durations or discrete-valued *signals* which are functions from time to some discrete domain. In this work we use Boolean signals as the semantic domain, but the extension of the results to time-event sequences (which are equivalent to the timed traces of [AD94]) need not be a difficult exercise.

Let the time domain $\mathbb{T}$ be the set $\mathbb{R}_{\geq 0}$ of non-negative real numbers and let $\mathcal{B} = \{0, 1\}$. An n-dimensional Boolean signal ξ is a partial function $\xi : \mathbb{T} \rightarrow \mathbb{B}^n$ whose domain of definition is an interval $I = [0, r)$, $r \in \mathbb{N} \cup \{\infty\}$. We say that the length of the signal is r and denote this fact by $|\xi| = r$ and let $\xi[t]$ stand for the value of the signal at time t. We use $t \oplus [a, b]$ to denote $[t + a, t + b)$, that is, the Minkowski sum of $\{t\}$ and $[a, b]$, and $t \ominus [a, b] = [t - b, t - a) \cap \mathbb{T}$ for the inverse operation with saturation at zero. In the sequel we will restrict our attention to well-behaving signals whose variability is bounded.

Definition 1 (Bounded Variability). *A signal ξ is of (Δ, k)-bounded variability if for every interval of the form $[t, t + \Delta]$ the number of changes in the value of ξ is at most k. A bounded-variability signal is a signal for which such $\Delta > 0$ and finite k exist.*

Proposition 1 (Preservation of Bounded Variability). *Let ξ_1 and ξ_2 be two infinite bounded variability signals characterized, respectively, by (Δ, k_1) and (Δ, k_2), and let $\xi = \xi_1 \text{ op } \xi_2$ be a signal obtained by applying the Boolean operation op to ξ_1 and ξ_2. Then, ξ is of $(\Delta, k_1 + k_2)$-bounded variability.*

This fact, which follows from the observation that for ξ to switch at time t, at least one of ξ_1 and ξ_2 should switch, implies that if we assume bounded variability of the propositional signals, we will also have bounded variability for the signals that indicate the truth values of subformulae. Hence we can build the automaton corresponding to the formula in an inductive and compositional manner based on the temporal testers introduced in [KP05] for discrete time and extended in [MNP05, MNP06] for dense time. In this construction bounded variability will be guaranteed at all levels.

We define the logic MTL-B as a bounded-horizon variant of the real-time temporal logic MTL [Koy90], such that *all* future temporal modalities are restricted to intervals of the form $[a, b]$ with $0 \leq a \leq b$ and $a, b \in \mathbb{N}$, but allow the unbounded past operator $\mathcal{S}$ (*since*) which is not really unbounded. Note that unlike MITL [AFH96], we allow "punctual" modalities with $a = b$ and in this case we will use a as a shorthand for $[a, a]$. Another deviation from MTL is the introduction of an additional past operator *precedes* ($\mathcal{P}$) which is roughly the bounded *until* operator from the point of view of the *end* of the relevant segment of the signal. This operator is *not* proposed for user-friendliness purposes, but rather to facilitate the translation from future to past. The basic formulae of MTL-B are defined by the grammar

$$\varphi := p \mid \neg\varphi \mid \varphi_1 \vee \varphi_2 \mid \varphi_1 \mathcal{U}_{[a,b]}\varphi_2 \mid \varphi_2 \mathcal{S}_{[a,b]}\varphi_1 \mid \varphi_2 \mathcal{S}\varphi_1 \mid \varphi_1 \mathcal{P}_{[a,b]}\varphi_2$$

where p belongs to a set $P = \{p_1, \ldots, p_n\}$ of propositions corresponding naturally to the coordinates of the n-dimensional Boolean signal considered. The *future fragment* of MTL-B uses only the $\mathcal{U}_{[a,b]}$ modality while the *past fragment* uses only the $\mathcal{S}_{[a,b]}$, $\mathcal{S}$ and $\mathcal{P}_{[a,b]}$ modalities. The satisfaction relation $(\xi,t) \models \varphi$, indicating that signal ξ satisfies φ at position t, is defined inductively below. We use $p[t]$ to denote the projection of $\xi[t]$ on the dimension that corresponds to variable p.

$$
\begin{aligned}
(\xi,t) &\models p && \leftrightarrow p[t] = \mathrm{T} \\
(\xi,t) &\models \neg\varphi && \leftrightarrow (\xi,t) \not\models \varphi \\
(\xi,t) &\models \varphi_1 \vee \varphi_2 && \leftrightarrow (\xi,t) \models \varphi_1 \text{ or } (\xi,t) \models \varphi_2 \\
(\xi,t) &\models \varphi_1 \mathcal{U}_{[a,b]} \varphi_2 && \leftrightarrow \exists t' \in t \oplus [a,b]\ (\xi,t') \models \varphi_2 \text{ and} \\
& && \quad \forall t'' \in [t,t'], (s,t'') \models \varphi_1 \\
(\xi,t) &\models \varphi_2 \mathcal{S}_{[a,b]} \varphi_1 && \leftrightarrow \exists t' \in t \ominus [a,b]\ (\xi,t') \models \varphi_1 \text{ and} \\
& && \quad \forall t'' \in [t',t], (\xi,t'') \models \varphi_1 \\
(\xi,t) &\models \varphi_2 \mathcal{S} \varphi_1 && \leftrightarrow \exists t' \in [0,t]\ (\xi,t') \models \varphi_1 \text{ and} \\
& && \quad \forall t'' \in (t',t], (\xi,t'') \models \varphi_1 \\
(\xi,t) &\models \varphi_1 \mathcal{P}_{[a,b]} \varphi_2 && \leftrightarrow \exists t' \in t \ominus [0,b-a]\ (\xi,t') \models \varphi_2 \text{ and} \\
& && \quad \forall t'' \in [t'-b,t']\ (\xi,t'') \models \varphi_1
\end{aligned}
$$

It is important to note the difference between the future and the past operators (see Figure 1): the *until* operator points from time t toward the future, while the *since* and *precedes* operators point from t backwards. On the other hand, the *until* and *precedes* operators differ from the *since* operators as they speak on the interval *before* the event that should be observed within a bounded time interval, while the latter refers to the interval immediately *after* its occurrence.

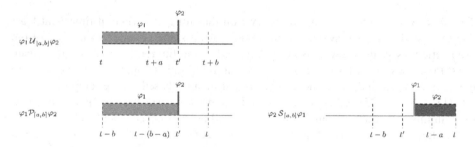

Fig. 1. The semantic definitions of *until*, *precedes* and *since*

From basic MTL-B operators one can derive other standard Boolean and temporal operators, in particular the time-constrained *sometime in the past*, *always in the past*, *eventually in the future* and *always in the future* operators whose semantics is defined as

$$
\begin{aligned}
(\xi,t) &\models \Diamondblack_{[a,b]} \varphi \leftrightarrow \exists t' \in t \ominus [a,b]\ (\xi,t') \models \varphi \\
(\xi,t) &\models \blacksquare_{[a,b]} \varphi \leftrightarrow \forall t' \in t \ominus [a,b]\ (\xi,t') \models \varphi \\
(\xi,t) &\models \Diamond_{[a,b]} \varphi \leftrightarrow \exists t' \in t \oplus [a,b]\ (s,t') \models \varphi \\
(\xi,t) &\models \Box_{[a,b]} \varphi \leftrightarrow \forall t' \in t \oplus [a,b]\ (\xi,t') \models \varphi
\end{aligned}
$$

Note that our definition of the semantics of the timed *until* and *since* operators differs slightly from their conventional definition since it requires a time instant t' where *both*

$(\xi, t') \models \varphi_2$ and $(\xi, t') \models \varphi_1$. For the untimed *since* operator we retain the standard semantics.

Each future MTL-B formula φ admits a number $D(\varphi)$ which indicates its *temporal depth*. Roughly speaking, to determine the satisfaction of φ by a signal ξ from any position t, it suffices to observe the value of ξ in the interval $[t, t + D(\varphi)]$. This property is evident from the semantics of the (bounded) temporal operators and admits the following recursive definition:

$$\begin{aligned}
D(p) &= 0 \\
D(\neg\varphi) &= D(\varphi) \\
D(\varphi_1 \vee \varphi_2) &= \max\{D(\varphi_1), D(\varphi_2)\} \\
D(\varphi_1 \mathcal{U}_{[a,b]}\varphi_2) &= b + \max\{D(\varphi_1), D(\varphi_2)\}
\end{aligned}$$

Note that D is a syntax-dependent *upper bound* on the actual depth: the satisfiability of a formula φ may be determined according to segments of ξ shorted than $D(\varphi)$. For example, $D(\Box_{[a,b]} \top) = b$, but the formula requires no part of ξ for its satisfiability to be determined. At the end of the day we are interested in properties of the form $\Box\,\varphi$ where φ is any (future, past or mixed) MTL-B formula. These properties are interpreted over infinite-duration signals and require that all segments of ξ of length $D(\varphi)$ satisfy φ.

3 From MTL-B to Deterministic Timed Automata

In [MP04, MNP05] we have studied the relation between real-time temporal logics and deterministic timed automata. It turns out that the non-determinism associated with real-time logics has two rather *independent* sources described below.

- *Acausality*: the semantics of future temporal logics is acausal in the sense that the satisfiability of a formula at position t may depend on the value of the sequence or signal at time $t' > t$. If the automaton has to output this value at time t, it has no choice but to "guess" at time t and abort later at time t' the computations that correspond to wrong predictions (see more detailed explanation in [MNP06]). This bounded non determinism is harmless and in the untimed case, that is, for LTL, it can be determinized away. We conjecture that such a detrmination procedure exists also for the timed case, but so far none has been reported. This problem does not exist for *past* temporal logic whose semantics is causal and hence it translates naturally into deterministic automata.
- *Unbounded variability*: when there is no bound on the variability of input signals, the automaton needs to remember the occurrence times of an unbounded number of events and use an unbounded number of clocks. All the pathological examples concerning non-determinizability and non-closure under complementation for timed automata [AD94] are based on this phenomenon.

In [MNP05] we have shown that the determinism of past MITL, compared to the non-determinism of future MITL, is a result of a syntactic accident which somehow imposes bounded variability (or indifference to small fluctuations) for the former but not the latter. The punctual version, past MTL, remains non deterministic (and of infinite memory) because the operator $\diamondsuit_a$ realizes an ideal delay element which requires unbounded memory.

The approach taken in this work in order to get rid of both sources of non determinism is the following: we use full MTL, that is, allow punctual modalities, but assume that we are dealing with signals of (Δ, k)-bounded variability, hence we can dispense with the severe form of non determinism.[2] We then transform future MTL-B formulae to past MTL-B formula which, under the bounded variability assumption, can be translated to deterministic timed automata. This part of the result is an extension of what we have shown in [MNP05] for the (non-punctual) *since* operator.

The key idea of the transformation is to change the time direction from future to past and hence eliminate the "predictive" aspect of the semantics. We will present an operator Π which takes as an argument a future formula φ and a displacement d, and transforms it to an "equivalent" past formula ψ such that φ is satisfied by a signal from position t iff ψ is satisfied by the same signal from $t + d$.

Definition 2 (Pastify Operator). *The operator Π on future MTL-B formulae φ and a displacement $d \geq D(\varphi)$ is defined recursively as:*

$$\Pi(p, d) = \diamondsuit_d p$$
$$\Pi(\neg\varphi, d) = \neg\Pi(\varphi, d)$$
$$\Pi(\varphi_1 \vee \varphi_2, d) = \Pi(\varphi_1, d) \vee \Pi(\varphi_2, d)$$
$$\Pi(\varphi_1 \mathcal{U}_{[a,b]}\varphi_2, d) = \Pi(\varphi_1, d - b)\mathcal{P}_{[a,b]}\Pi(\varphi_2, d - b)$$

Note that according the this definition $\Pi(\diamondsuit_{[a,b]} \varphi, d) = \diamondsuit_{[0,b-a]} \Pi(\varphi, d - b)$.

Proposition 2 (Relation between φ and $\Pi(\varphi, d)$). *Let φ be a bounded future formula and let $\psi = \Pi(\varphi, d)$ with $d \geq D(\varphi)$. Then for every ξ and $t \geq 0$ we have:*

$$(\xi, t) \models \varphi \text{ iff } (\xi, t + d) \models \psi \tag{1}$$

Proof: We proceed by induction on the structure of the formula. The base case, the atomic propositions, satisfy (1) trivially. Proceeding to the inductive case, we show that if (1) holds for formulae with complexity (nesting of operators) m, it holds as well for formulae of complexity $m + 1$. For Boolean operators this is straightforward. Assume now that φ_1 and φ_2 satisfy (1) and we will show that so does $\varphi = \varphi_1 \mathcal{U}_{[a,b]}\varphi_2$. Note that by definition, if $D(\varphi) = d$ then $D(\varphi_1) \leq d - b$ and $D(\varphi_2) \leq d - b$. Let $\psi_1 = \Pi(\varphi_1, d - b)$ and $\psi_1 = \Pi(\varphi_1, d - b)$. The fact the $(\xi, t) \models \varphi$ amounts to

$$\exists t' \in t \oplus [a, b] \, (\xi, t') \models \varphi_2 \wedge \forall t'' \in [0, t'] \, (\xi, t'') \models \varphi_1.$$

According to the inductive hypothesis we have that for such t' and t''

$$(\xi, t' + d - b) \models \psi_2 \text{ and } (\xi, t'' + d - b) \models \psi_1.$$

By letting $r' = t' + d - b$ and $r'' = t'' + d - b$ and substituting the constraints on t' and t'' we obtain

$$\exists r' \in t + d \ominus [0, b - a] \, (\xi, r) \models \psi_2 \wedge \forall r'' \in [t + d - b, r] \, (\xi, r'') \models \psi_1,$$

---

[2] It is worth noting that the procedure of [T02] for subset construction on-the-fly, that is, determinization with respect to a *given* (and hence of bounded variability) input, works due to the same reasons.

which is exactly the definition of $(\xi, t + d) \models \psi_1 \mathcal{P}_{[a,b]} \psi_2$.

For the other direction assume $(\xi, t + d) \models \psi_1 \mathcal{P}_{[a,b]} \psi_2$ which means that

$$\exists r' \in t + d \ominus [0, (b - a)] \, (\xi, r') \models \psi_2 \wedge \forall r'' \in [t + d - b, r'](\xi, r'') \models \psi_1.$$

By the inductive hypothesis such r' and r'' satisfy

$$(\xi, r' - (d - b)) \models \varphi_1 \text{ and } (\xi, r'' - (d - b)) \models \varphi_1.$$

Letting $t' = r' - (d - b)$ and $t'' = r'' - (d - b)$ and substituting the constraints on r' and r'' we obtain

$$\exists t' \in t \oplus [a, b] \, (\xi, t') \models \varphi_2 \wedge \forall t'' \in [t, t'] \, (\xi, t'') \models \varphi_1$$

which means that $(\xi, t) \models \varphi_1 \mathcal{U}_{[a,b]} \varphi_2$.   ⊿

Corollary 1 (Equisatifaction of $\square \, \varphi$ and $\square \, \psi$). *An infinite signal ξ satisfies $\square \, \varphi$ iff it satisfies $\square \, \psi$ where $\psi = \Pi(\varphi, D(\varphi))$.*

We now proceed to the construction of a deterministic timed automaton accepting exactly signals satisfying a past MTL-B formula ψ under a bounded-variability assumption. The construction, inspired by [KP05], is compositional in the sense that it yields a network of deterministic signal transducers (testers), each corresponding to a subformula of ψ. The output of every tester for ψ' at time t equals to the satisfaction of ψ' from t. A more formal description of this framework can be found in [MNP05, MNP06]. We first present a generic automaton, the *event recorder* which was first introduced in [MNP05] for the purpose of showing that the operator $\diamondsuit_{[a,b]}$ admits a deterministic timed automaton.

The automaton depicted in Figure 2 accepts signals satisfying $\diamondsuit_{[a,b]} \varphi$ by simply memorizing at any time instant t the value of φ in the past temporal window $[t - b, t]$. Assuming that φ is of bounded variability and cannot change more than $2m$ times in an interval of length b, the states of the automaton, $\{0, 01, \ldots, (01)^m 0\}$, correspond to the qualitative form of the value of φ in that time interval. Each clock x_i (respectively, y_i) measures the time elapsed since the ith rising (respectively, falling) of φ in the temporal window. When φ first becomes true, automaton moves from 0 to 01 and resets x_1. When φ becomes false it moves to 010 while resetting y_1 and so on. When clock $y_1 > b$, the first 01-episode of φ becomes irrelevant for the satisfaction of $\diamondsuit_{[a,b]} \varphi$ and can be forgotten. This is achieved by the "vertical" transitions which are accompanied by "shifting" the clocks values, that is, applying the operations $x_i := x_{i+1}$ and $y_i := y_{i+1}$ for all i. This allows us to use only a finite number of clocks.

The following proposition, first observed in [MN04], simplifies the construction of the automaton. It follows from the fact that if a bounded-variability signal is true at two close points, it has to be true throughout the interval between them.

Proposition 3. *If p is a signal of $(a, 1)$-bounded variability then*

- $(\xi, t) \models p \mathcal{U}_{[a,b]} q$ iff $(\xi, t) \models p \wedge \diamondsuit_{[a,b]} (p \wedge q)$
- $(\xi, t) \models p \mathcal{P}_{[a,b]} q$ iff $(\xi, t) \models \diamondsuit_b p \wedge \diamondsuit_{[0,b-a]} (p \wedge q)$

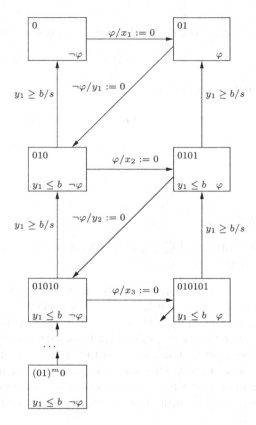

Fig. 2. An event recorder, an automaton which has φ as input and $\diamondsuit_{[a,b]}\,\varphi$ as output. The input labels and staying conditions are written on the bottom of each state. Transitions are decorated by the input labels of the target states and by clock resets. The clock shift operator is denoted by the symbol s. The automaton outputs 1 whenever $x_1 \geq a$.

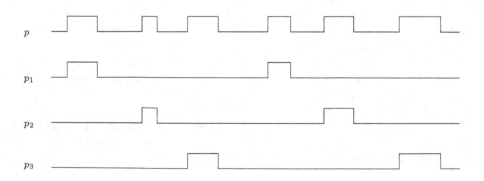

Fig. 3. Splitting p into $p_1 \vee p_2 \vee p_3$

Hence for a signal p satisfying this property, the automaton for $\mathcal{P}_{[a,b]}$ can be constructed from the event recorder by means of simple Boolean composition. Suppose now that p is of (a, k)-bounded variability with $k > 1$. We can decompose it into k signals $p_1, \ldots, p_k$ such that $p = p_1 \vee p_2 \cdots p_k$, $p_i \wedge p_j$ is always false for every $i \neq j$ and each p_i is of $(a, 1)$-bounded variability. This is achieved by letting p_i rise and fall only on the jth rising and falling of p, where $j = i \mod k$, as is illustrated, for $k = 3$, in Figure 3. It is not hard to see that for such p_i's we have

$$(\xi, t) \models p\mathcal{U}_{[a,b]}q \text{ iff } (\xi, t) \models \bigvee_{i=1}^{k} p_i\mathcal{U}_{[a,b]}q$$

and

$$(\xi, t) \models p\mathcal{P}_{[a,b]}q \text{ iff } (\xi, t) \models \bigvee_{i=1}^{k} p_i\mathcal{P}_{[a,b]}q.$$

The splitting of p can be done trivially using an automaton realizing a counter modulo k.

Corollary 2 (MTL-B **to Deterministic Timed Automata**). *Any* MITL-B *formulae can be transformed, under bounded-variability assumptions, into equivalent deterministic timed automata.*

4 Application to Synthesis

4.1 Discrete and Dense-Time Tools

What remains to be done is to transform the automaton into a timed game automaton by distinguishing controllable and uncontrollable actions and applying the synthesis algorithm. There are currently several choices for timed synthesis tools divided into two major families depending one whether discrete or dense time tools are used.[3]

- *Discrete time*: the logic and the automata are interpreted over the time domain $\mathbb{N}$. A major advantage of this approach is that the automaton becomes finite state and can be subject to symbolic verification and synthesis using BDDs, which is very useful when the discrete state space is large. On the other hand, the sensitivity of discrete time analysis to the size of the constants is much higher and will lead to explosion when they are large. Discrete-time synthesis of scheduler for fairly-large systems has been reported in [KY03].
- *Dense time*: here we have the opposite problem, namely there is a compact symbolic representation of subsets of the clock space, but the discrete states are enumerated. Several implementations of synthesis algorithms based on [MPS95] exist. One is the tool SynthKro included in the standard distribution of Kronos and described in [AT02], which works by standard fixpoint computation. Another alternative, which restricts the algorithm to work only on the reachable part of the

---

[3] Contrary to commonly-held beliefs, the important point of timed automata is not the density of time but the *symbolic* treatment of timing constraints using addition and inequalities rather than state enumeration.

state space is the tool `FlySynth` which refines the reachability graph of the game automaton according to the time-abstract bisimulation relation [TY01] yielding a finite quotient to which *untimed* synthesis algorithms can be applied [TA99]. Finally, the tool `Uppaal-Tiga` improves upon these ideas by combining forward and backward search, resulting in the most "on-the-fly" algorithm for timed synthesis [CDF$^+$05] and probably the most effective existing tool for timed synthesis.

We have conducted our first experiments in discrete time using a synthesis algorithm implemented on top of the tool TLV, while working on the implementation of an improved dense time algorithm combining ideas from [TY01] and [CDF$^+$05].

4.2 Example: Deriving an Arbiter

To demonstrate our approach we present a bounded-future specification of an *arbiter* module whose architectural layout is shown in Figure 4-(a). The arbiter is expected to allocate a single resource among n clients. The clients post their *requests* for the resource on the input ports $r_1, \ldots, r_n$ and receive notification of their *grants* on the arbiter's output ports $g_1, \ldots, g_n$. The protocol of communication between each client and the arbiter follows the cyclic behavior described in Figure 4-(b,c).

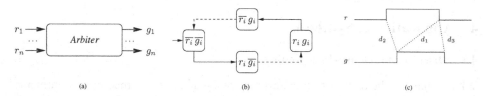

(a)   (b)   (c)

Fig. 4. (a) The architecture of an Arbiter; (b) The communication protocol between the arbiter and client i. Uncontrollable actions of the client (environment) are drawn as solid arrows, while controllable actions which are performed by the arbiter (controller) drawn as dashed arrows; (c) A typical interaction between the arbiter and a client.

In the initial state both r_i and g_i are low (0). Then, the client acts first by setting r_i to high (1) indicating a request to access the shared resource. Next, it is the turn of the arbiter to respond by raising the *grant* signal g_i to high. Sometimes later, the client terminates and indicates its readiness to relinquish the resource by lowering r_i. The arbiter acknowledges the release of the resource by lowering down the grant signal g_i.

We structure the specification into subformulae I^E, I^C, S^E, S^C, L^E and L^C denoting, respectively, the initial condition, safety component, and (bounded) liveness components of the environment (client) and the controller (arbiter). They are given by

$$
\begin{aligned}
I^E &: \bigwedge_i \overline{r_i} \\
I^C &: \bigwedge_i \overline{g_i} \\
S^E &: \bigwedge_i r_i \implies r_i \mathcal{S}(\overline{r_i} \wedge \overline{g_i})) \quad \wedge \quad \bigwedge_i (\overline{r_i} \implies \overline{r_i} \mathcal{B}(r_i \wedge g_i)) \\
S^C &: \bigwedge_i (g_i \implies g_i \mathcal{S}(r_i \wedge \overline{g_i})) \quad \wedge \quad \bigwedge_i (\overline{g_i} \implies \overline{g_i} \mathcal{B}(\overline{r_i} \wedge g_i))
\end{aligned}
$$

$$L^E : \bigwedge_i (g_i \implies \Diamond_{[0,d_1]} \overline{r_i})$$
$$L^C : \bigwedge_i (r_i \implies \Diamond_{[0,d_2]} g_i) \wedge \bigwedge_i (\overline{r_i} \implies \Diamond_{[0,d_3]} \overline{g_i})$$

The initial-condition requirements I^E and I^C state that initially all variables are low. The safety requirements S^E and S^C ensure that the environment and arbiter conform to the protocol as described in Figure 4-(b). In the untimed case, this is usually specified using the next-time operator $\bigcirc$ but in dense time specify these properties using the the untimed past $\mathcal{S}$ and $\mathcal{B}$ operators. Thus, the requirement $(r_i \implies r_i \mathcal{S}(\overline{r_i} \wedge \overline{g_i}))$ states that if r_i is currently high, it must have been continuously high since a preceding state in which both r_i and g_i were low. The reader can verify that the combination of the safety properties enforces the protocol.

The (bounded) liveness property $g_i \implies \Diamond_{[0,d_1]} \overline{r_i}$ requires that if g_i holds then within b time units, client C_i should release the resource by lowering r_i. The property $(r_i \implies \Diamond_{[0,d_2]} g_i)$ specifies quality of service by saying that every client gets the resource at most d_2 time after requesting it. Finally, property $\overline{r_i} \implies \Diamond_{[0,d_3]} \overline{g_i}$ requires that the arbiter senses the release of the resource within d_3 time and considers it available for further allocations. Note that the required response delays for the various properties employ different time constants. This is essential, because the specification is realizable only if d_2, the time bound on raising g, is at least $n(d_1 + d_3)$. This reflects the "worst-case" situation that all clients request the resource at about the same time, and the arbiter has to service each of them in turn, until it gets to the last one.

The various components are combined into a single MTL-B formula by transforming them to past formulae and requiring that the controller does not violate its requirements as long as the environment does not violate hers:

$$(I^E \implies I^C) \quad \wedge \quad \Box(\boxminus(\Pi(S^E) \wedge \Pi(L^E)) \implies (\Pi(S^C) \wedge \Pi(L^C))) \quad (2)$$

Below we report some preliminary experiments in automatic synthesis of the arbiter. Table 1 shows the results of applying the procedure to Equation (2) with $d_3 = 1$ and d_1 (the upper bound on the execution time of the client) varying between 2 and 4. The N column indicates the number of clients, the *Size* column indicate the number of BDD nodes in the symbolic representation of the transition relation of the synthesized automaton and *Time* indicates the running time (in seconds) of the synthesis procedure. As one can see, there is a natural exponential growth in N and also in d_2 as expected using discrete time.

Table 1. Results for $d_1 = 2, 3, 4$

N	d_1	d_2	Size	Time	d_1	d_2	Size	Time	d_1	d_2	Size	Time
2	2	4	466	0.00	3	5	654	0.01	4	6	946	0.02
3	2	8	1382	0.14	3	10	2432	0.34	4	12	4166	0.51
4	2	12	4323	0.63	3	15	7402	1.12	4	18	16469	2.33
5	2	16	13505	1.93	3	20	26801	4.77	4	24	50674	10.50
6	2	20	43366	8.16	3	25	84027	22.55	4	30	168944	64.38
7	2	24	138937	44.38	3	30	297524	204.56	4	36	700126	1897.56

5   Conclusions and Future Work

We have made an important step toward making synthesis a usable technology by suggesting MTL-B as a suitable formalism that can handle a variety of bounded response properties encountered in the development of real-time systems. We have provided a novel translation form real-time temporal logic to deterministic timed automata via transformation to past formulae and using the reasonable bounded-variability assumption. We have demonstrated the viability of this approach by deriving a non-trivial arbiter from specifications.

In the future we intend to focus on efficient symbolic algorithms in the spirit of [CDF+05] and conduct further experiments in order to characterize the relative merits of discrete and dense-time algorithms. We also intend to apply the synthesis algorithm to more complex specifications of real-time scheduling problems.

References

[AT02]   Altisen, K., Tripakis, S.: Tools for Controller Synthesis of Timed Systems. In: RT-TOOLS'02 (2002)

[AD94]   Alur, R., Dill, D.L.: A Theory of Timed Automata. Theoretical Computer Science 126, 183–235 (1994)

[AFH96]   Alur, R., Feder, T., Henzinger, T.A.: The Benefits of Relaxing Punctuality (first published in PODC'91). Journal of the ACM 43, 116–146 (1996)

[A04]   Asarin, E.: Challenges in Timed Languages. Bulletin of EATCS 83 (2004)

[ACM02]   Asarin, E., Caspi, P., Maler, O.: Timed Regular Expressions. The Journal of the ACM 49, 172–206 (2002)

[AMP95]   Asarin, E., Maler, O., Pnueli, A.: Symbolic Controller Synthesis for Discrete and Timed Systems. In: Antsaklis, P.J., Kohn, W., Nerode, A., Sastry, S.S. (eds.) Hybrid Systems II. LNCS, vol. 999, pp. 1–20. Springer, Heidelberg (1995)

[BL69]   Buchi, J.R., Landweber, L.H.: Solving Sequential Conditions by Finite-state Operators. Trans. of the AMS 138, 295–311 (1969)

[CDF+05]   Cassez, F., David, A., Fleury, E., Larsen, K.G., Lime, D.: Efficient On-the-Fly Algorithms for the Analysis of Timed Games. In: Abadi, M., de Alfaro, L. (eds.) CONCUR 2005. LNCS, vol. 3653, pp. 66–80. Springer, Heidelberg (2005)

[Chu63]   Church, A.: Logic, Arithmetic and Automata. In: Proc. of the Int. Cong. of Mathematicians 1962, pp. 23–35 (1963)

[KP05]   Kesten, Y., Pnueli, A.: A Compositional Approach to CTL* Verification. Theoretical Computer Science 331, 397–428 (2005)

[KY03]   Kloukinas, C., Yovine, S.: Synthesis of Safe, QoS Extendible, Application Specific Schedulers for Heterogeneous Real-Time Systems. In: ECRTS'03, pp. 287–294 (2003)

[Koy90]   Koymans, R.: Specifying Real-time Properties with Metric Temporal Logic. Real-time Systems 2, 255–299 (1990)

[M07]   Maler, O.: On Optimal and Reasonable Control in the Presence of Adversaries. In: Annual Reviews in Control (2007)

[MN04]   Maler, O., Nickovic, D.: Monitoring Temporal Properties of Continuous Signals. In: Lakhnech, Y., Yovine, S. (eds.) FORMATS 2004 and FTRTFT 2004. LNCS, vol. 3253, pp. 152–166. Springer, Heidelberg (2004)

[MNP05]   Maler, O., Nickovic, D., Pnueli, A.: Real Time Temporal Logic: Past, Present, Future. In: Pettersson, P., Yi, W. (eds.) FORMATS 2005. LNCS, vol. 3829, pp. 2–16. Springer, Heidelberg (2005)

[MNP06]   Maler, O., Nickovic, D., Pnueli, A.: From MITL to Timed Automata. In: Asarin, E., Bouyer, P. (eds.) FORMATS 2006. LNCS, vol. 4202, pp. 274–289. Springer, Heidelberg (2006)

[MP04]   Maler, O., Pnueli, A.: On Recognizable Timed Languages. In: Walukiewicz, I. (ed.) FOSSACS 2004. LNCS, vol. 2987, pp. 348–362. Springer, Heidelberg (2004)

[MPS95]   Maler, O., Pnueli, A., Sifakis, J.: On the Synthesis of Discrete Controllers for Timed Systems. In: Mayr, E.W., Puech, C. (eds.) STACS 95. LNCS, vol. 900, pp. 229–242. Springer, Heidelberg (1995)

[PPS06]   Piterman, N., Pnueli, A., Sa'ar, Y.: Synthesis of Reactive(1) Designs. In: Emerson, E.A., Namjoshi, K.S. (eds.) VMCAI 2006. LNCS, vol. 3855, pp. 364–380. Springer, Heidelberg (2005)

[PP06]   Piterman, N., Pnueli, A.: Faster Solutions of Rabin and Streett Games. In: LICS'06, pp. 275–284 (2006)

[PR89]   Pnueli, A., Rosner, R.: On the Synthesis of a Reactive Module. In: POPL'89, pp. 179–190 (1989)

[RW89]   Ramadge, P.J., Wonham, W.M.: The Control of Discrete Event Systems. Proc. of the IEEE 77, 81–98 (1989)

[TB73]   Trakhtenbrot, B.A., Barzdin, Y.M.: Finite Automata: Behavior and Synthesis. North-Holland, Amsterdam (1973)

[T02]   Tripakis, S.: Fault Diagnosis for Timed Automata. In: Damm, W., Olderog, E.-R. (eds.) FTRTFT 2002. LNCS, vol. 2469, pp. 205–224. Springer, Heidelberg (2002)

[TA99]   Tripakis, S., Altisen, K.: On-the-Fly Controller Synthesis for Discrete and Timed Systems, FM'99 1999. In: Woodcock, J.C.P., Davies, J., Wing, J.M. (eds.) FM 1999. LNCS, vol. 1709, Springer, Heidelberg (1999)

[TY01]   Tripakis, S., Yovine, S.: Analysis of Timed Systems using Time-abstracting Bisimulations. Formal Methods in System Design 18, 25–68 (2001)

An Accelerated Algorithm for 3-Color Parity Games with an Application to Timed Games[*]

Luca de Alfaro[1] and Marco Faella[2]

[1] Department of Computer Engineering, University of California, Santa Cruz, USA
[2] Dipartimento di Scienze Fisiche, Università di Napoli "Federico II", Italy

Abstract. Three-color parity games capture the disjunction of a Büchi and a co-Büchi condition. The most efficient known algorithm for these games is the progress measures algorithm by Jurdziński. We present an acceleration technique that, while leaving the worst-case complexity unchanged, often leads to considerable speed-ups in games arising in practice. As an application, we consider games played in discrete real time, where players should be prevented from stopping time by always choosing moves with delay zero. The time progress condition can be encoded as a three-color parity game. Using the tool TICC as a platform, we compare the performance of a BDD-based symbolic implementation of the progress measure algorithm with acceleration, and of the symbolic implementation of the classical μ-calculus algorithm of Emerson and Jutla.

1 Introduction

The parity acceptance condition for automata and games enjoys many interesting properties. Every ω-regular language can be recognized by a deterministic parity automaton [20]. The parity accepting condition is closed under complementation, and games with parity accepting conditions admit memoryless optimal strategies for both players. Moreover, parity games have received a great deal of attention due to their equivalence to the model checking of the modal μ-calculus. The complexity of this class of games is known to be in NP $\cap$ co-NP [11], and even in UP $\cap$ co-UP [14].

We are especially interested in parity conditions with three colors. which can express the disjunction of Büchi and co-Büchi conditions. As we shall see, 3-color parity games occur in the solution of *timed* games. For 3-color parity games, the algorithm with the best worst-case complexity is the progress measure algorithm of [13]. In this paper, we present an acceleration technique that greatly improves the performance of this algorithm in many cases, while retaining its worst-case behavior. We then show how the algorithm can be implemented symbolically, and how it compares in performance with more traditional, μ-calculus based algorithms [10].

We consider parity games with colors 0, 1, 2, where the goal of Player 1 is to ensure that the minimum color visited infinitely often is even. The progress measure algorithm works by updating a function assigning an integer value to each state of the game, called the *measure* of that state. The measure of each state starts at zero; each iteration

---

[*] This research was supported in part by the NSF grant CCR-0132780. The second author was supported by a scholar mobility program from Università di Napoli "Federico II".

W. Damm and H. Hermanns (Eds.): CAV 2007, LNCS 4590, pp. 108–120, 2007.

of the algorithm can either increase the measure at a state, or leave it unchanged. If the measure of a state exceeds the number n_1 of 1-color states, the state is losing for Player 1. The algorithm stops when the progress measure reaches a fixpoint. Even in the best case, the algorithm needs a number of iterations proportional to n_1.

We propose an acceleration scheme based on the following result. Suppose that, at a certain step of the algorithm, we find an integer k such that no state has measure k, but some states have measure greater than k. Call k a "gap" in the measure. We prove that all states having measure greater than the gap k are losing for Player 1; they can be immediately be assigned measure $n_1 + 1$. This enables us to solve many 3-color parity games in much fewer than n_1 iterations; as we shall see, this acceleration is especially effective for timed games.

In the second part of this paper, we show how the acceleration technique for three-color parity games can be applied to timed games, leading to efficient symbolic algorithms. Timed games are games played in such a way as to make explicit reference to the passage of time [15,3]. Generally, the players of a timed game specify in their moves both the action they want to execute and the time at which they want to execute it. Moreover, in the literature such games are usually played on timed-automata-like arenas, so that the game state is also made time-aware by the presence of clocks. As for standard games, the objective for a player is to obtain a game run belonging to a given set of desired runs, called *goal*. Common goals for timed games include reaching a given set of states (reachability) or staying forever in a given set of states (safety).

Most formulations of timed games allow players to "stop the progress of time" by proposing zero, or converging, time delays. Obviously, these physically impossible behaviors must be ruled out in order not to obtain artificial solutions to the game. Previous approaches differ in how they deal with this problem. Some papers make sure that non-physical behaviors cannot arise in the first place, by placing structural restrictions on the games they are willing to treat [3,12]. Other papers force a player to ensure time divergence [15] as a prerequisite for winning, with the result that players are precluded victory in many games where the goal can be achieved only with some delay. Still other papers ignore the issue, so that their solutions work only for sub-classes of games, such as safety [17,2] or reachability [5] games.

A technique that does not restrict the type of games that can be tackled is advocated in [9,7,1]. The approach distinguishes between the original *goal* of the game and the *winning condition*, which is a suitable modification of the goal ensuring that time-blocking strategies are not convenient for either player. The winning condition states, roughly, that in addition to achieving the goal, a player must ensure that either time diverges, or that the blame for stopping time lies with the other player [2,7]. As we shall see, for safety and reachability games, such winning condition can be captured by a 3-color deterministic parity automaton. Thus, solving safety and reachability timed games involves solving 3-color parity games.

We consider timed games played in discrete time, and we present a symbolic implementation of the progress measure algorithm, based on symbolic methods for updating the progress measure, finding the gaps, and achieving acceleration. We show that the acceleration is fundamental in achieving an efficient implementation of the progress measure algorithm: in the examples we tested, we achieved speed-up factors of several hundreds. We also compare the performance of the resulting algorithms with the classical μ-calculus-based fixpoint algorithm of [10]. The running times of the two algorithms were, in our experiments, within a factor of two of each other, with the classical μ-calculus algorithm generally being the fastest. However, our results are not conclusive, since minor implementation details, such as the choice of variable ordering and differences in the encoding of the game transition relation, seem to have a large effect on the performance of the algorithms.

2   Algorithms for 3-Color Parity Games

For an integer $d > 0$, a *parity game* with d *colors* is a tuple (S_1, S_2, E, c), where S_1 and S_2 are the finite sets of states of Player 1 and Player 2, respectively. We require $S_1 \cap S_2 = \emptyset$ and we set $S = S_1 \cup S_2$. $E \subseteq S^2$ is the set of edges, and $c : S \to \{0, 1, \ldots, d-1\}$ is a function assigning a color to each state. For all $i = 0, \ldots, d-1$, we set $C_i = c^{-1}(i)$. Moreover, let $n = |S|$ and $m = |E|$. A *strategy* for player $i \in \{1, 2\}$ is a function $\pi : S^* \to S$ such that, for all $\sigma \in S^*$, if the last state of σ is $s \in S_i$ then $(s, \pi(\sigma)) \in E$. Let Π^1 and Π^2 denote the sets of strategies of Player 1 and Player 2, respectively. A *trace* is an infinite path in the directed graph (S, E). Given $s \in S$, $\pi^1 \in \Pi^1$ and $\pi^2 \in \Pi^2$, the *outcome* $\delta(s, \pi^1, \pi^2)$ of π^1 and π^2 from s is the unique trace $s_0 s_1 \ldots$ such that $s_0 = s$ and for all $j > 0$, $s_j = \pi^i(s_0 s_1 \ldots s_{j-1})$ if and only if $s_{j-1} \in S_i$. We say that a strategy $\pi^1 \in \Pi^1$ is *winning* from state s iff for all $\pi^2 \in \Pi^2$, the smallest color that appears infinitely often in $\delta(s, \pi^1, \pi^2)$ is even. We denote by Win^1 the set of states from which Player 1 has a winning strategy.

In the following, we examine two algorithms for solving parity games with three colors. We consider a fixed parity game (S_1, S_2, E, c) with three colors. When discussing the complexity of the algorithms, we assume an adjacency list representation for the game.

2.1   Emerson-Jutla's μ-Calculus Algorithm

From [10], parity games can be solved using a fixpoint computation involving the so-called *controllable predecessor operators*.

Definition 1 (Controllable Predecessor Operator). For a set of states $X \subseteq S$, $Cpre^1(X)$ yields all states from which Player 1 can force the game into X in one step. Formally,

$$Cpre^1(X) = \{s \in S_1 \mid \exists(s, t) \in E . t \in X\} \cup \{s \in S_2 \mid \forall(s, t) \in E . t \in X\}.$$

For parity games with three colors, the set of winning states Win^1 can be characterized using the following formula [10], written in μ-calculus notation:

$$Win^1 = \nu Z.\mu Y.\nu X. \left[(Cpre^1(X) \cap C_2) \cup (Cpre^1(Y) \cap C_1) \cup (Cpre^1(Z) \cap C_0) \right].$$

Such fixpoint can be computed by Picard iteration, using three nested loops; we will refer to this algorithm as the *EJ algorithm*. An enumerative implementation of this algorithm takes time $O(m \cdot n^2)$: the inner loop can be computed in time $O(m)$ (the computation is analogous to the one used for solving safety games), while the outer loops can be performed at most n times each. On the other hand, a symbolic implementation requires time $O(m \cdot n^3)$, since the computation of $Cpre^1$ takes time $O(m)$, and it is performed $O(n^3)$ times.

2.2 Jurdziński's Progress Measure Algorithm

An alternative algorithm for computing Win^1 is the *progress measure* algorithm from [13]. For three-color parity games, this algorithm has the best worst-case complexity of all known algorithms. Let $n_1 = |C_1|$ and $M = \{0, 1, \ldots, n_1+1\}$. A *progress measure* is a function $\rho : S \to M$. The algorithm proceeds by building a monotonically increasing sequence $(\rho_i)_{i \geq 0}$ of progress measures, until a fixpoint is reached.

For $\alpha \in M$ and $j \in \{0, 1, 2\}$, we define

$$
Progr(\alpha, j) = \begin{cases} 0 & \text{if } j = 0 \text{ and } \alpha < n_1 + 1, \\ \alpha + 1 & \text{if } j = 1 \text{ and } \alpha < n_1 + 1, \\ \alpha & \text{otherwise.} \end{cases} \tag{1}
$$

We have $\rho_0(s) = 0$ for all $s \in S$. For all $i \geq 0$, the update from ρ_i to ρ_{i+1}, called *lift*, is dictated by the following rule, where $a \sqcup b$ denotes $\max\{a, b\}$.

$$
\rho_{i+1}(s) = \rho_i(s) \sqcup \begin{cases} \min_{(s,t) \in E} Progr(\rho_i(t), c(s)) & \text{if } s \in S_1, \\ \max_{(s,t) \in E} Progr(\rho_i(t), c(s)) & \text{if } s \in S_2. \end{cases} \tag{2}
$$

Denoting ρ^* the fixpoint of the sequence $(\rho_i)_{i \geq 0}$, the set of winning states Win^1 is characterized by:

$$
Win^1 = \{s \in S \mid \rho^*(s) < n_1 + 1\}.
$$

Given ρ_i, computing ρ_{i+1} requires time $O(m)$. Since at each step the measure of at least one state increases by at least one, our formulation of the algorithm requires time $O(m \cdot n^2)$. Notice that, by applying the complexity bound cited in Theorem 11 of [13], we obtain a time complexity of $O(m \cdot n)$. The difference is due to the fact that our formulation of the algorithm updates the progress measures for all states at once, while the original algorithm only updates the progress measure one state at a time. Moreover, the $O(m \cdot n)$ complexity can only be achieved if we can somehow efficiently determine which states need to be lifted. This presumably requires bookkeeping at every state and lift propagation algorithms, that are incompatible with the symbolic implementation we discuss in Section 5.

2.3 Gap Algorithm

We present the *gap acceleration technique* for the progress measure algorithm of Jurdziński. The resulting algorithm, which we call the *gap algorithm*, is often much faster than the original progress measure algorithm, while retaining its worst case complexity.

Informally, the idea is as follows. At any step of the algorithm, let k be an integer in $\{0, 1, \ldots, n_1\}$ such that no state has progress measure k, but some states have progress measure greater than k. We call such a value of k a "gap". We show that all states with progress measure greater than k are losing. Therefore, we can immediately set their measure to $n_1 + 1$, thus accelerating the convergence of the algorithm. In practice, after each update of the progress measure, we will seek the minimum gap k, and we will set to $n_1 + 1$ the progress measure of all states having progress measure above the gap k. The correctness of this optimization is proved by the following lemma and theorem.

Lemma 1. *For all $i \geq 0$ and $k > 0$, let $Z_i^k = \{s \in S \mid \rho_i(s) \geq k\}$. Then, for all $s \in Z_i^k$, Player 2 can enforce at least $\rho_i(s)$ visits to C_1. Moreover, only states in Z_i^k are visited before the first visit to C_1.*

Proof. Notice that, for all $i \leq j$, it holds $Z_i^k \subseteq Z_j^k$. We proceed by induction on i. For $i = 0$, the statement is trivially true, since $\rho_0(s) = 0$ for all $s \in S$. For $i > 0$, we distinguish the following cases.

- $s \in C_2$. If $s \in S_1$ (resp. $s \in S_2$), then all (resp. at least one) of the successors t of s are such that $\rho_{i-1}(t) \geq \rho_i(s) \geq k$; thus, $t \in Z_{i-1}^k$. By inductive hypothesis, Player 2 can enforce from t at least k visits to C_1, and the first visit occurs before Z_{i-1}^k is left. Since $Z_{i-1}^k \subseteq Z_i^k$, the thesis applies to s.
- $s \in C_1$. If $s \in S_1$ (resp. $s \in S_2$), then all (resp. at least one) of the successors t of s are such that $\rho_{i-1}(t) \geq \rho_i(s) - 1 \geq k - 1$; thus, $t \in Z_{i-1}^{k-1}$. By inductive hypothesis, Player 2 can enforce from t at least $k - 1$ more visits to C_1. Therefore, Player 2 can enforce from s at least k visits to C_1. The first visit to C_1 being s itself, it occurs trivially without leaving Z_i^k.
- $s \in C_0$. Then, $\rho_i(s) = 0$ or $\rho_i(s) = n_1 + 1$. If $\rho_i(s) = 0$, the result is trivial. If $\rho_i(s) = n_1 + 1$, the result follows by noticing that, if $s \in S_1$ (resp. $s \in S_2$), then all (resp. at least one) of the successors t of s are such that $\rho_i(t) = n_1 + 1$.   ∎

Theorem 1. *Given $i \geq 0$ and $k > 0$, assume that $\rho_i^{-1}(k - 1) = \emptyset$. Then, each state $s \in Z_i^k$ is a losing state for Player 1.*

Proof. First, we show that, starting from s, Player 2 can enforce infinitely many visits to C_1, while remaining in Z_i^k at all times. In particular, if $s \in Z_i^k \cap C_2$, by Lemma 1, Player 2 has a strategy to reach C_1 while staying in Z_i^k at all times. If instead $s \in Z_i^k \cap C_1$, Player 2 can enforce that the next state is still in Z_i^k, as the following argument shows. If $s \in S_1$, all successors t of s satisfy $\rho_i(t) \geq \rho_{i-1}(t) \geq \rho_i(s) - 1 \geq k - 1$. However, since it cannot be $\rho_i(t) = k - 1$, it must be $\rho_i(t) \geq k$, and so $t \in Z_i^k$. Finally, if $s \in S_2$, let t be the successor that maximizes $Progr(\rho_{i-1}(t), c(s))$. We have $\rho_i(t) \geq \rho_{i-1}(t) = \rho_i(s) - 1 \geq k - 1$. As before, it must be $\rho_i(t) \geq k$ and so $t \in Z_i^k$.

It remains to be proved that, while visiting C_1 infinitely often, C_0 is not visited infinitely often. Notice that for all $s \in Z_i^k \cap C_0$, it holds $\rho_i(s) = n_1 + 1$. Therefore, if a state in C_0 is ever visited, it is a losing state for Player 1.   ∎

It is not hard to devise an example where the gap acceleration does not decrease the total number of iterations. For all $k > 0$, consider the game G_k in Figure 1(a). States drawn as "◇" belong to S_1 while those drawn as "□" belong to S_2. The numbers in the states represent their color. The game G_k is a chain of k states of color one, leading to a sink state of color zero. The lock-step algorithm requires k global lifts to reach the

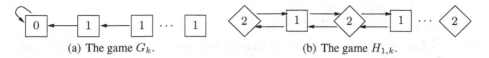

(a) The game G_k.   (b) The game $H_{1,k}$.

Fig. 1. Two game families illustrating different performance gains offered by the gap acceleration

fixpoint. During the process, the progress measure exhibits no gaps, thus neutralizing the proposed acceleration technique.

On the other hand, the gap acceleration technique can be responsible for an unbounded speed-up compared to both the original algorithm and our lock-step formulation of it. For all $k > 0$, consider the game $H_{1,k}$ from [13], depicted in Figure 1(b). The game is essentially a bi-directional chain made of k states of color one, alternating with $k + 1$ states of color 2. As proven in [13], the original algorithm has to lift each state k times before acknowledging that all states are losing, thus reaching a complexity of $O(k^2)$. Similarly, the lock-step formulation of the algorithm requires k global lifts, leading to a complexity of $O(k^2)$. However, after two global lifts all states have progress measure greater than zero. Therefore, if the gap acceleration is enabled, three lifts are enough to reach the fixpoint, for a total time complexity of $O(k)$.

3   Timed Interfaces with Variables

In this section, we present a model of real-time interfaces which is obtained from the *sociable interfaces* of [6], by adding discrete clocks in the spirit of [9].

The state space of our timed interfaces is represented by variables, interpreted over a given domain $\mathcal{D}$. Given a set of variables V, a *state* over V is a mapping $s : V \to \mathcal{D}$ that associates with each $x \in V$ a value $s(x) \in \mathcal{D}$. We denote by $[\![V]\!]$ the set of all states over V. For a set of variables $V' \subseteq V$, and a state $s \in [\![V]\!]$, the restriction of s to V' is a state $s' \in [\![V']\!]$ denoted by $s|_{V'}$. For two disjoint sets of variables V' and $V \setminus V'$, and two states $s' \in [\![V']\!]$ and $s'' \in [\![V \setminus V']\!]$, the operation $(s' \cdot s'')$ concatenates the two states resulting in a new state $s \in [\![V]\!]$. For two sets A and B, we write $f : A \rightrightarrows B$ to indicate that f is a function with domain A and codomain 2^B.

Definition 2 (Timed Interface). A *timed interface* is a tuple $M = (\Sigma_M, V_M^G, V_M^L, C_M, \tau_M^I, \tau_M^O, \varphi_M^I, \varphi_M^O)$, where:

- Σ_M is a set of *actions*.
- V_M^G is a set of *global variables*, V_M^L is a set of *local variables*, and C_M is the set of *clock variables*. Clock variables are interpreted over the set $\mathbb{N}_0$ of natural numbers including zero. We require $C_M \subseteq V_M^L$ and $V_M^G \cap V_M^L = \emptyset$. We set $V_M = V_M^G \cup V_M^L$.
- For all actions $a \in \Sigma_M$, $\tau_M^I(a) : [\![V_M]\!] \rightrightarrows [\![V_M]\!]$ is the *input transition relation* of a. We require this transition relation to be *deterministic* w.r.t. variables in V_M^L, that is,

$$\forall a \in \Sigma_M, s \in [\![V_M]\!], \forall s_1, s_2 \in \tau_M^I(a)(s). \ (s_1|_{V_M^L} = s_2|_{V_M^L}).$$

- For all actions $a \in \Sigma_M$, $\tau_M^O(a) : [\![V_M]\!] \rightrightarrows [\![V_M]\!]$ is the *output transition relation* of a.

- $\varphi_M^I \subseteq [\![V_M]\!]$ is the *input invariant*.
- $\varphi_M^O \subseteq [\![V_M]\!]$ is the *output invariant*.

The set of states $[\![V_M]\!]$ of a timed interface M is denoted by S_M. For $s \in S_M$, we denote by $s + 1$ the state which coincides with s, except that the clock variables have been incremented by one. Formally, $(s + 1)(v) = s(v) + 1$ for all $v \in C_M$, and $(s + 1)(v) = s(v)$ for all $v \in V_M \setminus C_M$.

The semantics of a timed interface is a game between players Input and Output. At each step, both players propose a move and the state of the interface evolves according to the following definitions. Each move can be *(i)* a state reachable from the current one by taking an action, *(ii)* the request to let time advance (move Δ_1), or *(iii)* the null move Δ_0. Each player can only play moves that maintain the player's invariant. In the following, we consider a fixed interface M.

Definition 3 (Moves). For all states $s \in S_M$ and $i \in \{I, O\}$, let $D^i(s) = \{\Delta_1\}$ if $s + 1 \in \varphi_M^i$, and $D^i(s) = \emptyset$ otherwise. The set of possible moves for player i at s is:

$$\Gamma_M^i(s) = \left(\bigcup_{a \in \Sigma_M} \tau_M^i(a)(s) \cap \varphi_M^i \right) \cup \{\Delta_0\} \cup D^i(s).$$

We also define $\Gamma_M^i = \bigcup_{s \in S_M} \Gamma_M^i(s)$.

Two Boolean variables bl^I and bl^O are used for specifying whether a player lets time elapse or not (i.e. proposes a Δ_1 action). bl^I (bl^O) is true if and only if the action proposed by the input (output) player is not Δ_1. An *extended state* $\hat{s}$ is a state $s \in S_M$ augmented with the truth values for the Boolean variables bl^O and bl^I. The set of all extended states of M is $\hat{S}_M = S_M \times \{T, F\}^2$.

Definition 4 (Moves Outcome). For all states $s \in S_M$ and moves $m^I \in \Gamma_M^I(s)$ and $m^O \in \Gamma_M^O(s)$, the *outcome* $\delta_M(s, m^I, m^O)$ of m^I and m^O at s is the set of extended states defined by the following table, where rows represent choices for m^I and columns represent choices for m^O.

	Δ_0	Δ_1	s''
Δ_0	$\{(s, \mathrm{bl}^I, \mathrm{bl}^O)\}$	$\{(s, \mathrm{bl}^I, \neg\mathrm{bl}^O)\}$	$\{(s'', \neg\mathrm{bl}^I, \mathrm{bl}^O)\}$
Δ_1	$\{(s, \neg\mathrm{bl}^I, \mathrm{bl}^O)\}$	$\{(s + 1, \neg\mathrm{bl}^I, \neg\mathrm{bl}^O)\}$	$\{(s'', \neg\mathrm{bl}^I, \mathrm{bl}^O)\}$
s'	$\{(s', \mathrm{bl}^I, \neg\mathrm{bl}^O)\}$	$\{(s', \mathrm{bl}^I, \neg\mathrm{bl}^O)\}$	$\{(s', \mathrm{bl}^I, \neg\mathrm{bl}^O), (s'', \neg\mathrm{bl}^I, \mathrm{bl}^O)\}$

Definition 5 (Strategy). A *strategy* for player $i \in \{I, O\}$ in M is a function $\pi^i : \hat{S}_M^* \to \Gamma_M^i$ that associates, with every finite sequence of extended states σ whose last state is $\hat{s} = (s, \mathrm{bl}^I, \mathrm{bl}^O)$, a move $\pi^i(\sigma) \in \Gamma_M^i(s)$. We denote by Π_M^I and Π_M^O the set of input and output strategies in M, respectively.

Definition 6 (Strategy Outcomes). Given a state $s \in S_M$, an input strategy $\pi^I \in \Pi_M^I$ and an output strategy $\pi^O \in \Pi_M^O$, the set of *outcomes* $\hat{\delta}_M(s, \pi^I, \pi^O)$ of π^I and π^O from s consists of all infinite sequences over extended states $\sigma = (s_0, \mathrm{bl}_0^I, \mathrm{bl}_0^O), \ldots, (s_i, \mathrm{bl}_i^I, \mathrm{bl}_i^O), \ldots$ such that $s_0 = s$, and for all $i \geq 0$ $(s_{i+1}, \mathrm{bl}_{i+1}^I, \mathrm{bl}_{i+1}^O) \in \delta_M(s_i, \pi^I(\sigma_{\leq i}), \pi^O(\sigma_{\leq i}))$ where $\sigma_{\leq i}$ denotes the prefix of σ up to the i-th extended state. Notice that bl_0^I and bl_0^O are arbitrarily defined.

In the following, we use *tick* as a shorthand for $\neg bl^O \wedge \neg bl^I$, which means that both players propose a time elapse step. Furthermore, we use the LTL notation [16] to denote sets of traces.

As discussed in [7], in order to take into proper account illegal behaviors that would lead to an artificial stopping of time, if player $i \in \{I, O\}$ has a certain goal *goal*, he should actually enforce the winning condition $WC^i(goal)$, defined as follows:

$$WC^I(goal) = (goal \wedge \Box \Diamond \text{tick}) \vee \Diamond \Box bl^O$$
$$WC^O(goal) = (goal \wedge \Box \Diamond \text{tick}) \vee \Diamond \Box \neg bl^O.$$

Intuitively, these conditions require a player to ensure that if time diverges, the goal is realized, and if time fails to diverge, the blame lies with the adversary. The conditions are asymmetrical, reflecting the fact that Input and Output do not behave in fully symmetrical ways during composition [9]. Given $s \in S_M$, a strategy $\pi^I \in \Pi^I_M$ is *I-winning* from s w.r.t. the goal *goal*, iff $\forall \pi^O \in \Pi^O_M . \hat{\delta}(s, \pi^I, \pi^O) \subseteq WC^I(goal)$. Similarly, a strategy $\pi^O \in \Pi^O_M$ is *O-winning* from s w.r.t. *goal*, iff $\forall \pi^I \in \Pi^I_M . \hat{\delta}(s, \pi^I, \pi^O) \subseteq WC^O(goal)$. A state $s \in S_M$ is *I-winning* (resp. O-winning) iff there exists an Input strategy that is I-winning (resp. O-winning) from s. The set of all I-winning (resp. O-winning) states is denoted by $Win^I_M(goal)$ (resp. $Win^O_M(goal)$).

A particularly important game is the *well-formedness* game, where the goals of the players are simply T, so that their winning conditions are $Win^I_M(\text{T})$ and $Win^O_M(\text{T})$, respectively. Intuitively, if a player can win the well-formedness game, it means that it can "keep the system going", without entering dead-end states from which time cannot progress [9,7].

4   Example: Scheduling as a Timed Game

We present an example of a periodical scheduling problem encoded as a timed interface. In the timed interface, the actions of Input represent scheduler decisions, such as the decision of starting a task. The actions of Output represent task nondeterminism, such as the variability in task execution times. The goal of Input is to ensure that no deadline is missed. If Input can win the game, the scheduler has a strategy that correctly schedules the tasks, ensuring that no deadline is missed regardless of task nondeterminism. Technically, the goal of not missing deadlines is a safety condition, stating that, while the tasks' execution has not completed, certain clocks should have values not exceeding the deadlines. We take this safety condition as the Input invariant, thus saddling the Input player, representing the scheduler, with the goal of meeting deadlines. We will see that taking into account for time progress in the winning condition is essential, if we wish to encode scheduling problems as timed games. Indeed, if the requirement for time progress is disregarded, the easiest way to ensure deadlines are met is to block the progress of time: as time cannot progress, deadlines cannot be missed!

The timed interface in Figure 2 encodes a periodical, non-preemptive scheduling problem involving two tasks, A and B. Task A has a period of 5s (measured by clock cA), and lasts up to 3s (measured by clock dA); task B has period 9s, and lasts up to 4s. The output invariant enforces the fact that neither task can be active for longer than

```
module Scheduling:
    var cpu, activeA, activeB, doneA, doneB: bool
    var cA, dA, cB, dB: clock

    oinv: (activeA -> dA <= 3) & (activeB -> dB <= 5)
    iinv: (cA <= 4) & (cB <= 9)

    input startA : { local: ~doneA & ~activeA & ~cpu ==>
                             activeA' := true, cpu' := true, dA' := 0 }
    input startB : { local: ~doneB & ~activeB & ~cpu ==>
                             activeB' := true, cpu' := true, dB' := 0 }

    output stopA : { activeA ==> ~activeA' & ~cpu' & doneA' }
    output stopB : { activeB ==> ~activeB' & ~cpu' & doneB' }

    input periodA: {local: doneA & cA = 4 ==> cA' := 0, doneA' := false}
    input periodB: {local: doneA & cB = 9 ==> cB' := 0, doneB' := false}
endmodule
```

Fig. 2. Timed interface representing the periodic scheduling problem of two non-preemptable tasks

its specified maximal duration. The input invariant states that the values of the clocks cA and cB cannot grow larger than the period lengths, namely, 5 and 9. This forces the scheduler to reset these clocks, via actions periodA and periodB, before they go beyond values 5 and 9. The action periodA signals the start of a new period for task A; its guard doneA specifies that periodA can be taken only once the execution of task A has completed. The situation for task B is similar. Therefore, to avoid violating the input invariant, Input (the scheduler) must issue actions startA, startB, periodA, periodB with a timing ensuring that jobs A and B terminate no later than the end of their respective periods. An Input strategy for doing this corresponds to a scheduling strategy for the task set.

This example illustrates why the winning condition needs to account for time divergence. Had we taken T as winning condition for Input, rather than $Win^I(\text{T}) = \Box\Diamond\text{tick} \vee \Diamond\Box\text{bl}^O$, Input could have won simply by stopping time progress, for instance, by playing always move Δ_0.

5   Symbolic Solution of the Well-Formedness Game

Consider the winning condition for the input player in the well-formedness game.

$$WC^I(\text{T}) = \Box\Diamond\text{tick} \vee \Diamond\Box\text{bl}^O.$$

Being the disjunction of a Büchi and a co-Büchi condition, it can be expressed as a parity condition with three colors, assigned as follows:

$$C_0 = \neg\text{bl}^I \wedge \neg\text{bl}^O; \qquad C_1 = \text{bl}^I \wedge \neg\text{bl}^O; \qquad C_2 = \text{bl}^O.$$

If ϕ is a safety, reachability, Büchi, or co-Büchi formula, it is similarly possible to obtain 3-color deterministic parity automata encoding $WC^I(\phi)$ and $WC^O(\phi)$.

We note that C_1 consists of the states where Input is forced to play either an action, or the 0-delay move Δ_0. Thus, in a timed game, the gap is related to the maximal number of times for which Input can be forced to play without letting time advance. This number is generally much smaller than the number of C_1 states, as these chains of forced 0-time transitions tend, in practical examples, to be fairly short (it is unusual for them to be longer than a dozen transitions). This explains the very large speedup provided by the gap acceleration in the analysis of timed games.

If we restrict the variable domain $\mathcal{D}$ to be finite, and we manage to let clock variables also range over a finite set, we can apply the EJ and gap algorithms to the problem of checking well-formedness of an interface. The tool TICC [8] allows the user to specify timed interfaces using a convenient syntax based on guarded commands. The tool is in the process of being extended to discrete real-time. In TICC, clock variables can only be compared to (or assigned from) constants. Under this assumption, it is well known that, for each clock x, it is sufficient to consider the range of values going from zero to the maximum constant to which x is ever compared (or assigned from), plus one.

We implemented in TICC both the EJ and the gap algorithms; we experimented with both algorithms for solving well-formedness games. In the tool, interfaces are internally represented using Multi-valued Decision Diagrams [19] (MDDs) as implemented by the CUDD library [18]. Therefore, in the following we discuss the issues regarding the symbolic implementation of both algorithms.

5.1 Gap Algorithm

Since the progress measure algorithm is tailored to turn-based games, we have to emulate the turns by providing separate transition relations for Input and Output. Input moves from the original (or *regular*) states of the concurrent game, while Output moves from intermediate *virtual* states. Notice that, if from a regular state s Input chooses to reach state s' via action a, Output in the next virtual state can decide to let a happen (by picking move Δ_0), or rather take an alternative action b from s. Thus, we have to store in the virtual state both the start state s and the proposed destination s'. Therefore, we end up having three copies of the state variables V_M, which we call V, V', and V''. The transition relation of Input in the turn-based game is represented by the predicate τ^I, of type $V \to V', V'', \mathrm{bl}^I$. The transition relation of Output is represented by the predicate τ^O, of type $V', V'', \mathrm{bl}^I \to V, \mathrm{bl}^O$. We need an extra variable ρ to represent the progress measure.

Next, we need to represent the function *Progr* from (1), used to update the progress measure. For states of color one, *Progr* has to increment the value of the progress measure by one. Consider the general problem of having a predicate α over the set of variables Z, and wanting to increment by one the variable $z \in Z$, unless the value of z is already equal to its maximum value z_{max}. Using standard MDD operators, this can be achieved by having an extra variable z' and performing the following computation:

$$incr(\alpha, z) = (\exists z(\alpha \wedge z' = z + 1))[z/z'] \vee (\alpha \wedge z = z_{max}).$$

However, the above computation leads to very poor performance: since ρ can have a very high maximum value, the computation of the predicate $\rho' = \rho + 1$ alone requires a very large amount of time. Thus, in place of the above computation, we developed a specific increment operator, as follows. Let $z_0, z_1, \ldots, z_k$ be the binary variables encoding variable z, ordered from the least significant (z_0) to the most. For $c \in \{0, \ldots, k\}$, and $\sim \in \{<, \leq, >, \geq\}$, let $z_{\sim c} = \{z_j \mid j \sim c\}$.

> **function Increment**(α, z)
> **vars:** $r, \overline{\alpha}, \underline{\alpha}, \mathrm{pos}, \mathrm{neg} : \mathrm{MDD}$
> $r := \textbf{false}$
> $\overline{\alpha} := \alpha \wedge (z = z_{max})$
> $\underline{\alpha} := \alpha \wedge (z \neq z_{max})$
>   **for** $i := 0$ **to** k **do**
> $\mathrm{neg} := \neg z_0 \wedge \neg z_1 \wedge \ldots \wedge \neg z_{i-1}$
> $\mathrm{pos} := z_0 \wedge z_1 \wedge \ldots \wedge z_{i-1}$
> $r := r \vee \left(\mathrm{neg} \wedge z_i \wedge \exists z_{\leq i} . (\underline{\alpha} \wedge \mathrm{pos} \wedge \neg z_i) \right)$
>   **done**
>   **return** $r \vee \overline{\alpha}$

Then, in order to implement the measure update step described by (2), we need the following symbolic operation. Let α be a predicate over the set of variables Z and let $z \in Z$. For each assignment to the variables in $Z \setminus \{z\}$, α may contain several different assignments to z. We want to preserve the minimum value of z only. We call this predicate $\min_z \alpha$. In set notation, we have:

$$\min_z \alpha = \left\{ s \in \alpha \mid s(z) = \min\{s'(z) \mid s' \in \alpha\} \right\}.$$

No efficient implementation of min exists using standard MDD operators. We thus developed a new "min" operator according to the following algorithm.

> **function Min**(α, z)
> **vars:** $r : \mathrm{MDD}$
> $r := \alpha$
>   **for** $i := k$ **down to** 0 **do**
> $r := r \wedge \left((\neg z_i \wedge \exists z_{>i} . r) \vee (z_i \wedge \forall z_{\geq i} . (\neg z_i \implies \neg r)) \right)$
>   **done**
>   **return** r

The "min" operator is also useful to determine the minimum gap in a measure. If α is the predicate over variables $(V, \mathrm{bl}^I, \mathrm{bl}^O, \rho)$ representing the measure of each regular state in the game, the equation $\min_\rho \forall V \forall \mathrm{bl}^I \forall \mathrm{bl}^O . \neg \alpha$ yields "false" if the measure has no unused values, or otherwise a predicate of the type $\rho = c$, where c is the minimum unused value of the measure (and thus a good candidate to be a gap). Such predicate can then be used to implement the acceleration technique presented in Section 2.3.

5.2 Emerson-Jutla's μ-Calculus Algorithm

To apply the EJ algorithm of Section 2.1, we do not need to consider the turn-based version of the game. Rather, we simply use as controllable predecessor operator the following.

Definition 7 (Concurrent Controllable Predecessor Operator). $Cpre^I : 2^{\hat{S}_M} \to 2^{S_M}$ assigns to each set of extended states X, the set of states from which Input can force the game into X in one step. Formally,

$$Cpre^I(X) = \{s \in S_M \mid \exists m^I \in \Gamma_M^I(s) . \forall m^O \in \Gamma_M^O(s) . \delta_M(s, m^I, m^O) \subseteq X\}.$$

The transition predicates τ^I and τ^O developed in the previous section can also be used to obtain a symbolic implementation of $Cpre^I$. Given a predicate α over variables $(V, \mathrm{bl}^I, \mathrm{bl}^O)$, we have:

$$Cpre^I(\alpha) = \exists V' \exists V'' \exists \mathrm{bl}^I . \tau^I \wedge (\forall V \forall \mathrm{bl}^O . \tau^O \implies \alpha).$$

Given the symbolic implementation of $Cpre^I$, the EJ algorithm can be implemented in a straightforward manner, using three nested loops that compute the fixpoint by Picard iteration.

5.3 Experimental Results

On the basis of the implementation discussed above, we compared the performance of the EJ and gap algorithms. Our results indicate that the performance improvement afforded by the gap acceleration is essential: for the scheduling example, for instance, the acceleration reduces the number of iterations from at least 73,920 in the original Jurdziński progress measure algorithm to 163 in the gap algorithm — a speed-up of over 450. Without acceleration, we believe that the progress measure algorithm is highly impractical for solving 3-color parity games.

Our results indicate that there is no clear winner between the EJ algorithm and the gap algorithm. The running times of the two algorithms were, in our experiments, within a factor of two of each other, with the EJ algorithm generally being the fastest. We suspect that the BDD variable ordering, and other details of the symbolic implementation, have a large influence on the results, so that we do not believe that our experiments are conclusive. For the scheduling example of Section 4, the input well-formedness of the interface can be computed in 144s with the EJ algorithm, and 302s with the gap algorithm, on an AMD Athlon 64 4400+ CPU running 32-bit linux. In the gap algorithm, the main expense occurs in the "lift" operation; we are investigating more efficient symbolic implementations of this operation.

In the same paper [13] that introduced the progress measure algorithm, the following acceleration is mentioned: in place of n_1, it suffices to take the maximum number n_1' of C_1-states belonging to a strongly-connected component (SCC) of the game graph (S, E); clearly, $n_1' \leq n_1$. In an enumerative setting, both this SCC-based acceleration, and our gap-based acceleration, are of interest, and each provides greater speed-ups on some games. In a symbolic setting, the time required to compute SCCs must be taken into account; the straightforward symbolic algorithm may require a quadratic number of iterations. In contrast, our gap-based acceleration can be performed at negligible cost.

References

1. Adler, B., de Alfaro, L., Faella, M.: Average reward timed games. In: Pettersson, P., Yi, W. (eds.) FORMATS 2005. LNCS, vol. 3829, pp. 65–80. Springer, Heidelberg (2005)
2. Alur, R., Henzinger, T.A.: Modularity for timed and hybrid systems. In: Mazurkiewicz, A., Winkowski, J. (eds.) CONCUR 1997. LNCS, vol. 1243, pp. 74–88. Springer, Heidelberg (1997)
3. Asarin, E., Maler, O., Pnueli, A., Sifakis, J.: Controller synthesis for timed automata. In: Proc. I.F.A.C. (ed.) Proc. IFAC Symposium on System Structure and Control, pp. 469–474. Elsevier, Amsterdam (1998)
4. Bouyer, P., Cassez, F., Fleury, E., Larsen, K.G.: Optimal strategies in priced timed game automata. In: Lodaya, K., Mahajan, M. (eds.) FSTTCS 2004. LNCS, vol. 3328, pp. 148–160. Springer, Heidelberg (2004)
5. Cassez, F., David, A., Fleury, E., Larsen, K.G., Lime, D.: Efficient on-the-fly algorithms for the analysis of timed games. In: Abadi, M., de Alfaro, L. (eds.) CONCUR 2005. LNCS, vol. 3653, pp. 66–80. Springer, Heidelberg (2005)
6. de Alfaro, L., da Silva, L.D., Faella, M., Legay, A., Roy, P., Sorea, M.: Sociable interfaces. In: Gramlich, B. (ed.) Frontiers of Combining Systems. LNCS (LNAI), vol. 3717, pp. 81–105. Springer, Heidelberg (2005)
7. de Alfaro, L., Faella, M., Henzinger, T.A., Majumdar, R., Stoelinga, M.: The element of surprise in timed games. In: Amadio, R.M., Lugiez, D. (eds.) CONCUR 2003. LNCS, vol. 2761, pp. 144–158. Springer, Heidelberg (2003)
8. de Alfaro, L., Faella, M., Legay, A.: An introduction to the tool TICC. In: Proc. of Workshop on Trustworthy Software, IBFI, Schloss Dagstuhl, Germany (2006)
9. de Alfaro, L., Henzinger, T.A., Stoelinga, M.: Timed interfaces. In: Sangiovanni-Vincentelli, A.L., Sifakis, J. (eds.) EMSOFT 2002. LNCS, vol. 2491, pp. 108–122. Springer, Heidelberg (2002)
10. Emerson, E.A., Jutla, C.S.: Tree automata, mu-calculus and determinacy (extended abstract). In: FOCS 91: Proc. 32nd IEEE Symp. Found. of Comp. Sci. pp. 368–377. IEEE Computer Society Press, Los Alamitos (1991)
11. Emerson, E.A., Jutla, C.S., Sistla, A.P.: On model checking for fragments of μ-calculus. In: Courcoubetis, C. (ed.) CAV 1993. LNCS, vol. 697, pp. 385–396. Springer, Heidelberg (1993)
12. Faella, M., La Torre, S., Murano, A.: Automata-theoretic decision of timed games. In: Cortesi, A. (ed.) VMCAI 2002. LNCS, vol. 2294, pp. 94–108. Springer, Heidelberg (2002)
13. Jurdziński, M.: Small progress measures for solving parity games. In: Reichel, H., Tison, S. (eds.) STACS 2000. LNCS, vol. 1770, pp. 290–301. Springer, Heidelberg (2000)
14. Jurdziński, M.: Deciding the winner in parity games is in UP ∩ co-UP. Information Processing Letters 68(3), 119–124 (1998)
15. Maler, O., Pnueli, A., Sifakis, J.: On the synthesis of discrete controllers for timed systems. In: Mayr, E.W., Puech, C. (eds.) STACS 95. LNCS, vol. 900, pp. 229–242. Springer, Heidelberg (1995)
16. Manna, Z., Pnueli, A.: The Temporal Logic of Reactive and Concurrent Systems: Specification. Springer, New York (1991)
17. Segala, R., Gawlick, G., Søgaard-Andersen, J., Lynch, N.: Liveness in timed and untimed systems. Information and Computation 141(2), 119–171 (1998)
18. F. Somenzi: CUDD: CU decision diagram package.
    `http://vlsi.colorado.edu/~{}fabio/CUDD/cuddIntro.html`
19. Srinivasan, A., Kam, T., Malik, S., Brayton, R.: Algorithms for discrete function manipulation. In: ICCAD 90: Proc. of IEEE Int. Conf. on Computer-Aided Design, pp. 92–95. IEEE Computer Society Press, Los Alamitos (1990)
20. Thomas, W.: Automata on Infinite Objects. In: Handbook of Theoretical Computer Science, Elsevier, Amsterdam (1990)

UPPAAL-Tiga: Time for Playing Games!
(Tool Paper)

Gerd Behrmann[1], Agnès Cougnard[1], Alexandre David[1], Emmanuel Fleury[2],
Kim G. Larsen[1], and Didier Lime[3]

[1] CISS, Aalborg University, Aalborg, Denmark
{behrmann,adavid,kgl}@cs.aau.dk
[2] LaBRI, Bordeaux-1 University, CNRS (UMR 5800), Talence, France
fleury@labri.fr
[3] IRCCyN, École Centrale de Nantes, CNRS (UMR 6597), Nantes, France
Didier.Lime@irccyn.ec-nantes.fr

Abstract. In 2005 we proposed the first efficient on-the-fly algorithm for solving games based on timed game automata with respect to reachability and safety properties. The first prototype presented at that time has now matured to a fully integrated tool with dramatic improvements both in terms of performance and the availability of the extended input language of UPPAAL-4.0. The new tool can output strategies or let the user play against them both from the command line and from the graphical simulator that was completely re-designed.

1 Introduction

For more than a decade timed, priced and hybrid games have been proposed and studied by various researchers [AMPS98, DAHM01, MPS95, BCFL04]. Though several decidability results and algorithms have been presented, so far only prototype tools have been developed [AT02]. UPPAAL-TIGA[1] is the first efficient tool supporting the analysis of timed games allowing synthesis of controllers for control problems modelled as timed game automata and with safety or liveness control objectives.

2 What Can Be Done with Uppaal-Tiga?

Control Problems. The modeling formalism of UPPAAL-TIGA consists of a network of timed game automata [MPS95] (NTGA). A timed game automaton is a timed automaton [AD94] in which the set of actions is partitioned into *controllable* actions and *uncontrollable* actions. The former are actions that can be triggered by the controller, the latter by the environment/opponent. The opponent has

---

[1] http://www.cs.aau.dk/~adavid/tiga/

W. Damm and H. Hermanns (Eds.): CAV 2007, LNCS 4590, pp. 121–125, 2007.
© Springer-Verlag Berlin Heidelberg 2007

priority over the controller. Given a NTGA, we are mainly interested in two types of control objectives:

The *reachability* objective: Is it possible to find a strategy for the triggering of controllable actions guaranteeing that a given set of (goal) states of the system is reached regardless of what and when uncontrollable actions are taken?

The *safety* objective: Is it possible to find a strategy for the triggering of controllable actions guaranteeing that a given set of (bad) states of the system are never reached regardless of what and when uncontrollable actions are taken?

Formally, control objectives are formulated as "control: P", where P is TCTL formula specifying either a safety property (A[] ϕ or A[ϕ_1 W ϕ_2]) or a liveness property (A<> ϕ or A[ϕ_1 U ϕ_2]). Given a control objective "control: P" the search engine of UPPAAL-TIGA will provide a strategy (if any such exists) under which the behaviour will satisfy P. Here a (winning) strategy is simply a function describing for each state of the system what the controller should do either in terms of "performing a particular controllable action" or to "delay".

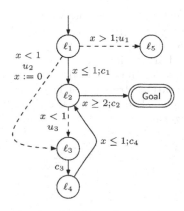

Fig. 1. Timed game automaton example

Example. To illustrate the use of UPPAAL-TIGA, consider the example in Fig. 1, consisting of a timed game automaton A with one clock x. It has two types of edges: controllable (c_i) and uncontrollable (u_i). A defines the rules of the game. In our current example (Fig. 1), we define the simple reachability objective "control: A<> A.Goal". UPPAAL-TIGA searches for a winning strategy on this game using the algorithm proposed in [CDF+05]. Each winning condition, entered in UPPAAL-TIGA as a regular query, is marked as "*satisfied*" if there exists a winning strategy and "*not satisfied*" if none exists. Hence, in our example, the query "control: A<> A.Goal" will be marked "*satisfied*". Moreover, the tool can output the corresponding strategy from the command line or let the user play against it in the simulator as shown in Fig. 2. For controllable games (here), UPPAAL-TIGA plays the controller and the user is the opponent. The first transition is for the controller (UPPAAL-TIGA), the second for the opponent (user), and the third is for the opponent but it will be countered by the controller (UPPAAL-TIGA takes the transition to ℓ_2), hence it is greyed – the opponent cannot take this action.

Applications. UPPAAL-TIGA has recently been used for an industrial case study with the company Skov A/S specializing in climate control systems used for modern pig and poultry stables [DJLR07]. The synthesis capability of the tool has been combined with Simulink and Real-Time Workshop to provide a complete tool chain for synthesis, simulation, and automatic generation of production code.

UPPAAL-TIGA has also been recently applied to check for (bi-)simulation between timed automata and timed game automata [CDL07]. Given two timed

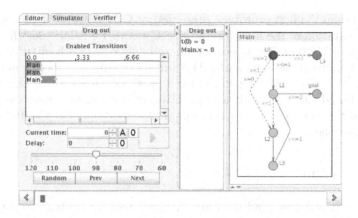

Fig. 2. View of the simulator when playing a strategy

automata, the tool can check if one (bi-)simulates the other and similarly for timed game automata with applications for controller synthesis with partial observability. This technique has been applied to the compositional verification of the ZeroConf protocol.

Our tool is being used in the AMAES project[2], a French national project on Advanced Methods for Autonomous Embedded Systems. UPPAAL-TIGA has been successfully applied for controlling the autonomous robot Dala [LC04] in charge of taking pictures and transmitting them back to Earth during limited transmission windows. It is desirable in such control problems to optimize the moves to save power.

3   What Is New?

Input Language. The new generation of UPPAAL-TIGA inherits the enriched input language of UPPAAL-4.0, with the only exception of priorities. The user has now access to C-like syntax to declare functions, custom types, *etc.* In addition, users can now define more complex winning conditions by means of logical formulas in the indicated subset of TCTL.

Strategies. UPPAAL-TIGA is able to generate a strategy for the controller, which ultimately corresponds to a control program, or a "counter-strategy" for the opponent as a proof that the controller cannot win. These strategies can now be output as decision graphs (hybrid BDD/CDD graphs). The discrete part of the states is represented as a BDD and the symbolic part as a CDD [LPWY99]. Finally, UPPAAL-TIGA allows the user to play against the strategy in both the GUI[3] and CLI.

Performances. UPPAAL-TIGA is faster by several orders of magnitude on large examples (more than 1000 times faster) and consumes much less memory (100

---

[2] http://www-verimag.imag.fr/~krichen/AMAES/
[3] This is a major new feature for the next major release.

times less) than the first prototype presented at CONCUR'05. This comes from
the full integration of the algorithm in the UPPAAL-4.0 [BDH+06][4] framework.
This brings to UPPAAL-TIGA some of the reliability and performances achieved
by years of UPPAAL developments. Also improvements have been made on the
DBM library, in particular on subtractions, partitions, federations, specific operations for timed games (*e.g.* the computation of controllable predecessors *w.r.t.*
delay), and the essential operation of merging several difference bound matrices
(DBMs) into one.

4   Conclusion

UPPAAL-TIGA is a new (and the only efficient) tool for controller synthesis for
control problems modeled as timed game automata. Its performance and usability has greatly been improved by its integration with UPPAAL-4.0. In a future
version methods for preventing synthesis of strategies generating zeno behaviour
will be provided. Also the computationally much more complex problem of synthesis under partial observability is under investigation.

References

[AD94]   Alur, R., Dill, D.: A Theory of Timed Automata. Theoretical Computer
           Science 126(2), 183–235 (1994)
[AMPS98]   Asarin, E., Maler, O., Pnueli, A., Sifakis, J.: Controller Synthesis for Timed
           Automata. In: Proc. IFAC Symp. on System Structure & Control, pp. 469–
           474. Elsevier, Amsterdam (1998)
[AT02]   Altisen, K., Tripakis, S.: Tools for controller synthesis of timed systems.
           In: RT-TOOLS'02 (2002)
[BCFL04]   Bouyer, P., Cassez, F., Fleury, E., Larsen, K.G.: Optimal Strategies
           in Priced Timed Game Automata. In: Lodaya, K., Mahajan, M. (eds.)
           FSTTCS 2004. LNCS, vol. 3328, pp. 148–160. Springer, Heidelberg (2004)
[BDH+06]   Behrmann, G., David, A., Håkansson, J., Hendriks, M., Larsen, K.G., Pet-
           tersson, P., Yi, W.: UPPAAL 4.0. In: Proc. of 3rd Int. Conf. on the Quanti-
           tative Evaluation of Systems, pp. 125–126. IEEE Computer Society Press,
           Los Alamitos (2006)
[CDF+05]   Cassez, F., David, A., Fleury, E., Larsen, K.G., Lime, D.: Efficient On-the-
           fly Algorithms for the Analysis of Timed Games. In: Abadi, M., de Alfaro,
           L. (eds.) CONCUR 2005. LNCS, vol. 3653, pp. 66–80. Springer, Heidelberg
           (2005)
[CDL07]   Chatain, T., David, A., Larsen, K.: Playing Games with Games (Unpub-
           lished)
[DAHM01]   De Alfaro, L., Henzinger, T.A., Majumdar, R.: Symbolic Algorithms for
           Infinite-State Games. In: Larsen, K.G., Nielsen, M. (eds.) CONCUR 2001.
           LNCS, vol. 2154, pp. 536–550. Springer, Heidelberg (2001)
[DJLR07]   David, A., Jessen, J.J., Larsen, K.G., Rasmussen, J.I.: Guided Controller
           Synthesis for Climate Controller Using UPPAAL-TIGA. Unpublished

---

[4] http://www.uppaal.com

[LC04]   Lemai-Chenevier, S.: IxTeT-eXeC: planification, réparation de plan et contrôle d'exécution avec gestion du temps et des ressources. PhD thesis, Institut National Polytechnique de Toulouse (2004)

[LPWY99]   Larsen, K.G., Pearson, J., Weise, C., Yi, W.: Clock Difference Diagrams. Nordic Journal of Computing 6(3), 271–298 (1999)

[MPS95]   Maler, O., Pnueli, A., Sifakis, J.: On the Synthesis of Discrete Controllers for Timed Systems. In: Mayr, E.W., Puech, C. (eds.) STACS 95. LNCS, vol. 900, pp. 229–242. Springer, Heidelberg (1995)

The TASM Toolset: Specification, Simulation, and Formal Verification of Real-Time Systems

(Tool Paper)

Martin Ouimet and Kristina Lundqvist

Embedded Systems Laboratory
Massachusetts Institute of Technology
Cambridge, MA, 02139, USA
{mouimet,kristina}@mit.edu

Abstract. In this paper, we describe the features of the Timed Abstract State Machine toolset. The toolset implements the features of the Timed Abstract State Machine (TASM) language, a specification language for reactive real-time systems. The TASM language enables the specification of functional and non-functional properties using a unified language. The toolset incorporates features to create specifications, simulate specifications, and verify formal properties of specifications. Properties that can be verified using the toolset include completeness, consistency, worst-case execution time, and best-case execution time. The toolset is being developed as part of an architecture-based framework for embedded real-time system engineering. We describe how the features of the toolset were used successfully to model and analyze case studies from the aerospace and automotive communities.

1 Introduction

The Timed Abstract State Machine (TASM) specification language is a specification language for reactive real-time systems. The TASM language aims to capture the three key aspects of real-time system behavior, namely, functional behavior, timing behavior and resource consumption. TASM is based on the theory of Abstract State Machines (ASM), a method for system design that can be applied at various levels of abstraction [1]. The TASM language has formal semantics, which makes its meaning precise and enables executable specifications. The time semantics of the language revolve around the concept of durative actions.

The TASM toolset implements the features of the TASM language through three main components - an editor, an analyzer, and a simulator. The toolset can be used during the early phases of development to understand behavior before the system is built, or it can be used throughout the development of the system to guide implementation. The type of analysis that can be performed with the toolset include verifying completeness and consistency of the specification [2] and verifying timing properties of the specification such as the absence of deadlocks and Worst-Case Execution Time (WCET). The philosophy of the toolset is to reuse the state of the art in analytical engines to perform formal verification. The TASM toolset integrates the UPPAAL tool suite [3] to verify

W. Damm and H. Hermanns (Eds.): CAV 2007, LNCS 4590, pp. 126–130, 2007.

timing properties of TASM specifications and uses the SAT4J SAT Solver [4] to verify completeness and consistency of TASM specifications [5]. The TASM toolset serves as the basis of a specification framework for real-time system engineering [6].

2   The Timed Abstract State Machine (TASM) Language

The TASM language is based on the theory of Abstract State Machines (ASM), a method for high-level system design [1]. In the ASM formalism, behavior is specified as the computation steps of an abstract machine and the effect of the computation steps on the global state. The TASM language extends the ASM language by providing constructs and semantics for time and resource consumption. In the TASM language, time is attached to the steps of the abstract machine in such a way that a finite amount of time elapses before the effect of the computation step is reflected on the global state. The semantics of *durative* actions are used to reflect the reality that actions are typically not instantaneous. In a similar fashion, resource consumption is attached to durative steps to denote the resources used by the machine to complete the computation step. Listing 1 shows a sample rule of a TASM machine from the production cell system describing the action of the robot picking up a block from the press. The execution of the rule takes between 1 and 3 time units to complete and consumes exactly 2000 units of power.

Listing 1. TASM Rule Describing the Robot Picking up a Block from the Press

```
R1: Pickup from Press
{
    t     := [1, 3];
    power := 2000;

    if armbpos = atpress and armb = empty and press_block = available then
        press_block := notavailable;
        press       := empty;
        armb        := loaded;
}
```

The TASM language also contains facilities for hierarchical composition, parallel composition, and synchronization channels. In the TASM language, *completeness* is defined as a machine having a rule enabled for all classes of inputs [5]. *Consistency* is defined as a machine having no more than one rule enabled for all classes of inputs [5]. Furthermore, because actions are durative in TASM, execution time refers to the time that it takes to reach a certain reachable state from a start state. Worst-Case Execution Time (WCET) is the maximum amount of time that the machine will take to reach a state. Conversely, Best-Case Execution Time (BCET) is the minimum amount of time between any two states.

3   The TASM Toolset

The TASM toolset uses literate and graphical facilities to edit, simulate, and verify TASM specifications. The toolset includes facilities for creating and editing TASM specifications, through the TASM Editor. The editor enables the specification of functional and non-functional behavior, with standard facilities for syntax highlighting and syntax checking. By definition, TASM specifications are executable. The execution semantics of the TASM language have been defined in [7]. The TASM Simulator enables the graphical visualization of the dynamic behavior expressed in the specification in a step-by-step fashion. Because time and resources can be specified using intervals, that is, using a lower bound and an upper bound, the simulation can use different semantics for time durations and resource consumption. For example, a given simulation can use the worst-case time (upper bound) for all steps, to visualize the system behavior under the longest running times. Other options include best-case time, average-case time, and using a time randomly selected within the specified interval. The same semantics can be selected for the resource consumption behavior.

The TASM Analyzer is the component of the TASM toolset that performs analysis of specifications. The analyzer can be used to verify basic properties of TASM specifications such as consistency and completeness [2]. In the TASM language, completeness ensures that for all classes of monitored variable values, a rule will be enabled. Consistency ensures that for all classes of monitored variable values, one and only one rule is enabled. In other words, verifying consistency means verifying that the rules of a given machine are mutually exclusive. Both completeness and consistency are verified at the machine specification level. The analysis of completeness and consistency is achieved by translating machine rule guard expressions into a boolean formula in conjunctive normal form [5]. The boolean formula can then be verified for satisfiability using a SAT solver. The TASM toolset uses the SAT4J solver, an open source SAT solver [4]. The completeness and consistency problem is formulated in such a way that an incomplete or inconsistent specification leads to a satisfiable boolean formula. Formulating the problem this way ensures that the SAT solver can automatically generate a counterexample if the specification is inconsistent or incomplete.

The TASM analyzer is also used to verify execution time of TASM specifications. The execution time is verified by mapping TASM specifications to the timed automata formalism of UPPAAL. The UPPAAL tool suite is used in conjunction with an approach we call *iterative bounded liveness*, to verify BCET and WCET. The approach uses the bounded liveness temporal logic pattern [3] in an iterative fashion to converge to an upper bound and to a lower bound from an initial time obtained through reachability analysis. For TASM specifications, execution times are bounded. Since the reachability problem is decidable for timed automata, verifying the execution times of TASM specifications is guaranteed to converge. The toolset is available, free of charge, from the TASM web site (http://esl.mit.edu/tasm).

4   Case Studies

The TASM language and toolset have been used to model and analyze three case studies. The toolset has been used to model an Electronic Throttle Controller (ETC) and to analyze the completeness and consistency of the mode switching logic of the controller [8]. The production cell, partially illustrated in Listing 1, was modeled and analyzed in the toolset. The production cell was analyzed to measure the minimum amount of time for the system to process 5 blocks. Using the model and BCET analysis, the optimal solution to process 5 blocks was automatically derived. The toolset was also used to model the Timeliner System, a scripting environment currently in use on the international space station. The model was used to analyze the WCET of one pass of the Timeliner system. The Timeliner system shares processor usage with other tasks using a fixed timeslice scenario. The execution time was analyzed to ensure that the assigned timeslice is adequate but not overly estimated, to ensure optimal processor usage. Future case studies will include a modular redundant avionics system, modeled and analyzed to understand the end-to-end latency of the system.

5   Conclusion and Future Work

The toolset and language have been used successfully to model and analyze embedded real-time systems as found in the avionics and automotive communities. Using specifications expressed in the TASM language, the toolset can verify properties of specifications such as completeness and consistency. The analysis is performed by translating the specification and using existing solvers. For completeness and consistency, this is achieved through a translation to boolean formulas and using the SAT4J SAT solver to automatically verify the property. Furthermore, the execution times of specifications can be analyzed using a translation of TASM specifications to UPPAAL's timed automata.

Future work on the toolset will investigate the use of theorem provers to verify properties of the models that cannot be handled because of state explosion problems. Furthermore, the toolset will be used to generate test cases based on TASM specifications. This will most likely be achieved by reusing the translation to boolean formulas and the translation to timed automata and using established algorithms to to generate test cases.

References

1. Börger, E.: The Origins and the Development of the ASM Method for High Level System Design and Analysis. Journal of Computer Science, vol. 8(5) (2001)
2. Heimdahl, M.P.E., Leveson, N.G.: Completeness and Consistency in Hierarchical State-Based Requirements. Software Engineering 22(6), 363–377 (1996)
3. Behrmann, G., David, A., Larsen, K.G.: A Tutorial on UPPAAL. In: Bernardo, M., Corradini, F. (eds.) Formal Methods for the Design of Real-Time Systems. LNCS, vol. 3185, Springer, Heidelberg (2004)
4. Leberre, D.: SAT4J: A Satisfiability Library for Java. presentation available from http://sat4j.objectweb.com
5. Ouimet, M., Lundqvist, K.: Automated Verification of Completeness and Consistency of Abstract State Machine Specifications using a SAT Solver. In: Proceedings of the 3rd International Workshop on Model-Based Testing (MBT '07), Satellite Workshop of ETAPS '07 (April 2007)
6. Ouimet, M., Lundqvist, K.: The Hi-Five Framework and the Timed Abstract State Machine Language. In: Proceedings of the 27th IEEE Real-Time Systems Symposium - Work in Progress Session, December 2006, IEEE Computer Society Press, Los Alamitos (2006)

7. Ouimet, M., Lundqvist, K.: The Timed Abstract State Machine Language: An Executable Specification Language for Reactive Real-Time Systems. In: Proceedings of the 15th International Conference on Real-Time and Network Systems (RTNS '07) (March (2007)
8. Ouimet, M., Berteau, G., Lundqvist, K.: Modeling an Electronic Throttle Controller using the Timed Abstract State Machine Language and Toolset. In: Kühne, T. (ed.) MoDELS 2006. LNCS, vol. 4364, Springer, Heidelberg (2007)

Systematic Acceleration in Regular Model Checking

Bengt Jonsson and Mayank Saksena

Dept. of Information Technology, P.O. Box 337, S-751 05 Uppsala, Sweden
{bengt,mayanks}@it.uu.se

Abstract. Regular model checking is a form of symbolic model checking technique for systems whose states can be represented as finite words over a finite alphabet, where regular sets are used as symbolic representation. A major problem in symbolic model checking of parameterized and infinite-state systems is that fixpoint computations to generate the set of reachable states or the set of reachable loops do not terminate in general. Therefore, *acceleration* techniques have been developed, which calculate the effect of arbitrarily long sequences of transitions generated by some action. We present a systematic method for using acceleration in regular model checking, for the case where each transition changes at most one position in the word; this includes many parameterized algorithms and algorithms on data structures. The method extracts a maximal (in a certain sense) set of actions from a transition relation. These actions, and systematically obtained compositions of them, are accelerated to speed up a fixpoint computation. The extraction can be done on any representation of the transition relation, e.g., as a union of actions or as a single monolithic transducer. Using this approach, we are for the first time able to verify completely automatically both safety and absence of starvation properties for a collection of parameterized synchronization protocols from the literature; for some protocols, we obtain significant improvements in verification time. The results show that symbolic state-space exploration, without using abstractions, is a viable alternative for verification of parameterized systems with a linear topology.

1 Introduction

A major approach in algorithmic verification of parameterized and infinite-state systems is to extend the paradigm of symbolic model checking [17] by appropriate symbolic representations; examples include Petri nets, timed automata, systems with unbounded communication channels, integers and reals. One direction is *regular model checking*, which considers systems whose states can be represented as finite words over a finite alphabet; regular sets are used to represent sets of states and transition relations. Regular model checking has been proposed as a uniform paradigm for algorithmic verification of several classes of parameterized and infinite-state systems [26,32,16,4].

In symbolic model checking of parameterized and infinite-state systems, a major problem is that fixpoint computations that generate the set of reachable

W. Damm and H. Hermanns (Eds.): CAV 2007, LNCS 4590, pp. 131–144, 2007.
© Springer-Verlag Berlin Heidelberg 2007

states or the set of reachable loops (for verifying liveness properties) do not terminate in general, since there is no uniform bound on the distance (in number of transitions) from an initial configuration to any reachable configuration. To make fixpoint computations converge more frequently, *acceleration* techniques have been developed, which calculate the effect of arbitrarily long sequences of transitions generated by some action (i.e., a subset of the transition relation). This has been done, e.g., for systems with unbounded FIFO channels [11,12,14,1], systems with counters [13,18], and for parameterized systems [6]. Acceleration is typically applied to small actions, e.g., corresponding to a single program statement or simple loop, since acceleration of larger actions or the entire transition relation is often intractable. Fixpoint computations can be sped up by using accelerated actions in each iteration, thereby allowing the fixpoint computation to converge in many practical cases (e.g., [1]).

For regular model checking, methods have been developed for computing the set of reachable configurations or reachable loops [25,16,19,8]. These algorithms typically work well for small system models, but have difficulties to cope with large transition relations. For instance, the automata-theoretic approach for parameterized systems [3] transforms verification of a liveness property into the problem of finding reachable loops for a system with a rather large transition relation. There has been no systematic way to to extract actions for acceleration from such a transition relation, and therefore liveness properties for several parameterized mutual exclusion protocols have not been proven automatically by this class of techniques.

In this paper, we present a systematic approach for using acceleration to speed up fixpoint computations in regular model checking. We consider *unary* systems, in which each computation step changes at most one position in the word; many models of parameterized algorithms and algorithms on data structures are unary. Our approach is based on accelerating a class of actions (called *separable*) which can be efficiently accelerated. We present techniques for

(a) systematically extracting a set of separable actions which is maximal in the sense that any other separable action is included in some extracted one; the extraction can be done on any representation of the transition relation, e.g., as a union of actions or as a single monolithic transducer,

(b) systematically composing actions to form separable actions that represent the effect of several transitions; such compositions are analogous to program loops; many verification examples require the acceleration of such compositions, rather than single actions, for termination.

We have implemented our approach in the context of our LTL(MSO) model checker for parameterized systems [3], and verified safety and liveness properties of several idealized parameterized protocols from the literature, including parameterized algorithms for mutual exclusion (e.g., the Bakery algorithm by Lamport, algorithms by Burns, Szymanski, and Dijkstra). The most important result is that, for the first time, liveness properties have been successfully verified for all of these algorithms; previous approaches have not been successfully applied to all of them. One should also note that our verification, following the automata theoretic approach, does not employ any form of abstraction: it computes an exact representation of the set of reachable states and reachable loops.

Related Work. Works on acceleration techniques in other contexts include techniques for systems with FIFO channels [1,12,14] and systems with counter variables [9,32]. Finkel, Leroux and colleagues have presented a systematic framework for acceleration techniques for programs with a finite number of variables, typically ranging over integers [10,23]. Their approach cannot be used for regular model checking, in which systems can not be modeled by a fixed number of integer variables. For regular model checking, Pnueli and Shahar [28] show how specific acceleration schemes can be defined in a version of S1S. They did not consider composition of actions, which is necessary in many cases, and they have reported verification of liveness for only one example, after applying a manually supplied abstraction. In our earlier work [6], we proved safety properties of several parameterized protocols by accelerating individual actions; this approach did not consider composition of actions and would therefore not have been able to verify liveness properties.

Proving liveness properties of parameterized systems has been considered also in other approaches. Pnueli, Xu, and Zuck [29] use a version of counter abstraction to prove absence of starvation properties for Szymanski's algorithm and the Bakery algorithm. Their abstractions are rather coarse, and lose information so that, e.g., safety properties can no longer be checked. Fang, Piterman, Pnueli, and Zuck [22,21] infer a ranking function and helpful directions of a certain form, by generalizing from the verification of finite instances. These approaches require that a system can be verified using assertions of a certain form. In our earlier work [5], we proved liveness properties by backwards reachability analysis from "terminated" configurations; this technique can be combined with other techniques for proving liveness, but can not be used to find counterexamples (bugs); our technique is based on state-space exploration, which is guaranteed to report counterexamples when they exist.

Abdulla et al. [2] verify safety properties of parameterized protocols by overapproximation of backwards reachable states; their approach can not be used for proving liveness properties. Other works apply abstraction [15] or regular inference [24] directly on the automata that represent reachable states or the transition relation.

Outline. In the next section, we introduce the framework of regular model checking and the fixpoint computations that are our concern. Section 3 presents our technique for extracting parts of a transition relation for acceleration. In Section 4, we present how to use our systematic acceleration in the verification of liveness properties. Experimental results from our implementation, and comparisons with other results are presented in Section 5. Section 6 presents conclusions and future work directions.

2   The Regular Model Checking Framework

Let Σ be a finite alphabet. A relation $\mathcal{R}$ on Σ^* (the set of finite words over Σ) is *length-preserving* if w and w' are of equal length whenever $(w, w') \in \mathcal{R}$. In this paper, we will only consider length-preserving relations on Σ^*. A relation $\mathcal{R}$ on Σ^* is *regular* if the set $\{(a_1, a_1') \cdots (a_n, a_n') \mid (a_1 \cdots a_n, a_1' \cdots a_n') \in \mathcal{R}\}$ is a regular subset of $(\Sigma \times \Sigma)^*$. A regular relation Σ^* can be represented by a finite-state transducer, i.e., a finite automaton over $(\Sigma \times \Sigma)$.

Regular relations are closed under union $\cup$, intersection $\cap$, relational composition $\circ$, as well as concatenation $\cdot$ defined by $\mathcal{R} \cdot \mathcal{R}' \overset{\triangle}{=} \{(w_1 \cdot w_1', w_2 \cdot w_2') \mid w_1 \, \mathcal{R} \, w_2 \text{ and } w_1' \, \mathcal{R}' \, w_2'\}$. For a (regular) set $\mathcal{S}$ of words, let $\mathcal{S} \circ \mathcal{R}$ denote the (regular) set $\{w \mid \exists w' \in \mathcal{S}. \ w' \, \mathcal{R} \, w\}$. We use $\mathcal{R}^+$ to denote the (not necessarily regular) transitive closure of $\mathcal{R}$; and $\mathcal{R}^*$ the reflexive-transitive closure. We denote by $Id = \{(w, w') \mid w = w'\}$ the identity relation on Σ^*.

Definition 1. A *regular transition system* (RTS for short) over Σ is a pair $(\mathcal{I}, \mathcal{R})$, where

$\mathcal{I}$ is a regular set over Σ, denoting a set of *initial configurations*, and
$\mathcal{R}$ is a regular relation on Σ^*, denoting the *transition relation*.

A *fair regular transition system* (FRTS for short) over Σ is a tuple $(\mathcal{I}, \mathcal{R}, \mathcal{F})$, where $(\mathcal{I}, \mathcal{R})$ is an RTS and $\mathcal{F}$ is a regular set over Σ, denoting the set of *accepting configurations*. Transition relations and regular sets are typically represented by transducers and automata, or by regular expressions.   □

A *configuration* w of an RTS $(\mathcal{I}, \mathcal{R})$ is a word $a_1 \, a_2 \, \cdots \, a_n \in \Sigma^*$. A *computation* of $(\mathcal{I}, \mathcal{R})$ is a finite or infinite sequence $w^0, w^1, w^2, \ldots$ of configurations such that $w^0 \in \mathcal{I}$ and $w^i \mathcal{R} w^{i+1}$ for all adjacent pairs of configurations. A configuration is *reachable* if it occurs in some computation. An infinite computation $w^0, w^1, w^2, \ldots$ of a FRTS is *accepting* if $w^i \in \mathcal{F}$ for infinitely many i.

Many parameterized systems with linear or ring-shaped topologies can be modeled as regular transition systems, by letting each position in a configuration model the local state of a system component. As an example of a parameterized system, we describe the mutual exclusion algorithm by Burns. In the algorithm, an arbitrary number of processes compete for a critical section. The processes are numbered, say from 1 to N. The *local state* of each process consists of a control state ranging over the integers from 1 to 7 and one Boolean flag, *flag*. A pseudo-code description of the behavior of process number i is shown in Figure 1. For instance, according to the code on line 4, if the control state of a process i is 4, and if the value of *flag* is 1 for some process $j < i$, then the control state of i may be changed to 1; otherwise to 5. Line 7 represents the critical section.

To model Burns' algorithm as an RTS, we let Σ be the set of possible local states, e.g., represented as tuples $\langle pc, flag \rangle$. A system configuration is a word in Σ^*. The effect of line j can be represented by a regular relation α_j. For instance, α_1 corresponds to $Id \cdot [(pc = 1) \longrightarrow (pc := 2, flag := 0)] \cdot Id$ where the notation $(pc = 1) \longrightarrow (pc := 2, flag := 0)$ represents the relation

1:	$flag[i] := 0$
2:	if $\exists j < i : flag[j] = 1$ then goto 1
3:	$flag[i] := 1$
4:	if $\exists j < i : flag[j] = 1$ then goto 1
5:	await $\forall j > i : flag[j] \neq 1$
6:	$flag[i] := 0$
7:	goto 1

Fig. 1. Burns' mutual exclusion algorithm

$\{(\langle pc_1, flag_1 \rangle, \langle pc_2, flag_2 \rangle) \mid pc_1 = 1, pc_2 = 2$ and $flag_2 = 0\}$. To distinguish between branches, let α_{ja}, α_{jb} denote the *if* and *else* branch of α_j, for $j = 2, 4$.

It is also possible to model programs that operate on linear unbounded data structures such as queues, stacks, integers, etc. For instance, a stack can be modeled by letting each position in the word represent a position in the stack. The stack should initially contain an arbitrary but bounded number of empty stack positions, which are "statically allocated". We can then faithfully model all finite computations of the system, by initially allocating sufficiently many empty stack positions. We will consider two verification problems:

Reachability: Compute the set of reachable states of a given RTS $(\mathcal{I}, \mathcal{R})$, i.e., the set $\mathcal{I} \circ \mathcal{R}^*$. The problem of verifying any safety property can in the standard way be reduced to that of computing the set of reachable states of a suitable RTS.

Repeated reachability: Does a given FRTS $(\mathcal{I}, \mathcal{R}, \mathcal{F})$ have an infinite accepting computation? The problem of verifying a liveness properties can, using the classical automata-theoretic framework [31] adapted to regular model checking [3], be reduced to the problem of repeated reachability of a suitable FRTS. A repeated reachability problem can be checked by computing the transitive closure of a transition relation, to be described in Section 4.

In general, these problems are undecidable, but techniques have been developed which are complete for certain classes of RTSs, and also verify examples from the literature (e.g., [25,8]).

3 Verification Using Acceleration

We can attempt to compute both reachable and repeatedly reachable configurations by standard fixpoint iterations. Let us describe this for the case of reachability. A naive computation of the set $\mathcal{I} \circ \mathcal{R}^*$ of reachable states is to compute the sequence $\mathcal{C}_0, \mathcal{C}_1, \mathcal{C}_2, \cdots$, where $\mathcal{C}_0 = \mathcal{I}$ and $\mathcal{C}_{i+1} = \mathcal{C}_i \cup (\mathcal{C}_i \circ \mathcal{R})$, until a fixpoint is reached, i.e., $\mathcal{C}_{k+1} = \mathcal{C}_k$ for some k. This approach is guaranteed to terminate for finite-state systems, but not in general for parameterized and infinite-state systems, since there is no uniform bound on the number of computation steps needed to reach any particular configuration. For RTSs, $\mathcal{I} \circ \mathcal{R}^*$

and $\mathcal{R}^+$ are in general not computable, but incomplete techniques have been developed [7,16,19], which are guaranteed to complete under conditions which are typically satisfied when $\mathcal{R}$ is "simple", but not when $\mathcal{R}$ is the entire transition relation of an RTS. We therefore present a method to compute $\mathcal{I} \circ \mathcal{R}^*$ or $\mathcal{R}^+$ by decomposing $\mathcal{R}$ into "simple" parts, compute the transitive closure of each part, and then use the results in a refined fixpoint computation.

To this end, let an *action* of the RTS $(\mathcal{I}, \mathcal{R})$ be any subset of $\mathcal{R}$. We use α to range over actions. By *acceleration*, we mean to compute α^+ from α. The fixpoint computation described in the previous paragraph is modified by instead defining $\mathcal{C}_{i+1}$ as the result of choosing an appropriate $\alpha_i \subseteq R^+$, and letting $\mathcal{C}_{i+1} = \mathcal{C}_i \cup (\mathcal{C}_i \circ \alpha_i^+)$. The test for convergence remains the same: is $\mathcal{C}_i = \mathcal{C}_i \cup (\mathcal{C}_i \circ \mathcal{R})$? The main problem is to decide how to choose the sequence of actions $\alpha_0 \, \alpha_1 \, \cdots$ to accelerate, in order to converge at $\mathcal{I} \circ \mathcal{R}^*$.

We will consider the class of *unary* RTS, in which each computation step changes at most one position in a configuration. This class contains many parameterized synchronization algorithms. For unary RTSs, there is a particular class of actions (called *separable*) which can be accelerated efficiently.

Definition 2. *A regular relation $\mathcal{R}$ is unary if w and w' differ in at most one position whenever $w \, \mathcal{R} \, w'$. A RTS $(\mathcal{I}, \mathcal{R})$ is unary if $\mathcal{R}$ is unary. A unary relation is separable if it is of form $\phi_L \cdot \tau \cdot \phi_R$, where $\phi_L, \phi_R \subseteq Id$, and τ is a relation on Σ. We call ϕ_L the left context and ϕ_R the right context of $\phi_L \cdot \tau \cdot \phi_R$.*

Separable unary actions are interesting, because there are efficient techniques for accelerating them, which are complete when ϕ_L and ϕ_R satisfy certain conditions that hold for a majority of separable unary actions encountered in practice [6,25], and yield good underapproximations otherwise. Our verification strategy is therefore to generate a sequence $\alpha_0 \, \alpha_1 \, \cdots$ of separable unary actions to drive the above modified fixpoint computation. To avoid overapproximation, we must obviously require $\alpha_i \subseteq \mathcal{R}^*$ for each i. To make the fixpoint computation as powerful as possible, we will generate as "large" actions as possible. By this, we will mean that any unary separable action in $\mathcal{R}$ is subsumed. We would also like to require the same for any composition of such actions, but this is not possible, since if α and α' are separable unary actions, then in general $\alpha \circ \alpha'$ is not unary and $\alpha \cup \alpha'$ is not separable. We therefore define restricted versions of these operations, *separable composition* $\circ_s$ and *separable union* $\cup_s$, as follows

$$(\phi_L \cdot \tau \cdot \phi_R) \; \circ_s \; (\phi'_L \cdot \tau' \cdot \phi'_R) \; \overset{\triangle}{=} \; (\phi_L \cap \phi'_L) \cdot \tau \circ \tau' \cdot (\phi_R \cap \phi'_R)$$

$$(\phi_L \cdot \tau \cdot \phi_R) \; \cup_s \; (\phi'_L \cdot \tau' \cdot \phi'_R) \; \overset{\triangle}{=} \; (\phi_L \cap \phi'_L) \cdot \tau \cup \tau' \cdot (\phi_R \cap \phi'_R)$$

where the changes in α and α' are constrained to occur in the same position. The resulting actions are separable, and can be efficiently accelerated.

Definition 3. *Let $\mathcal{R}$ be a regular relation. A set of actions $\mathcal{A}$ is separable-complete with respect to $\mathcal{R}$, if it satisfies:*
(U)   For any sequence $\alpha_1, \ldots, \alpha_n$ of separable unary actions, where $\alpha_j \subseteq \mathcal{R}$ for $j \in [1, n]$, there is an action $\alpha \in \mathcal{A}$ such that

$$(\alpha_1 \circ_s \ldots \circ_s \alpha_n)^+ \subseteq \alpha^+$$

If condition (U) is true for $n \leq k$, for some bound k, the set is separable-complete up to k, *and k is called the* composition depth.   □

As a special case, if $\mathcal{A}$ is separable-complete up to 1, then any separable unary action $\alpha' \subseteq \mathcal{R}$ is subsumed by some $\alpha \in \mathcal{A}$.

Let us see why separable-completeness is relevant for Burns' algorithm. Imagine that we are computing $\mathcal{I} \circ \mathcal{R}^*$ for Burns' algorithm, using a fixpoint computation. Consider a configuration where there are arbitrarily many processes on line 2, each with α_{2b} enabled. It is then possible for any single process to proceed to line 5, via lines 3 and 4. However, whenever α_3 is executed by some process i, all processes $j < i$ are blocked. Hence, in order for arbitrarily many processes to move from 2 to 5, they must act sequentially from higher to lower index. It follows that we need the accelerated sequential composition $(\alpha_{2b} \circ_s \alpha_3 \circ_s \alpha_{4b})^+$, to capture this behaviour; a fixpoint computation using only $\alpha_{2b}^+, \alpha_3^+, \alpha_{4b}^+$ would need unboundedly many computation steps. If (U) were true, we would have an action with $\alpha^+ \supseteq (\alpha_{2b} \circ_s \alpha_3 \circ_s \alpha_{4b})^+$, allowing us to compute the set of reachable configurations.

We are now ready to present our technique for generating actions to be accelerated in the fixpoint computation; it will automatically generate a finite set of actions which is separable-complete.

Generation Procedure. Our procedure for generating a sequence of actions that satisfy condition (U) has three steps.

1. We obtain any finite set of separable actions $\mathcal{A}'$ such that $\mathcal{R} = \cup \mathcal{A}'$.
   One way to do this is to extract such actions from a representation of $\mathcal{R}$ as a minimal deterministic automaton $\mathcal{T} = \langle S, \Sigma \times \Sigma, s_0, \delta, F \rangle$, as follows. Let $\mathcal{T}(s, Q)$ equal $\mathcal{T}$ but with $s_0 = s$ and $F = Q$. Then $\mathcal{R}$ is the union of actions $\{\phi_L \cdot \tau \cdot \phi_R\}$ where $\phi_L = \mathcal{T}(s_0, \{s\}) \cap Id$, and $\phi_R = \mathcal{T}(t, F) \cap Id$, and $\tau = \delta(s, t)$ for states $s, t \in S$ (and $\phi_L, \phi_R, \tau \neq \emptyset$).
2. We thereafter transform $\mathcal{A}'$ so that it has the property that any separable unary action $\alpha \subseteq \mathcal{R}$ is *in* (i.e., a subset of) the separable union of some actions in $\mathcal{A}'$. For this purpose, we define two operations on separable unary actions:

$$(\phi_L \cdot \tau \cdot \phi_R) \sqcap_L (\phi'_L \cdot \tau' \cdot \phi'_R) \triangleq (\phi_L \cap \phi'_L) \cdot (\tau \cap \tau') \cdot (\phi_R \cup \phi'_R)$$
$$(\phi_L \cdot \tau \cdot \phi_R) \sqcap_R (\phi'_L \cdot \tau' \cdot \phi'_R) \triangleq (\phi_L \cup \phi'_L) \cdot (\tau \cap \tau') \cdot (\phi_R \cap \phi'_R)$$

   Closing the set of actions under the operations $\sqcap_L$ and $\sqcap_R$ achieves the goal. As an optimization, we delete actions that are then subsets of other actions.
3. Finally, we close the set of actions $\mathcal{A}'$, from previous step, under $\cup_s$. Again, as an optimization, we delete actions that become subsets of other actions.

We motivate step **2** for Burns' algorithm. Suppose step **1** is applied to a deterministic representation of $\mathcal{R}$. We get $\mathcal{A}' \supseteq \{\alpha, \alpha'\}$, with $\alpha = \phi_{L4a} \cdot (\tau_3 \cup \tau) \cdot Id$, and $\alpha' = \phi_{L4b} \cdot (\tau_3 \cup \tau') \cdot Id$, for some τ, τ'. The desired property is false: α_3 is not in the separable union of α, α' (nor of $\mathcal{A}'$). The left context of α_3 has been divided. However, $\alpha_3 = (\alpha \sqcap_R \alpha')$, giving the desired property. Without step **2**, our procedure underapproximates α_3 and sequential compositions involving α_3.

The generated actions are separable-complete up to 1 by construction (by steps **2** and **3**). Let us now establish that they are even separable-complete. We use the following lemma, which establishes how $\circ_s$ and $\cup_s$ are related.

Lemma 1. *Let* $\mathcal{A}' = \{\alpha_1, \ldots, \alpha_m\}$ *be a set of separable unary actions, with* $\alpha_j = \phi_L^j \cdot \tau_j \cdot \phi_R^j$, *for* $j \in [1, m]$. *Let* $\sigma = \alpha_{i_1} \circ_s \alpha_{i_2} \circ_s \ldots \circ_s \alpha_{i_n}$ *be any composition such that each* $\alpha \in \mathcal{A}'$ *occurs at least once. Then:*

$$\sigma \subseteq \phi_L^1 \cap \ldots \cap \phi_L^m \cdot (\tau_1 \cup \ldots \cup \tau_m)^+ \cdot \phi_R^1 \cap \ldots \cap \phi_R^m \qquad \square$$

Theorem 1. *The set of actions generated by steps* **1**–**3** *is separable-complete.*

Proof. Given any sequence $\alpha_1, \ldots, \alpha_n$, where $\alpha_j \subseteq \mathcal{R}$ for $j \in [1, n]$. Let us denote the fact that the generated actions have composition depth 1 by (U$_1$). By (U$_1$), there are actions $\alpha_1', \ldots, \alpha_n'$ generated by our procedure such that $\alpha_j \subseteq \alpha_j'$, for each j. Again by (U$_1$), there exists a generated $\alpha = \phi_L \cdot \tau \cdot \phi_R$ such that $\alpha \supseteq \alpha_1' \cup_s \ldots \cup_s \alpha_n'$. Now, by the lemma, $\alpha_1' \circ_s \ldots \circ_s \alpha_n' \subseteq \phi_L \cdot \tau^+ \cdot \phi_R$. Finally, $(\phi_L \cdot \tau^+ \cdot \phi_R)^+ \subseteq \alpha^+$. $\qquad \square$

Note on complexity. Our procedure is essentially conjoining the guards of the actions; so an upper bound of the number of obtained actions is $2^{|\mathcal{A}'|}$, where $\mathcal{A}'$ is the least set satisfying the property of step **2**. For our benchmark (see Section 5), the actions can only be composed in a monotonic order, so the bound is only $|\mathcal{A}'|^2$. Nonetheless, in practice, we may choose to combine actions under $\cup_s$ a fixed number of iterations in step **3**, obtaining $\mathcal{A}$ with composition depth k.

4   Verifying Liveness

In this section, we describe how to verify liveness properties, which are reduced to the repeated reachability problem of a suitable FRTS. In particular, we describe how liveness properties of parameterized algorithms are verified using our *LTL(MSO)* model checker [3].

Recall that the falsification of a liveness property can be reduced to checking whether an FRTS has an infinite accepting run. Since the transition relation is length-preserving, so that each computation can visit only a finite set of configurations, this problem can be solved by repeated reachability, i.e., by checking whether there exists a reachable loop containing some configuration from $\mathcal{F}$. This is equivalent to checking whether there is a reachable configuration w in $\mathcal{F}$ such that $(w, w) \in Id \cap \mathcal{R}^+$, which can be checked as follows [27].

(1) Compute the set of *reachable configurations* $Inv = \mathcal{I} \circ \mathcal{R}^*$, as described in Section 3.
(2) Let $Inv_{\mathcal{F}} = \{(w, w') \mid w \in Inv \cap \mathcal{F}, (w, w') \in \mathcal{R}\}$, i.e., the *relation* containing all pairs of consecutive reachable configurations, where the first satisfies $\mathcal{F}$.

(3) Compute the relation $Inv_{\mathcal{F}} \circ \mathcal{R}^*$ as a fixpoint, which in the acceleration-based version constructs the sequence $\mathcal{C}_0, \mathcal{C}_1, \mathcal{C}_2, \cdots$, where $\mathcal{C}_0 = Inv_{\mathcal{F}}$ and $\mathcal{C}_{i+1} = \mathcal{C}_i \cup \mathcal{C}_i \circ \alpha_i^+$ for a suitable action $\alpha_i \subseteq \mathcal{R}^+$, until $\mathcal{C}_i = \mathcal{C}_i \cup \mathcal{C}_i \circ \mathcal{R}$.

(4) If the fixpoint computation in (3) converges, a repeatedly reachable config-uration w exists if and only if $(Inv_{\mathcal{F}} \circ \mathcal{R}^*) \cap Id$ is non-empty.

Note that if $\mathcal{C}_i \cap Id$ is non-empty for some approximation $\mathcal{C}_i$, we can abort the fixpoint computation of (3), and report that $\mathcal{C}_i$ contains a repeatedly reachable configuration.

The reachability phase (1) computes a fixpoint on sets of configurations, while the repeated reachability phase (3) computes a fixpoint on relations of configu-rations; the latter is significantly more difficult to compute.

We next show how this procedure specializes to verifying absence of starvation for parameterized systems. A typical liveness property, absence of starvation, is of form $\Box \forall i \, (\phi(i) \longrightarrow \Diamond \psi(i))$, where i ranges over processes modeled by positions in the configuration. For instance, for Burns' algorithm we check the property $\Box \forall i \, ((\mathrm{pc}[i] = 1 \wedge i = 0) \longrightarrow \Diamond \mathrm{pc}[i] = 7)$. This property is proven assuming *weak process fairness*, i.e., that in an infinite computation, each process is infinitely often either blocked or progressing, which can be expressed as $\forall i \, \Box \Diamond (\alpha(i) \vee \neg En(\alpha(i)))$, where $\alpha(i)$ is a disjunction of all actions process i can take, and $En(\alpha(i))$ is true if and only if process i is not blocked.

To verify absence of starvation using the automata-theoretic approach [31,3], the transition relation, fairness requirements and the negation of the liveness properties are conjoined and compiled into an FRTS, which accepts all fair computations of the system which violate the liveness property, i.e., satisfy $\Diamond \exists i \, (\phi(i) \wedge \Box \neg \psi(i))$. The negation of the liveness property is transformed into an extra boolean component $b_{violate}(i)$ in the local state of each position i, such that if $b_{violate}(i)$ is true, then process i satisfies $\Box \neg \psi(i)$. Process i may non-deterministically set $b_{violate}(i)$ to true. The weak fairness requirement is transformed into an extra boolean component $b_{fair}(i)$ in the local state of each position i and the set $\mathcal{F}$ of accepting configurations in which $b_{fair}(i)$ is 1 for all i and $b_{violate}(i)$ is 1 for some i. All components $b_{fair}(i)$ are set to 0 immediately after some configuration in $\mathcal{F}$ was visited, and each $b_{fair}(i)$ is thereafter set to 1 whenever process i satisfies $\alpha(i) \vee \neg En(\alpha(i))$. The repeated reachability prob-lem becomes to check whether there is an infinite computation which first visits a configuration where $b_{violate}(i)$ is 1 for some i, and thereafter infinitely often visits a configuration in $\mathcal{F}$.

The above procedure can be adapted to this setting by inserting a step $(1')$ between steps (1) and (2), which computes the set $Inv' = [Inv \wedge \exists i (\phi(i) \wedge b_{violate}(i))] \circ \mathcal{R}'^*$, where $\mathcal{R}'$ is $\mathcal{R}$ constrained to follow the semantics of $b_{violate}$, as described above. For the remaining steps, Inv' and $\mathcal{R}'$ take the roles of Inv and $\mathcal{R}$. For step (3), we further constrain $\mathcal{R}'$ to follow the semantics of b_{fair}. We have also added the following optimizations to our model checker.

– *Separating updates of* $b_{fair}(i)$. We separate the updates of $b_{fair}(i)$ into one action that sets it when $\alpha(i)$ is taken, and one action that sets it when

$\neg En(\alpha(i))$; this equivalent modeling makes the acceleration work more efficiently, since actions remain unary.

- *One violating witness.* We constrain the transition relation so that $b_{violate}(i)$ can be true for *at most* one process i; this simplifies the transition relation. Note that this does not forbid other processes from violating the property.

5   Experimental Results

We have implemented the systematic acceleration method described in this paper in our $LTL(MSO)$ model checker [3], and used it to generate the set of reachable states, as described in Section 3, and to check absence of individual starvation under weak fairness for parameterized synchronization algorithms from the literature, as described in Section 4. The models are described in detail in [27], and are available at http://user.it.uu.se/~mayanks/systematic/. For the Bakery algorithm, we verified the property Ba $\overset{\triangle}{=} \Box\forall i\,(q[i] = w \longrightarrow \Diamond q[i] = cs)$. All other checked liveness properties were of form $\Box\forall i\,(\phi(i) \longrightarrow \Diamond\psi(i))$, where $\psi(i)$, defined as $pc[i] = cs$, represents that process i is in the critical section, and where $\phi(i)$ expresses that process i intends to reach the critical section, and that also it is reasonable to suspect that process i is guaranteed to succeed in doing so. For each choice of $\phi(i)$ our implementation either reports a success in verification, or a counterexample. We checked several properties, whose $\phi(i)$ are given below, named after the initial letters of their corresponding protocols; Bakery, Burns, Szymanski, Dijkstra.

$$
\begin{array}{llll}
Bu_1 & : & pc[i] = 1 \wedge i = 0 & \qquad Sz_1 \;:\; pc[i] = 1 \\
Bu_2 & : & pc[i] = 1 \wedge i \neq 0 & \qquad Sz_2 \;:\; pc[i] = 2 \\
Bu_3 & : & pc[i] \neq 1 \wedge i \neq 0 & \qquad Sz_3 \;:\; pc[i] \neq 1 \\
Bu_4 & : & i = 0 \\
Di_1 & : & p[i] \wedge flag[i] \neq 0 \wedge \forall j \neq i \,.\, pc[j] \neq 3 \\
Di_2 & : & p[i] \wedge flag[i] = 0 \wedge \forall j \neq i \,.\, pc[j] \neq 3
\end{array}
$$

We used composition depth k as a parameter, successively using higher values if the verification did not succeed within a certain time bound. The times are given for the best values of k, not including "too low k" time. All protocols worked with some $k \in [2,5]$. Dijkstra's protocol needed 5, and Szymanski's protocol was significantly slower with $k > 2$, due to its actions using many different guards. If the generated actions become separable-complete for parameter k, using a higher value is not significantly slower, as testing for separable-completeness is quick. By Lemma 1, we need not consider k higher than the number of actions generated in step **2** of the generation procedure – that k gives the best approximation of $\mathcal{R}^+$, but can be suboptimal with respect to time. To handle the fact that one action of Dijkstra's protocol is not unary, we extended the composition techniques to a class of non-unary actions in the most straight-forward way. The experiments were run on a PC with a 2.4 GHz processor and 1 GB of RAM.

Table 1. Liveness (to the left) and safety (to the right) results

Property	This work	[27,3]	[5]
Ba	13	23	36
Bu_1	98		450
Bu_2	56 (f)		
Bu_3	60 (f)		
Bu_4	144		
Sz_1	540 (f)		
Sz_2	1369		435
Sz_3	1635		
Di_1	244		3311
Di_2	1031 (f)		

Protocol	This work	[27,3]
Bakery	4	5
Burns	15	39
Szymanski	19	34
Dijkstra	25	38

Results and Comparison with Related Work. Our verification results are presented in Table 1. The table contains time measured in seconds for the analysis, but does not include the translation from LTL(MSO) formulas into FRTSs. False properties, for which a counterexample was found, are marked "(f)". In the table, we compare our times with the works [27,3,5], as they use similar techniques, and were in fact timed on the same system. We also present related work, in alphabetical order with respect to authors. Note that works [27,3,28] could only have succeeded to verify Burns' and Dijkstra's protocols if the right sequential compositions were included; but they are difficult to find manually.

[2] Abdulla et al. use overapproximation for safety properties, obtaining times an order of magnitude better than ours (0.004–3.9 seconds), but the technique can not be extended to liveness properties.

[5] These techniques compute states which are guaranteed to satisfy $\psi(i)$ using backwards reachability, thus avoiding the repeated reachability problem. However, they are not able to produce counterexamples, and are sometimes slower (due to requiring many accelerations).

[15] Bouajjani et al. verify liveness of Bakery, as well as safety of all listed protocols, using counter-example guided abstractions, in 0.06–0.73 seconds.

[21,22,20] Fang et al. verify the Bakery protocol using automatically generated ranking functions, but do not report running times.

[27,3] The works of Nilsson et al. [27,3] report times for essentially the same technique, so we gave the best time for each protocol. The verification setting is as ours, but without the systematic addition of sequential compositions.

[28] Pnueli and Shahar, use user defined accelerations to verify safety properties of Szymanski's protocol in 0.2 seconds, as well as some protocols not in our benchmark.

[29] Pnueli et al. verify liveness of the Bakery and Szymanski protocols using manually supplied counter abstractions, in 1 and 96 seconds respectively. Their modeling of Szymanski's protocol is slightly different from ours, so we can not say which of the true properties were checked.

Using the techniques of this paper, we can compute an exact representation of the reachable loops for all the above protocols. It has, to our knowledge, never been done for Burns' and Dijkstra's protocols before.

6   Conclusions and Future Work

We have presented a systematic method for using acceleration to speed up fix-point computations in regular model checking. The method is defined for unary transition relations, and is independent of how the transition relation is represented. We show how to accelerate a set of actions which is maximal in a certain sense, in order to make the verification as powerful as possible. Using this approach, we have succeeded in verifying safety and liveness of parameterized synchronization protocols, whose verification has not been reported before.

Our work shows that acceleration-based symbolic state-space exploration can be used efficiently also in regular model checking, thus extending this approach from other classes of systems (e.g., [1,12,14,32,10,23]). Future work includes extending the approach to non-unary transition relations, in order to handle, e.g., systems with synchronous communication between adjacent processes.

References

1. Abdulla, P., Collomb-Annichini, A., Bouajjani, A., Jonsson, B.: Using forward reachability analysis for verification of lossy channel systems. Formal Methods in System Design 25(1), 39–65 (2004)
2. Abdulla, P., Delzanno, G., Henda, N.B., Rezine, A.: Regular model checking without transducers. In: Proc. TACAS '07 (to appear, 2007)
3. Abdulla, P., Jonsson, B., Nilsson, M., d'Orso, J., Saksena, M.: Regular model checking for MSO + LTL. In: Alur, R., Peled, D.A. (eds.) CAV 2004. LNCS, vol. 3114, pp. 348–360. Springer, Heidelberg (2004)
4. Abdulla, P., Jonsson, B., Nilsson, M., Saksena, M.: A survey of regular model checking. In: Gardner, P., Yoshida, N. (eds.) CONCUR 2004. LNCS, vol. 3170, pp. 35–48. Springer, Heidelberg (2004)
5. Abdulla, P., Jonsson, B., Saksena, M., Rezine, A.: Proving liveness by backwards reachability. In: Baier, C., Hermanns, H. (eds.) CONCUR 2006. LNCS, vol. 4137, pp. 95–109. Springer, Heidelberg (2006)
6. Abdulla, P.A., Bouajjani, A., Jonsson, B., Nilsson, M.: Handling global conditions in parameterized system verification. In: Halbwachs, N., Peled, D.A. (eds.) CAV 1999. LNCS, vol. 1633, pp. 134–145. Springer, Heidelberg (1999)
7. Abdulla, P.A., Jonsson, B., Nilsson, M., d'Orso, J.: Regular model checking made simple and efficient. In: Brim, L., Jančar, P., Křetínský, M., Kucera, A. (eds.) CONCUR 2002. LNCS, vol. 2421, pp. 116–130. Springer, Heidelberg (2002)
8. Abdulla, P.A., Jonsson, B., Nilsson, M., d'Orso, J.: Algorithmic improvements in regular model checking. In: Hunt Jr., W.A., Somenzi, F. (eds.) CAV 2003. LNCS, vol. 2725, pp. 236–248. Springer, Heidelberg (2003)
9. Annichini, A., Asarin, E., Bouajjani, A.: Symbolic techniques for parametric reasoning about counter and clock systems. In: Emerson, E.A., Sistla, A.P. (eds.) CAV 2000. LNCS, vol. 1855, pp. 419–434. Springer, Heidelberg (2000)

10. Bardin, S., Finkel, A., Leroux, J., Schnoebelen, P.: Flat acceleration in symbolic model checking. In: Peled, D.A., Tsay, Y.-K. (eds.) ATVA 2005. LNCS, vol. 3707, pp. 474–488. Springer, Heidelberg (2005)

11. Boigelot, B., Godefroid, P.: Symbolic verification of communication protocols with infinite state spaces using QDDs. In: Alur, R., Henzinger, T.A. (eds.) CAV 1996. LNCS, vol. 1102, pp. 1–12. Springer, Heidelberg (1996)

12. Boigelot, B., Godefroid, P., Willems, B., Wolper, P.: The power of QDDs. In: Van Hentenryck, P. (ed.) SAS 1997. LNCS, vol. 1302, Springer, Heidelberg (1997)

13. Boigelot, B., Wolper, P.: Symbolic verification with periodic sets. In: Dill, D.L. (ed.) CAV 1994. LNCS, vol. 818, pp. 55–67. Springer, Heidelberg (1994)

14. Bouajjani, A., Habermehl, P.: Symbolic reachability analysis of FIFO-channel systems with nonregular sets of configurations. Theoretical Computer Science 221(1-2), 211–250 (1999)

15. Bouajjani, A., Habermehl, P., Vojnar, T.: Abstract regular model checking. In: Alur, R., Peled, D.A. (eds.) CAV 2004. LNCS, vol. 3114, pp. 372–386. Springer, Heidelberg (2004)

16. Bouajjani, A., Jonsson, B., Nilsson, M., Touili, T.: Regular model checking. In: Emerson, E.A., Sistla, A.P. (eds.) CAV 2000. LNCS, vol. 1855, pp. 403–418. Springer, Heidelberg (2000)

17. Burch, J., Clarke, E., McMillan, K., Dill, D.: Symbolic model checking: 10^{20} states and beyond. Information and Computation 98, 142–170 (1992)

18. Comon, H., Jurski, Y.: Multiple counters automata, safety analysis and presburger arithmetic. In: Vardi, M.Y. (ed.) CAV 1998. LNCS, vol. 1427, Springer, Heidelberg (1998)

19. Dams, D., Lakhnech, Y., Steffen, M.: Iterating transducers. J. Log. Algebr. Program. 52-53, 109–127 (2002)

20. Fang, Y., McMillan, K.L., Pnueli, A., Zuck, L.D.: Liveness by invisible invariants. In: FORTE, pp. 356–371 (2006)

21. Fang, Y., Piterman, N., Pnueli, A., Zuck, L.: Liveness with incomprehensible ranking. In: Jensen, K., Podelski, A. (eds.) TACAS 2004. LNCS, vol. 2988, pp. 482–496. Springer, Heidelberg (2004)

22. Fang, Y., Piterman, N., Pnueli, A., Zuck, L.: Liveness with invisible ranking. In: Steffen, B., Levi, G. (eds.) VMCAI 2004. LNCS, vol. 2937, pp. 223–238. Springer, Heidelberg (2004)

23. Finkel, S., Leroux, J.: How to compose presburger-accelerations: Applications to broadcast protocols. In: Agrawal, M., Seth, A.K. (eds.) FST TCS 2002: Foundations of Software Technology and Theoretical Computer Science. LNCS, vol. 2556, pp. 145–156. Springer, Heidelberg (2002)

24. Habermehl, P., Vojnar, T.: Regular model checking using inference of regular languages. Electr. Notes Theor. Comput. Sci. 138(3), 21–36 (2005)

25. Jonsson, B., Nilsson, M.: Transitive closures of regular relations for verifying infinite-state systems. In: Schwartzbach, M.I., Graf, S. (eds.) ETAPS 2000 and TACAS 2000. LNCS, vol. 1785, Springer, Heidelberg (2000)

26. Kesten, Y., Maler, O., Marcus, M., Pnueli, A., Shahar, E.: Symbolic model checking with rich assertional languages. Theoretical Computer Science 256, 93–112 (2001)

27. Nilsson, M.: Regular Model Checking. PhD thesis, Uppsala University (2005)

28. Pnueli, A., Shahar, E.: Liveness and acceleration in parameterized verification. In: Emerson, E.A., Sistla, A.P. (eds.) CAV 2000. LNCS, vol. 1855, pp. 328–343. Springer, Heidelberg (2000)

29. Pnueli, A., Xu, J., Zuck, L.: Liveness with (0,1,infinity)-counter abstraction. In: Brinksma, E., Larsen, K.G. (eds.) CAV 2002. LNCS, vol. 2404, Springer, Heidelberg (2002)
30. Szymanski, B.K.: Mutual exclusion revisited. In: Proc. Fifth Jerusalem Conference on Information Technology, pp. 110–117. IEEE Computer Society Press, Los Alamitos (1990)
31. Vardi, M.Y., Wolper, P.: An automata-theoretic approach to automatic program verification. In: Proc. LICS '86, 1st LICS, pp. 332–344 (June 1986)
32. Wolper, P., Boigelot, B.: Verifying systems with infinite but regular state spaces. In: Vardi, M.Y. (ed.) CAV 1998. LNCS, vol. 1427, pp. 88–97. Springer, Heidelberg (1998)

Parameterized Verification of Infinite-State Processes with Global Conditions

Parosh Aziz Abdulla[1], Giorgio Delzanno[2], and Ahmed Rezine[1]

[1] Uppsala University, Sweden
parosh@it.uu.se, Rezine.Ahmed@it.uu.se
[2] Università di Genova, Italy
giorgio@disi.unige.it

Abstract. We present a simple and effective approximated backward reachability algorithm for parameterized systems with existentially and universally quantified global conditions. The individual processes operate on unbounded local variables ranging over the natural numbers. In addition, processes may communicate via broadcast, rendez-vous and shared variables. We apply the algorithm to verify mutual exclusion for complex protocols such as Lamport's bakery algorithm both with and without atomicity conditions, a distributed version of the bakery algorithm, and Ricart-Agrawala's distributed mutual exclusion algorithm.

1 Introduction

We consider the analysis of safety properties for *parameterized systems*. A parameterized system consists of an arbitrary number of processes. The task is to verify correctness regardless of the number of processes. This amounts to the verification of an infinite family; namely one for each size of the system. Most existing approaches to automatic verification of parameterized systems make the restriction that each process is finite-state. However, there are many applications where the behaviour relies on unbounded data structures such as counters, priorities, local clocks, time-stamps, and process identifiers.

In this paper, we consider parameterized systems where the individual processes operate on Boolean variables, and on numerical variables which range over the natural numbers. The transitions are conditioned by the local state of the process, values of the local variables; and by *global conditions* which check the local states and variables of the other processes. These conditions are stated as propositional constraints on the Boolean variables, and as *gap-order constraints* on the numerical variables. Gap-order constraints [20] are a logical formalism in which we can express simple relations on variables such as lower and upper bounds on the values of individual variables; and equality, and gaps (minimal differences) between values of pairs of variables. A global condition is either *universally* or *existentially* quantified. An example of a universal condition is "variable x of a given process i has a value which is greater than the value of variable y in all other processes inside the system". Process i is then allowed to

W. Damm and H. Hermanns (Eds.): CAV 2007, LNCS 4590, pp. 145–157, 2007.

perform the transition only if this condition is satisfied. In an existential condition we require that *some* (rather than *all*) processes satisfy the condition. In addition to these classes of transitions, processes may communicate through broadcast, rendez-vous, and shared variables.

There are at least two advantages with using gap-order constraints as a language for expressing the enabling conditions of transitions. First, they allow to handle a large class of protocols where the behaviour depends on the relative ordering of values among variables, rather than the actual values of these variables. The second reason is that they define a natural ordering on the set of system configurations. In fact, it can be shown, using standard techniques (such as the ones in [23]), that checking safety properties (expressed as regular languages) can be translated into the reachability of sets of configurations which are upward closed with respect to this ordering.

To check safety properties, we perform backward reachability analysis using gap-order constraints as a symbolic representation of upward closed sets of configurations. In the analysis, we consider a transition relation which is an over-approximation of the one induced by the parameterized system. To do that, we modify the semantics of universal quantifiers by eliminating the processes which violate the given condition. For instance in the above example, process i is always allowed to take the transition. However, when performing the transition, we eliminate each process j where the value of y is smaller or equal to the value of x in i. The approximate transition system obtained in this manner is *monotonic* with respect to the above mentioned ordering, in the sense that larger configurations can simulate smaller ones. In fact, it turns out that universal quantification is the only operation which does not preserve monotonicity and hence it is the only source of approximation in the model. The fact that the approximate transition relation is monotonic, means that upward closedness is maintained under the operation of computing predecessors. A significant aspect of the reachability procedure is that the number of copies of variables (both Boolean and numerical) which appear in constraints whose denotations are upward closed sets is not bounded a priori. The reason is that there is an arbitrary number of processes each with its own local copy of the variables. The whole verification process is fully automatic since both the approximation and the reachability analysis are carried out without user intervention. Observe that if the approximate transition system satisfies a safety property then we can conclude that the original system satisfies the property, too.

Termination of the approximated backward reachability analysis is not guaranteed in general. However, the procedure terminates on all the examples we report in this paper. Furthermore, termination is guaranteed in some restricted cases such as for systems with existential or universal global conditions but with at most one local integer variable.

In order to test our method we have selected a collection of challenging protocols in which integer variables are used either as identifiers, priorities, local clocks, or time-stamps. Almost all of the examples are outside the class for which termination is guaranteed. In particular, we automatically verify safety properties for parameterized versions of the following algorithms:

- Lamport's bakery algorithm [19] with atomicity conditions;
- A version of Lamport's bakery algorithm with non-atomic computation of tickets;
- A distributed version of Lamport's bakery in which tickets and entry conditions are computed and tested non-atomically by means of a handshake protocol run by each process;
- The Ticket mutual exclusion algorithm with a central monitor for distributing tickets [6];
- The Ricart-Agrawala distributed mutual exclusion algorithm based on the use of logical clocks and time-stamps [21].

We also consider a bogus version of the Lamport's bakery without atomicity conditions in the computation of tickets. In this version, the *choosing* flag is simply ignored in the entry section. For this example, our procedure returns symbolic traces (from initial to bad states) that explain the subtle race conditions that may arise when the flag is not tested.

Each one of these examples present challenging problems for parameterized verification methods in the following sense:

- Their underlying logic is already hard for manual or finite-state verification.
- They are all instances of multidimensional infinite-state systems in which processes have unbounded local variables and (apart from Ticket) an order over identifiers is used to break the tie in the entry section. For instance, they cannot be modelled without the use of abstractions in the framework of Regular Model Checking [17,5,8,4].
- In all examples, global conditions are needed to model the communication mechanisms used in the protocols (e.g. broadcasts, update, and entry conditions that depend on the local integer variables of other processes).

Related Work. The multi-dimensional parameterized models studied in the present paper cannot be analyzed without use of additional abstractions by methods designed for networks of finite-state processes, e.g., Regular Model Checking [17,5,8] and counter abstraction methods [12,16,13,14]. The approximation scheme we apply in our backward reachability procedure works well for a very large class of one-dimensional parameterized systems. In fact, the verification procedure used in [4] is a special case of the current one, where the processes are restricted to be finite-state systems.

Parameterized versions of Lamport's bakery algorithm have been tested using a semi-automated verification method based on *invisible invariants* in [7], with the help of *environmental abstractions* for a formulation with atomicity conditions in [11], and using heuristics to discover *indexed predicates* in [18]. A parameterized formulation of the Ricart-Agrawala algorithm has been verified semi-automatically in [22], where the STeP prover is used to discharge some of the verification conditions needed in the proof. We are not aware of other attempts of fully automatic verification of parameterized versions of the Ricart-Agrawala algorithm or of the distributed version (with no atomicity assumptions) of Lamport's bakery algorithm.

In contrast to the above mentioned methods, our verification procedure is fully automated and it is based on a generic approximation scheme. Furthermore, our method is applicable to versions of Lamport's bakery both with and without atomicity conditions and may return symbolic traces useful for debugging.

A parameterized formulation of an abstraction of the Ticket algorithm has been analyzed in [9]. The verification procedure in [9] does not handle parameterized universally quantified global conditions. Furthermore, in the abstraction of the Ticket algorithm studied in [9] the central monitor may forget tickets (the update of *turn* is defined by a jump to any larger value). Thus, the model does not keep the FIFO order of requests. With the help of universally quantified guards and of our approximation, we verify a more precise model in which the FIFO order of requests is always preserved.

In contrast to symbolic methods for finite, a priori fixed collections of processes with local integer variables, e.g., those in [10,15], our gap-order constraints are defined over an *infinite* collections of variables. The number of copies of variables needed during the backward search cannot be bounded a priori. This feature allows us to reason about systems with global conditions over any number of processes. Furthermore, the present method covers that of [2] which also uses gap-order constraints to reason about systems with unbounded numbers of processes. However, [2] cannot deal with global conditions which is the main feature of the examples considered here.

Outline. In the next two Sections we give some preliminaries and define a basic model for parameterized systems. Section 4 and 5 describe the induced transition system and the coverability (safety) problem. In Section 6 we define the approximated transition system. Section 7 defines the gap-order constraints and presents the backward reachability algorithm, while Section 8 describes the operations on constraints used in the algorithm. Section 9 explains how we extend the basic model to cover features such as shared variables, broadcast and binary communication. In Section 10 we report the results of running our prototypes on a number of examples. Finally, in Section 11, we give conclusions and directions for future work. In the appendix, we give some proofs and detailed descriptions of the case studies.

2   Preliminaries

In this section, we give some preliminary notations and definitions. We use $\mathcal{B}$ to denote the set $\{true, false\}$ of Boolean values; and use $\mathcal{N}$ to denote the set of natural numbers. For a natural number n, let $\overline{n}$ denote the set $\{1, \ldots, n\}$.

For a finite set A, we write a multiset over A as a list $[a_1, a_2, \ldots, a_n]$, where $a_i \in A$ for each $i : 1 \leq i \leq n$. We use $a \in A$ to denote that $a = a_i$ for some $i : 1 \leq i \leq n$. For multisets $M_1 = [a_1, \ldots, a_m]$ and $M_2 = [b_1, \ldots, b_n]$, we use $M_1 \bullet M_2$ to denote the union (sum) of M_1 and M_2 (i.e., $M_1 \bullet M_2 = [a_1, \ldots, a_m, b_1, \ldots, b_n]$).

We will work with sets of variables. Such a set A is often partitioned into two subsets: *Boolean* variables $A_\mathcal{B}$ which range over $\mathcal{B}$, and *numerical* variables $A_\mathcal{N}$ which range over $\mathcal{N}$. We denote by $\mathbb{B}(A_\mathcal{B})$ the set of Boolean formulas over $A_\mathcal{B}$. We will also use a simple set of formulas, called *gap formulas*, to constrain the numerical variables. More precisely, we let $\mathbb{G}(A_\mathcal{N})$ be the set of formulas which are either of the form $x = y$ or of the form $x \sim_k y$ where $\sim \in \{<, \leq\}$, $x, y \in A_\mathcal{N} \cup \mathcal{N}$, and $k \in \mathcal{N}$. Here $x <_k y$ stands for $x + k < y$. We use $\mathbb{F}(A)$ to denote the set of formulas which has members of $\mathbb{B}(A)$ and of $\mathbb{G}(\mathcal{N})$ as atomic formulas, and which is closed under the Boolean connectives $\wedge, \vee$. For instance, if $A_\mathcal{B} = \{a, b\}$ and $A_\mathcal{N} = \{x, y\}$ then $\theta = (a \supset b) \wedge (x + 3 < y)$ is in $\mathbb{F}(A)$. Sometimes, we write a formula as $\theta(y_1, \ldots, y_k)$ where $y_1, \ldots, y_k$ are the variables which may occur in θ; so we can write the above formula as $\theta(x, y, a, b)$.

Sometimes, we perform substitutions on logical formulas. A *substitution* is a set $\{x_1 \leftarrow e_1, \ldots, x_n \leftarrow e_n\}$ of pairs, where x_i is a variable and e_i is either a constant or a variable of the same type as x_i, for each $i : 1 \leq i \leq n$. Here, we assume that all the variables are distinct, i.e., $x_i \neq x_j$ if $i \neq j$. For a formula θ and a substitution S, we use $\theta[S]$ to denote the formula we get from θ by simultaneously replacing all occurrences of the variables $x_1, \ldots, x_n$ by $e_1, e_2, \ldots, e_n$ respectively. Sometimes, we may write $\theta[S_1][S_2] \cdots [S_m]$ instead of $\theta[S_1 \cup S_2 \cup \cdots \cup S_m]$. As an example, if $\theta = (x_1 < x_2) \wedge (x_3 < x_4)$ then $\theta[x_1 \leftarrow 3, x_4 \leftarrow 2][x_2 \leftarrow y] = (3 < y) \wedge (x_3 < 2)$.

3 Parameterized Systems

In this section, we introduce a basic model for parameterized systems. The basic model will be enriched by additional features in Section 9.

A parameterized system consists of an arbitrary (but finite) number of identical processes. Each process is modelled as an extended finite-state automaton operating on local variables which range over the Booleans and the natural numbers. The transitions of the automaton are conditioned by the values of the local variables and by *global* conditions in which the process checks, for instance, the local states and variables of all the other processes inside the system. A transition may change the value of any local variable inside the process (possibly deriving the new values from those of the other processes). A parameterized system induces an infinite family of (potentially infinite-state) systems, namely one for each size n. The aim is to verify correctness of the systems for the whole family (regardless of the number n of processes inside the system).

Formally, a *parameterized system* $\mathcal{P}$ is a triple (Q, X, T), where Q is a finite set of *local states*, X is a finite set of *local variables* partitioned into $X_\mathcal{B}$ (which range over $\mathcal{B}$) and $X_\mathcal{N}$ (which range over $\mathcal{N}$), and T is a finite set of *transition rules*. A transition rule t is of the form

$$t : [q \to q' \, \triangleright \, \theta] \tag{1}$$

where $q, q' \in Q$ and θ is either a *local* or a *global condition*. Intuitively, the process which makes the transition changes its local state from q to q'. In the meantime, the values of the local variables of the process are updated according to θ. Below, we describe how we define local and global conditions.

To simplify the definitions, we sometimes regard members of the set Q as Boolean variables. Intuitively, the value of the Boolean variable $q \in Q$ is *true* for a particular process iff the process is in local state q. We define the set $Y = X \cup Q$.

To define local conditions, we introduce the set X^{next} which contains the *next-value* versions of the variables in X. A variable $x^{next} \in X^{next}$ represents the next value of $x \in X$. A *local condition* is a formula in $\mathbb{F}(X \cup X^{next})$. The formula specifies how local variables of the current process are updated with respect to their current values.

Global conditions check the values of local variables of the current process, together with the local states and the values of local variables of the other processes. We need to distinguish between a local variable, say x, of the process which is about to perform a transition, and the same local variable x of the other processes inside the system. We do that by introducing, for each $x \in Y$, two new variables $\mathtt{self}\cdot x$ and $\mathtt{other}\cdot x$. We define the sets $\mathtt{self}\cdot Y = \{\mathtt{self}\cdot x | x \in Y\}$ and $\mathtt{other}\cdot Y = \{\mathtt{other}\cdot x | x \in Y\}$. The sets $\mathtt{self}\cdot X$, $\mathtt{other}\cdot X^{next}$, etc, are defined in the obvious manner. A *global condition* θ is of one of the following two forms:

$$\forall\, \mathtt{other} \neq \mathtt{self} \cdot \theta_1 \qquad \exists\, \mathtt{other} \neq \mathtt{self} \cdot \theta_1 \tag{2}$$

where $\theta_1 \in \mathbb{F}(\mathtt{self}\cdot X \cup \mathtt{other}\cdot Y \cup \mathtt{self}\cdot X^{next})$. In other words, the formula checks the local variables of the process which is about to make the transition (through $\mathtt{self} \cdot X$), and the local states and variables of the other processes (through $\mathtt{other}\cdot Y$). It also specifies how the local variables of the process in transition are updated (through $\mathtt{self}\cdot X^{next}$). A global condition is said to be *universal* or *existential* depending on the type of the quantifier appearing in it. As an example, the following formula

$$\forall\, \mathtt{other} \neq \mathtt{self} \cdot (\mathtt{self}\cdot a) \wedge (\mathtt{self}\cdot x^{next} > \mathtt{other}\cdot x) \wedge \mathtt{other}\cdot q_1$$

states that the transition may be performed only if variable a of the current process has the value *true*, and all the other processes are in local state q_1. When the transition is performed, variable x of the current process is assigned a value which is greater than the value of x in all the other processes.

4   Transition System

We describe the transition system induced by a parameterized system.

A *transition system* $\mathcal{T}$ is a pair $(D, \Longrightarrow)$, where D is an (infinite) set of *configurations* and $\Longrightarrow$ is a binary relation on D. We use $\overset{*}{\Longrightarrow}$ to denote the reflexive transitive closure of $\Longrightarrow$. Let $\preceq$ be an ordering on D. We say that $\mathcal{T}$ is *monotonic* with respect to $\preceq$ if the following property is satisfied: for all $c_1, c_2, c_3 \in D$ with $c_1 \Longrightarrow c_2$ and $c_1 \preceq c_3$, there is a $c_4 \in D$ such that $c_3 \Longrightarrow c_4$ and $c_2 \preceq c_4$. We will consider several transition systems in this paper.

First, a parameterized system $\mathcal{P} = (Q, X, T)$ induces a transition system $\mathcal{T}(\mathcal{P}) = (C, \longrightarrow)$ as follows. A configuration is defined by the local states and the values of the local variables in the processes. Formally, a *local variable state* v is a mapping from X to $\mathcal{B} \cup \mathcal{N}$ which respects variables' types. A *process state* u is a pair (q, v) where $q \in Q$ and v is a local variable state. As mentioned in Section 3, we may regard members of Q as Boolean variables. Thus, we can view a process state (q, v) as a mapping $u : Y \mapsto \mathcal{B} \cup \mathcal{N}$, where $u(x) = v(x)$ for each $x \in X$, $u(q) = true$, and $u(q') = false$ for each $q' \in Q - \{q\}$. A *configuration* is a multiset $[u_1, u_2, \ldots, u_n]$ of process states. Intuitively, the above configuration corresponds to an instance of the system with n processes. Notice that if c_1 and c_2 are configurations then so is their union $c_1 \bullet c_2$.

We define the transition relation $\longrightarrow$ on the set of configurations as follows. We start by describing the semantics of local conditions. Recall that a local condition corresponds to one process changing state without checking states of the other processes. Therefore, the semantics is defined in terms of two local variable states v, v' corresponding to the current resp. next values of the local variables of the process; and a formula $\theta \in \mathbb{F}(X \cup X^{next})$ (representing the local condition). We write $(v, v') \models \theta$ to denote the validity of the formula $\theta [\rho] [\rho']$ where the substitutions are defined by $\rho := \{x \leftarrow v(x)| \ x \in X\}$ and $\rho' := \{x^{next} \leftarrow v'(x)| \ x \in X\}$. In other words, we check the formula we get by replacing the current- resp. next-value variables in θ by their values as defined by v resp. v'. The formula is evaluated using the standard interpretations of the Boolean connectives, and the arithmetical relations $<, \leq, =$. For process states $u = (q, v)$ and $u' = (q', v')$, we use $(u, u') \models \theta$ to denote that $(v, v') \models \theta$.

Next, we describe the semantics of global conditions. The definition is given in terms of two local variable states v, v', a process state u_1, and a formula $\theta \in \mathbb{F} (\mathbf{self} \cdot X \cup \mathbf{other} \cdot Y \cup \mathbf{self} \cdot X^{next})$ (representing a global condition). The roles of v and v' are the same as for local conditions. We recall that a global condition also checks states of all (or some) of the other processes. Here, u_1 represents the local state and variables of one such a process. We write $(v, v', u_1) \models \theta$ to denote the validity of the formula $\theta [\rho] [\rho'] [\rho_1]$ where the substitutions are defined by $\rho := \{\mathbf{self} \cdot x \leftarrow v(x)| \ x \in X\}$, $\rho' := \{\mathbf{self} \cdot x^{next} \leftarrow v'(x)| \ x \in X\}$, and $\rho_1 := \{\mathbf{other} \cdot x \leftarrow u_1(x)| \ x \in Y\}$. The relation $(u, u', u_1) \models \theta$ is interpreted in a similar manner to the case of local conditions.

Now, we are ready to define the transition relation $\longrightarrow$. Let t be a transition rule of the form of (1). Consider two configurations $c = c_1 \bullet [u] \bullet c_2$ and $c' = c_1 \bullet [u'] \bullet c_2$ where $u = (q, v)$ and $u' = (q', v')$. We denote by $c \xrightarrow{t} c'$ that one of the following conditions is satisfied:

1. θ is a local condition and $(u, u') \models \theta$.
2. θ is a universal global condition of the form of (2), and $(u, u', u_1) \models \theta_1$ for each $u_1 \in c_1 \bullet c_2$.
3. θ is an existential global condition of the form of (2), and $(u, u', u_1) \models \theta_1$ for some $u_1 \in c_1 \bullet c_2$.

We use $c \longrightarrow c'$ to denote that $c \xrightarrow{t} c'$ for some $t \in T$.

5   Safety Properties

In this section, we introduce an ordering on configurations, and use it to define the safety problem. Given a parameterized system $\mathcal{P} = (Q, X, T)$, we assume that, prior to starting the execution of the system, each process is in an (identical) *initial* process state $u_{init} = (q_{init}, v_{init})$. In the induced transition system $\mathcal{T}(\mathcal{P}) = (C, \longrightarrow)$, we use *Init* to denote the set of *initial* configurations, i.e., configurations of the form $[u_{init}, \ldots, u_{init}]$. Notice that this set is infinite.

We define an ordering on configurations as follows. Consider two configurations, $c = [u_1 \cdot \ldots \cdot u_m]$ and $c' = [u'_1 \cdot \ldots \cdot u'_n]$, where $u_i = (q_i, v_i)$ for each $i : 1 \le i \le m$, and $u'_i = (q'_i, v'_i)$ for each $i : 1 \le i \le n$. We write $c \preceq c'$ to denote that there is an injection $h : \overline{m} \to \overline{n}$ such that the following four conditions are satisfied for each $i, j : 1 \le i, j \le m$:

1. $q_i = q'_{h(i)}$.
2. $v_i(x) = true$ iff $v'_{h(i)}(x) = true$ for each $x \in X_{\mathcal{B}}$.
3. $v_i(x) = v_j(y)$ iff $v'_{h(i)}(x) = v'_{h(j)}(y)$, for each $x, y \in X_{\mathcal{N}}$.
4. $v_i(x) <_k v_j(y)$ implies that there is a $l \ge k$ with $v'_{h(i)}(x) <_l v'_{h(j)}(y)$, for each $x, y \in X_{\mathcal{N}}$.

In other words, for each process in c there is a corresponding process in c'. The local states and the values of the Boolean variables coincide in the corresponding processes (Conditions 1 and 2). Regarding the numerical variables, the ordering preserves equality of variables (Condition 3), while gaps between variables in c' are at least as large as the gaps between the corresponding variables in c (Condition 4).

A set of configurations $D \subseteq C$ is *upward closed* (with respect to the ordering $\preceq$) if $c \in D$ and $c \preceq c'$ implies $c' \in D$. For sets of configurations $D, D' \subseteq C$ we use $D \longrightarrow D'$ to denote that there are $c \in D$ and $c' \in D'$ with $c \longrightarrow c'$.

The *coverability problem* for parameterized systems is defined as follows:

PAR-COV
Instance
  - A parameterized system $\mathcal{P} = (Q, X, T)$.
  - An upward closed set C_F of configurations.

Question *Init* $\overset{*}{\longrightarrow} C_F$?

It can be shown, using standard techniques (see e.g. [23]), that checking safety properties (expressed as regular languages) can be translated into instances of the coverability problem. Therefore, checking safety properties amounts to solving PAR-COV (i.e., to the reachability of upward closed sets).

6   Approximation

In this section, we introduce an over-approximation of the transition relation of a parameterized system. The aim of the over-approximations is to derive a new transition system which is *monotonic* with respect to the ordering $\preceq$ defined on configurations in Section 5. The only transitions which do not preserve monotonicity are those involving universal global conditions. Therefore, the approximate transition system modifies the behavior of universal quantifiers in such a manner that monotonicity is maintained. Roughly speaking, in the new semantics, we remove all processes in the configuration which violate the condition of the universal quantifier. Below we describe how this is done.

In Section 4, we mentioned that each parameterized system $\mathcal{P} = (Q, X, T)$ induces a transition system $\mathcal{T}(\mathcal{P}) = (C, \longrightarrow)$. A parameterized system $\mathcal{P}$ also induces an *approximate* transition system $\mathcal{A}(\mathcal{P}) = (C, \rightsquigarrow)$; the set C of configurations is identical to the one in $\mathcal{T}(\mathcal{P})$. We define $\rightsquigarrow = (\longrightarrow \cup \rightsquigarrow_1)$, where $\longrightarrow$ is defined in Section 4, and $\rightsquigarrow_1$ (which reflects the approximation of universal quantifiers) is defined as follows. For a configuration c, a formula $\theta \in \mathbb{F}(\texttt{self} \cdot X \cup \texttt{other} \cdot Y \cup \texttt{self} \cdot X^{next})$, and process states u, u', we use $c \ominus (\theta, u, u')$ to denote the configuration derived from c by deleting all process states u_1 such that $(u, u', u_1) \not\models \theta$. To explain this operation intuitively, we recall that a universal global condition requires that the current and next states of the current process (described by u resp. u') together with the state of each other process (described by u_1) should satisfy the formula θ. The operation then removes from c each process whose state u_1 does not comply with this condition.

Consider two configurations $c = c_1 \bullet u \bullet c_2$ and $c' = c_1' \bullet u' \bullet c_2'$, where $u = (q, v)$ and $u' = (q', v')$. Let t be a transition rule of the form of (1), such that θ is a universal global condition of the form of (2). We write $c \overset{t}{\rightsquigarrow}_1 c'$ to denote that $c_1' = c_1 \ominus (\theta_1, u, u')$ and $c_2' = c_2 \ominus (\theta_1, u, u')$. We use $c \rightsquigarrow c'$ to denote that $c \overset{t}{\rightsquigarrow} c'$ for some $t \in T$; and use $\overset{*}{\rightsquigarrow}$ to denote the reflexive transitive closure of $\rightsquigarrow$.

Lemma 1. *The approximate transition system $(C, \rightsquigarrow)$ is monotonic with respect to $\preceq$.*

We define the coverability problem for the approximate system as follows.

APRX-PAR-COV

Instance

- A parameterized system $\mathcal{P} = (Q, X, T)$.
- An upward closed set C_F of configurations.

Question *Init* $\overset{*}{\rightsquigarrow} C_F$?

Since $\longrightarrow \subseteq \rightsquigarrow$, a negative answer to APRX-PAR-COV implies a negative answer to PAR-COV.

7   Backward Reachability Analysis

In this section, we present a scheme based on backward reachability analysis for solving APRX-PAR-COV. For the rest of this section, we fix an approximate transition system $\mathcal{A}(\mathcal{P}) = (C, \rightsquigarrow)$.

Constraints. The scheme operates on *constraints* which we use as a symbolic representation for sets of configurations. For each natural number $i \in \mathcal{N}$ we make a copy Y^i such that $x^i \in Y^i$ if $x \in Y$. A *constraint* ϕ is a pair (m, ψ), where $m \in \mathcal{N}$ is a natural number, and $\psi \in \mathbb{F}(Y^1 \cup Y^2 \cup \cdots \cup Y^m)$. Intuitively, a configuration satisfying ϕ should contain at least m processes (indexed by $1, \ldots, m$). The constraint ϕ uses the elements of the set Y^i to refer to the local states and variables of process i. The values of these states and variables are constrained by the formula ψ. Formally, consider a configuration $c = [u_1, u_2, \ldots, u_n]$ and a constraint $\phi = (m, \psi)$. Let $h : \overline{m} \mapsto \overline{n}$ be an injection. We write $c \models_h \phi$ to denote the validity of the formula $\psi[\rho]$ where $\rho := \{ x^i \leftarrow u_{h(i)}(x) \mid x \in Y \text{ and } 1 \leq i \leq m \}$. In other words, there should be at least m processes inside c whose local states and variables have values which satisfy ψ. We write $c \models \phi$ to denote that $c \models_h \phi$ for some h; and define $\llbracket \phi \rrbracket = \{ c \mid \phi \models c \}$. For a (finite) set of constraints Φ, we define $\llbracket \Phi \rrbracket = \bigcup_{\phi \in \Phi} \llbracket \phi \rrbracket$. The following lemma follows from the definitions.

Lemma 2. *For each constraint ϕ, the set $\llbracket \phi \rrbracket$ is upward closed.*

In all the examples we consider, the set C_F in the definition of APRX-PAR-COV can be represented by a finite set Φ_F of constraints. The coverability question can then be answered by checking whether $Init \xrightarrow{*} \llbracket \Phi_F \rrbracket$.

Entailment and Predecessors. To define our scheme we will use two operations on constraints; namely *entailment*, and *computing predecessors*, defined below. We define an *entailment relation* $\sqsubseteq$ on constraints, where $\phi_1 \sqsubseteq \phi_2$ iff $\llbracket \phi_2 \rrbracket \subseteq \llbracket \phi_1 \rrbracket$. For sets Φ_1, Φ_2 of constraints, abusing notation, we let $\Phi_1 \sqsubseteq \Phi_2$ denote that for each $\phi_2 \in \Phi_2$ there is a $\phi_1 \in \Phi_1$ with $\phi_1 \sqsubseteq \phi_2$. Observe that $\Phi_1 \sqsubseteq \Phi_2$ implies that $\llbracket \Phi_2 \rrbracket \subseteq \llbracket \Phi_1 \rrbracket$.

For a constraint ϕ, we let $Pre(\phi)$ be a set of constraints, such that $\llbracket Pre(\phi) \rrbracket = \{ c \mid \exists c' \in \llbracket \phi \rrbracket . c \rightsquigarrow c' \}$. In other words $Pre(\phi)$ characterizes the set of configurations from which we can reach a configuration in ϕ through the application of a single rule in the approximate transition relation. In the definition of Pre we rely on the fact that, in any monotonic transition system, upward-closedness is preserved under the computation of the set of predecessors (see e.g. [1]). From Lemma 2 we know that $\llbracket \phi \rrbracket$ is upward closed; by Lemma 1, $(C, \rightsquigarrow)$ is monotonic, we therefore know that $\llbracket Pre(\phi) \rrbracket$ is upward closed. In fact, we show in Section 8 that this set is finite and computable. For a set Φ of constraints, we let $Pre(\Phi) = \bigcup_{\phi \in \Phi} Pre(\phi)$.

Scheme. Given a finite set Φ_F of constraints, the scheme checks whether $Init \xRightarrow{*} \llbracket \Phi_F \rrbracket$. We perform a backward reachability analysis, generating a sequence $\Phi_0 \sqsupseteq \Phi_1 \sqsupseteq \Phi_2 \sqsupseteq \cdots$ of finite sets of constraints such that $\Phi_0 = \Phi_F$, and $\Phi_{j+1} = \Phi_j \cup Pre(\Phi_j)$. Since $\llbracket \Phi_0 \rrbracket \subseteq \llbracket \Phi_1 \rrbracket \subseteq \llbracket \Phi_2 \rrbracket \subseteq \cdots$, the procedure terminates when we reach a point j where $\Phi_j \sqsubseteq \Phi_{j+1}$. Notice that the termination condition implies that $\llbracket \Phi_j \rrbracket = (\bigcup_{0 \leq i \leq j} \llbracket \Phi_i \rrbracket)$. Consequently, Φ_j characterizes the set of all predecessors of $\llbracket \phi_F \rrbracket$. This means that $Init \xrightarrow{*} \llbracket \Phi_F \rrbracket$ iff $(Init \cap \llbracket \Phi_j \rrbracket) \neq \emptyset$.

Observe that, in order to implement the scheme (i.e., transform it into an algorithm), we need to be able to (i) compute Pre; (ii) check for entailment between constraints; and (iii) check for emptiness of $(Init \cap \llbracket \phi \rrbracket) \neq \emptyset$ for a constraint ϕ.

8   Constraint Operations

In this section, we show how to perform the three operations on constraints which are used in the scheme presented in Section 7. In the rest of the section, we fix a parameterized systems $\mathcal{P} = (Q, X, T)$. Recall that $Y = X \cup Q$.

Entailment. Consider two constraints $\phi = (m, \psi)$, and $\phi' = (m', \psi')$. Let $\mathcal{H}(\phi, \phi')$ be the set of injections $h : \overline{m} \mapsto \overline{m'}$. We use ψ^h to denote the formula $\psi[\rho]$, where $\rho := \{x^i \leftarrow x^{h(i)} \mid x \in Y \text{ and } i \in \overline{m}\}$. The following lemma gives a logical characterization which allows the computation of the entailment relation.

Lemma 3. *Given constraints $\phi = (m, \psi)$, and $\phi' = (m', \psi')$, we have $\phi \sqsubseteq \phi'$ iff*

$$\forall y_1 \cdots y_k. \ \psi'(y_1, \ldots, y_k) \supset \bigvee_{h \in \mathcal{H}(\phi, \phi')} \psi^h(y_1, \ldots, y_k)$$

Pre The following lemma describes the computation of the function *Pre*.

Lemma 4. *For a constraint ϕ, we can compute $Pre(\phi)$ as a finite set of constraints.*

The complete proof of the lemma can be found in [3]. As an example, for a transition t with a universally quantified global condition θ, *Pre* applied to constraint (m, ψ) returns the constraint (m, ψ'), where

$$\psi' = \exists Y^\bullet. \bigwedge_{1 \le j \ne i \le m} \psi\left[\rho_1^i\right] \wedge \theta_1'\left[\rho_2^{i,j}\right] \tag{3}$$

Here, for each variable x, the substitution ρ_1^i maps variable x^i to a new variable $x^\bullet$ in $Y^\bullet$, while $\rho_2^{i,j}$ maps $\mathtt{self} \cdot x^{next}$ to $x^\bullet$, $\mathtt{self} \cdot x$ to x^i, and $\mathtt{other} \cdot x$ to x^j. The condition θ_1' is obtained from θ by adding information on q and q'. All fresh variables in $Y^\bullet$ are then projected away.

Intersection with Initial States. For a constraint $\phi = (m, \psi)$, we have $(Init \cap \llbracket \phi \rrbracket) \ne \emptyset$ iff $[u_{init}, \ldots, u_{init}] \models \phi$, where the multiset $[u_{init}, \ldots, u_{init}]$ is of size m.

9   Additional Features

We add a number of features to the model of Section 2, namely, *Binary Communication*, *Broadcast*, and *Shared Variables*. In Binary Communication, two processes satisfying some global conditions change their process states simultaneously. In Broadcast, a process satisfying a global condition, called the initiator, changes its process state, together with all other processes, called receptors, which satisfy another global condition. Shared Variables may have unbounded domain, and can be read and written by all processes in the system. For all the new features, we can use the same constraint system as in Section 7; consequently checking entailment and intersection with initial states need not be modified. Also, as shown in [3], the definition of the *Pre* operator can be extended to cope with the new classes of guards.

10   Experimental Results

We have built two different prototypes that implement our approximated backward reachability procedure, based on an integer resp. a real solver for handling the constraints over the process variables. The results are summarized in Figure 1. For each protocol we give the number of iterations and the time needed for performing the verification. The experiments are performed using a Pentium M 1.6 Ghz with 1G of memory (see [3] for more details).

Model	Iterations		Time		Safe		Trace	
	R	I	R	I	R	I	R	I
Simplified Bakery Alg.	6	6	0.8s	0.3s	√	√		
Lamport's Bakery Alg.	9	9	2.1s	2s	√	√		
Bogus Bakery	10	6	0.8s	11s			√	√
Ticket Mutex Alg.	9	8	0.3s	1.6s	√	√		
Ricart-Agrawala Distr. Mutex Alg.	9	11	3.4s	2mn40s	√	√		
Lamport's Distr. Mutex Alg.	21	27	9mn19s	146mn	√	√		

Fig. 1. Experimental results. R and I stand for the real resp. integer solver. Safe and Trace stand for checking safety properties resp. generating a counter-example.

11   Conclusion and Future Work

We have presented a method for approximate reachability analysis of systems which consist of an arbitrary number of processes each of which is infinite-state. Based on the method, we have implemented a prototype and automatically verified several non-trivial mutual exclusion protocols. The Bakery example describes a distributed protocol without atomicity assumptions on the transitions. One direction for future research is to develop a methodology for automatic verification of general classes of parameterized systems with non-atomic global conditions. Furthermore, our algorithm relies on an abstract ordering which can be naturally extended to several different types of data structures. We are currently developing similar algorithms for systems with more complicated topologies such as trees and general forms of graphs.

References

1. Abdulla, P.A., Čerāns, K., Jonsson, B., Yih-Kuen, T.: Algorithmic analysis of programs with well quasi-ordered domains. Information and Computation 160, 109–127 (2000)
2. Abdulla, P.A., Delzanno, G.: On the coverability problem for constrained multiset rewriting. In: Proc. AVIS'06
3. Abdulla, P.A., Delzanno, G., Rezine, A.: Parameterized Verification of Infinite-state Processes with Global Conditions, Technical Report 2007-014, Uppsala University (April 2007)

4. Abdulla, P.A., Henda, N.B., Delzanno, G., Rezine, A.: Regular model checking without transducers. In: Proc. TACAS '07, To appear (2007)
5. Abdulla, P.A., Jonsson, B., Nilsson, M., d'Orso, J.: Regular model checking made simple and efficient. In: Brim, L., Jančar, P., Křetínský, M., Kucera, A. (eds.) CONCUR 2002. LNCS, vol. 2421, Springer, Heidelberg (2002)
6. Andrews, G.: Foundations of Multithreaded, Parallel, and Distributed Programming. Addison-Wesley, Reading (2000)
7. Arons, T., Pnueli, A., Ruah, S., Xu, J., Zuck, L.: Parameterized verification with automatically computed inductive assertions. In *Proc. CAV 2001*. In: Agha, G.A., De Cindio, F., Rozenberg, G. (eds.) Concurrent Object-Oriented Programming and Petri Nets. LNCS, vol. 2102, Springer, Heidelberg (2001)
8. Boigelot, B., Legay, A., Wolper, P.: Iterating transducers in the large. In: Hunt Jr., W.A., Somenzi, F. (eds.) CAV 2003. LNCS, vol. 2725, Springer, Heidelberg (2003)
9. Bozzano, M., Delzanno, G.: Beyond parameterized verification. In: Katoen, J.-P., Stevens, P. (eds.) ETAPS 2002 and TACAS 2002. LNCS, vol. 2280, Springer, Heidelberg (2002)
10. Bultan, T., Gerber, R., Pugh, W.: Model-checking concurrent systems with unbounded integer variables. ACM TOPLAS 21(4), 747–789 (1999)
11. Clarke, E., Talupur, M., Veith, H.: Environment abstraction for parameterized verification. In: Emerson, E.A., Namjoshi, K.S. (eds.) VMCAI 2006. LNCS, vol. 3855, pp. 126–141. Springer, Heidelberg (2005)
12. Delzanno, G.: Automatic verification of cache coherence protocols. In: Wilhelm, R. (ed.) Informatics. LNCS, vol. 2000, Springer, Heidelberg (2001)
13. Emerson, E., Namjoshi, K.: On model checking for non-deterministic infinite-state systems. In: Proc. LICS' 98 (1998)
14. Esparza, J., Finkel, A., Mayr, R.: On the verification of broadcast protocols. In: Proc. LICS' 99, 14th IEEE Int. Symp., IEEE Computer Society Press, Los Alamitos (1999)
15. Fribourg, L., Richardson, J.: Symbolic verification with gap-order constraints. In: Gallagher, J.P. (ed.) LOPSTR 1996. LNCS, vol. 1207, Springer, Heidelberg (1997)
16. German, S.M., Sistla, A.P.: Reasoning about systems with many identical processes. Journal of the ACM 39(3), 675–735 (1992)
17. Kesten, Y., Maler, O., Marcus, M., Pnueli, A., Shahar, E.: Symbolic model checking with rich assertional languages. TCS 256, 93–112 (2001)
18. Lahiri, S.K., Bryant, R.E.: Indexed predicate discovery for unbounded system verification. In: Alur, R., Peled, D.A. (eds.) CAV 2004. LNCS, vol. 3114, pp. 135–147. Springer, Heidelberg (2004)
19. Lamport, L.: A new solution of dijkstra's concurrent programming problem. Commun. ACM 17(8), 453–455 (1974)
20. Revesz, P.: A closed form evaluation for datalog queries with integer (gap)-order constraints. Theoretical Computer Science 116(1), 117–149 (1993)
21. Ricart, G., Agrawal, A.K.: An optimal algorithm for mutual exclusion in computer networks. Communications of the ACM 24(1), 9–17 (1981)
22. Sedletsky, E., Pnueli, A., Ben-Ari, M.: Formal verification of the ricart-agrawala algorithm. In: Proc. FSTTCS'00 (2000)
23. Vardi, M.Y., Wolper, P.: An automata-theoretic approach to automatic program verification. In: Proc. LICS '86, June (1986)

CADP 2006: A Toolbox for the Construction and Analysis of Distributed Processes

(Tool Paper)

Hubert Garavel, Radu Mateescu, Frédéric Lang, and Wendelin Serwe

INRIA
Centre de recherche Rhône-Alpes / VASY
655, avenue de l'Europe, Montbonnot, 38 334 Saint Ismier Cedex, France
{Hubert.Garavel,Radu.Mateescu,Frederic.Lang,Wendelin.Serwe}@inria.fr

1   Introduction

CADP(*Construction and Analysis of Distributed Processes*)[1] [2,3] is a toolbox for specification, rapid prototyping, verification, testing, and performance evaluation of asynchronous systems (concurrent processes with message-passing communication). The developments of CADP during the last five years led to a new release named CADP 2006 *"Edinburgh"* (as a tribute to the achievements in concurrency theory of the Laboratory for Foundations of Computer Science) that supersedes the previous version CADP 2001.

2   Modular Integration of Verification Techniques

CADP 2006 includes a complete range of functionalities for the design of asynchronous systems: code generation, rapid prototyping, random, interactive, or guided simulation, explicit-state verification, test case generation, and performance evaluation. CADP accepts as input either networks of communicating automata or higher-level specification languages, such as the ISO standard LOTOS.

Many CADP tools operate on Labeled Transition Systems (LTSs), which are represented either *explicitly*, as compact binary files encoded in the BCG (*Binary Coded Graphs*) format, or *implicitly*, as C programs implementing the transition relation according to the OPEN/CÆSAR API (*Application Programming Interface*). Three forms of verification are supported by CADP: *visual checking* (graphical inspection of an LTS), *model checking* (satisfaction of a modal μ-calculus formula by an LTS), and *equivalence checking* (comparison of two LTSs with respect to some equivalence/preorder relation).

To address the state space explosion problem, CADP 2006 provides the following verification techniques[2]:

- *Compositional verification* builds the LTS of a concurrent system incrementally by generating, minimizing, and recomposing the LTSs of individual

---

[1] http://www.inrialpes.fr/vasy/cadp

[2] Related verification tools are listed at http://anna.fi.muni.cz/yahoda

W. Damm and H. Hermanns (Eds.): CAV 2007, LNCS 4590, pp. 158–163, 2007.

processes. Refined compositional verification uses interface constraints (specified manually or synthesized automatically) that restrict the behaviour of a process depending on its environment, thus limiting the size of intermediate LTSs.

- *On-the-fly verification* avoids the complete construction of an LTS by exploring only the portion relevant for verification. Model checking and equivalence checking are reformulated in terms of Boolean Equation Systems (BESs), which are solved on-the-fly using specialized linear-time algorithms.
- *Partial order reductions*, performed on-the-fly, reduce the LTS size by eliminating redundancies arising from the interleaving of independent transitions, still preserving various equivalence relations (branching bisimulation, weak trace equivalence, etc.).
- *Static analysis* aims at reducing the size of the LTSs generated from a system description, still preserving strong bisimulation.
- *Massively parallel verification* handles very large LTSs by using the computing resources of machine clusters and grids.

A key feature of CADP is to allow all these techniques to be combined in a highly modular way within the same software environment. Examples of such combinations that cumulate the reductions and scale up to larger systems are:

1. One can use a grid to generate the LTS corresponding to a LOTOS specification, while applying static analysis and on-the-fly τ-confluence reduction simultaneously.
2. One can model check on-the-fly whether a μ-calculus formula is satisfied by a network of communicating LTSs, while applying partial order reduction.
3. One can compare on-the-fly an LTS to a network of communicating LTSs that have been previously generated (taking into account refined interface constraints) and minimized for some bisimulation.

The tools of CADP can be invoked either interactively, by using the EUCALYPTUS graphical user interface, or in batch mode, by describing the desired verification scenario as a script in the SVL language.

3   New and Enhanced Tools in CADP 2006

CADP 2006 offers 42 tools and 20 generic software libraries dedicated to verification. Numerous tools existing in CADP 2001 were entirely rewritten or significantly improved, and 15 new tools and code libraries were added:

- BCG_GRAPH generates several useful kinds of LTSs in the BCG format, such as bags, FIFO queues, and chaos LTSs.
- BCG_MERGE [5] produces a single BCG file from a PBG file (see the DISTRIBUTOR tool below). It is equipped with a graphical tool to monitor the LTS generation interactively.

- BCG_STEADY and BCG_TRANSIENT [7] perform steady-state and transient analysis of an (extended) CTMC (*Continuous-Time Markov Chain*) encoded in the BCG format.
- BISIMULATOR [11,1] compares two LTSs on-the-fly modulo one out of 14 behavioural relations (strong, branching, observational, $\tau^*.a$, safety, trace, or weak trace equivalences — and their associated preorders). The equivalence checking problem is reformulated as a BES, which is solved using the CÆSAR_SOLVE library below. When both LTSs are not related, BISIMULATOR generates a counterexample, i.e., an acyclic LTS containing distinguishing transition sequences. Compared with former CADP tools, BISIMULATOR is more efficient and generates smaller counterexamples.
- CÆSAR 7.0 [6] is a compiler for the behaviour part of LOTOS. Among other improvements, CÆSAR 7.0 implements a static analysis based on live variable analysis, which assigns a canonical value to variables that are no longer used, thus avoiding to distinguish states that only differ by values of variables not used in the future. Compared to its previous version 6.2, CÆSAR 7.0 can reduce LTS size by several orders of magnitude (e.g., 10^4), thus allowing larger LOTOS specifications to be handled.
- CÆSAR.BDD uses Binary Decision Diagrams to perform various structural analyses on basic Petri nets, such as exploring reachable markings to determine the set of "*dead*" transitions and the pairs of "*concurrent*" units.
- CÆSAR_SOLVE [11] is a generic software library for on-the-fly resolution of BESs, represented as implicit boolean graphs similarly to LTSs in OPEN/CÆSAR. It offers 6 resolution algorithms, based on breadth-first search or depth-first search (with memory-efficient variants for acyclic or disjunctive/conjunctive BESs) strategies, which also generate diagnostics (boolean subgraphs) explaining the truth value of boolean variables.
- DETERMINATOR [7] takes as input an extended CTMC encoded in the BCG format and tries to extract on-the-fly a pure CTMC (i.e., containing only stochastic transitions). Doing so, the tool checks a sufficient condition ensuring that the resulting CTMC is unique, or returns an error otherwise.
- DISTRIBUTOR [5] performs distributed LTS generation and on-the-fly reduction by τ-compression and τ-confluence [10] using several machines connected by a network. It launches a remote process on each machine to generate a fragment of the entire LTS. The result of the distributed generation is a PBG (*Partitioned* BCG *Graph*), i.e., a set of LTS fragments located on remote machines. DISTRIBUTOR is equipped with a graphical tool to monitor the PBG generation in real-time.
- EVALUATOR 3.5 [12,11] evaluates on-the-fly, on an LTS, temporal properties expressed in regular alternation-free μ-calculus. The model checking problem is reformulated as a BES, which is solved using the CÆSAR_SOLVE library. The tool generates full diagnostics (examples and counterexamples) and optimizes memory consumption (i.e., does not store the transitions, but only the states of the LTS) for a large spectrum of properties. EVALUATOR 3.5 is 3 times faster and consumes 3 times less memory than EVALUATOR 3.0.

- EXP.OPEN 2.0 [8] maps communicating LTSs composed using synchronization vectors, parallel composition operators (from CCS, CSP, μCRL, LOTOS, and E-LOTOS), and/or generalized hide, rename, and cut operators onto the OPEN/CÆSAR API. It implements partial order reductions preserving various equivalences (e.g., branching, stochastic, weak trace equivalence). It can also translate communicating LTSs into the PEP, TINA, and FC2 formats, and can synthesize interface constraints for refined compositional verification [9]. EXP.OPEN 2.0 uses 2 times less memory and is up to 45 times faster than EXP.OPEN 1.0.
- PROJECTOR 2.0 [13] reduces an LTS on-the-fly with respect to interface constraints represented by another LTS and a set of labels. Among its new features, PROJECTOR 2.0 allows to describe the set of labels more compactly by the way of regular expressions. Experiments indicate that PROJECTOR 2.0 is up to 4 times faster than PROJECTOR 1.0.
- REDUCTOR 5.0 reduces an LTS on-the-fly, either partially or totally, modulo one out of 8 relations (trace, weak trace, $\tau^*.a$, and safety equivalences, τ-confluence, τ-compression, τ-divergence [10], and strong bisimulation), possibly displaying the equivalence classes of the quotient graph. Some of these reductions perform a local resolution of a BES using CÆSAR_SOLVE. The algorithm used by REDUCTOR 5.0 to eliminate invisible transitions has a lower average complexity than in earlier versions.
- SEQ.OPEN [4] maps traces onto the OPEN/CÆSAR API. It implements an optimized representation of a trace as an LTS without storing the whole trace in memory, which is also significantly more efficient (up to 50 times faster) than converting the trace first into a BCG file.

Notice that the ALDÉBARAN tool (available since the origin of CADP) was replaced in CADP 2006 by a (upward-compatible) shell script that invokes BISIMULATOR, BCG_INFO, BCG_MIN, and REDUCTOR to provide the same functionalities as ALDÉBARAN.

4   Conclusion

CADP 2006 "*Edinburgh*" is the result of five years of intensive R&D in verification technology. Four computing platforms are currently supported: SPARC/SOLARIS, INTEL/LINUX, INTEL/WINDOWS, and POWERPC/MAC OS. As regards impact, 366 organizations have signed the CADP license agreement already, and CADP has been installed on 820 machines in the world during year 2006. CADP was used for 94 case-studies[3] and 29 research tools[4] are connected to CADP. Most notably, in the FORMALFAME project, CADP was successfully used to validate crucial parts of Bull's NOVASCALE machines, which form the core of TERA10, Europe's most powerful supercomputer.

CADP will continue to be enhanced in the next years. In particular, we plan to apply CADP in three main areas: software environments for critical embedded

---

[3] listed at http://www.inrialpes.fr/vasy/cadp/case-studies
[4] listed at http://www.inrialpes.fr/vasy/cadp/software

systems (French projects OPENEMBEDD and TOPCASED), high-performance multiprocessor architectures (French project MULTIVAL), and bio-informatics (European project EC-MOAN, where CADP will contribute to the understanding of a bacterial model system).

Acknowledgements. Damien Bergamini, David Champelovier, Adrian Curic, Nicolas Descoubes, Holger Hermanns, Christophe Joubert, Bruno Ondet, Gordon Pace, Frédéric Perret, Irina Smarandache-Sturm, Gilles Stragier, Frédéric Tronel, and Marie Vidal contributed to CADP 2006. The authors are also grateful to the 79 CADP users[5] whose suggestions led to numerous CADP enhancements.

References

1. Bergamini, D., Descoubes, N., Joubert, C., Mateescu, R.: BISIMULATOR: A Modular Tool for On-the-Fly Equivalence Checking. In: Ziarko, W., Yao, Y. (eds.) RSCTC 2000. LNCS (LNAI), vol. 2005, Springer, Heidelberg (2001)
2. Fernandez, J.-C., Garavel, H., Kerbrat, A., Mateescu, R., Mounier, L., Sighireanu, M.: CADP (CÆSAR/ALDEBARAN Development Package): A Protocol Validation and Verification Toolbox. In: Alur, R., Henzinger, T.A. (eds.) CAV 1996. LNCS, vol. 1102, Springer, Heidelberg (1996)
3. Garavel, H., Lang, F., Mateescu, R.: An Overview of CADP 2001. EASST Newsletter 4, 13–24 (2002) Also available as INRIA Technical Report RT-0254
4. Garavel, H., Mateescu, R.: SEQ.OPEN: A Tool for Efficient Trace-Based Verification. In: Gelbukh, A. (ed.) CICLing 2001. LNCS, vol. 2004, Springer, Heidelberg (2001)
5. Garavel, H., Mateescu, R., Bergamini, D., Curic, A., Descoubes, N., Joubert, C., Smarandache-Sturm, I., Stragier, G.: DISTRIBUTOR and BCG_MERGE: Tools for Distributed Explicit State Space Generation. In: Hermanns, H., Palsberg, J. (eds.) TACAS 2006 and ETAPS 2006. LNCS, vol. 3920, Springer, Heidelberg (2006)
6. Garavel, H., Serwe, W.: State Space Reduction for Process Algebra Specifications. Theoretical Computer Science 351(2), 131–145 (2006)
7. Hermanns, H., Joubert, C.: A Set of Performance and Dependability Analysis Components for CADP. In: Garavel, H., Hatcliff, J. (eds.) ETAPS 2003 and TACAS 2003. LNCS, vol. 2619, Springer, Heidelberg (2003)
8. Lang, F.: EXP.OPEN 2.0: A Flexible Tool Integrating Partial Order, Compositional, and On-the-fly Verification Methods. In: Romijn, J.M.T., Smith, G.P., van de Pol, J. (eds.) IFM 2005. LNCS, vol. 3771, Springer, Heidelberg (2005)
9. Lang, F.: Refined Interfaces for Compositional Verification. In: Najm, E., Pradat-Peyre, J.F., Donzeau-Gouge, V.V. (eds.) FORTE 2006. LNCS, vol. 4229, Springer, Heidelberg (2006)
10. Mateescu, R.: On-the-fly State Space Reductions for Weak Equivalences. In: Proc. of FMICS '05, ACM Computer Society Press, New York (2005)
11. Mateescu, R.: CAESAR_SOLVE: A Generic Library for On-the-Fly Resolution of Alternation-Free Boolean Equation Systems. Springer International Journal on Software Tools for Technology Transfer (STTT) 8(1), 37–56 (2006)

---

[5] listed at http://www.inrialpes.fr/vasy/cadp/news6.html

12. Mateescu, R., Sighireanu, M.: Efficient On-the-Fly Model-Checking for Regular Alternation-Free Mu-Calculus. Science of Computer Programming 46(3), 255–281 (2003)
13. Pace, G., Lang, F., Mateescu, R.: Calculating τ-Confluence Compositionally. In: Hunt Jr., W.A., Somenzi, F. (eds.) CAV 2003. LNCS, vol. 2725, Springer, Heidelberg (2003)

jMoped: A Test Environment for Java Programs*
(Tool Paper)

Dejvuth Suwimonteerabuth, Felix Berger, Stefan Schwoon, and Javier Esparza

Technische Universität München, Boltzmannstr. 3, 85748 Garching, Germany**

1 Introduction

We present jMoped [1], a test environment for Java programs. Given a Java method, jMoped can simulate its execution for all possible arguments within a finite range and generate coverage information for these executions. Moreover, it checks for some common Java errors, i.e. assertion violations, null pointer exceptions, and array bound violations. When an error is found, jMoped finds out the arguments that lead to the error. A JUnit [2] test case can also be automatically generated for further testing.

Initially, jMoped was developed as a text-based translator from Java bytecode into symbolic pushdown systems (SPDS). Technical details about the translation process can be found in [3]. Since then, we have extended the tool with two goals:

- *Harnessing the model-checking technique to support testing.* Model checking can symbolically test many inputs at the same time, is useful for finding boundary cases, and can provide coverage metrics.
- *Giving more control to the user.* The tool must allow users to inspect the intermediate results and to interrupt and refine the analysis at any time. Partial results should also be useful for further analyses.

The resulting tool has been developed as a plug-in for Eclipse [4], which is again called jMoped. It now consists of a graphical user interface, the translator, and Moped [5] at the back-end. Moreover, the translator itself has been improved in many aspects. It supports not only almost all fundamental features, e.g. assignment, method call, and recursion, but is also able to handle inheritance, abstraction, and polymorphism. On the other hand, it still fails to translate negative numbers, floats, and multi-threading programs.

2 Testing and Model Checking

Traditionally, testing and model checking are seen as distinct methodologies; testing can detect bugs but not prove their absence, and model checking seeks to establish the absence of bugs, possibly at the cost of taking very long to complete (or not finishing at all). Recently, several efforts have been made at

---

* Partially supported by the DFG-Project "Algorithms for Software Model Checking".
** This work was done while the authors worked at the University of Stuttgart.

W. Damm and H. Hermanns (Eds.): CAV 2007, LNCS 4590, pp. 164–167, 2007.
© Springer-Verlag Berlin Heidelberg 2007

cross-fertilising between these two areas. Our tool falls into this line of work in the sense that we use a model checker to support the task of testing a program.

Internally, the tool translates a Java program into an SPDS, preserving the control flow of the program, but modelling only a finite amount of data. The size of variables and of the heap are bounded by user-defined (artificial) ranges. Thus, the model-checking procedure can be thought of as an extended symbolic testing procedure, which is still incomplete (because only runs within the given bounds are considered); however, once the bounds are established, the model checker will perform exact checks on *all* executions within these bounds.

We contend that this approach can complement traditional testing methods for two reasons: First, model checkers using compact data structures (such as BDDs) can simulate many executions at the same time, which can be more efficient than exhaustive testing. For example, our tool can test a Quicksort implementation for 60 array elements if each element has only one bit, whereas exhaustive testing for these parameters is infeasible. Secondly, model checking is suitable for finding boundary cases, i.e. inputs with special properties that are easily forgotten during testing, but are prone to cause bugs. E.g., two boundary cases for a sorting procedure would be an array where all elements are the same, or an array that is already sorted. Even relatively small bounds on the inputs are likely to contain many interesting boundary cases, and the model checker will test all of them (and find the faulty ones). Thus, the approach can greatly enhance the confidence in the correctness of a program, without strictly guaranteeing it.

The results of a model-checking procedure can support testing in other ways, too. The quality of a set of test cases is usually measured by so-called coverage metrics, e.g., counting how many lines of code were exercised by the test cases. We observe that such metrics can also be obtained by running a model checker on a set of inputs and checking which lines were found to be reachable. In jMoped, the user can observe the progress of these metrics while the checker is running. Moreover, the user may stop the checker at any time (e.g., if the attained level of coverage is deemed satisfactory), or ask it to specifically search for inputs that can reach a certain target in the program. Moreover, if the checker finds that bugs are caused by certain inputs, those inputs can be saved in a library of JUnit test cases, where they may be useful for future test runs.

3   Working with jMoped

jMoped consists of three parts: a graphical user interface, a translator from Java bytecode into SPDS, and an SPDS model checker. The translator and the checker are available as stand-alone tools, and the checker is capable of handling programs with thousands of lines, provided that the data complexity is low as is the case, for instance, with device drivers [5]. However, the graphical interface was developed for unit testing, with smaller, more data-intensive programs in mind. The interface is also described in more detail in [6].

The graphical interface takes the form of an Eclipse plug-in. Figure 1 shows an example when running with a Quicksort implementation taken from [7]. The

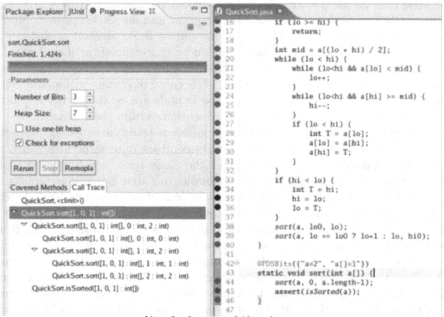

Fig. 1. A view of the plug-in

left-hand side is the plug-in interface, while the right-hand side shows parts of the code and the analysis results. Users select a method from which the analysis should start. In the example, the method **sort** starting at line 43 was chosen.

jMoped has two modes of operation. In the standard mode, jMoped exhaustively explores the program for all inputs within the bounds provided by the user. This is done in two steps. First, the program (which reads input from its user) is transformed into another program that nondeterministically generates an input. Then, the checker exhaustively explores all behaviours of the transformed program. In the second mode of operation, jMoped works backwards. Given a postcondition, jMoped computes the set of all states (within the given bounds) from which the states of the postcondition can be reached.

During the analysis, jMoped graphically displays its progress. First, black markers are placed in front of all statements. While the checker is running, the parts of the state space found to be reachable are mapped back to the Java program, and the appearance of the corresponding markers is changed. When a black marker turns green, it means that the corresponding Java statement is reachable from *some* argument values. A red marker means that an assertion statement has been violated by some argument values. Other markers indicate null pointer exceptions, array bound violations, and heap overflows (see below).

After the analysis, users can either create a *call trace* or a JUnit test case that reaches a given statement or violates some assertion. An example of the call trace can be seen in lower left part of Figure 1, where the assertion violation occured when the method **sort** was called with the array [1,0,1].

In a typical scenario, a user will want to achieve 100% coverage, i.e. the checker should test a set of inputs such that every statement is exercised at least once. The idea for achieving this is to combine the two modes of operation. First, one uses the standard mode to cover as many instructions as possible. Say all but three instructions were covered. Then, in a second phase, one applies three backward searches starting from these three particular instructions. Since these are specific searches with the "difficult" instructions as goal, the hope is that they have better success chances than the "blind" forward search.

For performance reasons, the user starts the checker in standard mode with small values for the parameters, in the hope of achieving a large coverage degree quickly. However, choosing small parameters may cause some (normally reachable) statements to be considered unreachable. (E.g., the body of an if-statement guarded by the condition x >= 8 would be unreachable with a specified bit size of less than 4.) Backward search can then be used to instruct the model checker to search for inputs that reach the remaining statements.

There are two important parameters to jMoped: the number of bits and the heap size. These determine the bounds for the inputs and executions that are to be tested. The number of bits restricts the range of every number that appears in a program, including constants, integer variables, and the lengths of arrays or strings. The heap size directly affects the number of objects that can be instantiated. jMoped simulates the Java heap when manipulating objects. For example, when an object is created, it occupies a part of the heap whose size depends on the size of the object. Note that these two parameters depend on each other, i.e. the heap size can be at most two to the number of bits minus one. For instance, the analysis in Figure 1 was performed with 3 bits and heap size 7. It is also possible to specify how many bits to use for individual variables, parameters, or fields. The annotation at line 42 of Figure 1 means that the length of array a has two bits, and each of its elements has one bit.

References

1. jMoped: A test environment for Java programs,
   http://www.fmi.uni-stuttgart.de/szs/ tools/moped/jmoped/
2. JUnit: Testing resources for extreme programming, http://www.junit.org/
3. Suwimonteerabuth, D., Schwoon, S., Esparza, J.: jMoped: A Java bytecode checker based on Moped (Tool paper). In: Halbwachs, N., Zuck, L.D. (eds.) TACAS 2005. LNCS, vol. 3440, pp. 541–545. Springer, Heidelberg (2005)
4. Eclipse: An open development platform, http://www.eclipse.org
5. Schwoon, S.: Model-Checking Pushdown Systems. PhD thesis, Technische Universität München (2002)
6. Berger, F.: A test and verification environment for Java programs. Master's thesis, University of Stuttgart (2007)
7. ParForCE Project Workshop: Performance comparison between Prolog and Java, http://www.clip.dia.fi.upm.es/Projects/ParForce/Final_review/slides/i ntro/node4.html

Hector: Software Model Checking with Cooperating Analysis Plugins

(Tool Paper)

Nathaniel Charlton and Michael Huth

Department of Computing, Imperial College London
{nac103,M.Huth}@doc.imperial.ac.uk

Abstract. We present HECTOR, a software tool for combining different abstraction methods to extract sound models of heap-manipulating imperative programs with recursion. Extracted models may be explored visually and model checked with a wide range of "propositional" temporal logic safety properties, where "propositions" are formulae of a first order logic with transitive closure and arithmetic ($\mathcal{L}$). HECTOR uses techniques initiated in [4,5] to wrap up different abstraction methods as modular *analysis plugins*, and to exchange information about program state between plugins through formulae of $\mathcal{L}$. This approach aims to achieve both (apparently conflicting) advantages of increased precision and modularity. When checking safety properties containing non-independent "propositions", our model checking algorithm gives greater precision than a naïve three-valued one since it maintains some dependencies.

1 Introduction

Abstraction has been proposed as the key to building systems which automatically verify the correctness of software programs. Software written in everyday languages such as Java typically has an enormous or infinite state space, but abstraction can reduce this to a finite space of (abstract) states. The software verification literature describes many abstraction methods; predicate abstraction [2] and three-valued shape analysis [9] are two important examples.

This paper presents HECTOR, a Prolog implementation of abstraction-based verification which allows users to experiment with three interesting new features:

F#1 Abstractions are pluggable: Abstraction methods are wrapped inside modules called *analysis plugins*, which implement a common interface; algorithms for constructing and checking models are generic and use whatever plugins are activated. By activating several analyses together we can verify programs with diverse behavior, e.g. those which use both linked data structures and arithmetic. Such programs may be beyond the reach of shape analysis (which lacks a systematic treatment of arithmetic), and also beyond the reach of predicate abstraction (which doesn't handle linked data structures well). But the combination of the two analyses may succeed. The modular structure of HECTOR makes it easy to integrate and investigate new analyses under such cooperation.

W. Damm and H. Hermanns (Eds.): CAV 2007, LNCS 4590, pp. 168–172, 2007.
© Springer-Verlag Berlin Heidelberg 2007

F#2 Plugins exchange information: Crucially, the interface which plugins implement allows them to exchange information about program state, expressed as formulae of a common logic $\mathcal{L}$. This information flow between the various plugins increases the precision of their respective analyses. Because there is a single common language, modularity is not broken. The implementor of a new abstraction method only has to make his plugin "understand" the common language, and the plugin will then automatically cooperate with existing ones.

F#3 Ad-hoc model checking: Because the abstraction process is generally costly, we maximize the utility of each abstract model generated by allowing the user to model check it with any property from an expressive safety language: the LTL fragment from [10], but where "propositions" are now any constraints on the program's current and initial states written in $\mathcal{L}$. Thus one can check for the absence of memory errors and assertion violations, but also much more.

The first two features were proposed and discussed in [4,5], where their formal basis is set out. We also refer to [4,5] for an account of related work. HECTOR's online version [6] can be used with plugins for monomial predicate abstraction, trivector predicate abstraction, three-valued shape analysis and constant propagation. (The predicate abstraction plugins call the theorem prover Simplify [11] and the shape analysis plugin calls the shape analyzer TVLA [12].) The web version offers some example programs to demonstrate various aspects; alternatively users may experiment with programs of their own.

2 Functionality of Hector

HECTOR maintains a list of models of (possibly different) programs; at any time users may build a new model, or select an existing one to draw graphically, model check, annotate with comments or delete.

2.1 Model Construction

To create a model, there are two steps.

S1 Enter the program to be analyzed: HECTOR analyses imperative, object-based programs, input as textual representations of control flow graphs (CFGs); this input language is sufficient to naturally express many simple Java-style programs. We currently don't handle inheritance, exceptions or concurrency.

S2 Configure the analyses: Firstly the user chooses which plugins to use. Secondly, the user configures each plugin; the settings for a plugin may tune the analysis it performs as well as how much information it propagates to other plugins. For the predicate abstraction plugins, for instance, a configuration consists of a choice of which abstraction predicates to use.

HECTOR then builds an abstract transition system which over-approximates the program, using a work-list algorithm which calls the selected plugins. Each abstract state is a tuple, containing one abstract value for each of the plugins; these are interpreted conjunctively. Recursion is handled by summarization,

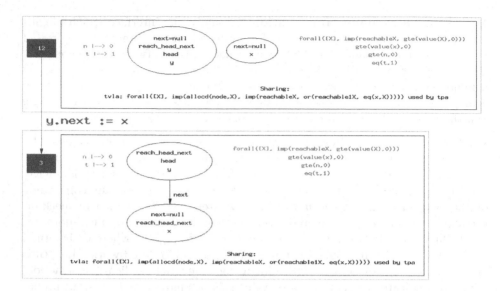

Fig. 1. Part of an abstract model, as generated and drawn by HECTOR. Program variables n and t are used for integers, *head*, x and y for addresses of list nodes.

as in [1]. As stated earlier, during model construction each plugin can propagate information about possible program states, expressed as formulae of the common logic $\mathcal{L}$; currently a round of propagation happens at every successor computation. Our choice of $\mathcal{L}$ for this purpose is discussed in [5].

To make it easier to create a new model, the program and configuration details can be copied from an existing model and then modified; alternatively HECTOR generates reasonable default configuration options.

2.2   Drawing Abstract Models

HECTOR can draw the generated models in graphical form[1], as in Fig. 1. Each abstract state is drawn as a box containing a list of the formulae propagated between plugins during successor computation, and an illustration of its component for each plugin: (left-to-right) for constant propagation a partial map from variables to integers, for shape analysis a three-valued heap graph, and for trivector predicate abstraction a collection of (here four) abstraction predicates or their negations. CFG nodes are also shown, each one being "boxed in" with the set of abstract states collected there. The user can ask for all propagated formulae to be shown, or (as in Fig. 1) just those that turn out to affect the analysis. The statement shown in Fig. 1 appends a new node to a linked list, currently of length one. The shape analysis plugin shares a fact about reachability of nodes from the list head, enabling predicate abstraction to maintain the constraint that reachable list nodes have nonnegative data values.

---

[1] The Graphviz toolkit [7] is used for graph layout.

2.3   Ad-Hoc Model Checking

Once a model has been built, safety properties can be checked against it. Our safety language is "two-level": we take the *syntactic safety* LTL fragment from Thm. 3.1 in [10], but allow the "propositions" to be arbitrary $\mathcal{L}$ constraints on the program's current and initial states. This language can express quite a lot: for example,

$$\mathsf{G}\,(allocd(node, x) \rightarrow \mathsf{G}\,(\exists Y : allocd(node, Y) \wedge next(Y) = x))$$

says that, if the variable x ever becomes a reference to a linked list node, then forever after, x is pointed to by the *next* field of some list node (but not necessarily the same one in each future state). For convenience, however, shortcuts are available in HECTOR's interface for commonly used idioms, such as the absence of memory errors and assertion violations.

Model checking is performed using automata (generated by invoking scheck [8]), where we reuse HECTOR's machinery of sharing and successor computation to look up the values of the $\mathcal{L}$ "propositions" in abstract states.

If a counterexample is found it is shown to the user. If no counterexample is found, then the property holds of the original program. However (as usual after abstraction) counterexamples may be spurious, in which case a refined model with a better configuration may suffice to verify the property. Optionally HECTOR can search for what we call a *strong* counterexample, one in which the evaluation of the $\mathcal{L}$ "propositions" of the safety property yielded a definite answer in every state (as opposed to the third value "unknown"). While this still does not guarantee that the counterexample is feasible (because the existence of transitions is still uncertain), we conjecture that a strong counterexample will typically be more informative to the user than a weak one, even if the latter is shorter.

Also, similarly to what was observed in [3], a naïve model checking algorithm will lose precision if "propositions" have dependencies; our algorithm sometimes delivers a definite answer in these cases. For an example of this see [6].

Future work may involve adding CEGAR (counterexample-guided abstraction refinement) features to HECTOR. We are particularly interested in the possibility of a generic CEGAR algorithm which would work with all plugins, perhaps along the lines of the ideas put forward in [13].

References

1. Ball, T., Rajamani, S.K.: Bebop: A symbolic model checker for boolean programs. In: Havelund, K., Penix, J., Visser, W. (eds.) SPIN Model Checking and Software Verification. LNCS, vol. 1885, pp. 113–130. Springer, Heidelberg (2000)
2. Ball, T., Podelski, A., Rajamani, S.K.: Boolean and Cartesian Abstraction for Model Checking C programs. In: Margaria, T., Yi, W. (eds.) ETAPS 2001 and TACAS 2001. LNCS, vol. 2031, Springer, Heidelberg (2001)
3. Bruns, G., Godefroid, P.: Generalized model checking: Reasoning about partial state spaces. In: Palamidessi, C. (ed.) CONCUR 2000. LNCS, vol. 1877, pp. 168–182. Springer, Heidelberg (2000)

4. Charlton, N.: Verification of Java Programs with Interacting Analysis Plugins. ENTCS 145, 131–150, Elsevier/Science Direct (2006)
5. Charlton, N.: Program Verification with Interacting Analysis Plugins. In: Formal Aspects of Computing, Springer, Heidelberg (2007), doi:10.1007/s00165-007-0029-4
6. Charlton, N.: HECTOR tool online, www.doc.ic.ac.uk/~nac103/hector/
7. GraphViz graph-drawing library: www.graphviz.org
8. Latvala, T.: scheck, www.tcs.hut.fi/~timo/scheck/
9. Sagiv, M., Reps, T., Wilhelm, R.: Parametric shape analysis via 3-valued logic. ACM TOPLAS 24, 217–298 (2002)
10. Sistla, A.P.: Safety, liveness and fairness in temporal logic. Formal Aspects of Computing 6(5), 495–512 (1994)
11. Simplify theorem prover: research.compaq.com/SRC/esc/Simplify.html
12. TVLA, 3-valued logic analyzer: www.cs.tau.ac.il/~tvla/
13. Gulavani, B.S., Rajamani, S.K.: Counterexample Driven Refinement for Abstract Interpretation. In: Hermanns, H., Palsberg, J. (eds.) TACAS 2006 and ETAPS 2006. LNCS, vol. 3920, Springer, Heidelberg (2006)

The Why/Krakatoa/Caduceus Platform for Deductive Program Verification*
(Tool Paper)

Jean-Christophe Filliâtre[1,3] and Claude Marché[2,3]

[1] CNRS, Lab. de Recherche en Informatique, UMR 8623, Orsay, F-91405
[2] INRIA Futurs, ProVal, Parc Orsay Université, F-91893
[3] Univ Paris-Sud, Orsay, F-91405

Abstract. We present the Why/Krakatoa/Caduceus set of tools for deductive verification of Java and C source code.

1 Introduction

Why/Krakatoa/Caduceus is a set of tools for deductive verification of Java and C source code. In both cases, the requirements are specified as *annotations* in the source, in a special style of comments. For Java (and Java Card), these specifications are given in the *Java Modeling Language* [1] and are interpreted by the *Krakatoa* tool. For C, we designed our own specification language, largely inspired from JML. Those are interpreted by the *Caduceus* tool. The tools are available as open source software at http://why.lri.fr/.

The overall architecture is presented on Figure 1. The general approach is to generate *Verification Conditions* (VCs for short): logical formulas whose validity implies the soundness of the code with respect to the given specification. This includes automatically generated VCs to guarantee the absence of run-time errors: null pointer dereferencing, out-of-bounds array access, etc. Then the VCs can be discharged using one or several theorem provers. The main originality of this platform is that a large part is common to C and Java. In particular there is a unique, stand-alone, VCs generator called Why, which is able to output VCs in the native syntax of many provers, either automatic or interactive ones.

Figure 2 shows a short example of annotated C code. Clauses `requires` introduces a precondition, `ensures` a postcondition, and `assigns` specifies the set of modified memory locations. `\valid` is a built-in predicate which specifies that the given pointer can be safely dereferenced, and `\old` denotes the value of the given expression at the function entry. Other kind of annotations include loop invariants and variants. VCs are generated modularly: when calling `credit` from `test`, only the specification of `credit` is used. To make this possible, the `assigns` clause is essential.

---

* This research is partly supported by ANR RNTL grant "CAT".

W. Damm and H. Hermanns (Eds.): CAV 2007, LNCS 4590, pp. 173–177, 2007.
© Springer-Verlag Berlin Heidelberg 2007

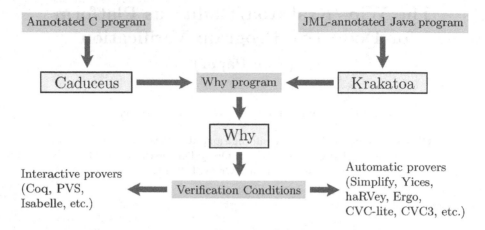

Fig. 1. Platform Architecture

```
typedef struct purse {
  int balance;
} purse;

/*@ requires \valid(p) && s >= 0
  @ assigns p->balance
  @ ensures p->balance ==
  @    \old(p->balance) + s
  @*/
void credit(purse *p,int s) {
  p->balance += s;
}
```

```
/*@ requires \valid(p1) && \valid(p2)
  @    && p1 != p2 && p1->balance == 0
  @ ensures p1->balance == 100
  @*/
void test(purse *p1, purse *p2) {
  credit(p1,100);
  p2->balance = 0;
  return p1->balance;
}
```

Fig. 2. Example of annotated C source code

2 The Why Verification Condition Generator

The input syntax of Why is a specific language dedicated to program verification. As a programming language, it is a 'WHILE' language which (1) has limited side-effects (only *mutable variables* that cannot be aliased), (2) provides no built-in data type, (3) proposes basic control statements (assignment, if, while) but also exceptions (throwing and catching). A Why program is a set of functions, annotated with pre- and postconditions. Those are written in a general purpose specification language: polymorphic multi-sorted first-order logic with built-in equality and arithmetic. This logic can be used to introduce abstract data types, by declaring new sorts, function symbols, predicates and axioms.

The VCs generation is based on a Weakest Precondition calculus, incorporating exceptional postconditions and computation of effects over mutable variables [2]. Last but not least, Why provides a multi-prover output as shown on

Figure 1. Actually Why can even by used only as a translator from first-order formulas to the syntax of those back-end provers. This translation includes a non-trivial removal of polymorphic sorts when the target logic does not support polymorphism [3].

3 Krakatoa and Caduceus

The common approach to Java and C source code is to translate them into Why programs. The Why specification language is then used both for the translation of input annotations and for the modeling of Java objects (resp. C pointers/structures). This model of the memory heap is defined by introducing abstract data types together with operations and an appropriate first-order axiomatization. Our heap memory models for C and Java both follow the principle of the Burstall-Bornat 'component-as-array' model [4]. Each Java object field (resp. C structure field) becomes a *Why mutable variable* containing a purely applicative map. This map is equipped with an access function *select* so that $select(f, p)$ denotes the field of the structure pointed-to by p; and an update function *store* so that $store(f, p, v)$ denotes a new map f' identical to f except at position p where it has value v. These two functions satisfy the so-called *theory of arrays*:

$$select(store(f, p, v), p) = p$$
$$p \neq p' \rightarrow select(store(f, p, v), p') = select(f, p')$$

For the example of Figure 2, the translation of the statement `p->balance += s` into the Why language is (1) $balance := store(balance, p, select(balance, p) + s)$. The translation of the postcondition `balance == \old(balance)+s` is $select(balance, p) = select(balance@, p) + s$ (where in Why, $x@$ denotes the old value of x) and its weakest precondition through (1) is $select(store(balance, p, select(balance, p) + s), p) = select(balance, p) + s$ which is a first-order consequence of the theory of arrays.

4 Past and Future Work

The heap memory models are original, in particular with the handling of assigns clauses [5], and C pointer arithmetic [6]. Since these publications, many improvements have been made on the platform:

- Improved efficiency, including a separation analysis [7].
- More tools, including a graphical interface.
- Support for more provers, e.g. SMT provers (Yices, RV-sat, CVC3, etc.) and Ergo, with encodings of polymorphic sorts as seen above.
- Enhancements of specification languages both for C and Java: ghost variables, axiomatic models

- Specifically to Krakatoa, more support for Java Card source: transactions [8].
- Support for floating-point arithmetic [9].

Several case studies have been conducted: Java Card applets provided by Axalto [10] and Trusted Logic companies; the Schorr-Waite graph-marking algorithm, considered as a challenge for program verification [11]; some avionics embedded code provided by Dassault aviation company, which leaded to an original analysis of memory separation [7]. Our intermediate first-order specification language was also used to design abstract models of programs [12].

To conclude, our platform is tailored to the proof of advanced behavioral specifications and proposes an original approach based on an intermediate first-order specification language. Its main characteristic is versatility: multi-prover output, multi-source input, on-the-fly generation of first-order models.

Future work includes the development of an integrated user environment. We are also designing an improved support for abstract modeling, by providing (UML-like) higher-level models and refinement. A key issue for the future is also the automatic generation of annotations. Long term perspective is to contribute to Grand Challenge 6 on Verified Software Repository: a key goal for us is to build libraries of verified software.

Acknowledgements. Many people have been involved in the design and development of the platform and the case studies: R. Bardou, S. Boldo, V. Chaudhary, S. Conchon, E. Contejean, J.-F. Couchot, M. Dogguy, G. Dufay, N. Guenot, T. Hubert, J. Kanig, S. Lescuyer, Y. Moy, A. Oudot, C. Paulin, J. Roussel, N. Rousset, X. Urbain.

References

1. Burdy, L., Cheon, Y., Cok, D., Ernst, M., Kiniry, J., Leavens, G.T., Leino, K.R.M., Poll, E.: An overview of JML tools and applications. International Journal on Software Tools for Technology Transfer (2004)
2. Filliâtre, J.C.: Verification of non-functional programs using interpretations in type theory. Journal of Functional Programming 13(4), 709–745 (2003)
3. Couchot, J.F., Lescuyer, S.: Handling polymorphism in automated deduction. In: CADE-21, Springer, Heidelberg (2007)
4. Bornat, R.: Proving pointer programs in Hoare logic. In: Mathematics of Program Construction, 102–126 (2000)
5. Marché, C., Paulin-Mohring, C.: Reasoning about Java programs with aliasing and frame conditions. In: Hurd, J., Melham, T. (eds.) TPHOLs 2005. LNCS, vol. 3603, Springer, Heidelberg (2005)
6. Filliâtre, J.C., Marché, C.: Multi-prover verification of C programs. In: Davies, J., Schulte, W., Barnett, M. (eds.) ICFEM 2004. LNCS, vol. 3308, pp. 15–29. Springer, Heidelberg (2004)
7. Hubert, T., Marché, C.: Separation analysis for deductive verification. In: Heap Analysis and Verification (HAV'07) (2007)
8. Marché, C., Rousset, N.: Verification of Java Card applets behavior with respect to transactions and card tears. In: SEFM'06, IEEE Computer Society Press, Los Alamitos (2006)

9. Boldo, S., Filliâtre, J.C.: Formal Verification of Floating-Point Programs. In: ARITH'07 (2007)
10. Jacobs, B., Marché, C., Rauch, N.: Formal verification of a commercial smart card applet with multiple tools. In: Rattray, C., Maharaj, S., Shankland, C. (eds.) AMAST 2004. LNCS, vol. 3116, Springer, Heidelberg (2004)
11. Hubert, T., Marché, C.: A case study of C source code verification: the Schorr-Waite algorithm. In: SEFM'05, IEEE Computer Society Press, Los Alamitos (2005)
12. Filliâtre, J.C.: Queens on a Chessboard: an Exercise in Program Verification (2007), http://why.lri.fr/queens/

Shape Analysis for Composite Data Structures

Josh Berdine[1], Cristiano Calcagno[2], Byron Cook[1], Dino Distefano[3],
Peter W. O'Hearn[3], Thomas Wies[4], and Hongseok Yang[3]

[1] Microsoft Research
[2] Imperial College
[3] Queen Mary
[4] University of Freiburg

Abstract. We propose a shape analysis that adapts to some of the complex composite data structures found in industrial systems-level programs. Examples of such data structures include "cyclic doubly-linked lists of acyclic singly-linked lists", "singly-linked lists of cyclic doubly-linked lists with back-pointers to head nodes", etc. The analysis introduces the use of generic higher-order inductive predicates describing spatial relationships together with a method of synthesizing new parameterized spatial predicates which can be used in combination with the higher-order predicates. In order to evaluate the proposed approach for realistic programs we have performed experiments on examples drawn from device drivers: the analysis proved safety of the data structure manipulation of several routines belonging to an IEEE 1394 (firewire) driver, and also found several previously unknown memory safety bugs.

1 Introduction

Shape analyses are program analyses which aim to be accurate in the presence of deep-heap update. They go beyond aliasing or points-to relationships to infer properties such as whether a variable points to a cyclic or acyclic linked list (*e.g.*, [6, 8, 11, 12]). Unfortunately, today's shape analysis engines fail to support many of the composite data structures used within industrial software. If the input program happens only to use the data structures for which the analysis is defined (usually unnested lists in which the field for forward pointers is specified beforehand), then the analysis is often successful. If, on the other hand, the input program is mutating a complex composite data structure such as a "singly-linked list of structures which each point to five cyclic doubly-linked lists in which each node in the singly-linked list contains a back-pointer to the head of the list" (and furthermore the list types are using a variety of field names for forward/backward pointers), most shape analyses will fail to deliver informative results. Instead, in these cases, the tools typically report false declarations of memory-safety violations when there are none. This is one of the key reasons why shape analysis has to date had only a limited impact on industrial code.

In order to make shape analysis generally applicable to industrial software we need methods by which shape analyses can adapt to the combinations of data structures used within these programs. Towards a solution to this problem,

W. Damm and H. Hermanns (Eds.): CAV 2007, LNCS 4590, pp. 178–192, 2007.

we propose a new shape analysis that dynamically adapts to the types of data structures encountered in systems-level code.

In this paper we make two novel technical contributions. We first propose a new abstract domain which includes a higher-order inductive predicate that specifies a family of linear data structures. We then propose a method that synthesizes new parameterized spatial predicates from old predicates using information found in the abstract states visited during the execution of the analysis. The new predicates can be defined using instances of the inductive predicate in combination with previously synthesized predicates, thus allowing our abstract domain to express a variety of complex data structures.

We have tested our approach on set of small (*i.e.* <100 LOC) examples representative of those found in systems-level code. We have also performed a case study: applying the analysis to data-structure manipulating routines found in a Windows IEEE 1394 (firewire) device driver. Our analysis proved safety of the data structure manipulation in a number of cases, and found several previously unknown memory-safety violations in cases where the analysis failed to prove memory safety.

Related work. A few shape analyses have been defined that can deal with more general forms of nesting. For example, the tool described in [7] infers new inductive data-structure definitions during analysis. Here, we take a different tack. We focus on a single inductive predicate which can be instantiated in multiple ways using higher-order predicates. What is discovered here is the predicates for instantiation. The expressiveness of the two approaches is incomparable. [7] can handle varieties of trees, where the specific abstraction given in this paper cannot. Conversely, our domain supports doubly-linked list segments and lists of cyclic lists with back-pointers, where [7] cannot due to the fact that these data structures require inductive definitions with more than two parameters and the abstract domain of [7] cannot express such definitions.

The parametric shape analysis framework of [9, 16] can in principle describe any finite abstract domain: there must exist some collection of instrumentation predicates that could describe a range of nested structures. Indeed, it could be the case that the work of [10], which uses machine learning to find instrumentation predicates, would be able in principle to infer predicates precise enough for the kinds of examples in this paper. The real question is whether or not the resulting collection of instrumentation predicates would be costly to maintain (whether in TVLA or by other means). There has been preliminary work on instrumentation predicates for composite structures [14], but as far as we are aware it has not been implemented or otherwise evaluated experimentally.

Work on analysis of complex structures using regular model checking includes an example on a list of lists [3]. The encoding scheme in [3] seems capable of describing many of the kinds of structure considered in this paper; again, the pertinent question is about the cost of the subsequent fixed-point calculation. It would be interesting to apply that analysis to a wider range of test programs.

A recent paper [17] also considers a generalized notion of linear data structure. It synthesizes patterns from heap configurations in a way that has some similarities with our predicate discovery method, in particular in generalizing repeated subgraphs with a kind of list structure. However, unlike ours, the abstract domain in [17] does not treat nested data structures such as lists of lists.

2 Synthesized Predicates and General Induction Schemes

The analysis described in this paper fits into the common structure of shape analyses based on abstract interpretation (*e.g.* [15, 16]) in which a fixed-point computation performs *symbolic execution* (*a.k.a.* update) together with *focusing* (*a.k.a.* rearrangement or coercion) to partially concretize abstract heaps and *abstraction* (*a.k.a.* canonicalization or blurring) to aid convergence to a fixed point. In this work we use a representation of abstract states based on separation logic formulæ, building on the methods of [1, 4].

There are two key technical ideas used in our new analysis:

Generic inductive spatial predicates: We define a new abstract domain which uses a higher-order generalization of the list predicates considered in the literature on separation logic.[1] In effect, we propose using a restricted subset of a higher-order version of separation logic [2]. The list predicate used in our analysis, ls Λ (x, y, z, w), describes a (possibly empty, possibly cyclic, possibly doubly-) linked list segment where each node in the segment itself is a data structure (*e.g.* a singly-linked list of doubly-linked lists) described by Λ. The ls predicate allows us to describe lists of lists or lists of structs of lists, for example, by an appropriate choice of Λ.

Synthesized parameterized non-recursive predicates: The abstraction phase of the analysis, which simplifies the symbolic representations of heaps, in our case is also designed to *discover new predicates* which are then fed as parameters to the higher-order inductive (summary) predicates, thereby triggering further simplifications. It is this predicate discovery aspect that gives our analysis its adaptive flavor.

Example. Fig. 1 shows a heap configuration typical of a Windows device driver. This configuration can be found, for example, in the Windows device driver supporting IEEE 1394 (firewire) devices, 1394DIAG.SYS. In this figure the pointer devObj is a pointer to a *device object*, defined by a Windows kernel structure called DEVICE_OBJECT. Each device object has a pointer to a *device extension*, which is used in essence as a method of polymorphism: device drivers declare their own driver-specific device extension type. In the case of 1394DIAG.SYS, the device extension is named DEVICE_EXTENSION and is defined to hold a number of locks, lists, and other data. For simplicity, in Fig. 1 we have depicted only three of the five cyclic doubly-linked lists in DEVICE_EXTENSION. Two of the three circular lists contain nested acyclic lists, and the nodes of these two lists have pointers back to the shared header DEVICE_EXTENSION. A subtle point is

---

[1] In this paper we concentrate on varieties of linked list, motivated by problems in device drivers, but the basic ideas might also be applied with other structures.

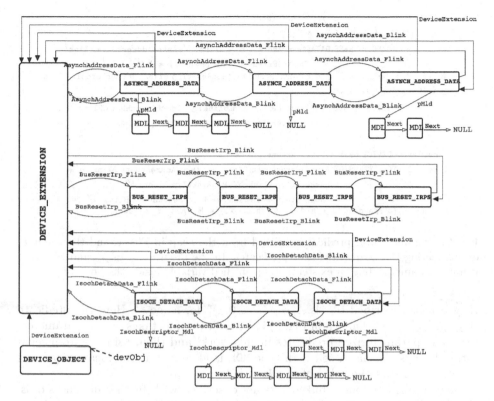

Fig. 1. Device driver-like heap configuration

that these nested lists (via `pMdl` or `IsochDescriptor_Mdl`) can be either empty or nonempty. This requires using a Λ in $\mathsf{ls}\ \Lambda\ (x, y, z, w)$ that covers both empty and nonempty linked lists; in contrast, when dealing with lists without nesting, it was possible to consider nonempty lists only [4].

There is further nesting that the kernel can see, that we have not depicted in the diagram. Each `DEVICE_OBJECT` participates in two further linked lists, one a list of all firewire drivers connected to a system, and the other a stack containing various drivers. This yields a "lists of lists of lists" nesting structure. More significantly, since `DEVICE_OBJECT` nodes participate in different linked lists we have overlapping structures, resulting in "deep sharing" reminiscent of that found in graphs. It is possible to write a logical formula to describe such structures. But, as far as we are aware, a tractable treatment of deep sharing remains an open problem in shape analysis. This paper is no different. Our abstract domain can describe nesting of disjoint sublists, but not overlapping structures. We state this just to be clear about this limitation of our approach.

When the abstraction step from our analysis is applied to the heap in Fig. 1 several predicates are discovered. Consider the singly-linked lists coming out of nodes in the first and third doubly-linked lists. Fig. 1 shows six of those lists, two of which are empty. These lists consist of C structures of type MDL, and

$\Lambda_{MDL} \triangleq \lambda[x', y', z', w', ()].\, x{=}w' \wedge x' \mapsto \text{MDL}(\text{Next}: z')$

$\Lambda_{Async} \triangleq \lambda[x', y', z', w', (e')].\, x'{=}w' \wedge$

$\qquad\qquad x' \mapsto \text{ASYNC\_ADDRESS\_DATA}(\text{AsyncAddressData\_Blink}: y', \text{AsyncAddressData\_Flink}: z',$

$\qquad\qquad\qquad\qquad\qquad \text{DeviceExtension}: \text{de}, \text{pMdl}: e') \,*\, \text{ls}\, \Lambda_{MDL}\, (e', \_, 0, \_)$

$\Lambda_{Bus} \triangleq \lambda[x', y', z', w', ()].\, x'{=}w' \wedge x'{\mapsto}\text{BUS\_RESET\_IRP}(\text{BusResetIrp\_Blink}: y', \text{BusResetIrp\_Flink}: z')$

$\Lambda_{Isoch} \triangleq \lambda[x', y', z', w', (e')].\, x'{=}w' \wedge$

$\qquad\qquad x' \mapsto \text{ISOCH\_DETACH\_DATA}(\text{IsochDetachData\_Blink}: y', \text{IsochDetachData\_Flink}: z',$

$\qquad\qquad\qquad\qquad\qquad \text{DeviceExtension}: \text{de}, \text{IsochDescriptor\_Mdl}: e') \,*$

$\qquad\qquad \text{ls}\, \Lambda_{MDL}\, (e', \_, 0, \_)$

$H \quad\triangleq \text{devObj} \mapsto \text{DEVICE\_OBJECT}(\text{DeviceExtension}: \text{de}) \,*$

$\qquad \text{de} \mapsto \text{DEVICE\_EXTENSION}(\text{AsyncAddressData\_Flink}: a', \text{AsyncAddressData\_Blink}: a'',$

$\qquad\qquad\qquad \text{BusResetIrp\_Flink}: b', \text{BusResetIrp\_Blink}: b'',$

$\qquad\qquad\qquad \text{IsochDetachData\_Flink}: i', \text{IsochDetachData\_Blink}: i'') \,*$

$\qquad \text{ls}\, \Lambda_{Async}\, (a', \text{de}, \text{de}, a'') \,*\, \text{ls}\, \Lambda_{Bus}\, (b', \text{de}, \text{de}, b'') \,*\, \text{ls}\, \Lambda_{Isoch}\, (i', \text{de}, \text{de}, i'')$

Fig. 2. Parameterized predicates inferred from the heap in Fig. 1, and the result H of abstracting the heap with those predicates. In the predicates Λ_{Async} and Λ_{Isoch}, e' is not a parameter, but an existentially quantified variable inside the body of Λ.

they can be described by "$\text{ls}\, \Lambda_{MDL}\, (e', \_, 0, \_)$" for some e'. Here the predicate $\Lambda_{MDL}(x', y', z', w')$ (shown in Fig. 2) is a predicate that takes in four parameters (as do all parameterized predicates in this work) and then, using $\mapsto$ from separation logic, says that a cell with type MDL is allocated at the location pointed to by x', and that the value of the Next field is equal to z'.

Next, the three doubly-linked lists are described with further instances of ls, obtained from predicates Λ_{Async}, Λ_{Bus}, and Λ_{Isoch} in Fig. 2. Λ_{Async} and Λ_{Isoch} describe nodes which have pointers to the header de, and which also point to nested singly-linked lists. Those predicates are built from Λ_{MDL}, a parameterized predicate for describing singly-linked lists.

The original heap is covered by the separation logic formula H in Fig. 2. The separating conjunction $*$ is used to describe three distinct doubly-linked lists which themselves are disjoint from structures de and devObj. In reading these formulæ, it is crucial to realize that the device extension, de, is not one of the nodes in the portion of memory described by any of the three $*$-conjuncts at the bottom. For instance, $\text{ls}\, \Lambda_{Async}\, (a', \text{de}, \text{de}, a'')$ describes a "partial" doubly-linked list from a' to a'', with an incoming pointer from de to a' and an outgoing pointer from a'' to de. Circularity in this case is decomposed into the $*$-composition of a single node, de, and an acyclic structure. The formula H is more abstract than the beginning heap in that the lengths of the doubly-linked lists and of nested singly-linked lists have been forgotten: this formula is also satisfied by heaps similar to that in Fig. 1 but of different size.

3   Symbolic Heaps with Higher-Order Predicates

We now define the abstract domain of symbolic heaps over which our analysis is defined. Let Var be a finite set of program variables, and Var' be an infinite set of variables disjoint from *Var*. We use *Var'* as a source of auxiliary variables to represent quantification, parameters to predicates, etc. Let *Fld* be a finite set of field names and *Loc* be a set of memory locations.

In this paper, we consider the storage model given by $Stack \triangleq (Var \cup Var') \rightarrow Val$, $Heap \triangleq Loc \rightarrow_{\mathsf{fin}} (Fld \rightharpoonup Val)$, and $States \triangleq Stack \times Heap$. Thus, a state consists of a stack s and a heap h, where the stack s specifies the values of program (non-primed) variables as well as those of auxiliary (primed) variables. In our model, each heap cell stores a whole structure; when $h(l)$ is defined, it is a partial function k where the domain of k specifies the set of fields declared in the structure l, and the action of k specifies the values of those fields.

Our analysis uses symbolic heaps specified by the following grammar:

$x \in Var$		variables
$x' \in Var'$		primed variables
$f \in Fld$		fields
$E ::= x \mid x' \mid \mathsf{nil}$		expressions
$\Pi ::= \mathsf{true} \mid E{=}E \mid E{\neq}E \mid \Pi \wedge \Pi$		pure formulæ
$\Sigma ::= \mathsf{emp} \mid \Sigma * \Sigma \mid E{\mapsto}T(\vec{f}\colon \vec{E}) \mid \mathsf{ls}\, \Lambda\, (E, E, E, E) \mid \mathsf{true}$	spatial formulæ
$H ::= \Pi \wedge \Sigma$		symbolic heaps
$\Lambda ::= \lambda[x', x', x', x', \vec{x}'].\, H$		par. symb. heaps

When $\Lambda = \lambda[x', y', z', w', \vec{v}'].\, H$, we could have written $\Lambda(x', y', z', w', \vec{v}') = H$. We write $\Lambda[D, E, F, G, \vec{C}]$ for the symbolic heap obtained by instantiating Λ's parameters: $(\lambda[x', y', z', w', \vec{v}'].\, H)[D, E, F, G, \vec{C}] = H[D/x', E/y', F/z', G/w', \vec{C}/\vec{v}']$.

The predicate "$\mathsf{ls}\, \Lambda\, (I_f, O_b, O_f, I_b)$" represents a segment of a (generic) doubly-linked list, where the shape of each node in the list is described by the first parameter Λ (*i.e.*, each node satisfies this parameter), and some links between this segment and the rest of the heap are specified by the other parameters. Parameters I_f (the *forward input link*) and I_b (the *backward input link*) denote the (externally visible) memory locations of the first and last nodes of the list segment. The analysis maintains the links from the outside to these exposed cells, so that the links can be used, say, to traverse the segment. Usually, I_f denotes the address of the "root" of a data structure representing the first node, such as the head of a singly-linked list. The common use of I_b is similar. Parameters O_b (called *backward output link*) and O_f (called *forward output link*) represent links from (the first and last nodes of) the list segment to the outside, which the analysis decides to maintain. Pictorially this can be viewed as:

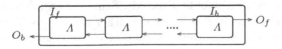

When lists are cyclic, we will have $O_f{=}I_f$ and $O_b{=}I_b$.

Generalized ls. The formal definition of ls is given as follows. For a parameterized symbolic heap Λ, ls Λ (I_f, O_b, O_f, I_b) is the least predicate that holds iff

$$(I_f = O_f \wedge I_b = O_b \wedge \mathsf{emp}) \vee (\exists x', y', \vec{z'}. \ (\Lambda[I_f, O_b, x', y', \vec{z'}]) * \mathsf{ls} \ \Lambda \ (x', y', O_f, I_b))$$

where $x', y', \vec{z'}$ are chosen fresh. A list segment is empty, or it consists of a node described by an instantiation of Λ and a tail satisfying ls Λ (x', y', O_f, I_b). Note that Λ is allowed to have free primed or non-primed variables. They are used to express the links from the nodes that are targeted for the same address, such as head pointers common to every element of the list.

Examples. The generic list predicate can express a variety of data structures:

- When Λ_s is $\lambda[x', y', z', x', ()]. \ (x' \mapsto \mathsf{Node}(\mathsf{Next}\colon z'))$ then the symbolic heap ls Λ_s (x, y', z, w') describes a standard singly-linked list segment from x to z. (Here note how we use the syntactic shorthand of including x' twice in the parameters instead of adding an equality to the predicate body.)
- A standard doubly-linked list segment is expressed by ls Λ_d (x, y, z, w) when Λ_d is $\lambda[x', y', z', x', ()]. \ x' \mapsto \mathsf{DNode}(\mathsf{Blink}\colon y', \mathsf{Flink}\colon z')$.
- If Λ_h is $\lambda[x', y', z', x', ()]. \ x' \mapsto \mathsf{HNode}(\mathsf{Next}\colon z', \mathsf{Head}\colon k)$, the symbolic heap ls Λ_h $(x, y', \mathsf{nil}, w')$ expresses a nil-terminated singly-linked list x where each element has a head pointer to location k.
- Finally, when Λ is

$$\lambda[x', y', z', x', (v', u')].$$
$$x' \mapsto \mathsf{SDNode}(\mathsf{Next}\colon z', \mathsf{Blink}\colon u', \mathsf{Flink}\colon v') * \mathsf{ls} \ \Lambda_d \ (v', x', x', u')$$

then ls Λ $(x, y', \mathsf{nil}, w')$ describes a singly-linked list of cyclic doubly-linked lists where each singly-linked list node is the sentinel node of the cyclic doubly-linked list.

Abstract domain. Let $\mathsf{FV}(X)$ be the non-primed variables occurring in X and $\mathsf{FV}'(X)$ be the primed variables. Let $\mathsf{close}(H)$ be an operation which existentially quantifies all the free primed variables in H (*i.e.* $\mathsf{close}(H) \triangleq \exists \mathsf{FV}'(H). H$). We use $\vDash$ to mean semantic entailment (*i.e.* that any concrete state satisfying the antecedent also satisfies the consequent). The meaning of a symbolic heap H (*i.e.* set of concrete states H represents) is defined to be the set of states that satisfy $\mathsf{close}(H)$ in the standard semantics [13]. Our analysis assumes a sound theorem prover $\vdash$, where $H \vdash H'$ implies $H \vDash \mathsf{close}(H')$. The abstract domain $\mathcal{D}^{\#}$ of our analysis is given by: $\mathcal{SH} \triangleq \{H \mid H \nvdash \mathsf{false}\}$ and $\mathcal{D}^{\#} \triangleq \mathcal{P}(\mathcal{SH})^{\top}$. That is, the abstract domain is the powerset of symbolic heaps with the usual subset order, extended with an additional greatest element $\top$ (indicating a memory-safety violation such as a double disposal). Semantic entailment $\vDash$ can be lifted to $\mathcal{D}^{\#}$ as follows: $d \vDash d'$ if d' is $\top$, or if neither d nor d' is $\top$ and any concrete state that satisfies the (semantic) disjunction $\bigvee d$ also satisfies $\bigvee d'$.

4   Canonicalization

As is standard, our shape analysis computes an invariant assertion for each program point expressed by an element of the abstract domain. This computation is accomplished via fixed-point iteration of an abstract post operator that over-approximates the concrete semantics of the program.

The abstract semantics consists of three phases: materialization, execution, and canonicalization. That is, the abstract post $[\![C]\!]$ for some loop-free concrete command C is given by the composition $materialize_C$; $execute_C$; $canonicalize$. First, $materialize_C$ partially concretizes an abstract state into a set of abstract states such that, in each, the footprint of C (that portion of the heap that C may access) is concrete. Then, $execute_C$ is the pointwise lift of symbolically executing each abstract state individually. Finally, $canonicalize$ abstracts each abstract state in effort to help the analysis find a fixed point.

The materialization and execution operations of [1, 4] are easily modified for our setting. In contrast, the canonicalization operator for our abstract domain significantly departs from [4] and forms the crux of our analysis. We describe it in the remainder of this section.

Canonicalization performs a form of over-approximation by soundly removing some information from a given symbolic heap. It is defined by the rewriting rules ($\leadsto$) in Fig. 3. Canonicalization applies those rewriting rules to a given symbolic heap according to a specific strategy until no rules apply; the resulting symbolic heap is called *canonical*.

The AppendLeft and AppendRight rules (for the two ends of a list) roll up the inductive predicate, thereby building new lists by appending one list onto another. Note that the appended lists may be single nodes (*i.e.* singleton lists). Crucially, in each case we should be able to use the same parameterized predicate Λ to describe both of the to-be-merged entities: The canonicalization rules build homogeneous lists of Λ's. The variable side-conditions on the rules are necessary for precision but not soundness; they prevent the rules from firing too often.

The Predicate Intro rule from Fig. 3 represents a novel aspect of our canonicalization procedure. It requires a predicate Λ that can be used to describe similar portions of heap, and two appropriately connected Λ nodes are removed from the symbolic heap and replaced with an ls Λ formula. The function Preds in the rule takes a symbolic heap as an argument and returns a set of predicates Λ. It is a parameter of our analysis. One possible choice for Preds is "fixed abstraction", where a fixed finite collection of predicates is given beforehand, and Λ is drawn from that fixed collection. Another approach is to consider an "adaptive abstraction", where the predicates Λ are inferred by scrutinizing the linking structure in symbolic heaps encountered during analysis. There is a tradeoff here: the fixed abstraction is simpler and can be effective, but requires more input from the user. We describe an approach to adaptive abstraction in the next section.

There is one further issue to consider in implementing the Predicate Intro rule. The first has to do with the entailment $H_0 \vdash -$ in the premise of the rule. We require a *frame inferring theorem prover* [1]—a prover for entailments $H_0 \vdash H_1 * H_2$ where only H_0 and H_2 are given and H_1 is inferred. While the aim

Define spatial$(\Pi \wedge \Sigma)$ to be Σ.

$$\frac{}{E{=}x' \wedge H \;\rightsquigarrow\; H[E/x']} \;(\text{Equality}) \qquad \frac{x' \notin \text{FV}'(\text{spatial}(H))}{E{\neq}x' \wedge H \;\rightsquigarrow\; H} \;(\text{Disequality})$$

$$\frac{\text{FV}(I_f, I_b) = \emptyset \qquad \text{FV}'(I_f, I_b) \cap \text{FV}'(\text{spatial}(H)) = \emptyset}{H * \text{ls } \Lambda \; (I_f, O_b, O_f, I_b) \;\rightsquigarrow\; H * \text{true}} \;(\text{Junk 1})$$

$$\frac{\text{FV}(E) = \emptyset \qquad \text{FV}'(E) \cap \text{FV}'(\text{spatial}(H)) = \emptyset}{H * (E \mapsto T(\vec{f}\colon \vec{E})) \;\rightsquigarrow\; H * \text{true}} \;(\text{Junk 2})$$

$$\frac{H_0 \;\vdash\; H_1 * \text{ls } \Lambda \; (I_f, O_b, x', y') \wedge I_f \neq x' \qquad \{x', y'\} \cap \text{FV}'(\text{spatial}(H_1)) \subseteq \{I_f, I_b\}}{H_0 * \text{ls } \Lambda \; (x', y', O_f, I_b) \;\rightsquigarrow\; H_1 * \text{ls } \Lambda \; (I_f, O_b, O_f, I_b)} \;(\text{Append Left})$$

$$\frac{H_0 \;\vdash\; H_1 * \text{ls } \Lambda \; (x', y', O_f, I_b) \wedge x' \neq O_f \qquad \{x', y'\} \cap \text{FV}'(\text{spatial}(H_1)) \subseteq \{I_f, I_b\}}{H_0 * \text{ls } \Lambda \; (I_f, O_b, x', y') \;\rightsquigarrow\; H_1 * \text{ls } \Lambda \; (I_f, O_b, O_f, I_b)} \;(\text{Append Right})$$

$$\frac{\begin{array}{c}\Lambda \in \text{Preds}(H_0) \qquad H_0 \;\vdash\; H_1 * \Lambda[I_f, O_b, x', y', \vec{u'}] * \Lambda[x', y', O_f, I_b, \vec{v'}] \\ (\{x', y'\} \cup \vec{u'} \cup \vec{v'}) \cap \text{FV}'(\text{spatial}(H)) \subseteq \{I_f, I_b\}\end{array}}{H_0 \;\rightsquigarrow\; H_1 * \text{ls } \Lambda \; (I_f, O_b, O_f, I_b)} \;(\text{Predicate Intro})$$

Fig. 3. Rules for Canonicalization

of a frame inferring theorem prover is to find a decomposition of H_0 into H_1 and H_2 such that the entailment holds, frame inference should just decompose the formula, not weaken it (or else frame inference could always return $H_1 = \text{true}$). So for a call to frame inference, we not only require the entailment to hold, but also require that there exists a disjoint extension of the heap satisfying H_2, and the extended heap satisfies H_0.[2]

There is a progress measure for the rewrite rules, so $\rightsquigarrow$ is strongly normalizing. The crucial fact underlying soundness is that all canonicalization rules correspond to true implications in separation logic, *i.e.* we have that $H \vDash H'$ whenever $H \rightsquigarrow H'$. This means that however we choose to apply the rules, we will always maintain soundness of the analysis. In particular, soundness is independent of the choice of the Preds function used in the Predicate Intro rule.

There are two sources of nondeterminism in the $\rightsquigarrow$ relation: the choice of order in which rules are applied, and the choice of which Λ to use in the Predicate Intro rule. The latter appears to be much more significant in practice than the former. In the implementation we have used a deterministic reduction strategy with no backtracking. But changes in the strategy for choosing Λ can have a dramatic impact on the performance and precision of the analysis algorithm.

5   Predicate Discovery

We now give a particular specification of the Preds function in the (Predicate Intro) rule, based on the idea of similar repeated subgraphs. We emphasize that the graph

---

[2] Different strengths of prover $\vdash$ can be considered. A weak one would essentially just do graph decomposition for frame inference.

view of a symbolic heap is intuitive but does not need semantic analysis here: as we indicated above, soundness of the analysis is independent of Preds. We are just describing one particular instance of Preds, which might be viewed as an heuristic constraint on the choice of new predicates.

The idea is to treat the spatial part of a symbolic heap H as a graph, where each atomic $*$-conjunct in H becomes a node in the graph; for instance, $E \mapsto T(\vec{f} \colon \vec{E})$ becomes a node E with outgoing edges $\vec{E}$. The algorithm starts by looking for nodes that are connected together by some fields, in a way that they can in principle become the forward and/or backward links of a list. Call these potential candidates root nodes, say E_l and E_r. Once root nodes are found, the procedure Preds(H) traverses the graph from E_l as well as from E_r simultaneously, and checks whether those two traverses can produce two disjoint isomorphic subgraphs. The shape defined by these subparts is then generalized to give the definition of the general pattern of their shape which provides the definition of the newly discovered predicate Λ. Preds(H) returns the candidate heaps for use in the (Predicate Intro) rule.

```
discover(H : symbolic heap) : predicate =
    let Σ = spatial(H)
    let Σ_Λ = emp
    let I = ∅ : set of expression pairs
    let C = ∅ : multiset of expression pairs
    choose (E_l, E_r) ∈ {(E_l, E_r) | Σ = E_l↦f : E_r * E_r↦f : E * Σ'}
    let W = {(E_l, E_r)} : multiset of expression pairs
    do
        choose (E_0, E_1) ∈ W
        if E_0 ≠ E_1 then
            if (E_0, E_1) ∉ C ∧ E_0 ∉ rng(I) ∧ E_1 ∉ dom(I) then
                if Σ ⊢ P(E_0, F⃗_0) * P(E_1, F⃗_1) * Σ' then
                    W := W ∪ {(F_{0,0}, F_{1,0}), . . . , (F_{0,n}, F_{1,n})}
                    I := I ∪ {(E_0, E_1)}
                    Σ := Σ'
                    Σ_Λ := Σ_Λ * P(E_0, F⃗_0)
                else fail
            C := C ∪ {(E_0, E_1)}
        W := W − {(E_0, E_1)}
    until W = ∅
    let I⃗_f, O⃗_f = [(E, F) | ∃G. (F, G) ∈ C ∧ (E, F) ∈ I]
    let I⃗_b, O⃗_b = [(E, F) | ∃G. (F, E) ∈ C ∧ (E, G) ∈ I]
    let x⃗' = FV'(Σ_Λ) − FV'(I⃗_f, O⃗_f, I⃗_b, O⃗_b)
    return (λ(I⃗_f, O⃗_b, O⃗_f, I⃗_b, x⃗'). Σ_Λ)
```

Fig. 4. Predicate discovery algorithm, where Preds(H) = {P | P = discover(H)}

Fig. 4 shows the pseudocode for the discovery algorithm. So far we have, in the interest of clarity, dealt with Λ's with parameters such as $x', y', z', w', \vec{v}'$, however in this section we admit that the analysis actually treats the more general situation where there are multiple links between nodes, and so predicates take parameters $\vec{x}', \vec{y}', \vec{z}', \vec{w}', \vec{v}'$. The algorithm is expressed as a nondeterministic

Table 1. Example run of discovery algorithm

Input symbolic heap
$H = x'_0 \mapsto T(f: x'_1, g: y'_0) * x'_1 \mapsto T(f: x'_2, g: y'_1) * x'_2 \mapsto T(f: x'_3, g: y'_2) *$
$\text{ls } \Lambda_1 (y'_0, \text{nil}, z'_1, \text{nil}) * y'_1 \mapsto S(f: \text{nil}, b: x'_0) * \text{ls } \Lambda_1 (y'_2, x'_1, z'_2, \text{nil})$
where $\Lambda_1 = (\lambda(x'_1, x'_0, x'_2, x'_1). x'_1 \mapsto S(f: x'_2, b: x'_0))$

#Iters	W	C	I	Σ_Λ
0	$\{(x'_1, x'_2)\}$	$\emptyset$	$\emptyset$	emp
1	$\{(x'_2, x'_3), (y'_1, y'_2)\}$	$\{(x'_1, x'_2)\}$	$\{(x'_1, x'_2)\}$	$x'_1 \mapsto T(f: x'_2, g: y'_1)$
2	$\{(y'_1, y'_2)\}$	$\{(x'_1, x'_2), (x'_2, x'_3)\}$	$\{(x'_1, x'_2)\}$	$x'_1 \mapsto T(f: x'_2, g: y'_1)$
3	$\{(x'_0, x'_1)\}$	$\{(x'_1, x'_2), (x'_2, x'_3),$ $(y'_1, y'_2)\}$	$\{(x'_1, x'_2), (y'_1, y'_2)\}$	$x'_1 \mapsto T(f: x'_2, g: y'_1) *$ $\text{ls } \Lambda_1 (y'_1, x'_0, z'_1, \text{nil})$
4	$\emptyset$	$\{(x'_1, x'_2), (x'_2, x'_3),$ $(y'_1, y'_2), (x'_0, x'_1)\}$	$\{(x'_1, x'_2), (y'_1, y'_2)\}$	$x_1 \mapsto T(f: x'_2, g: y'_1) *$ $\text{ls } \Lambda_1 (y'_1, x'_0, z'_1, \text{nil})$

Discovered predicate
$\lambda(x'_1, x'_0, x'_2, x'_1, (y'_1, z'_1)). x'_1 \mapsto T(f: x'_2, g: y'_1) * \text{ls } \Lambda_1 (y'_1, x'_0, z'_1, \text{nil})$

function, using **choose** twice. Preds then collects the set of all possible results, for instance by enumerating through the nondeterministic choices. The set I denotes the subgraph isomorphism between the already traversed subgraphs reachable from the chosen root nodes. The algorithm ensures that the two traverses are disjoint. Here $dom(I)$ denotes the projection of I to the left traverse starting from root node E_l, respectively $rng(I)$ denotes the right traverse starting from E_r. The set C marks how often each pair of nodes is reachable from the two root nodes. It is used for cycle detection and ensures termination of the traversal.

Whenever a new pair of nodes E_0, E_1 in the graph is discovered, the algorithm needs to check whether they actually correspond to $*$-conjuncts of the same shape. The simplest solution would be to check for syntactic equality. Unfortunately, this makes the discovery heuristic rather weak, *e.g.* we would not be able to discover the list of lists predicate from a list where the sublists are alternating between proper list segments and singleton instances of the sublist predicate. Instead of syntactic equality our algorithm therefore uses the theorem prover to check that the two nodes have the same shape. If they are not syntactically equal, then the theorem prover tries to generalize it via frame inference:

$$\Sigma \vdash P(E_0, \vec{F_0}) * P(E_1, \vec{F_1}) * \Sigma' .$$

Here the predicate $P(E, \vec{F})$ stands for either a points-to predicate or a list segment $\text{ls } \Lambda (\vec{I_f}, \vec{O_b}, \vec{O_f}, \vec{I_b})$ where $E \in \vec{I_f} \cup \vec{I_b}$ and $\vec{F} = \vec{O_f}, \vec{O_b}$. The generalized shape $P(E_0, \vec{F_0})$ of the node in the left traverse then contributes to the spatial part of the discovered predicate.

Once the body of the predicate is complete the parameter list is constructed to determine forward and backward links between instances of the predicate. The forward and backward links between the two traverses are encoded in sets I and C: *e.g.* if for a pair of nodes $(F, G) \in C$ we have that F is in the right traverse then there is a forward link going from the left traverse to node F. Thus F is an outgoing forward link and the node E which is isomorphic to F is the corresponding input link into the left traverse. If a pair (E, F) is reachable from the root nodes in more than one way, then C keeps track of all of them. Multiple occurrences of the same pair (E, F) in C then may contribute multiple links.

Table 2. Experimental results on IEEE 1394 (firewire) Windows device driver routines. "✓" indicates the proof of memory safety and memory-leak absence. "⊘" indicates that a genuine memory-safety warning was reported. The lines of code (LOC) column includes the struct declarations and the environment model code. The t1394Diag_PnpRemoveDevice* experiment used a precondition expressed in separation logic rather than non-deterministic environment code. Experiments conducted on a 2.0GHz Intel Core Duo with 2GB RAM.

Routine	LOC	Space (Mb)	Time (sec)	Result
t1394_BusResetRoutine	718	322.44	663	✓
t1394Diag_CancelIrp	693	1.97	0.56	⊘
t1394Diag_CancelIrpFix	697	263.45	724	✓
t1394_GetAddressData	693	2.21	0.61	⊘
t1394_GetAddressDataFix	698	342.59	1036	✓
t1394_SetAddressData	689	2.21	0.59	⊘
t1394_SetAddressDataFix	694	311.87	956	✓
t1394Diag_PnpRemoveDevice	1885	>2000.00	>9000	T/O
t1394Diag_PnpRemoveDevice*	1801	369.87	785	✓

Table 1 shows an example run of the discovery algorithm. The input heap H consists of a doubly-linked list of doubly-linked sublists where the backward link in the top-level list comes from the first node in the sublist. The discovery of the predicate describing the shape of the list would fail without the use of frame inference. Note that Λ_1 in the input symbolic heap could have been discovered by a previous run of the algorithm on a more concrete symbolic heap, possibly one containing no Λ's at all.

6   Experimental Results

Before applying our analysis to larger programs we first applied it to a set of small challenge problems reminiscent of those described in the introduction (*e.g.* "Creation of a cyclic doubly-linked list of cyclic doubly-linked lists in which the inner link-type differs from the outer list link-type", "traversal of a singly-linked list of singly-linked list which reverses each sublist twice", etc). These challenge problems were all less than 100 lines of code. We also intentionally inserted memory leaks and faults into variants of these and other programs, which were also correctly discovered.

We then applied our analysis to a number of data-structure manipulating routines from the IEEE 1394 (firewire) device driver. This was much more challenging than the small test programs. We used an implementation restricted to a simplified, singly-linked version of our abstract domain, in order to focus experimentation with the adaptive aspect of the analysis (we do not believe this restriction to be fundamental). As a result, our model of the driver's data structures was not exactly what the kernel can see. It turns out that the firewire code happens not to use reverse pointers (except in a single library call, which we were able to model differently) which means that our model is not too inaccurate for the purpose of these experiments. Also, the driver uses a small amount of address arithmetic in the way it selects fields (the "containing record idiom"), which we replaced with ordinary field selection, and our tool does not check array bounds errors, concentrating on pointer structures.

Our experimental results are reported in Table 2. We expressed the calling context and environment as non-deterministic C code that constructed five circular lists with common header, three of which had nested acyclic lists, and two of which contained back-pointers to the header; there were additionally numerous other pointers to non-recursive objects. In one case we needed to manually supply a precondition due to performance difficulties. The analysis proved safety of a number of driver routines' usage of these data structures, in a sequential execution environment (see [5] for notes on how we can lift this analysis to a concurrent setting). We also found several previously unknown bugs. As an example, one error (from t1394_CancelIrp, Table 2) involves a procedure that commits a memory-safety error on an empty list (the presumption that the list can never be empty turns out not to be justified). This bug has been confirmed by the Windows kernel team and placed into the database of device driver bugs to be repaired. Note that this driver has already been analyzed by SLAM and other analysis tools—These bugs were not previously found due to the limited treatment of the heap in the other tools. Indeed, SLAM *assumes* memory safety.

The routines did scanning of the data structures, as well as deletion of a single node or a whole structure. They did not themselves perform insertion, though the environment code did. Predicate discovery was used in handling nesting of lists. Just as importantly, it allowed us to infer predicates for the many pointers that led to non-recursive objects, relieving us of the need to write these predicates by hand. The gain was brought home when we wrote the precondition in the t1394Diag_PnpRemoveDevice* case. It involved looking at more than 10 struct definitions, some of which had upwards of 20 fields.

Predicate discovery proved to be quite useful in these experiments, but further work is needed to come to a better understanding of heuristics for its application. And, progress is needed on the central scalability problem (illustrated by the timeout observed for t1394Diag_PnpRemoveDevice) if we are to have an analysis that applies to larger programs.

7   Conclusion

We have described a shape analysis designed to fill the gap between the data structures supported in today's shape analysis tools and those used in industrial systems-level software. The key idea behind this new analysis is the use of a higher-order inductive predicate which, if given the appropriate parameter, can summarize a variety of composite linear data structures. The analysis is then defined over symbolic heaps which use the higher-order predicate when instantiated with elements drawn from a cache of non-recursive predicates. Our abstraction procedure incorporates a method of synthesizing new non-recursive predicates from an examination of the current symbolic heap. These new predicates are added into the cache of non-recursive predicates, thus triggering new rewrites in the analysis' abstraction procedure. These new predicates are expressed as the combination of old predicates, including instantiations of the higher-order predicates, thus allowing us to express complex composite structures.

We began this work with the idea sometimes heard, that systems code often "just" uses linked lists, and we sought to test our techniques on such code. We obtained encouraging, if partial, experimental results on routines from a firewire device driver. However, we also found that lists can be used in combination in subtle ways, and we even encountered an instance of sharing (described in Section 2) which, as far as we know, is beyond current automatic shape analyses. In general, real-world systems programs contain much more complex data structures than those usually found in papers on shape analysis, and handling the full range of these structures efficiently and precisely presents a significant challenge.

Acknowledgments. We are grateful to the CAV reviewers for detailed comments which helped us to improve the presentation. The London authors were supported by EPSRC.

References

[1] Berdine, J., Calcagno, C., O'Hearn, P.W.: Symbolic execution with separation logic. In: Yi, K. (ed.) APLAS 2005. LNCS, vol. 3780, Springer, Heidelberg (2005)

[2] Biering, B., Birkedal, L., Torp-Smith, N.: BI hyperdoctrines and higher-order separation logic. In: Sagiv, M. (ed.) ESOP 2005. LNCS, vol. 3444, Springer, Heidelberg (2005)

[3] Bouajjani, A., Habermehl, P., Rogalewicz, A., Vojnar, T.: Abstract tree regular model checking of complex dynamic data structures. In: Yi, K. (ed.) SAS 2006. LNCS, vol. 4134, Springer, Heidelberg (2006)

[4] Distefano, D., O'Hearn, P.W., Yang, H.: A local shape analysis based on separation logic. In: Hermanns, H., Palsberg, J. (eds.) TACAS 2006 and ETAPS 2006. LNCS, vol. 3920, Springer, Heidelberg (2006)

[5] Gotsman, A., Berdine, J., Cook, B., Sagiv, M.: Thread-modular shape analysis. In: To appear in PLDI (2007)

[6] Hackett, B., Rugina, R.: Region-based shape analysis with tracked locations. In: POPL (2005)

[7] Lee, O., Yang, H., Yi, K.: Automatic verification of pointer programs using grammar-based shape analysis. In: Sagiv, M. (ed.) ESOP 2005. LNCS, vol. 3444, Springer, Heidelberg (2005)

[8] Lev-Ami, T., Immerman, N., Sagiv, M.: Abstraction for shape analysis with fast and precise transfomers. In: Ball, T., Jones, R.B. (eds.) CAV 2006. LNCS, vol. 4144, Springer, Heidelberg (2006)

[9] Lev-Ami, T., Sagiv, M.: A system for implementing static analyses. In: Palsberg, J. (ed.) SAS 2000. LNCS, vol. 1824, Springer, Heidelberg (2000)

[10] Loginov, A., Reps, T., Sagiv, M.: Abstraction refinement via inductive learning. In: Etessami, K., Rajamani, S.K. (eds.) CAV 2005. LNCS, vol. 3576, Springer, Heidelberg (2005)

[11] Manevich, R., Yahav, E., Ramalingam, G., Sagiv, M.: Predicate abstraction and canonical abstraction for singly-linked lists. In: Cousot, R. (ed.) VMCAI 2005. LNCS, vol. 3385, Springer, Heidelberg (2005)

[12] Podelski, A., Wies, T.: Boolean heaps. In: Hankin, C., Siveroni, I. (eds.) SAS 2005. LNCS, vol. 3672, Springer, Heidelberg (2005)

[13] Reynolds, J.C.: Separation logic: A logic for shared mutable data structures. In: LICS (2002)

[14] Rinetzky, N., Ramalingam, G., Sagiv, M., Yahav, E.: Componentized heap abstraction. TR-164/06, School of Computer Science, Tel Aviv Univ. (December 2006)

[15] Sagiv, M., Reps, T., Wilhelm, R.: Solving shape-analysis problems in languages with destructive updating. ACM TOPLAS 20(1), 1–50 (1998)

[16] Sagiv, M., Reps, T., Wilhelm, R.: Parametric shape analysis via 3-valued logic. ACM TOPLAS 24(3), 217–298 (2002)

[17] Češka, M., Erlebach, P., Vojnar, T.: Generalised multi-pattern-based verification of programs with linear linked structures. Formal Aspects Comput (2007)

Array Abstractions from Proofs

Ranjit Jhala[1] and Kenneth L. McMillan[2]

[1] UC San Diego
[2] Cadence Berkeley Laboratories

Abstract. We present a technique for using infeasible program paths to automatically infer *Range Predicates* that describe properties of unbounded array segments. First, we build proofs showing the infeasibility of the paths, using axioms that precisely encode the high-level (but informal) rules with which programmers reason about arrays. Next, we mine the proofs for Craig Interpolants which correspond to predicates that refute the particular counterexample path. By embedding the predicate inference technique within a Counterexample-Guided Abstraction-Refinement (CEGAR) loop, we obtain a method for verifying data-sensitive safety properties whose precision is tailored in a program- and property-sensitive manner. Though the axioms used are simple, we show that the method suffices to prove a variety of array-manipulating programs that were previously beyond automatic model checkers.

1 Introduction

Counterexample-guided Abstraction-Refinement(CEGAR)-based techniques [8] have proven to be effective in the verification of control-dominated properties of software [2,15,7,16], chiefly because they precisely track only the small set of facts required to prove the property. However, CEGAR has not had success with data-sensitive properties which require the automatic discovery of abstractions for reasoning about unbounded structures. Consider for example, the following program `init` that initializes an array:

```
for(i=0;i != n; i++) M[i] = 0;
for(j=0;j != n; j++) assert(M[j] == 0);
```

CEGAR-based approaches fail on such programs as for each counterexample path corresponding to an unrolling of k iterations of the upper loop, they infer the atomic predicates: $sel(M, 0) = 0, \ldots, sel(M, k-1) = 0$, which state that the cells 0 through $k-1$ of the array M have the value 0. These predicates suffice to refute the particular path, but not other, longer paths. Thus, the inability to infer universally quantified predicates about unbounded segments of the array causes CEGAR-based approaches to diverge.

In this paper, we present a technique for using infeasible counterexample paths to infer predicates that describe properties of unbounded array segments and therefore prove many array manipulating programs correct. Our technique is

W. Damm and H. Hermanns (Eds.): CAV 2007, LNCS 4590, pp. 193–206, 2007.

based on two ingredients. The first ingredient is the notion of a *Range Predicate*, an implicitly universally quantified predicate, defined recursively as:

$$RP(t_1, t_2, p) \overset{\triangle}{=} p[t_1/\alpha] \wedge (t_1 + 1 = t_2 \vee RP(t_1 + 1, t_2, p))$$

where t_1 and t_2 are terms, respectively called the left and right index, p is an atomic first-order predicate, *i.e.*, an equality, disequality or inequality, which contains an implicitly bound variable α. Intuitively, the range predicate captures the fact that for each element t in the sequence $t_1, t_1 + 1, (t_1 + 1) + 1, \ldots$ upto, but not including, t_2, the fact $p[t/\alpha]$ holds. Thus, the range predicate: $RP(0, i, sel(M, \alpha) = 0)$ states that the first i elements of the array M are equal to 0. Similarly, $RP(0, n, \neg(sel(M, \alpha) \leq 0))$ stipulates that the first n elements of the array M are positive, and $RP(i, n, (sel(M, \alpha) \leq sel(M, \alpha + 1)))$ states that the segment of the array M from index i through n is sorted.

For range predicates to be useful for automatic verification, we require a way to automatically find range predicates relevant to the property being verified. The second ingredient of our technique, is an *axiom-based algorithm* for automatically finding relevant predicates as Craig Interpolants computed from proofs of infeasibility of counterexample paths. We instantiate the algorithm with axioms that precisely encode the high-level, but informal, rules with which which programmers reason about arrays, to obtain a method for automatically inferring range predicates tailored to the property to be proved. Thus, the two ingredients are combined to obtain a predicate inference technique which, when embedded within a CEGAR loop [14,17], results in automatic method for verifying data-sensitive safety properties of array-manipulating programs.

To address the challenge of computing range predicate interpolants instead of a divergent sequence of atomic predicates describing individual array cells, our axiom-based algorithm builds upon our previous technique of *L-restricted Interpolation* [18]. Consider the family of languages $L_0 \subseteq L_1 \subseteq \ldots$, where L_i is the language of predicates containing numeric constants with absolute value at most i. We set k to 0 and for each candidate counterexample path, try to find an interpolant belonging to L_k. If no such interpolant exists, we increase k and repeat. Thus, if there is an abstraction that suffices to prove the program infeasible, there is some k such that all the predicates of the abstraction belong to L_k, and so the abstraction-refinement loop is guaranteed to terminate. By *restricting* the language we force the solver to find interpolants (and therefore, abstraction predicates) that contain small constants, if these exist. Thus, in the example above, once the counterexample path contains more than $k + 1$ iterations of the first loop, the solver *cannot* return the interpolant $sel(M, 0) = 0, \ldots, sel(M, k) = 0$, and is instead forced to find the range predicate $RP(0, i, sel(M, \alpha) = 0)$, which yields an inductive invariant that proves the property.

To compute L-restricted interpolants it suffices to find L-restricted *split proofs* where each deduction belongs in L, and where for each deduction, there exists a time step such that the antecedents and consequence of the deduction are over program variables that are in scope at that time step. In Section 3 we show a *local* axiom based algorithm to generate split proofs of refutation, and therefore, interpolants. In Section 4 we present an instantiation of this framework using range predicate axioms. Though the axioms for reasoning about range predicates are simple, we present initial experiments in Section 5 that indicate that they are expressive enough to efficiently capture a variety of idiomatic uses of arrays, in a manner that is precise enough to prove data intensive properties.

Related Work. The problem of synthesizing abstractions and invariants for arrays and other unbounded data structures has received much attention. One line of research uses *templates* representing families of candidate loop invariants (*e.g.* affine constraints over program variables) to generate loop invariants [3,4,27]. These approaches use a template of quantified invariants derived from [6], where the problem of *checking* a given quantified invariant is studied. A second line of work uses abstract interpretation based techniques for shape analysis. Examples include those based on three-valued logic [26,21] and Separation Logic [10]. The abstract domain for arrays presented in [12] captures properties similar to range predicates. Predicate abstraction [13] based approaches for shape analysis [11,9,5,24,20,1] can also be viewed as an instance of abstract interpretation. In the approaches which work for unbounded structures an expert must supply appropriate predicates or instrumentation predicates which are combined via a fixpoint computation to obtain an inductive invariant. Several authors have proposed using specialized rules to build decision procedures [24], and more generally, program analyses [25].

2   Overview

We begin with an overview of safety verification via interpolant-based abstraction refinement.

Notation. In this paper, we use standard first-order logic (FOL). By $\mathcal{L}(\Sigma)$ we refer to the set of well-formed formulas over a vocabulary Σ of non-logical symbols, and for a given formula ϕ we use $\mathcal{L}(\phi)$ to denote the set of well-formed formulas over the vocabulary of non-logical symbols occurring in ϕ.

We assume that for every (non-logical) symbol s, there exists a unique symbol s', *i.e.*, s with one prime added. We use s with n primes added to represent the value of s at time step n. For any formula or term ϕ, we write $\phi^{\langle n \rangle}$ to denote the addition of n primes to every non-logical symbol in ϕ. Finally, for any set of symbols Σ, we write $\Sigma^{\langle n \rangle}$ to denote $\{s^{\langle n \rangle} \mid s \in \Sigma\}$ and Σ' to denote $\Sigma^{\langle 1 \rangle}$. For a term (resp. predicate) t we write $t[e/x]$ to denote the term (resp. predicate) obtained by substituting all occurrences of x in t with e.

Programs. We model programs abstractly using logical formulas, and restrict ourselves to single-procedure programs. Let S be a set of *state variables* corresponding to individual program variables. A *state formula* is a formula in $\mathcal{L}(S)$, which may contain interpreted symbols like $+, =, \leq$ in addition to the symbols in S. A *transition* is a formula in $\mathcal{L}(S \cup S')$. A *program* is a pair $(\mathcal{T}, \Pi)$ where $\mathcal{T}$ is a finite set of transitions and $\Pi \subseteq \mathcal{T}^*$ is a regular language of sequences of transitions. Intuitively, each command (basic block or branch condition) of the control-flow graph of the program corresponds to a transition, and the set of paths is the regular set of *syntactic* control-flow paths of the program.

The following are the transitions for the program `init` from Section 1. For each transition, we omit for clarity the implicit conjunction $x = x'$ for all program variables x whose primed version is not explicitly shown in the transition.

$T_1 : i' = 0 \qquad T_2 : i \neq n \land M' = upd(M, i, 0) \land i' = i + 1 \qquad T_3 : i \neq n$

$T_4 : j' = 0 \qquad T_5 : j \neq n \land sel(M, j) = 0 \land j' = j + 1 \qquad T_6 : j \neq n \land sel(M, j) \neq 0$

The set of syntactic paths of the program that lead to the `assert` failure are given by the regular expression: $T_1 \cdot T_2^* \cdot T_3 \cdot T_4 \cdot T_5^* \cdot T_6$.

Path Constraints. A *path* π is a sequence of transitions $T_0, \ldots, T_n$ in Π. For any path π, the *constraints* $\mathsf{Cons}(\pi)$ is the sequence of formulas $T_0^{\langle 0 \rangle}, \ldots, T_n^{\langle n \rangle}$. A path π is *infeasible* if the *path formula* $\bigwedge \mathsf{Cons}(\pi)$ is inconsistent, *i.e.*, unsatisfiable. A program $(\mathcal{T}, \Pi)$ is *infeasible* if every path in Π is infeasible.

The path formula represents all possible concrete program executions that follow the given control-flow path. A satisfying assignment for the path formula can be mapped back to the values taken by the program variables at each time step from 0 (the initial value) through $n + 1$ (at the end of the path). Thus, if the formula is satisfiable, the path corresponds to a feasible concrete execution of the program. The left side of Figure 1 shows the path constraints corresponding to the path where the upper and lower loops are unrolled twice. From top to bottom, the constraints shown are the formulas: $T_1^{\langle 0 \rangle}, T_2^{\langle 1 \rangle}, T_2^{\langle 2 \rangle}, T_3^{\langle 3 \rangle}, T_4^{\langle 4 \rangle}, T_5^{\langle 5 \rangle}, T_6^{\langle 6 \rangle}$. Using the standard axioms for equality and arithmetic, and McCarthy's axioms for *sel* and *upd*, one can check that the path formula shown on the left in Figure 1 is inconsistent.

Safety Verification. Informally, the safety verification problem is to determine whether the program always avoids entering a set of undesirable "error" states. We can reduce the safety verification problem to that of determining if a program is infeasible, by intersecting Π with the set of paths leading to the "error" states.

Interpolants. For a sequence of formulas $\Gamma = A_0, \ldots, A_n$, we say that $\hat{\Gamma} = \hat{A}_0, \ldots, \hat{A}_{n+1}$ is an interpolant for Γ if: (1) $\hat{A}_0 = \text{TRUE}$ and $A_{n+1} = \text{FALSE}$, and, (2) for all $0 \leq i \leq n$, $\hat{A}_i \land A_i$ implies $\hat{A}_{i+1}$, and, (3) for all $0 \leq i \leq n$, $A_{i+1} \in \mathcal{L}(A_i) \cap \mathcal{L}(A_{i+1})$

Interpolants are Abstractions. For any infeasible path, the sequence of formulas of the interpolant for the path constraints *overapproximate* the possible program configurations along the path in a manner that is *precise* enough to demonstrate the infeasibility of the path. To see this, observe that the interpolant for path formula $T_0^{\langle 0 \rangle}, \ldots, T_n^{\langle n \rangle}$ is a sequence of formulas $\hat{T}_0, \ldots, \hat{T}_{n+1}$, such that: (1) $\hat{T}_0$ is TRUE, representing all possible initial states and $\hat{T}_n$ is FALSE, indicating that there is no possible state at the end of the path, (2) for all $0 \leq i \leq n$, executing the transition T_i from a state in $\hat{T}_i$ takes the system into a state in

Path Constraints	Interpolant
	TRUE
$T_1^{\langle 0 \rangle} : i^{\langle 1 \rangle} = 0$	$i^{\langle 1 \rangle} = 0$
$T_2^{\langle 1 \rangle} : i^{\langle 1 \rangle} \neq n \wedge M^{\langle 2 \rangle} = upd(M^{\langle 1 \rangle}, i^{\langle 1 \rangle}, 0) \wedge i^{\langle 2 \rangle} = i^{\langle 1 \rangle} + 1$	$RP(0, i^{\langle 2 \rangle}, sel(M^{\langle 2 \rangle}, \alpha) = 0)$
$T_2^{\langle 2 \rangle} : i^{\langle 2 \rangle} \neq n \wedge M^{\langle 3 \rangle} = upd(M^{\langle 2 \rangle}, i^{\langle 2 \rangle}, 0) \wedge i^{\langle 3 \rangle} = i^{\langle 2 \rangle} + 1$	$RP(0, i^{\langle 3 \rangle}, sel(M^{\langle 3 \rangle}, \alpha) = 0)$
$T_3^{\langle 3 \rangle} : i^{\langle 3 \rangle} = n$	$RP(0, n, sel(M^{\langle 4 \rangle}, \alpha) = 0)$
$T_4^{\langle 4 \rangle} : j^{\langle 5 \rangle} = 0$	$RP(j^{\langle 5 \rangle}, n, sel(M^{\langle 5 \rangle}, \alpha) = 0)$
$T_5^{\langle 5 \rangle} : j^{\langle 5 \rangle} \neq n \wedge sel(M^{\langle 5 \rangle}, j^{\langle 5 \rangle}) = 0 \wedge j^{\langle 6 \rangle} = j^{\langle 5 \rangle} + 1$	$RP(j^{\langle 6 \rangle}, n, sel(M^{\langle 6 \rangle}, \alpha) = 0)$
$T_6^{\langle 6 \rangle} : j^{\langle 6 \rangle} \neq n \wedge sel(M^{\langle 6 \rangle}, j^{\langle 6 \rangle}) \neq 0$	FALSE

Fig. 1. On the left, we show the path constraints generated by the path leading to the assertion violation in `init` where each of the loops is unrolled twice. For $i \geq 3$ the i-th path constraint has an additional conjunct $M^{\langle i+1 \rangle} = M^{\langle i \rangle}$ omitted for brevity. The right column shows the interpolants generated using range predicates. We write the $i + 1$-th element of the interpolant sequence to the right of the i-th path constraint. Note that the $i + 1$-th element of the interpolant sequence is implied by the conjunction of the i-th element and the i-th path constraint.

$\hat{T}_{i+1}$, and, (3) for all $0 \leq i \leq n$, the set of possible states for time i is expressed as a state formula over the values of the variables at time i.

Thus, the interpolant corresponding to an infeasible path can be used to iteratively refine an abstract model of the program either directly [22], or indirectly by predicate abstraction over the set of atomic predicates appearing in the interpolant [14]. This process is repeated until all paths are shown infeasible or a feasible path is found [8]. For example, for the path constraints shown in Figure 1, a possible interpolant is the sequence of formulas: TRUE, $(i^{\langle 1 \rangle} = 0)$, $(i^{\langle 2 \rangle} = 1)$, $(sel(M^{\langle 3 \rangle}, 1) = 0)$, $(sel(M^{\langle 4 \rangle}, 1) = 0)$, $(sel(M^{\langle 5 \rangle}, 1) = 0 \wedge j^{\langle 5 \rangle} = 0)$, $(sel(M^{\langle 6 \rangle}, 1) = 0 \wedge j^{\langle 6 \rangle} = 1)$, FALSE. After dropping the superscripts, we get a set of predicates: $i = 0$, $i = 1, sel(M, 1) = 0$, $j = 0, j = 1$, that suffices to refute paths where the upper loop is unrolled at most two times.

(In)Completeness. Even though the atomic predicates suffice to eliminate the given path, more predicates may be needed for longer paths, *e.g.* those corresponding to more iterations through the loop. In our example, each path corresponding to j iterations of the upper loop will result in new predicates constraining the first j elements of the array to be zero, but which are insufficient to refute longer paths. As a result, the iterative abstraction-refinement diverges.

Range Predicates. We obtain the interpolant sequence shown on the right in Figure 1, by giving the interpolating procedure *axioms* for reasoning about range predicates and simultaneously restricting it to find interpolants in the language L_1 (using numeric constants of absolute value at most 1). Note that the restriction forces the solver to return an interpolant that states that all cells from 0 through n have have been initialized with zero for the point after the first loop has finished. After dropping the superscripts, we obtain the set of new abstraction predicates: $i = 0$, $RP(0, i, sel(M, \alpha) = 0)$, $RP(0, n, sel(M, \alpha) = 0)$,

$RP(j, n, sel(M, \alpha) = 0)$. Thus, perhaps counter-intuitively [4], from a finite path we can deduce predicates describing unbounded array segments, simply by restricting the language of the interpolants. Subsequent predicate abstraction over these predicates refutes this particular path and in fact, results in an inductive invariant that proves the program infeasible.

3   Generating Interpolants from Axioms

We now consider the problem of using a specialized set of axioms (in addition to the axioms belonging to the ground theories of equality, uninterpreted functions and difference constraints) to find L-restricted interpolants for a given sequence of formulas $\Gamma = A_0, \ldots, A_n$.

As shown in [18], this can be achieved by the following two-step process. First, we must find an L-restricted *split proof* where each deduction can be mapped to a time step i such that the antecedents and consequence of the deduction belong to $\mathcal{L}(A_i)$, and if there are no antecedents, the consequence is implied by A_i. Second, we can convert the split proof into a set of propositional clauses (by converting each atom into a literal) and then use propositional interpolation [23] to find an interpolant. The latter operation is polynomial in the size of the split-proof and results in interpolants whose atoms appear in the split proof and are thus from the restriction language L.

Split Proofs. An L-restricted split proof over a set of hypotheses $\Gamma = A_0, \ldots, A_n$ is a triple (V, E, N), where V is a set of formulas, (V, E) is a directed acyclic graph, and N is a labeling function from V to $[0 \ldots n]$ such that:

  – for each vertex $v \in V$, we have $A_{N(v)}, \{u \mid (u, v) \in E\} \models v$, and,
  – for each edge $(u, v) \in E$, we have $u, v \in \mathcal{L}(A_{N(v)})$, and,
  – for each edge $(u, v) \in E$, if $N(u) \neq N(v)$ then $u \in L$.

A L-restricted split refutation of Γ is an L-restricted split proof over Γ whose unique sink vertex (no out-edges) is FALSE.

Intuitively, a split proof is one where as before, each deduced formula (vertex) can be localized to a particular time step (the formula's label) – the formula is implied by the conjunction of previously deduced facts (the vertex's predecessors) and the hypotheses corresponding to the formula's time step. Moreover, if a formula is deduced at a time step different from those at which a predecessor was deduced, then the predecessor formula must belong to the restriction language L. In other words, within a time step (*e.g.* within the constraints corresponding to a large basic block of code), we may deduce formulas not in the restriction language L, as these formulas will not appear in the subsequent interpolant.

We call a sequence of hypotheses $\Gamma = A_0, \ldots, A_n$ strict if for all i, j such that $|i - j| > 1$ we have $\mathcal{L}(A_i) \cap \mathcal{L}(A_j) = \emptyset$. It is easy to check that the sequence of hypotheses corresponding to path constraints are strict.

Theorem 1. [18] *Given a strict sequence of hypotheses Γ and a propositionally closed language L, Γ has an L-restricted interpolant iff it has a L-restricted split refutation.*

Program	Time	Preds	Iter
init	1.190	18	7
vararg	1.520	14	8
copy	3.650	20	11
copy-prop	9.720	38	17
find	2.240	20	12
partition	7.960	37	14
part-init	4.630	32	12
producer	45.000	39	41
insert	91.220	74	36
scull	9.180	36	14

1: **Input:** Local axioms A
2: **Input:** Hypotheses $\Gamma = A_0, \ldots, A_n$
3: **Output:** A split refutation of Γ
4: indexed := Seed(Γ)
5: **while** FALSE $\notin$ pf.V **do**
6:     choose a, I, j from A, indexed, $[0, \ldots, n]$
7:     **match** Project(a, I, j) **with Some** (I', Q', c')
8:         **if** $c' \notin$ pf.V and $\forall q \in Q'$.Query(q) **then**
9:             pf.V := pf.$V \cup \{c'\}$
10:             pf.E := pf.$E \cup \{(h, c') \mid h \in I' \cup Q'\}$
11:             pf.$N(c')$:= j
12:             indexed := indexed $\cup c'$
13:             Assert(c')
14: **return** Cone(pf, FALSE)

Fig. 2. Procedure Generate

Fig. 3. Experimental Results: **Time** is the total number of seconds spent to prove the program safe, **Preds** is the number of predicates required, **Iter** is the number of iterations of the abstraction-refinement loop, Experiments were run on an IBM T42 Laptop with a 1.7GHz processor and 512Mb RAM

Generating Proofs from Local Axioms

Thus, to find L-restricted interpolants for Γ, we need to find L-restricted split refutations of Γ. The problem of generating L-restricted split refutations for formulas over theories of equality, uninterpreted functions, difference bounds and restricted use of the array operators "sel" and "upd" was addressed in [18]. Thus, we assume there is a "ground" procedure that handles the above theories and describe how this procedure can be *extended* with specialized axioms.

Local Axioms. A *local axiom* a is a partial function that takes as input a set of *index* formulas I and returns a pair of *query* formulas Q and a *consequence* formula c, such that (1) $I, Q \models c$, and, (2) $Q, c \in \mathcal{L}(I)$. Intuitively, for a given set of index formulas that is known to be true, there is a unique set of query formulas over the ground theory which if additionally true imply the consequence formula. To ensure that axiom instantiation results in split proofs, we require that the queries and consequence belong to the same language as the index formulas.

Algorithm Generate. Our non-deterministic algorithm Generate for finding split refutations for a sequence of hypotheses $\Gamma = A_0, \ldots, A_n$ is shown in Figure 2. The algorithm takes as input a set of local axioms A and a sequence of hypotheses Γ. It maintains a set of index formulas in the variable indexed, and a split proof pf whose vertices correspond to all the facts that have been deduced. The overall structure of the algorithm is similar to that of saturation-based provers [19]. First (line 4), it seeds the set of indexed formulas using the formulas that the ground procedure derives from Γ. Next, (lines 5–13) it goes into a loop where it repeatedly selects a set of index formulas and a candidate axiom and attempts to derive new facts by applying the axiom to the index formulas, until a contradiction is found (*i.e.*, FALSE is deduced).

Project. The main challenge in our setting is that we need to ensure that all the deductions can be *localized to a single time step* — we must ensure that whenever we deduce a consequence c from hypotheses I, Q, there must be some time step $j \in 0 \dots n$ such that I, Q, c belong in $\mathcal{L}(A_j)$, *i.e.*, contain symbols that are local to time step j. Note that the local axiom functions are defined only on index formulas belonging to some common time step. Thus, to make the procedure Generate complete, we would have to undertake the expensive task of maintaining different *representatives* for each formulas at each time step at which the formula has a congruent version. We avoid this by using a procedure Project that takes as input a set of formulas, possibly belonging to languages of different time steps, an axiom, and a target time step j and determines whether there is a set of formulas I' at time step j such that: (1) for each formula in I, there is a congruent version in I', and, (2) each formula in I' belongs to $\mathcal{L}(A_j)$, and, (3) the application of the axiom to the index formulas I' yields the query formulas Q' and a consequence c'. If a suitable I' exists, the procedure updates the split proof pf with congruence proofs (using the axioms for equality and uninterpreted functions) for the elements of I', and returns the tuple of (I', Q', c').

We use the Project function in the main loop as follows. In each iteration we choose an axiom a, a set of index formulas (from arbitrary time frames) I, and a target time frame j (line 6), and we call Project to determine if at time j there is a congruent version I' with query formulas Q' and consequence c', all of which belong to time step j. If Project succeeds (line 7), we check if the consequence c' is not a previously known fact, and invoke the ground procedure Query to determine whether each of the queries in Q' is true (line 8). For each provable query, the ground procedure updates the split proof pf with vertices for the query formula. If all the queries Q' are provable and the consequence c' is new, the split proof pf is updated with the new consequence (lines 9–12) and the consequence is asserted to the ground procedure (line 13). If this assertion yields a contradiction *i.e.*, causes the ground procedure to deduce FALSE, the algorithm returns a split refutation which is the backwards transitive closure of FALSE in the split proof pf.

Correctness and Termination. When the procedure Generate finishes, it returns a split refutation for the hypotheses Γ. The presented procedure is abstracted for clarity. In practice, by ensuring that we iterate over the indexed formulas exhaustively we can guarantee that the procedure will find a split refutation if one exists. The procedure can be terminated when it reaches a point where no new facts in the restriction language can be deduced. Termination follows as we restrict the language to bound the set of candidate formulas.

4   Axioms for Range Predicates

We now describe an instantiation of the framework of the previous section with axioms for reasoning about *Range Predicates* which describe properties of contiguous blocks of array elements. As range predicates capture facts that hold

$$\frac{\boxed{p}}{RP(t,\eta(t),p[\alpha/t])} \text{ Generalize} \qquad \frac{\boxed{RP(t_1,t_2,p)} \quad \boxed{RP(t_2,t_3,p)}}{RP(t_1,t_3,p)} \text{ Join}$$

$$\frac{\boxed{RP(t_1,t_2,p)}}{p[t_1/\alpha]} \text{ Instantiate-Left} \qquad \frac{\boxed{RP(t_1,\eta(t_2),p)}}{p[t_2/\alpha]} \text{ Instantiate-Right}$$

$$\frac{\boxed{RP(\eta(t_1),t_2,p)} \quad p[t_1/\alpha]}{RP(t_1,t_2,p)} \text{ Extend-Left} \qquad \frac{\boxed{RP(t_1,t_2,p)} \quad p[t_2/\alpha]}{RP(t_1,\eta(t_2),p)} \text{ Extend-Right}$$

$$\frac{\boxed{RP(t_1,t_2,p)} \quad \eta(t_1) \neq t_2}{RP(\eta(t_1),t_2,p)} \text{ Shrink-Left} \qquad \frac{\boxed{RP(t_1,\eta(t_2),p)} \quad t_1 \neq t_2}{RP(t_1,t_2,p)} \text{ Shrink-Right}$$

$$\frac{\boxed{RP(\eta(t_1),t_2,p)} \quad a \leq t[t_1/\alpha] \quad t \text{ is linear}}{RP(\eta(t_1),t_2,p[sel(upd(M,a,v),t)/sel(M,t)])} \text{ Preserve-Left}$$

$$\frac{\boxed{RP(t_1,t_2,p)} \quad t[t_2/\alpha] \leq a \quad t \text{ is linear}}{RP(t_1,t_2,p[sel(upd(M,a,v),t)/sel(M,t)])} \text{ Preserve-Right}$$

Fig. 4. Axioms for Reasoning about Range Predicates

for *sequences* of array indices, we devise axioms that: *generalize* range predicates from facts that hold about a single index, *instantiate* range predicates to individual indices, *extend* range predicates to longer sequences, *shrink* range predicates to shorter sequences, *join* range predicates over "adjacent" sequences, and, *preserve* range predicates in the presence of array updates.

Figure 4 shows a representative subset of the axioms used for reasoning about range predicates. We use η as an abbreviation for the map $\lambda t.t+1$ from terms to terms. Each axiom is shown as a proof rule, with the antecedents above the line and the consequence below the line. The antecedents within boxes are the index formulas, and those not in boxes are query formulas. Due to lack of space, we omit the meta-theorems that show the soundness of the range predicate axioms with respect to the recursive range predicate definition, and therefore show that the axioms only yield semantically valid derivations.

Generalize: The axiom Generalize for creating range predicates simply takes an ordinary formula and replaces occurrences of terms t inside the formula with α, to obtain a range predicate that holds from t to $\eta(t)$.

Instantiate: There are two rules for instantiating a range predicate: Instantiate-Left for instantiating with the left index, and Instantiate-Right for the right index. In either case, the consequence is p with α substituted with the appropriate index.

Extend: There are two rules for extending a range predicate: Extend-Left for extending at the left end and Extend-Right for extending at the right end. In either case, the axiom has an antecedent query formula that the predicate p hold at the appropriate index.

Shrink: There are two rules for shrinking a range predicate: Shrink-Left for shrinking at the left end and Shrink-Right for shrinking at the right end. In either case, the axiom has an antecedent query formula that ensures that in the result, the left and right indices are disequal. This ensures the soundness of the instantiation axioms.

Preserve: The trickiest rules are those that ensure that an update to the array preserves the properties captured by a given range predicate *i.e.*, the properties continue to hold in the updated array, as long as the update happens "outside" the range of indices of the range predicate. Both rules require a syntactic condition that the read address t be *linear*, *i.e.*, that α not appear under any function symbol inside t. The Preserve-Right rule states that for any linear read address t parameterized by α, if the address obtained by substituting α with the right index is less than (*i.e.*, to the left of) the address written to (a), then the reads return the same values in the updated array as the update does not affect the addresses read through t. The Preserve-Left rule is the symmetric version for writes to the left of the left index of the range predicate.

Join: The rule Join is used to join two adjacent range predicates.

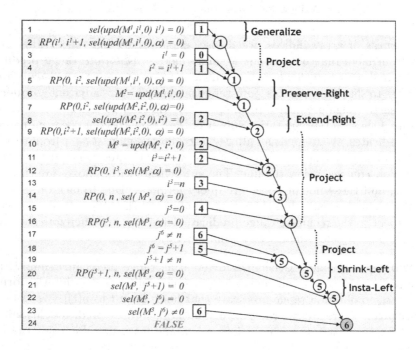

Fig. 5. Split proof generated by FOCI for the path constraints from Figure 1

Example Split Proof. Figure 5 shows a split proof generated by FOCI , to refute the path constraints from Figure 1. The constraints are simplified using Static Single Assignment form [14], which avoids the equality constraints that "copy" unmodified variables across a transition. In particular, we omit the copy constraints for M after time step 3 (as the array is not updated subsequently). For brevity, we write x^i for $x^{\langle i \rangle}$. On the left side we show the formulas corresponding to the split proof vertices on the right. Each square vertex is a hypothesis labeled by the time step to which the hypothesis belongs (*i.e.*, a hypothesis in A_j is labeled j). Each circular vertex is a deduction, made using the range predicate axioms or the axioms for equality, congruence or arithmetic, labeled by the time step at which the deduction was made. The curly braces describe how sub-proofs were generated, either by the application of a range predicate axiom (formulas at lines 1,7,9,20,22), or via Project which uses one or more applications of the axiom of congruence (formulas at lines 5,12,14,16,19). Notice that the formula at line 9 contains variables that do not belong in time step 5 where the Shrink-Left axiom can be applied, but which is congruent, and therefore is Project-ed to the formula at line 16 which does belong at time step 5.

5   Experiences

We now describe our experiences so far with implementing the technique and applying it to verify programs, some lessons drawn from our experiments and some possible avenues for future work.

Implementation. We have extended the FOCI split prover [18] with axioms for range predicates. Our current implementation is specialized to the axioms for range predicates and has an overall structure similar to procedure Generate from Section 3, but with a few differences. First, instead of applying the generalizing rule to all the atomic predicates deduced by the ground procedure, we only generalize from a set of predicates that are obtainable by some syntactic manipulation of the input constraints. Second, there are heuristics to bias the prover to find simpler proofs, with more general interpolants, *i.e.*, those which are less specific to the particular path whose constraints are fed to the prover. The extended prover is integrated with BLAST [14]. As the predicates found require disjunctive images, we use FOCI to iteratively refine the transition relation using the method presented in [17].

Experiments. In preliminary experiments, we have applied the model checker extended with range predicates to a variety of small array-intensive programs hitherto beyond the grasp of automatic refinement based tools. The results are summarized in Table 3. `init` is the example from Section 2. `vararg` is an instance of the common idiom in C programs for scanning the buffer of arguments to determine how many input parameters were passed into the program, by repeatedly increasing an index until a NULL cell is found, and then going backwards (decreasing the counter) dereferencing the contents of the array to extract the arguments. The property proved is that in the second phase, the values dereferenced are non-NULL. copy(from [12]) simply copies the contents of one array into another, and then asserts that the two are the same. copy-prop first checks that a given source array has only non-zero elements, then copies the array into a destination and asserts that the destination has only non-zero elements. find (from [11]) scans the array trying to find the index at which a particular value resides, and returns −1 if the value is not in the array. The property checks that if −1 is returned then the value is not in the array. partition (from [4]) copies the zero and non-zero elements of a source array into two different arrays and checks that the two destination arrays only have zeros and non-zeros respectively. part-init (from [12]) copies those indices of a source array for which the source array's value is positive, into a target array, and checks that at the index stored in the target array the source array's value is indeed positive. producer is a producer-consumer example, where a producer keeps generating a sequence of values and writes them into increasingly larger array indices via a head index that is incremented, while a consumer consumer uses a tail index to read the values stored in the array. The property checked is that the sequence of values written by the producer is the same as those read by the consumer. insert is an in-place insertion routine, that takes a sorted array and inserts a new element into the appropriate place by repeatedly swapping elements until the right position is found (*i.e.,* the inner loop in an insertion sort procedure). The property checked is that after the insertion, the extended array is sorted. scull is a text-book Linux device driver for which we check a property that requires an array of devices to be appropriately initialized.

Discussion and Future Work. Our experiments show that the axioms are expressive enough to capture many of the idiomatic uses of arrays, while yielding property-sensitive abstractions. However, there are several deficiencies in the approach that need to be remedied with future work. The main difficulty with the approach is that the prover may find proofs which refute short paths, but which do not generalize to longer paths, thereby delaying convergence, or worse, cluttering the abstraction with irrelevant facts about the program causing image computation to explode. This problem arose in our (as yet unsuccessful) attempt to prove that an implementation of insertion-sort correctly sorted an array. Though the range predicate axioms suffice to prove the property, BLAST is overwhelmed by irrelevant predicates generated by smaller paths. Thus, one possible line to pursue is to find ways to make the outer loop converge more rapidly. Finally, we view this work as first step towards an axiom-extensible technique for verifying data-sensitive properties. To this end, we would like to implement a generalized split-proof engine parameterized by axioms, and devise and instantiate it with axioms for other data structures like lists [24,20], hash tables and richer logical constructs like separating conjunctions [10].

Acknowledgements. We would like to thank Cormac Flanagan, Alan Hu, Rupak Majumdar, Zvonimir Rakamaric, Tom Reps, Andrey Rybalchenko, and the anonymous referees for extremely useful comments about a previous version of the paper. The first author was supported in part, by NSF grant CNS-0541606.

References

1. Balaban, I., Pnueli, A., Zuck, L.D.: Shape analysis by predicate abstraction. In: Cousot, R. (ed.) VMCAI 2005. LNCS, vol. 3385, pp. 164–180. Springer, Heidelberg (2005)
2. Ball, T., Rajamani, S.K.: The SLAM project: debugging system software via static analysis. In: POPL 02: Principles of Programming Languages, pp. 1–3. ACM Press, New York (2002)
3. Beyer, D., Henzinger, T., Majumdar, R., Rybalchenko, A.: Invariant synthesis in combination theories. In: Cook, B., Podelski, A. (eds.) VMCAI 2007. LNCS, vol. 4349, Springer, Heidelberg (2007)
4. Beyer, D., Henzinger, T., Majumdar, R., Rybalchenko, A.: Path invariants. In: PLDI 2007 (to appear)
5. Bouillaguet, C., Kuncak, V., Wies, T., Zee, K., Rinard, M.: Using first-order theorem provers in the Jahob data structure verification system. In: Verification, Model Checking and Abstract Interpretation (November 2007)
6. Bradley, A.R., Manna, Z., Sipma, H.B.: What's decidable about arrays? In: Emerson, E.A., Namjoshi, K.S. (eds.) VMCAI 2006. LNCS, vol. 3855, pp. 427–442. Springer, Heidelberg (2005)
7. Chaki, S., Clarke, E.M., Groce, A., Strichman, O.: Predicate abstraction with minimum predicates. In: Geist, D., Tronci, E. (eds.) CHARME 2003. LNCS, vol. 2860, pp. 19–34. Springer, Heidelberg (2003)
8. Clarke, E.M., Grumberg, O., Jha, S., Lu, Y., Veith, H.: Counterexample-guided abstraction refinement. In: Emerson, E.A., Sistla, A.P. (eds.) CAV 2000. LNCS, vol. 1855, pp. 154–169. Springer, Heidelberg (2000)
9. Dams, D., Namjoshi, K.S.: Shape analysis through predicate abstraction and model checking. In: Zuck, L.D., Attie, P.C., Cortesi, A., Mukhopadhyay, S. (eds.) VMCAI 2003. LNCS, vol. 2575, pp. 310–324. Springer, Heidelberg (2002)
10. Distefano, D., O'Hearn, P.W., Yang, H.: A local shape analysis based on separation logic. In: Hermanns, H., Palsberg, J. (eds.) TACAS 2006 and ETAPS 2006. LNCS, vol. 3920, pp. 287–302. Springer, Heidelberg (2006)
11. Flanagan, C., Qadeer, S.: Predicate abstraction for software verification. In: POPL 02: Principles of Programming Languages, pp. 191–202. ACM Press, New York (2002)
12. Denis Gopan, Thomas W. Reps, and Shmuel Sagiv. A framework for numeric analysis of array operations. In: POPL, pp. 338–350 (2005)
13. Graf, S., Saïdi, H.: Construction of abstract state graphs with PVS. In: Grumberg, O. (ed.) CAV 1997. LNCS, vol. 1254, pp. 72–83. Springer, Heidelberg (1997)
14. Henzinger, T.A., Jhala, R., Majumdar, R., McMillan, K.L.: Abstractions from proof. In: POPL 04, pp. 232–244. ACM Press, New York (2004)
15. Henzinger, T.A., Jhala, R., Majumdar, R., Sutre, G.: Lazy abstraction. In: POPL 02: Principles of Programming Languages, pp. 58–70. ACM Press, New York (2002)
16. Jain, H., Ivancic, F., Gupta, A., Ganai, M.K.: Localization and register sharing for predicate abstraction. In: Halbwachs, N., Zuck, L.D. (eds.) TACAS 2005. LNCS, vol. 3440, pp. 397–412. Springer, Heidelberg (2005)

17. Jhala, R., McMillan, K.L.: Interpolant-based transition relation approximation. In: Etessami, K., Rajamani, S.K. (eds.) CAV 2005. LNCS, vol. 3576, pp. 39–51. Springer, Heidelberg (2005)
18. Jhala, R., McMillan, K.L.: A practical and complete approach to predicate refinement. In: Hermanns, H., Palsberg, J. (eds.) TACAS 2006 and ETAPS 2006. LNCS, vol. 3920, pp. 298–312. Springer, Heidelberg (2006)
19. Lahiri, S.K., Ball, T., Cook, B.: Predicate abstraction via symbolic decision procedures. In: Etessami, K., Rajamani, S.K. (eds.) CAV 2005. LNCS, vol. 3576, pp. 24–38. Springer, Heidelberg (2005)
20. Shuvendu, K.: Lahiri and Shaz Qadeer. Verifying properties of well-founded linked list. In: POPL, pp. 115–126 (2006)
21. Lev-Ami, T., Sagiv, S.: TVLA: A system for implementing static analyses. In: Palsberg, J. (ed.) SAS 2000. LNCS, vol. 1824, Springer, Heidelberg (2000)
22. McMillan, K.L.: Lazy abstraction with interpolants. In: Ball, T., Jones, R.B. (eds.) CAV 2006. LNCS, vol. 4144, pp. 123–136. Springer, Heidelberg (2006)
23. McMillan, K.L.: An interpolating theorem prover. Theor. Comput. Sci. 345(1), 101–121 (2005)
24. Rakamaric, Z., Bingham, J.D., Hu, A.J.: An inference-rule-based decision procedure for verification of heap-manipulating programs with mutable data and cyclic data structures. In: Cook, B., Podelski, A. (eds.) VMCAI 2007. LNCS, vol. 4349, Springer, Heidelberg (2007)
25. Reps, T.W.: Demand interprocedural program analysis using logic databases. In: Workshop on Programming with Logic Databases (1993)
26. Sagiv, S., Reps, T.W., Wilhelm, R.: Parametric shape analysis via 3-valued logic. ACM Trans. Program. Lang. Syst. 24(3), 217–298 (2002)
27. Sankaranarayanan, S., Sipma, H.B., Manna, Z.: Scalable analysis of linear systems using mathematical programming. In: Cousot, R. (ed.) VMCAI 2005. LNCS, vol. 3385, pp. 25–41. Springer, Heidelberg (2005)

Context-Bounded Analysis of Multithreaded Programs with Dynamic Linked Structures

Ahmed Bouajjani[1], Séverine Fratani[1], and Shaz Qadeer[2]

[1] LIAFA, CNRS & University of Paris 7
{abou,fratani}@liafa.jussieu.fr
[2] Microsoft Research, Redmond
qadeer@microsoft.com

Abstract. Bounded context switch reachability analysis is a useful and efficient approach for detecting bugs in multithreaded programs. In this paper, we address the application of this approach to the analysis of multithreaded programs with procedure calls and dynamic linked structures. We define a program semantics based on concurrent pushdown systems with *visible heaps* as stack symbols. A visible heap is the part of the heap reachable from global and local variables. We use pushdown analysis techniques to define an algorithm that explores the entire configuration space reachable under given bounds on the number of context switches and the size of visible heaps.

1 Introduction

Automated analysis of software systems is a challenging problem. The behavior of these systems is usually complex and hard to predict due to aspects such as concurrency and memory management. Reasoning about these behaviors requires considering potentially infinite sets of configurations which makes verification problems undecidable in general. Therefore, approaches based on approximate analysis are needed. While over-approximations are useful for proving properties, under-approximations are useful for finding bugs. In this paper, we propose algorithmic (automata-based) techniques for under-approximate analysis of multithreaded programs that manipulate dynamic linked structures.

A simple way to get an under-approximate analysis is to bound the depth of the explored state space and use finite-state model checking techniques. This approach is interesting only if bugs appear after a small number of computation steps (e.g., [6]), which is unlikely to be the case for multithreaded programs. In such a program, processes interact through shared memory and are executed in alternation according to a schedule. Concurrency bugs appear only after a number of *context switches*, i.e, points in the execution where the active process is stopped and another one is resumed. Between context switches, a process may execute an unbounded number of computation steps. Therefore, a natural approach for under-approximate analysis of multithreaded program is to perform a (precise) analysis for a bounded number of context switches [9]. It has been demonstrated that this is indeed efficient for detecting bugs in multithread programs since they appear in many cases after a small number of context switches [7].

W. Damm and H. Hermanns (Eds.): CAV 2007, LNCS 4590, pp. 207–220, 2007.

However, bounding the number of context-switches does not allow the use of finite-state model checkers since each process may be infinite-state, and unbounded computations are possible between context switches. For example, in concurrent programs with procedure calls, each process may have an unbounded stack. In [9,2], automata-based techniques for symbolic analysis of pushdown systems have been used in order to define bounded context switch analysis of programs with finite data domains. In this paper, we consider the more general case of concurrent programs (with procedure calls) which can create shared objects and manipulate references to them.

In the spirit of under-approximate analysis, we could bound the heap size and reduce this verification problem to the case with finite data domains. This simple approach is unlikely to be effective at getting good state-space coverage for real programs, in which many heap-allocated objects are used either as local variables or for passing parameters to a called procedure. For such programs, it is better to bound only the *visible heap*, i.e., the part of the heap that is reachable from the global variables and the local variables of the running procedure in the active process. Indeed, a program's global heap might be unbounded in spite of its visible heap being bounded due to unbounded nesting of procedure calls.

It is nontrivial to obtain an algorithm for reachability analysis of multithreaded programs based on bounding the number of context switches and the size of the visible heap. In [10,11,8], the idea of visible heaps was used for interprocedural analysis of sequential programs; these techniques are based on procedure summarization and cannot be used for multithreaded programs since the (infinite) sets of stack configurations reached by processes must be stored at each context switch. Moreover, [10,11] consider abstract semantics, whereas we must consider an exact - sound and complete - semantics. Nevertheless, the idea of visible heaps can be used to define a program semantics where the heap is manipulated implicitly and not as a shared global structure: each procedure executed by some process manipulates a local heap structure which is a *copy* of its visible heap. Such an approach leads to a program model based on stack machines where locally visible heaps constitute the (potentially infinite) stack alphabet. To simulate correctly the "real" heap, our algorithm synchronizes the local views of procedures and processes at each procedure call or return and at each context switch. We prove that our new semantics is correct and use it to define an automata-based symbolic reachability analysis algorithm for bounded context switches and bounded visible heap. For lack of space, the proofs of our theorems are omitted here. They can be found in [3].

The contribution of our paper, although theoretical, has important practical applications. Since our algorithm constructs the set of reachable stack configurations, it allows the verification of reachability queries that require stack inspection. This expressiveness is important for specifying various resource-usage scenarios, e.g., user-space buffers are accessed by an operating system kernel only within the scope of an appropriate exception handler, or certain operations on security-critical objects are invoked only if a certain privileged procedure is present on the call stack. Our algorithm allows the verification of such expressive queries for multithreaded programs upto the context-switch and visible heap bounds and for single-threaded programs upto the visible heap bound. Of course, our algorithm can be used iteratively by systematically increasing the bounds in each iteration.

2 Multithreaded Programs with Dynamic Memory

We consider programs with multiple threads and procedure calls, which can dynamically create objects and manipulate pointers on these objects. A sequential program is given as a collection of control flow graphs, one graph for each of its procedures, defined by a set of control nodes N, and a set of transitions between these nodes labeled with actions and tests on the memory heap. We assume that the control flow graph of each procedure p has a unique initial control location n_{init}^p and a unique termination location n_{end}^p reachable after executing a return action. A multithread program consists of a parallel composition of a fixed number of sequential programs sharing the heap.

Let $\mathbb{A}$ be a countable (infinite) domain of memory addresses (pointers), and assume that $\mathbb{A}$ contains a special element $\perp$ representing the null address and a special element $\top$ representing an undefined address. Then, consider a class of objects where each object contains n successor fields $s_1, \ldots, s_n$ ranging over the pointer domain $\mathbb{A}$. Let $S = \{s_1, \ldots, s_n\}$. (We omit aspects related to data manipulation. Data values over finite data domains can of course be encoded in the successor fields.)

We assume that a program has a set of *global* pointer variables G ranging over $\mathbb{A}$. These variables are shared by all parallel threads, and all procedures. Moreover, we consider that each procedure has a set of *local* pointer variables (also ranging over $\mathbb{A}$). We assume w.l.o.g. that all the procedures have the same set of local variables L. Given a (global/local) pointer variable v and a successor field $s \in S$, we denote by $v.s$ the pointer stored in the field s of the object pointed by v. This notation can be extended to sequences of successor fields $\sigma \in S^*$ in the obvious manner. When σ is the empty sequence, we consider that $v.\sigma$ is identical to v.

Programs can perform the following operations on heaps: $v.\sigma := v'.\sigma'$ (*pointer assignment*), $v.\sigma := null$ (*pointer annihilation*), and $v.\sigma := new$ (*object creation*), where v, v' are pointer variables, and $\sigma \in S \cup \{\varepsilon\}, \sigma' \in S^*$. They can also perform the following tests: $v.\sigma \# v'.\sigma'$ with $\# \in \{=, \neq\}$ (*equality/disequality test*). In addition, they can perform the following actions: $call(p, v_1.\sigma_1, \ldots, v_m.\sigma_m)$ (*procedure call with parameters*), and *return* (*termination of a procedure call*), where p is a procedure name, $v_1, \ldots, v_m$ are pointer variables, and $\sigma_1, \ldots, \sigma_m \in S^*$. The effect of executing a statement $call(p, v_1.\sigma_1, \ldots, v_m.\sigma_m)$ is to call the procedure p after initialization of its local variables $\ell_1, \ldots, \ell_m$ with the pointer values $v_1.\sigma_1, \ldots, v_m.\sigma_m$ respectively where the variables $v_1, \ldots, v_m$ are either global variables or local variables of the calling procedure.

3 Program Semantics

Heaps as labeled graphs: A *global heap* is a finite directed graph where vertices correspond to memory addresses, edges are labeled by elements of S, and each element of G appears as a label of some vertex. Formally, a global heap is a tuple $GH = (A, \Delta, \Gamma)$ where (1) A is a finite subset of $\mathbb{A}$ containing $\perp$ and $\top$, (2) $\Delta : S \to (A \to A)$ associates with each $s \in S$ a successor mapping, and (3) $\Gamma : G \to A$ associates with a global variable g an object address. We assume that $\forall s \in S. \Delta(s)(\perp) = \top$ and $\Delta(s)(\top) = \top$, and $\forall a \in A$, $\Delta(s)(a)$ is defined.

Given $\sigma = s_{i_1} \cdots s_{i_m} \in S^*$, we denote by $\Delta(\sigma)$ the mapping $\Delta(s_{i_m}) \circ \cdots \circ \Delta(s_{i_1})$. When σ is the empty sequence, we consider that $\Delta(\sigma)$ is the identity mapping over A. Then, we define the reachability mapping to be $Reach_\Delta = \bigcup_{\sigma \in S^*} \Delta(\sigma)$.

Then, we consider that a *heap* is a global heap augmented by a mapping associating with each local variable an address. Formally, a heap is a pair $H = (GH, \Lambda)$, where $GH = (A, \Delta, \Gamma)$ is a global heap and $\Lambda : L \to A$.

Programs as concurrent heap pushdown systems: We associate with multithreaded programs concurrent stack machines which act on a (global) shared heap. The behavior of such concurrent stack machines is as follows: at each moment, there is one process which is running and has access to the heap through the global variables (shared by all processes), and its own local variables. Notice that due to nested procedure calls, the heap may be accessible from the local variables of the currently running procedure, and also from the local environments (of the pending procedure executions) stored in the stack of the process. While this process is running, all the other parallel processes are in an idle mode. When a context switch occurs, the active process is interrupted and some other one is resumed, becoming the new active process.

Let us sketch here the construction of the models associated with programs (details can be found in [3]). Let Σ be the (infinite) set of all pairs $\langle n, \Lambda \rangle$, where $n \in N$ and $\Lambda \in [L \to \mathbb{A}]$. We associate with each sequential program (given by a control flow graph) a *heap pushdown system* (H-PDS) which is a stack machine whose control states are global heaps, and whose stack alphabet is Σ: The semantics of basic operations and tests is defined by a transition relation $\xrightarrow{op}$ between heaps, and procedure calls and returns are modeled as usual by push and pop operations on the stack. Then, we associate with a multithreaded program with m parallel threads an m-dim *concurrent heap pushdown system* (CH-PDS). Control states of such a model are pairs (i, GH), where $i \in [1, m]$ is the index of the active process, and GH is a global heap. A configuration of a CH-PDS is a tuple $((i, GH), [u_1, \ldots, u_m])$ where $u_1, \ldots, u_m \in \Sigma^*$ are the local configurations of each of the threads, i.e., the contents of their stacks. A transition relation $\Rightarrow$ is defined between configurations: computations steps are either local to a process (the process i in the global state (i, GH)), or correspond to a context switch (i.e., substitution of i by some $j \neq i$ in the global state (i, GH)).

Bounded heap depth programs: Let $k \geq 1$. Let $c = ((i, GH), [u_1, \ldots, u_m])$ be a configuration, where $GH = (A, \Delta, \Gamma)$. Then, c is k-bounded iff for every $\langle n, \Lambda \rangle$ appearing in any u_i, for any $i \in \{1, \ldots, m\}$, we have $|Reach_\Delta(\Gamma(G) \cup \Lambda(L))| \leq k$. A program is k-bounded for a set of initial configurations C iff every $\Rightarrow$-reachable configuration from C is k-bounded. A program has *bounded heap depth* if it is k-bounded for some $k \geq 1$.

Notice that a heap with a bounded depth may have an unbounded size. Indeed, due to unbounded nesting of procedure calls, it is possible to have an unbounded stack of environments each of them pointing to a different but bounded part of the heap.

4   Program Semantics Based on Locally Visible Heaps

We define in this section a program semantics in terms of concurrent pushdown systems. The difference with the CH-PDS based semantics of the previous section is that the heap is not manipulated explicitly as a global shared structure, but rather implicitly: each procedure executed by some process manipulates a local heap structure which is a *copy* of the reachable part of the heap from its local and global variables. Therefore, we can associate with programs stack machines where locally visible heaps constitute the stack alphabet. However, to simulate correctly operations on the "real" heap, procedures and processes must exchange (pass/update) their local informations about the heap at each procedure call/return and context switch. These manipulations of the local heaps are quite delicate. Let us give an informal description of the main ideas behind them.

Consider first the case of a sequential program. At each procedure call, the caller passes to the callee a copy of a part of its local heap. At the return of the call, the callee gives back its new local heap, the last one before termination, to the caller which updates accordingly its own local heap (which corresponds to its view of the heap just before the call). To perform correctly these caller/callee communications, a relation between vertices in different copies of a same piece of the "real" heap must be maintained, relating vertices which are copies of each other, representing the same address in the heap. Moreover, since pointer manipulation may disconnect some vertices from the visible part of a procedure during its execution, the deletion of these vertices from the local structure can be problematic since these vertices may still be relevant for further executions of procedures in the call stack. To handle this problem, we introduce a notion of *cut points*: when a heap is passed from the caller to the callee, cut points represent the first vertices in the visible part by the callee which are reachable from the caller or from other procedures in the call stack. Then, during the execution of the procedure, a vertex can be removed from the locally visible heap only if it becomes unreachable from the local variables, the global variables, and the cut points.

In the case of parallel programs, an additional but similar mechanism has to be introduced for passing/updating locally visible heaps at context switches. Intuitively, parallel processes synchronize their views of the heap at each context switch. The active process passes its local heap to all of the other processes which can update accordingly their local heaps (corresponding to the configuration at the previous context switch), taking into account the modifications on the heap performed by the active process while they were idle. For that, the active process maintains in its control state, which is a global state for all its procedures, a relation between its current local heap and its initial local heap corresponding to the configuration at the last context switch, allowing to determine for each vertex in the (old) local heaps whether it has a copy in the (new) local heap returned by the active process. Also, to deal with vertex deletion, it is necessary to extend the use of cut points by considering the reachable vertices from the stacks of each process. In fact, each process needs to distinguish his own cut points from the ones of the other processes.

We prove that the new semantics is correct (sound and complete) w.r.t. the original semantics (in section 3) in the sense that they define bisimilar transition systems. An important property allowing to prove this fact is that isomorphism between locally visible heaps preserves bisimilarity (i.e., substitution of isomorphic local heaps does not modify behaviors). This holds because the performed operations and tests on the heaps do not refer to the precise values of the addresses. (Notice that there is an infinite number of isomorphic heaps of a same size since the address domain is infinite). Then, we consider a normalization operation for visible heaps which associates to each of them an equivalent heap modulo isomorphism, and we prove that the semantics based on normalized visible heaps is also correct w.r.t. the original semantics. Our normalization operation matches all the isomorphic visible heaps to a finite number of representatives. (We do not have a unique representative due to the presence of cut points.) Therefore, for sequential programs, our pushdown model construction terminates for bounded heap depth programs. For concurrent programs, the construction terminates for a finite number of a context switches, given a bound on the heap depth.

4.1 Locally Visible Heaps

A *cut heap* is a tuple $CH = (A, \Delta, \Gamma, \Lambda, \overrightarrow{C})$ where $(A, \Delta, \Gamma, \Lambda)$ is a heap and $\overrightarrow{C} \in (2^A)^m$ is a vector of sets of cut points. For each $i \in \{1, \dots, m\}$, $\overrightarrow{C}(i)$ is the set of cut points reachable from the local environments (of the pending procedure executions) stored in the stack of the process i. Then, a *visible heap* is a cut heap such that $A = Reach_\Delta(\Gamma(G) \cup \Lambda(L) \cup \bigcup_{i=1}^m \overrightarrow{C}(i) \cup \{\bot\})$, i.e., it is a cut heap without garbage. We define an operation of *garbage elimination* allowing to obtain a visible heap from a cut heap: given a cut heap $CH = (A, \Delta, \Gamma, \Lambda, \overrightarrow{C})$, the visible heap $Clean(CH)$ is given by $(A', \Delta', \Gamma, \Lambda, \overrightarrow{C})$ where $A' = A \cap Reach_\Delta(\Gamma(G) \cup \Lambda(L) \cup \bigcup_{i=1}^m \overrightarrow{C}(i) \cup \{\bot\})$ and $\forall s \in S. \Delta'(s) = \Delta(s) \cap [A' \to A']$, i.e., the restriction of $\Delta(s)$ to A'.

We define an equivalence relation $\simeq$ between visible heaps which is essentially graph isomorphism modulo renaming of vertices. Let $VH_1 = (A_1, \Delta_1, \Gamma_1, \Lambda_1, \overrightarrow{C_1})$ and $VH_2 = (A_2, \Delta_2, \Gamma_2, \Lambda_2, \overrightarrow{C_2})$ be two visible heaps and let $\beta : A_1 \to A_2$ be a bijection s.t. $\beta(\top) = \top$ and $\beta(\bot) = \bot$. Then, $VH_1 \simeq_\beta VH_2$ iff (i) $\forall s \in S. \forall a \in A_1. \beta(\Delta_1(s)(a)) = \Delta_2(s)(\beta(a))$, (ii) $\forall v \in G. \Gamma_2(v) = \beta(\Gamma_1(v))$, and $\forall v \in L. \Lambda_2(v) = \beta(\Lambda_1(v))$, and (iii) $\forall i \in [1, m]$, $\overrightarrow{C_2}(i) = \{\beta(c) : c \in \overrightarrow{C_1}(i)\}$. Then, $VH_1 \simeq VH_2$ if there is a β s.t. $VH_1 \simeq_\beta VH_2$.

4.2 Sequential Programs as Pushdown Systems

Let us define an *environment* to be a tuple $e = \langle n, VH, \pi \rangle$ where $n \in N$, VH is a visible heap, and $\pi \subseteq \mathbb{A} \times \mathbb{A}$ is an injective function (π relates vertices in the heap of the caller procedure with vertices in the current visible heap VH). Let $\mathbb{V}$ be the set of all environments. Then, we associate with each sequential process a *visible heap pushdown system* (VH-PDS) which is a stack machine whose stack alphabet is $\mathbb{V}$ and whose control states are injective functions from $\mathbb{A}$ to $\mathbb{A}$. These functions are used to maintain a link between the current visible heap of the running sequential process and its initial visible heap since its last activation (at the initial configuration of the system or at the last context switch). This information is needed at the next context switch for updating the visible heaps of the idle processes. (Informations in control states can be omitted in the case of a purely sequential program.) Now, let i be the index of a sequential process. We define the (infinite) set of transition rules R_i of the stack machine associated with process i by means of the three inference rules given hereafter.

Basic operations and test: We extend the relation $\xrightarrow{op}$ defined on heaps (see section 3) to a relation on visible heaps (which also informs about the correspondence between vertices in the original and final heaps). Let $VH_1 = (H_1, \vec{C_1})$, and $VH_2 = (H_2, \vec{C_2})$ be two visible heaps. For every function $\pi : \mathbb{A} \times \mathbb{A}$, we have $VH_1 \xrightarrow{op}_\pi VH_2$ iff there exists a heap H'_2 s.t. $H_1 \xrightarrow{op} H'_2$ and $Clean(H'_2, \vec{C_1}) \simeq_\pi VH_2$. Then:

$$\frac{n_1 \xrightarrow{op} n_2 \quad VH_1 \xrightarrow{op}_\pi VH_2}{(\Pi, \langle n_1, VH_1, \pi_1 \rangle) \hookrightarrow (\Pi \circ \pi, \langle n_2, VH_2, \pi_1 \circ \pi \rangle) \in R_i} \quad \text{HeapOp}$$

Procedure calls: Let $i \in [1, m]$ be the index of the active sequential process, let $VH_1 = (A_1, \Delta_1, \Gamma_1, \Lambda_1, \vec{C_1})$ be the visible heap of the caller procedure, and let $v_1.\sigma_1, \ldots, v_k.\sigma_k$ be the effective parameters which must be assigned respectively to the local variables $\ell_1, \ldots, \ell_k$ of the called procedure (considered as its formal parameters). The visible heap passed to the callee procedure (of the process i) is obtained as follows: (1) construct first the cut heap $CutPass_i(VH_1)$ which is a copy of VH_1, where local variables of the callee procedure are assigned with their new values, and local variables of the caller procedure are memorized as cut points, (2) then determine the new vector of sets of cut points: cut points of processes $j \neq i$ stay unchanged, cut points of the process i are the first addresses reachable from cut points of $CutPass_i(VH_1)$ in the sub-heap corresponding to reachable addresses from the new local variables, the global variables, and the cut points of all processes, (3) finally remove the garbage of $CutPass_i(VH_1)$ according to the new set of cut points.

Let us define formally the operation $CutPass_i$. Let $VH = (A, \Delta, \Gamma, \Lambda, \vec{C})$ be a visible heap. Then, $CutPass_i(VH, [\ell_1, v_1.\sigma_1], \ldots, [\ell_k, v_k.\sigma_k])$ is the cut heap $(A, \Delta, \Gamma, \Lambda', \vec{C'})$ where (1) $\forall j \in [1, k], \Lambda'(\ell_j) = \Delta(\sigma_j)((\Lambda \cup \Gamma)(v_j))$ and $\Lambda'(\ell) = \top$ for all other variables $\ell \in L$, (2) $\forall j \in [1, m], j \neq i$, we have $\vec{C'}(j) = \vec{C}(j)$, and (3) $\vec{C'}(i) = \vec{C}(i) \cup \Lambda(L)$.

We give now the formal definition of the visible heap passed by the caller to the callee. Consider $CH = (A, \Delta, \Gamma, \Lambda, \vec{C})$ to be any cut heap. Let $A' = Reach_\Delta(\Gamma(G) \cup \Lambda(L) \cup \bigcup_{j \neq i} \vec{C}(j))$ (the set A' is the visible part of the heap from local and global variables and from cut points in $\vec{C}(j)$, for $j \neq i$), and let Δ' be the restriction of Δ to vertices in A'. Then, let $Visible_i(CH) = Clean(A, \Delta, \Gamma, \Lambda, \vec{C'})$ where, for every $j \in [1, m]$ s.t. $j \neq i$, $\vec{C'}(j) = \vec{C}(j)$, and $\vec{C'}(i) = (A' \cap Reach_\Delta(\vec{C}(i))) \setminus \Delta'(S)(Reach_\Delta(\vec{C}(i)))$. The set $\vec{C'}(i)$ contains the first vertices in A' which are Δ-reachable from $\vec{C}(i)$. The cleaning operation removes all vertices which are Δ-reachable only from $\vec{C}(i)$, i.e., the set of vertices in $Visible_i(CH)$ is precisely A'.

Finally, given a visible heap VH, we define $\mathsf{Pass}_i(VH, p, v_1.\sigma_1, \ldots, v_k.\sigma_k)$ to be the set of pairs (VH_π, π) such that $Visible_i(CutPass_i(VH, [\ell_1, v_1.\sigma_1], \ldots, [\ell_k, v_k.\sigma_k])) \simeq_\pi VH_\pi$. The injective relation π allows to relate addresses in the visible heap of the caller with addresses in the new visible heap. It is used to update the heap of the caller after termination of the callee procedure. Then, we consider the inference rule:

$$\frac{n_1 \xrightarrow{call(p, v_1.\sigma_1, \ldots, v_k.\sigma_k)} n_2 \quad (VH_2, \pi_2) \in \mathsf{Pass}_i(VH_1, p, v_1.\sigma_1, \ldots, v_k.\sigma_k)}{(\Pi, \langle n_1, VH_1, \pi_1 \rangle) \hookrightarrow (\Pi \circ \pi_2, \langle n^p_{init}, VH_2, \pi_2 \rangle \langle n_2, VH_1, \pi_1 \rangle) \in R_i} \quad \text{Call}$$

Procedure returns: Given the current visible heap VH_2 of the terminating procedure and the visible heap VH_1 of the caller procedure stored in the stack, we define an operation updating VH_1 according to the effect of the procedure call on the heap.

Let $\pi_2 \subseteq A_1 \times A_2$ be an injective relation giving the correspondence between the vertices of VH_1 and VH_2 (i.e., if $(a_1, a_2) \in \pi$ and $(a'_1, a_2) \in \pi$, then $a_1 = a'_1$). We suppose that $A_1 \cap A_2 = \{\top, \bot\}$ (otherwise, instead of VH_2 and π_2, consider a new visible heap VH'_2 and $\pi_2 \circ \pi$ for some π s.t. $VH_2 \simeq_\pi VH'_2$).

Then, let $B_1 = \{a \in A_1 : \not\exists a' \in A_2. (a, a') \in \pi_2\}$, let $B_2 = \{a \in A_1 : \exists a' \in A_2. (a, a') \in \pi_2\}$, and let $B_3 = \{a' \in A_2 : \not\exists a \in A_1. (a, a') \in \pi_2\}$.

Intuitively, B_1 is the set of vertices in A_1 such that either they were not reachable in the initial visible heap passed to the called procedure, and therefore they should be restored in the heap of the caller procedure after the call return, or they became invisible during the call execution due to garbage deletion and therefore they should not appear in the heap after the call return since they were not reachable from cut points. (We explain below how to get rid of the vertices in this second category). Vertices in B_2 are those which were present before the call, and which are still present after termination of the call. Finally, B_3 is the set of the created vertices during the call.

It can be easily seen that these three sets are disjoint. Moreover, we have $B_3 \cup \pi_2(B_2) = A_2$. Let us consider the bijection $\beta : A_2 \to B_2 \cup B_3$ defined in the obvious way (for every $a \in A_2$, if $a \in B_3$ then $\beta(a) = a$, otherwise $\beta(a) = \pi_2^{-1}(a)$).

Let $(A'_1, \Delta'_1, \Gamma'_1, \Lambda'_1, \vec{C'_1})$ be the cut heap such that (1) $A'_1 = B_1 \cup B_2 \cup B_3$, (2) $\forall g \in G. \Gamma'_1(g) = \beta(\Gamma_2(g))$, (3) $\forall \ell \in L, \Lambda'_1(\ell) = \Lambda_1(\ell)$, (4) $\vec{C'_1}(i) = \vec{C_1}(i)$ and $\forall j \neq i, \vec{C'_1}(j) = \beta(\vec{C_2}(j))$, and (5) $\forall s \in S$, (i) $\forall a \in B_1. \Delta'_1(s)(a) = \Delta_1(s)(a)$, (ii) $\forall a \in B_2. \Delta'_1(s)(a) = \beta(\Delta_2(s)(\pi_2(a)))$, and (iii) $\forall a \in B_3. \Delta'_1(s)(a) = \beta(\Delta_2(s)(a))$.

Then, we define $\mathsf{Update\text{-}seq}_i(VH_1, VH_2, \pi_2)$ to be the set of all pairs (VH_π, π) such that $Clean(A'_1, \Delta'_1, \Gamma'_1, \Lambda'_1, \vec{C'_1}) \simeq_\pi VH_\pi$.

Notice that (1) the cleaning operation removes the vertices of A_1 which were garbage collected during the procedure call, and (2) for every VH'_2, and every β s.t. $VH_2 \simeq_\beta VH'_2$, $\mathsf{Update\text{-}seq}_i(VH_1, VH_2, \pi_2) = \mathsf{Update\text{-}seq}_i(VH_1, VH'_2, \pi_2 \circ \beta)$.

Then, we consider the inference rule:

$$\frac{n \xrightarrow{return} n_{end} \quad (VH'_1, \pi') \in \mathsf{Update\text{-}seq}_i(VH_1, VH_2, \pi_2)}{(\Pi, \langle n, VH_2, \pi_2\rangle \langle n', VH_1, \pi_1\rangle) \hookrightarrow (\Pi \circ \pi', \langle n', VH'_1, \pi_1 \circ \pi'\rangle) \in R_i} \quad \text{Return}$$

4.3   Multithreaded Programs as Concurrent Pushdown Systems

We associate with a multithreaded program with m parallel threads an m-dim *concurrent visible heap pushdown system* (CVH-PDS). The stack alphabet is $\mathbb{V}$, and the (infinite) set of control states is $\mathbb{S} = \{(i, \vec{\Pi}) : i \in [1, m], \vec{\Pi} = (\vec{\Pi}(1), \ldots, \vec{\Pi}(m)), \vec{\Pi}(j) : \mathbb{A} \to \mathbb{A}\}$. We define hereafter the set of transition rules $\mathcal{R}$ of the model.

Local transitions: Transitions of each sequential process are obviously transitions of the whole system. For every $i \in [1, m]$, let R_i be the set of transition rules associated with the process of index i (defined in the previous subsection). Then, we have:

$$\frac{(\Pi_i,w_i)\hookrightarrow(\Pi'_i,w'_i)\in R_i \quad \overrightarrow{\Pi}(i)=\Pi_i \quad \overrightarrow{\Pi'}(i)=\Pi'_i \quad \forall j\neq i. \; w_j\in V \text{ and } \overrightarrow{\Pi}(j)=\overrightarrow{\Pi'}(j)}{((i,\overrightarrow{\Pi}),[w_1,\ldots,w_i,\ldots,w_m]) \hookrightarrow ((i,\overrightarrow{\Pi'}),[w_1,\ldots,w'_i,\ldots,w_m]) \in \mathcal{R}} \quad \text{Local}$$

Context switches: Finally, consider the case of a context switch. Assume that process i was the last active process and let $VH_i = (A_i,\Delta_i,\Gamma_i,\Lambda_i,\overrightarrow{C_i})$ be its last visible heap. At the context switch, process i communicates to all the other ones (which were idle) informations about the new heap configuration. For that, the part which is *shared* by all processes is extracted from VH_i and passed to them. Then, each process $j \neq i$ updates accordingly its old visible heap (which corresponds to the heap configuration at the previous context switch) before the next active process starts its computation.

Formally, let us define $Shared_i(VH_i) = Visible_i(CutPass_i(VH_i,\forall\ell \in L. [\ell,\top]))$, and assume that $Shared_i(VH_i) = (A'_i,\Delta'_i,\Gamma'_i,\Lambda'_i,\overrightarrow{C'_i})$. Notice that we remove from A_i only vertices that are reachable from local variables in L or from cut points in $\overrightarrow{C_i}(i)$, but which are not reachable from global variables, nor from cut points of other threads. These vertices are not visible from other threads and therefore they do not belong to the shared part of the heap. The cut points in $\overrightarrow{C'_i}(i)$ allow to know which vertices in the shared part are reachable from local variables in the stack of the current thread. The removed vertices will be added to the heap when the current process will resume later. This is done by an updating operation described below.

Let $j \in [1,m]$, let $VH_j = (A_j,\Delta_j,\Gamma_j,\Lambda_j,\overrightarrow{C_j})$ be the visible heap of the process j, and suppose $\Pi \subseteq A_j \times A'_i$ is an injective relation connecting vertices in VH_j with vertices in $Shared_i(VH_i)$. We suppose that $A_i \cap A_j = \{\top,\bot\}$ (otherwise, instead of VH_j and Π, consider VH'_j and $\Pi \circ \pi$ for some π s.t. $VH_j \simeq_\pi VH'_j$).

Then, let $B_1 = \{a \in A_j : \nexists a' \in A'_i. (a,a') \in \Pi\}$, let $B_2 = \{a \in A_j : \exists a' \in A'_i. (a,a') \in \Pi\}$, and let $B_3 = \{a' \in A'_i : \nexists a \in A_j. (a,a') \in \Pi\}$. These sets are disjoint and we have $B_3 \cup \Pi(B_2) = A'_i$. Then, consider the bijection $\beta_j : A'_i \to B_2 \cup B_3$ defined in the obvious way (for every $a \in A'_i$, if $a \in B_3$ then $\beta_j(a) = a$, otherwise $\beta_j(a) = \Pi^{-1}(a)$).

We define the operation $\mathsf{Update\text{-}par}_j$, for $j \in [1,m]$, which updates the local heap of process j using the shared heap passed by process i. For $j \neq i$, let $(A'_j,\Delta'_j,\Gamma'_j,\Lambda'_j,\overrightarrow{C'_j})$ be the cut heap s.t. (1) $A'_j = B_1 \cup B_2 \cup B_3$, (2) $\forall g \in G. \; \Gamma'_j(g) = \beta_j(\Gamma'_i(g))$, (3) $\forall\ell \in L$, $\Lambda'_j(\ell) = \Lambda_j(\ell)$, (4) $\overrightarrow{C'_j}(j) = \overrightarrow{C_j}(j)$, and $\forall k \neq j, \; \overrightarrow{C'_j}(k) = \beta_j(\overrightarrow{C'_i}(k))$, and (5) $\forall s \in S$, (i) $\forall a \in B_1. \Delta'_j(s)(a) = \Delta_j(s)(a)$, (ii) $\forall a \in B_2. \Delta'_j(s)(a) = \beta_j(\Delta'_i(s)(\Pi(a)))$, and (iii) $\forall a \in B_3. \Delta'_j(s)(a) = \beta_j(\Delta'_i(s)(a))$. Then, $\mathsf{Update\text{-}par}_j(VH_j,VH_i,\Pi)$ is defined to be the set of all (VH'_j,π,Π_j) such that (1) $Clean(A'_j,\Delta'_j,\Gamma'_j,\Lambda'_j,\overrightarrow{C'_j}) \simeq_\pi VH'_j$, and (2) $\Pi_j = \pi^{-1} \circ \beta_j^{-1}$. Moreover, for every mapping $\Pi_i : \mathbb{A} \to \mathbb{A}$, we define $\mathsf{Update\text{-}par}_i(VH_i,VH_i,\Pi_i)$ to be the set of all (VH'_i,π,π^{-1}) such that $VH_i \simeq_\pi VH'_i$. Then, we consider the inference rule:

$$\frac{\begin{array}{ccc} i,k\in\{1,\ldots,m\} & i\neq k & \forall j\in\{1,\ldots,m\}. \; w_j=\langle n_j,VH_j,\pi_j\rangle \\[4pt] \multicolumn{3}{c}{\forall j\in\{1,\ldots,m\}. \; (VH'_j,\pi'_j,\Pi_j)\in\mathsf{Update\text{-}par}_j(VH_j,VH_i,\overrightarrow{\Pi}(j)\circ\overrightarrow{\Pi}(i))} \\[4pt] \multicolumn{3}{c}{\forall j\in\{1,\ldots,m\}. \; w'_j=\langle n_j,VH'_j,\pi_j\circ\pi'_j\rangle} \end{array}}{((i,\overrightarrow{\Pi}),[w_1,\ldots,w_m]) \hookrightarrow ((k,(\Pi_1,\ldots,\Pi_m)\circ\Pi_k^{-1}),[w'_1,\ldots,w'_m]) \in \mathcal{R}} \quad \text{Switch}$$

with the notational convention $(\Pi_1,\ldots,\Pi_m)\circ\Pi = (\Pi_1\circ\Pi,\ldots,\Pi_m\circ\Pi)$.

4.4 Associated Transition System and Correctness of the Semantics

A *configuration* of a CVH-PDS is a tuple $((i, \overrightarrow{\Pi}), [v_1, \ldots, v_m]) \in \mathbb{S} \times [\mathbb{V}^*]^m$ where $i \in [1, m]$ is the index of the active process, and $v_1, \ldots, v_m \in \mathbb{V}^*$ are the local configurations of all the processes. Let $\mathbb{C}$ be the set of all configurations.

Given $r = ((i_1, \overrightarrow{\Pi_1}), [u_1, \ldots, u_m]) \hookrightarrow ((i_2, \overrightarrow{\Pi_2}), [u'_1, \ldots, u'_m]) \in \mathcal{R}$, let $\mapsto_r \subseteq \mathbb{C} \times \mathbb{C}$ be the relation s.t. $b \mapsto_r b'$ iff $b = ((i_1, \overrightarrow{\Pi_1}), [v_1, \ldots, v_m])$, $b' = ((i_2, \overrightarrow{\Pi_2}), [v'_1, \ldots, v'_m])$, and $\forall k \in [1, m]$, $\exists w_k \in \mathbb{V}^*$ s.t. $v_k = u_k w_k$ and $v'_k = u'_k w_k$.

Let $\mapsto_{\mathsf{loc}}$ (resp. $\mapsto_{\mathsf{sw}}$) be the union of all relations $\mapsto_r$ where r is a Local rule (resp. Switch rule), and let $\mapsto$ be the union of all the relations $\mapsto_r$, for $r \in \mathcal{R}$. Then, we consider the relation $\rightsquigarrow = \mapsto_{\mathsf{loc}}^* \circ \mapsto_{\mathsf{sw}}$. For each $K \geq 1$, the relation $\rightsquigarrow^K$ (Kth power of $\rightsquigarrow$) corresponds to $\mapsto$-reachability with $K - 1$ context switches (or K consecutive contexts).

We extend the equivalence relation $\simeq$ defined on visible heaps to environments in $\mathbb{V}$: we consider that $\langle n_1, VH_1, \pi_1 \rangle \simeq_\beta \langle n_2, VH_2, \pi_2 \rangle$ iff (1) $n_1 = n_2$, and (2) β is a bijection from A_1 to A_2 such that $VH_1 \simeq_\beta VH_2$ and $\pi_2 = \pi_1 \circ \beta$. Given two environments e_1, e_2, we write $e_1 \simeq e_2$ iff there exists β such that $e_1 \simeq_\beta e_2$. We extend this equivalence relation to sequences of environments in the obvious manner ($e_1 \cdots e_j \simeq e'_1 \cdots e'_k$ iff $j = k$ and for every $i \in [1, j]$, $e_i \simeq e'_i$).

Finally, we extend $\simeq$ to configurations: let $b = ((i, \overrightarrow{\Pi}), [e_1 \alpha_1, \ldots e_m \alpha_m])$ and $b' = ((j, \overrightarrow{\Pi'}), [e'_1 \alpha'_1, \ldots, e'_m \alpha'_m])$ be two configurations. Then, $b \simeq b'$ iff (1) $i = j$, (2) $\forall k \in [1, m]$, $\alpha_k \simeq \alpha'_k$, and (3) $\exists \pi_k : \mathbb{A} \to \mathbb{A}$ s.t. $e'_k \simeq_{\pi_k} e_k$ and $\overrightarrow{\Pi'}(k) \circ \pi_k = \overrightarrow{\Pi}(k)$.

Proposition 1. *For every configurations b_0, b, b', if $b_0 \mapsto^* b$ and $b' \simeq b$, then $b_0 \mapsto^* b'$.*

We prove that given a multithreaded program, its associated CH-PDS and CVH-PDS are bisimilar. For that, we exhibit a bisimulation relation between configurations of the two systems. Intuitively, this relation maps a configuration of the CVH-PDS to a configuration of the CH-PDS by applying the updating operations through the configuration. (Indeed, visible heaps stored in the stacks of the CVH-PDS model are not up to date since they correspond to views of the heap at the moment of their memorization.)

Theorem 1. *The relations $\Rightarrow$ and $\mapsto$ define bisimilar transition systems.*

4.5 Program Semantics Based on Normalized Visible Heaps

Normalized visible heaps: Visible heaps in *normal form* are obtained by numbering nodes according to a depth-first traversal of the heap, for a given ordering of global and local variables, and the fixed order on the successor fields $\{s_1, \ldots, s_n\}$.

Let us consider a bijection $\eta : L \cup G \to [1, |L \cup G|]$. Then, given an environment $\langle n, VH, \pi \rangle$ with $VH = (A, \Delta, \Gamma, \Lambda)$, we define the class $[\![\langle n, VH, \pi \rangle]\!]_\eta$ to be the set of all environments $\langle n, VH', \pi \circ \beta \rangle$ with $VH' = (A', \Delta', \Gamma', \Lambda')$ s.t. (1) $VH \simeq_\beta VH'$, (2) $A' = [1, |A|]$, and (3) in the graph (V, Δ'_V) where $V = Reach_{\Delta'}(\Lambda'(L) \cup \Gamma'(G))$ and $\Delta'_V = \Delta' \cap [S \to (V \to V)]$, vertices correspond to the depth-first-traversal induced by the order η on root nodes (and the fixed order on successor fields labeling the edges of the graph).

Notice that, if all vertices in VH are reachable from $L \cup G$, then $[\![\langle n, VH, \pi \rangle]\!]_\eta$ contains a *single* element. Otherwise, there must be cut points (and may be other vertices reachable from them) which are not reachable from $L \cup G$. In that case, $[[\langle n, VH, \pi \rangle]]_\eta$ contains environments (with identical reachable parts from $L \cup G$) corresponding to different permutations of the vertices reachable from cut points but not from $L \cup G$.

Proposition 2. *For every* η, *the set* $[[\langle n, VH, \pi \rangle]]_\eta$ *is finite (if VH is finite).*

Concurrent pushdown systems on normalized visible heaps: Let us fix η. We define a program semantics where visible heaps are considered modulo the η-equivalence. Let $\mathbb{V}_\eta$ be the set of all $[[e]]_\eta$, for $e \in \mathbb{V}$. We consider the set of transition rules $\mathcal{R}_\eta$ corresponding to the restriction of the set $\mathcal{R}$ to the alphabet $\mathbb{V}_\eta$:

$$\mathcal{R}_\eta = \{((i, \overrightarrow{\Pi}), [\alpha_1, \ldots, \alpha_m]) \hookrightarrow ((j, \overrightarrow{\Pi'}), [\alpha_1', \ldots, \alpha_m']) \in \mathcal{R} \mid \forall j, \alpha_j, \alpha_j' \in \mathbb{V}_\eta^*\}.$$

Let $\mathbb{C}_\eta$ be the set of all configurations $((i, \overrightarrow{\Pi}), [\alpha_1, \ldots, \alpha_m])$ such that $\forall j, \alpha_j \in \mathbb{V}_\eta^*$. Then, let $\mapsto_{r,\eta}$ be the restriction of the transition relation $\mapsto_r$ to configurations in $\mathbb{C}_\eta$. Let $\mapsto_\eta$ be the union of the relations $\mapsto_{r,\eta}$ for all transition rules r. The relations $\mapsto_{\mathsf{loc},\eta}$, $\mapsto_{\mathsf{sw},\eta}$, and $\leadsto_\eta$ are also defined as previously in terms of the restricted relations $\mapsto_{r,\eta}$.

Theorem 2. *The relations* $\mapsto$ *and* $\mapsto_\eta$ *define bisimilar transition systems.*

5 Reachability Analysis

Bounded visible heap depth programs: Let $k \in \mathbb{N}$. A visible heap $VH = (A, \Delta, \Gamma, \Lambda, C)$ is k-bounded if (1) $|Reach_\Delta(\Lambda(L) \cup \Gamma(G))| \leq k$, and (2) $\forall i \in [1, m]. |Reach_\Delta(C(i))| \leq k$. Notice that k-boundedness does not imply that $|A| \leq k$ since there may exist vertices which are reachable from cut points but not from local/global variables. A sequence $\langle n_1, VH_1, \pi_1 \rangle \ldots \langle n_j, VH_j, \pi_j \rangle \in \mathbb{V}^*$ is k-bounded iff $\forall i \in [1, j], VH_i$ is k-bounded. A configuration $((i, \overrightarrow{\Pi}), [\alpha_1, \ldots, \alpha_m])$ is k-bounded iff $\forall j \in [1, m], \alpha_j$ is k-bounded.

Theorem 3. *Given* $k \geq 1$, *for every* k-*bounded* $\Rightarrow$-*computation in the CH-PDS model of a program there is a bisimilar* k-*bounded* $\mapsto$-*computation in its CVH-PDS model.*

Bounded heap depth reachability analysis of sequential programs: We extend to VH-PDS the automata-based construction of $post^*/pre^*$ images for pushdown systems (see, e.g., [1,5,4]). We assume in the sequel that visible heaps are in normal form according to some fixed ordering η on local and global variables. Sets of configurations are recognized by finite-state automata over the alphabet of normalized environments called *Conf-automata*. More precisely, initial states in these automata correspond to mappings Π, and edges are labeled by elements of $\mathbb{V}_\eta$. Then, a configuration (Π, α) is accepted by the automaton if starting from the initial state Π there is an accepting run for the sequence $\alpha \in \mathbb{V}_\eta^*$.

Given $k \geq 1$, and a regular set of k-bounded (local) configurations recognized by a Conf-automaton $\mathcal{A}$, we apply a saturation based algorithm $\mathsf{Closure}_\eta(\mathcal{A}, k)$ which constructs a sequence of Conf-automata with increasing languages, each of them being obtained from the previous one using one of the transition rules of the pushdown system. The difference here with the existing constructions for pushdown systems is that the stack alphabet of the built automata may increase at each step. Therefore, we restrict the construction to the k-bounded environments. Then, by Proposition 2, the algorithm terminates and produces a finite Conf-automaton representing all (forward/backward) reachable configuration by k-bounded $\hookrightarrow_\eta$-computations, which is a subset of the set of all reachable configurations from $L(\mathcal{A})$ (by Theorems 1 and 2), and which contains the set of all reachable configurations by k-bounded $\Rightarrow$-computations (by Theorem 3).

Reachability analysis of concurrent programs: Let us first introduce some definitions and notations: A *special* Conf-automaton is a Conf-automaton for which there exists a pair (Π, e) such that, for every local configuration $(\Pi', \alpha) \in L(\mathcal{A})$, $\Pi' = \Pi$ and there exists $\alpha' \in \mathbb{V}_\eta^*$ such that $\alpha = e\alpha'$, i.e., all words accepted by $\mathcal{A}$ start with (Π, e). The pair (Π, e) is then denoted $\widehat{\mathcal{A}}$. An *aggregate* is a tuple $(\mathcal{A}_1, \ldots, \mathcal{A}_m)$ of special Conf-automata. Such an aggregate defines the set of global configurations $L(\mathcal{A}_1, \ldots, \mathcal{A}_m) = \{((i, \overrightarrow{\Pi}), [\alpha_1, \ldots, \alpha_m]) : i \in [1, m], \forall j \in [1, m]. (\overrightarrow{\Pi}(j), \alpha_j) \in L(\mathcal{A}_j)\}$. A finite set of aggregates defines the union of the languages defined by all its elements.

Given a Conf-automaton $\mathcal{A}$ and (Π, e) with $e \in \mathbb{V}_\eta$, let $\mathcal{A}^{(\Pi, e)}$ be an automaton recognizing the language $L(\mathcal{A}) \cap (\Pi \times e\mathbb{V}_\eta^*)$. Clearly, $\mathcal{A}^{(\Pi, e)}$ is a special automaton. Given (Π, e) and a special automaton $\mathcal{A}$, we denote by $(\Pi, e) \rhd \mathcal{A}$ the special automaton recognizing the language $\{(\Pi, e\alpha) \mid (\Pi', e'\alpha) \in L(\mathcal{A})\}$, i.e., the language of $\mathcal{A}$ where the first symbol of every word is replaced by e and the initial state is replaced by Π.

We consider w.l.o.g. that the reachability analysis starts from a single initial configuration where the heap is empty and all pointer variables are equal to *null*: For each $i \in [1, m]$, let $\mathcal{A}_0^i$ be the special automaton recognizing the (singleton) language $\{(Id_{\{\top, \bot\}}, \langle n_{init}^i, VH_0, Id_{\{\top, \bot\}}\rangle)\}$, where n_{init}^i is the entry node of the main procedure of process i, and $VH_0 = (\{\top, \bot\}, \Delta_\top, \Gamma_\bot, \Lambda_\bot, \overrightarrow{0})$ with $\Delta_\top$ being the function mapping $\top$ to each address for all successor fields, $\Gamma_\bot$ (resp. $\Lambda_\bot$) being the functions mapping $\bot$ to each global (resp. local) variable, and $\overrightarrow{0}$ being the vector of functions mapping an empty set of cut points to each process.

Finally, given $h_1, \ldots, h_m$ such that for every $\ell \in [1, m]$, $h_\ell = (\overrightarrow{\Pi}(\ell), e_\ell)$, and given $i, j \in [1, m]$, $i \neq j$, we denote by $\mathsf{Update}_{i,j}(h_1, \ldots, h_m)$ the set of tuples $(h'_1, \ldots, h'_m)$ such that: (1) for every $\ell \in [1, m]$, $h'_\ell = (\overrightarrow{\Pi'}(\ell), e'_\ell)$, and (2) $((i, \overrightarrow{\Pi}), [e_1, \ldots, e_m]) \hookrightarrow_{\mathsf{SW}} ((j, \overrightarrow{\Pi'}), [e'_1, \ldots, e'_m])$, where $\hookrightarrow_{\mathsf{SW}}$ refers to the Switch inference rule (see section 4.3).

We are now ready to present our bounded reachability analysis algorithm. The algorithm is given in Figure 1. The input is a CVH-PDS, the bound on context switches K, and the bound on the size of visible heaps k. The algorithm computes (in *Reach*) the set of all reachable configurations by k-bounded $\leadsto_\eta^K$-computations: A set of *tasks* is maintained in a structure *todo*. A task is a triple $(\ell, i, \mathcal{A})$ where ℓ is the number of context switches done so far, i is the index of the process chosen to be active, and $\mathcal{A}$ is an aggregate. Initially, *todo* contains the initial configuration of the program with all possible starting active process (lines 2-3). Then, the treatment of a task is as follows: if ℓ has already reached K then $\mathcal{A}$ is added to *Reach* (lines 6-7). Otherwise, the set of reachable k-bounded configurations from $\mathcal{A}$ by process i is computed (line 9), and then new tasks are produced corresponding to all possible context switches from i to some other

---

Input: An m-dim CVH-PDS, and two integers $K, k \geq 1$
Output: The set of reachable configurations by k-bounded $\leadsto_\eta^K$-computations.

```
1    Reach ← ∅;
2    for all i ∈ {1,...,m}
3        todo ← {(0, i, 𝒜₀¹,..., 𝒜₀ᵐ)};
4    while todo ≠ ∅ do
5        pop (level, i, 𝒜₁,..., 𝒜ₘ) from todo with minimal level;
6        if level = K then
7            Reach ← Reach ∪ {(𝒜₁,..., 𝒜ₘ)};
8        else
9            let ℬᵢ = Closureη(𝒜ᵢ, k) in
10               for all (Π, eᵢ′) such that L(ℬᵢ^(Π,eᵢ′)) ≠ ∅
11                   for all j ∈ {1,...,m} such that j ≠ i
12                       for all (h₁,...,hₘ) ∈ Updateᵢ,ⱼ(𝒜̂₁,...,(Π,eᵢ′),...,𝒜̂ₘ)
13                           todo ← (level + 1, j, h₁ ⊳ 𝒜₁,..., hᵢ ⊳ ℬᵢ^(Π,eᵢ′),..., hₘ ⊳ 𝒜ₘ);
14   return Reach
```

Fig. 1. Algorithm for bounded context-switch/heap depth reachability on CVH-PDS

process j (lines 10-13). For that, a case splitting is performed according to all possible visible heaps reached by process i (line 10), corresponding to head environments of its possible stacks. Then, the local heaps of all processes are updated, and tasks (where ℓ is incremented) are defined for all possible next active processes $j \neq i$ (lines 11-12) and added to $todo$ (line 13).

References

1. Bouajjani, A., Esparza, J., Maler, O.: Reachability analysis of pushdown automata: Application to model-checking. In: Mazurkiewicz, A., Winkowski, J. (eds.) CONCUR 1997. LNCS, vol. 1243, Springer, Heidelberg (1997)
2. Bouajjani, A., Esparza, J., Schwoon, S., Strejcek, J.: Reachability analysis of multithreaded software with asynchronous communication. In: Ramanujam, R., Sen, S. (eds.) FSTTCS 2005. LNCS, vol. 3821, Springer, Heidelberg (2005)
3. Bouajjani, A., Fratani, S., Qadeer, S.: Bounded context switch analysis of mutithreaded programs with dynamic linked structures. Technical Report, 2007-02, LIAFA lab (January 2007) Available at http://www.liafa.jussieu.fr/~abou/publis.html
4. Esparza, J., Hansel, D., Rossmanith, P., Schwoon, S.: Efficient algorithms for model checking pushdown systems. In: Emerson, E.A., Sistla, A.P. (eds.) CAV 2000. LNCS, vol. 1855, Springer, Heidelberg (2000)
5. Finkel, A., Willems, B., Wolper, P.: A direct symbolic approach to model checking pushdown systems. Electr. Notes Theor. Comput. Sci., 9 (1997)
6. Godefroid, P.: Model checking for programming languages using Verisoft. In: POPL 1997, ACM Press, New York (1997)
7. Musuvathi, M., Qadeer, S.: Iterative context bounding for systematic testing of multithreaded programs. In: PLDI 1997, ACM Press, New York (2007)
8. Qadeer, S., Rajamani, S.: Deciding assertions in programs with references. Technical Report MSR-TR-2005-08, Microsoft Research (September 2005)

9. Qadeer, S., Rehof, J.: Context-bounded model checking of concurrent software. In: Halbwachs, N., Zuck, L.D. (eds.) TACAS 2005. LNCS, vol. 3440, Springer, Heidelberg (2005)
10. Rinetzky, N., Bauer, J., Reps, T., Sagiv, M., Wilhelm, R.: A semantics for procedure local heaps and its abstractions. In: POPL 2005, ACM Press, New York (2005)
11. Rinetzky, N., Sagiv, M., Yahav, E.: Interprocedural shape analysis for cutpoint-free programs. In: Hankin, C., Siveroni, I. (eds.) SAS 2005. LNCS, vol. 3672, Springer, Heidelberg (2005)

Revamping TVLA:
Making Parametric Shape Analysis Competitive
(Tool Paper)

Igor Bogudlov[1,*], Tal Lev-Ami[1,*], Thomas Reps[2,**], and Mooly Sagiv[1]

[1] School of Comp. Sci., Tel Aviv Univ.,
{igorbogu,tla,msagiv}@post.tau.ac.il
[2] Comp. Sci. Department, Univ. of Wisconsin, Madison
reps@cs.wisc.edu

Abstract. TVLA is a parametric framework for shape analysis that can be easily instantiated to create different kinds of analyzers for checking properties of programs that use linked data structures. We report on dramatic improvements in TVLA's performance, which make the cost of parametric shape analysis comparable to that of the most efficient specialized shape-analysis tools (which restrict the class of data structures and programs analyzed) without sacrificing TVLA's parametricity. The improvements were obtained by employing well-known techniques from the database community to reduce the cost of extracting information from shape descriptors and performing abstract interpretation of program statements and conditions. Compared to the prior version of TVLA, we obtained as much as 50-fold speedup.

1   Introduction

In this paper, we review recent improvements to TVLA (**T**hree-**V**alued-**L**ogic Analyzer), a system for automatically generating a static-analysis implementation from the operational semantics of a given program [1,2]. In TVLA, a language's small-step structural operational semantics is written in a meta-language based on First-Order Logic with Transitive Closure (FO(TC)). The main idea is that program states are represented as logical structures, and the program's transition system is defined using first-order logical formulas. The abstraction is controlled using a set of *Instrumentation Predicates*, which are defined using FO(TC) formulas and dictate what extra information is tracked for each program state. *Integrity constraints* can be provided in the form of FO(TC) formulas; these express invariant properties of the operational semantics (e.g., each program pointer can point to at most one concrete location).

TVLA is a parametric framework based on the theory of [2]. Given the concrete operational semantics, instrumentation predicates, and integrity constraints, TVLA automatically generates the abstract semantics, and, for each program point, produces a conservative abstract representation of the program states at that point. TVLA is intended as a testbed in which it is easy to try out new ideas for shape abstractions.

 * Supported by an Adams Fellowship through the Israel Academy of Sciences and Humanities.
** Supported in part by NSF under grants CCF-0540955 and CCF-0524051.

W. Damm and H. Hermanns (Eds.): CAV 2007, LNCS 4590, pp. 221–225, 2007.

A unique aspect of TVLA is that it automatically generates the abstract transformers from the concrete semantics; these transformers are (i) guaranteed to be sound, and (ii) rather precise—the number of false alarms reported in our applications is very small. The abstract transformers in TVLA are computed in 4 stages:

(i) *Focus*—a partial concretization operation in which each heap cell that will be updated is materialized as a singleton (non-summary) individual, so that it is possible to perform a strong update; (ii) *Update* — in which the update formulas are evaluated using Kleene semantics on the abstract structure to achieve a sound abstract transformer; (iii) *Coerce* — a semantic reduction in which an internal Datalog-style constraint solver uses the instrumentation predicates and integrity constraints to improve the precision of the analysis; and (iv) *Blur*—in which the abstraction function is re-applied (which ensures that the analyis terminates).

Compared to specialized shape-analysis approaches, the above operations incur interpretative overhead. In this paper, we show that using techniques taken from the realm of databases, such as semi-naive evaluation and query optimization [3], TVLA reduces this overhead, and thereby achieves performance comparable to that of state-of-the-art specialized shape analysis without changing TVLA's functionality.

Our technical report [4] contains more details about the implementation and related work; the new version of TVLA is available at [5].

2 Key Improvements

The bottleneck in previous versions of TVLA has been Coerce, which needs to consider interactions among all the predicates. The complexity of Coerce stems from the fact that the number of constraints is linear in the size of the program, and the number of tuples that need to be considered during the evaluation of a constraint is exponential in the number of variables in the constraint.

Coerce translates the definitions of instrumentation predicates and the integrity constraints to Datalog-like constraint rules of the form $\varphi \Rightarrow \psi$, where φ is called the base of the rule and is a conjunction of general formulas, and ψ is called the   head of the rule and is a literal. The head and the conjuncts of the base are called atoms. Each atom induces a relation of the tuples that satisfy it. Coerce then applies a constraint by searching for assignments to the free variables of the rule such that the base is known to hold (i.e., evaluates to 1), and the head either does not hold (i.e., evaluates to 0) or may not hold (i.e., evaluates to $\frac{1}{2}$). In the first case it safely discards the structure as inconsistent, and in the second case it attempts to coerce the value to 1 (more details can be found in [2]). This process continues until a fixed point is reached in a way similar to evaluation of Datalog rules in databases [3].

View Maintenance with Semi-Naive Evaluation. Semi-naive evaluation is a well-known technique in database view maintenance to speed up the bottom-up evaluation of Datalog rules [3]. On each iteration of the algorithm, it evaluates the rules in *incremental* fashion; i.e., it only considers variable assignments containing relation tuples that were changed during the previous iteration. All other assignments must have been examined during the previous iteration and thus cannot contribute any new information. Because the number of changed tuples is usually small compared to the size of the relation, this avoids a considerable amount of computation.

We take this idea one step further by using properties of the TVLA abstract trans-former step to avoid fully evaluating the constraints even once: all of the constraints hold before the *Focus* and *Update* steps, and thus the set of violating assignments for the structure is initially empty. Any assignment that violates the constraints must there-fore be due to a tuple changed by *Focus* or *Update*. We save the structure before and after the potentially violating step, and calculate the difference. This *delta structure* is used during the first iteration of *Coerce*.

Multi-Constraint Evaluation. TVLA integrity constraints are often symmetric, i.e., give rise to a set of rules, all consisting of the same atoms, such that for each such rule a different atom serves as the (negated) head of the rule and the rest remain in the base.

We introduced the notion of a *multi-constraint* to represent a set of rules that have the same set of atoms. Instead of evaluating these rules one-by-one, we can evaluate them all at once at a cost comparable to that of a single rule evaluation.

A constraint is violated when all of the atoms in the base evaluate to 1 while the negated head evaluates to either 1 or $\frac{1}{2}$. Similarly, a multi-constraint is violated when all of its atoms evaluate to 1, except at most one atom that evaluates to $\frac{1}{2}$ and is the head of some rule.

We evaluate the multi-constraint efficiently by keeping count of the number of $\frac{1}{2}$ values for an assignment while enumerating the relations' tuples.

This technique usually cuts the effective number of constraints in half, and affects the running time of *Coerce* accordingly.

Other Improvements. Many other improvements and techniques were introduced into TVLA, including the following: optimizing the query-evaluation order; precomputing information that only depends on constraint structure, such as atom types and depen-dencies; tracking modified predicates in each structure for quick constraint filtering; caching and on-demand recomputation of transitive closure; caching of recently-used predicate values and tuple lists for predicate negation.

In addition, we did extensive re-engineering and optimization of the TVLA core geared toward improved performance.

3   Experimental Results

We incorporated the above-mentioned techniques into TVLA. The empirical results from running the new tool on various benchmark examples are presented in Table 1. Table 1 compares the running time of each analysis with both the previously available TVLA version, as well as some specialized shape-analysis tools [6,7].

The benchmark suite consisted of the following examples: singly-linked lists op-erations, including Merge and Reverse; sorting of linked lists, including insertion sort, bubble sort, and a recursive version of Quicksort (using the extension of [8]); sorted-tree insertion and deletion; analysis of set data structures from [9]; analysis of the Lindstrom scanning algorithm [10,11]; insertion into an AVL tree [12].

For each program, Table 1 uses the following shorthand to indicate the set of prop-erties that the analysis established: CL—cleanness, i.e., absence of memory leaks and null-pointer dereferences; DI—data-structure invariants were maintained (e.g., treeness in the case of a tree-manipulation program); IS—the output result is isomorphic to the input; TE—termination; SO—the output result is sorted. The column labeled "Structs" indicates the total number of (abstracted) logical structures attached to the program's control-flow graph at the end of the analysis. "N/A" denotes absence of available empirical data for the tool. "B/S" denotes that the analysis is beyond the scope of the tool. The tests were done on a 2.6GHz Pentium PC with 1GB of RAM running XP.[1]

Table 1. Running time comparison results

Program	Properties	Structs	New TVLA	Old TVLA	[6]	[7]
LindstromScan	CL, DI	1285	8.21	63.00	10.85	B/S
LindstromScan	CL, DI, IS, TE	183564	2185.50	18154.00	B/S	B/S
SetRemove	CL, DI, SO	13180	106.20	5152.80	B/S	B/S
SetInsert	CL, DI, SO	299	1.75	22.30	B/S	B/S
DeleteSortedTree	CL, DI	2429	6.14	47.92	4.22	B/S
DeleteSortedTree	CL, DI, SO	30754	104.50	1267.70	B/S	B/S
InsertSortedTree	CL, DI	177	0.85	1.94	0.89	B/S
InsertSortedTree	CL, DI, SO	1103	2.53	12.63	B/S	B/S
InsertAVLTree	CL, DI, SO	1855	27.40	375.60	B/S	B/S
Merge	CL, DI	231	0.95	4.34	0.45	0.15
Reverse	CL, DI	57	0.29	0.45	0.07	0.06
InsertSort	CL, DI	712	3.02	23.53	0.09	0.06
BubbleSort	CL, DI	518	1.70	8.45	0.07	N/A
RecQuickSort	CL, DI	5097	3.92	16.04	B/S	0.30
RecQuickSort	CL, DI, SO	5585	9.22	75.01	B/S	B/S

Table 1 shows that our techniques indeed resulted in considerable speedup vis-a-vis the old version of TVLA: most of the examples run an order of magnitude faster, and in one case a factor of 50 is achieved. Moreover, the new tool's performance is comparable with that of specialized analysis tools, especially on larger examples.

More detailed explanations of the various algorithmic improvements, as well as additional data about the level of improved performance that we obtained, are available in a technical report [4]. The use of semi-naive-evaluation techniques improves the running time of Coerce by a factor of 2, and the total running time by about 50% (Table 2, page 9 of [4]). Various query-optimization techniques (Section 2.4 of [4]) also improve the running time significantly. An additional factor of about 3–4 in the running time comes from extensive engineering changes and code optimization (Section 2.2 of [4]).

References

1. Lev-Ami, T., Sagiv, M.: TVLA: A system for implementing static analyses. In: SAS (2000)
2. Sagiv, M., Reps, T., Wilhelm, R.: Parametric shape analysis via 3-valued logic. In: TOPLAS (2002)
3. Ullman, J.: Database and Knowledge Base Systems, vol. I. W.H. Freeman, New York (1988)

---

[1] Establishing total correctness of Lindstrom Scan was performed on a 2.4GHz Core 2 Duo with 4GB of RAM. The tests of [7] were done on a 2GHz Pentium Linux PC with 512MB of RAM.

4. Bogudlov, I., Lev-Ami, T., Reps, T., Sagiv, M.: Revamping tvla: Making parametric shape analysis competitive. Technical Report TR-2007-01-01, Tel-Aviv Univ. (2007) http://www.cs.tau.ac.il/~tla/2007/papers/TR-2007-01-01.pdf
5. TVLA system.
   (Available at http://www.cs.tau.ac.il/~tvla/#DownloadTVLA3)
6. Lev-Ami, T., Immerman, N., Sagiv, M.: Abstraction for shape analysis with fast and precise transformers. In: Ball, T., Jones, R.B. (eds.) CAV 2006. LNCS, vol. 4144, Springer, Heidelberg (2006)
7. Gotsman, A., Berdine, J., Cook, B.: Interprocedural shape analysis with separated heap abstractions. In: Yi, K. (ed.) SAS 2006. LNCS, vol. 4134, Springer, Heidelberg (2006)
8. Rinetzky, N., Sagiv, M., Yahav, E.: Interprocedural shape analysis for cutpoint-free programs. In: Hankin, C., Siveroni, I. (eds.) SAS 2005. LNCS, vol. 3672, Springer, Heidelberg (2005)
9. Reineke, J.: Shape analysis of sets. Master's thesis, Saarland University (2005)
10. Lindstrom, G.: Scanning list structures without stacks or tag bits. IPL vol. 2(2) (1973)
11. Loginov, A., Reps, T., Sagiv, M.: Automatic verification of the Deutsch-Schorr-Waite tree-traversal algorithm. In: Yi, K. (ed.) SAS 2006. LNCS, vol. 4134, Springer, Heidelberg (2006)
12. Parduhn, S.: Algorithm animation using shape analysis with special regard to binary trees. Master's thesis, Saarland University (2005)

Fast and Accurate Static Data-Race Detection for Concurrent Programs

Vineet Kahlon[1], Yu Yang[2], Sriram Sankaranarayanan[1], and Aarti Gupta[1]

[1] NEC Labs, Princeton, USA
[2] University of Utah, Salt Lake City, USA

Abstract. We present new techniques for fast, accurate and scalable static data race detection in concurrent programs. Focusing our analysis on Linux device drivers allowed us to identify the unique challenges posed by debugging large-scale real-life code and also pinpointed drawbacks in existing race warning generation methods. This motivated the development of new techniques that helped us in improving both the scalability as well as the accuracy of each of the three main steps in a race warning generation system. The first and most crucial step is the automatic discovery of shared variables. Towards that end, we present a new, efficient dataflow algorithm for shared variable detection which is more effective than existing correlation-based techniques that failed to detect the shared variables responsible for data races in majority of the drivers in our benchmark suite. Secondly, accuracy of race warning generation strongly hinges on the precision of the pointer analysis used to compute aliases for lock pointers. We formulate a new scalable context sensitive alias analysis that effectively combines a divide and conquer strategy with function summarization and is demonstrably more efficient than existing BDD-based techniques. Finally, we provide a new warning reduction technique that leverages lock acquisition patterns to yield provably better warning reduction than existing lockset based methods.

1 Introduction

The widespread use of concurrent software in modern day computing systems necessitates the development of effective debugging methodologies for multi-threaded software. Concurrent programs, however, are behaviorally complex involving subtle interactions between threads which makes them hard to analyze manually. This motivates the use of automated formal methods to reason about such systems. Particularly notorious to catch are errors arising out of data race violations. A data race occurs when two different threads in a given program can simultaneously access a shared variable, with at least one of the accesses being a write operation. Checking for data races is often a critical first step in the debugging of concurrent programs. Indeed, the presence of data races in a program typically renders its behavior non-deterministic thereby making it difficult to reason about it for more complex and interesting properties.

In this paper, we develop techniques for data race detection that are efficient, scalable and accurate. In order to identify the practical challenges posed by the debugging of large-scale real-life code, we focused our analysis on detecting data races in Linux device drivers. A careful study of bug reports and CVS logs at `kernel.org` revealed

W. Damm and H. Hermanns (Eds.): CAV 2007, LNCS 4590, pp. 226–239, 2007.

that the two main reasons for the presence of data races in drivers are incorrect locking and timing related issues. Since timing related data races are hard to analyze at the software level, we chose to focus only on locking related bugs.

The classical approach to data race detection involves three steps. The first and most critical step is the automatic discovery of shared variables, i.e., variables which can be accessed by two or more threads. Control locations where these shared variable are read or written determine potential locations where data races can arise. In fact, locking related data races arise if a common shared variable is accessed at simultaneously reachable program locations in two different threads where disjoint sets of locks are held. Since locks are typically accessed via pointers, in order to determine these locksets at program locations of interest, in the second step, a must-pointer alias analysis is carried out. Finally, the main drawback of static analysis is that a large number of bogus data race warnings can often be generated which do not correspond to true bugs. The last step, therefore, is to use warning reduction and ranking techniques in order to either filter out bogus warnings or prioritize them based on the degree of confidence.

The challenge lies in carrying out race detection while satisfying the conflicting goals of scalability and accuracy both of which depend on various factors. Key among them are (i) accuracy of shared variable discovery, and (ii) accuracy and scalability of the alias analyses for determining shared variables (may aliases) and locksets (must aliases). Wrongly labeling a variable as shared renders all warnings generated for it bogus. On the other hand, if we miss reporting a variable as shared then we fail to generate warnings for a genuine data race involving this variable.

Considerable research have been devoted to automatic shared variable discovery [7,14]. However, most existing techniques are based on the underlying assumption that when accessing shared variables, concurrent programs almost always follow a *locking discipline* by associating with each shared variable v a lock l_v which needs to be acquired before any access to v. Existing techniques focus on computing this association between locks and variables. Towards that end, various correlation based techniques have been developed – both statistical [7] and constraint based [14]. An advantage of statistical techniques is that they are scalable and do not depend on an alias analysis which can often be a bottleneck. However, the failure of correlation based techniques to detect the shared variables responsible for data races in majority of the drivers (8 out of 10) in our suite exposed the fact that their main weakness turns out to be this very reliance on the existence of locking discipline. Indeed, many data races arise precisely when the locking discipline is violated. Furthermore, it turns out that in most of the drivers that we considered, the original implementations correctly followed lock discipline. Data race bugs were introduced only when the programs were later modified by adding new code either for optimization purposes or in order to fix bugs. Typically, this newly added code was a "hack" that introduced lock-free accesses to shared variables that weren't present in the original code. Since the only occurrences of these variables were in regions unguarded by locks, no meaningful correlations could be developed for them and was the key reason why correlation-based techniques [7,14] failed to identify these variables as shared.

In order to ensure that no shared variable fails detection, we use a very liberal criterion to categorize variables as such. Our shared variable detection routine is based on the premise that all shared variables are either global variables of threads, aliases thereof, pointers passed as parameters to API functions or escape variables. Furthermore, we are only interested in identifying precisely the subset of variables from the above set that are written to in the given program as only these can participate in a data race. The main challenge here is that since global variables can be accessed via local pointers we need to track aliasing assignments leading to such local pointers. An additional complication is that not all assignments to aliases of global variables result in meaningful updates to global variables. Indeed, in a sequence of pointer assignments $p_1 = p, ..., q = p_k$, starting at a pointer p to a global structure S, say, we see that assignments in the above sequence merely pass aliasing information without updating the value of any (scalar) variable. If, however, the above sequence is followed by an assignment of the form $q \rightarrow f = exp$ to a field f of S, then it is a genuine update to f thus making it a variable of interest. We show that such update sequences can be detected via an efficient dataflow analysis. In fact, in most Linux drivers, data global to a thread is usually stored as global structures having a large number number of fields – typically 50 to 100. Only a small fraction of these are actually used for storing shared data which our new algorithm was able to isolate with high precision. Declaring all the fields of a global structure as shared would simply generate too many bogus warnings.

The second step in static race detection is to accurately determine locksets at program locations where shared variables are accessed. Since locks are typically accessed via pointers, this requires computation of must-aliases for these lock pointers. The accuracy of warning generation is therefore directly dependent on the precision of the must-alias pointer analysis. Moreover, for the sake of accuracy it is imperative that lock aliases be computed context sensitively. This is because most must-aliases in C programs arise from parameter passing of pointer arguments in functions, which alias to different pointers in different contexts. The result is that a context sensitive alias analysis produces drastically lesser bogus warnings than a context insensitive one. However, the key drawback of a context sensitive alias analysis is scalability as the number of possible contexts in a large program can easily explode. In recent years, considerable research has been devoted to ameliorating this problem by storing contexts symbolically using data structures like BDDs. Implementation of BDD-based context sensitive pointer analysis like BDDBDDB [18] have been shown to give good results for Java programs [13,12]. However, C programs, which are less structured than Java programs, typically have too many pointer variables and complex aliasing relations between them which, in our experience, became hard to handle using BDDBDDB as the program size grew. We therefore propose a new technique for scalable context sensitive pointer analysis that combines:

(i) **Divide and Conquer** which leverages the fact that we can partition the set of all pointers in a program into disjoint classes such that each pointer can only alias to a pointer within its class. While, in general, aliasing is not an equivalence relation, many widely used pointer analyses like Steensgaard [16] generate equivalence relations that are over-approximations of aliasing. Since we use this initial pointer analysis only for partitioning, scalability is more critical than accuracy and this is precisely what Steensgaard's analysis offers. There are two important consequences of this partitioning. First, since we are only interested in lock pointers, and since lock pointers can only alias to other lock pointers, we can ignore non-lock pointers. This drastically cuts down on the number of pointers we need to consider for our analysis. Secondly, since a given lock pointer can, in general, be aliased to a small subset of the total set of lock pointers, Steensgaard analysis provides us with a further decomposition of the set of lock pointers into yet smaller partitions. A second and more accurate context-sensitive alias analysis in then carried out on these final partitions and even though expensive in general, it becomes scalable on these small classes.

(ii) **Procedure Summarization** which exploits locality of reference, viz., the fact that locks and shared variables are accessed in a small fraction of functions. Our new summarization based must alias analysis procedure therefore needs to compute summaries only for these small number of functions thereby making our approach applicable to large programs. We emphasize that procedure summarization is extremely important in making any static analyses scalable. Indeed, typical real-life code has a large number of small functions that can be called from many different contexts. A non-summarization based technique like BDDBDDB can be overwhelmed as the program size grows. It is important to note that it is the synergy resulting by combining the two techniques that enables us to achieve scalability. Indeed, it is divide and conquer which allows us to exploit locality of reference thereby making summarization viable.

Finally, one of the main weaknesses of using static race detection techniques is that a large number of (bogus) race warnings can often be generated. In this paper, we show that tracking lock acquisition patterns, instead of locksets, results in a warning reduction technique that is more accurate than existing lockset based techniques [8] in two ways. First, by leveraging acquisition histories in addition to locksets we can filter out warnings generated by lockset based technique at the warning generation stage itself. Secondly, once the warnings are generated, we can use a dominator-based technique that leverages acquisition histories to give provably better warning reduction than [8]. Additionally, by using ranking, we can guarantee that our reduction technique is sound, viz., will not drop real data races in favor of bogus ones.

2 Shared Variable Discovery

So as not to miss any shared variable we use a very liberal definition of when a variable is declared as such. Essentially, we are interested in all *genuine* modifications to global variables, aliases thereof, pointers passed as parameters to API functions and escape variables. A global variable of a thread that is directly written to is declared as shared. Such variables can be determined merely by scanning through the program code. However, a global variable may also be accessed via a local pointer. Such a pointer q could occur at the end of a chain of pointer assignments $p_1 = p, p_2 = p_1, ..., q = p_k$ starting at a pointer p to, say, a global structure S, which is either global or passed as a parameter to an API function. Then any variable v modified via an access through p is also a variable of interest. However, simply declaring all pointers occurring in such sequence as shared could lead to a lot of bogus warnings. Indeed, in the above sequence, the assignments are not genuine updates but merely serve to propagate the values of fields of S. If, however, the above sequence is followed by an assignment of the form $q \to f = exp$, where exp is either a local variable or an expression other than simple propagation of a data value, it is a genuine update and should be declared a shared variable of interest. The above discussion motivates the following definition.

Algorithm 1. Dataflow Analysis for Shared Variable Detection

1: Initialize $V_{sh} = \emptyset$, G to the set of global variables of thread T, in to the entry statement of T, worklist W to the set $\{(in, G)\}$, and the set of processed tuples Pr to $\{(in, G)\}$.
2: **repeat**
3:     Remove a tuple $tup = (st, P_{sh})$ from W.
4:     **if** st is of the form $v = w$ where v and w are program variables **then**
5:        **if** $w \in P_{sh}$ **then**
6:           set $P_{sh} = P_{sh} \cup \{v\}$
7:        **else if** $v \in P_{sh}$ **then**
8:           set $V_{sh} = V_{sh} \cup \{v\}$.
9:        **end if**
10:    **else if** st is of the form $v = exp$ where exp is an expression other than a simple variable **then**
11:       **if** $v \in P_{sh}$ **then**
12:          set $V_{sh} = V_{sh} \cup \{v\}$.
13:       **end if**
14:    **end if**
15:    **for** each successor statement st' of st **do**
16:       **if** there does not exist a tuple in Pr of the form (st', S), where $P_{sh} \subseteq S$, **then**
17:          add (st', P_{sh}) to both W and Pr.
18:       **end if**
19:    **end for**
20: **until** W is empty
21: **return** V_{sh}

Definition 1. *A sequence of assignments $p_1 = p, p_2 = p_1, ..., q = p_k$ is called a complete update sequence from p to q iff for each i, there do not exist any assignments to p_i (in the given program) after it is written and before it is read in the sequence.*

Thus our goal is to detect complete update sequences from p to q that are followed by the modification of a scalar variable accessed via q, where p either points to a global variable or is passed as a parameter to an API function. We determine such sequences using our new dataflow analysis formulated as algorithm 1. Essentially, the procedure propagates the assignments in complete update sequences as discussed above till it hits a genuine update to a variable which is declared as shared. The algorithm keeps track of the potential shared variable as the set P_{sh}. To start with, P_{sh} contains variables of the given thread T that are pointers to global variables or passed as parameters to API functions. A separate variable V_{sh} keeps track of variables involving genuine updates which are therefore declared as shared. Each assignment of the form $v = w$ is a propagation if $w \in P_{sh}$. Thus if $v \notin P_{sh}$ it is added to P_{sh} (lines 4-6). A variable $v \in P_{sh}$ is included in V_{sh} only if there is an assignment of the form $v = w$, where v is potentially shared but w is not and is therefore a local variable (lines 7-9), or $v = exp$, where exp is a genuine update as discussed above (lines 10-14).

3 Scalable Context Sensitive Alias Analysis

As noted in the introduction, once the shared variables have been identified, the key bottleneck in generating accurate lockset based warnings is a scalable context-sensitive must alias analysis which is required to determine locksets at control locations where shared variables are accessed. In this section, we propose a new technique for scalable context sensitive alias analysis that is based on effectively combining a divide and conquer strategy with function summarization in order to leverage the benefits of both techniques.

3.1 Divide and Conquer Via Partitioning

We exploit the fact that, even though aliasing is not, in general, an equivalence relation, many alias analyses like Steensgaard's compute relations that are over-approximations of aliasing but are, importantly, equivalence relations. Additionally, an equally critical feature of Steensgaard's analysis is that it is highly scalable. This makes it ideally suitable for our purpose which is to partition the set of all pointers in the given program into disjoint classes that respect the aliasing relation, i.e., a pointer can only be aliased to pointers within the class to which it belongs. A drawback of Steensgaard's analysis is lack of precision. However, this is addressed next by focusing a more refined analysis on each individual Steensgaard partition. Indeed, partitioning, in effect, decomposes the pointer analysis problem into much smaller sub-problems where instead of carrying out the pointer analysis for all the pointers in the program, it suffices to carry out separate pointer analyses for each equivalence class. The fact that the partitioning respects the aliasing relation guarantees that we will not miss any aliases. The small size of each partition then offsets the higher computational complexity of a more precise analysis. As noted in the introduction, the Steensgaard generated equivalence class for a lock pointer typically contains only a small subset of lock pointers (typically 2-3) of the given program thus ensuring scalability of a context-sensitive alias analysis on each such partition.

3.2 Exploiting Locality of Reference Via Summarization

Using decomposition, once the set of pointers under consideration have been restricted to small sets of lock pointers, we can further exploit locality of reference which then allows us to effectively leverage procedure summarization for scalable context sensitive pointer analysis. Indeed, typically in real-life programs, shared variables, and as a consequence locks, are accessed in a very small number of functions. Thus instead of following the BDDBDDB approach that pre-computes aliases for all pointers in all contexts, it is much more scalable to instead use procedure summarization to capture all possible effects of executing a procedure on lock pointers. The reason it is more scalable is that we need to compute these summaries only for the small fraction of functions in which lock pointers are accessed. Once we have pre-computed the summaries, the aliases for a lock pointer at a program location in a given context can be generated efficiently on demand. We emphasize that it is the above decomposition that allows us to leverage locality of reference. Indeed, without decomposition we would have to compute summaries for each function with a pointer access, viz., practically every function in the given program. Additionally, for each function we would need to compute the summary for all pointers modified in the function not merely the lock pointers which could greatly increase the termination time of the algorithm. Thus by combining divide and conquer with summarization we can exploit the synergy between the two techniques.

3.3   Computing Procedure Summaries for Context-Sensitive Pointer Analysis

In order to formulate our new summarization based technique for demand driven context sensitive pointer analysis we need the following definition

Definition 2 (Maximally Complete Update Sequence). *Let* $\lambda : l_1, ..., l_m$ *be a sequence of successive program locations and let* π *be the sequence* $l_{i_1} : p_1 = p$, $l_{i_2} : p_2 = a_1,..., l_{i_k} : p_k = a_{k-1}, l_{i_{k+1}} : q = a_k$ *of pointer assignments occurring along* λ *with* $l_{i_1} = l_1$ *and* $l_{i_{k+1}} = l_m$. *Then* π *is called a maximally complete update sequence from p to q leading from locations* l_1 *to* l_m *iff it is the sequence of maximum length having the following properties (i) for each j,* $a_j = p_j$ *(semantically) at* $l_{i_{j+1}}$, *(ii) for each j, there does not exist any assignment to pointer* a_j *between locations* l_{i_j} *and* $l_{i_{j+1}}$ *along* λ, *and (iii) p is not modified between locations* l_{i_1} *and* $l_{i_{k+1}}$ *along* λ.

Then we have the following important observation.

Proposition 3. *Pointers p and q are aliased at control location l iff there exists a sequence* λ *of successive control locations starting at the entry location* l_0 *of the given program and ending at l such that either (i) there exists a complete update sequence from p to q along* λ, *or vice versa, or (ii) there exists a pointer a such that there exist maximally complete update sequences from a to both p and q along* λ.

A corollary of the above result is that in order to compute must-aliases of pointers, we need to construct function summaries that enable us to track maximally complete update sequences. The formal notion of function summaries that we use for our pointer analysis is given below.

Definition 4. *The summary for a function f in a given program is the set of all tuples of the form* (p, l, A), *where p is a pointer written to at location l in f and A is set of all pointers q such that there is a complete update sequence from q to p along each path starting at the entry location of f and ending at l. The set A is denoted by* $Sum(f, p, l)$.

As an example, consider the program in figure 1 with global pointers p and q. We see that $g_3 \in Sum(goo, 2c, p)$ and $g_4 \in Sum(goo, 2c, q)$. Similarly, $g_4 \in Sum(goo, 5c, q)$ but $g_5 \notin Sum(goo, 5c, p)$. This is because the control flow branches at location 3 c with p being set to g_5 in one branch and retaining the old value g_3 in the other. Statically, there is no way of deciding whether g_3 and g_5 are the same pointer. Thus $Sum(goo, 5c, p) = \emptyset$. Thus, $Sum(foo, 2a, p) = \{g_1\}$ and $Sum(foo, 2a, q) = \{g_2\}$, whereas $Sum(foo, 3a, p) = \emptyset$ and $Sum(foo, 3a, q) = \{g_4\}$.

Note that we do not need to cache the summary tuples for each program location of a function. Indeed, given a context *con* resulting from the sequence of function calls

```
foo(){                    bar(){                  goo(){
  1a: p = g₁;               1b: goo();              1c: p = g₃;
  2a: q = g₂;             }                         2c: q = g₄;
  3a: bar();                                        3c: if(global_var)
  4a: ... ;                                         4c:   p = g₅;
}                                                   5c: u = 1 ;
                                                  }
```

Fig. 1. An Example Program

$f_1, ..., f_n$, for function f_i, where $1 \leq i \leq n - 1$, all we need are the summary tuples for the locations where f_{i+1} is called. In addition, we also need to cache the summary tuple for the exit location as it might be required while performing the dataflow analysis. For the last function f_n in con, we need the summary tuples for each location in the function where a lock pointer is accessed. Since the number of such locations are typically few, the sizes of the resulting summaries are small.

The Algorithm. Given a pointer p and location l in function f, we perform a backward traversal on the CFG of the given program starting at l and track the complete update sequences as tuples of the form (m, A), where m is a program location and A is a set of lock pointers q such that there is a complete update sequence from q to p starting from m and ending at l. The algorithm maintains a set W of tuples that are yet to processed and a set P of tuples already processed. Initially, W contains the tuple $(l, \{p\})$ (line 2). Note that before processing a tuple (m, A) from W, since our goal is to compute must-aliases we need to make sure that each successor m' of m from which there exists a path in the CFG leading to l has already been processed during the backward traversal, viz., W currently has no tuples of the form (m', D). Such a tuple is called *ready* (line 4) (Note that if there are strongly connected components in the given CFG, the notion of a ready tuple is not well-defined. In that case, we first compute a spanning tree of the CFG on which the procedure is run while ignoring the back edges. Next we refine the tuples by processing each of the back edges one-by-one which may result in the (over approximated) aliases getting smaller till a fixpoint is reached. Since, in a given Steensgaard partition, the number of lock pointers is usually small (typically 2-3), this refinement step terminates quickly). If the statement at m is of the form $t = r$, where $t \in A$, then in processing (m, A), let A' be the set that we get from A by replacing t with r else $A' = A$ (lines 5-7).

In order to propagate the pointers in A' backwards, there are two cases to consider. First, assume that m is a return site of a function g that was called from within f. Then we have to propagate the effect of executing g backwards on each pointer in A'. Towards that end, we first check whether the summary tuples for g have already been computed for each of the pointers in A' for the exit location $exit_g$ of g. If they have, then we form the new tuple (m', B), where m' is the call site of g corresponding to the return site m and $B = \bigcup_{r \in A'} Sum(g, r, exit_g)$ (lines 12-14). If, on the other hand, the summary tuples have not been computed, we introduce the new tuple $(exit_g, A')$ in the worklist (line 16). For the second case, we assume that, m is not a function call

---

Algorithm 2. Summary Computation for Lock Pointer Analysis

1: **Input:** Lock Pointer: p, Control Location l, Function f.

2: Initialize W to $(l, \{p\})$.

3: **repeat**

4:     Remove a ready tuple $tup = (m, A)$ from W. Set $A' = A$.

5:     **if** lock pointer $t \in A$ and the statement at location m is of the form $t = r$ **then**

6:         $A' = (A \setminus \{t\}) \cup \{r\}$

7:     **end if**

8:     $NewTuples = \emptyset$

9:     **if** m is the entry location of function f **then**

10:         add (p, A) to the summary

11:     **else if** m is the call return site of a function call for g **then**

12:         **if** the summary tuples have already been computed for all lock pointers in A' for the exit location $exit_g$ of g **then**

13:             $B = \bigcup_{t \in A'} Sum(g, exit_g, t)$, where $Sum(g, exit_g, t)$ is the summary of pointer t with respect to $exit_g$ if it is written to in g else it is t

14:             Let $NewTuples = \{(m', B)\}$, where m' is the call site of g corresponding to m

15:         **else**

16:             Add $(exit_g, A')$ to W

17:         **end if**

18:     **else**

19:         $NewTuples = \bigcup_{m' \in Pred} \{(m', A')\}$, where $Pred$ is the set of predecessors of m

20:     **end if**

21:     **for** each tuple $(l, B) \in NewTuples$ that has not already been processed **do**

22:         **if** there exists a tuple of the form (l, C) in W **then**

23:             replace (l, C) by $(l, C \cap B)$

24:         **else**

25:             Add (l, B) to W

26:         **end if**

27:     **end for**

28: **until** W is empty

---

return site, we consider the set $Pred$ of all the predecessor locations of m in f (line 19). For each $m' \in Pred$, we form the tuple (m', A'). If tuple (m', A') has already been processed no action is required. Else, if there already exists a tuple of the form (m', C) in W, then we have discovered a new backward path to location m'. Since we are computing must aliases, viz., intersection of aliases discovered along all backwards CFG paths, we replace the tuple (m', C) with the tuple $(m', A' \cap C)$ (line 23). If there exists no such tuple, then we simply add the new tuple (m', A') to W.

4   Leveraging Acquisition Histories for Warning Reduction

We present two new race warning reduction techniques that are based on tracking lock acquisition patterns and are provably more accurate than existing lockset-based ones [8]. Our new reduction technique proceeds in two stages. In the first stage, we make use of the notion of consistency of lock acquisition histories which governs whether program locations in two different threads are simultaneously reachable. This allows us to discard, in a sound fashion, those warnings wherein lock acquisition histories are inconsistent even though disjoint locks are held at the corresponding program locations. Lockset based techniques alone could not remove such warnings. In the second stage, we use yet another warning reduction technique complementary to the first one which is based on defining an acquisition history based *weaker than* relation on the remaining warnings that is more refined than the lockset based weaker than relation defined in [8].

The lockset based *weaker than relation* technique of [8] defines an *access event* as a 4-tuple of the form (v, T, L, a, c), where v is a shared variable accessed at control location c of thread T with lockset L and a denotes the type of accesses, i.e., whether it is a read or a write. Let e_1, e_2 and e_3 be access events such that e_2 and e_3 occur along same local computation path of a thread. Then if the occurrence of a race between e_1 and e_2 implies the occurrence of a race between e_1 and e_3, we need not generate a warning for the pair (e_1, e_2). In this case, the event e_3 is said to be *weaker than* e_2, denoted by $e_3 \sqsubseteq e_2$. The relation $\sqsubseteq$ is hard to determine precisely without exploring the state space of the given program which, in general, may not be scalable. Instead, it is typically over-approximated via static analysis. A lockset based approximation, $\sqsubseteq_l$, given in [8] is defined below.

Definition 5 (Lockset Based Weaker Than [8]). *For access event $p = (v, T, L_1, a_1, c_1)$ occurring before access event $q = (v, T, L_2, a_2, c_2)$ along a common local computation x of thread T, $p \sqsubseteq_l q$ iff $L_1 \subseteq L_2$ and either $a_1 = a_2$ or a_1 is a write operation.*

4.1 Acquisition History Based Warning Reduction

We motivate our technique with the help of a simple concurrent program $\mathcal{CP}$ comprised of the two threads T_1 and T_2 shown in figure 2 that access shared variable x. Let e_1, e_2, e_3 and e_4 denote accesses to x at locations 6a, 6b, 9b and 2b, respectively. Note that the locksets at control locations 6b and 9b are $L_2 = \{lk2\}$ and $L_3 = \{lk2\}$, respectively. Since $L_2 \subseteq L_3$, $e_2 \sqsubseteq_l e_3$ and so the lockset based reduction technique would drop (e_1, e_3) in favor of (e_1, e_2).

However, control locations 6a and 6b are not simultaneously reachable whereas 6a and 9b are, even though in both cases disjoint locksets are held at the two locations.

```
                              1b:  lock(lk2);
        1a:  a = 1;           2b:  x = 0;
        2a:  lock(lk1);       3b:  lock(lk1);
        3a:  lock(lk2);       4b:  b = 2;
        4a:  y = 1;           5b:  unlock(lk1);
        5a:  unlock(lk2);     6b:  x = 2;
        6a:  x = 3;           7b:  unlock(lk2);
        7a:  unlock(lk1);     8b:  lock(lk2);
                              9b:  x = 1;
```

Fig. 2. Threads T_1 and T_2 with shared variable x

The key reason is that simultaneous reachability of two control locations in separate threads depends not merely on the locks held at these locations but also on the patterns in which they were acquired in the individual threads. Indeed, in order for T_2 to reach 6b it needs to execute the statements at locations 3b and 5b, viz., acquire and release lock $lk1$. Note, however, that once T_1 acquires $lk1$ at location 2a it does not release it until after it has exited 6a. Thus in order for the two threads to simultaneously reach 6a and 6b, T_2 must first acquire and release $lk1$, viz., must already have executed 5b before T_1 executes 2a. However, in that case T_2 holds lock $lk2$ (via execution of 1b) which it cannot release, thus preventing T_2 from executing 3a and transiting further. This proves our claim. The simultaneous reachability of 6a and 9b, on the other hand, is easy to check. Thus the $\sqsubseteq_l$-based reduction of [8] drops a warning corresponding to a real data race in favor of a bogus one. In general, when testing for reachability of control states c and c' of two different threads we need to test whether there exist paths x and y in the individual threads leading to states c and c' holding lock sets L and L' which can be acquired in a compatible fashion so as to prevent the scenario above. Compatibility can be captured using the notion of acquisition histories defined below. Let $Lock\text{-}Set(T_i, c)$ denote the set of locks held by thread T_i at control location c.

Definition 6 (Acquisition History) [9]. *Let x be a global computation of a concurrent program CP leading to global configuration c. Then for thread T_i and lock l of CP such that $l \in Lock\text{-}Set(T_i, c)$, we define $AH(T_i, l, x)$ to be the set of locks that were acquired (and possibly released) by T_i after the last acquisition of l by T_i along x.*

If L is the set of locks, each acquisition history AH is a map $L \rightarrow 2^L$ associating which each lock a lockset, i.e., the acquisition history of that lock. We say that acquisition histories AH_1 and AH_2 are *consistent* iff there do not exist locks l_1 and l_2, such that $l_1 \in AH_2(l_2)$ and $l_2 \in AH_1(l_1)$. Then the above discussion can formalized as follows.

Theorem 7 (Decomposition Result) [9]. *Let CP be a concurrent program comprised of the two threads T_1 and T_2. Then for control states a_1 and b_2 of T_1 and T_2, respectively, a_1 and b_2 are simultaneously reachable only if there are local computations x and y of threads T_1 and T_2 leading to control states a_1 and b_2, respectively, such that (i) $Lock\text{-}Set(T_1, s) \cap Lock\text{-}Set(T_2, t) = \emptyset$, and (ii) the acquisition histories AH_1 and AH_2 at a_1 and b_2, respectively, are consistent. If the threads communicate solely via nested locks then the above conditions are also sufficient.*

These acquisition histories can be tracked via static analysis much like locksets. To leverage the Decomposition result, we therefore define an ah-augmented access event as a tuple of the form (v, T, L, AH, a, c), where (v, T, L, a, c) is an access event and AH is the current acquisition history. Our warning reduction proceeds in two stages.

Stage I. Since consistency of acquisition histories is a necessary condition for simultaneous reachability, we drop all warnings (e_1, e_2), where $e_i = (v, T, L_i, AH_i, a_i)$ and AH_1 and AH_2 are inconsistent. In our example, (e_1, e_3) will be dropped at this stage.

Stage II. On the remaining warnings, we impose a new *acquisition history based weaker than* relation $\sqsubseteq_a$. Towards that end, given two acquisition histories AH_1 and AH_2, we say that $AH_1 \sqsubseteq AH_2$ iff for each lock l, $AH_1(l) \subseteq AH_2(l)$. An immediate, but important, consequence is the following

Proposition 8. *Given acquisition history tuples AH, AH_1 and AH_2, such that $AH_1 \sqsubseteq AH_2$, AH is consistent with AH_2 implies that AH is consistent with AH_1.*

Definition 9 (Acquisition History based Weaker Than). *For access event $e_1 = (v, T, L_1, AH_1, a_1, c_1)$ occurring before $e_2 = (v, T, L_2, AH_2, a_2, c_2)$ along a common computation of thread T, $e_1 \sqsubseteq_a e_2$ iff $L_1 \subseteq L_2$, $AH_1 \sqsubseteq AH_2$ and either $a_1 = a_2$ or a_1 is a write operation.*

In our example, the acquisition histories for events e_1, e_3 and e_4 are $AH_1 = \{(lk1, \{lk2\})\}$, $AH_3 = \{(lk2, \emptyset)\}$ and $AH_4 = \{(lk2, \emptyset)\}$, respectively. Clearly, $AH_4 \sqsubseteq AH_3$, and so $e_4 \sqsubseteq_a e_3$. Thus we drop (e_1, e_3) and retain (e_1, e_4). The intuition behind this is that any local computation of T_2 leading to accesses e_3 has to pass through the access e_4. Moreover, since $AH_3 \sqsubseteq AH_4$, it follows that if AH_1 and AH_3 are consistent then so are AH_1 and AH_4. Thus, since T_1 and T_2 communicate only via nested locks, by the decomposition result, if there is a computation realizing the data race corresponding to the warning (e_1, e_3), then there also exists one realizing (e_1, e_4). Thus we may drop (e_1, e_3) is favor of (e_1, e_4).

Acquisition History-based Covers. Note that is general there might be multiple paths leading to an access event e_k, in which case before dropping a pair (e_i, e_k), we need to make sure that along each path in the program leading to e_k there exists an accesses event $e_j \sqsubseteq_a e_k$. This can be accomplished by using the notion of a *cover* for an access event. Given an access event e, a *Cover* for e is a set of access events c such that $c \sqsubseteq_a e$. Such a cover can be easily determined via a backwards dataflow analysis from the program location corresponding to e.

Making Reduction Sound via Ranking. Finally, we note that if the thread synchronization is not merely lock based, a reduction strategy based on either $\sqsubseteq_a$ or $\sqsubseteq_l$ is not sound. In [8], a manual inspection routine is proposed in order to identify real warnings that may have been dropped which may not be practical. We propose using ranking in order to ensure soundness. Towards that end, we do not drop any warning based on $\sqsubseteq_a$ but merely rank them lower. Then whether a warning lower in the order in inspected is contingent on the fact that the warning higher in the order turns out to be a bogus one.

5   Experimental Results

The experimental results for our suite of 10 Linux device drivers downloaded from `kernel.org` are tabulated below. The results clearly demonstrate (i) the effectiveness of our shared variable discovery routine, (ii) the scalability and efficiency (*Time* column) of our new summary based pointer analysis, and (iii) the effectiveness and hence the importance of leveraging warning reduction techniques. The *Time* column refers to the time taken (not including the time taken for building the CFG - typically less than a minute) when using our new summary based technique for must-alias analysis. The BDDBDDB engine was run only on the first three drivers and took respectively, 15min, 1 hr and 30 min, respectively, thus clearly demonstrating the improvement in running time when using our new alias analysis. The columns labeled *War* and *Aft. Red.* refer, respectively, to the total number of warnings generated originally and after applying reduction based on the $\sqsubseteq_a$ relation. Even after applying these reductions, there could still be a lot of warnings generated as Linux drivers usually have a large number of small functions resulting a large number of contexts. Thus the same program location may generate many warnings that result from essentially the same data race but different contexts. The column *Aft. Con.* refers to the number of warnings left after generating only one warning for each program location and abstracting out the contexts.

Driver	KLOC	# *ShVars*	#War	#Aft.Red.	#Aft.Con.	Time(secs)
hugetlb	1.2	5	4	1	1	3.2
ipoib_multicast	26.1	10	33228	6	6	7
plip	13.7	17	94	51	51	5
sock	0.9	6	32	21	13	2
ctrace_comb	1.4	19	985	218	58	6.7
autofs_expire	8.3	7	20	8	3	6
ptrace	15.4	3	9	1	1	15
tty_io	17.8	1	6	3	3	4
raid	17.2	6	23	21	13	1.5
pci_gart	0.6	1	3	1	1	1

6   Conclusion and Related Work

Data race detection being a problem of fundamental interest has been the subject of extensive research. Many techniques have been leveraged in order to attack the problem including dynamic run-time detection, static analysis and model checking.

Early work on dynamic data race detection includes the Eraser data race detector [15] which is based on computing locksets. There has been much work that improves upon the basic Eraser methodology. One such approach [8] leverages the use of static analysis to reduce the number of data race warnings that need to be validated via a run-time analysis. Other run-time detection tools based on Lamport's happened before model restrict the number of interleavings that need be explored [6,11]. The advantage of run-time techniques is the absence of false warnings. On the other hand, the disadvantages are the extra cost incurred in instrumenting the code and poor coverage both of which become worse as the size of code increases especially in the context of concurrent programs. Additionally, run time detection techniques presume that the given code can be executed which may not be an option for applications like device drivers.

Model Checking [3], which is an efficient exploration of the state space of the given program, is another powerful technique that has been employed in the verification of concurrent programs [1,4]. However, the state space explosion has made it hard to verify concurrent programs beyond 10K lines of code and is thus not, with the current state-of-the-art, an option for debugging large-scale real-life code.

Recently, there has been a spurt of activity in applying static analysis techniques for data race detection [5,10,17,2,13,12,7,14,8]. An advantage of such techniques is that they can be made to scale to large programs. The key disadvantage is that since static analysis works on heavily abstracted versions of the original program, they are not refined enough and can produce a large number of false warnings.

A credible approach is to strengthen static analysis to make it more refined with the goal of reducing the number of bogus warnings. The key steps to an accurate race detection procedure are (i) accurate shared variable discovery, (ii) scalable context sensitive pointer analysis to determine must locksets, and (iii) effective warning reduction. In this paper, we have proposed a new shared variable detection analysis that can be used to enhance existing correlation based techniques [7,14]. Secondly, we have proposed a new scalable context sensitive must alias analysis which is critical in ensuring both scalability and accuracy of our race detection analysis. Prior context-sensitive alias analysis techniques have been shown to be more successful for Java [13,12,18] than C, whereas other techniques [7] simply do not use any pointer analysis which limits their accuracy. Finally, we have proposed a new two stage acquisition history based warning reduction technique which is provably more accurate than existing lockset based techniques given in [8]. Experimental results on a suite of Linux drivers demonstrate the efficacy, viz., both the accuracy and scalability, of our new techniques.

References

1. Brat, G., Havelund, K., Park, S., Visser, W.: Model checking programs. In: ASE 2000
2. Burrows, M., Leino, K.: Finding stale-value errors in concurrent programs. In: Compaq Systems Research Center SRC-TR-2002-004 (2002)
3. Clarke, E.M., Emerson, E.A.: Design and synthesis of synchronization skeletons using branching time temporal logic. In: Workshop on Logics of Programs, pp. 52–71 (1981)
4. Corbett, J., Dwyer, M., Hatcliff, J., Laubach, S., Robby, C.P., Zheng, H.: Bandera: Extracting finite-state models from java source code. In: ICSE 2000
5. Detlefs, D., Leino, K.R.M., Nelson, G., Saxe, J.: Extended static checking. In: TR SRC-159 Compaq SRC (1998)
6. Dinning, A., Schonberg, E.: An empirical comparison of monitoring algorithms for access anomaly detection. In: PPoPP 1990
7. Engler, D., Ashcraft, K.: RacerX: Effective, Static Detection of Race Conditions and Deadlocks. In: SOSP 2003
8. Choi, J., Lee, K., Loginov, A., O'Callahan, R., Sarkar, V., Sridharan, M.: Efficient and precise datarace detection for multithreaded object-oriented programs. In: PLDI 2002
9. Kahlon, V., Ivančić, F., Gupta, A.: Reasoning about threads communicating via locks. In: Etessami, K., Rajamani, S.K. (eds.) CAV 2005. LNCS, vol. 3576, Springer, Heidelberg (2005)
10. Leino, R., Neslon, G., Saxe, J.: Esc/java users' manual. Technical Note 2000-002, Compaq Systems Research Center (2001)
11. Mellor-Crummey, J.: One-the-fly detection of data races for programs with nested fork-join parallelism. In: Proceedings of the 1991 Supercomputer Debugging Workshop (1991)
12. Naik, M., Aiken, A.: Conditional must not aliasing for static race detection. In: POPL 2007
13. Naik, M., Aiken, A., Whaley, J.: Effective static race detection for java. In: PLDI 2006
14. Pratikakis, P., Foster, J.S., Hicks, M.: LOCKSMITH: Context-Sensitive Correlation Analysis for Race Detection. In: PLDI 2006
15. Savage, S., Burrows, M., Nelson, G., Sobalvarro, P., Anderson, T.: Eraser: A dynamic data race detector for multithreaded programming. In: ACM TCS, vol. 15(4), ACM Press, New York (1997)
16. Steensgaard, B.: Points-to analysis in almost linear time. In: POPL 1996
17. Sterling, N.: Warlock: A static data race analysis tool. In: USENIX Winter Technical Conference (1993)
18. Whaley, J., Lam, M.: Cloning-based context-sensitive pointer alias analysis using binary decision diagrams. In: PLDI 2004

Parametric and Sliced Causality

Feng Chen and Grigore Roşu

Department of Computer Science
University of Illinois at Urbana - Champaign, USA
{fengchen,grosu}@uiuc.edu

Abstract. Happen-before causal partial orders have been widely used in concurrent program verification and testing. This paper presents a parametric approach to happen-before causal partial orders. Existing variants of happen-before relations can be obtained as instances of the parametric framework. A novel causal partial order, called *sliced causality*, is then defined also as an instance of the parametric framework, which loosens the obvious but strict happen-before relation by considering static and dynamic dependence information about the program. Sliced causality has been implemented in a runtime predictive analysis tool for JAVA, named JPREDICTOR, and the evaluation results show that sliced causality can significantly improve the capability of concurrent verification and testing.

1 Introduction

Concurrent systems are notoriously difficult to verify, test and debug due to their inherent nondeterminism. The *happen-before* causality, first introduced in [14], provides an effective way to analyze the potential dynamic behaviors of concurrent systems and has been widely used in concurrent program verification and testing [21,16,18,19,9]. Approaches based on happen-before causality extract causal partial orders by analyzing process or thread communication at runtime; the extracted causal partial order can be regarded as an abstract model of the runtime behaviors of the program and thus can be checked against the desired property. This way, one analyzes *a class of executions* that are characterized by the same causal partial order. Therefore, for verification, the state space to explore can be reduced, while for testing, one can predict potential errors without re-execute the program. Happen-before based approaches are sound (no false alarms) and can handle general purpose properties, e.g., temporal ones.

Several variants of happen-before causalities have been introduced for applications in different domains [14,16,19]. Although these notions are similar in principle, there is however no adequate unifying framework for all of them. A proof of soundness has to be re-done for every variant of happen-before causality, which typically involves sophisticate details of the specific domain. This may slow future developments, in particular defining new, or domain-specific causalities. The first contribution of this paper is a *parametric framework* for causal partial orders, which is purposely designed to facilitate defining and proving correctness of happen-before causalities. The proof of correctness of a happen-before relation is reduced to proving a simple, easy to check closed local property of causal dependence. Existing variants of happen-before relations can be obtained and proved sound as instances of our parametric framework.

W. Damm and H. Hermanns (Eds.): CAV 2007, LNCS 4590, pp. 240–253, 2007.

The second contribution of this paper consists of using the above framework to define a novel causal partial order relation, called *sliced causality*, which aims at improving coverage of analysis without giving up soundness or genericity of properties to check: it works with any *monitorable* (safety) properties, including regular patterns, temporal assertions, data-races, atomicity, etc. Previous approaches based on happen-before (such as [16,18,19]) extract causal partial orders from analyzing *exclusively* the dynamic thread communication in executions. Since they consider *all* interactions among threads, e.g., all reads/writes of shared variables, the obtained causal partial orders are rather *restrictive*, or *rigid*, in the sense of allowing a reduced number of linearizations and thus of errors that can be detected. In general, the larger the causality (as a binary relation) the fewer linearizations it has, i.e., the more restrictive it is.

Let us consider a simple and common safety property for a shared resource, that any access should be authenticated. Figure 1 shows a buggy multi-threaded program using the shared resource. The main thread authenticates and then the task thread uses the authenticated resource. They communicate via the `flag` variable. Synchronization is unnecessary, since only the main thread modifies

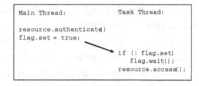

Fig. 1. Multi-threaded execution

`flag`. However, the developer makes a (rather common [7]) mistake by using `if` instead of `while` in the task thread. Suppose now that we observed a successful run of the program, as shown by the arrow. The traditional happen-before will not be able to find the bug because of the causality induced by write/read on `flag`. But since `resource.access()` is *not* controlled by `if`, our technique will be able to correctly predict the violation from the successful execution. When the bug is fixed by replacing `if` with `while`, `resource.access()` will be controlled by `while` because it is a non-terminating loop; then no violation will be reported by our technique.

In summary, based on an apriori static analysis, sliced causality drastically cuts the usual happen-before causality by removing unnecessary dependencies; this way, a significantly larger number of consistent runs can be inferred and thus analyzed. Experiments show that, on average, the sliced causality relation has about 50% direct inter-thread causal dependencies compared to the more conventional happen-before partial order (Section 5). Since the number of linearizations of a partial order tends to be exponential with the size of the *complement* of the partial order, any linear reduction in size of the sliced causality compared to traditional happen-before relations is expected to *increase exponentially the coverage* of the corresponding analysis, still avoiding any false alarms. Indeed, the use of sliced causality allowed us to detect concurrency errors that would be very little likely detected using the conventional happen-before causalities.

This paper is organized as follows. Section 2 introduces existing happen-before causalities. Section 3 defines our parametric framework. Section 4 proposes sliced causality. Section 5 discusses the evaluation of sliced causality and Section 6 concludes. Most proofs are omitted because of limited space; they can be found in [4].

2   Happen-Before Causalities

The first happen-before relation was introduced almost 3 decades ago by Lamport [14], to formally model and reason about concurrent behaviors of distributed systems. Since then, a plethora of variants of happen-before causal partial order relations have been introduced in various frameworks and for various purposes. The basic idea underlying happen-before relations is to observe the events generated by the execution of a distributed system and, based on their order, their type and a straightforward causal flow of information in the system (e.g., the receive event of a message follows its corresponding send event), to define a partial order relation, the happen-before causality. Two events related by the happen-before relation are causally linked in that order.

When using a particular happen-before relation for (concurrent) program analysis, the crucial property of the happen-before relation is that, for an observed execution trace τ, other *sound permutations* of τ, also called *linearizations* or *linear extensions* or *consistent runs* or even *topological sortings* in the literature, are also possible computations of the concurrent system. Consequently, if any of these linearizations violates or satisfies a property φ, then the system can indeed violate or satisfy the property, regardless of whether the particular observed execution that generated the happen-before relation violated or satisfied the property, respectively. For example, [6] defines formulae *Definitely*(φ) and *Possibly*(φ), which hold iff φ holds in all and, respectively, in some possible linearizations of the happen-before causality.

The soundness/correctness of a happen-before causality can be stated as follows: given a happen-before causal partial order extracted from a run of the concurrent system under consideration, all its linearizations are *feasible*, that is, they correspond to other possible execution of the concurrent system. To prove it, one needs to formally define the actual computational model and what a concurrent computation is; these definitions tend to be rather intricate and domain-specific. For that reason, proofs need to be redone in different settings facing different "details", even though they follow conceptually the same idea. In the next section we present a simple and intuitive property on traces, called *feasibility*, which ensures the desired property of the happen-before causality and which appears to be easy to check in concrete situations.

To show how the various happen-before causalities fall as special cases of our parametric approach, we recall two important happen-before partial orders, one in the context of distributed systems where communication takes place exclusively via message passing, and another in the context of multithreaded systems, where communication takes place via shared memory. In the next section we show that their correctness [2,19] follow as corollaries of our main theorem. In Section 4 we define another happen-before causality, called *sliced causality*, which non-trivially uses static analysis information about the multithreaded program. The correctness of sliced causality will also follow as a corollary of our main theorem in the next section.

In the original setting of [14], a distributed system is formalized as a collection of processes communicating only by means of asynchronous message passing. A process is a sequence of events. An event can be a *send* of a message to another process, a *receive* of a message from another process, or an *internal* (local) event.

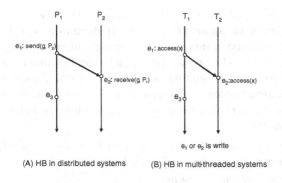

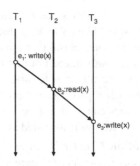

(A) HB in distributed systems

(B) HB in multi-threaded systems

Fig. 2. Happen-before partial-order relations

Fig. 3. Happen-before causality in multi-threaded systems

Definition 1. *Let τ be an execution trace of a distributed system consisting of a sequence of events as above. Let E be the set of all events appearing in τ and let the* **happen-before** *partial order "$\rightarrow$" on E be defined as follows:*

1. *if e_1 appears before e_2 in some process, then $e_1 \rightarrow e_2$;*
2. *if e_1 is the send and e_2 is the receive of the same message, then $e_1 \rightarrow e_2$;*
3. *$e_1 \rightarrow e_2$ and $e_2 \rightarrow e_3$ implies $e_1 \rightarrow e_3$.*

A space-time diagram to illustrate the above definition is shown in Figure 2 (A), in which e_1 is a send message and e_2 is the corresponding receive message; $e_1 \rightarrow e_2$ and $e_1 \rightarrow e_3$, but e_2 and e_3 are not related. It is easy to prove that $(E, \rightarrow)$ is a partial order. The soundness of this happen-before relation, i.e., all the permutations of τ consistent with $\rightarrow$ are possible computations of the distributed system, was proved in [2] using a specific formalization of the global state of a distributed system. This property will follow as an immediate corollary of our main theorem in the next section.

Happen-before causalities have been devised in the context of multithreaded systems for various purposes. For example, [15,16] propose datarace detection techniques based on intuitive multi-threaded variants of happen-before causality, [19] proposes a happen-before relation that drops read/read dependencies, and [20] even drops the write/write conflicts but relates each write with all its subsequent reads atomically.

Finding appropriate happen-before causalities for multithreaded systems is a non-trivial task. The obvious approach would be to map the inter-thread communication in a multi-threaded system into send/receive events in some corresponding distributed system. For example, starting a new thread generates two events, namely a send event from the parent thread and a corresponding receive event from the new thread; releasing a lock is a send event and acquiring a lock is a receive event. A write on a shared variable is a send event while a read is a receive event. However, such a simplistic mapping suffers from several problems related to the semantics of shared variable accesses. First, every write on a shared variable can be followed by multiple reads whose order should not matter; in other words, some "send" events now can have multiple corresponding "receive" events. Second, consider the example in Figure 3. Since e_3 may write a different value into x other than e_1, the value read at where e_2 occurs may change if we observe e_3 after e_1 but before e_2 appears. Therefore, $e_1 e_3 e_2$ may not be a trace of some feasible execution since e_2 will not occur any more. Hence, a causal order between e_2 and e_3 should be enforced, which cannot be captured by the original definition in [14].

The various causalities for multithreaded systems address these problems (among others). However, each of them still needs to be proved correct: any sound permutation of events results in a feasible execution of the multithreaded system. If one does not prove such a property for one's desired happen-before causality, then one's analysis techniques can lead to false alarms. We next recall one of the simplest happen-before relations for multi-threaded systems [19]:

Definition 2. *Let τ be an execution of a multithreaded system, let E be the set of all events in τ, and let the **happen-before** partial order "$\rightsquigarrow$" on E be defined as follows:*

1. *if e_1 appears before e_2 in some thread, then $e_1 \rightsquigarrow e_2$;*
2. *if e_1 and e_2 are two accesses on the same shared variable such that e_1 appears before e_2 in the execution and at least one of them is a write, then $e_1 \rightsquigarrow e_2$;*
3. *$e_1 \rightsquigarrow e_2$ and $e_2 \rightsquigarrow e_3$ implies that $e_1 \rightsquigarrow e_3$.*

In Figure 2 (B), $e_1 \rightsquigarrow e_2$ and $e_1 \rightsquigarrow e_3$, but e_2 and e_3 are not comparable under $\rightsquigarrow$.

3   Parametric Framework for Causality

We here define a parametric framework that axiomatizes the notion of causality over events and *feasibility* of traces in a system-independent manner. We show that proving the feasibility of the linearizations of a causal partial order extracted from an execution can be reduced to checking a simpler "closure" local property on feasible traces.

Let *Events* be the set of all events. A trace τ is a finite ordered set of (distinct) events $\{e_1 < e_2 < \cdots < e_n\}$, usually identified with the *Events** word $e_1 \cdots e_n$. Let $\xi_\tau = \{e_1, e_2, \ldots, e_n\}$ be called the alphabet of τ and $<_\tau$ be the total order on ξ_τ induced by τ. Let *Traces* denote the set of all such traces. Given a set X, let $\mathcal{PO}(X)$ denote the set of partial orders defined on subsets of X, that is, the set of pairs $(\xi, <)$ where $\xi \subseteq X$ and $< \subseteq \xi \times \xi$ is a partial order.

Definition 3. *A causality operator is a partial function C : Traces-↠$\mathcal{PO}$(Events) s.t.:*

1. *If $C(\tau) = (\xi, <)$, then $\xi = \xi_\tau$ and $< \subseteq <_\tau$; and*
2. *For any $\tau = \tau_1 e_1 e_2 \tau_2$ such that $C(\tau) = (\xi, <)$ with $e_1 \not< e_2$, $C(\tau_1 e_2 e_1 \tau_2)$ is also defined and equal to $C(\tau)$.*

Let Dom(C) denote the domain of C.

Note that condition (ii) in the definition above is closely related to that of trace equivalence introduced by Mazurkiewicz in [11]. However, the theory of Mazurkiewicz traces starts with a given dependency relation on events and considers equivalence of traces according to that fixed dependency, while in our framework, we prefer to associate a separate dependency relation to each trace, assuming that only at runtime we can get enough information about the causality for a given trace; for example, acquiring lock l and writing shared variable x can be or not dependent events, depending on the particular execution of the program. This allows us to be more precise while still using part of the generic Mazurkiewicz trace theory to simplify our correctness proofs.

Any concurrent system can produce only a particular subset of *feasible* traces, which are in the following relationship with the corresponding causality operator:

Definition 4. *Given a causality operator C, a set $\mathcal{F}$ of traces is C-feasible iff C is defined on $\mathcal{F}$ and for any $\tau \in \mathcal{F}$ with $C(\tau) = (\xi, <)$, $\mathcal{F}$ contains all the linearizations of $C(\tau)$ (i.e., all traces τ' such that $\xi_{\tau'} = \xi$ and $< \subseteq <_{\tau'}$).*

Theorem 1. *$Dom(C)$ is C-feasible, More precisely, if $C(\tau) = (\xi, <)$ then for any τ', $C(\tau') = C(\tau)$ if and only if $\xi_{\tau'} = \xi$ and $< \subseteq <_{\tau'}$.*

Corollary 1. *$\mathcal{F}$ is C-feasible iff C is defined on $\mathcal{F}$ and for any $\tau = \tau_1 e_1 e_2 \tau_2$ such that $C(\tau) = (\xi, <)$, $e_1 \not< e_2$ implies $\tau_1 e_2 e_1 \tau_2 \in \mathcal{F}$.*

The two variants of happen-before relations discussed in Section 2 can be captured as instances of our parametric framework. For the happen-before relation defined in Definition 1, let Events$_{hb}$ be the set of all the send, receive and internal events.

Corollary 2. *For an observed trace τ, any permutation of τ consistent with $\rightarrow$ is a possible computation of the distributed system.*

Proof: Let C_{hb} be the partial function Traces$_{hb} \nrightarrow \mathcal{PO}($Events$_{hb})$ with $C_{hb}(\tau) = (\xi_\tau, \rightarrow)$ for any $\tau \in$ Traces$_{hb}$. Let $\mathcal{F}_{hb}$ be the set of computation traces of the distributed system as defined in [2]. The result follows from Corollary 1, noticing that C_{hb} is a causality operator and $\mathcal{F}_{hb}$ is C_{hb}-feasible. □

For the happen-before relation in Definition 2, let Events$_{mhb}$ be the set of all the write and read events on shared variables as well as all internal events.

Corollary 3. *For an observed trace τ of a multi-threaded system, any permutation of τ consistent with $\rightsquigarrow$ is a possible execution of the multi-threaded system.*

Proof: Let C_{mhb} be the partial function Traces$_{mhb} \nrightarrow \mathcal{PO}($Events$_{mhb})$ with $C_{mhb}(\tau) = (E_\tau, \rightsquigarrow)$ for any $\tau \in$ Traces$_{mhb}$. Let $\mathcal{F}_{mhb}$ be the set of traces that are generated by all feasible executions of the multi-threaded system (see, e.g., [19] for a formalization of multi-threaded systems). The result follows from Corollary 1, noticing that C_{mhb} is a causality operator and $\mathcal{F}_{mhb}$ is C_{mhb}-feasible. □

4   Sliced Causality

Without additional information about the structure of the program that generated the event trace τ, the least restrictive causal partial order that an observer can extract from τ is the one which is total on the events generated by each thread and in which each write event of a shared variable precedes all the corresponding subsequent read events. This is investigated and discussed in detail in [20]. In what follows we show that one can construct a much more general causal partial order, called *sliced causality*, by making use of dependence information obtained statically and dynamically. Briefly, instead of computing the causal partial order on all the observed events like in the traditional happen-before based approaches, our approach first slices τ according to the desired property and then computes the causal partial order on the achieved slice; the slice contains all the events relevant to the property, as well as all the events upon which the relevant events depend. This way, irrelevant causality on events is trimmed without breaking the soundness of the approach, allowing more permutations of relevant events to be analyzed and resulting in better coverage of the analysis.

We employ dependencies among events to assure the correct slicing. The dependence discussed here somehow relates to *program slicing* [12], but we focus on finer grained units here, namely events, instead of statements. Our analysis keeps track of actual memory locations in every event, available at runtime, avoiding inter-procedural analysis. Also, we need *not* maintain the entire dependence relation, since we only need to compute the causal partial order among events that are relevant to the property to check. This leads to an effective vector clock (*VC*) algorithm ([3]).

Intuitively, event e' *depends upon* event e in τ, written $e \sqsubset e'$, iff a change of e may change or eliminate e'. This tells the observer that e *should occur before e' in any consistent permutation of τ*. There are two kinds of dependence: (1) *control dependence*, written $e \sqsubset_{ctrl} e'$, when a change of the state of e may eliminate e'; and (2) *data-flow dependence*, written $e \sqsubset_{data} e'$, when a change of the state of e may lead to a change in the state of e'. While the control dependence only relates events generated by the same thread, the data-flow dependence may relate events generated by different threads: e may write some shared variable in a thread t, which is then read in another thread t'.

4.1   Events and Traces

Events represent atomic steps observed in the execution of the program. In this paper, we focus on multi-threaded programs and consider the following types of events (other types can be easily added): write/read of variables, beginning/ending of function invocations, acquiring/releasing locks, and starts and exits of threads. A statement in the program may produce multiple events. Events need to store enough information about the program state in order for the observer to perform its analysis.

Definition 5. *An **event** is a mapping of **attributes** into corresponding **values**. A **trace** is a sequences of events. We let τ, τ', etc., denote traces. From now on in the paper, we assume an arbitrary but fixed trace τ and let ξ denote ξ_τ (recall $\xi_\tau = \{e \mid e \in \tau\}$) for simplicity; events in ξ are called **concrete events**.*

For example, one event can be e_1 : (*counter* $= 8$, *thread* $= t_1$, *stmt* $= L_{11}$, *type* $=$ *write*, *target* $= a$, *state* $= 1$), which is a write on location a with value 1, produced at statement L_{11} by thread t_1. One can easily include more information into an event by adding new attribute-value pairs. We use *key(e)* to refer to the value of attribute *key* of event e. The attribute *state* contains the value associated to the event; specifically, for the write/read on a variable, *state(e)* is the value written to/read from the variable; for ending of a function call, *state(e)* is the return value if there is one; for the lock operation, *state(e)* is the lock object; for other events, *state(e)* is undefined. To distinguish among different occurrences of events with the same attribute values, we add a designated attribute to every event, *counter*, collecting the number of previous events with the same attribute-value pairs (other than the *counter*). This way, all events appearing in a trace can be assumed different.

4.2 Control Dependence on Events

Informally, if a change of *state(e)* may affect the occurrence of e', then we say that e' has a *control dependence* on e, and write $e \sqsubset_{ctrl} e'$. For example, in Figure 4, the write on x at S_1 and the write on y at S_2 have a control dependence on the read on i at C_1, while the write on z at S_3 does not have such control dependence. Control dependence occurs inside of a thread, so we first define the total order within one thread:

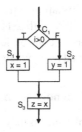

Fig. 4. Control dependence

Definition 6. *Let* < *denote the union of the total orders on events of each thread, i.e.,* $e < e'$ *iff thread(e) = thread(e') and* $e <_\tau e'$.

The control dependence among events in sliced causality is parametric in a control dependence relation among statements. In particular, one can use off-the-shelf algorithms for classic [8] or for weak [17] control dependence. We chose to use the termination-sensitive control dependence (TSCD) introduced in [5] in our implementation of jPRE-DICTOR[3]. Nevertheless, all we need to define sliced causality is a function returning the *control scope* of any statement C, say *scope* (C), which is the set of statements whose reachability depends upon the choice made at C, that is, the statements that control depend on C, for some appropriate or preferred notion of control dependence. Our approach also regards the lock acquire statement as a control statement that controls all the following statements, since the thread has to wait for the lock to continue its execution.

We assume that any control statement generates either a *read* event (the lock acquire is regarded as a read on the lock) or no event (the condition is a constant) when checking its condition. For the control statement with a complex condition, e.g., involving function calls and side effects, we can always transform the program to simplify its condition to a simple check of a boolean variable: one can compute the original condition before the control statement, store its result in a fresh boolean variable, and then modify the control statement to check only that variable in its condition.

Definition 7. $e \sqsubset_{ctrl} e'$ *iff* $e < e'$, *stmt(e')* ∈ *scope(stmt(e)), and e is "largest" with this property, i.e., there is no* e'' *such that* $e < e'' < e'$ *and stmt(e')* ∈ *scope(stmt(e'')).*

Intuitively, an event e is control dependent on the *latest* event issued by some statement upon which *stmt(e)* depends. For example, in Figure 4, a write of x at S_1 is control dependent on the most recent read of i at C_1 and not on previous reads of i at C_1.

The *soundness* of analysis based on sliced causality is contingent to the *correctness* (no false negatives) of the employed control dependence: the analysis produces no false alarms when the *scope* function returns for each statement *at least* all the statements that control-depend on it. An extreme solution is to include all the statements in the program in each scope, in which case sliced causality becomes precisely the classic happen-before relation. As already pointed out in Section 1 and empirically shown in Section 5, such a choice significantly reduces the coverage of analysis. A better solution, still over-conservative, is to use weak dependence when calculating the control scopes. If termination information of loops is available, termination-sensitive control dependence can be utilized to provide correct and more precise results. One can also try to use the classic control dependence instead, but one should be aware that false bugs may be reported (e.g., when synchronization is implemented based on "infinite" loops).

4.3 Data Dependence on Events

If a change of $state(e)$ may affect $state(e')$ then we say e' has a *data dependence* on e and write $e \sqsubset_{data} e'$. Formally,

Definition 8. *For events e and e', $e \sqsubset_{data} e'$ iff $e <_\tau e'$ and one of the following holds:*

1. $e < e'$, $type(e) = read$ and $stmt(e')$ uses $target(e)$ to compute $state(e')$;
2. $type(e) = write$, $type(e') = read$, $target(e) = target(e')$, and there is no other e'' with $e <_\tau e'' <_\tau e'$, $type(e'') = write$, and $target(e'') = target(e')$;
3. $e < e'$, $type(e') = read$, $stmt(e') \notin scope \, (stmt(e))$, and there exists a statement S in $scope \, (stmt(e))$ such that S can change the value of $target(e')$.

The first case in this definition encodes the common data dependence. For example, for an assignment $x := E$, the write of x has data dependence on the reads generated by the evaluation of E. The second case in Definition 8 captures the interference dependence [13] in multithreaded programs, saying that a read depends on *the most recent* write of the same memory location. For instance, in Figure 4, if the observed execution is $C_1 S_1 S_3$ then the read of x at S_3 is data dependent on the most recent write of x at S_1. We treat lock release as a write on the lock and lock acquire as a read. The third case in Definition 8 is more intricate and relates to the relevant dependence in [10]. Assuming another execution of Figure 4, say $C_1 S_2 S_3$, no data dependence defined in cases *1* and *2* can be found in this run. However, the change of the value of the read of i at C_1 can potentially change the value of the read of x at S_3: if the value of i changes then C_1 may choose to execute the branch of S_1, resulting in a new write of x that may change the value of the read of x at S_3. Therefore, we say that the read of x at S_3 is data dependent on the read of i at C_1, as defined in case *3*. Note that although this dependence is caused by a control statement, it can *not* be caught by the control dependence; for example, the read of x at S_3 is *not* control dependent on the read of i at C_1 since $S_3 \notin scope(C_1)$. Aliasing information is needed to correctly compute dependence defined in case *3*, which one can obtain using any available techniques.

An important observation of Definition 8 is that there are no write-write, read-read, read-write data dependencies. Specifically, case 2 only considers the write-read data dependence, enforcing the read to depend upon only the latest write of the same variable. In other words, a write and the following reads of the same variable form an *atomic* block of events. This captures in a more general setting the work in [20].

4.4 Slicing Causality Using Relevance

When checking a trace τ against a property φ, not all the events in τ are relevant to φ; for example, to check dataraces on a variable x, accesses to other variables or function calls are irrelevant. Moreover, the *state* attributes of some relevant events may not be relevant; for example, the particular values written to or read from x for datarace (on x) detection. We next assume a generic *filtering function* that can be instantiated, usually automatically, to concrete filters depending upon the property φ under consideration:

Definition 9. *Let* α: Events $\rightarrow$ Events *be a partial function, called a **filtering function**. The image of* α*, that is* α(Events)*, is written more compactly* Events$_\alpha$*; its elements are called **abstract relevant events**, or simply just **relevant events**. All thread start and exit events are relevant:* $\alpha(e)$ *defined whenever* $type(e) = start$ *or* $type(e) = exit$.

Let us assume an arbitrary but fixed property φ in what follows. Intuitively, $\alpha(e)$ is defined if and only if e is relevant to φ; if $\alpha(e)$ is defined, then $key(\alpha(e)) = key(e)$ for any attribute $key \neq state$, while $state(\alpha(e))$ is either undefined or equal to $state(e)$.

Definition 10. *Let* $\alpha(\tau)$*, written more compactly as* τ_α*, be the trace of relevant events achieved by applying* α *on events in* τ*. Let* ξ_α *denote* ξ_{τ_α} *for simplicity.*

This relevance-based abstraction plays a crucial role in increasing the predictive power of our analysis approach: in contrast to the concrete event set ξ, the corresponding abstract event set ξ_α allows more permutations of abstract events; instead of calculating permutations of ξ and then abstracting them into permutations of ξ_α like in traditional happen-before based approaches, we will calculate valid permutations of a *slice* of $\xi \cup \xi_\alpha$ that contains only events (directly or indirectly) relevant to φ. This slice is defined using the dependence on concrete and abstract events.

Definition 11. *All dependence relations are extended to abstract relevant events: If* $e < / \sqsubset_{ctrl} / \sqsubset_{data} e'$ *then also* $\alpha(e) < / \sqsubset_{ctrl} / \sqsubset_{data} e'$, $e < / \sqsubset_{ctrl} / \sqsubset_{data} \alpha(e')$, *and* $\alpha(e) < / \sqsubset_{ctrl} / \sqsubset_{data} \alpha(e')$*, whenever* $\alpha(e)$ *and/or* $\alpha(e')$ *is defined;* $\sqsubset_{data}$ *is extended only when* $state(\alpha(e'))$ *is defined.*

We next define a novel dependence relation, called *relevance dependence*, which is concerned with *potential* occurrences of relevant events. Consider Figure 4 again. Suppose that relevant events include writes of y and z. For the execution $C_1 S_1 S_3$, only one relevant event is observed, namely the write of z at S_3 (e'), which is not control dependent on the read of i generated at C_1 (e). Consider now another execution $C_1 S_2 S_3$; in addition to e', a new relevant event will be generated, namely the write of y at S_2, caused by the different choice made at C_1. Hence, a change of $state(e)$ *may affect the number of generated relevant events*. Formally, we define *relevance dependence* as follows:

Definition 12. *For* $e \in \xi, e' \in \xi_\alpha$*, we write* $e \sqsubset_{rlvn} e'$ *iff* $e < e'$*,* $stmt(e') \notin scope(stmt(e))$*, and there is a statement* $S \in scope(stmt(e))$ *that may generate a relevant event.*

Intuitively, if $e \sqsubset_{rlvn} e'$ then e' is not control dependent on e, but when $state(e)$ changes, some new relevant events may occur before e'. This may invalidate some permutations of ξ_α since valid permutations should preserve the *exact* number of relevant events.

Definition 13. *Let* $\sqsubset$ *be the relation* $(\sqsubset_{data} \cup \sqsubset_{ctrl} \cup \sqsubset_{rlvn})^+$*. If* e *and* e' *are concrete or relevant events such that* $e \sqsubset e'$*, then we say that* e' ***depends upon*** e.

Definition 14. *Let* $\overline{\xi_\alpha} \subseteq \xi \cup \xi_\alpha$ *be the relevant slice of events, extending* ξ_α *with events* $e \in \xi$ *such that* $e \sqsubset e'$ *for some* $e' \in \xi_\alpha$*. Let* $\overline{\tau_\alpha}$ *be the **abstract trace** of* τ*, i.e., the permutation of* $\overline{\xi_\alpha}$ *consistent with* $<_\tau$.

Intuitively, $\overline{\xi}_\alpha$ contains all the events that are directly or indirectly relevant to the property α. Our goal here is to define an appropriate notion of causal partial order on $\overline{\xi}_\alpha$ and then to show that any permutation consistent with it is sound. Recall that we fixed a trace τ; in what follows, τ' is used to refer to any arbitrary trace.

Definition 15. *Let $<^\tau \subseteq \overline{\xi}_\alpha \times \overline{\xi}_\alpha$ be the relation $(< \cup \sqsubset)^+$, which we call the **sliced causality** (or **sliced causal partial order**) of τ.*

From here on, by "causal partial order" we mean the sliced one. We next show that sliced causality is an instance of the parametric framework in Section 3.

Definition 16. *Let C_α: Traces$\rightharpoonup PO(\mathsf{Events})$ be the partial function defined as $C_\alpha(\tau') = (\xi_{\tau'}, <^{\tau'})$ for each $\tau' \in$ Traces. Let $\mathcal{F}_\alpha \subseteq$ Traces be the set of all possible abstract traces: for each $\tau_\mathcal{F} \in \mathcal{F}_\alpha$, there is some execution generating τ' such that $\overline{\tau'_\alpha} = \tau_\mathcal{F}$.*

Theorem 2. *C_α restricted to $\mathcal{F}_\alpha$ is total and a causality operator. That is, for any abstract trace $\tau_\mathcal{F} \in \mathcal{F}_\alpha$, each linieazation of $<^{\tau_\mathcal{F}}$ corresponds to some possible execution of the multi-threaded system.*

Proof (Sketch). The first condition of the causality operator definition can be easily verified. The more intricate part is to show that the trace obtained by permuting two consecutive independent events in an abstract trace is in $\mathcal{F}_\alpha$, that is, it corresponds to a possible execution. This is achieved by definning partial executions and feasible prefix traces, i.e., (abstract) traces corresponding to partial executions. The technical details of this proof can be found in the companion technical report.

We can therefore analyze the permutations of relevant events consistent with sliced causality to detect potential violations *without* re-executing the program.

5   Evaluation

We implemented a vector clock algorithm for computing sliced causality as part of jPre-dictor, a prototype tool for concurrency error detection of Java programs. To measure the effectiveness of sliced causality in contrast with more conventional happen-before causalities, we also implemented the algorithm in [19] for extracting happen-before causality from Java programs. Interested readers are referred to [3] for more details about the algorithm and the implementation of jPredictor. jPredictor has been evaluated on several concurrent programs. Two measurements were used during the evaluation to compare the sliced causality with the conventional happen-before causality, namely the size of the partial order and the prediction capability to detect data races. The results of our evaluation are shown in Table 1.

The first part of Table 1 shows the benchmarks that we used, along with their size (LOC abbreviates "lines of code"), number of shared variables (S.V.), and number of threads created during their executions. Banking and Http-Server are two simple examples showing relatively classical concurrent bug patterns discussed in detail in [7]. Elevator, sor, and tsp come from [22]. Daisy is a small highly concurrent file system proposed to challenge and evaluate software verification tools. Raytracer is a program from the Java Grande benchmark suite, and SystemLogHandler and WebappLoader are

Table 1. Evaluation of sliced causality

Benchmarks				Causality Size		Races	
Program	LOC	S. V.	Threads	H.B.	S.C.	S.C.	H.B.
Banking	150	10	11	18	2	1	1
Http-Server	170	2	7	22	2	2	1
Elevator	530	20	4	240	2	0	0
sor	600	42	4	21	8	0	0
tsp	1.1k	15	3	5	2	1	0
Daisy	1.5K	312	3	41	23	1	0
Raytracer	1.8k	4	4	7	3	1	1
SystemLogHandler	320	3	3	2	1	1	0
WebappLoader	3k	10	3	9	5	3	0

two components of Tomcat 5.0.28. The property under verification is the datarace of the shared variable. The test cases used in experiments were manually generated using *fixed* inputs. More bugs could be found if more effective test generation techniques were employed, but that was not our objective here.

The second part of the table shows the coverage improvement of the analysis when using sliced causality versus the happen-before causality. A more precise measure of coverage would be the number of all the sound linearizations of the causal partial order; unfortunately, counting sound linearizations is a #P-complete problem [1], so it may be no easier than the problem of generating them. Note that a fully constrained partial order, that is, a total order, admits only one linearization, while a fully unconstrained partial order, that is, a set, admits an exponential number of linearizations. Extrapolating, even though it should not be taken as an absolute measure in all situations, we can say that the fewer causal dependencies a partial order has, the larger the number of sound permutations; moreover, we can also say that the number of linearizations is exponential in the number of unordered elements in the partial order. This simplistic and admittedly informal reasoning leads us to an important insight: any reduction in the number of causal dependencies may have a significant impact on coverage; in particular, a linear reduction of the number of causal dependencies can lead to an *exponential* increase in the coverage of the analysis. Since the total orders on the events of each thread are enforced by both sliced causality and happen-before, we only measure the causal dependencies due to direct inter-thread communication. Therefore, the following dependencies are counted, their number declared the *size of the causality*, and then used as a measurement metric: $e_1 \sqsubset e_2$, $thread(e_1) \neq thread(e_2)$, and there is no e_3 such that $e_1 \sqsubset e_3$ and $e_3 \sqsubset e_2$. Our experiments illustrate that sliced causality is significantly smaller than the conventional happen-before, indicating a magnificent increase in the number of covered potential executions.

The third part of Table 1 directly compares the effectiveness of race detection using sliced causality versus happen-before. The first column in this part is the number of races detected by sliced causality, while the second column gives the number of races detected by the standard, unsliced happen-before causality using the *same* execution traces. As expected, sliced causality is more effective in detecting dataraces, since it covers more potential runs. Even though, in theory, the standard happen-before technique may also be able to detect, through many executions of the system, the errors detected from one run using sliced causality, we were not able to find any of the races in some programs, e.g., in tsp and Tomcat, without enabling the sliced causality. Moreover, in these experiments, sliced causality did *not* produce any false alarms and, except for Tomcat, it found *all* the previously known dataraces. For Tomcat, two bugs were revealed from the detected dataraces, both of which had been submitted to and confirmed by the developers of Tomcat. More details can be found in [3].

6   Conclusion

We presented a parametric approach to happen-before causal partial orders, which facilitates defining and proving correctness of happen-before relations. Existing variants of happen-before causalities can be obtained as instances of this parametric framework. A novel causal partial order relation, called sliced causality, was also defined and shown correct within our parametric framework. Sliced causality employs static and dynamic analysis to filter out unnecessary dependencies on events in order to improve the coverage of analysis without losing soundness. Evaluation shows that sliced causality can significantly increase the coverage of concurrent program analysis and testing.

References

1. Brightwell, G., Winkler, P.: Counting linear extensions is #p-complete. In: Annual ACM symposium on Theory of computing (STOC) (1991)
2. Chandy, K.M., Lamport, L.: Distributed snapshots: determining global states of distributed systems. ACM Trans. Comput. Syst. 3(1), 63–75 (1985)
3. Chen, F., Roşu, G.: Predicting concurrency errors at runtime using sliced causality. Technical Report UIUCDCS-R-2005-2660, Department of Computer Science at UIUC (2005)
4. Chen, F., Roşu, G.: Parametric and sliced causality. Technical Report UIUCDCS-R-2007-2807, Department of Computer Science at UIUC (2007)
5. Chen, F., Roşu, G.: Parametric and termination-sensitive control dependence - extended abstract. In: International Static Analysis Symposium (SAS) (2006)
6. Cooper, R., Marzullo, K.: Consistent detection of global predicates. In: ACM/ONR workshop on Parallel and distributed debugging (PADD) (1991)
7. Farchi, E., Nir, Y., Ur, S.: Concurrent bug patterns and how to test them. In: International Parallel and Distributed Processing Symposium (IPDPS) (2003)
8. Ferrante, J., Ottenstein, K.J., Warren, J.D.: The program dependence graph and its use in optimization. ACM Trans. Program. Lang. Syst. 9(3), 319–349 (1987)
9. Flanagan, C., Godefroid, P.: Dynamic partial-order reduction for model checking software. In: ACM SIGPLAN symposium on Principles of programming languages (POPL), ACM Press, New York (2005)
10. Gyimothy, T., Beszedes, A., Forgacs, I.: An efficient relevant slicing method for debugging. In: ACM SIGSOFT Symposium on Foundations of Software Engineering (FSE), ACM Press, New York (1999)
11. Hoogeboom, H.J., Rozenberg, G.: Dependence graphs. In: Diekert, V., Rozenberg, G. (eds) The Book of Traces, pp. 43–67. World Scientific (1995)
12. Horwitz, S., Reps, T.W.: The use of program dependence graphs in software engineering. In: International Conference on Software Engineering (ICSE) (1992)

13. Krinke, J.: Static slicing of threaded programs. In: Workshop on Program Analysis for Software Tools and Engineering (PASTE) (1998)
14. Lamport, L.: Time, clocks, and the ordering of events in a distributed system. Comm. of ACM 21(7), 558–565 (1978)
15. Netzer, R.H.B., Miller, B.P.: Improving the accuracy of data race detection. In: ACM SIGPLAN symposium on Principles and practice of parallel programming (PPoPP), ACM Press, New York (1991)
16. O'Callahan, R., Choi, J.-D.: Hybrid dynamic data race detection. In: ACM SIGPLAN Symposium on Principles and Practice of Parallel Programming (PPoPP), ACM Press, New York (2003)
17. Podgurski, A., Clarke, L.A.: A formal model of program dependences and its implications for software testing, debugging, and maintenance. IEEE Transactions on Software Engineering 16(9), 965–979 (1990)
18. Sen, A., Garg, V.K.: Detecting temporal logic predicates in distributed programs using computation slicing. In: Proceedings of the Seventh International Conference on Principles of Distributed Systems (OPODIS) (2003)
19. Sen, K., Roşu, G., Agha, G.: Runtime safety analysis of multithreaded programs. In: ACM SIGSOFT Symposium on Foundations of Software Engineering (FSE), ACM Press, New York (2003)
20. Sen, K., Roşu, G., Agha, G.: Detecting errors in multithreaded programs by generalized predictive analysis of executions. In: Steffen, M., Zavattaro, G. (eds.) FMOODS 2005. LNCS, vol. 3535, Springer, Heidelberg (2005)
21. Stoller, S.D., Unnikrishnan, L., Liu, Y.A.: Efficient detection of global properties in distributed systems using partial-order methods. In: Emerson, E.A., Sistla, A.P. (eds.) CAV 2000. LNCS, vol. 1855, Springer, Heidelberg (2000)
22. von Praun, C., Gross, T.R.: Object race detection. In: ACM SIGPLAN Conference on Object Oriented Programming, Systems, Languages, and Applications (OOPSLA), ACM Press, New York (2001)

SPADE: Verification of Multithreaded Dynamic and Recursive Programs[*]

(Tool Paper)

Gaël Patin[1], Mihaela Sighireanu[2], and Tayssir Touili[2]

University of Paris 7, Case 7014, 2 place Jussieu, 75251 Paris 05, France
LIAFA, CNRS & University of Paris 7, Case 7014, 2 place Jussieu, 75251 Paris 05, France
{sighirea,touili}@liafa.jussieu.fr

1 Introduction

Recently, there are a lot of tools that have been considered for software verification. We can for example mention BLAST [HJMS02], SLAM [BR01], KISS [QW04,QR05], ZING [QRR04], and MAGIC [CCG+03,CCG+04,CCK+06]. However, none of these tools can deal with parallelism, communication between parallel processes, dynamic process creation, and recursion at the same time. The tool we propose, called SPADE, allows to analyse automatically boolean programs presenting all these features. As far as we know, this is the first software model checking tool based on an expressive model that *accurately* models all these aspects in programs.

SPADE checks safety properties of programs by iteratively refining abstractions of the sets of the program execution paths that violate the property. Since property checking is undecidable for programs presenting all the features mentioned above, the SPADE refinement algorithm may not converge. In case of convergence, it can either find a bug in the program and returns a counterexample to the user, or certify that the program is correct.

We have applied SPADE to different case studies. Our results are encouraging and are reported in Section 4. In particular, we were able to *automatically* find two bugs in two versions of a Windows NT Bluetooth driver. The bugs were already found in [CCK+06]. But there, the verification was not *completely* automatic since the authors needed to *guess* the number of processes for which the bugs occur. Whereas with SPADE, the verification process was done in a *completely* automatic manner. Indeed, we don't need to make any guess since our tool handles *dynamic creation of processes*.

The current version of SPADE is available at http://www.liafa.jussieu.fr/~sighirea/spade.

2 The Underlying Techniques

SPADE is based on the SPAD model [Tou05]. A SPAD is a finite set of rules of the form $t \xrightarrow{a} t'$, where a is a synchronisation action, t and t' are terms built up from the

---

[*] This work has been supported by the French Governement program ACI Jeunes Chercheurs, Contract No.02 2 0205.

W. Damm and H. Hermanns (Eds.): CAV 2007, LNCS 4590, pp. 254–257, 2007.
© Springer-Verlag Berlin Heidelberg 2007

null process "0", a finite number of variables (X), the sequential composition "·", and the asynchroneous parallel composition "$\|$", where the operators "·" and "$\|$" are respectively associative and associative/commutative, and where each action a has its corresponding co-action $\bar{a}$. Intuitively, the process "0" represents termination, a process variable X corresponds to a control point of the program, and a process term t describes the control structure of the program. A procedure call is represented by a rule of the form $X \to Y \cdot Z$, where the program at control point X calls the procedure Y and goes to control point Z. This control point Z becomes active when Y terminates. Dynamic creation of parallel processes is modeled by rules of the form $X \to Y \| Z$, expressing that a process in control point X can create two parallel processes in control points Y and Z, respectively. Finally, handshakes between parallel processes are represented according to the CCS style by rules of the form $t_1 \xrightarrow{a} t_1'$ and $t_2 \xrightarrow{\bar{a}} t_2'$, meaning that two parallel processes t_1 and t_2 can synchronize and move simultaneously to t_1' and t_2', respectively.

SPADE deals with rechability queries for SPAD models. More precisely, given two (possibly infinite) sets of configurations *Init* and *Bad*, the problem is to know whether the set of bad configurations *Bad* can be reached from the initial configurations *Init*. The approach implemented in SPADE consists in computing abstractions of the execution path language that leads form *Init* to *Bad* and iteratively refining these abstractions [Tou05]. Our techniques are based on (1) the representation of the sets of configurations with binary tree automata, (2) the use of these automata to compute a set of constraints whose least fixpoint characterize the set of execution paths of the program, and (3) the resolution of this set of constraints in an abstract domain. Our algorithm is generic and can deal with different abstract domains. In particular, we considered the domains D_n of finite action words of length less or equal to n. These domains allow to compute abstractions of the execution paths that are exact up to the depth n. These abstractions are called n-prefix abstractions. The refinement step consists in considering a "more precise" abstract domain by incrementing the depth n.

3   The SPADE Tool

SPADE has two inputs. The first input is an ASCII file describing (1) the SPAD model of the program (names of processes, names of actions, rewriting rules), (2) the (possibly infinite) set of initial configurations *Init* (given by a tree automaton), and (3) the bad configuration *Bad* (a tree automaton). The second input is optional and consists of an integer that represents the depth n of the prefix abstraction. If this parameter is not given by the user, the tool starts with a prefix abstration of depth one, and automatically increases the abstraction depth until either an error is found or the program is proven to be correct.

SPADE outputs (a) the language $reach_n$ representing the n-prefix abstraction of the paths between *Init* and *Bad*, and (b) the result of the intersection of $reach_n$ with the set of *good* execution paths. This result may be either (CANNOT) if the intersection is empty (i.e., the n-prefix abstraction does not allow to find an execution leading from *Init* to *Bad*), (MAYBE) if the intersection is not empty but the path found has been cut by the abstraction, (CAN) if a *real* path (i.e., not cut by abstraction) has been found between *Init* and *Bad*.

SPADE implements in OCAML the algorithm described in [Tou05]. OCAML provides a rich and efficient built-in library of data structures (e.g., hash tables, maps, sets), a powerful system of modules, and garbage collection facilities. Due to these features, the algorithm is implemented as a *generic* module parameterized by two *signatures* (interfaces): the first signature collects types and operations dealing with tree automata, and the second signature collects types and operations of the abstract domain of execution paths. The current version of SPADE instantiates the first parameter of the algorithm with the OCAML implementation of tree automata provided by the TIMBUK tool [GT01]. This implementation provides a large list of operations on tree automata (union, intersection, emptiness test, minimization, etc) and an easy access to the states and the transitions of automata. For the second parameter, we implemented in OCAML a library for the abstract domain D_n (i.e., finite sets of finite words of length less or equal to n). The library provides efficient implementation of operations intensively used by the algorithm: union, concatenation, shuffle, prefix, and inclusion.

4   Summary of the Results

SPADE has been applied to several examples. The performances are given in Table 1. The experiments were obtained on a 4GHz Pentium IV with 4GB of memory.

Table 1. Performances of SPADE

Example	Time	Space
BlueTooth v1	1623mn28s	50 MB
BlueTooth v2	1216mn28s	46 MB
ConcVector v1	7s	3.4 MB
ConcVector v2	14s	14.8 MB
Lock/unlock	8s	3.6MB

The *BlueTooth* v1 is the SPAD model of the BlueTooth driver program used by Windows NT and given in [QW04]. We were able to find a bug in this program. To find this error, the [QW04] authors needed to guess the number of driver's requests for which the error occurs, and then run their tool; whereas with SPADE, the verification was done in a *completely* automatic manner, since we did not have to guess the number of requests for which the error occurs because our tool can deal with *dynamic creation of processes*.

The *BlueTooth* v2 is a corrected version of *BlueTooth* v1 proposed by the authors of [QW04]. SPADE finds an error in this version as well. This bug was already found in [CCK$^+$06]. Again, to be able to find the bug, the authors of [CCK$^+$06] needed to guess the number of requests that causes the bug before running their tool, whereas SPADE did not need to perform this guess.

ConcVector is a SPAD model of a multithreaded program using concurrently methods of the class `java.util.Vector` from the Java Standard Collection Framework. The program's threads create and remove the elements of a `Vector` object. Wand and Stoller [WS03] reported a high-level data race that occurs on such programs because the constructor of the Vector class is not atomic. SPADE found this bug for a program with an unbounded number of threads (ConcVector v1). Version v2 fixes the bug by taking an atomic implementation of the constructor. SPADE was able to prove that this version is correct.

The *Lock/unlock* example is a system that handles an *arbitrary* number of concurrent insertions on a binary search tree. The algorithm was proposed in [KL80], and can be applied to handle simultaneous insertions (done by several users) into a database, or to reduce the time necessary for a single insertion. We considered a buggy version of the algorithm where one or several processes do not adhere to the required lock and unlock policy. This version was considered in [CCK+06], where the bug was found *only* for systems where the number of concurrent processes is less or equal to 7. With SPADE, we were able to check this buggy program for *arbitrary* number of concurrent insertion processes.

References

BR01.   Ball, T., Rajamani, S.K.: Automatically validating temporal safety properties of interfaces. In: Dwyer, M.B. (ed.) Model Checking Software. LNCS, vol. 2057, Springer, Heidelberg (2001)

CCG+03. Chaki, S., Clarke, E., Groce, A., Jha, S., Veith, H.: Modular verification of software components in C. In: International Conference on Software Engineering (ICSE), pp. 385–395 (2003)

CCG+04. Chaki, S., Clarke, E., Grumberg, O., Ouaknine, J., Sharygina, N., Touili, T., Veith, H.: An expressive framework for state/event systems. Technical report, Carnegie Mellon University (2004)

CCK+06. Chaki, S., Clarke, E., Kidd, N., Reps, T., Touili, T.: Verifying concurrent message-passing C programs with recursive calls. In: TACAS (2006)

GT01.   Genet, T., Viet Triem Tong, V.: Reachability analysis of term rewriting systems with timbuk. In: Nieuwenhuis, R., Voronkov, A. (eds.) LPAR 2001. LNCS (LNAI), vol. 2250, pp. 695–706. Springer, Heidelberg (2001)

HJMS02. Henzinger, T.A., Jhala, R., Majumdar, R., Sutre, G.: Lazy abstraction. In: Symposium on Principles of Programming Languages, pp. 58–70 (2002)

KL80.   Kung, H.T., Lehman, P.L.: Concurrent manipulation of binary search trees. ACM Trans. Database Syst. 5(3), 354–382 (1980)

QR05.   Qadeer, S., Rehof, J.: Context-bounded model checking of concurrent software. In: Halbwachs, N., Zuck, L.D. (eds.) TACAS 2005. LNCS, vol. 3440, Springer, Heidelberg (2005)

QRR04.   Qadeer, S., Rajamani, S.K., Rehof, J.: Summarizing procedures in concurrent programs. In: POPL 04: ACM Principles of Programming Languages, pp. 245–255 (2004)

QW04.   Qadeer, S., Wu, D.: Kiss: Keep it simple and sequential. In: PLDI 04: Programming Language Design and Implementation, pp. 14–24 (2004)

Tou05.   Touili, T.: Dealing with communication for dynamic multithreaded recursive programs. In: 1st VISSAS workshop, Invited Paper (2005)

WS03.   Wang, L., Stoller, S.D.: Run-time analysis for atomicity. In: Proceedings of the Third Workshop on Runtime Verification (RV). Electronic Notes in Theoretical Computer Science, vol. 89(2), Elsevier, Amsterdam, Netherlands (2003)

Anzu: A Tool for Property Synthesis[*]

(Tool Paper)

Barbara Jobstmann, Stefan Galler, Martin Weiglhofer, and Roderick Bloem

Graz University of Technology

Abstract. We present the tool ANZU. ANZU takes a formal specification of a design and generates a functionally correct system if one exists. The specification is given as a set of linear temporal logic (LTL) formulas belonging to the class of *generalized reactivity* of rank 1. Such formulas cover the majority of the formulas used in practice. ANZU is an implementation of the symbolic reactive(1) approach to synthesis by Piterman, Pnueli, and Sa'ar. If the specification is *realizable* ANZU provides the user with a Verilog module that represents a correct finite-state system.

1 Introduction

Automatically constructing a system from a logical specification has been one of the more ambitious dreams in computer science for almost half a century [Chu62]. Given a specification over the signals $\mathcal{I} \cup \mathcal{O}$ the Synthesis Problem is to construct a reactive system with input signals $\mathcal{I}$ and output signal $\mathcal{O}$ such that all infinite input-output sequences produces by this system adhere to φ, in case such a system exists.

Rabin [Rab69] and Büchi and Landweber [BL69] were the first to provide solutions to the Synthesis Problem for S1S. Pnueli and Rosner [PR89] reconsidered the problem for specifications in *linear temporal logic* (LTL) and provided an algorithm to construct *open systems*, systems that behave correctly independent of the surrounding environment. Furthermore, they proved that synthesis of LTL formulas is 2EXPTIME-complete [Ros92].

In order to overcome the complexity issues, research concentrated in part on subsets of LTL. Recently, Pnueli, Piterman, and Sa'ar [PPS06] proposed an efficient symbolic algorithm to synthesize specification of reactive(1) designs, in time N^3 where N is the size of the state space of the design. ANZU implements this approach and extends it to generate compact circuits.

Anzu can be found at http://www.ist.tugraz.at/staff/jobstmann/anzu/

2 Case Studies

We start by describing our case studies as we will use parts of them to show how ANZU works. We have tried ANZU on two examples. The first is an arbiter for ARM's AMBA Advanced High-Performance Bus (AHB). The AHB is an on-chip bus that connects

---

[*] This work was supported in part by the European Union under contract 507219 (PROSYD).

W. Damm and H. Hermanns (Eds.): CAV 2007, LNCS 4590, pp. 258–262, 2007.

```
[INPUT_VARIABLES]                    [OUTPUT_VARIABLES]
  RtB0;                                BtR0;
  ...                                  ...
[ENV_INITIAL]                        [SYS_INITIAL]
  ...                                  ...
[ENV_TRANSITIONS]                    [SYS_TRANSITIONS]
  G((BtR0=1 * RtB0=1) -> X(RtB0=1));   G((RtB0=1 * BtR0=1) -> X(BtR0=1));
  G( BtR0=0 -> X(RtB0=0));             G( RtB0=1 -> X(BtR0=0));
  ...                                  ...
[ENV_FAIRNESS]                       [SYS_FAIRNESS]
  ...                                  ...
```

Fig. 1. Part of the input file to synthesis GenBuf with ANZU

components like processor cores, DMA controllers, and cache. It has up to 16 masters, which initiate transfers, and up to 16 clients, which are mostly passive. The AHB supports different transfer types, including different length bursts. From the official specification for the bus [ARM99], which is written in English, we have distilled a set of 4 assumptions and 11 guarantees.

The second case study is a generalized buffer (henceforth *GenBuf*) from IBM[1]. This design forwards data from n senders to two receivers using a handshake protocol on either side and a FIFO to store data temporarily. The design is used at IBM and came with a very clear and relatively complete (although not fault-free) formal specification. Our full specification consists of 13 guarantees and 5 assumptions.

3   Technical Approach

ANZU is written in Perl and the symbolic algorithms rely on PerlDD, a Perl extension of the the the CUDD BDD Package [Som]. We use the handshake protocol between GenBuf and a receiver to illustrate a specification. Genbuf communicates with receiver i using the signals BtoRi and RtoBi. The handshake between GenBuf and a receiver consists of four phases: (1) GenBuf requests receiver i (by raising BtoRi) and may not cancel the request. (2) Receiver i eventually answers the request (by raising RtoBi). (3) In the next step, GenBuf lowers the request, and (4) after a further step the receiver deasserts the signal RtoBi. In order to ensure a correct handshake, GenBuf and the receiver have to meet the following requirements. GenBuf has to guarantee $\bigwedge_{i \in \{0,1\}}(G((\text{BtoRi} \wedge \neg\text{RtoBi}) \to X\,\text{BtoRi}) \wedge G(\text{RtoBi} \to X\,\neg\text{BtoRi}))$. Receiver i has to fulfill $G(\text{BtoRi} \to F\,\text{RtoBi}) \wedge G((\text{BtoRi} \wedge \text{RtoB}) \to X\,\text{RtoBi}) \wedge G(\neg\text{BtoRi} \to X\,\neg\text{RtoBi})$. Fig.1 shows part of the requirements as we write them for ANZU.

ANZU takes a text file holding the definitions of the input and output signals (see Fig.1, Line 1-3) and a specification in a subset of LTL. The specification needs to comply with simple syntax rules [PPS06]: A specification consists of two parts: *assumptions* on the environment (Fig.1, Col.1) and *guarantees* the system has to keep, if the environment fulfills its assumptions (Fig.1, Col.2). Each part is defined by a set of LTL formulas over input signals $\mathcal{I}$ and output signals $\mathcal{O}$. The signals in $\mathcal{I}$ are controlled by

---

[1] See http://www.haifa.ibm.com/projects/verification/RB_Homepage/tutorial3/.

the environment, signals in $\mathcal{O}$ are controlled by the system. An assumption or a guarantee defines either allowed *initial* states, possible *transitions*, or *fairness* obligations that all accepting runs have to fulfill.

A formula that does not fall in one of these three classes can usually (but not always) be transformed to a suitable format by using *deterministic monitors*. For such a formula we construct a deterministic Büchi word automaton We create a Boolean encoding of the state space of the automaton using a new set of variables, and describe its behavior using an initial constraint, a constraint on the transition relation, and a fairness constraint, as before. For instance, for the formula $\mathsf{G}(\mathrm{BtoR0} \to \mathsf{F}\,\mathrm{RtoB0})$ we add a variable s and encode a corresponding deterministic monitor with the formulas $\neg s$, $\mathsf{G}((\neg s \wedge (\neg\mathrm{BtoR0} \vee \mathrm{RtoB0})) \to \mathsf{X}\,\neg s)$, $\mathsf{G}((\neg s \wedge \mathrm{BtoR0} \wedge \neg\mathrm{RtoB0}) \to \mathsf{X}\,s)$, $\mathsf{G}((s \wedge \neg\mathrm{RtoB0}) \to \mathsf{X}\,s)$, $\mathsf{G}((s \wedge \mathrm{RtoB0}) \to \mathsf{X}\,\neg s)$, and $\mathsf{G}\,\mathsf{F}\,\neg s$.

ANZU follows the approach of [PPS06]: it builds a transition system over the input and output variables from the formulas restricting the transitions. On the transition system ANZU searches for states from which the system can force an accepting run independent of the input values the environment chooses. A run is accepting if either a fairness obligation of the environment is violated or all fairness obligation of the system are fulfilled. If the initial states belong to this set of states, the specification is realizable and ANZU builds a BDD representing a set of possible implementations. Otherwise, ANZU reports that the specification is not realizable and quits. From the BDD, ANZU extracts a circuit with $|\mathcal{I}| + |\mathcal{O}|$ flip flops and combinational logic expressed on the gate level. The relation between the variables of the specification and the signals of the circuit are depict in Fig.2. (Primed variables denote next-state values.) The construction of the combinational circuitry turns out to be the most time consuming part of synthesis. We have tried approaches based on [KS00] and on the use of cofactors [BGJ+07] and we are actively researching better ways of constructing the circuits.

Results. We have synthesized GenBuf for upto 10 senders. (Ten senders seem enough considering that the original circuit handles only four.) The specification for 10 senders consists of 13 fairness formulas (2 for the environment and 11 for the system) and 121 guarantees and 27 assumptions that restrict the transition relation. Figure 3 shows how the size of the circuit grows as a function of the number of senders for two different

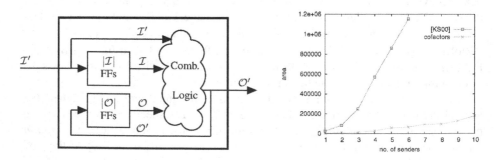

Fig. 2. Design of the generated circuits   **Fig. 3.** Size of the generalized buffer

methods of constructing the circuit. (The y axis shows the "standard cell grid count" for the synthesized circuit, which allows for a fair comparison of the sizes of different circuits, even though the absolute values may not be very informative.) Note that even with the cofactor method, the circuit is still about a factor of 10 larger than a hand-written one. The number of latches needed in the circuit grows from 13 to 40 and synthesis goes through in under a minute for 10 masters.

The AHB arbiter is harder. We are able to synthesize it for up to 10 masters, after which our tool runs out of memory. The case study is described in detail in [BGJ$^+$07]. The number of latches needed for the largest arbiter is 60 and the time for synthesis is 6.5 hours, 85% of which is spent reordering BDDs.

4   Benefits and Drawbacks of Synthesis

The generalized reactivity(1) framework in which we stated the specification turned out to be expressible enough for anything we wanted state. Deciding realizability is relatively simple in comparison to building a circuit. Furthermore, the specifications are relatively small and easy to read.

On the other hand, writing a (complete!) formal specification is sometimes hard, although the introduction of new signals usually helped. (We see great potential for tools that help the user debug the specification.) Furthermore, the performance of the tool depends heavily on the formulation of the specification. The circuits produced by ANZU are relatively large and their size depends heavily on the value of the parameter, much more strongly than is expected for manually coded circuits.

Concluding, ANZU allows for synthesis of real, though modest sized, industrial examples from specifications and ANZU's performance is improving rapidly.

Acknowledgments. The authors would like to thank Karin Greimel and Milan Milinkovic for their help with the implementation, and Nir Piterman and Amir Pnueli for interesting discussions.

References

[ARM99]   ARM Ltd. AMBA Specification (Rev. 2) (1999) Available from www.arm.com

[BGJ$^+$07]   Bloem, R., Galler, S., Jobstmann, B., Piterman, N., Pnueli, A., Weiglhofer, M.: Automatic hardware synthesis from specifications: A case study. In: Proceedings of the Conference on Design, Automation and Test in Europe (to Appear)

[BL69]   Büchi, J.R., Landweber, L.H.: Solving sequential conditions by finite-state strategies. Transactions of the American Mathematical Society 138, 295–311 (1969)

[Chu62]   Church, A.: Logic, arithmetic and automata. In: Proceedings International Mathematical Congress (1962)

[KS00]   Kukula, J.H., Shiple, T.R.: Building circuits from relations. In: Emerson, E.A., Sistla, A.P. (eds.) CAV 2000. LNCS, vol. 1855, pp. 113–123. Springer, Heidelberg (2000)

[PPS06]   Piterman, N., Pnueli, A., Sa'ar, Y.: Synthesis of reactive(1) designs. In: Proc. Verification, Model Checking, and Abstract Interpretation, pp. 364–380 (2006)

[PR89]   Pnueli, A., Rosner, R.: On the synthesis of a reactive module. In: Proc. Symposium on Principles of Programming Languages (POPL '89), pp. 179–190 (1989)

[Rab69]   Rabin, M.O.: Decidability of second-order theories and automata on infinite trees. Transactions of the American Mathematical Society 141, 1–35 (1969)

[Ros92]   Rosner, R.: Modular Synthesis of Reactive Systems. PhD thesis, Weizmann Institute of Science (1992)

[Som]   Somenzi, F.: CUDD: CU Decision Diagram Package. University of Colorado at Boulder ftp://vlsi.colorado.edu/pub/

RAT: A Tool for the Formal Analysis of Requirements*

(Tool Paper)

Roderick Bloem[1], Roberto Cavada[2], Ingo Pill[1], Marco Roveri[2], and Andrei Tchaltsev[2]

[1] Graz University of Technology — Inffeldgasse 16b/II - 8010 Graz - Austria
{rbloem, ipill}@ist.tugraz.at
[2] Fondazione Bruno Kessler - irst — Via Sommarive, 18 - 38050 Povo (Trento) - Italy
{cavada, roveri, tchaltsev}@itc.it

Abstract. Formal languages are increasingly used to describe the functional requirements of circuits. Although formal requirements can be hard to understand and subtle, they are seldom the object of verification. In this paper we present our requirement analysis tool, RAT. Our tool supports quality assurance of formal specifications. A designer can interactively explore the requirements' semantics and automatically check the specification against *assertions* (which must be satisfied) and *possibilities* (which describe allowed corner-case behavior). Using RAT, a designer can also investigate the realizability of a specification. RAT was successfully examined in several industrial projects.

1 Introduction

Formal specifications are becoming increasingly important, not only for verification, but also to describe design intent.

Traditionally, the verification effort focuses mainly on the design. A design is verified using either a golden model or a set of properties. This can be done either by simulation or by static verification. Either requires a large amount of effort on behalf of the user and is a time consuming part of the design cycle. Requirements, however, are seldom the *object* of verification. This is somewhat surprising, since industrial data show that about 50 percent of product defects originate in flawed requirements and that around 80 percent of rework effort can be traced back to requirement defects [12].

The use of formal requirements is a first and substantial step towards high quality specifications, but is obviously not enough to ensure the desired quality. RAT, our requirements analysis tool, supports the designer in the crucial task of writing high quality formal requirements of circuits. (We use specifications as a synonym for formal functional requirements.) RAT can be downloaded from http://rat.itc.it. It supports PSL [1], and provides a convenient graphical interface for the development, analysis, and management of a specification. Our current version draws from complementary techniques to explore requirement semantics, assure system traits, and check for realizability: *property simulation* [10], *property assurance* [10], and *property realizability*.

In the remainder of this paper we show how these techniques integrate, present a methodological guideline, give technical details, and report feedback from industry.

---

* Supported by the European Commission under contract 507219 (PROSYD).

W. Damm and H. Hermanns (Eds.): CAV 2007, LNCS 4590, pp. 263–267, 2007.

2   Requirements Analysis

Property Simulation provides the designer with an interactive method to understand the semantics of formal requirements by exploring their behavior one trace at a time. A designer can ask for an example behavior, *constrain* it by fixing the value of any signal for any given time step, and then check whether the altered trace is still allowed by the requirements. If not, the designer can ask for a different trace that is correct and adheres to the user-specified constraints. Although a property does not differentiate between inputs and outputs, the designer may do so. Based on such a classification she can perform a "what-if" analysis by setting inputs and asking to be presented with corresponding outputs. Dually, a "how-can" analysis can be performed by setting output signals and asking how, if at all, these outputs can be achieved. We provide an explanation of derived traces in the form of the property syntax tree plus the truth values of each subformula at every step. This helps the designer to understand how the subformulas and the property itself are evaluated along the trace. In a way, property simulation allows for a reverse-engineering of the property semantics much like a hardware design would be simulated.

Property Assurance provides the designer with a general means to assess whether she has written the right set of properties. First, property assurance can check that the requirements are consistent and do not contain a contradiction. Second, the designer can provide two sets of properties: Φ_A, a set of *assertions* that must be guaranteed, and Φ_P, a set of *possibilities* that describes corner cases that must be allowed by the requirements. Using assertions, a designer can check whether the requirements are strict enough to exclude any undesired behavior. With possibilities, she can check that they are not overly strict, and desirable behavior is allowed.

Property Realizability aims to verify whether there is a system that behaves according to the specification for any provided input sequence. To decide realizability, we split the requirements into assumptions on the environment and guarantees on the system behavior. Then we check for the existence of a system which can provide correct outputs for any inputs that are consistent with the environment assumptions. This problem can be seen as a two player game (the players being the environment and the system), where we have to determine a winning strategy (an implementation) for the system. Realizability is much more demanding than logical consistency. Indeed, there are logical consistent specifications that are unrealizable.

Figure 1 depicts a requirements analysis process that integrates the three proposed techniques. First, the designer comes up with initial approximations of the requirements Γ, assertions Φ_A, and possibilities Φ_P. We propose an iterative approach, checking whether the requirements are consistent, whether they allow for all possibilities stated in Φ_P, and whether they do not contradict any assertion in Φ_A. For any problem, the designer is presented with diagnosis information, and consequently refines Γ, Φ_A, and Φ_P to fix it. After any change, the requirements are verified again for consistency and for adherence to Φ_A and Φ_P. Finally, realizability of the specification is checked. If the requirements are unrealizable, the designer is requested to revise the specification.

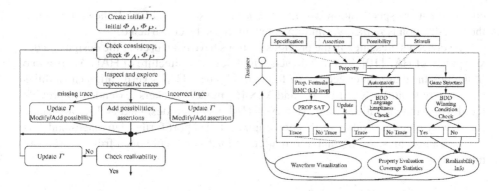

Fig. 1. Guidelines

Fig. 2. RAT architecture

3   Technical Aspects

Property simulation and assurance rely on *Automata-based* and *Bounded Model Checking* (BMC) techniques [9,3]. For both approaches we derive an automaton and check its language for emptiness, for a (bounded) witness or counterexample for the task at hand.

To decide the realizability of a specification we construct a two-player game between the system and the environment [11]. The goal of the system is to satisfy the specification by delivering correct outputs considering the so far encountered input, regardless of the input sequence provided by the environment. Realizability can be decided by checking whether this game is winning for the system or the environment. For a winning

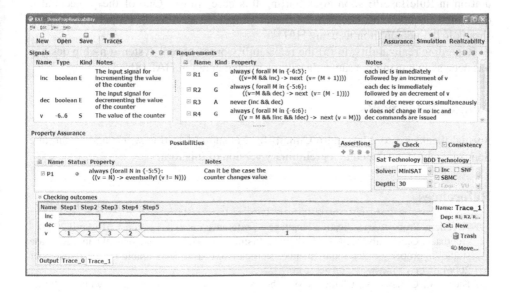

Fig. 3. RAT's GUI

environment, the specification is *unrealizable* and must be modified. If the system wins, the specification is *realizable*: an implementation can be constructed.

The concepts presented in the previous sections have been used in the design and development of RAT [10]. Figure 2 depicts a high level architecture of RAT. An example of the graphical user interface can be found in Figure 3. RAT's verification capabilities currently rely on the NuSMV [7] and VIS [6] model checkers, extended to provide the devised functionalities [4,8]. However, RAT has been designed and implemented for an easy plug in of other verification engines, to support further languages and verification algorithms. Additional information on RAT can be obtained from its web site http://rat.itc.it

4   Experimental Analysis

In [2] IBM, Infineon, STMicroelectronics, and OneSpin examined several new techniques and tools for property-based requirements specification, including a RAT prototype supporting property simulation and assurance. The case studies included transport frontends, protocols, a bridge, SOC interconnects, and other industrial design blocks.

Although our tool was a prototype when the case studies were done, our technology appeals to designers: "We found the concept of property simulation attractive as it allows a developer to debug her/his own PSL code easily, quickly and independently". Several bugs in the properties were found, and property assurance has been "used effectively in specific cases to prove that one set of properties can be substituted by another". The interface and usability features provided by RAT "make the development process easier and provide an enjoyable development experience". IBM's experience with the tool prompted them to start "to design and develop a feature similar to property simulation in RuleBasePE soon after starting this case study". One of the projects also quantified an economical benefit; estimated 1.5 person months for property debugging shrank to 0.5 person months using RAT.

Regarding realizability, in [5] the realizability proof of real system-on-chip designs has been shown using the same algorithms implemented in RAT [8].

Acknowledgements

Special thanks go to Alessandro Cimatti for his support in this work, and to Simone Semprini who contributed to a preliminary version of this tool.

References

1. Accellera. Property specification language — reference manual, version 1.01 (April 2003)
2. Auerbach, G., Benalycherif, L., Fedeli, A., Fisman, D., McIsaac, A., Winkelmann, K.: Case studies in property-based requirements specification, Prosyd Delivarable D1.4/1 (November 2006) http://www.prosyd.org
3. Biere, A., Cimatti, A., Clarke, E.M., Zhu, Y.: Symbolic model checking without BDDs. In: Cleaveland, W.R. (ed.) ETAPS 1999 and TACAS 1999. LNCS, vol. 1579, pp. 193–207. Springer, Heidelberg (1999)

4. Bloem, R., Cavada, R., Eisner, C., Pill, I., Roveri, M., Semprini, S.: Manual for property simulation and property assurance tool, Prosyd Delivarable D1.2/4-5 (November 2005) http://www.prosyd.org
5. Bloem, R., Galler, S., Jobstman, B., Weiglhofer, M., Piterman, N., Pnueli, A.: Automatic hardware synthesis from specifications: A case study. In: Proceeding of DATE'07 (to appear)
6. Brayton, R.K., et al.: A system for verification and synthesis. In: Henzinger, T., Alur, R. (eds.) CAV 1996. LNCS, vol. 1102, pp. 428–432. Springer, Heidelberg (1996)
7. Cimatti, A., Clarke, E.M., Giunchiglia, F., Roveri, M.: NuSMV: a new Symbolic Model Verifier. In: Halbwachs, N., Peled, D.A. (eds.) CAV 1999. LNCS, vol. 1633, pp. 495–499. Springer, Heidelberg (1999)
8. Cimatti, A., Roveri, M., Tchaltsev, A.: Manual for property realizability tool, Prosyd Delivarable D1.2/8 (December 2006) http://www.prosyd.org
9. Kurshan, R.: Computer-Aided Verification of Coordinating Processes: the automata theoretic approach. Princeton University Press, Princeton, NJ (1994)
10. Pill, I., Semprini, S., Cavada, R., Roveri, M., Bloem, R., Cimatti, A.: Formal analysis of hardware requirements. In: Design Automation Conference, pp. 821–826 (2006)
11. Piterman, N., Pnueli, A., Sa'ar, Y.: Synthesis of reactive(1) designs. In: VMCAI, pp. 364–380 (2006)
12. Wiegers, K.E.: Inspecting requirements. StickyMinds Weekly Colum (July 2001)

Parallelising Symbolic State-Space Generators*

Jonathan Ezekiel[1], Gerald Lüttgen[1], and Gianfranco Ciardo[2]

[1] University of York, York, YO10 5DD, U.K.
{jezekiel,luettgen}@cs.york.ac.uk
[2] University of California, Riverside, CA 92521, U.S.A.
ciardo@cs.ucr.edu

Abstract. Symbolic state-space generators are notoriously hard to parallelise, largely due to the irregular nature of the task. Parallel languages such as Cilk, tailored to irregular problems, have been shown to offer efficient scheduling and load balancing. This paper explores whether Cilk can be used to efficiently parallelise a symbolic state-space generator on a shared-memory architecture. We parallelise the Saturation algorithm implemented in the SMART verification tool using Cilk, and compare it to a parallel implementation of the algorithm using a thread pool. Our experimental studies on a dual-processor, dual-core PC show that Cilk can improve the run-time efficiency of our parallel algorithm due to its load balancing and scheduling efficiency. We also demonstrate that this incurs a significant memory overhead due to Cilk's inability to support pipelining, and conclude by pointing to a possible future direction for parallel irregular languages to include pipelining.

1 Introduction

Automated verification, such as temporal-logic model checking [8], relies on efficient algorithms for computing state spaces of complex system models. To avoid the well-known state-space explosion problem, symbolic algorithms working on *decision diagrams*, usually BDDs, have proved successful in practise [7, 16]. Several efforts have been made to implement these algorithms on parallel computer platforms, most notably on networks of workstations and on PC clusters [11, 12, 13, 17, 19]. The efforts range from simple approaches that essentially implement BDDs as two-tiered hash tables [17, 19], to sophisticated approaches relying on *slicing* BDDs [12] and techniques for *workstealing* [11]. However, the resulting implementations show only limited speedups.

While parallel implementations of symbolic model checkers are often successful in increasing available memory, limited speedups can largely be attributed to the irregular nature of the state-space generation task and the resulting high parallel overheads such as load imbalance and scheduling of small computations. When combined with the extra overheads incurred from synchronisation on the symbolic data structure, it is possible for irregularity to severely decrease run-time efficiency. Irregular problems have been addressed in the parallel literature,

---

* Research funding was provided by the EPSRC under grant no. GR/S86211/01.

W. Damm and H. Hermanns (Eds.): CAV 2007, LNCS 4590, pp. 268–280, 2007.

resulting in languages such as *Cilk* [1, 10] for shared memory architectures. Cilk has been shown to alleviate the irregular overheads by offering efficient scheduling and load balancing. When successfully applied, it offers potential improvements in time efficiency, and a large reduction in effort with respect to deriving and implementing scheduling and load balancing techniques. To date, Cilk has been used for other irregular problems involving searches, but overlooked for parallelising state-space generation, which underlies model checking.

Saturation [5], as implemented in the verification tool SMART [4], is a symbolic state-space generation algorithm with unique features (cf. Sec. 2). It is intended for asynchronous system models with interleaving semantics, and exploits the local effect of firing events on state vectors by locally manipulating MDDs, which are a generalisation of BDDs [14]. Saturation has proved to be orders of magnitude more time-efficient and memory-efficient than other symbolic algorithms [5], including the one in NuSMV [7], when applied to asynchronous system models. Like other symbolic algorithms, Saturation is irregular in nature and suffers from high parallelisation overheads. Hence, the question arises as to whether using a proven parallel language for irregular problems is beneficial to the time efficiency of a parallel implementation of Saturation. A previous approach to parallelising Saturation [2] on a PC cluster used a message-passing library, but not a language tailored to irregular problems.

This paper investigates the parallelisability of the Saturation algorithm for shared-memory architectures using Cilk and reports on our experiences made. Our implementation (cf. Sec. 3) focuses on shared-memory architectures, but due to the increasing popularity of *distributed shared-memory* libraries, our results are also of significance for parallelisations of Saturation on PC clusters. To put our results into context, we contrast our Cilk algorithm with our own thread pool parallelisation of Saturation for shared memory architectures [9], which is based on the POSIX Pthreads library [15], and compare run-time and memory efficiency. We extend our investigation to optimise the parallel ordering in which the state space is generated, and determine the effects on run-time and memory for both parallel implementations. Our experimental studies (cf. Sec. 4) using a PC with two dual-core Intel processors show that the efficiency of Cilk improves the run-time of the parallel algorithm when compared to our thread pool implementation, but incurs a significant increase in memory due to Cilk's inability to support pipelining. Our experiences show how parallel irregular languages can be considered when parallelising symbolic state-space generators, and we conclude by pointing to a potential future direction within the parallel community which may allow parallel irregular languages to improve the time-efficiency of parallel state-space generation without severely impacting on memory (cf. Sec. 6).

2   Background

A discrete-state model is a triple $(\widehat{\mathcal{S}}, \mathbf{s}^0, \mathcal{N})$, where $\widehat{\mathcal{S}}$ is the set of *potential states* of the model, $\mathbf{s}^0 \in \widehat{\mathcal{S}}$ is the *initial state*, and $\mathcal{N} : \widehat{\mathcal{S}} \rightarrow 2^{\widehat{\mathcal{S}}}$ is the *next-state function* specifying the states reachable from each state in one step. Assuming that the model contains K *submodels*, a *(global)* state $\mathbf{i}$ is a K-tuple $(i_K,...,i_1)$, where i_k is the *local* state of submodel k, for $K \geq k \geq 1$, and $\widehat{\mathcal{S}} = \mathcal{S}_K \times \cdots \times \mathcal{S}_1$ is the cross-product of K *local state-spaces*. This allows us to use *symbolic* techniques based on decision diagrams to store sets of states. We decompose $\mathcal{N}$ into a disjunction of next-state functions, so that $\mathcal{N}(\mathbf{i}) = \bigcup_{e \in \mathcal{E}} \mathcal{N}_e(\mathbf{i})$, where $\mathcal{E}$ is a finite set of *events* and $\mathcal{N}_e$ is the next-state function for event e. We seek to build the *reachable state-space* $\mathcal{S} \subseteq \widehat{\mathcal{S}}$, the smallest set containing $\mathbf{s}^0$ and closed with respect to $\mathcal{N}$: $\mathcal{S} = \{\mathbf{s}^0\} \cup \mathcal{N}(\mathbf{s}^0) \cup \mathcal{N}(\mathcal{N}(\mathbf{s}^0)) \cup \cdots = \mathcal{N}^*(\mathbf{s}^0)$, where "*" denotes reflexive and transitive closure and $\mathcal{N}(\mathcal{X}) = \bigcup_{\mathbf{i} \in \mathcal{X}} \mathcal{N}(\mathbf{i})$.

Symbolic Encodings of $\mathcal{S}$ and $\mathcal{N}$. In the sequel, we assume that each $\mathcal{S}_k$ is finite and known a priori. In practise, the local state spaces $\mathcal{S}_k$ can actually be generated on-the-fly by interleaving symbolic global state-space generation with explicit local state-space generation [6]. Without loss of generality, we assume that $\mathcal{S}_k = \{0, 1, \ldots, n_k-1\}$, with $n_k = |\mathcal{S}_k|$. We then encode any set $\mathcal{X} \subseteq \widehat{\mathcal{S}}$ in a *(quasi-reduced ordered) MDD* over $\widehat{\mathcal{S}}$. Formally, an MDD is a directed acyclic edge-labelled multi-graph where:

- Each node p belongs to a *level* $k \in \{K, ..., 1, 0\}$, denoted $p.lvl$.
- There is a single *root* node r at level K.
- Level 0 can only contain the two *terminal* nodes *Zero* and *One*.
- A node p at level $k > 0$ has n_k outgoing edges, labelled from 0 to n_k-1. The edge labelled by i_k points to a node q at level $k-1$; we write $p[i_k] = q$.
- Given nodes p and q at level k, if $p[i_k] = q[i_k]$ for all $i_k \in \mathcal{S}_k$, then $p = q$, i.e., there are no *duplicates*.

The set encoded by an MDD node p at level $k > 0$ is $\mathcal{B}(p) = \bigcup_{i_k \in \mathcal{S}_k} \{i_k\} \times \mathcal{B}(p[i_k])$, letting $\mathcal{X} \times \mathcal{B}(\mathbf{0}) = \emptyset$ and $\mathcal{X} \times \mathcal{B}(\mathbf{1}) = \mathcal{X}$ for any set $\mathcal{X}$

For storing $\mathcal{N}$, we adopt a representation inspired by work on Markov chains. This requires the model to be *Kronecker consistent* [5], a restriction that can often be automatically satisfied by concurrency models such as Petri nets. Each $\mathcal{N}_e$ is conjunctively decomposed into K local next-state functions $\mathcal{N}_{k,e}$, for $K \geq k \geq 1$, satisfying $\mathcal{N}_e(i_K, \ldots, i_1) = \mathcal{N}_{K,e}(i_K) \times \cdots \times \mathcal{N}_{1,e}(i_1)$, in any global state $(i_K, \ldots, i_1) \in \widehat{\mathcal{S}}$. Using $K \cdot |\mathcal{E}|$ matrices $\mathbf{N}_{k,e} \in \{0,1\}^{n_k \times n_k}$ with $\mathbf{N}_{k,e}[i_k, j_k] = 1 \Leftrightarrow j_k \in \mathcal{N}_{k,e}(i_k)$, we encode $\mathcal{N}_e$ as a boolean Kronecker product: $\mathbf{j} \in \mathcal{N}_e(\mathbf{i}) \Leftrightarrow \bigotimes_{K \geq k \geq 1} \mathbf{N}_{k,e}[i_k, j_k] = 1$, where $\otimes$ indicates the Kronecker product of matrices. The $\mathbf{N}_{k,e}$ matrices are extremely sparse; when encoding a Petri net, for example, each row contains at most one nonzero entry.

Saturation-Based Iteration Strategy. In addition to efficiently representing $\mathcal{N}$, the Kronecker encoding allows us to recognise *event locality* [5] and employ *Saturation* [5]. We say that event e is *independent* of level k if $\mathbf{N}_{k,e} = \mathbf{I}$, the identity matrix. Let $Top(e)$ denote the highest level for which $\mathbf{N}_{k,e} \neq \mathbf{I}$. An MDD node p at level k is *saturated* if it is a fixed point with respect to all $\mathcal{N}_e$ such that $Top(e) \leq k$, i.e., $\mathcal{S}_K \times \cdots \times \mathcal{S}_{k+1} \times \mathcal{B}(p) = \mathcal{N}_{\leq k}(\mathcal{S}_K \times \cdots \times \mathcal{S}_{k+1} \times \mathcal{B}(p))$, where $\mathcal{N}_{\leq k} = \bigcup_{e: Top(e) \leq k} \mathcal{N}_e$. To saturate MDD node p once all its descendants are saturated, we *update it in place* so that it encodes also any state in $\mathcal{N}_{k,e} \times \cdots \times \mathcal{N}_{1,e}(\mathcal{B}(p))$, for all events e such that $Top(e) = k$. This can create new MDD nodes at levels below k, which are saturated immediately, prior to completing the saturation of p. If we start with the MDD encoding the initial state $\mathbf{s}^0$ and saturate its nodes bottom up, the root r will encode $\mathcal{S} = \mathcal{N}^*(\mathbf{s}^0)$ at the end, as shown in [5].

Saturation consists of many "lightweight" nested fixed-point iterations and is completely different from the traditional breadth-first approach that employs a single "heavyweight" global fixed-point iteration. The algorithm contains two main mutually recursive functions (cf. Sec. 3): *Saturate* calls *Fire* to recursively perform the event firings while saturating nodes, while *Fire* calls *Saturate* to saturate nodes that are created as a result of event firings. The algorithm also uses supporting functions for creating and deleting nodes, performing a union on two nodes, storing saturated nodes by checking them into a hash table, and caching results to previous calls of *Fire*. Experimental results reported in [3, 5, 6] consistently show that Saturation outperforms breadth-first symbolic state-space generation by orders of magnitude in both memory and time, making it arguably the most efficient state-space generation algorithm for globally-asynchronous locally-synchronous discrete event systems.

Cilk. Symbolic state-space generation algorithms incur significant overheads from parallelisation, making gains in time-efficiency difficult to achieve. The main overheads are *synchronisation overheads* due to frequent locking on the symbolic structure (i.e., nodes stored in hash tables), *load imbalance* from the irregular sizes of computations during state-space generation, and *scheduling overheads* since state-space generation computations can be small. Parallel tools to reduce these overheads are thus desirable. To the best of our knowledge, Cilk [1, 10] is the only parallel language that offers both efficient scheduling and load balancing. The Cilk language simplifies parallel programming by allowing the use of C-based functions to express control over the parallelism of a program. The language is powerful enough to facilitate mutually recursive algorithms such as Saturation [5]. It is designed to run efficiently on symmetric processors, e.g., those found in shared-memory machines, and includes a scheduler employing randomised work-stealing, that is theoretically and practically efficient. To achieve efficiency, Cilk employs its own model of multithreaded computation.

Cilk uses call/return semantics to enable parallelism, and provides keywords that enable the programmer to easily express parallelism. A Cilk function can be specified by using the keyword **cilk** in front of a C function, and can be *spawned* to run in parallel by using the keyword **spawn** when calling it. The C function semantics is preserved by allowing the return value of the spawned function to be stored by the parent. Multiple functions can be spawned within the calling function, and the calling function continues its computation while the spawned functions work in parallel. To permit controlled synchronisation of spawned threads, the **sync** keyword prevents the calling function from continuing its computation until all of its spawned functions have completed. Cilk functions contain an implicit **sync** before they are allowed to return.

The return value of the calling function can either be stored by the parent once the function completes, or can be handled by the parent in a more complex way via the use of an **inlet**. An inlet can be specified as an internal function to a Cilk function, which handles the result of a spawned function. To preserve atomicity, only one completed Cilk function can be handled at a time by the inlet, and further computation by the parent is prevented until the inlet has returned. The spawn and sync keywords cannot be used within an inlet. This restriction arises from Cilk's inability to support pipelining, making it difficult to express *producer/consumer* problems such as state-space generation.

3   Parallel Saturation

Using Cilk we can easily interpret Saturation as a parallel algorithm in *divide and conquer* format. The algorithm in Fig. 1 shows the original Saturation algorithm [5] expressed as a parallel algorithm in Cilk. The algorithm is parallelised via *task parallelism* in exactly the same way as in our thread pool implementation using POSIX Pthreads [9], where the *Fire* function is defined as a parallel task, so that event firings can execute in parallel. We therefore choose to spawn the function *Fire* on line 16 of the algorithm, while the return value of the spawned function is handled using an inlet we call *DoUnion*, specified in lines 1 to 9 of the algorithm. The inlet performs the *Union* on the node being saturated if the firing returns a non-zero node. The calling function synchronises on the spawned firings in line 17 of the Cilk algorithm using the keyword sync. The firing loop continues again when all of the currently spawned firings have completed. Access to the hash table and caches is granted on a per-level basis via a mutex lock that

---

cilk *Saturate*(in k:lvl, p:node)

> Update p, a node at level k not in the hash table, in–place, to encode $\mathcal{N}^*_{\leq k}(\mathcal{B}(p))$.

declare $pCng$: bool; e : event; i, j : lcl;
declare $\mathcal{L}$: set of lcl; u : node;
1. inlet void $DoUnion(f : lcl)$ {
2.   if $f \neq 0$ then
3.   foreach $j \in \mathcal{N}_{k,e}(i)$ do
4. $u \Leftarrow Union(k-1, f, p[j])$;
5.   if $u \neq p[j]$ then
6. $p[j] \Leftarrow u$; $pCng = true$;
7.   if $\mathcal{N}_{k,e}(j) \neq 0$ then
8. $\mathcal{L} = \mathcal{L} \cup \{j\}$;
9. }
10. repeat
11. $pCng \Leftarrow false$;
12.   for each $e \in \mathcal{E}_k$ do
13. $\mathcal{L} = Locals(e,k,p)$;
14.   while $\mathcal{L} \neq \emptyset$ do
15. $i = Pick(\mathcal{L})$;
16. $DoUnion(\text{spawn } Fire(e, k-1, p[i]))$;
17.   sync;
18. until $pCng = false$;

cilk *Fire*(in e:event, l:lvl, q:node):node

> Build an MDD rooted at level l, encoding $\mathcal{N}^*_{\leq l}(\mathcal{N}_e(\mathcal{B}(q)))$.

declare $\mathcal{L}$: set of lcl;
declare i, j : lcl;
declare f, u, s : node;
declare $sCng$: bool;
1. if $l < Last(e)$ then return q;
2. if $Find(FireCache[l], \{q, e\}, s)$ return s;
3. $s \Leftarrow NewNode(l)$; $sCng \Leftarrow false$;
4. $\mathcal{L} \Leftarrow Locals(e, l, q)$;
5. while $\mathcal{L} \neq \emptyset$ do
6. $i \Leftarrow Pick(\mathcal{L})$;
7. $f \Leftarrow Fire(e, l-1, q[i])$;
8.   if $f \neq 0$ then
9.   foreach $j \in \mathcal{N}_{l,e}(i)$ do
10. $u \Leftarrow Union(l-1, f, s[j])$;
11.   if $u \neq s[j]$ then
12. $s[j] \Leftarrow u$; $sCng \Leftarrow true$;
13.   if $sCng$ then $Saturate(l, s)$;
14. $CheckIntoHashTable(l, s)$;
15. $Insert(FireCache[l]\{q, e\}, s)$;
16. return s;

Fig. 1. Cilk based Saturation using inlets

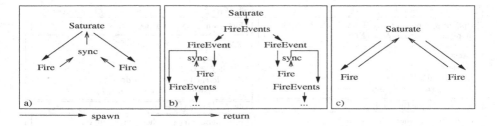

Fig. 2. Calling order for spawns

can be specified in Cilk. We argued the correctness of this way of parallelising Saturation in [9].

Unfortunately, this parallelisation approach creates a load imbalance since all firings must be completed before performing the union operation. The ordering can be shown in Fig. 2(a), where function *Saturate* must wait for the two spawned *Fire* calls to synchronise before spawning more work. It would be more efficient to perform the union operation and then immediately spawn new work using the ordering in Fig. 2(c).

Expressing a Producer/Consumer Problem. The call/return semantics of Cilk means that we cannot elegantly deal with a spawned function as soon as it has completed, since we cannot tell when an individual firing has completed outside of an inlet. It is desirable to use an inlet to spawn off more work as soon as a firing completes; however, inlets are restricted to prevent new functions being spawned from within them. We could attempt to let the calling function know when a firing has completed via an inlet through the use of a flag or a queue, but Cilk does not allow us to suspend the calling function outside of a sync statement, which means that the calling function would have to continue monitoring for completed child functions. It is undesirable to tie up the processor with a function that is polling in this manner, since it largely performs useless work. This means that the ordering of work shown in Fig. 2(c) cannot be achieved using Cilk, due to the restrictions arising from Cilk's lack of pipelining in its multithreaded computational model.

We can rewrite the algorithm to continue spawning firings when they have completed by utilising the spawn keyword, without exploiting the call/return semantics of Cilk. An example algorithm is shown in Fig. 3, which breaks the original Saturation function into sub-functions. Once a spawned firing has been completed, it performs the union in *DoUnion* and then immediately spawns further firings on the updated state. Expressing our producer/consumer problem by bypassing the call/return semantics is not ideal. When the functions complete, they do not have any further work to do, yet they are left on the Cilk function stack after spawning more work, waiting for it to complete. This ordering is shown in Fig. 2(b). A large number of functions can be unnecessarily left on the stack during the state-space generation process, which potentially increases

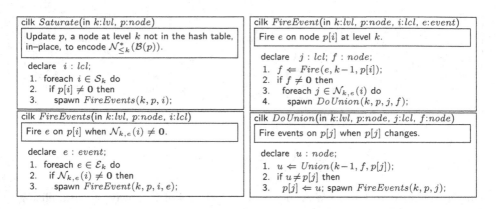

Fig. 3. Cilk based Saturation without exploiting call/return semantics

the amount of memory required for the process. The problem is compounded because of the mutually recursive calls between *Saturate* and *Fire*.

Using a Thread Pool. To achieve the ideal ordering in Fig. 2(c), we must relinquish functions from the stack while spawned work executes. Since a function frame requires its own storage, a smaller amount of memory could be used by storing only the variables that are required once a spawned child is complete, instead of storing the calling function. We can use a thread pool for load balancing purposes, an auxiliary structure to store required variables, and structure our algorithm to relinquish functions, leaving the child functions to complete the work of the calling function. In our thread pool algorithm [9], we store the variables in *upward arcs* in the MDD structure. Children can be spawned using *tasks* allocated to threads in the thread pool via the use of a FIFO queue. An available thread will pick up a task from the queue and execute it. Tasks can restore the status of their calling function using the upward arcs, which allows calling functions to terminate, leaving spawned tasks to complete their work.

A snippet of the pseudo-code from the thread pool algorithm is shown in Fig. 4. The algorithm behaves (or acts) in much the same way as the sequential Saturation algorithm, except that, when a firing is performed in function *Fire*, an upward arc is set to the node that needs to be updated as a result of the firing. This allows the *Fire* call to terminate since the upward arc contains the information required for spawned tasks to complete the *Fire* function. The mutual recursion on the function stack is broken as *Fire* spawns *Saturate* tasks, i.e., once the node created by *Fire* is ready to be saturated, a saturation task is added to the queue and *Fire* terminates. To determine whether a node has been saturated, the number of tasks performing computations on the node needs to be stored. When all tasks have completed, the node is saturated and the function *NodeSaturated* is called. *NodeSaturated* picks up where *Fire* left off, updating any of the nodes which have upward arcs set to them, and continues to fire events on any updated node until the node is saturated.

Saturate(in k:lvl, p:node)	Fire(in e:event, k:lvl, p:node, q:node, i:lcl):node
declare i : lcl;	declare s : node; j : lcl;
	...
1. foreach $i \in S_k$ do	4. $s = CreateNode(k-1)$;
2. if $p[i] \neq 0$ then	5. foreach $j \in \mathcal{N}_{k,e}(i)$ do
3. $FireEvents(k, p, i)$;	6. $AddTask(k, p)$; $SetUpArc(k-1, s, j, p)$;
4. if $Tasks(k, p) = 0$ then	...
5. $NodeSaturated(k, p)$;	14. $AddQueue(Saturate(k-1, s))$;
	...

FireEvents(in k:lvl, p:node, i:lcl)	NodeSaturated(in k:lvl, p:node)
declare e : event;	declare q : node;
1. foreach $e \in \mathcal{E}_k$ do	1. while $GetUpArc(k, p, i, q)$
2. if $\mathcal{N}_{k,e}(i) \neq 0$ then	2. $DoUnion(k+1, q, i, p)$;
3. $Fire(e, k, p, p[i], i)$;	3. if $Tasks(k+1, q) = 0$ then
	4. $NodeSaturated(k+1, q)$;

Fig. 4. Thread pool Saturation [9]

The use of upward arcs introduces its own overheads [9]: additional locks, task management, and the thread pool queue. The upward arcs also require extra memory for both the arcs and the locks to synchronise the arcs. The thread pool is not as efficient as Cilk, due to the time required to add and remove a task from the queue. When we compare Cilk to a thread pool using the functionally lightweight *Fibonacci* problem in [10] on a dual-processor, dual-core machine, Cilk reports a 3× speedup whereas the thread pool reports a 2× slowdown due to the time spent adding and removing tasks from the queue. Our thread pool is, however, very efficient compared to creating threads on demand, where the allocation of work to a thread is over 10× faster than creating one. [9].

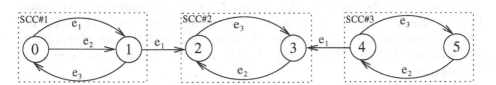

Fig. 5. The effect of events with $Top = k$ on the states $\{0, 1, 2, 3, 4, 5\}$ of S_k

Optimising the Ordering of Events. The study of the thread pool algorithm in [9] revealed that the ordering in which events are fired in parallel can significantly affect Saturation's run-time and memory requirements. Fig. 5 shows the effect of events e_1, e_2, and e_3, with $Top(e_1) = Top(e_2) = Top(e_3) = k$, on the local states at level k (these events may of course affect lower levels as well). When saturating a node p at level k, we must repeatedly fire e_1, e_2, and e_3 in p, until no more new states are found, i.e., until p encodes a fixed point. However, Saturation does not dictate the order in which these events should be fired. For example, firing $0 \xrightarrow{e_1} 1$ followed by $1 \xrightarrow{e_3} 0$ might be sub-optimal, since we might have to fire $1 \xrightarrow{e_3} 0$ again once $0 \xrightarrow{e_2} 1$ has been fired, if this causes $p[1]$ to point to a different node encoding more states. Similarly, if we fire $1 \xrightarrow{e_1} 2$ before firing $0 \xrightarrow{e_2} 1$, all transitions in $SCC\#2$ may have to be fired again.

To address this problem, we use the *chaining heuristic* of [3], which extracts the strongly connected components (SCCs) from a *dynamic transition graph* that is built from the static graph of Fig. 5 and the dynamic pattern of non-zero children of node p. We use these SCCs to enhance the order of parallel event firings. However, while this chaining heuristic tends to improve run-time and memory in a sequential implementation, it also reduces the potential parallelism and introduces time and memory overheads due to storing the SCC graphs, traversing them and managing parallel access.

4   Experimental Results

We implemented four experimental algorithms, two using Cilk and two utilising a thread pool, which either fire events using the unoptimised ordering or the chaining heuristic. Our thread pool algorithms were implemented using C and the POSIX Pthreads library [15]. The machine used for this evaluation is a dual-processor, dual-core PC with 2GB of memory and Intel Xeon CPU 3.06GHz processors with 512KB cache sizes, running Redhat Linux AS 4, Redhat kernel 2.6.9-22.ELsmp, with glibc 2.3.4-2.13. We applied the algorithms to a set of parameterised models previously used to evaluate Saturation [3, 5, 6], where the parameter controls the size of a model's state space. One of our models is the Runway Safety Monitor (RSM) designed by Lockheed Martin and NASA to reduce aviation accidents [18]. For each model, Table 1 shows the run-time and memory when executing our experimental algorithms on four cores, where N is the parameter and $|S|$ is the approximate size of the final state space. The thread pool algorithms are denoted by *TP*, the Cilk algorithms are denoted by *Cilk*, and a *C* at the end of these names indicates the use of chaining. We ran only non-chained versions of the algorithms on the FMS and Philosophers models since the SCC graphs using the chaining heuristic were too large to fit into memory.

The *run-time speedup* shows the comparative speed of the parallel algorithms against the sequential version, where a value greater (less) than 1 indicates a speedup (slowdown). The ideal speedup on our machine is approximately 3.2, since the speedup obtained from a secondary core is less than that of a secondary processor. A speedup greater than 3.2 is a superlinear speedup, which occurs when the parallelism introduced into an algorithm causes it to be more optimal than its sequential counterpart. It is difficult to achieve an ideal speedup for any parallel search algorithm due to the *search overhead factor*. For Saturation this includes synchronisation overheads on the symbolic structure, where the MDD has to be locked frequently, and model specific factors such as how small the computations are. In contrast to standard breadth-first state exploration techniques, Saturation is heavily optimised. Hence, many of its computations are extremely small and are thus difficult to parallelise efficiently [9].

Our experimental results reflect these overheads and model specific factors, since only seven of the models exhibit parallelism, varying from small speedups of just over 1 to a superlinear speedup of over 4. The results, however, also show

Table 1. Run-time and memory results on a dual-processor, dual-core machine

N	$\lvert S \rvert$	Run-time speedup					Memory increase				
		Seq (s)	Tp	TpC	Cilk	CilkC	Seq (b)	Tp	TpC	Cilk	CilkC
Slotted ring network protocol (Slot) N = no. of nodes in the network											
90	5.9×10^{94}	6.79	0.26	0.31	0.28	0.42	5923040	11.84	5.55	2.52	1.40
120	5.1×10^{126}	15.80	0.29	0.33	0.29	0.44	13405440	12.00	5.67	2.68	1.44
150	4.5×10^{158}	30.84	0.30	0.37	0.31	0.45	25441840	12.10	5.88	2.73	1.52
Round robin mutex protocol (Robin) N = no. of processors											
180	6.2×10^{56}	7.94	0.94	0.49	1.15	0.69	1165764	1.88	1.82	18.01	17.51
210	7.8×10^{65}	15.43	0.96	0.50	1.18	0.70	1574304	1.91	1.90	18.10	17.58
240	9.5×10^{74}	41.71	0.99	0.50	1.22	0.72	2044044	1.94	1.92	18.13	17.59
Kanban manufacturing system (Kanban) N = no. of each type of parts											
25	7.6×10^{12}	2.79	0.65	0.57	0.22	0.65	7334600	1.92	1.22	1.48	1.16
30	5.0×10^{13}	5.07	0.69	0.57	0.24	0.66	13784976	2.00	1.27	1.49	1.18
35	2.5×10^{14}	10.25	0.71	0.58	0.25	0.66	23957940	2.08	1.31	1.54	1.19
Flexible manufacturing system (FMS) N = no. of each type of parts											
11	1.1×10^{9}	12.22	2.11	N/A	2.19	N/A	3148980	1.72	N/A	22.89	N/A
13	5.8×10^{9}	55.54	2.18	N/A	2.35	N/A	8173844	1.88	N/A	23.56	N/A
14	1.3×10^{10}	119.87	2.26	N/A	2.47	N/A	12591300	1.97	N/A	24.35	N/A
Queen problem (Queens) N = no. of queens on an $N \times N$ chessboard											
11	166926	1.78	0.52	0.53	1.22	0.60	4248776	1.91	2.05	17.68	17.99
12	856189	19.38	0.56	0.54	1.52	0.62	19920672	2.01	2.15	18.27	18.20
13	4674890	438.59	0.61	0.59	2.48	0.67	99807456	2.24	2.56	19.01	18.62
Runway safety monitor (RSM) Targets = 1, Speeds = 2, X=N, Y=3, Z=2											
3	1.3×10^{10}	5.41	0.49	0.78	0.54	0.93	6267568	2.21	1.63	16.22	15.95
5	3.8×10^{10}	37.62	0.55	1.42	0.84	1.75	23307704	2.36	1.72	16.91	16.55
8	1.0×10^{11}	316.77	0.67	2.99	0.93	4.47	74024440	2.55	1.89	17.67	16.93
Aloha network protocol (Aloha) N = no. of nodes in the network											
40	2.3×10^{13}	2.69	0.79	0.71	1.55	0.80	15879556	1.52	1.44	12.14	11.91
70	4.3×10^{22}	22.20	0.86	0.84	1.69	0.89	82907316	1.66	1.63	13.22	12.90
100	6.5×10^{31}	66.28	0.87	0.85	1.74	0.91	239179076	1.78	1.75	14.38	14.33
Randomised leader election protocol (Leader) N = no. of processors											
6	1.9×10^{6}	3.72	0.48	0.71	0.89	0.97	2422704	2.81	2.01	14.34	13.71
7	2.4×10^{7}	24.34	0.44	0.65	0.81	1.1	7063232	3.29	2.17	15.89	14.43
8	3.0×10^{8}	128.08	0.43	0.63	0.82	1.24	16107968	3.61	2.52	16.70	15.61
Bounded open queueing network (BQ) N = no. of customers											
30	2.4×10^{8}	2.1	0.36	0.41	0.82	0.90	2241036	2.08	1.96	18.66	17.59
50	4.6×10^{9}	24.25	0.39	0.44	0.85	0.91	15112996	2.14	2.05	18.93	17.92
70	3.3×10^{10}	146.01	0.41	0.45	0.87	0.94	54895356	2.50	2.23	19.20	18.36
Dining philosophers (Philosophers) N = philosophers, phil./level = 6											
20	3.5×10^{12}	14.82	1.12	N/A	1.26	N/A	569608	1.82	N/A	14.07	N/A
40	1.2×10^{25}	33.32	1.13	N/A	1.32	N/A	1097560	1.96	N/A	14.40	N/A
80	1.4×10^{50}	77.35	1.19	N/A	1.35	N/A	2321768	2.28	N/A	14.93	N/A

that the efficient load balancing and scheduling of Cilk is superior to our thread pool in exploiting parallelism where parallelism exists. In comparison, Cilk is able to obtain a speedup for seven of the models instead of three for the thread pool. Where models can be parallelised, the larger the size of the model, the greater the parallelism. The models of particular interest due to their comparatively high speedups against the other models, are the Queens, FMS, and RSM models. On a four processor 2.4GHz Intel Operon machine, the speedups for these models increase to over 3 for the Queens and FMS models and over 5 for the RSM model, demonstrating that all of the cores are being utilised. The RSM model exhibits a superlinear speedup due to the combined effects of chaining and the effective parallelisation using Cilk.

Chaining is practically effective in improving the run-time on both the RSM and Leader models, although it may conceptually hinder run-time due to the synchronisation overhead from managing access and updates to the chaining graphs. This is because chaining can also decrease the overall amount of work by finding an event ordering that leads to firing fewer events. This effect also leads to the use of less memory across all of the models, as shown in the *memory increase* column indicating the relative increase in memory for the parallel algorithms against the sequential version. The column also shows that the Cilk algorithms require significantly more memory than the sequential algorithm, due to the size of the Cilk stack. The only model where Cilk requires less memory than the thread pool algorithm when using chaining is the slotted ring model. For this model, chaining helps the thread pool algorithm, halving the memory used by the non-chained version. Overall, however, the thread pool algorithm significantly outperforms the Cilk algorithm regarding memory, which is due to the fact that it does not have to allocate memory for a waiting stack.

Our results show that Cilk is more effective in exploiting parallelism than our hand-crafted thread pool algorithm, but incurs a significant memory overhead due to its lack of support for pipelining. This is a relevant and timely observation due to the increasing popularity of multi-core machines. However, the scalability of our algorithm across a larger number of processors (or processor cores) requires further study in order to fully understand the impact of the synchronisation overhead introduced by each processor (core). We leave this to future work.

5   Related Work

Research on symbolic model checking has primarily focused on networks of workstations (NOWs) [2, 11, 12, 13, 17, 19], using message-passing libraries to communicate between workstations. None of the existing approaches uses a parallel language to facilitate scheduling and load balancing; approaches to dealing with these overheads are implemented by hand. Also, most work on parallel state-space generation considers how to parallelise the underlying data structure. These approaches target the increased memory available on a NOW by slicing data structures and distributing them across processors. The structure of decision diagrams has previously been sliced horizontally [2] and vertically [13, 17, 19]. Horizontal slicing scales well but prevents significant speedups, since each slice has to complete its work before the next slice can begin.

Grumberg, Heyman, Ifergan, and Schuster [11] parallelised symbolic state-space generation algorithms to gain speedups by developing vertical slices on different processors of a NOW. If the algorithm controlling the slices has to frequently synchronise on the application of the next-state function, each round of computation is only as fast as the slowest time it takes for a slice to develop on a processor. To achieve speedups, the parallel algorithm allows slices to develop asynchronously while the next-state function is applied to create more work. The algorithm is load-balanced using workstealing techniques implemented by hand [12]. For very large circuits, these techniques can lead to efficient parallelisation, showing up to an order of magnitude improvement in time-efficiency.

Our approach is unique in that we consider how to functionally decompose the Saturation algorithm rather than its data structures. In comparing a proven efficient parallel language to our own hand-crafted approach, we determined how efficient both implementations are in terms of run-time and memory. We expect that our observations can be extrapolated to PC clusters when utilising distributed shared-memory (DSM) techniques.

6   Conclusions

We investigated whether the parallel language Cilk could improve the efficiency of a parallel variant of the MDD-based Saturation algorithm for computing reachable state spaces of asynchronous systems on shared-memory architectures, such as modern multi-processor multi-core PCs. Our experimental studies showed that Cilk is much more effective than a hand-crafted implementation for addressing load balancing and scheduling. However, while the usage of Cilk led to considerable improvements in time-efficiency, the restrictions imposed by the Cilk language implied an enormous memory overhead.

The results from running our hand-crafted solution demonstrated that preventing idle functions from inhabiting the stack removes this memory overhead. Pipelining is therefore an essential feature of any language for parallelising symbolic state-space generators. To the best of our knowledge, there is currently no parallel language fitting this description. However, a possible future direction of parallel irregular languages extending the Cilk model of multithreaded computation to include pipelining is proposed in [20]. This would enable the truly efficient parallelisation of symbolic state-space generators, thereby making significant progress in utilising parallel architectures in automated verification.

Acknowledgements. We wish to thank the anonymous reviewers for their detailed comments and suggestions.

References

[1] Blumofe, R.D., Joerg, C.F., Kuszmaul, B.C., Leiserson, C.E., Randall, K.H., Zhou, Y.: Cilk: An efficient multithreaded runtime system. In: PPOPP, pp. 207–216. ACM, New York (1995)

[2] Chung, M.-Y., Ciardo, G.: Saturation NOW. QEST, pp. 272–281. IEEE (2004)

[3] Chung, M.-Y., Ciardo, G., Yu, A.J.: A fine-grained density-guided chaining heuristic for symbolic reachability analysis. In: Graf, S., Zhang, W. (eds.) ATVA 2006. LNCS, vol. 4218, pp. 51–66. Springer, Heidelberg (2006)

[4] Ciardo, G., Jones, R.L., Miner, A.S., Siminiceanu, R.: Logical and Stochastic Modeling with SMART. Performance Evaluation 63, 578–608 (2006)

[5] Ciardo, G., Lüttgen, G., Siminiceanu, R.: Saturation: An efficient iteration strategy for symbolic state-space generation. In: TACAS, vol. 2031, pp. 328–348. LNCS (2001) An extended version is to appear in the FMSD journal

[6] Ciardo, G., Marmorstein, R., Siminiceanu, R.: Saturation unbound. In: Garavel, H., Hatcliff, J. (eds.) ETAPS 2003 and TACAS 2003. LNCS, vol. 2619, pp. 379–393. Springer, Heidelberg (2003)

[7] Cimatti, A., Clarke, E.M., Giunchiglia, F., Roveri, M.: NuSMV: A new symbolic model checker. STTT 2(4), 410–425 (2000)

[8] Clarke, E.M., Grumberg, O., Peled, D.: Model Checking. MIT Press, Cambridge (1999)

[9] Ezekiel, J., Lüttgen, G., Siminiceanu, R.: Can Saturation be parallelised? In: Brim, L., Haverkort, B., Leucker, M., van de Pol, J. (eds.) FMICS 2006 and PDMC 2006. LNCS, vol. 4346, Springer, Heidelberg (2007)

[10] Frigo, M., Leiserson, C.E., Randall, K.H.: The implementation of the Cilk-5 multithreaded language. In: SIGPLAN, pp. 212–223. ACM, New York (1998)

[11] Grumberg, O., Heyman, T., Ifergan, N., Schuster, A.: Achieving speedups in distributed symbolic reachability analysis through asynchronous computation. In: Borrione, D., Paul, W. (eds.) CHARME 2005. LNCS, vol. 3725, pp. 129–145. Springer, Heidelberg (2005)

[12] Grumberg, O., Heyman, T., Schuster, A.: A work-efficient distributed algorithm for reachability analysis. FMSD 29(2), 157–175 (2006)

[13] Heyman, T., Geist, D., Grumberg, O., Schuster, A.: Achieving scalability in parallel reachability analysis of very large circuits. In: Emerson, E.A., Sistla, A.P. (eds.) CAV 2000. LNCS, vol. 1855, pp. 20–35. Springer, Heidelberg (2000)

[14] Kam, T., Villa, T., Brayton, R., S-Vincentelli, A.L.: Multi-valued decision diagrams: Theory and applications. Multiple-Valued Logic 4(1-2), 9–62 (1998)

[15] Lewis, B., Berg, D.: Multithreaded Programming with Pthreads. Prentice-Hall, Englewood Cliffs (1998)

[16] McMillan, K.L.: Symbolic Model Checking. Kluwer Academic Publishers, Dordrecht (1993)

[17] Milvang-Jensen, K., Hu, A.J.: BDDNOW: A parallel BDD package. In: Gopalakrishnan, G.C., Windley, P. (eds.) FMCAD 1998. LNCS, vol. 1522, pp. 501–507. Springer, Heidelberg (1998)

[18] Siminiceanu, R., Ciardo, G.: Formal verification of the NASA runway safety monitor. STTT 9(1), 63–76 (2007)

[19] Stornetta, T., Brewer, F.: Implementation of an efficient parallel BDD package. In: DAC, pp. 641–644. ACM, New York (1996)

[20] Yong, X., Wen-Jing, H.: Aligned multithreaded computations and their scheduling with performance guarantees. Par. Proc. Let. 13(3), 353–364 (2003)

I/O Efficient Accepting Cycle Detection*

Jiri Barnat, Lubos Brim, and Pavel Šimeček

Department of Computer Science, Faculty of Informatics
Masaryk University Brno, Czech Republic

Abstract. We show how to adapt an existing non-DFS-based accepting cycle detection algorithm OWCTY [10,15,29] to the I/O efficient setting and compare its I/O efficiency and practical performance to the existing I/O efficient LTL model checking approach of Edelkamp and Jabbar [14]. The new algorithm exhibits similar I/O complexity with respect to the size of the graph while it avoids quadratic increase in the size of the graph. Therefore, the number of I/O operations performed is significantly lower and the algorithm exhibits better practical performance.

1 Introduction

Model checking became one of the standard technique for verification of hardware and software systems even though the class of systems that can be fully verified is fairly limited due to the well known *state explosion problem* [12]. The automata-theoretic approach [33] to model checking finite-state systems against linear-time temporal logic (LTL) reduces to the detection of reachable accepting cycles in a directed graph. Due to the state explosion problem, the graph tends to be extremely large and its size poses real limitations to the verification process. Many more-or-less successful techniques have been introduced [12] to reduce the size of the graph advancing thus the frontier of still tractable systems. Nevertheless, for real-life industrial systems these techniques are not efficient enough to fit the data into the main memory. An alternative solution is to increase the computational resources available to the verification process. The two major approaches include the usage of clusters of workstations and the usage of external memory devices (disks).

Regarding external memory devices, the goal is to develop algorithms that minimize the number of I/O operations an algorithm has to perform to complete its task. This is because the access to information stored on an external device is orders of magnitude slower than the access to information stored in the main memory. Thus the complexity of I/O efficient algorithms is measured in the number of I/O operations [1].

A lot of effort has been put into research on I/O efficient algorithms working on explicitly stored graphs [11,20,24,25]. For an explicitly stored graph, an I/O efficient algorithm typically has to perform a random access operation every

---

* This work has been partially supported by the Grant Agency of Czech Republic grant No. 201/06/1338 and the Academy of Sciences grant No. 1ET408050503.

W. Damm and H. Hermanns (Eds.): CAV 2007, LNCS 4590, pp. 281–293, 2007.

time it needs to enumerate edges incident with a given vertex. However, in model checking, the graphs are often given implicitly which means that the edges incident with a given vertex are computed on demand from the vertex itself. Thus, an algorithm working on an implicitly given graph may save up to $|V|$ random access operations, which may have significant impact on the performance of the algorithm in practice.

A distinguished technique that allows for an I/O efficient implementation of a graph traversal procedures is the so called *delayed duplicate detection* [21,22,26,32]. A traversal procedure has to maintain a set of visited vertices to prevent their re-exploration. Since the graphs are large, the set cannot be completely kept in the main memory and must be stored on the external memory device. When a new vertex is generated it is checked against the set to avoid its re-exploration. The idea of the delayed duplicate detection technique is to postpone the individual checks and perform them together in a group for the price of a single scan operation.

Unfortunately, the delayed duplicate detection technique is incompatible with the depth-first search (DFS) of a graph [14]. Therefore, most approaches to I/O efficient (LTL) model checking suggested so far, have focused on the state space generation and verification of safety properties only. The first I/O efficient algorithm for state space generation has been implemented in Murφ [32]. Later on, several heuristics for the state space generation were suggested and implemented in various verification tools [16,18,23]. The first attempt to verify more than safety properties was described in [19], however, the suggested approach uses the random search to find a counterexample to a given property. Therefore, it is incomplete in the sense that it is not able to prove validity of the property.

To the best of our knowledge, the only *complete* I/O efficient LTL model checker was suggested by Edelkamp and Jabbar in [14] where the problematic DFS-based algorithm was avoided by the reduction of the accepting cycle detection problem to the reachability problem [7,31] whose I/O efficient solution was further improved by using the directed (A^*) search and parallelism. The algorithm works in the on-the-fly manner meaning that only a part of the state space is constructed, which is needed in order to check the desired property. The reduction transforms the graph so that the size of the graph after the transformation is asymptotically quadratic with respect to the original one. More precisely, the size of the resulting graph is $|F| \times |G|$, where $|G|$ is the size of the original graph and $|F|$ is the number of accepting vertices. As the external memory algorithms are meant to be applied to large scale graphs, the quadratic increase in the size of the graph is significant and, according to our experience, it often aborts due to the lack of space. This is especially the case when the model is valid and the entire graph has to be traversed to prove the absence of an accepting cycle. The approach is thus mainly useful for finding counterexamples in the case a standard verification tool fails due to the lack of memory. However, completeness is a very important aspect of LTL model checking as well. A typical scenario is that if the system is invalid and the counterexample found, the system is corrected and the property verified again. In the end, the graph must be traversed completely anyway.

Since DFS-based algorithms cannot be used for I/O efficient solution to the accepting cycle detection, a non-DFS algorithm is required. The situation very much resembles a similar one encountered in cluster-based approach to LTL model checking [2]. The main problem of the approach is that the optimal sequential algorithm (e.g. Nested DFS [17]) is inherently sequential and hence difficult to be parallelized [30]. Consequently, several new parallel algorithms that do not build on top of the depth-first search have been introduced [3,4,8,9,10].

In this paper we show how to adapt a parallel enumerative version of the *One Way Catch them Young Algorithm* (OWCTY) [10,15,29] to the I/O efficient setting and compare its I/O efficiency and practical performance with the I/O efficient LTL model checking algorithm by Edelkamp and Jabbar [14].

2   I/O Efficient OWCTY Algorithm

As discussed above, an I/O efficient solution to LTL model checking has to build upon a non-DFS algorithm. A particularly suitable algorithm for enumerative LTL model checking was described in [10]. The goal of the algorithm is to compute the set of vertices that are reachable from a vertex on an accepting cycle. If the set is empty, there is no accepting cycle in the graph, otherwise the presence of an accepting cycle is ensured [15,29].

The algorithm repeatedly computes approximations of the target set until a fixpoint is reached. All reachable vertices are inserted into the approximation set (*ApproxSet*) within the procedure INITIALIZE-APPROXSET. After that, vertices violating the condition are gradually removed from the approximation set using procedures ELIM-NO-ACCEPTING and ELIM-NO-PREDECESSORS. Procedure ELIM-NO-ACCEPTING removes those vertices from the approximation set that have no accepting ancestors in the set, i.e. vertices that lie on leading non-accepting cycles. Procedure ELIM-NO-PREDECESSORS removes vertices that have no ancestors at all, i.e. leading vertices lying outside a cycle. The pseudo-code is given as Algorithm 1.

Algorithm 1. DETECTACCEPTINGCYCLE

Require: Implicit definition of G=(V,E,ACC)
 1: INITIALIZE-APPROXSET()
 2: $oldSize \leftarrow \infty$
 3: **while** $(ApproxSet.size \neq oldSize) \wedge (ApproxSet.size > 0)$ **do**
 4:     $oldSize \leftarrow ApproxSet.size$
 5:     ELIM-NO-ACCEPTING()
 6:     ELIM-NO-PREDECESSORS()
 7: **return** $ApproxSet.size > 0$

The approximation set induces an approximation graph. The in-degree of a vertex in the approximation graph corresponds to the number of its immediate predecessors in the approximation set. To identify vertices without ancestors in the approximation set, the in-degree is maintained for every vertex of the approximation graph. Procedure ELIM-NO-PREDECESSORS then works as follows. All vertices from the set with a zero in-degree are moved to a queue from where they are dequeued one by one. Dequeued vertices are eliminated from the set, and the in-degrees of its descendants are updated. If an in-degree drops to zero, the corresponding vertex is inserted into the queue to be eliminated as well. The procedure eliminates vertices in a topological order and hence the queue becomes empty as soon as all vertices preceding a cycle are eliminated.

Procedure ELIM-NO-ACCEPTING works as follows. If a vertex has an accepting ancestor in the approximation set, it has to be reachable from some accepting vertex in the set. Therefore, the procedure first removes all non-accepting vertices from the set and sets the numbers of predecessors of all vertices remaining in the set to zero. Then a forward search is performed starting from the vertices remaining in the set. During the search all visited vertices are re-inserted to the approximation set and the numbers of immediate predecessors of vertices in the set are re-counted.

There are three major data structures used by the algorithm. These are *Candidates*, *ApproxSet*, and *Open*. *Candidates* is the set of vertices strictly kept in memory that is used for the delayed duplicate detection technique. It keeps vertices that have been processed and are waiting to be checked against the set of vertices stored on the external device. *ApproxSet* is the set of vertices belonging to the current approximation set. It is implemented as a linear list and stored externally. Together with *Candidates*, it is used as the set of vertices already visited during the forward exploration of the graph in procedure ELIM-NO-ACCEPTING. For that purpose, both *Candidates* and *ApproxSet* data structures are modified to keep not only vertices, but also the corresponding numbers of relevant immediate predecessors. The number associated with a particular vertex s is referred to as the *appendix* of the vertex and is set and read with methods *setAppendix(s)* and *getAppendix(s)*, respectively. Finally, the data structure *Open* is a queue of vertices. It is used to keep open vertices during the breadth-first exploration of the graph within procedure ELIM-NO-ACCEPTING, and vertices to be eliminated (vertices without any predecessors) during the execution of procedure ELIM-NO-PREDECESSORS. The data structure *Open* is stored in the external memory, the vertices are, however, inserted into and taken from it in a strict FIFO manner. Thus, a possible I/O overhead could be minimized using an appropriate buffering mechanism.

In some of its phases, the algorithm performs a *scan* through the externally stored set of vertices (*ApproxSet*) and decides about every vertex if it should be removed from the set or not. To preserve the I/O efficiency of such an operation, a temporary external data structure *ApproxSet'* is introduced. In particular, vertices that should remain in the set are copied to the temporary structure.

Algorithm 2. MERGE

```
1: if mode = Elim-No-Accepting then
2:      for all s ∈ ApproxSet do
3:          if s ∈ Candidates then
4:              app ← Candidates.getAppendix(s)
5:              app' ← ApproxSet.getAppendix(s)
6:              Candidates ← Candidates \ {s}
7:              ApproxSet.setAppendix(s, app + app')
8:      for all s ∈ Candidates do
9:          Open.pushBack(s)
10:         ApproxSet ← ApproxSet ∪ {s}
11: else
12:     ApproxSet' ← ∅
13:     for all s ∈ ApproxSet do
14:         app' ← ApproxSet.getAppendix(s)
15:         if s ∈ Candidates then
16:             app ← Candidates.getAppendix(s)
17:             if (app + app') = 0 then
18:                 Open.pushBack(s)
19:             else
20:                 ApproxSet' ← ApproxSet' ∪ {s}
21:                 ApproxSet'.setAppendix(s, app + app')
22:         else
23:             ApproxSet' ← ApproxSet' ∪ {s}
24:             ApproxSet'.setAppendix(s, app')
25:     ApproxSet ← ApproxSet'
26: Candidates ← ∅
```

Once the scan is complete, the content of the original *ApproxSet* is discarded and replaced with the content of the temporary structure *ApproxSet'*.

Having described the data structures we are ready to introduce several auxiliary subroutines. The most important one is procedure MERGE that is responsible for merging information about vertices stored in the internal memory (*Candidates*) and vertices stored externally (*ApproxSet*). The procedure can operate in two different modes according to the value of the variable *mode*. The two modes correspond to the top most procedures ELIM-NO-ACCEPTING and ELIM-NO-PREDECESSORS. In the mode **Elim-No-Accepting**, vertices from set *Candidates* are merged with vertices from *ApproxSet* and the result is stored externally to *ApproxSet*. For already visited vertices the corresponding appendices are just combined and stored externally. Moreover, newly discovered vertices are inserted into the queue of vertices to be further processed (*Queue*). In the mode **Elim-No-Predecessors**, no new vertices are discovered, hence only the appendices are combined. Vertices with zero in-degree are removed from the external memory and in-degree of their immediate descendants is appropriately decreased. For the details see Algorithm 2.

Algorithm 3. STOREORCOMBINE

Require: s, app
1: **if** $s \in Candidates$ **then**
2:     $app' \leftarrow Candidates.getAppendix(s)$
3:     $Candidates.setAppendix(s, app+app')$
4: **else**
5:     $Candidates \leftarrow Candidates \cup \{s\}$
6:     $Candidates.setAppendix(s, app)$
7:     **if** MEMORYISFULL() **then**
8:         MERGE()

Another auxiliary procedure is procedure STOREORCOMBINE whose purpose is to insert a vertex into the candidate set if the vertex is not yet present in the set, or update the corresponding appendix of the vertex, otherwise. Once the main memory becomes full, vertices from the candidate set are processed and the candidate set is emptied by procedure MERGE.

Algorithm 4. OPENISNOTEMPTY

1: **if** $Open.isEmpty()$ **then**
2:     MERGE()
3: **return** $\neg Open.isEmpty()$

The last auxiliary function is a function for checking the emptiness of the queue of vertices to be processed ($Open$). If the queue is empty, procedure OPENISNOTEMPTY calls procedure MERGE to perform the delayed duplicate detection. The procedure returns **False**, if $Open$ is empty and merging has not brought any new vertices to be processed.

Algorithm 5 and Algorithm 6 give pseudo-codes of the two main procedures. Note that algorithm DETECTACCEPTINGCYCLE uses functions GETINITIALVERTEX, GETSUCCESSORS, and ISACCEPTING to traverse the graph and to check whether a vertex is accepting or not. These functions are part of the implicit definition of the graph. Procedure ELIM-NO-ACCEPTING has actually two goals. First, to eliminate those vertices from the approximation set that are unreachable from accepting vertices in the set, and second, to properly count the in-degrees in the approximation graph. Procedure ELIM-NO-PREDECESSORS employs the in-degrees to recursively remove vertices without predecessors from the approximation set.

An important observation is that it is not necessary to initialize the approximation set with the set of all vertices. Since the first procedure in the very first iteration of the while loop performs forward exploration of the graph starting from accepting vertices in the set, it is enough to initialize the set with "leading" accepting vertices only, i.e. those accepting vertices that have no accepting ancestors. Such vertices can be identified with a simple forward traversal that is

Algorithm 5. ELIM-NO-ACCEPTING

1: $mode \leftarrow$ **Elim-No-Accepting**
2: $ApproxSet' \leftarrow \emptyset$
3: **for all** $s \in ApproxSet$ **do**
4:     **if** ISACCEPTING(s) **then**
5:         $Open.pushBack(s)$
6:         $ApproxSet' \leftarrow ApproxSet' \cup \{s\}$
7:         $ApproxSet'.setAppendix(s, 0)$
8: $ApproxSet \leftarrow ApproxSet'$
9: **while** OPENISNOTEMPTY() **do**
10:     $s \leftarrow Open.popFront()$
11:     **for all** $t \in$ GETSUCCESSORS(s) **do**
12:         STOREORCOMBINE($t, 1$)

Algorithm 6. ELIM-NO-PREDECESSORS

1: $mode \leftarrow$ **Elim-No-Predecessors**
2: $ApproxSet' \leftarrow \emptyset$
3: **for all** $s \in ApproxSet$ **do**
4:     **if** $ApproxSet.getAppendix(s) = 0$ **then**
5:         $Open.pushBack(s)$
6:     **else**
7:         $ApproxSet' \leftarrow ApproxSet' \cup \{s\}$
8: $ApproxSet \leftarrow ApproxSet'$
9: **while** OPENISNOTEMPTY() **do**
10:     $s \leftarrow Open.popFront()$
11:     **for all** $t \in$ GETSUCCESSORS(s) **do**
12:         STOREORCOMBINE($t, -1$)

Algorithm 7. INITIALIZE-APPROXSET

1: $mode \leftarrow$ **Elim-No-Accepting**
2: $Candidates \leftarrow \emptyset$
3: $s \leftarrow$ GETINITIALVERTEX()
4: $ApproxSet \leftarrow \{s\}$
5: **if** $\neg$ISACCEPTING(s) **then**
6:     $Open.pushBack(s)$
7:     **while** OPENISNOTEMPTY() **do**
8:         $s \leftarrow Open.popFront()$
9:         **for all** $t \in$ GETSUCCESSORS(s) **do**
10:             **if** ISACCEPTING(t) **then**
11:                 $ApproxSet \leftarrow ApproxSet \cup \{t\}$
12:             **else**
13:                 STOREORCOMBINE($t, 0$)

allowed to explore descendants of non-accepting vertices only. See the pseudo-code given as Algorithm 7.

3   Complexity Analysis

A widely accepted model for the analysis of the complexity of I/O algorithms is the model of Aggarwal and Vitter [1], where the complexity of an I/O algorithm is measured in terms of the numbers of external I/O operations only. This is motivated by the fact that a single I/O operation is by approximately six orders of magnitude slower than a computation step performed in the main memory [34]. Therefore, an algorithm that does not perform the optimal amount of work but has a lower I/O complexity, may be faster in practice compared to an algorithm that performs the optimal amount of work, but has a higher I/O complexity. The complexity of an I/O algorithm in the model of Aggarwal and Vitter is further parametrized by M, B, and D, where M denotes the number of items that fits into the internal memory, B denotes the number of items that can be transferred in a single I/O operation, and D denotes the number of blocks that can be transferred in parallel, i.e. the number of independent parallel disks available. The abbreviations $sort(n)$ and $scan(n)$ stand for $\theta(N/(DB)log_{M/B}(N/B))$ and $\theta(N/(DB))$, respectively. In this section we give the I/O complexity of our algorithm and compare it with the complexity of the algorithm from [14].

We use the following notation. *BFS tree* is a tree given by the graph traversal from the initial set of vertices in the breadth-first order. Its height h_{BFS} is called *BFS height*, its levels are called *BFS levels*. *SCC graph* is a directed acyclic graph, whose vertices are maximal strongly connected components of the graph and the edges are given according to the reachability relation between the components. Let l_{SCC} denote the length of the longest path in the SCC graph. The I/O complexity of the algorithm is given in Theorem 1. The proof of the complexity can be found in the full version of the paper [6].

Theorem 1. *The I/O complexity of algorithm* DETECTACCEPTINGCYCLE *is*

$$\mathcal{O}(l_{SCC} \cdot (h_{BFS} + |p_{max}| + |E|/M) \cdot scan(|V|)),$$

where p_{max} is the longest path in the graph going through trivial strongly connected components (without self-loops).

For the purpose of comparison we denote our new algorithm as *DAC* and the algorithm of Edelkamp and Jabbar [14] as *EJ*. Theorem 1 of [14] claims that *EJ* is able to detect accepting cycles with I/O complexity $\mathcal{O}(sort(|F||E|) + l \cdot scan(|F||V|))$, where $|F|$ is the number of accepting states and l is the length of the shortest counterexample.

The complexity of *EJ* is not easy to compare with our results, because the two algorithms use different ways to maintain the set of candidates. The candidate set can be either stored externally (*EJ*) or internally (*DAC*). In the case that the candidate set is stored externally, it is possible to perform the merge operation on a BFS level independently of the size of the main memory. Therefore, this approach is suitable for those cases where memory is small or the graph is by orders of magnitude larger. The disadvantage of the approach is that it needs *sort* operations and it cannot be combined with heuristics, such as bit-state hashing and a lossy hash table [16]. Fortunately, both *EJ* and *DAC* are modular enough to be able to work in both modes. Table 1 gives I/O complexities of all four variants, where *EJ'* denotes algorithm *EJ* modified so that the candidate set is kept in the internal memory, and *DAC'* denotes algorithm *DAC* modified so that the candidate set is stored externally.

Table 1. I/O complexity of algorithms for both modes of storage of the candidate set

Candidate set in the main memory:

EJ'	$\mathcal{O}((l + |F||E|/M) \cdot scan(|F||V|))$
DAC	$\mathcal{O}(l_{SCC} \cdot (h_{BFS} + |p_{max}| + |E|/M) \cdot scan(|V|))$

Candidate set in the external memory:

EJ	$\mathcal{O}(l \cdot scan(|F||V|) + sort(|F||E|))$
DAC'	$\mathcal{O}(l_{SCC} \cdot ((h_{BFS} + |p_{max}|) \cdot scan(|V|) + sort(|E|)))$

In the worst case the values of l_{SCC}, $|p_{max}|$, and h_{BFS} are equal to $|V|$. Thus the worst case I/O complexity of *DAC* is better than that of *EJ'* and the worst case I/O complexity of *DAC'* is equal to that of *EJ*, provided that $l = |V|$ and $|F| = |V|$.

Note that for graphs of verified systems the numbers l_{SCC}, $|p_{max}|$, and h_{BFS} are typically smaller by several orders of magnitude than the number of vertices. l_{SCC} (giving the upper bound to the number of iterations of the loop of Algorithm 1) usually ranges from 1 to 20 [15]. h_{BFS} is not proportional to the size of the state space and oscillates around several hundreds [27], so the $|p_{max}|$ according to our own measurements. However, the number of accepting vertices (F) is quite often in the same order of magnitude as the number of vertices. Therefore, *EJ'* and *EJ* suffer from the graph blow-up and perform much more I/O operations compared to *DAC* and *DAC'*, respectively. On the other hand, *EJ'* and *EJ* work on-the-fly and can thus outperform *DAC* and *DAC'* on the graphs with small number of accepting vertices and short counterexamples. Nevertheless, short counterexamples are also easy to find using on-the-fly internal memory model checkers which outperform both external memory approaches.

Regarding space complexity, *DAC* is more space efficient than *EJ*. Since *EJ'* needs to remember all visited pairs of vertices, where a pair consists of one accepting and one arbitrary vertex, the space complexity of the algorithm is $\mathcal{O}(|F||V|)$, i.e. asymptotically quadratic in the size of the graph. On the other hand, the space complexity of *DAC* is $\mathcal{O}(|V|)$, as it only maintains the approximation set, queue and the candidate set whose sizes are always bounded by the number of vertices. The same holds for the pair *EJ* and *DAC'*.

4   Experimental Evaluation

In order to obtain experimental evidence about how our algorithm behaves in practice, we implemented both algorithms and compared them mutually as well as with the model checker SPIN with all the default reduction techniques (including partial order) turned on.

Algorithm *DetectAcceptingCycle* (*DAC*) has been implemented upon DiVinE Library [5], providing the state space generator, and STXXL Library [13], providing the necessary I/O primitives. Algorithm *EJ* was implemented as a procedure that performs the graph transformation as suggested in [14] and then employs I/O efficient breadth-first search to check for the counterexample. Note that our implementation of [14] does not have the A^* heuristics and so it can be less efficient in the search for the counterexample. The procedure is referred to as *Liveness as Safety with BFS* (*LaS-BFS*).

We have measured run times and a memory consumption of SPIN, *LaS-BFS* and *DAC* on a collection of systems and their LTL properties taken from the BEEM project [28]. The models were selected so that the state spaces generated by SPIN and DiVinE were exactly of the same size. The experimental results are listed in Table 2. Note that just before the unsuccessful termination of *LaS-BFS* due to exhausting the disk space the size of BFS levels exhibited growing

Table 2. Run times and memory consumption on a single workstation with 2 GB of RAM and 60 GB of available hard disk space. The time is given in `hh:mm:ss` format.

		SPIN		LaS-BFS		DAC	
	States	Time	RAM	Time	Disk	Time	Disk
Phils(16,1),P3	61,230,206	Out of memory		Out of disk space		02:01:11	5.5 GB
MCS(5),P4	119,663,657	Out of memory		Out of disk space		03:32:41	8 GB
Szymanski(5),P4	419,183,762	Out of memory		Out of disk space		44:49:36	32 GB
Elevator2(16),P4	76,824,540	Out of memory		Out of disk space		11:37:57	9.2 GB
Leader Fil.(7),P2	431,401,020	00:01:35	1369 MB	Out of disk space		32:03:52	42 GB

Valid properties on large models.

		SPIN		LaS-BFS		DAC	
	States	Time	RAM	Time	Disk	Time	Disk
Lamport(3),P4	56,377	00:00:01	18 MB	00:55:34	799 MB	00:00:19	6,1 MB
Anderson(4),P2	58,205	00:00:01	20 MB	00:11:11	153 MB	00:00:18	6,1 MB
Peterson(4),P4	2,239,039	00:00:08	85 MB	Out of disk space		00:04:44	159 MB

Valid properties on small models.

		SPIN		LaS-BFS		DAC	
	States	Time	RAM	Time	Disk	Time	Disk
Bakery(5,5),P3	506,246,410	00:00:01	16 MB	01:34:13	5,4 GB	69:27:58	38 GB
Szymanski(4),P2	4,555,287	00:00:01	18 MB	00:59:00	203 MB	00:19:55	205 MB
Elevator2(7),P5	43,776	00:00:01	17 MB	00:01:15	121 MB	00:00:18	6,1 MB

Invalid properties.

tendency. This suggests that the computation would last substantially longer if sufficient disk space was available. For the same input graphs, algorithm *DAC* manage to perform the verification using a few GBs of space only.

Measurements on large systems with valid formulas demonstrate that *DAC* is able to successfully prove the correctness of systems, on which SPIN and *LaS-BFS* fail. However, there are systems and valid formulas, which take a long time to verify by our algorithm, but can be verified quickly using SPIN (e.g. model *Leader Filters*). This is due to the partial order reduction technique, which is extraordinarily efficient in this case. Results on small systems show the state space blow-up in case of *LaS-BFS*. E.g. on the model *Lamport*, 6,1 MB of disk space is enough for *DAC* to store the entire state space while *LaS-BFS* needs 799 MB. As for systems with invalid formulas, the new algorithm is slow, since it does not work on-the-fly. Nevertheless, it is able to finish if the state space fits in the external memory. Moreover, it is faster than *LaS-BFS* on systems with long counterexamples as the space space blow-up takes effect when *LaS-BFS* has to traverse a substantial part of the state space (e.g. model *Elevator2*).

In summary, the new algorithm is especially useful for verification of large systems with valid formulas where SPIN fails due to the limited size of the main memory and *LaS-BFS* runs out of the available external memory because of a large amount of accepting states. On systems with invalid formulas, algorithm *DAC* finishes if the state space fits in the external memory, but it may take quite a long time as it does not work on-the-fly.

5   Conclusions and Future Work

In this paper we presented a new I/O efficient algorithm for accepting cycle detection on implicitly given graphs. The algorithm exhibits linear space complexity while preserving practically reasonable I/O complexity. Another indirect contribution of the paper is that it introduces an I/O efficient procedure to compute the topological sort on implicitly given graphs (procedure ELIM-NO-PREDECESSORS).

Our experimental evaluation confirmed that the new algorithm is able to fully solve instances of the LTL model checking problem that cannot be solved either with the standard LTL model checker SPIN or using so far the best I/O efficient approach of Edelkamp and Jabbar [14]. The approach of [14] fails especially if the verified formula is valid, which is because after the transformation, the graph becomes too large to be kept even in the external memory.

On the other hand, unlike SPIN and the approach of [14] our algorithm does not work on-the-fly. The on-the-fly algorithms are particularly successful if the property is violated and the counterexample can be found early during the state space exploration.

As our algorithm is based on the algorithm which can be easily parallelized [10], it is straightforward to develop a parallel version of the algorithm that can further speed up verification of large systems. It also seems promising to design I/O efficient variants of other BFS-based verification algorithms [3,4,8,9,10].

Some of them work on-the-fly and hence could outperform both the new algorithm and the algorithm of Edelkamp and Jabbar.

An open problem for which we still do not know a practically good solution, is the inefficiency of the delayed duplicate detection technique as used in procedure ELIM-NO-PREDECESSORS. Since procedure MERGE is called every time a BFS level is explored, merging a small level into a large set can slow down the exploration speed of a few vertices per minute. The question is, if this can be avoided.

References

1. Aggarwal, A., Vitter, J.S.: The Input/Output Complexity of Sorting and Related Problems. Communications of the ACM 31(9), 1116–1127 (1988)
2. Barnat, J.: Distributed Memory LTL Model Checking. PhD thesis, Faculty of Informatics, Masaryk University Brno (2004)
3. Barnat, J., Brim, L., Chaloupka, J.: Parallel Breadth-First Search LTL Model-Checking. In: Automated Software Engineering (ASE'03), pp. 106–115. IEEE Computer Society Press, Los Alamitos (2003)
4. Barnat, J., Brim, L., Stříbrná, J.: Distributed LTL Model-Checking in SPIN. In: Dwyer, M.B. (ed.) Model Checking Software. LNCS, vol. 2057, pp. 200–216. Springer, Heidelberg (2001)
5. Barnat, J., Brim, L., Černá, I., Šimeček, P.: DiVinE – The Distributed Verification Environment. In: PDMC'05, pp. 89–94 (2005)
6. Barnat, J., Brim, L., Šimeček, P.: LTL Model Checking with I/O-Efficient Accepting Cycle Detection. Technical Report FIMU-RS-2007-01, Faculty of Informatics, Masaryk University (2007)
7. Biere, A., Artho, C., Schuppan, V.: Liveness Checking as Safety Checking. Electr. Notes Theor. Comput. Sci. 66(2) (2002)
8. Brim, L., Černá, I., Moravec, P., Šimša, J.: Accepting Predecessors are Better than Back Edges in Distributed LTL Model-Checking. In: Hu, A.J., Martin, A.K. (eds.) FMCAD 2004. LNCS, vol. 3312, pp. 352–366. Springer, Heidelberg (2004)
9. Brim, L., Černá, I., Krčál, P., Pelánek, R.: Distributed LTL Model Checking Based on Negative Cycle Detection. In: Hariharan, R., Mukund, M., Vinay, V. (eds.) FST TCS 2001: Foundations of Software Technology and Theoretical Computer Science. LNCS, vol. 2245, pp. 96–107. Springer, Heidelberg (2001)
10. Černá, I., Pelánek, R.: Distributed Explicit Fair Cycle Detection. In: Ball, T., Rajamani, S.K. (eds.) SPIN'03. LNCS, vol. 2648, pp. 49–73. Springer, Heidelberg (2003)
11. Chiang, Y., Goodrich, M., Grove, E., Tamassia, R., Vengroff, D., Vitter, J.: External-Memory Graph Algorithms. In: SODA'95, pp. 139–149. Society for Industrial and Applied Mathematics (1995)
12. Clarke Jr, E., Grumberg, O., Peled, D.: Model Checking. MIT press, Cambridge (1999)
13. Dementiev, R., Kettner, L., Sanders, P.: STXXL: Standard Template Library for XXL Data Sets. In: Brodal, G.S., Leonardi, S. (eds.) ESA 2005. LNCS, vol. 3669, pp. 640–651. Springer, Heidelberg (2005)
14. Edelkamp, S., Jabbar, S.: Large-Scale Directed Model Checking LTL. In: SPIN'06, pp. 1–18 (2006)

15. Fisler, K., Fraer, R., Kamhi, G., Vardi, M.Y., Yang, Z.: Is There a Best Symbolic Cycle-Detection Algorithm? In: Margaria, T., Yi, W. (eds.) ETAPS 2001 and TACAS 2001. LNCS, vol. 2031, pp. 420–434. Springer, Heidelberg (2001)
16. Hammer, M., Weber, M.: To Store Or Not To Store Reloaded: Reclaiming Memory On Demand. In: FMICS 2006 and PDMC 2006. LNCS, vol. 4346, pp. 51–66. Springer, Heidelberg (2006)
17. Holzmann, G.J., Peled, D., Yannakakis, M.: On Nested Depth First Search. In: The SPIN Verification System, pp. 23–32. American Mathematical Society (1996)
18. Jabbar, S., Edelkamp, S.: I/O Efficient Directed Model Checking. In: Cousot, R. (ed.) VMCAI 2005. LNCS, vol. 3385, pp. 313–329. Springer, Heidelberg (2005)
19. Jones, M., Mercer, E.: Explicit State Model Checking with Hopper. In: Graf, S., Mounier, L. (eds.) SPIN'04. LNCS, vol. 2989, pp. 146–150. Springer, Heidelberg (2004)
20. Katriel, I., Meyer, U.: Elementary Graph Algorithms in External Memory. In: Algorithms for Memory Hierarchies, pp. 62–84 (2002)
21. Korf, R.: Best-First Frontier Search with Delayed Duplicate Detection. In: AAAI'04, pp. 650–657. AAAI Press / The MIT Press, Cambridge, MA (2004)
22. Korf, R., Schultze, P.: Large-Scale Parallel Breadth-First Search. In: AAAI'05, pp. 1380–1385. AAAI Press / The MIT Press, Cambridge, MA (2005)
23. Kristensen, L., Mailund, T.: Efficient Path Finding with the Sweep-Line Method Using External Storage. In: Dong, J.S., Woodcock, J. (eds.) ICFEM 2003. LNCS, vol. 2885, pp. 319–337. Springer, Heidelberg (2003)
24. Kumar, V., Schwabe, E.: Improved Algorithms and Data Structures for Solving Graph Problems in External Memory. In: 8th IEEE Symposium on Parallel and Distributed Processing (SPDP'96), IEEE Computer Society Press, Los Alamitos (1996)
25. Mehlhorn, K., Meyer, U.: External-Memory Breadth-First Search with Sublinear I/O. In: Möhring, R.H., Raman, R. (eds.) ESA 2002. LNCS, vol. 2461, pp. 723–735. Springer, Heidelberg (2002)
26. Munagala, K., Ranade, A.: I/O-Complexity of Graph Algorithms. In: SODA'99, pp. 687–694, Philadelphia, PA, USA, Society for Industrial and Applied Mathematics (1999)
27. Pelánek, R.: Typical Structural Properties of State Spaces. In: Graf, S., Mounier, L. (eds.) SPIN'04. LNCS, vol. 2989, pp. 5–22. Springer, Heidelberg (2004)
28. Pelánek, R.: BEEM: BEnchmarks for Explicit Model checkers (February 2007) http://anna.fi.muni.cz/models/index.html
29. Ravi, K., Bloem, R., Somenzi, F.: A Comparative Study of Symbolic Algorithms for the Computation of Fair Cycles. In: Johnson, S.D., Hunt Jr., W.A. (eds.) FMCAD 2000. LNCS, vol. 1954, pp. 143–160. Springer, Heidelberg (2000)
30. Reif, J.H.: Depth-First Search is Inherrently Sequential. Information Processing Letters 20(5), 229–234 (1985)
31. Schuppan, V., Biere, A.: Efficient Reduction of Finite State Model Checking to Reachability Analysis. International Journal on Software Tools for Technology Transfer (STTT) 5(2–3), 185–204 (2004)
32. Stern, U., Dill, D.L.: Using Magnetic Disk Instead of Main Memory in the Murphi Verifier. In: CAV'98, pp. 172–183 (1998)
33. Vardi, M., Wolper, P.: An Automata-Theoretic Approach to Automatic Program Verification. In: Logic in Computer Science (LICS'86), pp. 332–344. IEEE Computer Society Press, Los Alamitos (1986)
34. Vitter, J.: External Memory Algorithms and Data Structures: Dealing with Massive Data. ACM Comput. Surv. 33(2), 209–271 (2001)

C32SAT: Checking C Expressions
(Tool Paper)

Robert Brummayer and Armin Biere

Institute for Formal Models and Verification
Johannes Kepler University Linz, Austria
{robert.brummayer,armin.biere}@jku.at

Abstract. C32SAT is a tool for checking C expressions. It can check whether a given C expression can be satisfied, is tautological, or always defined according to the ISO C99 standard. C32SAT can be used to detect nonportable expressions where program behavior depends on the compiler. Our contribution consists of C32SAT's functional representation and the way it handles undefined values. Under-approximation is used as optimization.

1   Introduction

Formal verification of C programs is an active area of research [6,7,8,11]. C32SAT[1] addresses a verification problem not explicitly considered by other verification tools. It detects situations where, according to the C99 standard [9], the behavior upon an operation on certain values is undefined, e.g. the behavior upon dividing an integer by zero. The C99 standard [9] describes undefined behavior as "behavior, upon use of a nonportable or erroneous program construct or of erroneous data, for which this International Standard imposes no requirements" [9]. The execution of such an undefined operation ranges from ignoring the situation to terminating the execution in the worst case.

In contrast to other programming languages, e.g. Java, there are many cases in the C programming language where undefined behavior can occur. This situation makes it hard to write secure and portable programs where the behavior is fully defined and does not depend on compiler semantics.

If the behavior upon an operation is undefined, then C32SAT raises a flag that marks the result to be *undefined*. This flag propagates and can only be masked out by short circuit evaluation of the logical conjunction &&, logical disjunction || and the conditional operator ?:. Note that except for these three operations the order of evaluation of subexpressions is undefined as in the C99 standard.

C32SAT takes as input one C expression. It can check whether it can be satisfied, is tautological or always defined according to the C99 standard. C32SAT supports all main C operators, including multiplication, division and modulo. Additionally, C32SAT supports logical implication and equivalence. Pointer related operators are scheduled as future work.

---

[1] http://fmv.jku.at/c32sat/

W. Damm and H. Hermanns (Eds.): CAV 2007, LNCS 4590, pp. 294–297, 2007.

2   System Architecture

The core of C32SAT version 1.4 consists of approximately 7500 lines of C code. Figure 1 shows the core components of C32SAT. The frontend mainly consists of the components `Parser` and `Parse Tree`. The remaining components are part of the backend. The architecture is similar to that of a compiler except that the backend generates a Conjunctive Normal Form (CNF) instead of machine code.

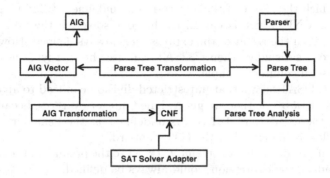

Fig. 1. Core architecture of C32SAT

3   Internal Functionality

C32SAT treats the type of every variable as *signed* integer. The bit width $w \in \{4, 8, 16, 32, 64\}$ can be globally configured. A variable is internally represented by a vector of And-Inverter Graphs (AIGs) [10] where every AIG represents exactly one bit.

Each C operator is mapped to a circuit that takes the AIG vector operands as input. For example the result of the word level XOR operator ^ is an AIG vector where the AIG vectors of the operands are bitwise combined by boolean XOR. This functional representation is in contrast to COGENT [8], which uses a relational representation. Our approach allows the application of sophisticated circuit simplification techniques like local two-level AIG rewriting [4] and the application of structural SAT solvers.

Every integer is actually represented by $w + 1$ AIGs. The additional AIG represents the *undefined* value. In general an expression is undefined when a subexpression is undefined. The only exception is short-circuit evaluation of &&, || and ?:.

Regarding C32SAT's set of operators the result of every operation is either fully defined or fully undefined. It is never the case that only a part of the bits is undefined while the remaining bits are defined. Therefore, C32SAT handles undefined values on the AIG vector level and not on the AIG level.

The general flow of C32SAT is the following. C32SAT parses the input expression and builds a parse tree, which is analyzed and transformed into an AIG. Afterwards, the AIG is transformed into Conjunctive Normal Form (CNF) using

Tseitin Transformation [12] and passed to a SAT solver. Alternatively, the AIG can be dumped in the AIGER [2] format.

The default SAT solver of C32SAT is PicoSAT [2]. Additionally, C32SAT supports the SAT solvers NanoSAT [1], BooleForce and CompSAT [3] [3]. The SAT solver computes if the CNF is satisfiable or not and returns a model in the satisfiable case. C32SAT uses this model to generate a word level model, which is printed out as part of the result. As an example consider the C expression y != 0 => x / y. We want to determine if there exists an assignment to x and y, for which the result of the expression is undefined. C32SAT generates a corresponding CNF, which is passed to the SAT solver. If the SAT instance is unsatisfiable, then the result of the expression is always defined. However, if the SAT instance is satisfiable, then C32SAT can use the satisfying assignment to generate a useful counter example.

Actually, C32SAT shows that unrestricted division can lead to an overflow. If we divide INT_MIN by -1, then we get a signed integer overflow, because in two's complement the negation of INT_MIN is undefined, as the behavior upon signed integer overflow is undefined in the C99 standard.

Note that if we added the constraint y != -1 to the premise of the implication, then the result of the expression would always be defined.

4   Under-Approximation Optimization

Inspired by [5], we added an under-approximation optimization technique to the latest version of C32SAT. Instead of encoding an n-bit integer variable with n AIGs, we simply restrict the number of AIGs used for encoding. For example we encode a 32 bit integer variable in the following way. We represent the least significant bit by one AIG variable and all other bits by another. This AIG vector represents the values from -2 to 1 instead of -2147483648 to 2147483647.

If the under-approximated SAT instance is satisfiable, then also the original formula is satisfied by the same assignment. However, if the under-approximated SAT instance is unsatisfiable, then the approximation has to be refined. In this case C32SAT doubles the precision of the under-approximation. In the worst case no satisfying assignment can be found during under-approximation and C32SAT has to generate the full CNF.

Using this under-approximation technique leads to smaller AIGs. This results in a smaller CNF, which is typically easier to solve. Beside speeding up the search for satisfying assignments, the under-approximation technique produces assignments that are easier to interpret.

5   Conclusion

We presented C32SAT, a tool for checking C expressions. It can be used to detect nonportable expressions where program behavior depends on the compiler.

---

[2] http://fmv.jku.at/aiger/

[3] The SAT solvers are available at http://fmv.jku.at/software/

We presented C32SAT's functional representation, the way it handles undefined values and its under-approximation optimization technique. As future work we want to support pointers and over-approximation techniques.

References

1. Biere, A.: The evolution from LIMMAT to NANOSAT. Technical Report 444, Dept. Computer Science, ETH Zürich (2004)
2. Biere, A.: Occurrence lists for 2-watched literal schemes (submitted)
3. Biere, A., Sinz, C.: Decomposing sat problems into connected components. Journal on Satisfiability, Boolean Modeling and Computation (JSAT), 2 (2006)
4. Brummayer, R., Biere, A.: Local two-level And-Inverter Graph minimization without blowup. In: Proceedings of the 2nd Doctoral Workshop on Mathematical and Engineering Methods in Computer Science (MEMICS'06) (2006)
5. Bryant, R.E., Kroening, D., Ouaknine, J., Seshia, S.A., Strichman, O., Brady, B.: Deciding bit-vector arithmetic with abstraction. In: Proceedings of TACAS 2007, Springer, Heidelberg (to appear)
6. Clarke, E., Kroening, D., Lerda, F.: A tool for checking ANSI-C programs. In: Jensen, K., Podelski, A. (eds.) TACAS 2004. LNCS, vol. 2988, pp. 168–176. Springer, Heidelberg (2004)
7. Clarke, E., Kroening, D., Sharygina, N., Yorav, K.: SATABS: SAT-based predicate abstraction for ANSI-C. In: Halbwachs, N., Zuck, L.D. (eds.) TACAS 2005. LNCS, vol. 3440, pp. 570–574. Springer, Heidelberg (2005)
8. Cook, B., Kroening, D., Sharygina, N.: Cogent: Accurate theorem proving for program verification. In: Etessami, K., Rajamani, S.K. (eds.) CAV 2005. LNCS, vol. 3576, pp. 296–300. Springer, Heidelberg (2005)
9. ISO/IEC. Programming languages - C (ISO/IEC 9899:1999(E)) (1999)
10. Kuehlmann, A., Paruthi, V., Krohm, F., Ganai, M.K.: Robust boolean reasoning for equivalence checking and functional property verification. IEEE Trans. on CAD of Integrated Circuits and Systems 21(12), 1377–1394 (2002)
11. Sethi, N., Barret, C.: Cascade: C assertion checker and deductive engine. In: Ball, T., Jones, R.B. (eds.) CAV 2006. LNCS, vol. 4144, pp. 166–169. Springer, Heidelberg (2006)
12. Tseitin, G.S.: On the complexity of derivation in the propositional calculus. Studies in constructive mathematics and mathematical logic, pp. 115–125 (1968)

CVC3

(Tool Paper)

Clark Barrett[1] and Cesare Tinelli[2]

[1] New York University
barrett@cs.nyu.edu
[2] University of Iowa
tinelli@cs.uiowa.edu

Abstract. CVC3, a joint project of NYU and U Iowa, is the new and latest version of the Cooperating Validity Checker. CVC3 extends and builds on the functionality of its predecessors and includes many new features such as support for additional theories, an abstract architecture for Boolean reasoning, and SMT-LIB compliance. We describe the system and discuss some applications and continuing work.

1 Introduction

Like its predecessors, SVC [5], CVC [12], and CVC Lite [1], CVC3 is an automatic theorem prover for the *Satisfiability Modulo Theories* (SMT) problem: given an input formula ϕ in first order logic, CVC3 attempts to determine the validity (or dually, the satisfiability) of ϕ with respect to one or more background theories.

CVC3 builds on the architecture and features of the successful CVC and CVC Lite systems, but it also differs in important ways. First of all, the project is under new management: it is being developed at NYU and the University of Iowa (unlike its predecessors, all of which were hosted at Stanford University). Second, the system is mature enough now that it seemed best to drop the "Lite" moniker. It is called CVC3 because it is the third major release of a system with the CVC name. Most importantly, many new features have been added and most of the code has been revised or rewritten. For these reasons, a new major release and accompanying system description seemed appropriate.

2 System Description

A high-level view of CVC3's architecture is shown in Fig. 1. CVC3 provides several different user interfaces including high-level API's for both C and C++, an interactive command-driven interface, and a file interface. The Main API supports two main types of operations: formula creation and methods for validity/satisfiability checking. The main deduction engine is called the Search Engine. Its role is to link the Boolean reasoning capabilities of the DPLL engine with the theory reasoning capabilities of the Theory Solver. The DPLL engine relies on a Boolean SAT solver to do its work and the Theory Solver relies on a set of decision procedures, one for each supported theory.

W. Damm and H. Hermanns (Eds.): CAV 2007, LNCS 4590, pp. 298–302, 2007.
© Springer-Verlag Berlin Heidelberg 2007

Because of space limitations, we focus on new features in this paper, referring the reader to previous work for a discussion of the more basic features of the system. The new features can be broadly partitioned into three categories: the search engine, new theories, and enhanced usability.

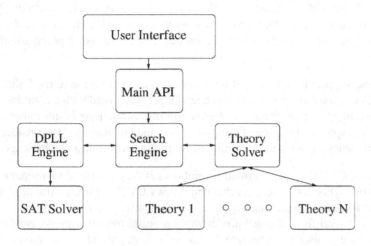

Fig. 1. CVC3 System design

2.1   The Search Engine

CVC3 features a new Search Engine. The Search Engine processes incoming queries, first using standard techniques to convert them into equisatisfiable formulas in conjunctive normal form. The Boolean structure is then fed to the DPLL Engine. One of the primary reasons for developing a new Search Engine was to make it easy to plug in different implementations of the DPLL Engine. To do this, a simple abstract API was developed based on the Extended Abstract DPLL Modulo Theories framework [3]. Ideas developed in this theoretical framework, such as theory propagation and splitting on demand, made it possible to implement a simple API that was rich enough to be practical and efficient. Implementations of this API are largely shielded from the rest of the system and communicate with the Search Engine using a simple minimal interface which references only basic data-structures for Boolean variables, literals, and clauses.

One measure of success is that we were quickly able to integrate two different SAT solvers. In fact, our experience has been that the main difficulty is not in implementing the API, but in adapting the SAT solvers to support necessary features like dynamic addition of clauses and variables. The SAT solvers currently available in CVC3 are zchaff [11] and MiniSat [7]. Another measure of success is that with the new Search Engine, CVC3 outperforms CVC Lite on nearly all benchmarks, typically by a factor of 2 or 3, but up to an order of magnitude on benchmarks with significant Boolean structure.

2.2   New Theories

Abstract Data Types. While its predecessors could reason about simple aggregate data types like records and tuples, CVC3 has the ability to reason about arbitrary recursive and mutually recursive data types. A simple example of a recursive data type is the *list* type from LISP with constructors *null* and *cons* and selectors *car* and *cdr*. A simple example of a query that CVC3 can solve over this type is: $\forall x : list. x = null \lor \exists yz. x = cons(y,z)$. The implementation is based on our abstract decision procedure described in [4].

Bitvectors. Support for a theory of bitvectors was a late addition to the CVC Lite system. In CVC3, the bitvector theory has been largely reworked with a resulting substantial improvement in performance. However, the implementation is still rather naive and based on a simple combination of pre-processing and bit-blasting. We consider improving the efficiency of bitvector reasoning to be an important research challenge.

Quantifiers. CVC3 treats quantified formulas as if they belonged to a separate "quantifier" theory. This convenient mechanism allows CVC3 to use a special strategy for quantified formulas: existential formulas are skolemized and then passed back to the main theory solver for additional processing; universal formulas are accumulated and a set of heuristics is used to instantiate the formulas with ground terms from other literals known to the theory solver. CVC3 contains a new instantiation mechanism that extends the "matching" techniques of the Simplify theorem prover [6]. CVC3 is significantly better than CVC Lite on formulas with quantifiers and our experiments on the SMT-LIB benchmarks indicate that it can solve more problems than other instantiation-based systems [9].

2.3   Enhanced Usability

SMT-LIB. In order to support the SMT-LIB initiative, a powerful translation module was added to CVC Lite. It has been updated and improved in CVC3. This module is capable of translating benchmarks to and from the SMT-LIB format. The most difficult part of this is inferring the correct SMT-LIB logic based on syntactic properties of the benchmark. CVC3 has been used to verify the correct logic categorization of all benchmarks currently in the SMT-LIB library, and it is currently the standard for checking the syntax and categorization of new benchmarks submitted to the library.

Model Generation. An important feature of CVC3 is that it can produce concrete models after a satisfiable query. For example, instead of reporting $x \neq y$, CVC3 can assign actual values to x and y, such as $x = 0$ and $y = 1$. This is useful for tools that use CVC3 as a back-end and need to provide meaningful feedback to the user. It should be mentioned that this feature was already present in CVC Lite, but it was added after the system description was published and so is worth emphasizing here.

Incremental Use. It has always been possible to use the CVC tools incrementally using a stack-based push and pop mechanism. Several new features have been added to aid incremental use. First of all, the Minisat implementation of the DPLL Engine has been enhanced to be incremental. This means that it is possible to reuse lemmas learned from one query in another related query. Second, it is possible to search for additional models after a model has been found by using a "continue" command. Finally, it is also possible to search for models that satisfy an additional assumption. This is implemented with a command called "restart". The restart command is is useful for refining abstractions and has been implemented in such a way that the work done in finding the first model can be reused, which is important for efficiency.

3 Conclusion

CVC3 aims to continue the tradition of its predecessors by providing a free, robust, automatic, and feature-rich tool suitable for a variety of research and industrial applications. Some applications of previous versions of CVC include a proof-producing decision procedure for HOL Light [10]; a verification tool for C programs [8], a translation validator for optimizing compilers [2], and a study on the verification of clock synchronization algorithms [13].

We expect that these and similar future applications will find CVC3 even more useful. In particular, we currently have collaborations in place with research groups at the University of Dublin, Microsoft Research, and Rockwell-Collins on using CVC3 respectively within an extended static checker for Java, an automated unit test generator for .NET programs, and a model checker for programs written in the dataflow language Lustre.

There is still much that we plan to do to improve CVC3. Current work includes improvements to the arithmetic, bitvector, and quantifier theories. New theories under consideration include a theory of strings, a theory of sets, and a theory of subtypes. One important enhancement we expect to make soon is to allow user-defined symbols to have polymorphic types. We also plan to improve the current support for proofs and models. Finally, of course, we would like to continue to improve overall performance of the system.

CVC3 has an active user and development community. More information, including instructions for downloading and installing the tool, can be found on the CVC3 web site at http://www.cs.nyu.edu/acsys/cvc3.

References

1. Barrett, C., Berezin, S.: CVC Lite: A new implementation of the cooperating validity checker. In: CAV, pp. 515–518 (2004)
2. Barrett, C., Fang, Y., Goldberg, B., Hu, Y., Pnueli, A., Zuck, L.: TVOC: A translation validator for optimizing compilers. In: CAV, pp. 291–295 (2005)
3. Barrett, C., Nieuwenhuis, R., Oliveras, A., Tinelli, C.: Splitting on demand in SAT modulo theories. In: LPAR (2006)
4. Barrett, C., Shikanian, I., Tinelli, C.: An abstract decision procedure for satisfiability in the theory of recursive data types. In: PDPAR (2006)
5. Barrett, C.W., Dill, D.L., Levitt, J.R.: Validity checking for combinations of theories with equality. In: FMCAD, pp. 187–201 (1996)

6. Detlefs, D.L., Nelson, G., Saxe, J.B.: Simplify: A theorem-prover for program checking. Technical Report HPL-2003-148, HP System Research Center (2003)
7. Eén, N., Sörensson, N.: An extensible sat-solver. In: SAT (2003)
8. Filliâtre, J.-C., Marché, C.: Multi-Prover Verification of C Programs. In: ICFEM, pp. 15–29 (2004)
9. Ge, Y., Barrett, C., Tinelli, C.: Solving quantified verification condisions using satisfiability modulo theories. In: CADE July 2007 (to appear)
10. McLaughlin, S., Barrett, C., Ge, Y.: Cooperating theorem provers: A case study combining HOL-Light and CVC Lite. In: PDPAR, pp. 43–51 (2006)
11. Moskewicz, M.W., Madigan, C.F., Zhao, Y., Zhang, L., Malik, S.: Chaff: Engineering an Efficient SAT Solver. In: DAC (2001)
12. Stump, A., Barrett, C.W., Dill, D.L.: CVC: A cooperating validity checker. In: CAV, pp. 500–504 (2002)
13. Tiu, A., Barsotti, D., Prensa, L.: Verification of clock synchronization algorithms: Experiments on a combination of deductive tools. In: AVOCS (2005)

BAT: The Bit-Level Analysis Tool[*]
(Tool Paper)

Panagiotis Manolios[1], Sudarshan K. Srinivasan[2], and Daron Vroon[1]

[1] College of Computing
[2] School of Electrical & Computer Engineering
Georgia Institute of Technology
Atlanta, GA-30313
manolios@cc.gatech.edu, darshan@ece.gatech.edu,
vroon@cc.gatech.edu

Abstract. While effective methods for bit-level verification of low-level properties exist, system-level properties that entail reasoning about a significant part of the design pose a major verification challenge. We present the Bit-level Analysis Tool (BAT), a state-of-the-art decision procedure for bit-level reasoning that implements a novel collection of techniques targeted towards enabling the verification of system-level properties. Key features of the BAT system are an expressive strongly-typed modeling and specification language, a fully automatic and efficient memory abstraction algorithm for extensional arrays, and a novel CNF generation algorithm. The BAT system can be used to automatically solve system-level RTL verification problems that were previously intractable, such as refinement-based verification of RTL-level pipelined machines.

1 Introduction

The Bit-level Analysis Tool (BAT) [5] is a system for verifying bit-level problems arising from hardware, software, and security domains. BAT implements a state-of-the-art decision procedure for solving quantifier-free formulas over the extensional theory of fixed-size bit-vectors and fixed-size bit-vector arrays (memories). BAT is a publicly available tool that can be downloaded from the BAT Webpage [5].

Our primary goal in developing BAT is to enable the verification of high-level properties of complex systems described at the bit-level, such as the verification of bit-level pipelined machine models. We have been able to use BAT to verify a 32-bit 5 stage pipelined machine in approximately 2 minutes [4]. Key features of BAT that enable the verification of complex systems such as pipelined machines are a fully automatic and efficient algorithm for abstracting bit-level memories [4] and a novel method for generating CNF (Conjunctive Normal Form) from a high-level circuit representation [6].

2 The BAT Specification Language

The BAT specification language is a strongly typed, Lisp-like language whose types include bit-vectors, bit-vector memories, and sequences over these types (multiple value

---

[*] This research was funded in part by NSF grants CCF-0429924, IIS-0417413, and CCF-0438871.

W. Damm and H. Hermanns (Eds.): CAV 2007, LNCS 4590, pp. 303–306, 2007.

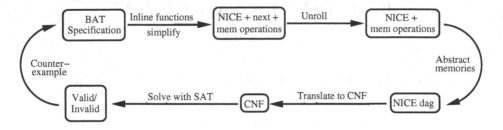

Fig. 1. The Bit-level Analysis Tool (BAT) decision procedure

types). We invested much effort in designing a powerful, general, and usable language that can be the target for synthesizable subsets of VHDL or Verilog. The language also allows for a clear separation of concerns between models and specifications, a feature that drastically simplifies the effort required to describe system-level properties of complex hardware models such as pipelined machines.

An important feature of the BAT language is that memories are treated as first class objects. Memories can be compared for equality and inequality in all contexts, and they can be passed as arguments to functions and returned by functions. Other key features of the language include a type inference algorithm that can determine the type of any expression; this alone finds many silly mistakes, especially when one is experimenting with parametrized modes. The language allows users to define functions that can be used not only to model systems, but to specify their correctness. BAT also provides multiple value types, *i.e.*, users can create a sequence of any types. Finally, BAT provides support for easily defining parametrized models.

The BAT language supports a variety of bit-vector operations including bit-vector comparisons such as equality, less than, and greater than; various types of shift operations; arithmetic operations including modular and machine addition, subtraction, and multiplication; bitwise operations such as bitwise conjunction, disjunction, negation, implication. The language also supports temporal operators AG and AF. Applicative functions for reading and updating memories are also supported.

3   The BAT Decision Procedure

BAT can be used as a decision procedure, a bounded model checker, or as a k-induction engine. BAT takes a specification described using the BAT language as input, and compiles this specification to a SAT problem in four high-level steps. The SAT problem is then checked with a SAT solver. If a bug is found, BAT generates a counterexample in terms of the original BAT specification. The compilation to CNF is performed using a novel data structure for representing circuits, known as the NICE dag, because it contains Negations, Ites, Conjunctions, and Equivalences.

We now describe the four high-level compilation steps. First, BAT inlines functions, propagates constants, and performs a simplification step to transform the original specification to a NICE dag extended with *next* operators (used to specify the transition relation) and memory operators. Second, the transition relation is unrolled, resulting in a NICE dag extended with memory operations. Third, the memories are abstracted using BAT's memory reduction algorithm and the memory operations for the resulting reduced memories are replaced with their equivalent Boolean circuits, resulting in a NICE dag. Fourth, the NICE dag is translated to a SAT problem in CNF. Note that BAT can make a decision after any of the above steps. For example, during simplification, BAT may simplify the problem to true or false.

3.1 Memory Abstraction

BAT implements a sound, complete, fully automatic, and efficient memory abstraction algorithm that can deal with an extensional theory of finite bit-vector memories [4]. The use of memory abstraction is crucial in bit-level verification problems as the presence of large memories would otherwise lead to intractable SAT problems.

The key idea of the BAT memory abstraction algorithm is to reduce memories to manageable sizes in a sound and complete way. This is possible because, even for very large memories, correctness conditions tend to refer to only a relatively small collection of memory references, which can be to any part of memory, however.

The complexity of the resulting verification problem depends heavily on the size of the abstracted memory, which is based on the number of unique memory accesses. Our memory abstraction algorithm includes term-rewriting techniques that are very effective in simplifying expressions containing memory operations. This allows us to recognize when syntactically distinct expressions correspond to the same memory address, which leads to more efficient memory abstractions and eventually to simpler SAT problems.

We deal with extensionality by keeping the abstract memories around. The intuition is that this allows us to compare memories for equality or inequality by comparing the abstract memories directly. To make this sound and efficient, a more sophisticated analysis is required, which is presented in our previous work on memory abstraction [4].

3.2 Efficient Translation to CNF

BAT uses a novel and efficient approach to generate SAT problems based on the use of NICE dags, a new data structure for representing circuits [6]. This is an important problem because, while modern SAT solvers have become proficient at solving Boolean satisfiability problems in CNF, these problems mostly arise from general Boolean circuits that are then translated to CNF. Furthermore, the CNF translation algorithm can significantly impact verification times. Experimental evaluation based on over 8,000 benchmarks showed that our CNF generation algorithm leads to significant time savings over both the widely used Tseitin algorithm [7] and Jackson and Sheridan's state-of-the-art algorithm [2]. For example, Minisat2 was able to handle all the SAT problems generated by the BAT CNF translation algorithm, whereas, it timed out on many of the SAT problems generated by both the Tseitin and Jackson/Sheridan algorithms.

4 Applications

BAT is the first bit-level reasoning tool that has been used successfully to verify non-trivial bit-level pipelined machines automatically [4]. Pipelined machine verification entails showing that the pipelined machine refines its instruction set architecture. This is a computationally demanding problem as it requires reasoning about a large part of the control logic of the system. The problem also involves comparing large memories for equality. With previous work, it was only possible to automatically solve pipelined machine verification problems at the term-level.

Using BAT we have been able to prove automatically that a 32-bit 5 stage pipelined machine refines its ISA in about 125 seconds. Other state-of-the-art tools that we have tried, including Yices [1] (winner of the 2006 SMT competition), cannot solve simple 2-stage pipelined machine problems. Such problems can be solved with BAT in less than a second. We have also been able to use BAT in a compositional verification flow to check complex pipelined machines with as many as 10 stages [3].

5   Conclusions

We have presented the Bit-level Analysis Tool (BAT), a state-of-the-art decision procedure for bit-level reasoning. We have used BAT to solve system-level verification problems, including the verification of pipelined machine which cannot be handled by other verification tools. For example, BAT can be used to verify that a 32-bit 5-stage pipelined machine model refines its instruction set architecture in approximately 2 minutes. The BAT language is feature-rich and enables users to effectively model systems and to specify properties. From an algorithm point of view, we described two key advances that are implemented in BAT. One is an efficient, automatic, sound, and complete memory abstraction algorithm for extensional arrays that is further improved with term-rewriting techniques. The second is a novel circuit to CNF conversion algorithm that provides significant improvements over other available CNF conversion algorithms. For future work, we plan to extend BAT with a counterexample guided abstraction-refinement framework, explore the use of more advanced term-rewriting techniques, and consider methods for automatically abstracting data paths.

References

[1] Dutertre, B., de Moura, L.M.: A fast linear-arithmetic solver for DPLL(T). In: Ball, T., Jones, R.B. (eds.) CAV 2006. LNCS, vol. 4144, pp. 81–94. Springer, Heidelberg (2006)
[2] Jackson, P., Sheridan, D.: Clause form conversions for boolean circuits. In: Hoos, H.H., Mitchell, D.G. (eds.) SAT 2004. LNCS, vol. 3542, pp. 183–198. Springer, Heidelberg (2005)
[3] Manolios, P., Srinivasan, S.K.: A complete compositional reasoning framework for the efficient verification of pipelined machines. In: International Conference on Computer-Aided Design (ICCAD'05), pp. 863–870. IEEE Computer Society Press, Los Alamitos (2005)
[4] Manolios, P., Srinivasan, S.K., Vroon, D.: Automatic memory reductions for RTL-level verification. In: ICCAD 2006. ACM-IEEE International Conference on Computer Aided Design, ACM, California (2006)
[5] Manolios, P., Srinivasan, S.K., Vroon, D.: BAT: The Bit-level Analysis Tool (2006) Available from http://www.cc.gatech.edu/~manolios/bat/
[6] Manolios, P., Vroon, D.: Efficient circuit to CNF conversion. In: International Conference on Theory and Applications of Satisfiability Testing (2007)
[7] Tseitin, G.S.: On the complexity of derivation in propositional calculus. In: Slisenko, A.O. (ed.) Studies in Constructive Mathematics and Mathematical Logic, Part2, pp. 115–125. Consultants Bureau, New York-London (1962)

LIRA: Handling Constraints of Linear Arithmetics over the Integers and the Reals*

(Tool Paper)

Bernd Becker[1], Christian Dax[2], Jochen Eisinger[1], and Felix Klaedtke[2]

[1] Albert-Ludwigs-Universität Freiburg, Germany
[2] ETH Zurich, Switzerland

1 Introduction

The mechanization of many verification tasks relies on efficient implementations of decision procedures for fragments of first-order logic. Interactive theorem provers like PVS also make use of such decision procedures to increase the level of automation. Our tool LIRA[1] implements decision procedures based on automata-theoretic techniques for first-order logics with linear arithmetic, namely, for $FO(\mathbb{N}, +)$, $FO(\mathbb{Z}, +, <)$, and $FO(\mathbb{R}, \mathbb{Z}, +, <)$.

The theoretical foundations for using automata to decide logics like Presburger arithmetic, i.e., $FO(\mathbb{N}, +)$ were laid in the 1960s [4]: For Presburger arithmetic, the elements of the domain are represented by finite words, and for a given formula, one constructs recursively over the formula structure an automaton that accepts precisely the words that represent the natural numbers that satisfy the formula. Automata constructions handle the logical connectives and quantifiers. A similar approach works for $FO(\mathbb{Z}, +, <)$ and $FO(\mathbb{R}, \mathbb{Z}, +, <)$. To represent reals, one uses infinite words. In [2], it is shown that weak deterministic Büchi automata (WDBAs) suffice to decide $FO(\mathbb{R}, \mathbb{Z}, +, <)$. WDBAs are a restricted class of Büchi automata, which can be handled algorithmically almost as efficiently as deterministic finite automata (DFAs).

LIRA also provides an automata library that efficiently represents and manipulates DFAs and WDBAs. LIRA's automata library can be compared to a BDD library for representing and manipulating finite sets encoded by booleans. Instead of BDDs, LIRA uses DFAs to represent and manipulate sets that are definable in $FO(\mathbb{N}, +)$ and $FO(\mathbb{Z}, +, <)$, and uses WDBAs for sets definable in $FO(\mathbb{R}, \mathbb{Z}, +, <)$. Efficiently representing and manipulating such definable sets has applications beyond deciding these logics efficiently. For instance, in the safety verification of integer-counter systems and hybrid systems one has to cope with such sets. Furthermore, approaches like regular model checking rely on manipulating automata efficiently. LIRA's automata library can be used in all these applications.

Closely related to LIRA are LASH [13], PRESTAF [5], and MONA [12]. Like LIRA's automata library, LASH provides operations for automata over finite and infinite

---

* This work was supported by the German Research Foundation (DFG) and the Swiss National Science Foundation (SNF).
[1] LIRA is available at http://lira.gforge.avacs.org/ under the GNU public licence.

W. Damm and H. Hermanns (Eds.): CAV 2007, LNCS 4590, pp. 307–310, 2007.
© Springer-Verlag Berlin Heidelberg 2007

words. LIRA outperforms LASH by several orders of magnitude. One reason for the speedup are novel automata constructions. PRESTAF's and MONA's automata libraries only support automata over finite words and can only handle Presburger definable sets. Moreover, MONA's automata library is not tailored to the representation and manipulation of Presburger definable sets. The OMEGA library [14] is related to LIRA since it allows one to represent and manipulate sets definable in $FO(\mathbb{Z}, +, <)$. In contrast to LIRA, it does not support the reals and uses a formula-based set representation, which does not have a canonical form. Heuristics are used to simplify the set representations. SMT solvers like MATHSAT [3] and YICES [9] are also related to LIRA since they provide decision procedures for fragments of linear arithmetic over the integers and reals. However, these solvers do not handle quantifiers at all or only in a limited way. Note that most current SMT solvers also handle other fragments of first-order theories and combinations thereof.

In the following, in §2, we give implementation details and list some features of LIRA, and in §3, we report on applications and performance.

2   Implementation Details and Features

LIRA is implemented in C++. Given a formula, LIRA's decision procedures construct the minimal DFA or WDBA according to the selected logic. By analyzing the automaton, LIRA determines whether the formula is satisfiable. Additionally, it can output a satisfying assignment and a counterexample if they exist, or it can output the constructed automaton.

LIRA defines a flexible high-level API for the decision procedures. A formula is represented as a tree structure and generic functions implement syntactic transformations on such a tree representation. LIRA's decision procedures use the high-level API to generate from such a tree representation a sequence of abstract operations. The decision procedures can easily be modified and extended to generate sequences that exploit domain specific information or include certain heuristics. The sequence of operations is then executed by using LIRA's automata library to check whether the given formula is satisfiable. LIRA's automata library provides efficient implementations of standard automata constructions for DFAs and WDBAs and specific automata constructions for the supported logics, like for equations and inequations. The automata library is accessible through a low-level API.

LIRA uses a similar automata representation as MONA [12], where shared multi-terminal binary decision diagrams (MTBDDs) are used to compactly represent the transition function of an automaton. In our implementation we use CUDD [6] to represent and to manipulate these MTBDDs. We benefit here from CUDD's cache-optimized algorithms. Similar to MONA, our automata representation supports boolean variables. Our automata representation also utilizes don't care states, which were introduced in [11] for DFAs and can also be used for WDBAs. The advantage of don't care states is that automata constructions usually become conceptually cleaner and more efficient.

To reduce the number of states of a WDBA, we use don't care words as described in [10]. We use an automaton construction that handles quantifiers in $FO(\mathbb{R}, \mathbb{Z}, +, <)$ more efficiently than previous proposed constructions: it copes with don't care words efficiently and is based on the powerset construction for DFAs instead of the more involved breakpoint construction for determinizing co-Büchi automata (see [8] for details).

3 Applications and Performance

We carried out the following case studies to evaluate LIRA's applicability and performance.[2]

(1) We ran LIRA and the frontends of PRESTAF and LASH on randomly generated formulas with a quantifier prefix $\exists$ and $\forall\exists$. LIRA outperformed PRESTAF and LASH. Moreover, LIRA succeeded to build the automaton for all given formulas whereas PRESTAF and LASH sometimes exceeded the time limit or ran out of memory.

(2) We tested LIRA on formulas that arise in the verification of hybrid systems. The test formulas have one quantifier alternation and are generated by a model checker when accelerating the reachability computation [7]. Although some of the formulas are large (the formula sizes range from under 1 Mbyte up to 39 Mbytes), the constructed WDBAs remain rather small and LIRA handles the quantifiers quickly. Note that in [7] another data-structure, based on and-inverter graphs (AIGs), is used to represent and manipulate the formulas. In contrast to DFAs and WDBAs, this data-structure does not have a canonical form and heuristics are applied for minimization. Their representations usually grow with the number of applied operations and contain redundancies.

(3) We wrote a plugin for the model checker FAST [1] that uses LIRA's automata library. We used FAST's benchmark suite to compare the running times of our plugin with other FAST plugins based on MONA, PRESTAF, LASH, and the OMEGA library. The plugins based on MONA, PRESTAF, and LIRA have competitive performance, LIRA is in most cases the fastest, whereas the LASH plugin is on all examples significantly slower. The OMEGA plugin has, on few examples, competitive running times. However, on most examples it is either outperformed, exceeds the time limit, or crashes.

Acknowledgements. We thank Stefan Disch, Florian Pigorsch, and Viorica Sofronie-Stokkermans for providing benchmark formulas from the domain of hybrid system verification. We also thank Jérôme Leroux and Gérald Point for assisting us with PRESTAF and FAST related issues.

References

1. Bardin, S., Leroux, J., Point, G.: FAST extended release. In: Ball, T., Jones, R.B. (eds.) CAV 2006. LNCS, vol. 4144, pp. 63–66. Springer, Heidelberg (2006)

---

[2] Experimental results are available at `http://lira.gforge.avacs.org/toolpaper/`.

2. Boigelot, B., Jodogne, S., Wolper, P.: An effective decision procedure for linear arithmetic over the integers and reals. ACM Trans.Comput. Log 6, 614–633 (2005)
3. Bozzano, M., Bruttomesso, R., Cimatti, A., Junttila, T.A., van Rossum, P., Schulz, S., Sebastiani, R.: The MathSAT 3 system. In: Ziarko, W., Yao, Y. (eds.) RSCTC 2000. LNCS (LNAI), vol. 3632, pp. 315–321. Springer, Heidelberg (2001)
4. Büchi, J.: Weak second-order arithmetic and finite automata. Zeitschrift der mathematischen Logik und Grundlagen der Mathematik 6, 66–92 (1960)
5. Couvreur, J.-M.: A BDD-like implementation of an automata package. In: Domaratzki, M., Okhotin, A., Salomaa, K., Yu, S. (eds.) CIAA 2004. LNCS, vol. 3317, pp. 310–311. Springer, Heidelberg (2005)
6. CUDD, Colorado university Decision Diagram package.
   http://vlsi.colorado.edu/~fabio/CUDD/
7. Damm, W., Disch, S., Hungar, H., Pang, J., Pigorsch, F., Scholl, C., Waldmann, U., Wirtz, B.: Automatic verification of hybrid systems with large discrete state space. In: Graf, S., Zhang, W. (eds.) ATVA 2006. LNCS, vol. 4218, pp. 276–291. Springer, Heidelberg (2006)
8. Dax, C., Eisinger, J., Klaedtke, F.: Mechanizing the powerset construction for restricted classes of ω-automata, Tech. Report 228, Institut für Informatik, Albert-Ludwigs-Universität Freiburg (2007)
9. Dutertre, B., de Moura, L.: The Yices SMT solver (2006) Available at http://yices.csl.sri.com/tool-paper.pdf
10. Eisinger, J., Klaedtke, F.: Don't care words with an application to the automata-based approach for real addition. In: Ball, T., Jones, R.B. (eds.) CAV 2006. LNCS, vol. 4144, pp. 67–80. Springer, Heidelberg (2006)
11. Klarlund, N.: A theory of restrictions for logics and automata. In: Halbwachs, N., Peled, D.A. (eds.) CAV 1999. LNCS, vol. 1633, pp. 406–417. Springer, Heidelberg (1999)
12. Klarlund, N., Møller, A., Schwartzbach, M.I.: MONA implementation secrets. Int. J. Found. Comput. Sci. 13, 571–586 (2002)
13. lash, The Liège Automata-based Symbolic Handler
    http://www.montefiore.ulg.ac.be/~{}boigelot/research/lash/
14. omega, The Omega project. http://www.cs.umd.edu/projects/omega/

Three-Valued Abstraction
for Continuous-Time Markov Chains[*]

Joost-Pieter Katoen[1], Daniel Klink[1], Martin Leucker[2], and Verena Wolf[3]

[1]RWTH Aachen University
[2]TU Munich
[3]University of Mannheim, Germany

Abstract. This paper proposes a novel abstraction technique for continuous-time Markov chains (CTMCs). Our technique fits within the realm of three-valued abstraction methods that have been used successfully for traditional model checking. The key idea is to apply abstraction on uniform CTMCs that are readily obtained from general CTMCs, and to abstract transition probabilities by intervals. It is shown that this provides a conservative abstraction for both *true* and *false* for a three-valued semantics of the branching-time logic CSL (Continuous Stochastic Logic). Experiments on an infinite-state CTMC indicate the feasibility of our abstraction technique.

1 Introduction

Continuous-time Markov chains (CTMCs) are an important class of stochastic processes that are extensively used in a wide range of application domains ranging from planning of production lines and safety-critical systems to systems biology. Model checking of CTMCs has been proved to extend and complement long-standing analysis techniques for Markov processes. Tools for stochastic Petri nets such as SMART [8] and GreatSPN [9], the PEPA Workbench [12] (a stochastic variant of the CWB), and Statemate [7] have adopted model checkers to analyse CTMCs, and temporal logics for Markov chains became prominent property specification techniques in performance and dependability analysis.

Like for traditional model checking, one of the main challenges in the automated verification of CTMCs is the state-space explosion problem. This paper proposes a novel *abstraction* technique for CTMCs. Abstraction amounts to obtain smaller models by collapsing sets of concrete states to abstract states. In two-valued semantics, abstraction is typically conservative in the sense that affirmative verification results for abstract models carry over to concrete models. False negatives may occur due to overapproximation. Promising results in traditional model checking have been obtained for a three-valued semantics of temporal logic formulae, i.e., an interpretation in which a formula evaluates to either true, false or indefinite. In this setting, abstraction is conservative for both

[*] The research has been partially funded by the DFG Research Training Group 1298 (AlgoSyn).

W. Damm and H. Hermanns (Eds.): CAV 2007, LNCS 4590, pp. 311–324, 2007.
© Springer-Verlag Berlin Heidelberg 2007

positive and negative verification results. Only if the verification of the abstract model yields an indefinite answer, the validity in the concrete model is unknown. The abstraction technique proposed here follows this three-valued approach.

We consider abstractions for the branching-time logic CSL [3], a real-time probabilistic variant of CTL. CSL is a powerful logic for expressing quantitative time-bounded constrained reachability properties such as the probability to reach a set of goal states (by avoiding bad states) within a maximal time span exceeds $\frac{7}{8}$. Existing abstraction techniques in this setting that have been applied in practice consider either bisimulation [16], matrix bounding [6], simulation [24] or symmetry reduction [19]. (Due to the absence of nondeterminism, techniques such as partial-order reduction do not yield substantial reductions.) Despite the fact that fairly large reductions have recently been reported, more aggressive abstraction techniques are needed. Such techniques would also be useful to obtain finite abstractions for a larger class of infinite-state CTMCs.

In traditional model checking, abstract models contain may and must transitions as over- and under-approximation, respectively of the concrete transition relation. This concept can be lifted to discrete-time Markov chains (DTMCs) in a rather natural way [11,14,15] by replacing transition probabilities by *intervals* where lower and upper bounds act as under- and over-approximation, respectively. In this paper we investigate such techniques for CTMCs. The main technical complication is that besides transition probabilities, one has to determine the residence time of an abstract state that results from concrete states with distinct residence times. We show that intervals of transition probabilities, intervals on residence times (or combinations thereof) are not satisfactory in terms of precision. Instead, we suggest to overcome this imprecision by using *uniform* CTMCs, i.e., CTMCs in which all states have equal residence times and use transition probability intervals. Note that this is not a restriction, as any CTMC can be transformed into a weak bisimilar uniform CTMC in linear time. The abstraction is shown to preserve simulation: concrete states are simulated by their abstract counterparts. Then we show that extreme schedulers suffice, i.e., schedulers that only consider lower- and upper bounds. This allows to compute reachability probabilities up to a given tolerance ε rather efficiently [2]. Using a three-valued semantics of CSL it is shown that the abstraction is indeed conservative for affirmative and negative verification results. Besides, we show the relationship with the approach in [11] for DTMCs. The feasibility of the approach is shown by considering abstractions of different granularity for an unbounded stochastic Petri net.

Related work. Abstraction-refinement has been applied to reachability problems in MDPs [10], partial-order reduction techniques using Peled's ample-set method have been generalised to MDPs [13], abstract interpretation has been applied to MDPs [20], and various bisimulation equivalences and simulation pre-orders allow model aggregation prior to model checking, see e. g., [4,23]. Recent techniques that have been proposed include abstraction of MDPs by two-player stochastic games [18], and symmetry reduction [19]. To our knowledge, three-valued abstraction of continuous-time stochastic models has not been considered.

2   Preliminaries

Let X be a finite set. For $Y, Y' \subseteq X$ and function $Q : X \times X \to \mathbb{R}_{\geq 0}$ let $Q(Y, Y') = \sum_{y \in Y, y' \in Y'} Q(y, y')$. The function $Q(x, \cdot)$ is given by $x' \mapsto Q(x, x')$ for all $x' \in X$. Furthermore a function f is called a *distribution on* X iff $f : X \to [0, 1]$ and $f(X) := \sum_{x \in X} f(x) = 1$. Let AP be a fixed, finite set of atomic propositions and $\mathbb{B}_2 = \{\bot, \top\}$ the two-valued truth domain.

Definition 1 (DTMC). *A DTMC is a tuple* $(S, \mathbf{P}, L)$ *with a finite non-empty set of states* S, *transition probability function* $\mathbf{P} : S \times S \to [0, 1]$ *satisfying* $\mathbf{P}(s, S) = 1$ *for all* $s \in S$, *and labeling function* $L : S \times AP \to \mathbb{B}_2$.

$\mathbf{P}(s, s')$ is the one-step probability to move from s to s' and $L(s, a)$ states if atomic proposition a holds in s. A DTMC is time-abstract; in contrast, CTMCs are time-aware, as they have an explicit reference to time, in the form of exit rates which determine, together with the transition probabilities, the stochastic evolution of the system in time.

Definition 2 (CTMC). *A CTMC* $\mathcal{M}$ *is a tuple* $(S, \mathbf{P}, E, L)$ *with* S, $\mathbf{P}$ *and* L *as before, and* exit rate $E : S \to \mathbb{R}_{>0}$.

The quantity $E(s)$ determines the random residence time of s, i.e. $1 - e^{-E(s) \cdot t}$ is the probability to take a transition emanating from s within the next t time units. (Note that self-loops are admitted.) The probability to move from s to s' within t time units is now given by $\mathbf{P}(s, s', t) := \mathbf{P}(s, s') \cdot (1 - e^{-E(s) \cdot t})$.

The time-abstract probabilistic behaviour of CTMC $\mathcal{M}$ is described by its embedded DTMC. The *embedded* DTMC of CTMC $\mathcal{M} = (S, \mathbf{P}, E, L)$ is simply given by $emb(\mathcal{M}) = (S, \mathbf{P}, L)$. A CTMC is *uniform* if all its states have the same exit rate, i.e., $E(s) = E(s') = e$ for all states $s, s' \in S$. Each CTMC can be transformed into a uniformized CTMC by adding self-loops:

Definition 3 (Uniformisation). *Let* $\mathcal{M} = (S, \mathbf{P}, E, L)$ *be a CTMC and let* *(uniformisation rate)* $e \in \mathbb{R}_{>0}$ *such that* $e \geq \max_{s \in S} E(s)$. *Then,* $unif(\mathcal{M}) = (S, \overline{\mathbf{P}}, \overline{E}, L)$ *is a uniform CTMC with* $\overline{E}(s) = e$ *for all* $s \in S$ *and*

$$\overline{\mathbf{P}}(s, s') = \mathbf{P}(s, s') \cdot \frac{E(s)}{e} \text{ for } s' \neq s \quad \text{and} \quad \overline{\mathbf{P}}(s, s) = 1 - \overline{\mathbf{P}}(s, S \setminus \{s\}).$$

The minimal appropriate value of e is determined by the state in $\mathcal{M}$ with the shortest mean residence time[1]. In $unif(\mathcal{M})$ all rates of self-loops are "normalized" with respect to e. Thus, transitions occur with an average "pace" of e, uniform for all states. A CTMC is weak bisimilar to its uniformized CTMC [4].

Continuous Stochastic Logic. CSL [1,3] extends CTL by replacing existential and universal path quantification by a probability operator (as in PCTL) and by equipping the until-operator with a time bound (as in timed CTL):

$$\varphi ::= true \mid a \mid \varphi \wedge \varphi \mid \neg \varphi \mid \mathcal{P}_{\bowtie p}(\Psi) \qquad \Psi ::= \varphi \mathcal{U}^I \varphi$$

---

[1] Strictly speaking, we should write $unif_e(\mathcal{M})$ as the uniformization depends on e.

Table 1. Semantics of CSL

$$
\begin{aligned}
&[\![s, \mathit{true}]\!] &&= \top && [\![s, a]\!] &&= L(s, a) \\
&[\![s, \varphi_1 \wedge \varphi_2]\!] &&= [\![s, \varphi_1]\!] \sqcap [\![s, \varphi_2]\!] && [\![s, \neg\varphi]\!] &&= [\![s, \varphi]\!]^c \\
&[\![s, \mathcal{P}_{\bowtie p}(\Psi)]\!] &&= \top, \text{ iff } \mathit{Prob}(\{\sigma \in \mathit{Paths}_s^{\mathcal{M}} \mid [\![\sigma, \Psi]\!] = \top\}) \bowtie p
\end{aligned}
$$

$$
[\![\sigma, \varphi_1 \mathcal{U}^I \varphi_2]\!] = \top, \text{ iff } \exists\, t \in I : ([\![\sigma@t, \varphi_2]\!] = \top \wedge \forall\, t' \in [0, t) : [\![\sigma@t', \varphi_1]\!] = \top)
$$

where $\bowtie \in \{<, \leq, \geq, >\}, p \in [0,1], I = [0,t) \mid [0,t] \mid [0, \infty)$ for $t \in \mathbb{R}_{>0}$ and $a \in AP$. φ is a *state-formula*, whereas Ψ is a *path-formula*. State formulas are ranged over by $\varphi, \psi, \ldots$ and path formulas are ranged over by $\Psi, \Phi, \ldots$.

A *path* in a CTMC is an alternating sequence $\sigma = s_0\, t_0\, s_1\, t_1\, s_2 \ldots$ with $\mathbf{P}(s_i, s_{i+1}) > 0$ and $t_i \in \mathbb{R}_{>0}$ for all i. The time stamps t_i denote the amount of time spent in state s_i. $\sigma@t$ denotes the state of σ occupied at time t, i.e. $\sigma@t = s_i$ with i the smallest index such that $t < \sum_{j=0}^{i} t_j$. Let *Prob* denote the unique probability measure on sets of paths and let $\mathit{Paths}_s^{\mathcal{M}}$ denote the set of all paths of $\mathcal{M}$, starting in s. The subscript s is omitted when s is clear from the context; the same applies to superscript $\mathcal{M}$. Note that the probability measure of the set of infinite paths $s_0 t_0 s_1 t_1 \ldots$ with $\sum_{i=0}^{\infty} t_i$ is converging, is zero [3].

The semantics of CSL is given in Table 1. $\top$ and $\bot$ form a complete lattice such that $\bot < \top$ and *meet* $\sqcap$ as well as *complement* $\cdot^c$ are defined as usual.

Measures of interest can now be expressed as CSL formula in a convenient way. For example, the liveness property to reach a *down* state in a system within 52 time units, via *premium* states, with probability at most 0.01 would be formulated as $\mathcal{P}_{\leq 0.01}(\mathit{premium}\, \mathcal{U}^{[0,52]}\, \mathit{down})$. Another typical example would be to check, if some designated *goal* state is reachable at all times: $\mathcal{P}_{>0}(\mathit{true}\, \mathcal{U}^{[0,\infty)}\, \mathit{goal})$.

As in our abstraction, states may be grouped that satisfy distinct atomic propositions, we resort to a three-valued interpretation. Let $\mathbb{B}_3 = \{\bot, ?, \top\}$ with ordering $\bot < ? < \top$ and let $?^c = ?$. When a formula evaluates to $\bot$ or $\top$, the result is *definitely* true or false respectively, otherwise it is *indefinite*.

3 Abstraction

Our aim is to provide an abstraction of CTMCs which is conservative for both positive and negative verification results of CSL formulas. This is established by adopting a three-valued interpretation. The basic principle is to collapse sets of concrete states into single abstract states such that concrete states are simulated by abstract ones. As opposed to abstract interpretation only disjoint sets of concrete states are collapsed. That is, we consider a partitioning $\mathcal{A} = \{A_1, \ldots, A_n\}$ of the state space S of a CTMC $\mathcal{M} = (S, \mathbf{P}, E, L)$. The probability to evolve from abstract state A_i to A_j, $i, j \in \{1, \ldots, n\}$ within some time interval is represented by the functions: $\mathbf{P}(A_i, A_j) = \{\mathbf{P}(s, s', \cdot) \mid s \in A_i, s' \in A_j\}$.

Taking minimal and maximal probabilities as under- and over-approximation, respectively, suggests to define

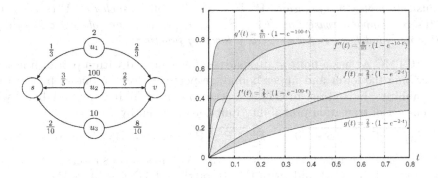

Fig. 1. Abstraction for non-uniform CTMCs

$$\mathbf{P}^l(A_i, A_j, t) = \inf_{f \in \mathbf{P}(A_i, A_j)} f(t) \quad \text{and} \quad \mathbf{P}^u(A_i, A_j, t) = \sup_{f \in \mathbf{P}(A_i, A_j)} f(t).$$

The functions $\mathbf{P}^l(A_i, A_j, t)$ and $\mathbf{P}^u(A_i, A_j, t)$ (considered as functions ranging over t) are in general not of the form $p \cdot (1 - e^{-E \cdot t})$ for fixed $p \in [0, 1]$ and $E > 0$.

Example 1. Consider the non-uniform CTMC $\mathcal{M} = (\{s, u_1, u_2, u_3, v\}, \mathbf{P}, E, L)$ in Fig. 1 (left). We focus on the transition probabilities of the states u_1, u_2, u_3 (indicated as labeled edges) and their exit rates which appear above the corresponding vertices. Further details of $\mathcal{M}$ are omitted in Fig. 1. Let $\mathcal{A} = \{A_s, A_u, A_v\}$ with $A_u = \{u_1, u_2, u_3\}$, $A_s = \{s\}$ and $A_v = \{v\}$. The set $\mathbf{P}(A_u, A_v) = \{f, f', f''\}$ is plotted in Fig. 1 (right). Note that $\mathbf{P}^l(A_u, A_v, t)$ and $\mathbf{P}^u(A_u, A_v, t)$ are not of the form $p \cdot (1 - e^{-E \cdot t})$. In general, the complexity of these functions grows when the number of transitions between states aggretated to A_u and A_v increases.

One might combine the infimum (supremum) of an abstract state's exit rates with the infimum (supremum) of the one-step transition probabilities to define an appropriate under- and over-approximation, yielding a rather coarse abstraction as indicated in Fig. 1 (right) which shows the plot of the functions g and g' resulting from this approach. But increasing the number of parameters to obtain a more accurate approximation results in a far too complex abstraction.

Therefore, we propose to abstract a CTMC by generating its uniformised CTMC (cf. Def. 3), and apply abstraction on the uniform CTMC, i.e., CTMCs in which all exit rates are equal to, say, E_{unif}. The advantage of uniform CTMCs is that $p_l \cdot (1 - e^{-E_{unif} \cdot t}) \leq p_u \cdot (1 - e^{-E_{unif} \cdot t})$ iff $p_l \leq p_u$ where p_l, p_u are the lower and upper bounds of time-abstract transition probabilities. Note that CTMC $\mathcal{M}$ and $unif(\mathcal{M})$ are weak bisimilar, and as weak bisimulation preserves CSL equivalence[2] [4], the shift to the uniformized CTMC is correct for CSL. Our abstract model now becomes:

Definition 4 (Abstract CTMC). *An abstract CTMC (ACTMC for short) is a tuple* $\mathcal{M} = (S, \mathbf{P}^l, \mathbf{P}^u, E_{unif}, L)$ *with a non-empty finite set of states S,*

---

[2] Recall that we consider the fragment of CSL without the next-step operator.

transition probability functions $\mathbf{P}^l, \mathbf{P}^u : S \times S \mapsto [0,1]$ *such that* $\mathbf{P}^l(s,S) \leq 1 \leq \mathbf{P}^u(s,S)$ *componentwise for all* $s \in S$. $E_{unif} \in \mathbb{R}_{>0}$ *is the (global) exit rate for all states, and* $L : S \times AP \mapsto \mathbb{B}_3$ *is a labeling function.*

An ACTMC $\mathcal{M}$ has a finite state space and is equipped with a pair of functions describing the lower and upper bound, respectively for the one-step transition probabilities. In contrast to CTMCs, states in an ACTMC may be labeled with ? . The set of transition probability functions is given by

$$\mathbf{P}_{\mathcal{M}} = \{\bar{\mathbf{P}} : S \times S \mapsto [0,1] \mid \mathbf{P}^l \leq \bar{\mathbf{P}} \leq \mathbf{P}^u \text{ and } \bar{\mathbf{P}}(s,S) = 1 \text{ for all } s \in S\},$$

where $\leq$ is to be interpreted element-wise. We may drop subscript $\mathcal{M}$ if $\mathcal{M}$ is clear from the context and write $\mathbf{P}(s,\cdot)$ for the set $\{\bar{\mathbf{P}}(s,\cdot) \mid \bar{\mathbf{P}} \in \mathbf{P}\}$.

An ACTMC $(S, \mathbf{P}^l, \mathbf{P}^u, E_{unif}, L)$ with $\mathbf{P}^l = \mathbf{P}^u$ and $L(s,a) \in \mathbb{B}_2$ for any $s \in S$ and $a \in AP$ is a uniform CTMC.

Definition 5 (Abstraction). *For ACTMC* $\mathcal{M} = (S, \mathbf{P}^l, \mathbf{P}^u, E_{unif}, L)$, *partitioning* $\mathcal{A} = \{A_1, \ldots, A_n\}$ *of* S *and* $1 \leq i, j \leq n$, *the abstraction of* $\mathcal{M}$ *induced by* $\mathcal{A}$ *is the ACTMC* $abstr(\mathcal{A}, \mathcal{M}) := (\mathcal{A}, \tilde{\mathbf{P}}^l, \tilde{\mathbf{P}}^u, E_{unif}, \tilde{L})$ *given by:*

- $\tilde{\mathbf{P}}^l(A_i, A_j) = \min_{s \in A_i} \mathbf{P}^l(s, A_j)$ *and* $\tilde{\mathbf{P}}^u(A_i, A_j) = \min\{1, \max_{s \in A_i} \mathbf{P}^u(s, A_j)\}$,

- $\tilde{L}(A_i, a) = \begin{cases} \top & \text{if } L(s,a) = \top & \text{for all } s \in A_i, a \in AP, \\ \bot & \text{if } L(s,a) = \bot & \text{for all } s \in A_i, a \in AP, \\ ? & \text{otherwise.} \end{cases}$

Example 2. Consider the CTMC in Fig. 2 (left) with exit rate 12, $AP = \{a\}$, $L(s_0, a) = L(s_1, a) = \top$ and $L(s_0', a) = L(s_2, a) = \bot$. The ACTMC induced by partition $\{\{s_0, s_0'\}, \{s_1\}, \{s_2\}\}$ is depicted in Fig. 2 (right) with $L(A_0, a) = ?$, $L(A_1, a) = \top$, $L(A_2, a) = \bot$.

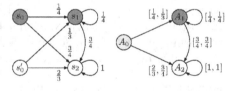

Fig. 2. Abstracting a CTMC

The probability to move from s to s' in an ACTMC may be any probability in $[\mathbf{P}^l(s, s'), \mathbf{P}^u(s, s')]$ and is chosen nondeterministically. As for Markov decision processes, *schedulers* are used to resolve nondeterminism. We consider (time-abstract) history-dependent schedulers that given a time-abstract path nondeterministically select a transition probability function from the set $\mathbf{P}$.

Definition 6 (Scheduler). *A history-dependent scheduler for ACTMC* $\mathcal{M}$ *is a function* $D : Paths_{abs}(\mathcal{M}) \mapsto \mathbf{P}_{\mathcal{M}}$.

Here, $Paths_{abs}(\mathcal{M})$ denotes the set of time-abstract paths in $\mathcal{M}$. A time-abstract path in $\mathcal{M}$ is a finite sequence of states $s_0 s_1 s_2 \ldots s_n$ such that $\bar{\mathbf{P}}(s_i, s_{i+1}) > 0$ for some $\bar{\mathbf{P}} \in \mathbf{P}$ for all $i \in \{0, 1, \ldots, n\}$. The set of history-dependent schedulers for ACTMC $\mathcal{M}$ is denoted by $Sched^{\mathcal{M}}$.

If only lower and upper bounds on transition probabilities are given, it may happen that not every combination is possible. For instance, in Example 2, a possible choice in state A_0 is to select A_1 with $\frac{1}{4}$ and A_2 with $\frac{2}{3}$, but $\frac{1}{4} + \frac{2}{3} < 1$.

Definition 7 (Delimited ACTMC). *An ACTMC* $\mathcal{M} = (S, \mathbf{P}^l, \mathbf{P}^u, E_{unif}, L)$ *is delimited iff for any* $s, s' \in S$ *and* $p \in [\mathbf{P}^l(s, s'), \mathbf{P}^u(s, s')]$, *there exists* $\bar{\mathbf{P}} \in \mathbf{P}$ *with* $\bar{\mathbf{P}}(s, s') = p$.

In the following, we define an operation, called *cut*, that transforms a given ACTMC into a delimited one. It basically strips off combinations of probabilities in the intervals that do not yield transition probabilities. A similar function has been defined for abstractions of DTMCs (see Def. 11) in [11].

Definition 8 (Cut). *Let* $\mathcal{M} = (S, \mathbf{P}^l, \mathbf{P}^u, E_{unif}, L)$ *be an ACTMC. We define the functions* $cut(\mathbf{P}^l, \mathbf{P}^u) = (\tilde{\mathbf{P}}^l, \tilde{\mathbf{P}}^u)$ *by* $\tilde{\mathbf{P}}^l(s, s') = \max\{\mathbf{P}^l(s, s'), 1 - \mathbf{P}^u(s, S \setminus \{s'\})\}$ *and* $\tilde{\mathbf{P}}^u(s, s') = \min\{\mathbf{P}^u(s, s'), 1 - \mathbf{P}^l(s, S \setminus \{s'\})\}$ *for all* $s, s' \in S$.
The cut *of* $\mathcal{M}$ *is defined as* $cut(\mathcal{M}) = (S, \tilde{\mathbf{P}}^l, \tilde{\mathbf{P}}^u, E_{unif}, L)$.

Lemma 1. *For ACTMC* $\mathcal{M}$, $cut(\mathcal{M})$ *is delimited and* $Sched^{\mathcal{M}} = Sched^{cut(\mathcal{M})}$.

A finite subset of the transition probability distributions, which will prove useful when considering lower and upper bounds of reachability properties, is the set of extreme distributions. Intuitively they result from a one by one minimisation/maximisation of transition probabilities. Note that different priorities for minimising/maximising yield different minimal/maximal probabilities. Actually, the number of extreme distributions grows exponentially in the state space size.

Definition 9 (Extreme distributions). *Let* $s \in S$ *and* $S' \subseteq S$. *We define* $extr(\mathbf{P}^l, \mathbf{P}^u, S', s) \subseteq \mathbf{P}$ *such that* $\mu \in extr(\mathbf{P}^l, \mathbf{P}^u, S', s)$ *iff either* $S' = \emptyset$ *and* $\mu = \mathbf{P}^l(s, \cdot) = \mathbf{P}^u(s, \cdot)$ *or one of the following conditions is true*[3]

$$\exists s' \in S' : \mu(s') = \mathbf{P}^l(s, s') \text{ and } \mu \in extr(\mathbf{P}^l, \mathbf{P}^u[s' \mapsto \mu(s')], S' \setminus \{s'\}, s)$$
$$\exists s' \in S' : \mu(s') = \mathbf{P}^u(s, s') \text{ and } \mu \in extr(\mathbf{P}^l[s' \mapsto \mu(s')], \mathbf{P}^u, S' \setminus \{s'\}, s)$$

We call $\mu \in \mathbf{P}(s, \cdot)$ *an* extreme distribution *if* $\mu \in extr(\mathbf{P}^l, \mathbf{P}^u, S, s)$.

To compare the behavior described by two ACTMCs, we introduce the notion of probabilistic simulation which is a variant of probabilistic simulation for CTMCs as it can be found in [4].

Definition 10 (Probabilistic simulation). *Let* $\mathcal{M} = (S, \mathbf{P}^l, \mathbf{P}^u, E_{unif}, L)$ *be an ACTMC. We call* $\mathcal{R} \subseteq S \times S$ *a* probabilistic simulation *iff* $s\mathcal{R}s'$ *implies:*

1. $L(s', a) \neq ? \Rightarrow L(s', a) = L(s, a)$ *for all* $a \in AP$.
2. *For all distributions* $\mu \in \mathbf{P}(s, \cdot)$, *there is a distribution* $\mu' \in \mathbf{P}(s', \cdot)$ *and a weight function* $\Delta : S \times S \to [0, 1]$ *with:*
   (a) $\Delta(u, v) > 0 \Rightarrow u\mathcal{R}v$, (b) $\Delta(u, S) = \mu(u)$, (c) $\Delta(S, v) = \mu'(v)$.

State s *is simulated by* s' *(written* $s \preceq s'$*) if there exists a probabilistic simulation* $\mathcal{R}$ *with* $(s, s') \in \mathcal{R}$. *We lift* $\preceq$ *to the union of two ACTMCs in the usual way.*

---

[3] Here, $f[s \mapsto x]$ denotes the function that agrees everywhere with f except at s where it is equal to x.

Theorem 1. *For ACTMC $\mathcal{M}$ with state space S, and $\mathcal{A}$ a partitioning on S inducing the ACTMC $\mathrm{abstr}(\mathcal{A}, \mathcal{M})$ with state space $\mathcal{A}$*

$$s \in A \Rightarrow s \preceq A \text{ for all } s \in S, A \in \mathcal{A}$$

Example 3. Consider the CTMC in Fig. 2(a), the partitioning leading to 2(b) (see Ex. 2) with $\mathcal{R} = \{(s_0, A_0), (s_0', A_0), (s_1, A_1), (s_2, A_2)\}$. Note that A_i should be considered as a single abstract state. We have $s_0 \mathcal{R} A_0$ because condition 1 of Def. 10 is trivially fulfilled since $L(A_0, a) = ?$. For condition 2 we observe that in s_0 there is only one possible distribution $\mu = (0, 0, \frac{1}{4}, \frac{3}{4})$ to choose. The only distribution in $\mathbf{P}(A_0, \cdot)$, for which there is a weight function Δ fulfilling condition 2, is $\mu' = (0, \frac{1}{4}, \frac{3}{4})$ with $\Delta(s_1, A_1) = \frac{1}{4}$, $\Delta(s_2, A_2) = \frac{3}{4}$ and 0 otherwise. The conditions of Def. 10 can be checked for the remaining elements of $\mathcal{R}$ similarly.

In the following we show that our abstraction of CTMCs can be regarded as a conservative extension of abstraction of DTMCs as recently proposed in [11].

Definition 11 (Abstract DTMC). *An abstract DTMC (ADTMC) is a tuple $(S, \mathbf{P}^l, \mathbf{P}^u, L)$ with S, $\mathbf{P}^l$, $\mathbf{P}^u$, and L as before.*

Abstract DTMCs are thus abstract CTMCs without exit rates. The theorem below shows that the following diagram commutes:

$$
\begin{array}{ccccc}
\mathcal{M} & \xrightarrow{\text{abstr.}} & \mathcal{M}_{abstr} & \xrightarrow{\text{cut}} & \mathcal{M}_{del} \\
\text{embedded} \downarrow & & & & \downarrow \text{embedded} \\
\mathcal{N} & \xrightarrow{\text{abstr.}} & \mathcal{N}_{abstr} & \xrightarrow{\text{cut}} & \mathcal{N}_{del}
\end{array}
\quad
\begin{array}{l}
\} \text{ (A)CTMCs} \\
\\
\} \text{ (A)DTMCs}
\end{array}
$$

Theorem 2. *For delimited uniform CTMC $\mathcal{M}$ and partitioning $\mathcal{A}$:*

$$emb(cut(abstr(\mathcal{A}, \mathcal{M}))) = cut_{ADTMC}(abstr_{DTMC}(\mathcal{A}, emb(\mathcal{M})))$$

where cut_{ADTMC} and $abstr_{\mathrm{DTMC}}$ are the counterparts of cut and $abstr$ in the setting of (A)DTMCs [11].

4   Model Checking Three-Valued CSL

Now, we develop a three-valued version of CSL which is interpreted over ACTMCs. The simulation relation allows us to reason about more concrete systems.

For an ACTMC $\mathcal{M}$, every scheduler $D \in Sched^{\mathcal{M}}$ induces a probability space with a probability measure $Prob^D$ in the same manner as for CTMCs (see [3] for details). When interested in the infimum of probabilities of measurable sets with regard to all schedulers, it suffices to consider only extreme distributions. A scheduler which only chooses such distributions is an *extreme* scheduler. The set of all extreme schedulers for $\mathcal{M}$ is denoted as $Sched^{\mathcal{M}}_{extr}$.

Theorem 3. *Let $\mathcal{M} = (S, \mathbf{P}^l, \mathbf{P}^u, E_{unif}, L)$ be an ACTMC. For every measurable set Q of the induced probability space:*

$$\inf\nolimits_{D \in Sched^{\mathcal{M}}_{extr}} Prob^D(Q) = \inf\nolimits_{D \in Sched^{\mathcal{M}}} Prob^D(Q).$$

The proof for the above theorem is rather technical and goes along the structure of the generated Borel field of the induced probability space. Note that the number of choices at a state is finite for extreme schedulers, whereas this is uncountable for arbitrary schedulers.

Before discussing CSL, let us first consider *time-dependent reachability probabilities* in ACTMCs, i. e., the probabilities to reach some state in set B within t time units, formally $Reach_{\leq t}(s, B) = \{\sigma \in Paths_s^{\mathcal{M}} \mid \sigma@t' \in B$ for some $t' \in [0, t]\}$. When computing the semantics of CSL formulas, the main challenge is to determine lower bounds of reachability properties, as we will see. Therefore, we will now analyse how to compute $\inf_{D \in Sched^{\mathcal{M}}} Prob^D(Reach_{\leq t}(s, B))$. $Prob^l(Q)$ will be used as abbreviation for $\inf_{D \in Sched^{\mathcal{M}}} Prob^D(Q)$.

We start with an algorithm for the approximation of probability bounds for timed reachability properties in uniform CTMDPs (see [2]). By Theorem 3, it suffices to consider extreme schedulers if one is interested in lower bounds. We interpret an ACTMC as a CTMDP, where each extreme distribution can be chosen by some action. From [2], we know that an ε-approximation of transient probabilities q_0 can efficiently be computed in an iterative way[4]:

$$
\begin{aligned}
q_0 &= \psi_{E_{unif},t}(0) \cdot i_B + q_1 \\
q_i &= \psi_{E_{unif},t}(i) \cdot i_B + \mathbf{P}_i \cdot q_{i+1}, \text{ for } i \in \{1, ..., k(\varepsilon, E_{unif}, t)\}, \\
q_{k(\varepsilon, E_{unif}, t)+1} &= \underline{0}, \text{ where } k(\varepsilon, E_{unif}, t) \text{ is a proper truncation point,} \\
&\quad \text{and } \psi_{E_{unif},t}(n) \text{ is the probability that} \\
&\quad n \text{ events occur in a Poisson process of rate } E_{unif \cdot t}
\end{aligned}
$$

Therefore, instead of checking for all extreme distributions in each iteration, we can find a minimizing distribution in polynomial time, by minimizing the vector-product $\mathbf{P}_i(s, \cdot) \cdot q_{i+1}$ with additional constraint $q_{i+1}(S) = 1$. This can be done by successively assigning as much proportion as possible to the transition leading to the successor s' for which $q_{i+1}(s')$ is minimal. For $N := |S|$, sorting the q-vector can be done in $\mathcal{O}(N \log(N))$ and assertion of probabilities takes $O(N^3)$ since the cut has to be applied N times and the *cut* itself has a complexity of $\mathcal{O}(N^2)$. This yields a worst-case complexity of $\mathcal{O}(N^2 \cdot (N \log(N) + N^3) + N) = \mathcal{O}(N^5)$ for every iteration step.

The following theorem, which states that the above algorithm yields an ε-accurate approximation of reachability properties, follows directly from [2].

Theorem 4. *For ACTMC $\mathcal{M} = (S, \mathbf{P}^l, \mathbf{P}^u, E_{unif}, L)$, $s \in S$, $B \subseteq S$, $t \in \mathbb{R}_{>0}$ and error margin ε:*

$$Prob^l(Reach_{\leq t}(s, B)) - \varepsilon \leq q_0(s) \leq Prob^l(Reach_{\leq t}(s, B))$$

Three-valued CSL-semantics. We define the satisfaction function $[\![\cdot]\!] : (S \cup Paths^{\mathcal{M}}) \times CSL \rightarrow \mathbb{B}_3$ inductively as shown in Table 2, where $Prob^l(s, \Phi, \alpha) = Prob^l(\{\sigma \in Paths_s^{\mathcal{M}} \mid [\![\sigma, \Phi]\!] = \alpha\})$ for $\alpha \in \mathbb{B}_3$.

---

[4] The truncation point $k(\varepsilon, E_{unif}, t)$ depends linearly on E_{unif} and t and can easily be computed on-the-fly.

Table 2. Three-valued semantics of CSL

$$\llbracket s, \mathit{true} \rrbracket = \top \qquad\qquad \llbracket s, \mathit{false} \rrbracket = \bot \qquad \llbracket s, a \rrbracket = L(s,a)$$

$$\llbracket s, \varphi_1 \wedge \varphi_2 \rrbracket = \llbracket s, \varphi_1 \rrbracket \sqcap \llbracket s, \varphi_2 \rrbracket \qquad\qquad \llbracket s, \neg \varphi \rrbracket = \llbracket s, \varphi \rrbracket^c$$

$$\llbracket \sigma, \varphi_1 \mathcal{U}^I \varphi_2 \rrbracket = \begin{cases} \top & \text{if } \exists\, t \in I : (\llbracket \sigma @ t, \varphi_2 \rrbracket = \top \wedge \forall\, t' \in [0,t) : \llbracket \sigma @ t', \varphi_1 \rrbracket = \top) \\ \bot & \text{if } \forall\, t \in I : (\llbracket \sigma @ t, \varphi_2 \rrbracket = \bot \vee \exists\, t' \in [0,t) : \llbracket \sigma @ t', \varphi_1 \rrbracket = \bot) \\ ? & \text{otherwise} \end{cases}$$

$$\llbracket s, \mathcal{P}_{\unrhd p}(\Psi) \rrbracket = \begin{cases} \top & \text{if } \mathit{Prob}^l(s, \Psi, \top) \unrhd p \\ \bot & \text{if } \mathit{Prob}^l(s, \Psi, \bot) \rhd 1 - p \\ ? & \text{otherwise} \end{cases} \qquad \unrhd \in \{>, \geq\}, \rhd = \begin{cases} > & \text{if } \unrhd\, = \geq \\ \geq & \text{if } \unrhd\, = > \end{cases}$$

$$\llbracket s, \mathcal{P}_{\unlhd p}(\Psi) \rrbracket = \begin{cases} \top & \text{if } 1 - p \unlhd \mathit{Prob}^l(s, \Psi, \bot) \\ \bot & \text{if } \qquad p \lhd \mathit{Prob}^l(s, \Psi, \top) \\ ? & \text{otherwise} \end{cases} \qquad \unlhd \in \{<, \leq\}, \lhd = \begin{cases} < & \text{if } \unlhd\, = \leq \\ \leq & \text{if } \unlhd\, = < \end{cases}$$

Let us have a closer look at the semantics. For the propositional fragment the semantics is clear. A path σ satisfies until-formula $\varphi_1 \mathcal{U}^{[0,t]} \varphi_2$ if φ_1 holds for sure until φ_2 holds for sure at the latest at time t. The until-formula $\varphi_1 \mathcal{U}^{[0,t]} \varphi_2$ is violated, if either before φ_2 holds, φ_1 is violated, or if φ_2 is violated for sure. Otherwise, the result is indefinite.

To determine the satisfaction of $\mathcal{P}_{\leq p}(\Psi)$ we consider the probability of the paths for which Ψ is surely violated. If this probability is greater than $1 - p$, then paths where Ψ holds may have measure at most p. Similarly, to show that $\mathcal{P}_{\leq p}(\Psi)$ is violated, we have to consider the measure of all paths surely satisfying Ψ. If this measure is greater than p, then obviously $\mathcal{P}_{\leq p}(\Psi)$ is violated. The semantics of $\mathcal{P}_{\unlhd p}(\Psi)$ for $\unlhd\, \in \{<, >, \geq\}$ follows from a similar argumentation.

Example 4. Consider the CTMC in Fig. 2(a). Starting in s_0 (s_1), the probability to reach a non-a-state in 0.3 time units is about 0.9037 (0.9328, respectively). Thus, formula $\varphi = a \rightarrow \mathcal{P}_{\geq 0.9}(\mathit{true}\, \mathcal{U}^{\leq 0.3} \neg a)$ is true in all states. Consider the abstraction in Fig. 2(b): The lower and upper probability bounds to reach a non-a-state in 0.3 time units from A_0 are about 0.8807 respectively 0.9037. Hence, $\llbracket A_0, a \rightarrow \mathcal{P}_{\geq 0.9}(\mathit{true}\, \mathcal{U}^{\leq 0.3} \neg a) \rrbracket = ? \sqcup \llbracket t_0, \mathcal{P}_{\geq 0.9}(\mathit{true}\, \mathcal{U}^{\leq 0.3} \neg a) \rrbracket = ? \sqcup\, ? = ?$. For $\mathcal{P}_{\geq 0.88}$ instead of $\mathcal{P}_{\geq 0.9}$, the formula would have been satisfied in the abstraction as well, while for $\mathcal{P}_{\geq 0.91}$ the result would still be ? since $? \sqcup \bot =\, ?$.

The following theorem states that our framework developed so far can indeed be used for abstraction based model checking. It can be shown by structural induction on the CSL formulas. Intuitively, the theorem asserts that the result of checking a CSL formula in the abstract CTMC agrees with the one for the more concrete model, unless it is indefinite.

Theorem 5 (Preservation of CSL). *Let s and s' be two states of an ACTMC $\mathcal{M}$ with $s \preceq s'$. Then for all CSL formulas φ:*

$$\llbracket s', \varphi \rrbracket \neq\, ? \quad \text{implies} \quad \llbracket s, \varphi \rrbracket = \llbracket s', \varphi \rrbracket.$$

Observe that the 3-valued CSL semantics on a CTMC (viewed as ACTMC) coincides with the 2-valued CSL semantics for CTMCs (see Section 2), showing that our abstraction is *conservative* for positive and negative verification results.

Model checking. As for CTL, model checking works bottom-up the parse tree of the CSL formula φ. Boolean combinations of formulas as well as the $\mathcal{P}$-formulas are evaluated, as expected. For the latter, however, we need the lower probability bounds for the satisfaction/violation of an until-formula, which remains the only operator to discuss.

The idea of dealing with until-operators is similar as in [11]: For getting the measure of paths surely satisfying $\Psi = \varphi_1\,\mathcal{U}^{[0,t]}\varphi_2$, it suffices to compute the measure of reaching states satisfying φ_2 in time bounded by t along paths of states satisfying φ_1. By induction, we know which states do not satisfy φ_1. Removing these from the CTMC, a path satisfies $\varphi_1\mathcal{U}^{[0,t]}\varphi_2$ iff a state φ_2 is reached within time bound t. In other words, it remains to solve a time-bounded reachability problem in the reduced graph. Getting the measure of paths violating Ψ for sure, is done similarly by exchanging $\top$ and $\bot$ in the argumentation above.

Recall that the given algorithm for computing time-bounded reachability approximates only with error margin ε. However, it can easily be guaranteed that the error due to approximation only yields ? in cases where a definite value could be obtained given a smaller error margin.

Theorem 6. *Given an ACTMC $\mathcal{M}$, a CSL formula φ, and an error margin ε, we can approximate $[\![\mathcal{M},\varphi]\!]$ in time polynomial in size of $\mathcal{M}$ and linear in size of φ, E_{unif} and the highest time bound t occurring in φ (dependency on ε is omitted as ε is linear in $E_{unif} \cdot t$). In case the approximation yields $\top$ or $\bot$, the result is correct, while ? is correct with an error of at most ε.*

5   Case Study: Quasi-Birth-Death Processes

Let us consider a simple system with a fixed number m of available processors and an infinite queue for storing job requests. The processing speed of the processors is described by an exponential distribution with rate γ and λ is the incoming rate of jobs. When all processors are being utilized, new jobs are added to the infinite queue. As soon as processors are getting available again, jobs from the queue

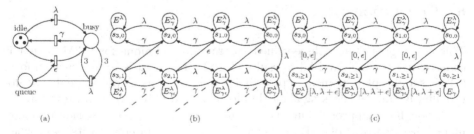

Fig. 3. (a) SPN, (b) uniformized underlying infinite CTMC, (c) finite abstraction

are processed. To model these spontaneous transitions, we choose a high rate $\epsilon \gg \lambda$. In our experiments about 10 times the incoming rate for tasks has been a sufficiently precise approximation. The system initially has no job to process, i.e. all three processors are available and the queue is empty. For $m = 3$, this is being formally described by the *stochastic Petri net* (SPN) [5] in Fig. 3(a). Numbers at edges denote that the corresponding transition consumes or produces the given number of tokens and can not be fired until there are enough token to consume. The semantics of this SPN is equal to an infinite CTMC. Uniformization with rate E results in the infinite uniform CTMC (Fig. 3(b)). For $E, x, y, z \in \mathbb{R}_{\geq 0}$, we shortly write $E_{yz}^x = E_y^x - z$, $E_y^x = E^x - y$ and $E^x = E - x$. State $s_{i,j}$ represents the marking of the SPN, where i tokens are at *idle*, $m - i$ at *busy* and j at *queue*. Aggregating $\{s_{i,j} \mid j \geq n\}$ by $s_{i,\geq n}$ for all $i \in \{0, ..., m\}$ yields Fig. 3(c) ($n = 1$).

Consider $\varphi = (\langle l_1 = 0 \rangle \wedge \langle l_2 = 0 \rangle) \rightarrow \mathcal{P}_{\leq p}(true\,\mathcal{U}^{[0,t]}(\langle l_1 = m \rangle \wedge \langle l_2 = 0 \rangle))$ where $\langle l_1 = i \rangle$, $\langle l_2 = j \rangle \in AP$ hold in all states $s_{i,j}$ of the infinite CTMCs.

In Fig. 4, for $\lambda \in \{1, ..., 6\}$, lower and upper probability bounds for φ for abstractions with $n \in \{1, ..., 9\}$ are plotted. As expected, by increasing n, lower and upper bounds are closer, i.e. the accuracy of the abstraction improves.

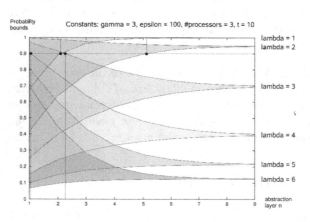

Fig. 4. Probability bounds for φ

Increasing m improves the system performance. The probability for which φ holds decreases for increasing m. If the system is upgraded with m' additional processors then the requirement is not about m jobs anymore, but about $m + m'$. Note that CSL model-checking algorithms for quasi-birth-death processes have also been considered in [21]. Our abstraction technique, though, is not restricted to these (regular) infinite CTMCs.

6   Conclusion

This paper presented a three-valued abstraction technique for CTMCs that is conservative for true and false results of CSL. The idea is to abstract uniform CTMCs and replace transition probabilities by intervals. A polynomial-time approximative model-checking algorithm for 3-valued CSL has been provided.

Although our approach intends to combat the state-space explosion problem, model checking of probabilistic interval models is of interest in its own, when the exact values are not known and e.g., estimated by experiments, cf. [22].

Our experiments indicate that—like for most other abstraction techniques—the partitioning of the state space determines the accuracy of the abstraction; e.g., merging "slow" and "fast" states typically yields too coarse abstractions. To conduct more experiments, we currently incorporate the abstraction into the model checker MRMC [17]. Besides we plan to work on refinement techniques to improve abstractions when the verification yields indefinite results.

References

1. Aziz, A., Sanwal, K., Singhal, V., Brayton, R.: Model-checking continuous time Markov chains. ACM TOCL 1, 162–170 (2000)
2. Baier, C., Hermanns, H., Katoen, J.P., Haverkort, B.R.H.M.: Efficient computation of time-bounded reachability probabilities in uniform continuous-time Markov decision processes. TCS 345, 2–26 (2005)
3. Baier, C., Haverkort, B., Hermanns, H., Katoen, J.-P.: Model-checking algorithms for continuous-time Markov chains. IEEE TSE 29, 524–541 (2003)
4. Baier, C., Katoen, J.-P., Hermanns, H., Wolf, V.: Comparative branching-time semantics for Markov chains. Information and Computation 200, 149–214 (2005)
5. Bause, F., Kritzinger, P.S.: Stochastic Petri nets: An introduction to the theory. SIGMETRICS Performance Evaluation Review 26 (1998)
6. Ben Mamoun, M., Pekergin, N., Younès, S.: Model checking of continuous-time Markov chains by closed-form bounding distributions. In: QEST, pp. 189–198. IEEE CS, Los Alamitos (2006)
7. Böde, E., Herbstritt, M., Hermanns, H., Johr, S., Peikenkamp, T., Pulungan, R., Wimmer, R., Becker, B.: Compositional performability evaluation for Statemate. In: QEST, pp. 167–178. IEEE CS, Los Alamitos (2006)
8. Ciardo, G.I.R.L.J., Miner, A., Siminiceanu, R.: Logical and stochastic modeling with SMART. In: Kemper, P., Sanders, W.H. (eds.) TOOLS 2003. LNCS, vol. 2794, pp. 78–97. Springer, Heidelberg (2003)
9. D'Aprile, D., Donatelli, S., Sproston, J.: CSL model checking for the GreatSPN tool. In: Aykanat, C., Dayar, T., Körpeoğlu, İ. (eds.) ISCIS 2004. LNCS, vol. 3280, pp. 543–553. Springer, Heidelberg (2004)
10. D'Argenio, P.R., Jeannet, B., Jensen, H.E., Larsen, K.G.: Reachability analysis of probabilistic systems by successive refinements. In: de Luca, L., Gilmore, S.T. (eds.) PROBMIV 2001, PAPM-PROBMIV 2001, and PAPM 2001. LNCS, vol. 2165, pp. 39–56. Springer, Heidelberg (2001)
11. Fecher, H., Leucker, M., Wolf, V.: Don't know in probabilistic systems. In: Valmari, A. (ed.) Model Checking Software. LNCS, vol. 3925, pp. 71–88. Springer, Heidelberg (2006)
12. Gilmore, S., Hillston, J.: The PEPA workbench: A tool to support a process algebra-based approach to performance modelling. In: Haring, G., Kotsis, G. (eds.) Computer Performance Evaluation. LNCS, vol. 794, pp. 353–368. Springer, Heidelberg (1994)
13. Groesser, M., Baier, C.: Partial order reduction for Markov decision processes: a survey. In: de Boer, F.S., Bonsangue, M.M., Graf, S., de Roever, W.-P. (eds.) FMCO 2005. LNCS, vol. 4111, pp. 408–427. Springer, Heidelberg (2006)
14. Huth, M.: An abstraction framework for mixed non-deterministic and probabilistic systems. In: Baier, C., Haverkort, B., Hermanns, H., Katoen, J.-P., Siegle, M. (eds.) Validation of Stochastic Systems. LNCS, vol. 2925, pp. 419–444. Springer, Heidelberg (2004)

15. Huth, M.: On finite-state approximants for probabilistic computation tree logic. TCS 346, 113–134 (2005)
16. Katoen, J.-P., Kemna, T., Zapreev, I., Jansen, D.N.: Bisimulation minimisation mostly speeds up probabilistic model checking. In: TACAS. LNCS, vol. 4424, pp. 87–102. Springer, Heidelberg (2007)
17. Katoen, J.-P., Khattri, M., Zapreev, I.S.: A Markov reward model checker. In: QEST, pp. 243–244. IEEE Computer Society Press, Los Alamitos (2005)
18. Kwiatkowska, M., Norman, G., Parker, D.: Game-based abstraction for Markov decision processes. In: QEST, pp. 157–166. IEEE Computer Society Press, Los Alamitos (2006)
19. Kwiatkowska, M., Norman, G., Parker, D.: Symmetry reduction for probabilistic model checking. In: Ball, T., Jones, R.B. (eds.) CAV 2006. LNCS, vol. 4144, pp. 234–248. Springer, Heidelberg (2006)
20. Monniaux, D.: Abstract interpretation of programs as Markov decision processes. Science of Computer Programming 58, 179–205 (2005)
21. Remke, A., Haverkort, B.R., Cloth, L.: Model checking infinite-state Markov chains. In: Halbwachs, N., Zuck, L.D. (eds.) TACAS 2005. LNCS, vol. 3440, pp. 237–252. Springer, Heidelberg (2005)
22. Sen, K., Viswanathan, M., Agha, G.: Model-checking Markov chains in the presence of uncertainties. In: Hermanns, H., Palsberg, J. (eds.) TACAS 2006 and ETAPS 2006. LNCS, vol. 3920, pp. 394–410. Springer, Heidelberg (2006)
23. Sproston, J., Donatelli, S.: Backward bisimulation in Markov chain model checking. IEEE TSE 32, 531–546 (2006)
24. Zhang, L., Hermanns, H., Eisenbrand, F., Jansen, D.N.: Flow faster: efficient decision algorithms for probabilistic simulations. In: TACAS. LNCS, vol. 4424, pp. 155–170. Springer, Heidelberg (2007)

Magnifying-Lens Abstraction
for Markov Decision Processes*

Luca de Alfaro and Pritam Roy

Computer Engineering Department
University of California, Santa Cruz, USA

Abstract. We present a novel abstraction technique which allows the analysis of reachability and safety properties of Markov decision processes with very large state spaces. The technique, called *magnifying-lens abstraction,* (MLA) copes with the state-explosion problem by partitioning the state-space into regions, and by computing upper and lower bounds for reachability and safety properties on the regions, rather than on the states. To compute these bounds, MLA iterates over the regions, considering the concrete states of each region in turn, as if one were sliding across the abstraction a magnifying lens which allowed viewing the concrete states. The algorithm adaptively refines the regions, using smaller regions where more detail is needed, until the difference between upper and lower bounds is smaller than a specified accuracy. We provide experimental results on three case studies illustrating that MLA can provide accurate answers, with savings in memory requirements.

1 Introduction

Markov decision processes (MDPs) provide a model for systems with both probabilistic and nondeterministic behavior, and they are widely used in probabilistic verification, planning, optimal control, and performance analysis [13,4,26,8,10]. MDPs that model realistic systems tend to have very large state spaces, and the main challenge in their analysis consists in devising algorithms that work efficiently on such large state spaces. In the non-probabilistic setting, abstraction techniques have been successful in coping with large state-spaces: abstraction enables to answer questions about a system by considering a smaller, more concise abstract model. This has spurred research into the use of abstraction techniques for probabilistic systems [7,18,22,19]. We present a novel abstraction technique, called *magnifying-lens abstraction* (MLA), for the analysis of reachability and safety properties of MDPs with very large state spaces. We show that the technique can lead to substantial space savings in the analysis of MDPs.

An MDP is defined over a state space S. At every state $s \in S$, one or more *actions* are available; with each action is associated a probability distribution over the successor states. We focus on *safety* and *reachability* properties of MDPs. A safety property specifies that the MDP's behavior should not leave a *safe* subset of states $T \subseteq S$; a reachability property specifies that the behavior should reach a set $T \subseteq S$ of *target* states. A controller can choose the actions available at each state so as to maximize, or minimize, the probability of satisfying reachability and safety properties. MLA computes

---

* This research was sponsored in part by the grant NSF-CCR-0132780.

W. Damm and H. Hermanns (Eds.): CAV 2007, LNCS 4590, pp. 325–338, 2007.

converging upper and lower bounds for the maximal reachability or safety probability; the minimal probabilities can be obtained by duality. In its ability to provide both upper and lower bounds for the quantities of interest, MLA is similar to [19].

In the analysis of large MDPs, the main challenge lies in the representation of the value $v(s)$ of the reachability or safety probability at all $s \in S$. In contrast, actions and transition probabilities from each state s can usually be either computed on the fly, or represented in a compact fashion, via Kronecker representations or probabilistic guarded commands [23,10,17]. The goal of MLA is to reduce the space required for storing v and, secondarily, the running time of the analysis. To this end, MLA partitions the state space S of the MDP into *regions;* for each region r, it stores upper and lower bounds $v^+(r)$, $v^-(r)$ for the maximal reachability or safety probability. The values $v^+(r)$, $v^-(r)$ constitute bounds for all states $s \in r$. In order to update these estimates, MLA iterates over the regions, "magnifying" one of them at a time. When the region r is magnified, MLA computes $v^+(s)$, $v^-(s)$ at all concrete states $s \in r$ via value iteration, and then summarizes these results by setting $v^+(r) = \max_{s \in r} v^+(s)$ and $v^-(r) = \min_{s \in r} v^-(s)$. Figuratively, MLA slides a magnifying lens across the abstraction, enabling the algorithm to see the concrete states of one region at a time when updating the region values. Given a desired accuracy ε for the answer, MLA periodically splits regions r with $v^+(r) - v^-(r) > \varepsilon$ into smaller regions. In this way, the abstraction is refined in an adaptive fashion: smaller regions are used where finer detail is needed, guaranteeing the convergence of the bounds, and larger regions are used elsewhere, saving space. When splitting regions, MLA takes care to re-use information gained in the analysis of the coarser abstraction in the evaluation of the finer one. MLA can be adapted to the problem of computing a control strategy by recording the optimal actions for the concrete states of interest, when they are magnified.

Related work on MDP abstraction. Compared with other approaches to MDP abstraction, MLA has two distinctive features:

1. it clusters states based on value, rather than based on the similarity in their transition function;
2. it updates the valuation of abstract states by considering the concrete states associated with the abstract states, rather than by considering an abstract model only.

The second of the above points underlines how MLA is a semi-abstract, rather than fully abstract, approach to verification: the abstract computation still involves consideration of the concrete states, even though this is done in a way that provides space savings.

For the most part, approaches to MDP abstraction in the literature have followed another route, which we call very broadly the *full abstraction* approach: an abstract model is constructed, and then analyzed on the basis of an abstract transition structure, without further reference to the concrete model. These fully abstract approaches generally rely on clustering states that are similar not only in value, but also in transition structure: in this way, every region of concrete states can be summarized via an abstract state with an associated abstract transition structure. The abstract transition structure may, or may not, be similar to the concrete one. For instance, [19] bases the abstract transition structure on games, rather than MDPs: in this fashion, player 1 can represent the choice of action of the MDP, and player 2 can represent the uncertainty about the concrete state corresponding to the abstract state. This approach enables the computation of lower and upper bounds for properties of interest, similarly to MLA. In a somewhat related spirit, but using entirely different technical means, [14] proposes to abstract Markov chains into *abstract Markov chains* whose transitions are labeled with intervals of probability, representing the uncertainty about the concrete state. Clustering states based on the similarity in their transition probabilities has also been used in [12], which proposes to find the coarsest refinement of an MDP where for each action, states in the same region have the same probability of going to other regions. An approach for the verification of probabilistic reachability properties via abstraction has been proposed in [7]. The abstraction is built through successive refinements starting from a coarse partition based on the property. Several other approaches also, in fact, rely on constructing MDP abstractions based on simulation or abstract interpretation [18,22,21]; all of these approaches rely on clustering states with similar transition structure, and representing these clusters of states, and their transition structures, via compact abstract representations.

The full-abstraction approach outlined above, and the partial value-based approach followed by MLA, each have advantages. The full-abstraction result can handle unbounded, and (depending on the specific approach) even infinite state spaces. In contrast, the space savings afforded by MLA are limited to a square-root factor (a system of size n can be studied in $O(\sqrt{n})$ space), due to the need to consider the concrete states corresponding to each abstract one. Furthermore, the full-abstraction approaches typically need to construct the abstract model only once; in contrast, MLA needs to refer to concrete states (albeit not all of them at once) during the computation.

On the other hand, the ability of MLA to cluster states based on value only, disregarding differences in their transition relation, can lead to compact abstractions for systems where full abstraction provides no benefit. We will give below an example supporting this. Furthermore, in MLA the abstraction is refined dynamically, depending on the required accuracy of the analysis; there is no need to "guess" the right state partition in advance. In our experience, MLA is particularly well-suited to problems where there is a notion of *locality* in the state space, so that it makes sense to cluster states based on variable values — even though their transition relations may not be similar. Many planning and control problems are of this type. MLA instead is not as well-suited to problems where clustering states based on variable values is less effective. Approaches based on predicate abstraction could lend the MLA approach more generality.

An example of Magnifying-Lens Abstraction. To illustrate MLA, and its potential benefits, we give a simple example. We consider the problem of navigating an $n \times n$ minefield. The minefield contains m mines, each with coordinates (x_i, y_i), for $1 \leq i \leq m$, where $1 \leq x_i < n$, $1 \leq y_i < n$. We consider the problem of computing the maximal probability with which a robot can reach the target corner (n, n), from all $n \times n$ states. At interior states of the field, the robot can choose among four actions: *Up, Down, Left, Right;* at the border of the field, actions that lead outside of the field are missing. From a state $s = (x, y) \in \{1, \ldots, n\}^2$ with coordinates (x, y), each action causes the robot to move to square (x', y') with probability $q(x', y')$, and to "blow up" (move to an additional sink state) with probability $1 - q(x', y')$. For action *Right*, we have $x' = x + 1$, $y' = y$; similarly for the other actions. The probability $q(x', y')$ depends on the proximity to mines, and is given by

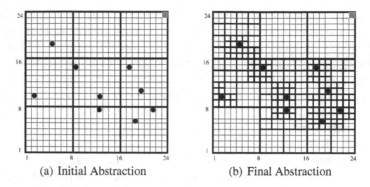

(a) Initial Abstraction   (b) Final Abstraction

Fig. 1. Initial, and final refined abstraction, for the problem of motion planning in a 24 × 24 minefield. The circles denote the mines

$$q(x', y') = \prod_i^m \exp\left(-0.7 \cdot \left((x' - x_i)^2 + (y' - y_i)^2\right)\right).$$

The problem, for $n = 24$, is illustrated in Figure 1.

Intuitively, it is desirable to group the 8×8 states in the top-middle area into a single region r_0: since no mines are nearby, the robot can freely roam in r_0, so that the maximal probability of reaching the target corner is essentially constant across r_0. Indeed, to a human trying to determine a best path to the target corner, the states in r_0 are essentially equivalent. When the 8×8 concrete states are grouped in r_0, MLA leads to accurate results, since it can analyze the dynamics inside r_0 when r_0 is magnified. We also note how, in this example, the ability of MLA to refine the abstraction adaptively is crucial. As shown in Figure 1(b), MLA is able to use small regions close to mines, and large regions elsewhere. If we insisted on a uniform region size, then we would have to adopt the smallest size throughout, and no space savings would be possible.

On the other hand, the full-abstraction approaches described earlier, such as [7,22,19], based on probabilistic simulation [27], are not well suited to this example. Such techniques would associate with an abstract state, such as r_0, a summary of the transition structure from states $s \in r_0$, and use that summary to analyze the abstraction. The problem is that the states in r_0, while similar in value, are not similar in transition structure: the states on the border of r_0 can transition outside of r_0, while those in the interior cannot. In the abstraction, the probability of going from r_0 to the region at the right hand side will be modeled as being in an interval $[0, q]$, for some q close to 1 (all mines are far away). Consequently, previous techniques would have yielded a lower bound of 0, and an upper bound close to 1, for the maximum probability of reaching the target corner. Similarly, the technique of [12] would lead to recursively splitting the MDP, until the regions consisted of only one concrete state each.

Other related work. MLA is reminiscent to methods that represent value functions via ADDs or MTBDDs [6,1] with an approximation factor used to merge leaves. The similarity, however, is superficial: MLA leads to far more precise results in the analysis; we discuss this in the conclusions, where the appropriate notation will be available.

MLA is also loosely reminiscent of *adaptive mesh refinement* (AMR) methods used in the solution of partial differential equations [3]. There are, however, two important differences between MLA and AMR. In AMR, separate lower and upper bounds are not kept. AMR methods perform computation at the finest mesh sizes only where needed. In MLA, due to the discrete nature of MDPs, we have no way of computing over a "coarse mesh" only: to update valuations over a region, we need to "magnify" the region to its individual states. Thus, MLA is forced to consider the individual states over the whole system, and it summarizes and returns the results in terms of lower and upper bounds, which are well-suited to answering verification questions.

2 Preliminary Definitions and Algorithms

For a countable set S, a *probability distribution* on S is a function $p : S \mapsto [0, 1]$ such that $\sum_{s \in S} p(s) = 1$; we denote the set of probability distributions on S by $D(S)$. A *valuation* over a set S is a function $v : S \mapsto \mathbb{R}$ associating a real number $v(s)$ with every $s \in S$. For $x \in \mathbb{R}$, we denote by $\mathbf{x}$ the valuation with constant value x; for $T \subseteq S$, we indicate by $[T]$ the valuation having value 1 in T and 0 elsewhere. For two valuations v, u on S, we define $\|v - u\| = \sup_{s \in S} |v(s) - u(s)|$.

A *partition* of a set S is a set $R \subseteq 2^S$, such that $\bigcup \{s | s \in R\} = S$, and such that for all $r, r' \in R$, if $r \neq r'$ then $r \cap r' = \emptyset$. For $s \in S$ and a partition R of S, we denote by $[s]_R$ the element $r \in R$ with $s \in r$. We say that a partition R' is *finer* than a partition R if the elements of R can be written as unions of the elements of R'.

A *Markov decision process* (MDP) $M = \langle S, A, \Gamma, p \rangle$ consists of the following components:

- A finite state space S.
- A finite set A of actions (moves),
- A move assignment $\Gamma : S \to 2^A \setminus \emptyset$.
- A probabilistic transition function $p : S \times A \to D(S)$.

At every state $s \in S$, the controller can choose an action $a \in \Gamma(s)$; the MDP then proceeds to the successor state t with probability $p(s, a, t)$, for all $t \in S$. A *path* of G is an infinite sequence $\bar{s} = s_0, s_1, s_2, \ldots$ of states of S; we denote by S^ω the set of all paths, and we denote by $\bar{s}_k$ the k-th state s_k of $\bar{s} = s_0, s_1, s_2, \ldots$.

We model the choice of actions, on the part of the controller, via a *strategy* (strategies are also variously called *schedulers* [26] or *policies* [13]). A *strategy* is a mapping $\pi : S^+ \mapsto D(A)$: given a past history $\sigma s \in S^+$ for the MDP, a strategy π chooses each action $a \in \Gamma(s)$ with probability $\pi(\sigma s)(a)$; we obviously require $\pi(\sigma s)(b) = 0$ for all $b \in A \setminus \Gamma(s)$. Thus, strategies can be both history-dependent, and randomized. We denote by Π the set of all strategies.

We consider *safety* and *reachability* goals. Given a subset $T \subseteq S$ of states, the reachability goal $\Diamond T = \{\bar{s} \in S^\omega \mid \exists k. \bar{s}_k \in T\}$ consists in the paths that reach T, and the safety goal $\Box T = \{\bar{s} \in S^\omega \mid \forall k. \bar{s}_k \in T\}$ consists in the paths that stay always in T. These sets of paths are measurable [28], so that given a strategy $\pi \in \Pi$, we can define the probabilities $\Pr_s^\pi(\Diamond T)$, $\Pr_s^\pi(\Box T)$ of following a path in these sets from an initial state $s \in S$ under strategy π. By choosing appropriate strategies, the

---

Algorithm 1. VallIter($T, f, g, \varepsilon_{float}$)   Value iteration

---

1. $v := [T]$
2.   **repeat**
3. $\hat{v} := v$
4.   **for all** $s \in S$ **do** $v(s) := f\Big([T](s), \; g\{\sum_{s' \in S} p(s, a, s') \cdot \hat{v}(s') \mid a \in \Gamma(s)\}\Big)$
5.   **until** $||v - \hat{v}|| \le \varepsilon_{float}$
6.   **return** v

---

controller can maximize or minimize these probabilities. Thus, we consider the problem of computing, at all $s \in S$, the quantities:

$$V_{\Box T}^{\max}(s) = \max_{\pi \in \Pi} \Pr_s^{\pi}(\Box T) \qquad V_{\Diamond T}^{\max}(s) = \max_{\pi \in \Pi} \Pr_s^{\pi}(\Diamond T)$$
$$V_{\Box T}^{\min}(s) = \min_{\pi \in \Pi} \Pr_s^{\pi}(\Box T) \qquad V_{\Diamond T}^{\min}(s) = \min_{\pi \in \Pi} \Pr_s^{\pi}(\Diamond T).$$

The fact that on the right-hand side we have max, min rather than sup, inf is a consequence of the existence of optimal (and memoryless) strategies [13]. In the remainder of the paper, unless explicitly noted, we present algorithms and definitions for a fixed MDP $M = \langle S, A, \Gamma, p \rangle$.

Reachability and safety probabilities on an MDP can be computed via a classical value-iteration scheme [13,4,11]. The algorithm, depicted as Algorithm 1, is parametrized by two operators $f, g \in \{\max, \min\}$. The operator f specifies how to merge the valuation of the current state with the expected next-state valuation; we use $f = \max$ for reachability goals, and $f = \min$ for safety ones. The operator g specifies whether to select the action that maximizes, or minimizes, the expected next-state valuation; we use $g = \max$ to compute maximal probabilities, and $g = \min$ to compute minimal probabilities, The algorithm is also parametrized by $\varepsilon_{float} > 0$: this is the threshold below which we consider value iteration to have converged. The following facts are well-known (see, e.g., [13,8,9]). For all $\varepsilon_{float} > 0$ and for all $f, g \in \{\min, \max\}$, the call VallIter($T, f, g, \varepsilon_{float}$) terminates. Moreover, consider any $g \in \{\max, \min\}$ and any $\triangle \in \{\Box, \Diamond\}$, and let $f = \min$ if $\triangle = \Box$, and $f = \max$ if $\triangle = \Diamond$. Then, for all $\delta > 0$, there is $\varepsilon_{float} > 0$ such that, at all $s \in S$:

$$v(s) - \delta \le V_{\triangle T}^{g}(s) \le v(s) + \delta$$

where $v = $ VallIter($T, f, g, \varepsilon_{float}$). We note that can replace statement 1 of Algorithm 1 with the following initialization: **if** $f = \max$ **then** $v := \mathbf{0}$ **else** $v := \mathbf{1}$.

3   Magnifying-Lens Abstraction

Magnifying-lens abstractions (MLA) is a technique for the analysis of reachability and safety properties of MDPs. Let v^* be the valuation on S that is to be computed: v^* is one of $V_{\Box T}^{\min}, V_{\Box T}^{\max}, V_{\Diamond T}^{\min}, V_{\Diamond T}^{\max}$. Given a desired accuracy $\varepsilon_{abs} > 0$, MLA computes upper

---

Algorithm 2. $\mathrm{MLA}(T, f, g, \varepsilon_{float}, \varepsilon_{abs})$ Magnifying-Lens Abstraction

---

1. $R :=$ some initial partition.
2.   **if** $f = \max$ **then** $u^- := 0; u^+ := 0$ **else** $u^- := 1; u^+ := 1$
3.   **loop**
4.   **repeat**
5. $\hat{u}^+ := u^+; \hat{u}^- := u^-;$
6.   **for** $r \in R$ **do**
7. $u^+(r) := \mathrm{MagnifiedIteration}(r, R, T, \hat{u}^+, \hat{u}^-, \hat{u}^+, \max, f, g, \varepsilon_{float})$
8. $u^-(r) := \mathrm{MagnifiedIteration}(r, R, T, \hat{u}^-, \hat{u}^-, \hat{u}^+, \min, f, g, \varepsilon_{float})$
9.   **end for**
10.   **until** $\|u^+ - \hat{u}^+\| + \|u^- - \hat{u}^-\| \leq \varepsilon_{float}$
11.   **if** $\|u^+ - u^-\| \geq \varepsilon_{abs}$
12.   **then** $R, u^-, u^+ := \mathrm{SplitRegions}(R, u^-, u^+, \varepsilon_{abs})$
13.   **else return** R, u^-, u^+
14.   **end if**
15. **end loop**

---

and lower bounds for v^*, spaced less than ε_{abs}. MLA starts from an initial partition R of S, and computes the lower and upper bounds as valuations u^- and u^+ over R. The partition is refined, until the difference between u^- and u^+, at all regions, is below a specified threshold. To compute u^- and u^+, MLA iteratively considers each r in turn, and performs a *magnified iteration:* it improves the estimates for $u^-(r)$ and $u^+(r)$ using value iteration on the concrete states $s \in r$.

The MLA algorithm is presented as Algorithm 2. The algorithm has parameters T, f, g, which have the same meaning as in Algorithm ValIter. The algorithm also has parameters $\varepsilon_{float} > 0$ and $\varepsilon_{abs} > 0$. Parameter ε_{abs} indicates the maximum difference between the lower and upper bounds returned by MLA. Parameter ε_{float}, as in ValIter, specifies the degree of precision to which the local, magnified value iteration should converge. MLA should be called with ε_{abs} greater than ε_{float} by at least one order of magnitude: otherwise, errors in the magnified iteration can cause errors in the estimation of the bounds. Statement 2 initializes the valuations u^- and u^+ according to the property to be computed: reachability properties are computed as least fixpoints, while safety properties are computed as greatest fixpoints [11]. A useful time optimization, not shown in Algorithm 2, consists in executing the loop at lines 6–9 only for regions r where at least one of the neighbor regions has changed value by more than ε_{float}.

Magnified iteration. The algorithm performing the magnified iteration is given as Algorithm 3. The algorithm is very similar to Algorithm 1, except for three points.

First, the valuation v (which here is local to r) is initialized not to $[T]$, but rather, to $u^-(r)$ if $f = \max$, and to $u^+(r)$ if $f = \min$. Indeed, if $f = \max$, value iteration converges from below, and $u^-(r)$ is a better starting point than $[T]$, since $[T](s) \leq u^-(r) \leq v^*(s)$ at all $s \in r$. The case for $f = \min$ is symmetrical.

Second, for $s \in S \setminus r$, the algorithm uses, in place of the value $v(s)$ which is not available, the value $u^-(r')$ or $u^+(r')$, as appropriate, where r' is such that $s \in r'$. In other words, the algorithm replaces values at concrete states outside r with the

---

Algorithm 3. MagnifiedIteration($r, R, T, u, u^-, u^+, h, f, g, \varepsilon_{float}$)

---

v: a valuation on r

1. **if** $f = \max$
2.   **then for** $s \in r$ **do** $v(s) = u^-(r)$
3.   **else for** $s \in r$ **do** $v(s) = u^+(r)$
4. **repeat**
5. $\hat{v} := v$
6.   **for all** $s \in r$ **do**

$$v(s) = f\left([T](s), g\left\{\sum_{s' \in r} p(s, a, s') \cdot \hat{v}(s') + \sum_{s' \in S \setminus r} p(s, a, s') \cdot u([s]_R) \,\middle|\, a \in \Gamma(s)\right\}\right)$$

7. **until** $||v - \hat{v}|| \leq \varepsilon_{float}$
8. **return** $h\{v(s) \mid s \in r\}$

"abstract" values of the regions to which the states belong. To this end, we need to be able to efficiently find the "abstract" counterpart $[s]_R$ of a state $s \in S$. We use the following scheme, similar to schemes used in AMR [3]. Most commonly, the state-space S of the MDP consists in value assignments to a set of variables $X = \{x_1, x_2, \ldots, x_l\}$. We represent a partition R of S, together with the valuations u^+, u^-, via a binary decision tree. The nodes of the tree are labeled by $\langle y, i \rangle$, where $y \in X$ is the variable according to which we split, and i is the position of the bit (0 =LSB) of the variable according to whose value we split. The leaves of the tree correspond to regions, and they are labeled with u^-, u^+ values. Given s, finding $[s]_R$ in such a tree requires time logarithmic in $|S|$.

Third, once the concrete valuation v is computed at all $s \in r$, Algorithm 3 returns the minimum (if $h = \min$) or the maximum (if $h = \max$) of $v(s)$ at all $s \in r$, thus providing a new estimates for $u^-(r)$, $u^+(r)$, respectively.

Adaptive abstraction refinement. We denote the *imprecision* of a region r by $\Delta(r) = u^+(r) - u^-(r)$. MLA adaptively refines a partition R by splitting all regions r having $\Delta(r) > \varepsilon_{abs}$. This is perhaps the simplest possible refinement scheme. We experimented with alternative refinement schemes, but none of them gave consistently better results. In particular, we considered splitting the regions with high Δ-value, all whose successors, according to the optimal moves, have low Δ-value: the idea is that such regions are the ones where precision degrades. While this reduces somewhat the number of region splits, the total number of refinements is increased, and the resulting algorithm is not clearly superior, at least in the examples we considered. We also experimented with splitting all regions $r \in R$ with $\Delta(r) > \delta$, for a threshold δ that is initially set to $\frac{1}{2}$, and that is then gradually decreased to ε_{abs}. This approach, inspired by simulated annealing, also failed to provide consistent improvements.

In the minefield example, each region is *squarish* (horizontal and vertical sizes differ by at most 1); we split each such squarish region into 4 smaller squarish regions. In more general cases, the following heuristic for splitting regions is widely applicable, and has worked well for us. The user specifies an ordering $x_0, x_1, \ldots, x_l$ for the state variables X defining S: this specifies a priority order for splitting regions. As previously mentioned, we represent a partition R via a decision tree, whose leaves correspond to the regions. In the refinement phase, we split a leaf according to the value of a new variable (not present in that leaf), following the variable ordering given by the user. Precisely, to split a region r, we look at the label $\langle x_j, i \rangle$ of its parent node. If $i > 0$, we split according to bit $i - 1$ of x_j; otherwise, we split according to the MSB of x_{j+1}. A refinement of this technique allows the specification of groups of variables, whose ranges are split in interleaved fashion. Once a region r has been split into regions r_1, r_2, we set $u^-(r_j) = u^-(r)$ and $u^+(r_j) = u^+(r)$ for all $j = 1, 2$. A call to SplitRegions($R, u^+, u^-, \varepsilon_{abs}$) returns a triple $\tilde{R}, \tilde{u}^-, \tilde{u}^+$, consisting of the new partition with its upper and lower bounds for the valuation.

Correctness. The following theorem summarizes MLA correctness.

Theorem 1. *For all MDPs* $M = \langle S, A, \Gamma, p \rangle$, *all* $T \subseteq S$, *and all* $\varepsilon_{abs} > 0$, *the following assertions hold.*

1. *Termination. For all* $\varepsilon_{float} > 0$, *and for all* $f, g \in \{\min, \max\}$, *the call MLA* $(T, f, g, \varepsilon_{float}, \varepsilon_{abs})$ *terminates.*
2. *(Partial) correctness. Consider any* $g \in \{\max, \min\}$, *any* $\varepsilon_{abs} > 0$, *and any* $\triangle \in \{\Box, \Diamond\}$, *and let* $f = \min$ *if* $\triangle = \Box$, *and* $f = \max$ *if* $\triangle = \Diamond$. *The following holds. For all* $\delta > 0$, *there is* $\varepsilon_{float} > 0$ *such that:*

$$\forall r \in R: \qquad u^+(r) - u^-(r) \leq \varepsilon_{abs}$$
$$\forall s \in S: \qquad u^-([s]_R) - \delta \leq V_{\triangle T}^g(s) \leq u^+([s]_R) + \delta$$

where $(R, u^-, u^+) = MLA(T, f, g, \varepsilon_{float}, \varepsilon_{abs})$.

We note that the theorem establishes the correctness of lower and upper bounds only within a constant $\delta > 0$, which depends on ε_{float}. This limitation is inherited from the value-iteration scheme used over the magnified regions. If linear programming [13,4] were used instead, then MLA would provide true lower and upper bounds. However, in practice value iteration is preferred over linear programming, due to its simplicity and great speed advantage, and the concerns about δ are solved — in practice, albeit not in theory — by choosing a small $\varepsilon_{float} > 0$.

4   Experimental Results

In order to evaluate the time and space performance of MLA, we have implemented a prototype, and we have used it for three case studies: the minefield navigation problem, the Bounded Retransmission Protocol [7], and the ZeroConf protocol for the autonomous configuration of IP addresses [5,19].

When comparing MLA to ValIter, we compute the space needs of the algorithms as follows. For ValIter, we take the space requirement to be equal to $|S|$, the domain of v. For MLA, we take the space requirement to be the maximum value of $2 \cdot |R| + \max_{r \in R} |r|$ that occurs every time MLA is at line 4 of Algorithm2: this gives the maximum space required to store the valuations u^+, u^-, as well as the values v for the largest magnified region. Since $\max_{r \in R} |r| \geq (|S|/|R|)$, the space complexity of the algorithm is (lower) bounded by a square-root function $\sqrt{8 \cdot |S|}$.

Algorithm	Space	Time
ValIter	16,384	21.97
MLA	7,926	123.54

MLA Iteration Details			
#Abs	$|R|$	D	Time
1	144	0.994	9.21
2	576	0.837	38.48
3	2,312	0.663	47.36
4	3,256	0.645	11.39
5	3,566	0.020	14.59
6	3,899	0.007	2.52

(a) $n = 128, m = 128$

Algorithm	Space	Time
ValIter	65,536	130.18
MLA	7,944	185.13

MLA Iteration Details			
#Abs	$|R|$	D	Time
1	256	0.983	49.48
2	985	0.656	76.27
3	1,513	0.776	12.61
4	2,341	0.605	17.58
5	3,844	0.007	29.19

(b) $n = 256, m = 128$

Algorithm	Space	Time
ValIter	262,144	1,065.36
MLA	30,180	3,199.31

MLA Iteration Details			
#Abs	$|R|$	D	Time
1	576	0.999	299.02
2	2,295	0.777	1648.67
3	4,347	0.777	206.64
4	7,171	0.659	228.95
5	11,678	0.525	362.70
6	14,862	0.007	453.33

(c) $n = 512, m = 512$

Fig. 2. Comparison between MLA and ValIter for $n \times n$ minefields with m mines, for $\varepsilon_{abs} = 10^{-2}$ and $\varepsilon_{float} = 10^{-4}$. Mine densities (m/n^2) are (a) $1/64$, (b) $1/512$, and (c) $1/512$. All times are in seconds. #Abs is the number of abstraction steps (number of loops 3–15 of MLA), and $D = \max_{r \in R}(u^+(r) - u^-(r))$.

Algorithm	Space	Time
ValIter	16,384	20.51
MLA	3,672	54.51

(a) $n = 128, m = 128$

Algorithm	Space	Time
ValIter	65,536	130.08
MLA	4,548	126.40

(b) $n = 256, m = 128$

Algorithm	Space	Time
ValIter	262,144	1,065.65
MLA	15,476	1,853.01

(c) $n = 512, m = 512$

Fig. 3. Comparison between MLA and ValIter for $n \times n$ minefields with m mines, for $\varepsilon_{abs} = 10^{-1}$ and $\varepsilon_{float} = 10^{-2}$. Mine densities (m/n^2) are (a) $1/64$, (b) $1/512$, and (c) $1/512$. All times are in seconds.

4.1 Minefield Navigation

We experimented with different-size minefields in the mine-field example. In all cases, the mines were distributed in a pseudo-random fashion across the field. The performance of algorithms ValIter and MLA, for $\varepsilon_{abs} = 0.01$, are compared in Figure 2. As we can see, the space savings are 2.06 for a mine density of $1/64$, and an average of 8.47 for a mine density of $1/512$. This comes at a cost in running time, which is of 5.67 for a mine density of $1/64$, and 1.42 to 3.00 for a mine density of $1/512$. Especially for lower mine densities, MLA provides space savings that are larger than the incurred time penalty. The space savings are even more pronounced when we decrease the desired precision of the result to $\varepsilon_{abs} = 0.1$, as indicated in Figure 3.

4.2 The ZeroConf Protocol

The ZeroConf protocol [5] is used for the dynamic self-configuration of a host joining a network; it has been used as a testbed for the abstraction method considered in [19]. We consider a network with 4 existing hosts, and 32 total IP addresses; protocol messages have a certain probability of being lost during transmission. We consider the problem of determining the worst-case probability of a host eventually acquiring an IP address: this is a probabilistic reachability problem.

N	MAX	ValIter time	#Reachable states	MLA space	MLA time
16	3	0.08	1,966	918	27.38
32	5	0.21	5,466	2,604	140.79
64	5	0.40	10,650	5,380	266.53

Fig. 4. Comparison between MLA and ValIter for BRP. N denotes number of chunks and MAX denotes the maximum number of retransmissions. All times are in seconds.

The abstraction approach of [19] reduces the problem from $26,121$ concrete reachable states to 737 abstract states. MLA reduces the problem to 131 regions, requiring a total space of 1267 (including also the space to perform the magnification step) for $\varepsilon_{abs} = 10^{-3}$ and $\varepsilon_{float} = 10^{-6}$. We cannot compare the running times, due to the absence of timing data in [19].

4.3 Bounded Retransmission Protocol

We also considered the Bounded Retransmission Protocol described in [7]. We compared the performance of algorithms ValIter and MLA on "Property 1" from [7], stating that the sender eventually does not report a successful transmission. The results are compared in Figure 4, for $\varepsilon_{abs} = 10^{-2}$ and $\varepsilon_{float} = 10^{-4}$. MLA achieves a space saving of a factor of 2, but at the price of a great increase in running time.

4.4 Discussion

From these examples, it is apparent that MLA does well on problems where there is some notion of "distance" between states, so that "nearby" states have similar values for the reachability or safety property of interest. These problems are common in planning and control. As we discussed in the introduction, many of these problems do not lend themselves to abstraction methods based on the similarity of transition relations, such as [19,7], and other methods based on simulation. We believe the MLA algorithm is valuable for the study of this type of problems. We note that each mine affects a region of size 5×5 by more than the desired precision $\varepsilon_{abs} = 10^{-2}$. Therefore, while the mine density is only 1/512, the ratio of "disturbed" vs. "undisturbed" state space is 25/512, or 1/20. This is a typical value in planning problems with sparse obstacles.

On the other hand, for problems where simulation-based methods can be used, these methods tend to be more effective than MLA, as they can construct, once and for all, a small abstract model on which all properties of interest can be analyzed.

5 Conclusions

A natural question about MLA is the following: why does MLA consider the concrete states at each iteration, as part of the "magnification" steps, rather than constructing an abstract model once and for all, and then analyze it, as other approaches to MDP abstraction do [7,18,22,19]? The answer has two parts. First, we cannot build an abstract model once and for all: our abstraction refinement approach would require the computation of several abstractions. Second, we have found that the cost of building abstractions that are sufficiently precise, without resorting to a "magnification" step, is substantial, negating any benefits that might derive from the ability to perform computation on a reduced system.

To understand the performance issues in constructing precise abstractions, consider the problem of computing the maximal reachability probability. To summarize the maximal probability of a transition from a region r to r_1, we need to compute $P_r^+(r_1) = \min_{s \in r} \max_{\pi \in \Pi} \Pr_s^\pi(r \, \mathcal{U} \, r_1)$, where $\mathcal{U}$ is the "until" operator of linear temporal logic [20]; this quantity is related to building abstractions via *weak simulation* [27,2,24]. These probability summaries are not additive: for $r_1 \neq r_2$, we have that $P_r^+(r_1) + P_r^+(r_2) \leq P^+(r_1 \cup r_2)$, and equality does not hold in general. Indeed, these probability summaries constitute *capacities,* and they can be used to analyze maximal reachability properties via the Choquet integral [25,15,16]. To construct a fully precise abstraction, one must compute $P_r^+(R')$ for all $R' \subseteq R$, clearly a daunting task. In practice, in the minefield example, it suffices to consider those $R' \subseteq R$ that consist of neighbors of r. To further lower the number of capacities to be computed, we experimented with restricting R' to unions of no more than k regions, but for all choices of k, the algorithm either yielded grossly imprecise results, or proved to be markedly less efficient than MLA.

The space savings provided by MLA are bounded by a square-root function of the state space. We could improve this bound by applying MLA hierarchically, so that each magnified region is studied, in turn, with a nested application of MLA.

Symbolic representations such as ADDs and MTBDDs [6,1] have been used for representing the value function compactly [10,17]. The decision-tree structure used by MLA to represent regions and abstract valuations is closely related to MTBDDs, and in future work we intend to explore symbolic implementations of MLA, where separate MTBDDs will be used to represent lower and upper bounds.

References

1. Bahar, R.I., Frohm, E.A., Gaona, C.M., Hachtel, G.D., Macii, E., Pardo, A., Somenzi, F.: Algebraic decision diagrams and their applications. Journal of Formal Methods in System Design 10(2/3), 171–206 (1997)
2. Baier, C., Hermanns, H.: Weak bisimulation for fully probabilistic processes. In: Grumberg, O. (ed.) CAV 1997. LNCS, vol. 1254, pp. 119–130. Springer, Heidelberg (1997)
3. B., J., Berger, J.O.: Adaptive mesh refinement for hyperbolic partial differential equations. Journal of Computational Physics 53, 484–512 (1984)
4. Bertsekas, D.: Dynamic Programming and Optimal Control. Athena Scientific, Volumes I and II (1995)
5. Cheshire, S., Adoba, B., Gutterman, E.: Dynamic configuration of ipv4 link local addresses (internet draft).
6. Clarke, E., Fujita, M., McGeer, P., Yang, J., Zhao, X.: Multi-terminal binary decision diagrams: An efficient data structure for matrix representation. In: International Workshop for Logic Synthesis (1993)

7. D'Argenio, P., Jeannet, B., Jensen, H., Larsen, K.: Reachability analysis of probabilistic systems by successive refinements. In: de Luca, L., Gilmore, S.T. (eds.) PROBMIV 2001, PAPM-PROBMIV 2001, and PAPM 2001. LNCS, vol. 2165, pp. 39–56. Springer, Heidelberg (2001)

8. de Alfaro, L.: Formal Verification of Probabilistic Systems. PhD thesis, Stanford University, Technical Report STAN-CS-TR-98-1601 (1997)

9. Alfaro, L.d.: Computing minimum and maximum reachability times in probabilistic systems. In: Baeten, J.C.M., Mauw, S. (eds.) CONCUR 1999. LNCS, vol. 1664, pp. 66–81. Springer, Heidelberg (1999)

10. L.,, Kwiatkowska, M., Norman, G., Parker, D., Alfaro, R.S.d.: Symbolic model checking of concurrent probabilistic processes using MTBDDs and the Kronecker representation. In: Schwartzbach, M.I., Graf, S. (eds.) ETAPS 2000 and TACAS 2000. LNCS, vol. 1785, pp. 395–410. Springer, Heidelberg (2000)

11. Alfaro, L.d., Majumdar, R.: Quantitative solution of omega-regular games. Journal of Computer and System Sciences 68, 374–397 (2004)

12. Dean, T., Givan, R.: Model minimization in markov decision processes. In: AAAI/IAAI, pp. 106–111 (1997)

13. Derman, C.: Finite State Markovian Decision Processes. Academic Press, London (1970)

14. Fecher, H., Leucker, M., Wolf, V.: Don't know in probabilistic systems. In: Valmari, A. (ed.) Model Checking Software. LNCS, vol. 3925, Springer, Heidelberg (2006)

15. Gilboa, I.: Expected utility with purely subjective non-additive probabilities. Journal of Mathematical Economics 16, 65–88 (1987)

16. Gilboa, I., Schmeidler, D.: Additive representations of non-additive measures and the choquet integral. Discussion Papers 985, Northwestern University, Center for Mathematical Studies in Economics and Management Science (1992), available at http://ideas.repec.org/p/nwu/cmsems/985.html.

17. Hinton, A., Kwiatkowska, M., Norman, G., Parker, D.: PRISM: A tool for automatic verification of probabilistic systems. In: Hermanns, H., Palsberg, J. (eds.) TACAS 2006 and ETAPS 2006. LNCS, vol. 3920, pp. 441–444. Springer, Heidelberg (2006)

18. Huth, M.: On finite-state approximations for probabilistic computational-tree logic. Theor. Comp. Sci. 346(1), 113–134 (2005)

19. Kwiatkowska, M., Norman, G., Parker, D.: Game-based abstraction for markov decision processes. In: Proc. of QEST: Quantitative Evaluation of Systems, pp. 157–166. IEEE Computer Society Press, Los Alamitos (2006)

20. Manna, Z., Pnueli, A.: The Temporal Logic of Reactive and Concurrent Systems: Specification. Springer, New York (1991)

21. McIver, A., Morgan, C.: Abstraction, Refinement, and Proof for Probabilistic Systems. In: Monographs in Computer Science, Springer, Heidelberg (2004)

22. Monniaux, D.: Abstract interpretation of programs as Markov decision processes. Science of Computer Programming 58(1–2), 179–205 (2005)

23. Plateau, B.: On the stochastic structure of parallelism and synchronization models for distributed algorithms. In: SIGMETRICS '85: Proceedings of the 1985 ACM SIGMETRICS conference on Measurement and modeling of computer systems, pp. 147–154. ACM Press, New York, NY, USA (1985)

24. Plilippou, A., Lee, I., Sokolsky, O.: Weak bisimulation for probabilistic systems. In: Palamidessi, C. (ed.) CONCUR 2000. LNCS, vol. 1877, pp. 334–349. Springer, Heidelberg (2000)

25. Schmeidler, D.: Integral representation without additivity. Proceedings of the American Mathematical Society 97, 255–261 (1986)

26. Segala, R.: Modeling and Verification of Randomized Distributed Real-Time Systems. PhD thesis, MIT, Technical Report MIT/LCS/TR-676 (1995)
27. Segala, R., Lynch, N.A.: Probabilistic simulations for probabilistic processes. In: Jonsson, B., Parrow, J. (eds.) CONCUR 1994. LNCS, vol. 836, pp. 481–496. Springer, Heidelberg (1994)
28. Vardi, M.Y.: Automatic verification of probabilistic concurrent finite-state systems. In: Proc. 26th IEEE Symp. Found. of Comp. Sci. pp. 327–338. IEEE Computer Society Press, Los Alamitos (1985)

Underapproximation for Model-Checking Based on Random Cryptographic Constructions

Arie Matsliah[1,2] and Ofer Strichman[1,3]

[1] IBM Haifa Research Laboratory, Haifa, Israel
[2] Faculty of Computer Science, Technion, Haifa, Israel
ariem@cs.technion.ac.il
[3] Information Systems Engineering, IE, Technion, Haifa, Israel
ofers@ie.technion.ac.il

Abstract. For two naturals m, n such that $m < n$, we show how to construct a circuit C with m inputs and n outputs, that has the following property: for some $0 \leq k \leq m$, the circuit defines a k-universal function. This means, informally, that for every subset K of k outputs, every possible valuation of the variables in K is reachable (we prove that k is very close to m with an arbitrarily high probability). Now consider a circuit M with n inputs that we wish to model-check. Connecting the inputs of M to the outputs of C gives us a new circuit M' with m inputs, that its original inputs have freedom defined by k. This is a very attractive feature for underapproximation in model-checking: on one hand the combined circuit has a smaller number of inputs, and on the other hand it is expected to find an error state fast if there is one.

We report initial experimental results with bounded model checking of industrial designs (the method is equally applicable to unbounded model checking and to simulation), which shows mixed results. An interesting observation, however, is that in 13 out of 17 designs, setting m to be $n/5$ is sufficient to detect the bug. This is in contrast to other underapproximation that are based on reducing the number of inputs, which in most cases cannot detect the bug even with $m = n/2$.

1 Introduction

Experience with model-checking of industrial hardware designs shows that when the model violates a specification, it is frequently the case that the values of only some of the inputs is important for triggering an erroneous behavior (as the saying goes: "when it rains - it pours!"). Based on this observation it is appealing to underapproximate the model, attempting to make it easier to check, yet not eliminating the problematic behavior altogether. In other words, the challenge is to underapproximate by finding those restrictions that do not prevent all error states from being reached. Designing a fully automatic model-checking algorithm based on underapproximation that is still sound and complete requires an iterative process of underapproximation and refinement.

Automatic underapproximation/refinement for model-checking is not nearly as popular as its dual, automated overapproximation/refinement. An

W. Damm and H. Hermanns (Eds.): CAV 2007, LNCS 4590, pp. 339–351, 2007.
© Springer-Verlag Berlin Heidelberg 2007

overapproximating abstraction may result in a false negative, accompanied by a spurious (abstract) counterexample. This counterexample can then be used to guide the refinement process, as in the CEGAR [8,4,5,3] and proof-based [1] frameworks (in the latter only the length of the counterexample is used). All of these works are based on overapproximation.

An underapproximation, on the other hand, may result in a false positive: here, good refinements are harder to achieve, as there is no equivalent to the counterexample that can guide it. An exception to this rule is in SAT-based Bounded Model-Checking (BMC), where the unsatisfiable core can guide the refinement: Grumberg et al. [6] used this fact in their work on underapproximation-refinement for bounded model checking of multi-process systems. We are only aware of few works on underapproximations with BDDs (e.g., [10,11,2]), all of which are based on the size of the BDD (e.g., restricting the growth of the reachable state-space when the BDD size becomes too large), but none of them are fully automatic and complete.

In this paper we focus on underapproximations that are based on reducing the number of inputs to the model. In theory this should make the model easier to solve, at least in the worst-case, since the number of computation paths has exponential dependency on the number of inputs[1]. The most basic technique is to restrict some of the inputs to constants. Such naive underapproximation, combined with a gradual lifting of these restrictions (typically in a manual manner) is a common practice in the industry probably from the very first days of industrial model-checking. If no user-guidance is provided, however, an automated refinement based on some arbitrary order of lifting the restrictions has a small chance to succeed, unless the bug is ubiquitous enough to be very simple to find. It is enough for one of the inputs necessary for exposing the error-trace to be falsely restricted, to potentially make the model too big for model-checking by the time this input is released. Another option is to combine inputs (arbitrarily) and refining by splitting the combined sets. In Section 2.2 we analyze these options in more depth.

What is this article about? The current work suggests an underapproximation which reduces the number of inputs as well, but it is based on adding circuitry to the model, while maintaining a measurable and uniform degree of freedom to the original inputs. This technique is automatic, easy to combine in an underapproximation-refinement method, and is applicable to any form of model-checking or simulation, whether it is SAT-based or BDD-based. The technique is inspired by theoretical constructions of cryptographic circuits, the Pseudo Random Generators (PRGs). These PRGs can expand a short truly random Boolean sequence into a longer one, which is almost random (more details are given in Section 2). Based on constructions of these PRGs, we build simple Boolean circuits and prove that they have the universality property as defined below.

---

[1] In the context of SAT this is less obvious because SAT does not distinguish between inputs and other variables. But the reduction in the number of inputs implies that it has a smaller upper-bound on the size of the smallest back-door set [13], namely the inputs, which suggest a better upper-bound on the run-time.

Consider a model M with n inputs that we wish to model-check. We build a Boolean circuit with m inputs and n outputs, $0 < m < n$, which is k-*universal*. Informally, this means that the circuit implements a function such that any valuation of at most k outputs can be reached under some assignment to the inputs. We then connect the outputs of C to the inputs of M (see Figure 1). The composed model M' has less inputs and underapproximates the original model M. One of the challenges in such a construction is to guarantee high values of k for a given value of m. We discuss this question in detail in Section 3.1.

Universality was also used in [7], in the context of simulation. The authors constructed vectors that have a certain degree of universality and showed that this indeed has a better chance to expose problems in comparison to alterative vector sets of the same size.

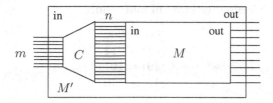

Fig. 1. Since the attached Boolean circuit is k-universal, *any* assignment on *any* k out of the n inputs of the original model M, can be achieved under some assignment on the inputs of M'

The main contribution of this paper is theoretical: we show how to construct M' and derive lower-bounds on the value of k as a function of m. Since the construction is based on a random function, the results are probabilistic. We also define a weaker version of universality, called (k, ϵ)-universality, in which for only a $1 - \epsilon$ fraction of the subsets of size k, any assignment is possible (k-universality corresponds to $\epsilon = 0$). With this relaxation we prove that for $k = \max(0, m - \log \frac{1}{\epsilon \cdot \delta})$, where δ is the confidence level, the circuit C is (k, ϵ)-universal with probability at least $1 - \delta$. For example, with probability 0.99, for 99% of the subsets of size $k = \max(0, m - 14)$, any assignment can be achieved.

In Section 4 we describe our experiments, which attempt to check whether k-universality can be useful in the context of model-checking. In other words, whether the freedom on the original inputs as guaranteed by this method is indeed helpful in detecting bugs in real designs, in comparison to other forms of underapproximation that have the same search-space. The answer is conclusive: it is able to find bugs with far less inputs. The results are less conclusive, but still positive, when it comes to comparing to a run without underapproximation at all. This is probably due to the fact that our construction is based on a XOR function, which is notoriously hard for SAT solvers. We conclude in Subsection 4.1 by pointing to several practical issues in applying this method that are still open.

2   Local Universality

2.1 k-Universal Circuits and Upper-Bound on k

Let C be a Boolean circuit with m inputs and n outputs, $m \leq n$, implementing a corresponding function $C : \{0,1\}^m \to \{0,1\}^n$.

Definition 1 (k-universal functions). *The function C is k-universal if for every subset $K \subset \{1,\ldots,n\}$ of k outputs and every partial assignment $\alpha_K \in \{0,1\}^k$ on K, there is a full assignment $\alpha \in \{0,1\}^m$ on the inputs of C such that $C(\alpha)|_K = \alpha_K$.*   □

In other words, any subset of k output bits can take all 2^k possible assignments in a k-universal function C.

Example 1. The following function $C : \{0,1\}^2 \to \{0,1\}^3$ is 2-universal, since every two output coordinates have all four values:

$$
\begin{aligned}
C(00) &= 000 \\
C(01) &= 011 \\
C(10) &= 101 \\
C(11) &= 110
\end{aligned}
\tag{1}
$$

□

In Section 3 we present a method for constructing k-universal circuits.

2.2   Universality of Some Known Underapproximations

Underapproximations based on restricting the inputs can be seen as functions mapping inputs of the restricted model to inputs of the original model. It is worthwhile to check how universal these functions are. Recall that if the model is unrestricted, it is n-universal, where n is the number of inputs.

- *Underapproximation by restricting a subset of the inputs to constant values.* Regardless of the method for choosing these inputs and their values, or whether it is part of a refinement process or not, it is clear that the underlying set of possible assignment vectors to the restricted model is not even 1-universal, since there are inputs that cannot have both values.
- *Underapproximation by combining inputs.* In this method the set of inputs is partitioned, and all inputs in the same partition class are forced to agree on their value. Regardless of the partitioning method, this method guarantees 1-universality, but not 2-universality, because two inputs in the same partition class cannot have all 4 valuations.

3   The PRG-Like Construction

The structure of our k-universal circuits, as mentioned earlier, were inspired by constructions of Pseudo Random Generators. PRG is a circuit that, given a short sequence of truly random bits, outputs a longer sequence of pseudo random bits. More formally:

Definition 2 (PRG). Pseudo Random Generator (PRG) *is a deterministic polynomial time function* $G : \{0,1\}^m \rightarrow \{0,1\}^n$, *where* $n > m$, *such that the following distributions are not distinguishable by circuits of size* n:

- *Distribution* G_n *defined as the output of function* G *on a uniformly selected input in* $\{0,1\}^m$.
- *Distribution* U_n *defined as the uniform distribution on* $\{0,1\}^n$. □

The original motivation for constructing PRG's was derandomizing probabilistic algorithms[2].

In this section we sketch briefly how the original PRG of [9] is constructed, and introduce a slightly different (random) construction that, as we prove later, provides with arbitrarily high probability, k-universal circuits. The parameter k here is almost linear in m, with practically small coefficients. Without going into the details, based on a result in [12] it can be shown that ($2^k \log n \leq 2^m$), which means that an upper bound on k is $m - \log \log n$. Hence, the circuit we construct has nearly optimal parameters.

Definition 3 (System[3]). *A family* $S = (S_1, S_2, \ldots, S_n)$ *of equally-sized subsets* $S_i \subset \{1, 2, \ldots, m\}$ *is a* (l, ρ, m, n)-*system if*

- $\forall i, \quad |S_i| = l$
- $\forall i, j \quad |S_i \cap S_j| \leq \rho$ □

Given a Boolean function $f : \{0,1\}^l \rightarrow \{0,1\}$ and a system $S = (S_1, S_2, \ldots, S_n)$, we construct the circuit $C = C(S, f)$ as follows:

- $I_C = \{i_1, \ldots, i_m\}$ are the inputs of C.
- $O_C = \{o_1, \ldots, o_n\}$ are the outputs of C.
- For $j \in \{1, \ldots, n\}$,
  - Let $I(o_j) = \{i_h : h \in S_j\}$ be a set of l inputs chosen according to the system S.
  - Set $o_j = f(I(o_j))$.

In the original paper [9] the existence of systems with "good" parameters is proved, and the PRG's are constructed based on these "good" systems using functions f that have some specific cryptographic properties. Further details are given in the above reference.

Now we define our random systems, based on which we will build k-universal circuits.

---

2 For instance, a "perfect" PRG would be a function $G : \{0,1\}^{\log n} \rightarrow \{0,1\}^n$. If we have such a PRG, then we can deterministically simulate any probabilistic algorithm by going over all $2^{\log n} = n$ possible seeds for G, running the probabilistic algorithm and taking the majority vote.

3 In the original terminology this set system is called a *Design*. We avoid this term to prevent ambiguity.

Definition 4 (Random System). *Let n, m be naturals such that $1 \leq m \leq n$. An (m, n)-Random System is a family $RS = (S_1, S_2, \ldots, S_n)$ of n uniformly chosen random subsets $S_i \subset \{1, 2, \ldots, m\}$. Namely, for every $1 \leq i \leq n$ (independently of each other), the set S_i is chosen uniformly at random out of all 2^m possible subsets of $\{1, 2, \ldots, m\}$.* □

Similarly to the previous construction, we build the circuit $C = C(RS, f)$ where we set f to be the XOR function ($\oplus$). Formally,

- $I_C = \{i_1, \ldots, i_m\}$ are the inputs of C.
- $O_C = \{o_1, \ldots, o_n\}$ are the outputs of C.
- For $j \in \{1, \ldots, n\}$,
  - Let $I(o_j) = \{i_h : h \in S_j\}$ be the randomly chosen set of inputs from RS.
  - Set $o_j = \oplus(I(o_j))$.

In the following section we prove that with arbitrary high probability these circuits are k-universal for relatively high k.

3.1   Lower Bounds on k

First we prove that if the family RS has certain algebraic properties, then the circuit C that is built from RS is k-universal.

Lemma 1. *Let A be an $n \times m$ Boolean matrix defined by the family RS. Formally, the entry $a_{ij} \in A$ is 1 if $j \in S_i$ and 0 otherwise. Then if every k rows of A are linearly independent[4], the circuit $C = C(RS, \oplus)$ as above is k-universal.*

Proof (of Lemma 1). First notice that the i'th output of C implements a XOR function on the inputs that correspond to the '1' entries of the i'th row in the matrix A. So we can think of C as a linear transformation in field $GF(2)$ (Galois Field), induced by multiplying the matrix A with the input vector (recall that addition in $GF(2)$ is equivalent to the XOR operator). In other words, for every $\alpha_1 \alpha_2 \cdots \alpha_m \in \{0, 1\}^m$ and $\beta_1 \beta_2 \cdots \beta_n \in \{0, 1\}^n$, $C(\alpha_1 \alpha_2 \cdots \alpha_m) = \beta_1 \beta_2 \cdots \beta_n$ if and only if the following holds:

$$
\begin{pmatrix}
a_{11} & a_{12} & \ldots & a_{1m} \\
a_{21} & a_{22} & \ldots & a_{2m} \\
 & & & \\
 & \cdot & \cdot & \\
 & \cdot & \cdot & \\
 & & & \\
a_{n1} & a_{n2} & \ldots & a_{nm}
\end{pmatrix}
\times
\begin{pmatrix}
\alpha_1 \\
\alpha_2 \\
\vdots \\
\alpha_m
\end{pmatrix}
=
\begin{pmatrix}
\beta_1 \\
\beta_2 \\
\cdot \\
\cdot \\
\cdot \\
\beta_n
\end{pmatrix} .
\tag{2}
$$

Let $K = \{o_1, o_2, \ldots, o_k\} \subset \{1, 2, \ldots, n\}$ be arbitrary set of k outputs, and let $\beta_{o_1} \beta_{o_2} \cdots \beta_{o_k}$ be any partial assignment on K. Notice that for any $\alpha_1 \alpha_2 \cdots \alpha_m$ the value $C(\alpha_1 \alpha_2 \cdots \alpha_m)$ restricted to K equals $\beta_{o_1} \beta_{o_2} \cdots \beta_{o_k}$ if and only if

---

[4] Equivalently, every k rows of A form a full rank matrix.

$$\begin{pmatrix} a_{o_1 1} & a_{o_1 2} & \cdots & a_{o_1 m} \\ a_{o_2 1} & a_{o_2 2} & \cdots & a_{o_2 m} \\ \cdot & & & \cdot \\ \cdot & & & \cdot \\ \cdot & & & \cdot \\ a_{o_k 1} & a_{o_k 2} & \cdots & a_{o_k m} \end{pmatrix} \times \begin{pmatrix} \alpha_1 \\ \alpha_2 \\ \vdots \\ \alpha_m \end{pmatrix} = \begin{pmatrix} \beta_{o_1} \\ \beta_{o_2} \\ \cdot \\ \cdot \\ \cdot \\ \beta_{o_k} \end{pmatrix}. \tag{3}$$

We denote this restricted $k \times m$ matrix by B. Recall that our purpose is to prove that such an assignment $\alpha_1 \alpha_2 \cdots \alpha_m$ indeed exists. Here we use the fact that every k rows in A are linearly independent, and thus the matrix B is invertible. Therefore such an assignment exists, and it can be computed by:

$$\begin{pmatrix} \alpha_1 \\ \alpha_2 \\ \vdots \\ \alpha_m \end{pmatrix} = \begin{pmatrix} a_{o_1 1} & a_{o_1 2} & \cdots & a_{o_1 m} \\ a_{o_2 1} & a_{o_2 2} & \cdots & a_{o_2 m} \\ \cdot & & & \cdot \\ \cdot & & & \cdot \\ \cdot & & & \cdot \\ a_{o_k 1} & a_{o_k 2} & \cdots & a_{o_k m} \end{pmatrix}^{-1} \times \begin{pmatrix} \beta_{o_1} \\ \beta_{o_2} \\ \cdot \\ \cdot \\ \cdot \\ \beta_{o_k} \end{pmatrix}. \tag{4}$$

$\square$

The next lemma states that with probability $1 - \delta$ (wher $\delta > 0$ is an arbitrary confidence parameter), in the matrix A defined by the family RS, every k rows are linearly independent.

Lemma 2. *Let $k > 1$, $a > 1$, $b > 1$ be natural numbers and let $\delta > 0$ be a fixed confidence parameter. Set $b = m/k$ and $a = n/m$. Let RS be a family of subsets in (m, n)-Random System and let A be the underlying matrix as above. If $b > \log(e \cdot ab(1/\delta)^{1/k}) + 1$ then with probability at least $1 - \delta$ every k rows in A are linearly independent[5].*

Before proving the lemma, we list some known useful inequalities:

(i) Let $x_1, x_2, \ldots, x_n$ be non negative reals. Then $\prod_{i=1}^{n} \left(1 - x_i\right) > 1 - \sum_{i=1}^{n} x_i$.

(ii) $\binom{n}{k} < (\frac{en}{k})^k$.

(iii) Let m, k be naturals such that $m > k$. Then $\sum_{i=1}^{k} 2^{i-m} \leq 2 \cdot 2^{k-m}$.

Proof (of Lemma 2). According to the construction of random systems, every row in A is a random Boolean vector of length m. Let $K = \{o_1, o_2, \ldots, o_k\} \subset \{1, 2, \ldots, n\}$ be any sequence of k rows in A. Now we define a sequence of "bad" event indicators: $I_j = 1$ if and only if the j'th row $o_j \in K$ is a linear combination of the rows $o_1, \ldots, o_{j-1}$. Obviously if $(\sum_{j=1}^{k} I_j) = 0$ then the rows in K are linearly independent. Note that in every step j, the $j - 1$ preceding vectors span

---

[5] $e = 2.718\ldots$ is the Euler constant.

a linear space of size at most 2^{j-1}. Since the rows of A are chosen uniformly at random (independently of each other), we have $\Pr[I_j = 0] \geq \frac{2^m - 2^{j-1}}{2^m}$. Therefore,

$$\Pr\left[\left(\sum_{j=1}^{k} I_j\right) = 0\right] = \prod_{j=1}^{k} \frac{2^m - 2^{j-1}}{2^m} = \tag{5}$$

$$= \prod_{j=1}^{k}(1 - 2^{j-1-m}) \geq 1 - \sum_{j=1}^{k} 2^{j-1-m} \geq 1 - 2^{k-m}. \tag{6}$$

The last two inequalities follow from (i) and (iii). We can now conclude that

$$\Pr\left[\left(\sum_{j=1}^{k} I_j\right) > 0\right] \leq 2^{k-m}. \tag{7}$$

There are $\binom{n}{k} \leq \left(\frac{en}{k}\right)^k$ possible sets of k rows, and by the Union Bound[6] the probability that some set of k rows is not linearly independent is at most

$$\left(\frac{en}{k}\right)^k \cdot 2^{k-m} = (eab)^k \cdot 2^{(1-b)k} \leq (eab)^k \cdot 2^{-\log(eab(1/\delta)^{1/k}) \cdot k} = \delta. \tag{8}$$

$\square$

Sample Values of Universality. It is worthwhile to see some values of k given n, m and δ. For instance, for $n = 140$, $m = 70$ and $\delta = 0.02$ we can get $k = 10$-universality with probability at least 0.98. This means that we can reduce the number of inputs to the model by half, and still get 10-universality in a very high probability.

In general δ has negligible effect on k, hence the probability of success can be made very close to 1. The chart in Figure 2 refers to a fixed value $\delta = 0.02$. The chart shows the value of k for $n = 100, 200, \ldots, 500$, where m is sampled 9 times for each value of n, in the range $n/10 \ldots 9n/10$. It is clear from the graph that k is close to linear in m, and that it has a constant factor of about 5. In fact, the equation $b = \log(e \cdot ab(1/\delta)^{1/k}) + 1$ from Lemma 2 implies that $k \sim \frac{m}{\log(n/k)}$, which means that k is linear in m for all practical n.

Corollary 1. *Let $k > 1$, $a > 1$, $b > 1$ be natural numbers and let $\delta > 0$ be a fixed confidence parameter, such that $b > \log(e \cdot ab(1/\delta)^{1/k}) + 1$. Set $b = m/k$ and $a = n/m$. Then with probability at least $1 - \delta$, a circuit C based on the family RS of a random system as described above (with parameters m, n) is k-universal.*

Proof. By Lemma 2 we know that with these parameters, in the underlying matrix A every k rows are linearly independent with probability $1 - \delta$ or higher. On the other hand, by Lemma 1 we know that if every k rows in A are linearly independent, then the circuit $C = C(RS, \oplus)$ is k-universal. $\square$

---

[6] Union Bound: For a countable set $A_1, A_2, A_3, \ldots$ of events, $\Pr\left[\bigcup_i A_i\right] \leq \sum_i \Pr\left[A_i\right]$.

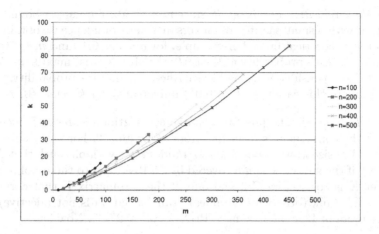

Fig. 2. The value of k for different values of m and n, and a fixed value of δ (0.02)

Based on Corollary 1, it is left to show how we construct the underapproximating model M'. The construction is as follows:

- Let $\{i_1, \ldots, i_n\}$ be the primary inputs of M. Construct the k-universal circuit C based on a random system $RS = (S_1, \ldots, S_n)$.
- For each $j \in \{1, \ldots, n\}$, connect the j'th input of M to the j'th output of C.

The inputs of the underapproximating model M' are the m inputs of C.

3.2 A Better Lower Bounds on k for "Almost" k-Universality

In practice, given n and m the parameter of universality (k) is expected to be significantly higher than what our analytic lower bound provides. But it is quite challenging to estimate the gap between the lower bound and the actual values of k, since checking k universality of a circuit $C : \{0,1\}^m \to \{0,1\}^n$ is hard for reasonably large n, m and k. But if we slightly relax our notion of universality we can get much better bounds on k. Formally, let m, n, k and $C = C(RS, \oplus)$ be as above. Given a subset $K \subset \{1, \ldots, n\}$ of k outputs, we say that the subset K is *covered* by C if for every partial assignment $\alpha_K \in \{0,1\}^k$ on K, there is a full assignment $\alpha \in \{0,1\}^m$ on the inputs of C such that $C(\alpha)|_K = \alpha_K$.

Definition 5 ((k, ϵ)-**universality**). *A circuit C is (k, ϵ)-universal if C covers at least $(1 - \epsilon)\binom{n}{k}$ subsets $K \subset \{1, \ldots, n\}$ of k outputs.*   □

Recall that our previous bounds on k were valid for circuits that cover *all* $\binom{n}{k}$ subsets K, i.e. $(k, 0)$-universal circuits. The following result is another lower-bound, which is better than the previous one as long as ϵ is not too small.

Lemma 3. *Let $m < n$ be naturals and let $C = C(RS, \oplus)$ be a circuit as defined above. Fix $0 < \delta$, $0 < \epsilon < 1$ and set $k = \max(0, m - \log \frac{1}{\epsilon \cdot \delta})$. The circuit C is (k, ϵ)-universal with probability at least $1 - \delta$.*

Observe the implication of this result: since m is an absolute upper bound on k, it means that with a small sacrifice of universality and confidence we obtain a value close to this theoretical limit. For example, for $\delta = \epsilon = 0.1$ (and $m \geq 7$), we get $k = m - 7$, i.e., with probability at least 0.9, the circuit C is $(\max(0, m-7), 0.1)$-universal. Now consider a negligible sacrifice and failure probability, such as $\delta = \epsilon = 0.01$. In this case we get $(k, 0.01)$-universality for $k = \max(0, m - 14)$.

Proof (of Lemma 3). The proof is a simple application of Markov's inequality[7] on one of the consequences from the proof of Lemma 2. For every subset $K \subset \{1, 2, \ldots, n\}$ of size k, we define X_K as a random 0, 1 variable, such that $X_K = 1$ if and only if the subset K is *not* covered by C. Referring to the proof of Lemma 1, the set K is covered by C if and only if the sub-matrix B that corresponds to K has full rank (otherwise the linear transformation is not injective). Then from the proof of Lemma 2 we have $\Pr[X_K = 1] \leq 2^{k-m}$. Now let

$$X = \sum_{K \subset \{1, \ldots, n\}, |K| = k} X_K$$

be the sum of these variables. By linearity of expectation[8],

$$E[X] = \sum_K E[X_K] \leq \binom{n}{k} \cdot 2^{k-m}, \tag{9}$$

and by Markov's inequality,

$$\Pr\left[X \geq \epsilon \cdot \binom{n}{k}\right] = \Pr\left[X \geq \epsilon \cdot 2^{m-k} \cdot \binom{n}{k} \cdot 2^{k-m}\right] \leq \frac{1}{\epsilon \cdot 2^{m-k}} = \delta. \tag{10}$$

From (10) we derive $k \geq m - \log \frac{1}{\epsilon \cdot \delta}$. $\qquad\square$

4   Experimental Results

We interfaced our tool with IBM's model-checker RuleBase. We experimented with bounded model-checking of 17 different real designs (after Rulebase has applied numerous optimizations on them in the front-end, hence the relatively small number of inputs) that had previously known bugs. The tables show our results *without* an automatic refinement procedure. The reason we are giving the tables in this form is that we want to show the influence of m on run-time and chances to find the bug with each underapproximation technique. The tables show run-times in seconds until detecting the bug, for different values of m, where m in all techniques represent the number of inputs to the underapproximated

---

[7] Markov inequality: Let X be a random variable assuming only non-negative values. Then for all $c > 0$, $\Pr\left[X \geq c \cdot E[X]\right] \leq \frac{1}{c}$.

[8] Linearity of Expectation: For any n random variables $X_1, \ldots, X_n$ the following holds: $E\left[\sum_{i=1}^{n} X_i\right] = \sum_{i=1}^{n} E[X_i]$.

model. A sign '-' denotes that the bug was not found up to a bound of 100. 'TO' denotes a timeout of 6 hours.

The table in Figure 3 summarizes results with our construction, hence m is the number of inputs to the circuit. The column S denotes run-time with no underapproximation. It is clear from this table that while $m = n/10$ is too low, $m = n/5$ is high enough to find the bug in 13 out of 17 cases, and typically in less time comparing to the S column, despite the complexity of the XOR function in the PRG-like circuit. Thus, our refinement procedure is set to begin with this value. The last three designs indicate that there are cases in which underapproximation does not work (in all three methods – see Figure 4 as well). Since Rulebase activates various engines in parallel, this is not a serious issue: the contribution of a tool is mainly measured by the number of wins rather than by the average run-time. This is also the reason it is acceptable that such a method has no value if the design satisfies the property.

Design	inputs (n)	S	(PRG) $m = ...$			
			$n/2$	$n/3$	$n/5$	$n/10$
IBM#1	45	96	66	63	66	63
IBM#2	76	173	149	76	72	68
IBM#3	76	191	127	77	79	-
IBM#4	85	211	170	121	105	140
IBM#5	68	61	65	20	592	-
IBM#6	68	73	59	14	661	-
IBM#7	68	482	308	46	52	-
IBM#8	68	122	152	16	90	-
IBM#9	64	2101	1915	1966	1654	1208
IBM#10	80	1270	1392	1830	1137	-
IBM#11	83	2640	2364	2254	1845	-
IBM#12	6	8201	7191	-	-	-
IBM#13	60	942	453	432	351	-
IBM#14	218	965	735	778	510	396
IBM#15	52	1206	-	-	-	-
IBM#16	157	953	-	-	-	-
IBM#17	68	21503	TO	TO	TO	TO

Fig. 3. Run-times with the PRG construction. The second column indicates the number of inputs in the design, i.e., n. The column 'S' stands for run-times without any underapproximation.

In Figure 4 we show results for the two alternative underapproximations described in Subsection 2.2. It is clear from these tables that universality matters: both of these underapproximations need far more inputs than the PRG construction in order to find the bug. Somewhat surprisingly even in the cases they are able to find the bug, they do so in time comparable or longer than without underapproximation at all. The reason seems to be that the underapproximation

Design	inputs (n)	S	(FIX) $m = ...$				(Group) $m = ...$			
			$n/2$	$n/3$	$n/5$	$n/10$	$n/2$	$n/3$	$n/5$	$n/10$
IBM#1	45	96	246	-	-	-	223	229	227	231
IBM#2	76	173	-	-	-	-	361	446	-	-
IBM#3	76	191	373	-	-	-	168	317	-	-
IBM#4	85	211	191	317	-	-	306	289	405	-
IBM#5	68	61	-	-	-	-	410	-	-	-
IBM#6	68	73	-	-	-	-	-	-	-	-
IBM#7	68	482	-	-	-	-	561	491	-	-
IBM#8	68	122	-	-	-	-	113	-	-	-
IBM#9	64	2101	1693	-	-	-	2150	-	-	-
IBM#10	80	1270	-	-	-	-	-	-	-	-
IBM#11	83	2640	-	-	-	-	-	-	-	-
IBM#12	6	8201	-	-	-	-	-	-	-	-
IBM#13	60	942	1206	-	-	-	413	407	-	-
IBM#14	218	965	-	-	-	-	969	1102	-	-
IBM#15	52	1206	-	-	-	-	-	-	-	-
IBM#16	157	953	-	-	-	-	-	-	-	-
IBM#17	68	21503	-	-	-	-	TO	-	-	-

Fig. 4. Run-times when (left) fixing $n - m$ inputs to an arbitrary value and (right) grouping the inputs into m sets, and forcing inputs in the same set to be equal. See Section 2.2 for more details on these underapproximations. The column 'S' stands for run-times without any underapproximation.

delays the finding of the bug to deeper cycles, which in general affects negatively the run time of SAT.

4.1 Further Directions

There are various directions in which this research can progress. First, it has to be evaluated with unbounded model-checking and simulation. Simulation is insensitive to the XOR circuit, which indicates that it might show a stronger influence on the results. Second, our current implementation of refinement is very naive, as it simply increases m. There are probably better alternatives for refinement, and we leave it for future work to find them. In the case of SAT-based model checking, for example, the unsatisfiable core can guide the refinement.

Finally, the fact that in Bounded Model Checking the inputs of each time-frame are represented by different variables can be exploited for reducing m further. The PRG construction can be attached to the *unrolled* circuit. This construction will now have m inputs for $0 < m < n \cdot \mathcal{K}$, where $\mathcal{K}$ is the unrolling bound. It is very likely that errors can be found this way with a smaller set of inputs per cycle.

Acknowledgements. We thank E. Ben-Sasson, M. Shamis and K. Yorav for useful discussions.

References

1. Amla, N., McMillan, K.: Automatic abstraction without counterexamples. In: Garavel, H., Hatcliff, J. (eds.) ETAPS 2003 and TACAS 2003. LNCS, vol. 2619, Springer, Heidelberg (2003)
2. Barner, S., Grumberg, O.: Combining symmetry reduction and upper-approximation for symbolic model checking. In: Brinksma, E., Larsen, K.G. (eds.) CAV 2002. LNCS, vol. 2404, Springer, Heidelberg (2002)
3. Clarke, E., Grumberg, O., Jha, S., Lu, Y., Veith, H.: Counterexample-guided abstraction refinement. J. ACM 50(5), 752–794 (2003)
4. Clarke, E., Gupta, A., Strichman, O.: SAT based counterexample-guided abstraction-refinement. Transactions on Computer Aided Design (TCAD) 23(7), 1113–1123 (2004)
5. Glusman, M., Kamhi, G., Mador-Haim, S., Fraer, R., Vardi, M.Y.: Multiple-counterexample guided iterative abstraction refinement: An industrial evaluation. In: Garavel, H., Hatcliff, J. (eds.) ETAPS 2003 and TACAS 2003. LNCS, vol. 2619, pp. 176–191. Springer, Heidelberg (2003)
6. Grumberg, O., Lerda, F., Strichman, O., Theobald, M.: Proof-guided underapproximation-widening for multi-process systems. In: POPL '05: Proceedings of the 32nd ACM SIGPLAN-SIGACT sysposium on Principles of programming languages, pp. 122–131. ACM Press, New York (2005)
7. Hartman, A., Raskin, L.: Problems and algorithms for covering arrays. Discrete Math 284, 149–156 (2004)
8. Kurshan, R.: Computer aided verification of coordinating processes. Princeton University Press, Princeton, NJ (1994)
9. Nisan, N., Wigderson, A.: Hardness vs randomness. Journal of Computer and System Sciences 49, 146–167 (1994)
10. Ravi, K., Somenzi, F.: High-density reachability analysis. In: Proc. Intl. Conf. on Computer-Aided Design, pp. 154–158 (November 1995)
11. Ravi, K., Somenzi, F.: Hints to accelerate symbolic traversal. In: Pierre, L., Kropf, T. (eds.) CHARME 1999. LNCS, vol. 1703, pp. 250–264. Springer, Heidelberg (1999)
12. Seroussi, G., Bshouty, N.: Vector sets for exhaustive testing of logic circuits. IEEE Transactions on Information Theory, 34 (1988)
13. Williams, R., Gomes, C.P., Selman, B.: Backdoors to typical case complexity. In: IJCAI, pp. 1173–1178 (2003)

Using Counterexamples for Improving the Precision of Reachability Computation with Polyhedra

Chao Wang[1], Zijiang Yang[2], Aarti Gupta[1], and Franjo Ivančić[1]

[1] NEC Laboratories America, Princeton, NJ 08540, U.S.A
[2] Western Michigan University, Kalamazoo, MI 49008, U.S.A

Abstract. We present an *extrapolation with care set* operator to accelerate termination of reachability computation with polyhedra. At the same time, a counterexample guided refinement algorithm is used to iteratively expand the care set to improve the precision of the reachability computation. We also introduce two heuristic algorithms called *interpolate* and *restrict* to minimize the polyhedral representations without reducing the accuracy. We present some promising experimental results from a preliminary implementation of these techniques.

1 Introduction

Static analysis based on abstract interpretation [9] and model checking [7, 27] are popular techniques for program verification. They both rely on fixpoint computation, with the former heavily employing widening [11] to ensure termination. The precision of a widening operator is crucial for the effectiveness of abstract interpretation. Often a widening operator is carefully designed by the user *a priori* for an abstract domain, and if it does not provide enough precision, the user either accepts the result as inconclusive or has to redesign the operator. In this paper, we use counterexample guided refinement developed in model checking to automatically improve the precision of reachability computation using the polyhedral abstract domain.

Widening for convex polyhedra was introduced in [11] for numerical relational analysis and later extended to verification of integer-valued programs [15] and linear hybrid systems [16]. The operator was generalized in [5] and in [2] to powersets (or finite unions) of convex polyhedra. Approximation techniques were also studied in [17], where an *extrapolation* operator is introduced. The difference between widening and extrapolation is that the latter does not guarantee termination. The widening precision can be increased by partitioning methods [20]. In [1], a widening algorithm was introduced by combining several known heuristics and using convex widening as a last resort. In all these previous works, there is no automatic refinement involved.

In model checking, counterexample guided refinement [21, 6, 3] has been used together with predicate abstraction [13] to verify software programs. Predicate abstraction relies on finite sets of predicates to define abstract domains, and therefore can be viewed as an instance of domain refinement in abstract interpretation. However, finite abstractions in general are not as powerful as an infinite abstract domains with widening for Turing equivalent programming languages [10]. Although our new procedure uses a backward counterexample analysis similar to those in [3], our goal is to refine

W. Damm and H. Hermanns (Eds.): CAV 2007, LNCS 4590, pp. 352–365, 2007.
© Springer-Verlag Berlin Heidelberg 2007

the care set in the same abstract domain instead of creating a new abstract model (or a new abstract domain).

In a recent work [14], Gulavani and Rajamani also proposed a counterexample driven refinement method for abstract interpretation, which identifies the fixpoint steps at which precision loss happens due to widening in forward fixpoint computation, and then use the least upper bound (convex hull for convex polyhedra) instead of widening at those steps. In effect, their refinement procedure simply skips the widening at particular steps (the least upper bound of two consecutive sets P and Q of a fixpoint computation is actually Q, since $P \sqsubseteq Q$). Our refinement procedure does not merely skip the over-approximation; instead, it produces a refined care set to guide the *direction-of-growth* in over-approximation at the next iteration of the refinement loop.

We define a new operator called *extrapolation with a care set*. Given two sets $P \sqsubseteq Q$ and a *care set* C such that $Q \cap C = \emptyset$, the extrapolation of P with respect to Q under C is a set S such that $Q \sqsubseteq S$ and $S \cap C = \emptyset$. In reachability computation, the care set C is initially empty—in this case the new operator can be substituted by normal widening whose result $S = P \nabla Q$ satisfies both $Q \sqsubseteq S$ and $S \cap C = \emptyset$. If a given invariant property ψ holds in the over-approximated reachable set, then the property is proved. Otherwise, we intersect this over-approximated set with $\neg\psi$, pick a subset, and start a precise backward analysis in order to build a counterexample. If a counterexample can be found, then we report it as a real error; otherwise, it remains to be decided. In the latter case, we analyze the spurious counterexample and produce a new care set C. The expanded care set C is used with extrapolation to compute a new reachability fixpoint. This iterative refinement process continues until either enough precision is achieved to derive a conclusive result, or the computing resources are exhausted. Note that the entire procedure is automatic, whereas for the existing widening techniques, typically the user has to redesign the widening operator manually when a false bug is reported.

We propose a set of algorithms for implementing the new operator in the domain of convex polyhedra. For two powersets P and Q of convex polyhedra, we apply the proposed operator to individual pairs $P_i \in P$ and $Q_i \in Q$ only when $P_i \sqsubseteq Q_i$. In practice, the use of a care set can significantly increase the precision of program analysis in the polyhedral powerset domain. We also introduce two new operators called *interpolate* and *restrict* to heuristically simplify the polyhedral representations. Applying these two operators during forward and backward reachability fixpoint computations does not cause a loss in precision.

There is an analogy between our widening criterion and the over-approximation in interpolant-based model checking [24]. That is, both are goal-directed and may over-approximate the reachable states by adding any state that cannot reach an error in a given number of steps, or along a given path. Our method can benefit from other recent improvements in widening-based approaches, such as lookahead widening [12]. Improved ways of selecting extrapolation points can benefit us also. Overall, we believe that our goal-directed approach for improving precision is complementary to these approaches based mostly on program structure.

2 Preliminaries

2.1 Abstract Interpretation

Within the general framework of abstract interpretation [9], the abstract postcondition and precondition operations, as well as the least upper bound, may all induce approximations. Widening is used to enforce and/or to accelerate the termination of fixpoint computations since in general the computation may not have a fixpoint or have one that cannot be reached in a finite number of iterations.

Widening (cf. [9]). A widening operator on a partial order set $(L, \sqsubseteq)$ is a partial function $\nabla : L \times L \to L$ such that

1. for each $x, y \in L$ such that $x \nabla y$ is defined, $x \sqsubseteq x \nabla y$ and $y \sqsubseteq x \nabla y$;
2. for all ascending chains $y_0 \sqsubseteq y_1 \sqsubseteq \ldots$, the ascending chain defined by $x_0 := y_0$ and $x_{i+1} := x_i \nabla y_{i+1}$ for $i \geq 0$ is not strictly increasing.

An operator satisfying the first condition but not the *strictly increasing* requirement of the second condition is called an *extrapolation* [17]. In the sequel, we use ∇ to denote both widening and extrapolation when the context is clear. Since there is more freedom in choosing an actual implementation of an extrapolation operator than widening, it is possible for extrapolation to produce a tighter upper-bound set than widening.

For program verification, we consider a powerset domain of convex polyhedra over a linear target program, where only ∇ causes the precision loss (i.e., precondition, postcondition, and least upper bound are precise). We want to compute the reachability fixpoint $F = \mu Z \, . \, I \cup post(Z)$, where I is the initial predicate and $post(Z)$ is the postcondition of Z with respect to a set of transfer functions. In general, Z is a finite union of convex polyhedra. We define ψ as a predicate that is expected to hold in the program (i.e., the property of interest), then program verification amounts to checking whether $F \sqsubseteq \psi$. To apply widening/extrapolation in the reachability computation, let $y_{i+1} = x_i \cup post(x_i)$; that is,

$$
\begin{aligned}
y_0 &= I & x_0 &= I \\
y_1 &= I \cup post(I) & x_1 &= I \,\nabla y_1 \\
y_2 &= x_1 \cup post(x_1) & x_2 &= x_1 \nabla y_2 \\
y_3 &= \ldots
\end{aligned}
$$

Reachability computation in the concrete domain, as is often used in symbolic model checking [23], can be viewed as a special case (by making $x_i = y_i$ for all $i \geq 0$).

2.2 Polyhedral Abstract Domain

The polyhedral abstract domain was first introduced in [11] to capture numerical relations over integers. Let $\mathbb{Z}$ be the set of integer numbers and $\mathbb{Z}^n$ be the set of all n-tuples. A linear inequality constraint is denoted by $\mathbf{a}^T \cdot \mathbf{x} \leq b$, where $\mathbf{x}, \mathbf{a} \in \mathbb{Z}^n$ are n-tuples ($\mathbf{x}$ is the variable) and $b \in \mathbb{Z}$ is a scalar constant. A polyhedron P is a subset of $\mathbb{Z}^n$ defined by a finite conjunction of linear inequality constraints, $P = \{\mathbf{x} \in \mathbb{Z}^n \mid \forall i : \mathbf{a}_i^T \cdot \mathbf{x} \leq b_i\}$. We choose to use this *constraint system representation* in order to be consistent with our actual implementation, which is based on the Omega library [25]. An alternative would be to define P as a generator system comprising a finite set of vertices, rays, and lines. Some implementations (e.g., [22]) choose to maintain both to take advantages of their complementing strengths and to avoid the conversion overhead between the two.

The first widening operator for this abstract domain was introduced in [11], often being termed as *standard widening* (we follow this convention for ease of reference).

Standard Widening. Let P and Q be two polyhedra such that $P \sqsubseteq Q$; the widening of P with respect to Q, denoted by $P \nabla Q$, is computed as follows: when P is empty, return Q; otherwise, remove from P all inequalities not satisfied by Q and return.

The intuition behind standard widening is to predict the *directions of growth* from P to Q and then drop any constraint of P in these directions. The finiteness of the first polyhedron (where widening starts) ensures termination.

Widening Up-to. Let P and Q be two polyhedra such that $P \sqsubseteq Q$, and let M be a finite set of linear constraints. The widening up-to operator, denoted by $P \nabla_M Q$, is the conjunction of the standard widening $P \nabla Q$ with all the constraints in M that are satisfied by both P and Q.

The *widening up-to* operator was introduced in [15, 16] to improve standard widening whenever the result is known to lie in a known subset. This subset, or *up-to set* M, is defined as a set of constraints associated with each control state of a program. For instance, if a variable x is declared to be of subrange type 1..10, then $x \geq 1$ and $x \leq 10$ are added into M. If there exists a loop for (x=0; x<5; x++), then the constraint $x < 5$ is also added into M. It is worth pointing out that the up-to set in [15, 16] is fixed. It does not consider automatic refinement adaptive to the property under verification.

3   Extrapolation with a Care Set

We define the *care set* to be an area within which no extrapolation result should reside in order to avoid false bugs. We use a precise counterexample guided analysis to gradually expand the care set and therefore improve the precision of the extrapolation with care set operator (defined below).

Definition 1. *An extrapolation with a care set C on a partial order set $(L, \sqsubseteq)$ is a partial function $\overset{\neg C}{\nabla} : L \times L \to L$ such that*

1. *for each $x, y \in L$ such that $x \overset{\neg C}{\nabla} y$ is defined, $x \sqsubseteq x \overset{\neg C}{\nabla} y$ and $y \sqsubseteq x \overset{\neg C}{\nabla} y$;*
2. *for all ascending chains $y_0 \sqsubseteq y_1 \sqsubseteq \dots$ such that $y_i \cap C = \emptyset$, the ascending chain defined by $x_0 := y_0$ and $x_{i+1} := x_i \overset{\neg C}{\nabla} y_{i+1}$ for $i \geq 0$ satisfies $x_i \cap C = \emptyset$.*

Definition 1 is generic since it is not restricted to any particular abstract domain. In this paper, we consider an implementation for the domains of convex polyhedra and their powersets. Figure 1 provides a motivating example, in which P_1 and Q_1 are two polyhedra and C is the care set. P_1 is represented by the shaded area in the middle, and Q_1 is represented by the solid thick lines. From P_1 to Q_1 there are two directions of

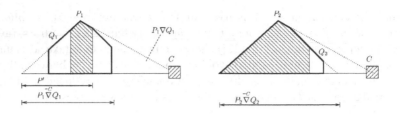

Fig. 1. An example of using a care set with extrapolation

growth. The standard widening $P_1 \nabla Q_1$ would generate the outer triangle that intersects C, thereby introducing false bugs.

We prohibit the growth to the right by using the care set C in extrapolation. By expanding only towards the left, the extrapolation result, denoted by $P_1 \overset{\neg C}{\nabla} Q_1$ on the left, and P_2 (shaded area) on the right, does not intersect C. In the next fixpoint step, we consider the extrapolation of P_2 with respect to Q_2 (solid thick lines) under the care set C. This time, the standard widening result would not intersect C. Therefore, we prefer that the result of extrapolation with a care set is the same as $P_2 \nabla Q_2$.

3.1   Using the Care Set

We now present an algorithm to compute the extrapolation with care set for convex polyhedra. In the sequel, a linear inequality constraint c is also referred to as a *half-space* since it represents a set $\{\mathbf{x} \in \mathbb{Z}^n | \mathbf{a}^T \cdot \mathbf{x} \leq b\}$. Let c be a constraint of a polyhedron P, and let c' be another constraint (may or may not be in P); we use $P_{c'}^c$ to denote the new polyhedron after replacing c with c' in P, and use P_{true}^c to denote the new polyhedron after dropping c from P.

Algorithm 1. *Let $P \sqsubseteq Q$ be two polyhedra, and C be a non-empty powerset such that $Q \cap C = \emptyset$. The extrapolation of P with respect to Q under C is computed as follows:*

1. *build a new polyhedron P': for each constraint c of P whose half-space does not contain Q, if $P_{\text{true}}^c \cap C = \emptyset$, then drop c.*
2. *build a new polyhedron Q': drop any constraint c of Q whose half-space does not contain P'.*

Return Q' as the result.

An example of applying this algorithm is the extrapolation of P_1 with respect to Q_1 under the care set C to generate P_2 in Figure 1. In this example, P' is the polyhedron formed by dropping the left-most constraint of P_1; then all but the left-most constraint of Q are satisfied by P', so the result Q' is the polyhedron obtained by dropping the left-most constraint of Q_1. It is clear that the result does not intersect with C. In general, the result S of Algorithm 1 satisfies $Q \sqsubseteq S \sqsubseteq P \nabla Q$.

Using this algorithm together with an iterative framework to improve the care set can guarantee that after refinement, the previous precision loss will not appear again. However, if all the *directions of growth* (indicated by standard widening) are forbidden by the care set C, then Algorithm 1 will return Q. This may lead to postponing the widening operation forever (which may produce a non-terminating sequence). In theory, if desired, we could remedy the termination problem by switching from Algorithm 1 back to standard widening after a sufficiently large (but finite) number of fixpoint steps. Another alternative is to use the *widening up-to* operator instead of extrapolation, by accepting the fact that the refinement of care set may stop making progress. However, there is a trade-off between precision and termination, since program verification in general is undecidable in the polyhedral domain. In practice, it is often possible for the proposed technique to achieve both termination and increased precision.

This algorithm is defined for two convex polyhedra. In program verification, we intend to represent reachable state sets by finite unions of convex polyhedra. We extend the extrapolation operator to the powerset domain as follows: given two powersets P and Q, we apply Algorithm 1 only to individual convex polyhedra pairs $P_i \in P$ and $Q_i \in Q$ such that $P_i \sqsubseteq Q_i$. If $P_i \in P$ is not contained in any $Q_i \in Q$ (no matching pair), we simply use P_i. The extrapolation result is also a powerset. This is similar to the approach of Bultan *et al.* [5], except that their work does not use the care set.

3.2 Refinement for Improving the Care Set

Let $\hat{F}$ be the fixpoint of reachability computation achieved with extrapolation, and $F \sqsubseteq \hat{F}$ be the set of actual reachable states. If the invariant property ψ holds in $\hat{F}$, then ψ also holds in F. If there exists $s \in (\hat{F} \cap \neg\psi)$, it remains to be decided whether $s \in F$, or s is introduced because of extrapolation. If $s \in F$, then we can compute a concrete counterexample. Otherwise, there is a precision loss due to extrapolation.

We compute $\hat{F}$ by extrapolation with care set as follows,

- $\hat{F}_0 = I$;
- $\hat{F}_{i+1} = \hat{F}_i \overset{\neg C}{\nabla} (\hat{F}_i \cup post(\hat{F}_i))$, for $i \geq 0$ until fixpoint.

When the care set C is empty, the extrapolation with care set is equivalent to normal widening. If there is an index fi such that $\hat{F}_{fi} \cap \neg\psi \neq \emptyset$, we stop reachability computation and start the backward counterexample analysis (using precondition computations),

- $B_{fi} = \hat{F}_{fi} \cap \neg\psi$;
- $B_{i-1} = \hat{F}_{i-1} \cap pre(B_i)$ for all $i \leq fi$ and $i > 0$, if $B_i \neq \emptyset$.

If $B_0 \neq \emptyset$, we have found a concrete counterexample inside the sequence $B_0, \ldots, B_{fi}$. If $B_{i-1} = \emptyset$ for an index $i > 0$, then the set B_i is introduced by extrapolation.

Theorem 1. *If there exists an index $0 < i < fi$ such that $B_{i-1} = \emptyset$, then B_i must have been introduced into $\hat{F}_i$ by extrapolation during forward fixpoint computation.*

Proof. Since $\hat{F}_i = \hat{F}_{i-1} \overset{\neg C}{\nabla} (\hat{F}_{i-1} \cup post(\hat{F}_{i-1}))$, the set $B_i \subseteq \hat{F}_i$ is added either by postcondition or by extrapolation. Since $B_{i-1} = \emptyset$ and $B_{i-1} = \hat{F}_{i-1} \cap pre(B_i)$, B_i is not reached from $\hat{F}_{i-1}$ in one step. Therefore B_i is introduced by extrapolation. $\square$

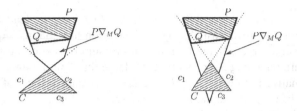

Fig. 2. Two examples of applying widening up-to operator: $M = \{\neg c_1, \neg c_2, \neg c_3\}$

We expand the care set (initially empty) by making $C = C \cup B_i$. After that, extrapolation is allowed only if it does not introduce any erroneous state in B_i. Recall that extrapolation estimates directions of growth and then over-approximates growth in these directions. B_i provides hints about directions in which over-approximation should be prohibited. With the expanded care set C, we can re-start reachability fixpoint computation from $\hat{F}_{i-1}$ where $B_{i-1} = \emptyset$ and $B_i \neq \emptyset$. The bad states in set $\hat{F} \cap \neg\psi$ can no longer be reached through the same counterexample. This set may either become empty, or remain non-empty due to a different sequence of $\hat{F}_i$'s. In the latter case, we keep expanding the care set until one of the following happens: (1) a concrete counterexample is found and we report that the property ψ fails; (2) the set $\hat{F} \cap \neg\psi$ is empty and we report that the property ψ holds; (3) the limit of computing resources (CPU time or memory) is exceeded; in this case, the property remains undecided.

The correctness of the iterative refinement method is summarized as follows: (1) Since $\hat{F}$ remains an upper-bound of F, if a property fails in F, then it must fail in $\hat{F}$ as well. Therefore, a failing property will never be reported as true in our analysis. (2) Since we report bugs only when the precise backward analysis reaches an initial state, only failing properties can produce concrete counterexamples. Therefore, a passing property will never be reported as false in our analysis.

We have kept union exact in order to simplify the presentation of our refinement algorithm. However, only the requirement of exact postcondition/precondition is necessary. Union can be made less precise by, for instance, selectively merging convex polyhedra in a powerset, as long as the resulting powerset does not immediately intersect the care set. This precision loss can be recovered by using the same counterexample guided refinement (the argument is similar to Theorem 1).

3.3 Improving the Up-to Set

Once the care set C is computed, it can be used to derive the up-to set M for the *widening up-to* operator. In our iterative refinement framework, the extrapolation operator can be replaced by ∇_M—this is an alternative way of implementing our iterative widening refinement procedure. In [15, 16], the original ∇_M operator relies on a fixed set M of linear constraints, which are often derived statically from control conditions of the target program. Given a care set C, we can negate individual constraints of its polyhedra and add them into the *up-to set M*; that is, $M = \{\neg c_i \mid c_i$ is a constraint of a polyhedron in $C\}$.

In widening up-to computation $P \nabla_M Q$, the half-space of a constraint in M, or $\neg c_i$, does not have to contain P and Q. If $\neg c_i$ contains P and Q, the definition of ∇_M

demands that $\neg c_i$ also contains $P\nabla_M Q$. However, if $\neg c_i$ does not contain P and Q, then $\neg c_i$ does not need to contain $P\nabla_M Q$ either. Figure 2 shows two examples for this computation, where C is the care set and M is the derived up-to set. In the left example, since both $\neg c_1$ and $\neg c_2$ (representing areas above the two lines) contain Q (hence P), the result of $P\nabla_M Q$ is the conjunction of $\neg c_1$, $\neg c_2$, and standard widening $P\nabla Q$; the constraint $\neg c_3$ (representing the area below the line) does not contain Q. In the right example, since none of the three constraints $\neg c_1, \neg c_2, \neg c_3$ contains Q, the widening result is simply $P\nabla Q$ itself, and therefore $(P\nabla_M Q) \cap C \neq \emptyset$.

In general, the *up-to set* M is weaker than the care set C in restricting the ways to perform overapproximation, so there is no guarantee that the widing up-to result does not intersect C. Therefore, it is possible that the reachability fixpoint computation (with widening up-to) after the refinement of care set generates a previously inspected spurious counterexample. As a result, although each individual forward reachability fixpoint computation always terminates, the overall iterative refinement loop may stop making progress (a tradeoff).

4 Optimizations

Counterexample analysis using precise precondition computations may become computationally expensive. In this section, we present several optimizations to make it faster.

4.1 Under-Approximating Backward Analysis

The overhead of counterexample analysis can be reduced by under-approximating the set B_i for $i \leq fi$ and $i > 0$; that is, at each backward step, we use a non-empty subset $B_i' \sqsubseteq B_i$. For instance, B_i' could be a single convex polyhedron when B_i is a finite union of polyhedra. The simplified counterexample analysis is given as follows:

1. $B_{fi} = (\hat{F}_{fi} \cap \neg\psi)$ and $B_{fi}' = \text{SUBSET}(B_{fi})$;
2. $B_{i-1} = \hat{F}_{i-1} \cap pre(B_i')$ and $B_{i-1}' = \text{SUBSET}(B_{i-1})$ for all $i \leq fi$, if $B_i' \neq \emptyset$.

The correctness of this simplification, that the proof of Theorem 1 still holds after we replace B_i with B_i', is due to the following two reasons. First, the precondition is precise in our powerset domain (it would not hold, for instance, in the convex polyhedral lattice where LUB may lose precision). Second, the overall iterative procedure remains correct by adding each time B_i' instead of B_i into the care set C—the difference between this simplified version and the original counterexample analysis is that the simplified one uses a more lazy approach for refinement, and it may need more than one refinement pass to achieve the same effect as using B_i. When using B_i' instead of B_i to compute the care set, we may not be able to remove the spurious set $B_i \setminus B_i'$ right away. However, if spurious counterexamples leading to $B_i \setminus B_i'$ appear again after refinement, $\text{SUBSET}(B_i \setminus B_i')$ will be picked up to start computing the new care set.

Finally, if $B_0' \neq \emptyset$, it guarantees that there is a real counterexample since all precondition computation results, although underapproximated, are accurate. What we miss is the guarantee to find a concrete counterexample during the earliest possible pass, because there may be cases where $B_i \neq \emptyset$ but $B_i' = \emptyset$.

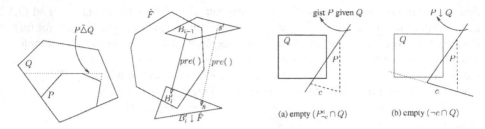

Fig. 3. (a) *interpolate* and (b) *restrict*

Fig. 4. comparing *gist* with *restrict*

4.2 Simplifications of Polyhedral Representations

We now present two heuristic algorithms for simplifying the representations of polyhedra without reducing the accuracy of fixpoint computation. These are orthogonal to the use of extrapolation with a care set.

Definition 2 (Interpolate). *Let P and Q be two sets such that $P \sqsubseteq Q$. The interpolate $P\tilde{\triangle}Q$ is a new set such that $P \sqsubseteq (P\tilde{\triangle}Q) \sqsubseteq Q$.*

The interpolate can be used to simplify the *from set*, i.e., the set for which we compute the postcondition during the reachability computation. Let $\hat{F}_{i-1} \sqsubseteq \hat{F}_i$ be two consecutive sets in this computation. We use $(\hat{F}_i \setminus \hat{F}_{i-1})\tilde{\triangle}\hat{F}_i$ instead of $\hat{F}_i$ (or the frontier $\hat{F}_i \setminus \hat{F}_{i+1}$) to compute the postcondition. In principle, any set S such that $P \sqsubseteq S \sqsubseteq Q$ can be used as the *from set* without reducing the accuracy of the reachability result. We prefer one with a simpler polyhedral representation.

Algorithm 2. *Let $P \sqsubseteq Q$ be two convex polyhedra. We compute a new polyhedron S by starting with $S = P$ and keep dropping its constraints c as long as $S^c_{\text{true}} \sqsubseteq Q$. We return, between Q and S, the one with the least number of constraints.*

This heuristic algorithm tries to minimize the representation of P by inspecting every constraint greedily. Figure 3 (a) gives an example for applying this algorithm, where dropping any constraints in $P\tilde{\triangle}Q$ makes the result grow out of Q.

We note that similar ideas and algorithms exist for BDDs [4] and are routinely used in symbolic model checking [23]. Our definition of $\tilde{\triangle}$ is a generalization of these ideas for abstract domains. Also note that since the purpose here is heuristic simplification, any cheap convex over-approximation technique (instead of a tight convex-hull) can be used to first compute a convex set from $\hat{F}_i \setminus \hat{F}_{i+1}$.

Definition 3 (Restrict). *Let P and Q be two sets. The restrict $P \downarrow Q$ is defined as the new set $\{\mathbf{x} \in \mathbb{Z}^n \mid \mathbf{x} \in P \cap Q, \text{ or } \mathbf{x} \notin Q\}$.*

Restrict computes a simplified set S for P such that (1) its intersection with Q, or $S \cap Q$, equals $P \cap Q$ and (2) S may contain an arbitrary subset of $\neg Q$. Restrict can be used to simplify the *from set* in precondition computation, with respect to a known $\hat{F}$. In counterexample analysis, when computing $B_{i-1} = \hat{F}_{i-1} \cap pre(B'_i)$, we use $pre(B'_i \downarrow \hat{F})$ instead of $pre(B'_i)$. As is shown in Figure 3 (b), adding $s \in \neg\hat{F}$ does not add any erroneous states into $\hat{F}_k$ for $0 \le k < (i-1)$.

Algorithm 3. *Let P and Q be convex polyhedra. We define the computation of $(P \downarrow Q)$ as follows: If $P = \mathbb{Z}^n$ or if $Q = \emptyset$, return $\mathbb{Z}^n$. Otherwise, in the recursive step, choose a constraint c from P: if $\neg c \cap Q$ is empty, return $(P_{\text{true}}^c \downarrow Q)$, else return $c \cap (P_{\text{true}}^c \downarrow (Q \cap c))$.*

This algorithm is inspired by the *gist* operator [26], which itself is a restrict operator on polyhedra. In particular, *gist* P *given* Q returns a conjunction containing a minimal subset of constraints in P such that $(gist\ P\ given\ Q) \cap Q = P \cap Q$. However, *gist* in its original form is expensive and not suitable for fast heuristic simplification. In Algorithm 3, we have safely dropped the *minimal subset* requirement by checking the emptiness of $\neg c \cap Q$ (instead of $P_{\neg c}^c \cap Q$ as in [26]). This may sometimes produce a less compact representation: in Figure 4, for example, $P \downarrow Q$ (right) has two constraints while the *gist* result has only one. However, the computation of $P \downarrow Q$ is more efficient and the result remains a generalized cofactor [29].

5 Application in Program Verification

We have implemented the proposed techniques in the F-SOFT [19, 18] platform. F-SOFT is a tool for analyzing safety properties in C programs by using both static analysis and model checking. Static analysis is used to quickly filter out properties that can be proved in a numerical abstract domain [28]. Unresolved properties are then given to the model checker. Despite the combination of different analysis engines, in practice there are still many properties that (1) cannot be proved by static analysis techniques with standard widening, and (2) symbolic model checking takes a long time to terminate because of the large sequential depth and state explosion. Our work aims at resolving these properties using extrapolation with an iteratively improved care set.

Implementation. We incorporated the proposed technique into a symbolic analysis procedure built on top of CUDD [30] and the Omega library [25], as described in [32]. It begins with a C program and applies a series of source-level transformations [18], until the program state is represented as a collection of simple scalar variables and each program step is represented as a set of parallel assignments to these variables (each program step corresponds to a *basic block*). The transformations produce a control flow structure that serves as the starting point for both static analysis and model checking. We use BDDs to track the control flow logic (represented as Boolean functions) and polyhedral powersets to represent numerical constraints of the target program.

The reachable sets (e.g. $\hat{F}_i$) are decomposed and maintained as powersets at the individual program locations (basic blocks), so that each location l is associated with a subset F_i^l. Each location l is also associated with a care set C^l. Extrapolation with the care set C^l is applied only locally to F_i^l and $F_i^l \cup post^l(F_i)$, where $post^l(F_i)$ denotes the subset of postcondition of F_i that resides at the program location l.

During forward reachability computation, we apply extrapolation selectively at certain program locations: We identify back-edges in the control flow graph whose removal will break all the cycles in the control flow. Tails of back-edges serve as the *synchronization points* in the fixpoint computation. A *lock-step* style [32] fixpoint computation

Table 1. Comparing methods for computing reachability fixpoint (? means unknown)

Test Program				Analysis Result				Total CPU Time (s)			
name	loc	vars	blks	widen only	extra refine	MIX m.c.	BDD m.c.	widen only	extra refine	MIX m.c.	BDD m.c.
bakery	94	10	26	?	true	true	true	18	5	13	2
tcas-1	1652	59	133	?	true	true	true	18	34	128	433
tcas-2	1652	59	133	?	true	true	true	18	37	132	644
tcas-3	1652	59	133	?	true	true	true	18	49	135	433
tcas-4	1652	59	133	?	true	true	true	18	19	137	212
tcas-5	1652	59	133	?	false	false	false	18	80	150	174
appl-a	1836	78	307	true	true	?	?	17	22	>1800	>1800
appl-b	1836	78	307	?	false	false	?	11	94	277	>1800
appl-c	1836	78	307	?	false	false	?	13	111	80	>1800
appl-d	1836	78	307	?	false	false	?	13	68	78	>1800

is conducted as follows: we use transfer functions on the forward-edges only in the fix-point computation until it terminates; we propagate the reached state set simultaneously through the back-edges; we then perform forward computation again. Inside this reachability computation framework, we apply extrapolation only at the tails of back-edges and only when we propagate the state sets through back-edges.

Experiments. Our experiments were conducted on a set of control intensive C programs. Among the test cases, *bakery* is a C model of Leslie Lamport's bakery protocol, with a mutual exclusion property. The *tcas* examples are various versions of the Traffic alert and Collision Avoidance System [8] with properties originally specified in linear temporal logic; we model these properties by adding assertions to the source code to trap the corresponding bugs, i.e., an error exists only if an unsafe statement becomes reachable. The *appl* examples are from an embedded software application for a portable device. Most of the properties cannot be resolved directly by conventional static analysis techniques (due to the low widening precision).

Our experiments were conducted on a Linux machine with 3 GHz Pentium 4 CPU and 2GB of RAM. The results are given in Table 1, wherein we list in Columns 1-4 the name, the lines of C code, the number of variables, and the number of basic blocks. These numbers are collected after the test programs have been aggressively simplified using program slicing and constant value propagation. Columns 5-8 indicate the analysis result of four different methods: *widen-only* denotes an implementation of the standard widening algorithm, *extra-refine* denotes our new iterative refinement method with the use of care set, *MIX-mc* denotes a model checking procedure using a combination of BDDs and finte unions of polyhedra [32], and *BDD-mc* denotes a symbolic model checker using only BDDs that has been tuned specifically for sequential programs [31]. We have tried SAT-based BMC also, but our BDD-based algorithm outperforms BMC on these examples (experimental comparison in [31, 32]). Columns 9-12 compare the runtime of different methods.

Among the four methods, *widen-only* is the fastest but also the least precise in terms of the analysis result—it cannot prove any of true properties except *appl-a*. BDD and

MIX are symbolic model checking algorithms, which often take a longer time to complete and are in general less scalable. In contrast, the new method *extra-refine* achieves a runtime comparable to *widen-only* and at the same time is able to prove all these true properties. For false properties, *widen-only* always reports them as "potential errors." The other three methods, *extra-refine*, *MIX*, and *BDD*, are able to produce concrete counterexamples if they complete. Due to state explosion and the large sequential depth of the software models, *BDD* does not perform well on these properties. Both *MIX* and *extra-refine* find all the counterexamples, due to their use of Integer-level representations internally. The method *extra-refine* has a run time performance comparable to (often slightly better than) that of *MIX* on these properties, although in *appl-c* it takes more time to produce a counterexample than *MIX* due to the overhead of performing multiple forward-backward refinement passes.

Unlike common programming errors such as array bound violations, most properties in the above examples are at the functional level and are harder to prove by using a general-purpose static analyzer only. Although our new method is also based on abstract interpretation, the precision of its extrapolation operator is adaptive and *problem-specific*, i.e., it adapts to the property at hand through use of counterexamples.

6 Conclusions

We have presented a new refinement method to automatically improve the precision of extrapolation in abstract interpretation by iteratively expanding a care set. We propose, for the polyhedral domain, a set of algorithms for implementing *extrapolation with a care set* and for refining the care set using counterexample guided analysis. Our preliminary experimental evaluation shows that the new extrapolation based method can retain the scalability of static analysis techniques and at the same time achieve an accuracy comparable to model checking. For future work, we plan to investigate the use of care sets in other numerical abstract domains including the octagon and interval domains.

References

[1] Bagnara, R., Hill, P.M., Ricci, E., Zaffanella, E.: Precise widening operators for convex polyhedra (LNCS 2694). In: Cousot, R. (ed.) SAS 2003. LNCS, vol. 2694, pp. 337–354. Springer, Heidelberg (2003)

[2] Bagnara, R., Hill, P.M., Zaffanella, E.: Widening operators for powerset domains. In: Steffen, B., Levi, G. (eds.) VMCAI 2004. LNCS, vol. 2937, pp. 135–148. Springer, Heidelberg (2004)

[3] Ball, T., Majumdar, R., Millstein, T., Rajamani, S.K.: Automatic predicate abstraction of C programs. In: Programming Language Design and Implementation (2001)

[4] Bryant, R.E.: Graph-based algorithms for Boolean function manipulation. IEEE Trans. on Computer C-35(8), 677–691 (1986)

[5] Bultan, T., Gerber, R., League, C.: Verifying systems with integer constraints and boolean predicates: A composite approach. In: Symposium on Software Testing and Analysis, pp. 113–123 (1998)

[6] Clarke, E., Grumberg, O., Jha, S., Lu, Y., Veith, H.: Counterexample-guided abstraction refinement. In: Emerson, E.A., Sistla, A.P. (eds.) CAV 2000. LNCS, vol. 1855, pp. 154–169. Springer, Heidelberg (2000)

[7] Clarke, E.M., Emerson, E.A.: Design and synthesis of synchronization skeletons using branching time temporal logic. In: Kozen, D. (ed.) Logics of Programs. LNCS, vol. 131, pp. 52–71. Springer, Heidelberg (1982)

[8] Coen-Porisini, A., Denaro, G., Ghezzi, C., Pezze, M.: Using symbolic execution for verifying safety-critical systems. In: European Software Engineering Conference/Foundations of Software Engineering, pp. 142–151 (2001)

[9] Cousot, P., Cousot, R.: Static determination of dynamic properties of programs. In: International Symposium on Programming, pp. 106–126 (1976)

[10] Cousot, P., Cousot, R.: Comparing the galois connection and widening/narrowing approaches to abstract interpretation. In: Bruynooghe, M., Wirsing, M. (eds.) PLILP 1992. LNCS, vol. 631, pp. 269–295. Springer, Heidelberg (1992)

[11] Cousot, P., Halbwachs, N.: Automatic discovery of linear restraints among variables of a program. In: Principles of Programming Languages, pp. 84–96 (1978)

[12] Gopan, D., Reps, T.W.: Lookahead widening. In: Ball, T., Jones, R.B. (eds.) CAV 2006. LNCS, vol. 4144, pp. 452–466. Springer, Heidelberg (2006)

[13] Graf, S., Saïdi, H.: Construction of abstract state graphs with PVS. In: Grumberg, O. (ed.) CAV 1997. LNCS, vol. 1254, pp. 72–83. Springer, Heidelberg (1997)

[14] Gulavani, B.S., Rajamani, S.K.: Counterexample driven refinement for abstract interpretation. In: Hermanns, H., Palsberg, J. (eds.) TACAS 2006 and ETAPS 2006. LNCS, vol. 3920, pp. 474–488. Springer, Heidelberg (2006)

[15] Halbwachs, N.: Delay analysis in synchronous programs. In: Courcoubetis, C. (ed.) CAV 1993. LNCS, vol. 697, pp. 333–346. Springer, Heidelberg (1993)

[16] Halbwachs, N., Proy, Y.E., Roumanoff, P.: Verification of real-time systems using linear relation analysis. Formal Methods in Systems Design 11(2), 157–185 (1997)

[17] Henzinger, T.A., Ho, P.-H.: A note on abstract interpretation strategies for hybrid automata. In: Hybrid Systems II. LNCS, vol. 999, pp. 252–264. Springer, Heidelberg (1995)

[18] Ivančić, F., Shlyakhter, I., Gupta, A., Ganai, M.K., Kahlon, V., Wang, C., Yang, Z.: Model checking C program using F-Soft. In: IEEE International Conference on Computer Design, pp. 297–308 (2005)

[19] Ivančić, F., Yang, Z., Shlyakhter, I., Ganai, M.K., Gupta, A., Ashar, P.: F-Soft: Software verification platform. In: Etessami, K., Rajamani, S.K. (eds.) CAV 2005. LNCS, vol. 3576, pp. 301–306. Springer, Heidelberg (2005)

[20] Jeannet, B., Halbwachs, N., Raymond, P.: Dynamic partitioning in analyses of numerical properties. In: Cortesi, A., Filé, G. (eds.) SAS 1999. LNCS, vol. 1694, pp. 39–50. Springer, Heidelberg (1999)

[21] Kurshan, R.P.: Computer-Aided Verification of Coordinating Processes. Princeton University Press, Princeton, NJ (1994)

[22] The Parma Polyhedra Library. University of Parma, Italy, http://www.cs.unipr.it/ppl/

[23] McMillan, K.L.: Symbolic Model Checking. Kluwer Academic Publishers, Boston, MA (1994)

[24] McMillan, K.L.: Interpolation and SAT-based model checking. In: Hunt Jr., W.A., Somenzi, F. (eds.) CAV 2003. LNCS, vol. 2725, pp. 1–13. Springer, Heidelberg (2003)

[25] The Omega Project. University of Maryland, http://www.cs.umd.edu/projects/omega/

[26] Pugh, W., Wonnacott, D.: Going beyond integer programming with the Omega test to eliminate false data dependences. IEEE Trans. on Parallel and Distributed Systems 6(2), 204–211 (1994)

[27] Quielle, J.P., Sifakis, J.: Specification and verification of concurrent systems in CESAR. In: Symposium on Programming (1981)

[28] Sankaranarayanan, S., Ivančić, F., Shlyakhter, I., Gupta, A.: Static analysis in disjunctive numerical domains. In: Symposium on Static Analysis (2006)

[29] Shiple, T.R., Hojati, R., Sangiovanni-Vincentelli, A.L., Brayton, R.K.: Heuristic minimization of BDDs using don't cares. In: Design Automation Conference, pp. 225–231 (1994)

[30] Somenzi, F.: CUDD: CU Decision Diagram Package. University of Colorado at Boulder, ftp://vlsi.colorado.edu/pub/

[31] Wang, C., Yang, Z., Ivančić, F., Gupta, A.: Disjunctive image computation for embedded software verification. In: Design, Automation and Test in Europe, pp. 1205–1210 (2006)

[32] Yang, Z., Wang, C., Ivančić, F., Gupta, A.: Mixed symbolic representations for model checking software programs. In: Formal Methods and Models for Codesign, pp. 17–24 (2006)

Structural Abstraction of
Software Verification Conditions*

Domagoj Babić and Alan J. Hu

Department of Computer Science
University of British Columbia

Abstract. Precise software analysis and verification require tracking the exact
path along which a statement is executed (path-sensitivity), the different contexts from which a function is called (context-sensitivity), and the bit-accurate
operations performed. Previously, verification with such precision has been considered too inefficient to scale to large software. In this paper, we present
a novel approach to solving such verification conditions, based on an automatic abstraction-checking-refinement framework that exploits natural abstraction boundaries present in software. Experimental results show that our approach
easily scales to over 200,000 lines of real C/C++ code.

1 Introduction

Verification conditions (VCs) are logical formulas, constructed from a system and desired correctness properties, such that the validity of verification conditions corresponds
to the correctness of the system. Proving validity of verification conditions is an essential step in software verification, and is the focus of this paper.

In general, proving software VCs requires interprocedural analysis, e.g. of the propagation of data-flow facts. Some properties, like proper nesting of lock-unlock calls, tend
to be localized to a single function and are amenable to simpler analysis. Many others,
especially pointer-related properties, tend to span through many function calls.

To handle the complexity of interprocedural analysis, the software analysis community has developed a number of increasingly expensive abstractions. For instance,
path-insensitive analysis does not track the exact path along which a certain statement
is executed, while context-insensitive analysis does not differentiate the contexts from
which a function is called. These abstractions work well in optimizing compilers, but
are not precise enough for verification purposes. Software verification analysis has to
be both path- and context-sensitive (*-sensitive) to keep the number of false errors low.

Precise *-sensitive software verification has two components: (1) we need an analysis
that takes a piece of software as input and computes VCs as logical formulas in some
logic, and (2) once the VCs are computed, we need to check their validity. This paper
proposes a novel approach to checking the validity of *-sensitive VCs.

Our approach is an abstraction-checking-refinement framework that exploits the natural function-level abstraction boundaries present in software. Programmers organize
code into functions and use them as abstractions. They tend to ignore the details of the

---

* Research supported by a Microsoft Graduate Fellowship and an NSERC Discovery Grant.

W. Damm and H. Hermanns (Eds.): CAV 2007, LNCS 4590, pp. 366–378, 2007.

effects of the function on the caller's context — the easiest invariant to remember is to remember no invariant at all. Analogously, our approach initially treats individual effects of a function call as unconstrained variables and incrementally adds constraints corresponding to the effects of the function call. We demonstrate that such a structural refinement approach works well, even on large general-purpose C/C++ applications.

1.1 Related Work

Interprocedural analysis can have many forms, and is commonly based on some form of summarization. Usually, the more expressive the summaries are, the higher the computational complexity. For instance, if the set of data-flow facts is a finite set, and the data-flow functions distribute over the confluence, interprocedural data-flow analysis can be done in polynomial time [21]. If the summaries are composed of predicates over arbitrary logic the analysis gets more complex, depending on the underlying logic.

If the number of predicates is relatively small, predicate abstraction [14] makes it possible to represent summaries compactly as BDDs [5]. This approach has been effectively used in SLAM [3] and BLAST [15,16]. Predicate abstraction is very coarse, and hasn't been shown to scale well to large applications for data-intensive properties. Its advantage is that the VCs given to the theorem prover are relatively simple, corresponding to a conjunction of conditions on some path in the program. Saturn [25] handles lock-properties in a similar way — by computing summaries as projections onto a set of predicates, with the difference that it does not abstract VCs before passing them to the theorem prover. In contrast to the above-mentioned approaches, the technique presented in this paper allows summaries to be arbitrary expressions, rather than just projections onto a set of predicates.

Livshits and Lam [20] proposed a path- and context-sensitive points-to analysis and used it for simple security checks. Their summaries represent definition-use chains required for tracking pointers interprocedurally. They demonstrated their analysis on small programs up to 13 thousand lines of code. Whaley and Lam [23] stressed the importance of context-sensitive analysis and proposed a brute force approach to context-sensitive, inclusion-based pointer alias analysis. Their analysis, implemented in the bddbdd system, represents input-output relations as BDDs [5]. The BDD-based approach seems to work well for tracking a set of locations, but it is not applicable to verification of assertions because BDDs are known to suffer from exponential blow-up on multiplication, division, and barrel shifters — all frequent operations in software. Both works focused on the software analysis side, while our focus is on proving *-sensitive VCs. We believe that our results could improve the scalability of their approach.

The CBMC tool [7,6] verifies C programs, to bounded depth, with bit-accuracy and *-sensitivity. The approach is direct symbolic execution of the C into a SAT instance, unrolling all loops and inlining all function calls, so solving the generated VC is the performance bottleneck for large software. Our results address that bottleneck.

In the domain of programs limited to static memory allocation, Astrée [4] has been successfully applied to verification of mission-critical software systems. Although context-sensitive over the chosen abstract domain(s), Astrée was designed for systems that contain no goto statements, no dynamic memory allocation, no recursive calls, no recursive data structures, and no pointer arithmetic. Since our focus is verification of assertions in general purpose software, these constraints were not acceptable.

Context-sensitivity is only one component of the problem. Path-sensitivity is the other. The BLAST and SLAM software model checkers enumerate paths one-by-one, hoping that refinement will refute many paths with each added predicate. For each path, the model checker constructs an abstracted theorem prover query, which can correspond to a path that spans through many functions. Such path enumeration during the abstraction-checking-refinement loop seems wasteful — SAT solvers are extremely efficient in path enumeration and refutation of infeasible paths, so we believe that path enumeration should be left to the SAT solver.

Others have realized the importance of letting the theorem prover enumerate the paths as well. For instance, software verification systems like Boogie [18] and ESC/Java [12] do construct a single formula and let the theorem prover enumerate the paths. However, these systems rely on the user to provide interface abstractions, and do not attempt to abstract the formulas before calling the theorem prover.

Our approach to proving *-sensitive VCs merges both SAT-solver-based path enumeration and abstraction, yielding a precise, but practically efficient alternative to previous methods.

2   A Review of Verification Condition Generation

Traditionally, VCs are computed by Dijkstra's weakest precondition transformer [10], as is done for example in ESC/Java [12] and Boogie [18]. A naïve representation of VCs computed by the weakest precondition can be exponential in the size of the code fragment being checked, but this blow-up can be avoided by the introduction of fresh variables to represent intermediate expressions [22,13,19]. Here, we give a quick overview of weakest-precondition-based VC computation to illustrate the process, some common problems, and an efficient representation.

Consider the following simple program (modified from [19]):

```
S1:  if (x < 0) { y = −2*x − y; }
S2:  y = x + y;
S3:  assert(0 <= y);
```

The VC can be computed as the weakest liberal precondition wlp() of a sequential composition of those three statements with respect to true, giving:

$$\mathsf{wlp}(S1;S2;S3,\mathrm{true}) = \mathsf{wlp}(S1,\mathsf{wlp}(S2,\mathsf{wlp}(S3,\mathrm{true}))) \qquad (1)$$

$$= \mathsf{wlp}(S1,\mathsf{wlp}(S2,0 \le y)) \qquad (2)$$

$$= \mathsf{wlp}(S1,0 \le x+y) \qquad (3)$$

$$= 0 \le ITE(x < 0, -(x+y), x+y) \qquad (4)$$

where *ITE* is the if-then-else operator. Obviously, continuous application of wlp() can lead to exponential blowup in the size of the formula. To avoid the blowup, we can perform renaming, which guarantees a single point of definition for each variable (as in Single Static Assignment (SSA) form [9]):

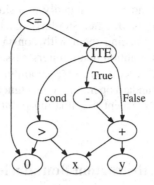

Fig. 1. Graph Representation of the Verification Condition. Non-leaf nodes are labeled with operators; leaf nodes, with variables and constants. Operator nodes are connected to their operands by edges.

```
S1:  if (x0 < 0) { y1 = -2*x0 - y0; } else { y1 = y0; }
S2:  y2 = x0 + y1;
S3:  assert(0 <= y2);
```

Since each variable has a single point of definition, assignments can be replaced with equivalences (*passive commands* in [19]), and then $\text{wlp}(S1;S2;S3, 0 \leq y_2)$ boils down to:

$$(x_0 < 0 \Rightarrow (y1 \equiv -2x_0 - y_0)) \land (x_0 \geq 0 \Rightarrow (y_1 \equiv y_0)) \land (y_2 \equiv x_0 + y_1) \land (0 \leq y_2)$$

Exponential blowup is avoided at the expense of introduction of fresh variables.

The same VC can be represented in the form of a graph. In particular, we simply represent a logical formula as a directed, acyclic graph, in which non-leaf nodes are labeled with operators, their children are their operands, and the leaves are labeled with variables or constants. A graph representation of a logical formula such that all common subexpression nodes have been merged will be called a maximally-shared graph. Figure 1 depicts a maximally shared graph representation of the computed VC in Eq. 4. The advantage of using maximally-shared graphs for VC representation is that the elimination of common subexpressions is simple, while the graph is still linear in the size of the code fragment.

The work in this paper is to support our static checker CALYSTO, which is being designed to be a general-purpose, bit-precise assertion checker. CALYSTO implements an efficient interprocedural symbolic execution algorithm [1] that converts SSA (computed using the LLVM compiler framework [17]) into function summaries and VCs in the form of acyclic maximally-shared graphs. For each location that a function modifies, CALYSTO computes the resulting expression in terms of the function inputs (including globals). Each such expression is represented as a separate summary expression, which gives fine-grained control during the refinement process (Sec. 3.2). Like other static checkers, CALYSTO makes a few unsound approximations. For example, loops are unrolled a fixed number of times, with the additional assumption that the loop test fails at the loop exit, as is done in ESC/Java [12], Saturn [25], and older versions of

Boogie [18]. We could also handle loops soundly by using loop invariants (computed by any technique), as is done in Boogie. Similarly, CALYSTO handles non-constant array indices by unsoundly replacing them with constant indices. In addition, CA-LYSTO makes the unsound assumption that pointers passed as function parameters are not aliased, as in [20,25]. However, CALYSTO's computed VCs are *-sensitive, fully bit-accurate, and support all standard operators (e.g., signed/unsigned division and multiplication on bit-vectors, etc.), except that floating-point arithmetic is not yet implemented.

3 Exploiting Natural Abstraction Boundaries

We begin with an example that provides intuition about how our approach solves *-sensitive VCs. The code used in the example is a simplified and slightly modified piece of code from a real application.[1] To prove an assertion, we need to prove either that the assertion itself is unreachable, or that it always evaluates to true. Through the example, we shall follow a sequence of steps needed to prove the assertion on line 22.

```
1        int global1 , global2 ;
2
3        // If *data<0, returns true and computes *data=abs(*data).
4        bool flip(int *data) {
5            if (*data < 0) {
6                *data = -(*data);
7                return true;
8            }
9            return false;
10       }
11
12       // Assume init is a pure function (no side-effects).
13       int init(int x) {
14           // Some expensive computation ...
15       }
16
17       // If global1 is positive and global2 is negative, scales
18       // global1 by abs(global2).
19       void scale() {
20           global2 = init(global1);
21           if (flip(&global2)) {
22               assert(global2 != 0); // Div by zero.
23               global1 /= global2;
24           }
25       }
```

$$(5)$$

---

[1] The example is modified from our modular arithmetic theorem prover SPEAR.

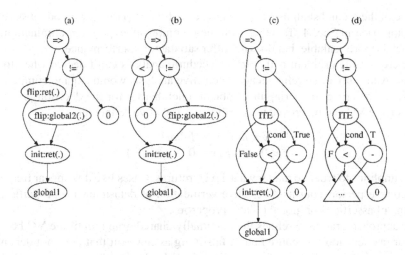

Fig. 2. Sequence of Refinements of the Computed VC. Summary nodes are structurally refined in the following sequence: `flip:ret`, `flip:global2`, and finally `init:ret`. The subgraph obtained by the refinement of `init:ret` is represented by a triangle. For simplicity, these figures do not show pointer references and dereferences.

As mentioned earlier, the symbolic execution will compute a graph representing each effect of each function in terms of its parameters (and globals). For example, the function `flip` has two effects: a boolean return value and its effect on the location pointed to by its parameter. At the caller's side, the symbolic execution initially denotes effects of a function call by a placeholder operator node. For example, the return value of a call to `flip` will be an operator node labeled *flip : ret* whose child is the argument to `flip`.

The VC will be an implication: if line 22 is reachable, then the asserted condition must hold. Let us ponder the structure of the computed VC. The antecedent contains two nested function calls. The consequent is a simple comparison of zero with the effect of `flip` on the global variable. Observe that the expression is written in terms of the initial values of all involved variables, facilitating common subexpression elimination by simple graph rewriting. Graphically, the VC can be represented as a maximally-shared graph (Fig. 2a). Summaries of the individual effects of each called function are at first represented as unconstrained fresh variables. Those nodes will be called summary nodes. Interpretation of a summary node corresponds to replacing the node with a node that represents the summarized expression. Such expansion corresponds to a round of inlining.

To be fully context-sensitive, the obvious approach is to completely inline all calls. Such inlining leads to exponential blow-up even on small applications. We found that aggressive inlining of non-recursive function calls works only on several very small applications, resulting in roughly 50-180X increase in the size of the code.

A better approach is to track the individual effects of a function separately. This fine-grained approach makes it possible to expand only the slice of the called function that is actually in the cone of influence of the verified property. We consider this approach to be the state of the art and shall use it as the base case for comparison with our abstraction-based approach in Sec. 4. Together with the common subexpression elimination, this approach is more scalable, but does not offer satisfactory performance.

The crux of the problem is that interprocedural analysis can't decide when to stop inlining. After only three refinements, *-sensitive analysis would expand computationally expensive `init`, rendering the problem much harder for the decision procedure. However, the VC can be proved to be valid after only two refinements

$$\text{Let } x = init : ret(global1)$$
$$x < 0 \Rightarrow ITE(x < 0, -x, x) \neq 0$$

which simplifies to true, no matter what `init` returns. Cases like this appear frequently in practice, especially during *-sensitive verification of data-intensive properties, like checking of assertions or global pointer properties.

Our approach gradually refines the maximally-shared graph, until the VC becomes valid, or the decision procedure finds a falsifying assignment that does not depend on any summary nodes. The rest of this section gives the details of our approach.

3.1 Algorithm Overview

The proposed approach follows the general paradigm of automatic, counter-example-guided, abstraction refinement [8], but unlike typical CEGAR approaches, our abstraction and refinement operations are entirely structural, and the refinement works incrementally on abstract counterexamples (rather than concretizing the abstract counterexample, proving it spurious, and then analyzing the proof). Locations modified by a function call (either indirectly through a pointer, or directly via returned values) are initially considered to be unconstrained variables. Those unconstrained variables are incrementally refined until the formula represented by the graph becomes valid, or the falsifying assignment does not depend on any unconstrained variables. In our case, incremental refinement is structural refinement on the maximally-shared graph. The refinement step replaces an unconstrained variable with a subgraph that represents the summary expression and the edges that were pointing to the unconstrained variable are relinked to point to the newly constructed expression. We shall say that refinement *expands* summary nodes.

Algorithm 1. Main abstraction-checking-refinement loop.

1: Let F be a node in the maximally-shared graph representing some VC.
2: $f = encode(F)$
3: **while** $\neg solve(f)$ **do**   ▷ *solve* returns false if a solution (falsifying assignment) is found.
4:     **if** $\neg$REFINE$(F, current\_solution)$ **then**
5:         Report solution and exit.
6: Report VALID and exit.

An abstract rendition of our algorithm is given in Alg. 1. The checked verification condition is represented by a root F in the maximally-shared graph. The algorithm encodes F on the fly into formula f and passes it to the decision procedure (*solve()*). In our case, F is bit-accurately translated to CNF by the standard Tseitin transform [22], but from the maximally shared graph after common subexpressions have been eliminated. Summary nodes are encoded as unconstrained variables. If the decision procedure proves f valid, we are done. Otherwise, refinement takes F and the table of current assignments to variables represented by nodes in the support of F, and returns true if the graph was refined, and false otherwise. If the graph was not refined, then all the summary nodes related to the falsifying assignment have been expanded, and the main loop terminates. Otherwise, the abstraction-checking-refinement cycle continues. Since maximally-shared graphs are acyclic, the algorithm necessarily terminates.

The algorithm interacts gracefully with incremental decision procedures — each expansion of a summary node replaces only a single node with the expression represented by the summary node, monotonically increasing the set of constraints.

Our lazy approach to interpretation of function summaries resembles the intuition behind lazy proof explication [11], a technique used to bridge between different theories in a theorem prover. The shared intuition is to abstract away expensive reasoning — expanding a function summary or solving a sub-theory query — as unconstrained variables, and then constrain them lazily, only as needed to refute solutions to the abstracted problem. The specifics of what to abstract and how to refine, of course, are different, since we are solving different problems.

Since critical software bugs (e.g. [2]) are often caused by the finite nature of bit-vector arithmetic, it is important to maintain the bit-level behavior of the verified software. CALYSTO computes bit-precise VCs, which are translated to CNF directly — even expensive 64-bit arithmetic operations, like division and remainder, are handled precisely. The bit-vectors are represented with the same bit-width as in the compiled code. In our case that means that integers and pointers are represented with 64 bits.

Path enumeration is completely left to the SAT solver. We found that it is important for the SAT solver to process the variables in an order that roughly corresponds to reverse preorder traversal (all predecessors are visited before the successors). If the opposite traversal is used, the solving phase typically requires 7-10X more time. This supports our conclusion that most of the paths become infeasible close to the VC root node.

3.2 Structural Refinement

The first few iterations of the main loop of Alg. 1 will likely return false counterexamples, since the initial abstraction is usually very crude. So, the refinement algorithm has to identify very quickly a set of summary nodes that are relevant to the found solution.

The algorithm attempts to minimize the number of expanded summaries to avoid expensive computation. Given a falsifying assignment, our refinement scheme searches the graph and selects a single summary node to expand, thereby refining the model. In particular, the algorithm starts traversing the formula from the VC root. During the traversal, the algorithm detects don't-care values — values that are irrelevant to the current solution and can therefore be ignored.[2] To formalize the concept of don't-care values, we define absorptive element as:

---

[2] The anonymous reviewers noted a connection between our analysis and strictness analysis in functional programming, as well as the work of Wilson and Dill [24]. The commonality is

Definition 1 (Absorptive Element). *If there exists an element a for some operator $\star$, such that $\forall x : a \star x = a$, then a is an absorptive element of $\star$, denoted as* abelem $(\star) = a$.

For instance, abelem $(\wedge) = $ false, abelem $(*) = 0$, and so on.

If the decision procedure returns a falsifying assignment, each node F in the graph representing the checked VC has some assigned value, which we shall denote as val (F). If F is an operator $\star$, our algorithm checks val (x) for each operand x of F. If val (x) is an absorptive element of $\star$, it is a sufficient explanation of the value of F in the falsifying assignment (the other operand is a don't-care). Hence, it suffices to refine only x. Our refinement procedure is given in Alg. 2. As is usual for graph traversal, visited nodes are marked during traversal to avoid re-visiting nodes; marking is not shown in the pseudocode.

Algorithm 2. Structural Refinement Algorithm. F is a node in the maximally-shared graph, and x and y are its operands. The return value indicates whether a summary has been expanded.

```
 1: function REFINE(graph node F, values assigned to nodes)
 2:     if F is a summary node then
 3:         expand the summary for F; return true
 4:     else if F is a leaf node then
 5:         return false
 6:     else if F ≡ x⋆y then
 7:         if val (x) = abelem (⋆) then
 8:             return REFINE(x)
 9:         else if val (y) = abelem (⋆) then
10:             return REFINE(y)
11:     else
12:         return REFINE(x) or REFINE(y)
13:         (The or is lazy: if either call succeeds, the other is skipped.)
14:         (The order is arbitrary. Either x or y can be refined first.)
```

Some operators (like implication and if-then-else) do not have absorptive elements, but allow similar don't-care analysis. Our implementation performs such reductions according to the rules in Alg. 3.

Returning to the example in Fig. 2, in 2a, the checker treats the placeholder nodes as unconstrained variables and finds a falsifying assignment where $flip : ret$ is true and the $!=$ is false. Alg. 3 will derive the refinement in 2b, where a possible falsifying solution gives the $init : ret$ node a negative value. Next, the algorithm might choose to expand the $flip : global2$ node, yielding the refinement in 2c, which is valid. We were able to avoid the expensive expansion of the $init : ret$ node.

---

the goal of finding cases in which a value is not used or needed. For example, in an ITE in a functional programming language, the condition argument is strict because it is always evaluated, whereas the other two arguments are non-strict. In our case, we are refining a falsifying solution, so we have much more don't-care information available, e.g., we know the value of the condition argument, so we know exactly which branch need not be refined.

Algorithm 3. Additions to the Basic Refinement Algorithm

1: **if** $F \equiv (x \Rightarrow y)$ and val $(x) \equiv$ false **then** return REFINE(x)
2: **else if** $F \equiv (x \Rightarrow y)$ and val $(y) \equiv$ true **then** return REFINE(y)
3: **else if** $F \equiv (x \Rightarrow y)$ return REFINE(x) **or** REFINE(y)
4:
5: **if** $F \equiv ITE(c,x,y)$ and val $(c) \equiv$ true return REFINE(c) **or** REFINE(x)
6: **else if** $F \equiv ITE(c,x,y)$ return REFINE(c) **or** REFINE(y) ▷ val (c) must be true or false.

Unlike other approaches, our approach to refinement does not require a theorem prover. The downside is that our refinement might be less precise and result in more refinement cycles. However, each refinement cycle only adds additional constraints to the decision procedure incrementally, making the solving phase more efficient as well.

4   Experimental Results

To test our approach, we used CALYSTO to generate VCs for six real-world, publicly-available C/C++ applications, ranging in size from 9 to 228 thousand lines of code (KLOC) before preprocessing. The benchmarks are the Dspam spam filter, our boolean satisfiability solver HYPERSAT, the Licq ICQ chat client, the OpenLDAP implementation of the Lightweight Directory Access Protocol, the Wine Windows OS emulator, and the Xchat IRC client. For each program, for each pointer dereference, we generated a VC to check that the pointer is non-NULL (omitting VCs that were solved trivially by our expression simplifier).

CALYSTO has a simple, non-recursive expression simplifier that runs during symbolic execution. The simplifier rules are numerous, but straightforward. We noticed that performing constant propagation during the simplification reduces the memory footprint, but does not drastically speed-up the solving phase because our modular arithmetic theorem prover SPEAR (like many others) performs aggressive constant propagation on its own. Other, slightly more complex rules, like $ITE(c,x,\neg c \wedge y) \equiv ITE(c,x,y)$ do speed up the solving phase, but not drastically.

As the basis for comparison, we also solved the VCs using eager expansion of sliced summaries (described in Sec. 3). The approaches were tested under equal conditions: the same simplification and common subexpression elimination were applied to both approaches after every summary expansion, before calling the SAT solver. The same SAT solver was used for both the base case and our approach.

Table 1 and Fig. 3 summarize the results. In a large majority of cases, the structural abstraction approach is superior to the eager approach, which suffers 81% more timeouts, and 75% longer runtime. There are some cases, however, where the eager approach performs significantly better. Analyzing those cases, we found that occasionally our simplifier can simplify some expanded summaries to trivial constants, which in turn can make the VC trivially easy to solve. For example, the most frequent case we have seen is when an expanded summary, which is an antecedent in an implication, trivially simplifies to false, rendering the whole implication true. A priori, there is no way to know whether or not an expanded summary will drastically simplify the VC

Table 1. The first column gives the name and version of the benchmark, KLOC is the number of source code lines (in thousands) before preprocessing, and #VCs is the number of checked VCs. The next four columns give the total run time in seconds (including timeouts) and the number of timeouts, for the base approach and for our new structural abstraction and refinement method. The timeout limit was 300 seconds. Experiments were performed on a dual-processor AMD X2 4600+ machine with 2 GB RAM, running Linux 2.6.15.

Benchmark	KLOC	#VCs	Base Approach		with Struct. Abs./Ref.	
			Time (sec)	Timeouts	Time (sec)	Timeouts
Dspam v3.6.5	37	8003	4451	12	3758	10
HyperSAT v1.7	9	427	32602	108	27025	81
Licq v1.3.4	20	5165	24103	50	4072	4
OpenLDAP v2.3.30	228	4935	738	0	572	0
Wine v0.9.27	126	8831	2598	0	2145	0
Xchat v2.6.8	76	24045	18914	13	10024	6
Total	496	55583	83406	183	47596	101

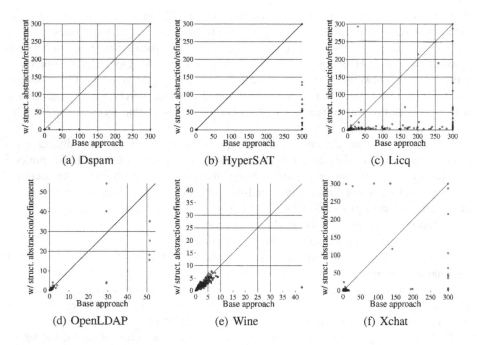

Fig. 3. Results presented as scatter plots. Timeouts are plotted at 300secs.

(akin to the classic debate of eager vs. lazy constraint propagation in SMT solvers). Our experimental results, though, show that for solving software VCs, laziness wins.

Overall, our structural abstraction-checking-refinement approach is able to quickly verify *-sensitive, bit-accurate VCs from large software. Moving forward, we believe there is additional structure to be exploited, and that is the direction of future work.

5 Discussion

We believe there are two main reasons behind the success of our approach: efficient path enumeration and exploiting natural abstraction boundaries in software.

In our experience, path enumeration dominates the cost of software verification, even when the loops are abstracted away. In the worst case, any path-sensitive analysis has to analyze all the paths. We use our SAT-solver-based prover SPEAR to enumerate paths efficiently, but the order in which any SAT solver processes constraints is important. Most solvers add variables to the decision queue in the order in which the variables are found in the clauses. So, by starting the SAT solver from a root of the VC graph and letting it enumerate paths, we explore paths in a breadth-first manner. In analyzing several open-source applications, we realized that most paths in an average program are infeasible, and this breadth-first path exploration prunes more paths more quickly. Contemporary software model checkers do not exploit this fact, but rather rely on depth-first search, performing numerous calls to the theorem prover through a counterexample-driven refinement process, just to refute a path that is most likely to be infeasible anyway. Similarly, the lazy summary expansion prunes obviously infeasible paths before function summaries are expanded and analyzed, decreasing the number of paths that need to be explored even further.

The proposed abstraction-refinement approach exploits the natural abstraction boundaries in software that correspond closely to the programmer's mental model. To manage complexity, programmers tend to organize code into structural units (functions) and use them as abstractions — whatever a function returns, the rest of the code should work. This common programming tactic, which reduces the mental load on the programmer, inspired our approach. To the extent that programmers use functions effectively as abstractions, our refinement algorithm can avoid expanding the details that were abstracted away.

Our simple abstraction does not rely on the standard abstraction domains. Hence, the contributions of this paper can be applied to a wide range of software analysis tools that require interprocedural analysis and a decision procedure. If further complexity reduction is needed, we believe our approach should be compatible with classical abstract domains and other abstraction techniques.

References

1. Babić, D., Hu, A.: Fast Symbolic Execution for Static Checking (submitted for publication)
2. Babić, D., Musuvathi, M.: Modular Arithmetic Decision Procedure. Technical Report TR-2005-114, Microsoft Research Redmond (2005)
3. Ball, T., Majumdar, R., Millstein, T., Rajamani, S.: Automatic Predicate Abstraction of C Programs. Programming Language Design and Implementation, pp. 203–213 (2001)
4. Blanchet, B., Cousot, P., Cousot, R., Feret, J., Mauborgne, L., Miné, A., Monniaux, D., Rival, X.: A static analyzer for large safety-critical software. Programming Language Design and Implementation, pp. 196–207 (2003)
5. Bryant, R.: Graph-based algorithms for boolean function manipulation. IEEE Trans. Comput. 35(8), 677–691 (1986)

6. Clarke, E., Kroening, D., Lerda, F.: A tool for checking ANSI-C programs. In: Jensen, K., Podelski, A. (eds.) TACAS 2004. LNCS, vol. 2988, pp. 168–176. Springer, Heidelberg (2004)
7. Clarke, E., Kroening, D., Yorav, K.: Behavioral consistency of C and Verilog programs using bounded model checking. In: Design Automation Conference, pp. 368–371 (2003)
8. Clarke, E.M., Grumberg, O., Jha, S., Lu, Y., Veith, H.: Counterexample-guided abstraction refinement. In: Emerson, E.A., Sistla, A.P. (eds.) CAV 2000. LNCS, vol. 1855, pp. 154–169. Springer, Heidelberg (2000)
9. Cytron, R., Ferrante, J., Rosen, B.K., Wegman, M.N., Zadeck, F.K.: Efficiently Computing Static Single Assignment Form and the Control Dependence Graph. ACM Trans Programming Languages and Systems 13(4), 451–490 (1991)
10. Dijkstra, E.W., Scholten, C.S. (eds.): Predicate Calculus and Program Semantics. Springer, Heidelberg (1990)
11. Flanagan, C., Joshi, R., Ou, X., Saxe, J.B.: Theorem proving using lazy proof explication. In: Hunt Jr., W.A., Somenzi, F. (eds.) CAV 2003. LNCS, vol. 2725, pp. 355–367. Springer, Heidelberg (2003)
12. Flanagan, C., Leino, K.R.M., Lillibridge, M., Nelson, G., Saxe, J.B., Stata, R.: Extended static checking for Java. Programming Language Design and Implementation, pp. 234–245 (2002)
13. Flanagan, C., Saxe, J.B.: Avoiding exponential explosion: generating compact verification conditions. Principles of Programming Languages, pp. 193–205 (2001)
14. Graf, S., Saidi, H.: Construction of abstract state graphs with PVS. In: Grumberg, O. (ed.) CAV 1997. LNCS, vol. 1254, pp. 72–83. Springer, Heidelberg (1997)
15. Henzinger, T., Jhala, R., Majumdar, R., Sutre, G.: Lazy Abstraction. Principles of Programming Languages, pp. 58–70 (2002)
16. Henzinger, T.A., Jhala, R., Majumdar, R., McMillan, K.L.: Abstractions from proofs. Principles of Programming Languages, pp. 232–244 (2004)
17. Lattner, C., Adve, V.: LLVM: A Compilation Framework for Lifelong Program Analysis & Transformation. In: CGO '04: Proceedings of the International Symposium on Code Generation and Optimization, p. 75. IEEE Computer Society, Washington, DC, USA (2004)
18. Leino, K.R.M., Müller, P.: A verification methodology for model fields. In: Sestoft, P. (ed.) ESOP 2006 and ETAPS 2006. LNCS, vol. 3924, pp. 115–130. Springer, Heidelberg (2006)
19. Leino, K.R.M.: Efficient weakest preconditions. Inf. Process. Lett. 93(6), 281–288 (2005)
20. Livshits, V.B., Lam, M.S.: Tracking Pointers with Path and Context Sensitivity for Bug Detection in C Programs. In: European Software Engineering Conference/International Symposium on Foundations of Software Engineering, pp. 317–326 (2003)
21. Reps, T., Horwitz, S., Sagiv, M.: Precise interprocedural dataflow analysis via graph reachability. Principles of Programming Languages, pp. 49–61 (1995)
22. Tseitin, G.S.: On the complexity of derivation in propositional calculus. In: Siekmann, J., Wrightson, G. (eds.) Automation of Reasoning 2: Classical Papers on Computational Logic 1967-1970, pp. 466–483. Springer, Heidelberg (1983)
23. Whaley, J., Lam, M.S.: Cloning-based context-sensitive pointer alias analysis using binary decision diagrams. Programming Language Design and Implementation, pp. 131–144 (2004)
24. Wilson, C., Dill, D.L.: Reliable verification using symbolic simulation with scalar values. In: 37th Design Automation Conference, pp. 124–129. ACM/IEEE (2000)
25. Xie, Y., Aiken, A.: Scalable error detection using boolean satisfiability. Principles of Programming Languages, pp. 351–363 (2005)

An Abstract Domain for Analyzing
Heap-Manipulating Low-Level Software*

Sumit Gulwani[1] and Ashish Tiwari[2]

[1] Microsoft Research, Redmond, WA 98052
sumitg@microsoft.com
[2] SRI International, Menlo Park, CA 94025
tiwari@csl.sri.com

Abstract. We describe an abstract domain for representing useful invariants of heap-manipulating programs (in presence of recursive data structures and pointer arithmetic) written in languages like C or low-level code. This abstract domain allows representation of must and may equalities among pointer expressions. Pointer expressions contain existentially or universally quantified integer variables guarded by some base domain constraint. We allow quantification of a special form, namely $\exists\forall$ quantification, to balance expressiveness with efficient automated deduction. The existential quantification is over some *dummy* non-program variables, which are automatically made explicit by our analysis to express useful program invariants. The universal quantifier is used to express properties of collections of memory locations. Our abstract interpreter automatically computes invariants about programs over this abstract domain. We present initial experimental results demonstrating the effectiveness of this abstract domain on some common coding patterns.

1 Introduction

Alias analysis attempts to answer, for a given program point, whether two pointer expressions e_1 and e_2 are always equal (must-alias) or may be equal (may-alias). Keeping precise track of this information in the presence of recursive data-structures is hard because the number of expressions, or aliasing relationships, becomes potentially infinite. The presence of pointer arithmetic makes this even harder.

We describe an abstract domain that can represent precise must and may-equalities among pointer expressions that are needed to prove correctness of several common code patterns in low-level software. It is motivated by the early work on representing aliasing directly using must-alias and may-alias pairs of pointer expressions [2, 15, 4, 5]. However, there are two main differences. (a) The language of our pointer expressions is richer: The earlier work built on constructing pointer expressions from (pre-defined) field dereferences; however our

---

* The second author was supported in part by the National Science Foundation under grant CCR-0326540.

W. Damm and H. Hermanns (Eds.): CAV 2007, LNCS 4590, pp. 379–392, 2007.

```
struct List {int Len, *Data; List* Next;}
ListOfPtrArray(struct List* x)
1    for (y := x; y ≠ null; y := y→next)
2        t :=?; y→len := t; y→data := malloc(4t);
3    for (y := x; y ≠ null; y := y→next)
4        for (z := 0; z < y→len; z := z + 1) y→data→(4z) := ...;
```

Fig. 1. An example of a pattern of initializing the pairs of dynamic arrays and their lengths inside each list element and later accessing the array elements

expressions are built from dereferencing at arbitrary integer (expression) offsets. This gives our abstract domain the ability to handle arrays, pointer arithmetic, and recursive structures in one unified framework. (b) Apart from the integer program variables, we also allow integer variables (in our expressions) that are existentially or universally quantified. This allows our abstract domain to represent nontrivial properties of data-structures in programs. [1]

We allow only a special form of quantification in our abstract domain, namely $\exists\forall$ quantification, to balance expressiveness with potential for automated deduction. The quantification is over integer variables that are *not* program variables. The existentially quantified variables can be seen as *dummy* program variables that are explicitly needed to express common program invariants. The universally quantified variables describe properties of (potentially unbounded) collections of memory locations.

Our abstract domain uses only two base predicates, must and may equality, unlike the common approach of using a pre-defined set of richer predicates [13,20, 19,14]. As a result, reasoning in our abstract domain does not require any special deduction rules, thereby yielding comparative simplicity and easier automation.

Consider, for example, the program shown in Figure 1. The input variable x points to a list (unless qualified, list refers to an acyclic singly-linked list in this paper), where each list element contains two fields, **Data** and **Len**, apart from the **Next** field. **Data** is a pointer to some array, and **Len** is intended to be the length of that array. In the first while loop, the iterator y iterates over each list element, initializing **Data** to point to a newly created array and **Len** to the length of that array. In the second while loop, the iterator y iterates over each list element accessing the array pointed to by **Data**. The proof of memory safety of this commonly used code pattern requires establishing the invariant that for all list elements in the list pointed to by x, **Len** is the length of the array **Data**. This *quantified* invariant is expressed in our abstract domain as

$$\exists i.\mathbf{List}(x, i, \mathtt{next}) \wedge \forall j [0 \leq j < i \Rightarrow \mathbf{Array}(x \to \mathtt{next}^j \to \mathtt{data}, 4 \times x \to \mathtt{next}^j \to \mathtt{len})] \quad (1)$$

where $x \to \mathtt{next}^j$ is an (pointer) expression in our language that denotes the memory location obtained by performing j dereferences at offset **next** starting from x. The predicates **List** and **Array** are abbreviations for the following definitions.

---

[1] A limited form of quantification over integer variables was implicitly hidden in the set representation used for representing may-aliases in the work by Deutsch [5].

$$\texttt{List}(x, i, \texttt{next}) \;\equiv\; i \geq 0 \wedge x{\to}\texttt{next}^i = \texttt{null} \wedge \forall j[0 \leq j < i \Rightarrow \texttt{Valid}(x{\to}\texttt{next}^j)]$$
$$\texttt{Array}(x, t) \;\equiv\; \forall j[(0 \leq j < t) \Rightarrow \texttt{Valid}(x + j)]$$

Intuitively, $\texttt{List}(x, i, \texttt{next})$ denotes that x points to a list of length i (with $\texttt{next}$ as the next field) and $\texttt{Array}(x, t)$ denotes that x points to a region of memory of length t. The predicate $\texttt{Valid}(e)$ is intended to denote that e is a valid pointer value, which is safe to dereference (provided the subexpressions of e are safe to dereference)[2], and can be encoded as the following must-equality:

$$\texttt{Valid}(e) \;\equiv\; e{\to}\beta = \texttt{valid}$$

where β is a special symbolic integer offset that is known to not alias with any other integer expression, and $\texttt{valid}$ is a special constant in our expression language. We automatically generate invariants, like the one described in Equation 1, by performing abstract interpretation (whose transfer functions are described in a full version of this paper [11]) over our abstract domain.

This paper is organized as follows. Section 2 describes our program model, which closely reflects the memory model of C modulo some simple assumptions. We then formally describe our abstract domain and present its semantics in relation to our program model (Section 3). We then describe the procedure to check implication in this abstract domain (Section 4). Section 5 discusses preliminary experimental results, while Section 6 describes some related work.

2 Program Model

Values. A value v is either an integer, or a pointer value, or is undefined. A pointer value is either $\texttt{null}$ or a pair of a region identifier and a positive offset.

$$v \;::=\; c \mid \langle r, d \rangle \mid \texttt{null} \mid \bot$$

Program State. A *program state* ρ is either undefined, or is a tuple $\langle D, R, V, P \rangle$, where D represents the set of valid region identifiers, R is a *region map* that maps a region identifier in D to a positive integer (which denotes size of that region), V is a *variable map* that maps program variables to values, and P is a *memory* that maps non-$\texttt{null}$ pointer values to values. We say that a pointer value $\langle r, d \rangle$ is *valid* in a program state $\langle D, R, V, P \rangle$ if $r \in D$ and $0 \leq d < R(r)$. We say that a pointer value is *invalid* if it is neither valid nor $\texttt{null}$.

Expressions. The program expressions e that occur on the right side of an assignment statement are described by the following language.

$$e \;::=\; c \mid x \mid e_1 \pm e_2 \mid c \times e \mid e_1{\to}e_2 \mid \texttt{null} \mid ?$$

---

[2] This assumption is important because we want to treat $\texttt{Valid}$ as an uninterpreted unary predicate, which allows us to encode it as a simple must-equality. However this necessitates that validity of all valid subexpressions be described explicitly.

$$\frac{}{[\![\text{null}]\!]\rho = \text{null}}\ \text{null} \qquad \frac{[\![e_1]\!]\rho = \langle r,d\rangle \quad [\![e_2]\!]\rho = c \quad r \in D \quad 0 \le d+c < R(r)}{[\![e_1 \!\to\! e_2]\!]\rho = P(\langle r, d+c\rangle)}\ \text{deref}$$

$$\frac{[\![e_1]\!]\rho \text{ and } [\![e_2]\!]\rho \text{ are ints}}{[\![e_1 \pm e_2]\!]\rho = [\![e_1]\!]\rho + [\![e_2]\!]\rho}\ \text{intArith} \qquad \frac{[\![x_1]\!]\rho \text{ and } [\![x_2]\!]\rho \text{ are ints}}{[\![x_1 \text{ rel } x_2]\!]\rho = [\![x_1]\!]\rho \text{ rel } [\![x_2]\!]\rho}\ \text{IntCompare}$$

$$\frac{}{[\![c]\!]\rho = c}\ \text{cons} \qquad \frac{\text{rel} \in \{\neq,=\} \quad [\![x_1]\!]\rho, [\![x_2]\!]\rho \text{ are null or valid pointers}}{[\![x_1 \text{ rel } x_2]\!]\rho = [\![x_1]\!]\rho \text{ rel } [\![x_2]\!]\rho}\ \text{ptrCompare}$$

$$\frac{[\![e_1]\!]\rho = \langle r,d\rangle \quad [\![e_2]\!]\rho = \text{int } c}{[\![e_1 \pm e_2]\!]\rho = \langle r, d \pm c\rangle}\ \text{ptrArith} \qquad \frac{V(y) = \langle r,i\rangle \quad r \in D \quad 0 \le i < R(r)}{[\![\text{free}(y)]\!]\rho = \langle D - \{r\}, R, V, P\rangle}\ \text{Free}$$

$$\frac{\text{Let } c \text{ be a non-det int}}{[\![?]\!]\rho = c}\ \text{nonDet} \qquad \frac{}{[\![x := e]\!]\rho = \langle D, R, V[x \mapsto [\![e]\!]\rho],\ P\rangle}\ \text{varUpdate}$$

$$\frac{}{[\![x]\!]\rho = V(x)}\ \text{var} \qquad \frac{V(x) = \langle r,i\rangle \quad [\![e_1]\!]\rho = j \quad r \in D \quad 0 \le i+j < R(r)}{[\![x \!\to\! e_1 := e_2]\!]\,\rho = \langle D, R, V, P[\langle r, i+j\rangle \mapsto [\![e_2]\!]\rho]\rangle}\ \text{MemUpdate}$$

$$\frac{[\![e]\!]\rho \ge 0 \quad \text{Let } r \text{ be some fresh region identifier}}{[\![x := \text{malloc}(e)]\!]\rho = \langle D \cup \{r\},\ R[r \mapsto [\![e]\!]\rho],\ V[x \mapsto \langle r,0\rangle],\ P\rangle}\ \text{Malloc}$$

Fig. 2. Semantics of Expressions, Predicates, and Statements in our language. ρ denotes the state $\langle D, R, V, P\rangle$. In a program state, an expression is evaluated to a value, a predicate is evaluated to a boolean value, and a statement is evaluated to a program state. Evaluation of an expression, or statement in a state s.t. none of the above rules apply yields a $\bot$ value or $\bot$ state respectively.

$e_1 \!\to\! e_2$ represents dereference of the region pointed to by e_1 at offset e_2 (i.e., $*(e_1 + e_2)$ in C language syntax). The above expressions have the usual expected semantics with the usual restrictions that it is not proper to add or subtract two pointer values, and that only a valid pointer value can be dereferenced. ? denotes a non-deterministic integer and is used to conservatively model other program expressions whose semantics we do not precisely capture (e.g., those that involve bitwise arithmetic). Given a program state ρ, an expression e evaluates to some value, denoted by $[\![e]\!]\rho$, according to the formal semantics given in Figure 2.

Statements. The assignment statements, $x := e$ and $*x := e$, have standard semantics. The memory allocation assignment, $x := malloc(e)$, assigns a pointer value with a fresh region identifier to x. The statement $free(e)$ frees the region pointed to by e. The formal semantics of these statements is given in Figure 2.

Predicates. The predicates that occur in conditionals are of the form $x_1 \text{ rel } x_2$, where $\text{rel} \in \{<, \le, \neq, =\}$. Without loss of any generality, we assume that x_1 and x_2 are either program variables or constants. These predicates have the usual semantics: Given a program state ρ, a predicate evaluates to either **true** or **false**. Pointer-values can be compared for equality or disequality, while integer values can be compared for inequality too; see Figure 2.

Memory Safety and Leaks. We say that a procedure is *memory-safe* and *leak-free* under some precondition, if for any program state ρ satisfying the precondition, the execution of the procedure yields program states ρ' that have the following properties respectively: (a) $\rho' \neq \bot$, (b) if $\rho' = \langle D, R, V, P \rangle$, then for all region identifiers $r \in D$, there exists an expression e s.t. $[\![e]\!]\rho' = \langle r, d \rangle$.

Intuitively, a procedure is memory-safe if all memory dereferences and free operations are performed on valid pointer values. Observe that our definition of memory safety precludes dangling pointer dereferences also. Similarly, a procedure is leak-free if all allocated regions can be traced by means of some expression.

Relation with C programs. The semantics of our program model closely reflects the C language semantics under the following assumptions: (a) All memory accesses are at word-boundaries and the size of each object read or written is at most a word. (b) The free(x) call frees a valid region returned by malloc even if x points somewhere in middle of that region (some implementations of C insist that x point to the beginning of a region returned by malloc). Our program model can be easily adapted to capture other possible semantics of C while not depending on the above assumptions. The current choice has been made to simplify presentation. We can thus test if a C program is memory-safe and leak-free by checking for the respective properties in our model.

3   Abstract Domain

The elements of our abstract domain describe must and may equalities between expressions. However, we need a richer language of expressions (as compared to the language of program expressions described in Section 2) to describe useful program properties. Hence, we extend the expression language as follows:

$$e ::= c \mid x \mid e_1 \pm e_2 \mid c \times e \mid e_1{\rightarrow}e_2^{e_3} \mid \textbf{valid} \mid \textbf{null}$$

valid is a special constant in our domain that satisfies **valid** $\neq$ **null**. The constant **valid** is used to represent that certain expressions contain a valid pointer value (as opposed to null or uninitialized or dangling etc) in the **Valid** predicate defined on Page 381 in Section 1.

The new construct $e_1{\rightarrow}e_2^{e_3}$ denotes e_3 de-references of expression e_1 at offset e_2, as is formalized by following semantics (If e_3 is 1, we write $e_1{\rightarrow}e_2^{e_3}$ as $e_1{\rightarrow}e_2$).

$$[\![e_1{\rightarrow}e_2^{e_3}]\!]\rho = \begin{cases} [\![e_1]\!]\rho & \text{if } [\![e_3]\!]\rho = 0 \\ [\![(e_1{\rightarrow}e_2){\rightarrow}e_2^{e_3-1}]\!]\rho & \text{if } [\![e_3]\!]\rho > 0 \\ \bot & \text{otherwise} \end{cases}$$

Must-equality is a binary predicate over *pointer* expressions denoted using "=" and is used in an infix notation. This predicate describes equalities between expressions that have the same value at a given program point (in all runs of the program). May-equality is also a binary predicate over *pointer* expressions. It is denoted using "∼" and is used in an infix notation. This predicate describes an over-approximation of all possible expression equalities at a given program point (in any run of the program). Disequalities are deduced from absence of (transitive closure of) may-equalities. The reason for keeping may-equalities instead of disequalities is that the former representation is often more succinct in the common case when most memory locations are not aliased (i.e., have only one incoming pointer).

3.1   Abstract Elements

An abstract element F in our domain is a collection of must-equalities M, and may-equalities Y, together with some arithmetic constraints C on *integer* expressions. Apart from the program variables, the expressions in M, Y, and C may contain extra integer variables that are existentially or universally quantified. Each must-equality and may-equality is universally quantified over integer variables U_f that satisfy some constraints C_f. The collection of these must-equalities M, may-equalities Y and constraints C may further be existentially quantified over some variables. Thus, the abstract element is a $\exists\forall$ formula. The constraints C and C_f are arithmetic constraints on expressions in a *base constraint domain* that is a parameter to our algorithm.

$$
\begin{aligned}
F &::= \quad \exists U : C, M, Y \\
M &::= \quad \texttt{true} \mid M \ \wedge \ \forall U_f(C_f \Rightarrow (e_1 = e_2)) \\
Y &::= \quad \texttt{true} \mid Y \ \wedge \ \forall U_f(C_f \Rightarrow (e_1 \sim e_2))
\end{aligned}
$$

The existentially quantified variables, U, can be seen as *dummy* program variables that are needed to express the particular program invariant. The universal quantification allows us to express properties of collections of entities (expressions in our case).

Formal Semantics of Abstract Elements. An abstract element F represents a collection of program states ρ, namely those states ρ that *satisfy* F (as defined below). A program state $\rho = \langle D, R, V, P \rangle$ satisfies the formula $F = \exists U : C, M, Y$ (denoted as $\rho \models F$) if there exists an integer substitution σ for variables in U such that the following holds: If $\rho_e = \langle D, R, V\sigma, P \rangle$, (where $V\sigma$ denotes the result of mapping v to $\sigma(v)$, for all v, in V) then,

- $\rho_e \models C$, i.e., for each predicate e_1 rel $e_2 \in C$, $[\![e_1 \text{ rel } e_2]\!]\rho_e$ evaluates to $\texttt{true}$.
- $\rho_e \models M$, i.e., for all facts $(\forall U_f(C_f \Rightarrow (e_1 = e_2))) \in M$, for every integer assignment σ_f to variables in U_f, if $\rho_f \models C_f$ then $[\![e_1]\!]\rho_f = [\![e_2]\!]\rho_f$, where $\rho_f = \langle D, R, V\sigma\sigma_f, P \rangle$. In the special case when $e_1 = e_2$ is of the form $e \to \beta = \texttt{valid}$, then $[\![e]\!]\rho_f = \langle r, c \rangle$, $r \in D$, and $0 \le c + [\![\beta]\!]\rho_f < R(r)$.
- For all expressions e_1 and e_2, if there is a state ρ' s.t. $\rho' \models C$, $\rho' \models Y$ (treating may-equality as must-equality and using the above definition of $\models$), $[\![e_1]\!]\rho' \ne \bot$, $[\![e_2]\!]\rho' \ne \bot$, and $[\![e_1]\!]\rho' \ne [\![e_2]\!]\rho'$, then $[\![e_1]\!]\rho_e \ne [\![e_2]\!]\rho_e$. Informally, if $e_1 \sim e_2$ is not implied by Y, then $[\![e_1]\!]\rho_e \ne [\![e_2]\!]\rho_e$.

The top element $\top$ in our abstract domain is represented as:

$$\bigwedge_{x,y} \forall i_1, i_2, j_1, j_2[(x \rightarrow i_1^{j_1}) \sim (y \rightarrow i_2^{j_2})]$$

In standard logic with equality and disequality predicates, this would be represented as true. However, since we represent the disequality relation by representing its dual, we have to explicitly say that anything reachable from any variable x may be aliased to anything reachable from any variable y.

Observe that the semantics of must-equalities and may-equalities is *liberal* in the sense that a must-equality $e_1 = e_2$ or may-equality $e_1 \sim e_2$ does not automatically imply that e_1 or e_2 are valid pointer expressions. Instead the validity of an expression needs to be explicitly stated using Valid predicates (defined on Page 381 in Section 1).

Observe that there cannot be any program state that satisfies a formula whose must-equalities are not a subset of (implied by the) may-equalities. Hence, any useful formula will have every must-equality also as a may-equality. Therefore, we assume that in our formulas all must-equalities are also may-equalities, and avoid duplicating them in our examples.

3.2   Expressiveness

In this section, we discuss examples of program properties that our abstract elements can express.

(a) x points to an (possibly null) acyclic list: $\exists i : \text{List}(x, i, \text{next})$. The predicate List is as defined on Page 381.

(b) x points to a region (array) of t bytes: $\text{Array}(x, t)$. The predicate Array is as defined on Page 381.

(c) x points to a cyclic list: $\exists i : i \geq 1 \wedge x = x \rightarrow \text{next}^i \wedge \forall k (0 \leq k < i \Rightarrow \text{Valid}(x \rightarrow \text{next}^k))$

(d) Lists x and y share a common tail: $\exists i, j : i \geq 0 \wedge j \geq 0 \wedge x \rightarrow \text{next}^i = y \rightarrow \text{next}^j$

(e) y *may* point to some node in the list pointed to by x.

$$\exists i : x \rightarrow \text{next}^i \sim y \quad \text{or, equivalently,} \quad \forall i (x \rightarrow \text{next}^i \sim y)$$

Observe that existential quantification and forall quantification over may-equalities has the same semantics.

(f) The (reachable) heap is completely disjoint, i.e., no two distinct reachable memory locations point to the same location: true. Observe that disjointedness comes for free in our representation, i.e., we do not need to say anything if we want to represent disjointedness.

(g) y may be reachable from x, but only by following left or right pointers. Such invariants are useful to prove that certain iterators over data-structures do not update certain kinds of fields. The expression language described above is insufficient to represent this invariant precisely. However, a simple extension in which disjunctions of offsets (as opposed to a single offset) are allowed can represent this invariant precisely as follows: $\forall i \geq 0 : x \rightarrow (\text{left} \| \text{right})^i \sim y$. The semantics of the abstract domain can be easily extended to accomadate disjunctive offsets as above. A formal treatment of disjunctive offsets was avoided in this paper for the purpose of simplified presentation.

Regarding limitations of the abstract domain, we can not express arbitrary disjunctive facts and invariants that requires $\forall\exists$ quantification (such as the invariants required to analyze the Schorr-Waite algorithm [12]). We plan to enrich our abstract domain in the future.

4   Automated Deduction over the Abstract Domain

In this section, we briefly describe the key ideas behind our sound procedure for checking implication in our abstract domain.[3] For lack of space, the remaining transfer functions (namely, Join, Meet, Widen, and Strongest Postcondition operations) needed for performing abstract interpretation over our abstract domain are described in a full version of this paper [11].

The first step in deciding if F implies F', where F, F' are abstract elements, is to instantiate the existentially quantified variables in F' in terms of existentially quantified variables in F. We do this by means of a heuristic that we have found to be effective for our purpose. After this step, we can treat the existential variables as constants. Now consider the simpler problem of checking whether F implies $e_1 = e_2$ or whether F implies $e_1 \neq e_2$. For the former, we compute an under-approximation of must-aliases of e_1 from the must-equalities of F and then check whether e_2 belongs to that set. For that latter, we compute an over-approximation of may-aliases of e_1 from the may-equalities of F and then check whether e_2 does not belong to that set.

The function MustAliases(e, F) returns an under-approximation A of all must-aliases of expression e such that for every $e' \in A$, we can deduce that $F \Rightarrow e = e'$. Similarly, the function MayAliases(e, F) returns an over-approximation A of all may-aliases of expression e such that if $F \Rightarrow e \sim e'$, then $e' \in A$. Since these alias sets may have an infinite number of expressions, we represent the alias sets of an expression e using a finite set of pairs (C, e'), where (C, e') denotes all expressions e' that satisfy the constraint C. [4]

The pseudo-code for MustAliases and MayAliases is described in Figure 3. The key idea in our algorithm for MustAliases is to do a bounded number of transitive inferences on the existing must-equalities. The key idea in MayAliases

---

[3] We have not investigated decidability of the entailment relation in our abstract domain. Results about $\exists\forall$ fragment of first-order logic are not directly applicable because of integer variables in our terms. In this work, the focus was on obtaining an abstract domain for building a sound abstract interpreter that can generate useful invariants. Theoretical issues, such as decidability, are left for future work.

[4] This representation is motivated by the one used by Deutsch [5] except that the constraints in his formalism were pure linear arithmetic facts with no support for uninterpreted function subterms, and the expressions did not have support for pointer arithmetic. Moreover Deutsch used this representation only for computing may-aliases, and there was no support for must-aliases in his framework.

MustAliases(e, F)
  $A := \{\langle \text{true}, e \rangle\}$
  While change in A and not tired
    Forall $(\forall V(C \Rightarrow e_1 = e_2)) \in F$ and
      $\langle C', e' \rangle \in A$
      If $((\sigma, \gamma) := \text{MatchExpr}(e', e_1) \neq \bot)$
        $A := A \cup \{\langle C' \wedge C\sigma, (e_2\sigma) \rightarrow \gamma \rangle\}$
  return A

MayAliases(e, F)
  $A := \{\langle \text{true}, e \rangle\}$
  While change in A
    Forall $(\forall V(C \Rightarrow e_1 \sim e_2)) \in F$ and
      $\langle C', e' \rangle \in A$
      If $((\sigma, \gamma) := \text{MatchExpr}(e', e_1) \neq \bot)$
        $A := A \cup \{\langle C' \wedge C\sigma, (e_2\sigma) \rightarrow \gamma \rangle\}$
        $A := \text{OverApprox}(A)$
  return A

(a) Algorithm

Inputs:

$e = x$
$F_1 = \{x = x \rightarrow \mathbf{n}^j\}$
$F_2 = \{\forall i((0 \leq i < j) \Rightarrow$
        $x \rightarrow \mathbf{n}^i = x \rightarrow \mathbf{n}^{i+1} \rightarrow \mathbf{p})\}$

Outputs:

MustAliases$(e, F_1) =$
  $\{x \rightarrow \mathbf{n}^j, x \rightarrow \mathbf{n}^{2j}\}$
MustAliases$(e, F_2) =$
  $\{x \rightarrow \mathbf{n} \rightarrow \mathbf{p}, x \rightarrow \mathbf{n} \rightarrow \mathbf{p} \rightarrow \mathbf{n} \rightarrow \mathbf{p}\}$
MayAliases$(e, F_1) =$
  $\{x \rightarrow \mathbf{n}^t \mid t \geq j\}$
MayAliases$(e, F_2) =$
  $\{x \rightarrow (\mathbf{n}\|\mathbf{p})^t \mid 0 \leq t\}$ or
  $\{x \rightarrow (t_1)^{t_2} \mid 0 \leq t_2 \wedge \ell \leq t_1 \leq u\}$
  where $\ell = \min(\mathbf{n}, \mathbf{p}), u = \max(\mathbf{n}, \mathbf{p})$

(b) Examples

Fig. 3. The functions MustAliases and MayAliases. In (b), the first choice for MayAliases(e, F_2) is better than the second choice (if the $\mathbf{n}$ and $\mathbf{p}$ fields are not laid out successively), but will be generated only if we allow disjunctive offsets, as addressed in Section 3.2. Even though MayAliases is a conservative overapproximation it helps us prove that x does not alias with, for example, $x \rightarrow \text{data}$.

is to do transitive inferences on may-equalities until fixed-point is reached. A function, OverApprox, for over-approximating the elements in the set is used to guarantee termination in a bounded number of steps. (Similar widening techniques have been used for over-approximating regular languages [21].) Due to the presence of universal variables, the application of transitive inference requires matching and substitution, as in the theory of rewriting. The function MatchExpr(e', e_1) returns either $\bot$ or a substitution σ (for the universally quantified variables in e_1) and a subterm γ s.t. e' and $e_1\sigma \rightarrow \gamma$ are syntactically equal.

Observe that the above algorithm for MustAliases lacks the capability for inductive reasoning. For example, even if the transitive inference goes on forever, it cannot deduce, for example, that $x \rightarrow \mathbf{n}^i \rightarrow \mathbf{p}^i$ is a must-alias of x, for any i, given F_2 of Figure 3. However, such inferences are not usually required.

5 Experiments

We have implemented a tool that performs an abstract interpretation of programs over the abstract domain described in this paper. Our tool is implemented in C++ and takes two inputs: (i) some procedure in a low-level three-address code format (without any typing information) (ii) precondition for the inputs of that procedure expressed in the language of our abstract domain.

Program	Property Discovered (apart from memory safety)	Precondition Used
`ListOfPtrArray`		Input is a list
`ListReverse`	Reversed list has length n	Input is list of size n
`List2Array`	Corresponding array and list elmts are same	Input is a list

Fig. 4. Examples on which we performed our experiments. Our prototype implementation took less than 0.5 seconds for automatic generation of invariants on these examples. We also ran our tool in a verification setting in which we provided the loop invariants and the tool took less than 0.1 seconds to verify the invariants.

Our experimental results are encouraging. We chose the base constraint domain to be the conjunctive domain over *combination* of linear arithmetic and uninterpreted function terms [10]. We were successfully able to run our tool on the example programs shown in the table in Figure 4. These examples have been chosen for the following reasons: (i) These examples represent very common coding patterns. (ii) We do not know of any automatic tool that can verify memory safety of these programs automatically in low-level form, where pointer arithmetic is used to compute array offsets and even field dereferences.

ListOfPtrArray. This is the same example as described in Figure 1. Our tool generates the following non-trivial loop invariant required to establish the property in Equation 1, which is required to prove memory safety in the second loop.

$$\exists i, j' : \texttt{List}(x, i, \texttt{next}) \ \land \ 0 \leq j' \leq i \ \land \ y = x{\rightarrow}\texttt{next}^{j'} \ \land$$
$$\forall j[(0 \leq j < j') \Rightarrow \texttt{Array}(x{\rightarrow}\texttt{next}^j{\rightarrow}\texttt{data}, 4 \times (x{\rightarrow}\texttt{next}^j{\rightarrow}\texttt{len}))]$$

We now briefly describe how the above invariant is automatically generated. We denote $\texttt{Array}(x{\rightarrow}\texttt{next}^i{\rightarrow}\texttt{data}, 4 \times (x{\rightarrow}\texttt{next}^i{\rightarrow}\texttt{len}))$ by the notation $S(i)$. For simplicity, assume that the length of the list x is at least 1 and the body of the loop has been unfolded once. The postcondition operator generates the following must-equalities F^1 and $F^{\textrm{r}}$ (among other must-equalities) before the loop header and after one loop iteration respectively.

$$F^1 \ = \ (y = x{\rightarrow}\texttt{next} \land S(0)) \qquad F^{\textrm{r}} \ = \ (y = x{\rightarrow}\texttt{next}^2 \land S(0) \land S(1))$$

Our join algorithm computes the join of these must-equalities as

$$\exists j' : 1 \leq j' \leq 2 \land y = x{\rightarrow}\texttt{next}^{j'} \land \forall j(0 \leq j < j' \Rightarrow S(j))$$

which later gets widened to the desired invariant. Note the power of our join algorithm [11] to generate quantified facts from quantifier-free inputs.

ListReverse. This procedure performs an in-place list reversal. The interesting loop invariant that arises in this example is that the sum of the lengths of the list pointed to by the iterator y (i.e., the part of the list that is yet to be reversed) and the list pointed to by the current result `result` (i.e., the part of the list that has been reversed) is equal to the length n of the original input list.

$$\exists i_1, i_2 : i_1 + i_2 = n \ \land \ \texttt{List}(y, i_1, \texttt{next}) \ \land \ \texttt{List}(\texttt{result}, i_2, \texttt{next})$$

```
List2Array(x)
  struct {int Data, *Next}*x;
1  ℓ := 0;
2  for(y := x; y ≠ null; y := y→n)
3    ℓ := ℓ + 1;
4  A := malloc(4ℓ);  y := x;
5  for(k := 0;  k < ℓ;  k := k + 1)
6    A→(4k) := y→d;  y := y→n;
7  return A
```

π	Invariant at π
1	$\exists i : \mathtt{List}(x, i, \mathtt{n})$
2	$\exists i : \ell = 0, \mathtt{List}(x, i, \mathtt{n})$
3	$\exists i : 0 \leq \ell < i, \mathtt{List}(x, i, \mathtt{n}), y = x{\to}\mathtt{n}^\ell$
4	$\mathtt{List}(x, \ell, \mathtt{n})$
5	$\mathtt{List}(x, \ell, \mathtt{n}), \mathtt{Array}(A, 4\ell)$
6	$\mathtt{List}(x, \ell, \mathtt{n}), \mathtt{Array}(A, 4\ell), 0 \leq k < \ell, y = x{\to}\mathtt{n}^k$
	$\forall j((0 \leq j < k) \Rightarrow x{\to}\mathtt{n}^j{\to}\mathtt{d} = A{\to}(4j + \mathtt{d})$
7	$\mathtt{List}(x, \ell, \mathtt{n}), \mathtt{Array}(A, 4\ell), y = \mathtt{null}$
	$\forall j((0 \leq j < \ell) \Rightarrow x{\to}\mathtt{n}^j{\to}\mathtt{d} = A{\to}(4j + \mathtt{d}))$

Fig. 5. List2Array example. We assume that the structure fields Data and Next are at offsets $\mathtt{d} = 0$ and $\mathtt{n} = 4$ respectively. The table on the right lists *selected* invariants at the corresponding program points that were discovered by our implementation. The List and Array predicates are as defined on Page 381.

List2Array. This example flattens a list into an array by using two *congruent* loops - one to compute the length of the input list to determine the size of the array, and the second to copy each list elements in the allocated array. Figure 5 describes this example and the useful invariants generated by our tool.

This example reflects a common coding practice in which memory safety relies on inter-dependence between different loop iterations. In this example, it is crucial to compute the invariant that ℓ stores the length of the input list.

6 Related Work

Alias/Pointer analysis. Early work on alias analysis used two main kinds of approximations to deal with recursive data-structures: *summary nodes* that group together several concrete nodes based on some criteria such as same allocation site (e.g., [2]), or *k-limiting* which does not distinguish between locations obtained after k dereferences (e.g., [15]), or a combination of the two (e.g., [4]). However, such techniques had limited expressiveness and precision. Deutsch proposed reducing the imprecision that arises as a result of *k*-limiting by using suitable representations to describe pointer expressions (and hence alias pairs) with potentially unbounded number of field dereferences [5]. The basic idea was to use new variables to represent the number of field dereferences and then describe arithmetic constraints on those variables. Deutsch analysis did not have any *must* information.

Most of the new techniques that followed focused on defining logics with different kinds of predicates (other than simple must-equality and may-equality predicates, which were used by earlier techniques) to keep track of shape of heap-structures [13, 20, 19, 14]. There is a lot of recent activity on building abstract interpreters using these specialized logics [6, 17, 9]. In this general approach, the identification of the "right" abstract predicates and automation of the analysis are challenging tasks. In some cases, the analysis developer has to provide the transfer functions for each of these predicates across different flowchart nodes.

Additionally, the focus of the above mentioned techniques has been on recursive data structures, and they do not provide good support for handling arrays and pointer arithmetic. Recently though, there has been some work in this area. Gopan, Reps, and Sagiv have suggested using canonical abstraction [20] to create a finite partition of (potentially unbounded number of) array elements and using summarizing numeric domains to keep track of the values and indices of array elements [8]. However, the description of their technique has been limited to reasoning about arrays of integers. Calcagno et al. have used separation logic to reason about memory safety in presence of pointer arithmetic, albeit with use of a special predicate tailored for a specific kind of data-structure (multi-word lists) [1]. Chatterjee et al. have given a formalization of the reachability predicate in presence of pointer arithmetic in first-order logic for use in a modular verification environment where the programmer provides the loop invariants [3].

The work presented in this paper tries to address some of the above-mentioned limitations. Our use of quantification over two simple (must and may-equality) predicates offers the benefits of richer specification as well as the possibility of automated deduction. Additionally, our abstract domain has good support for pointer arithmetic in presence of recursive data structures.

Data-structure Specifications. McPeak and Necula have suggested specifying and verifying properties of data-structures using local equality axioms [18]. For example, the invariant associated with the program List2Array (after execution of the first loop) in Figure 5 might be specified at the data-structure level as saying that the field Len is the length of the array field Data. Similar approaches have been suggested to specify and verify properties of object-oriented programs [16], or locking annotations associated with fields of concurrent objects [7].

These approaches might result in simpler specifications that avoid universal quantification (which has been made implicit), but they also have some disadvantages: (a) They require source code with data-structure declarations, while our approach also works on low-level code without any data-structure declarations. (b) Sometimes it may not be feasible to provide specifications at the data-structure level since the related fields may not be local (i.e., not present in the same data-structure). (c) Programmers have to provide the intended specifications for the data-structures which can be a daunting task for large legacy code-bases, (d) It is not clear what such a specification would mean when these fields are set only after some computation has been performed. Perhaps something like pack/unpack of Boogie methodology [16] or the temporary invariant breakage approach [18] may be used for a well-defined semantics, but this requires additional annotations for updates to additional (non-program) variables.

7 Conclusion and Future Work

This paper describes an abstract domain that gives first-class treatment to pointer arithmetic and recursive data-structures. The proposed abstract domain can be used to represent useful quantified invariants. These quantified invariants can be automatically discovered by performing an abstract interpretation of programs over this domain - without using any support in the form of user-specified list of predicates. Future work includes performing more experiments and extending these techniques to an interprocedural analysis.

References

1. Calcagno, C., Distefano, D., O'Hearn, P., Yang, H.: Beyond reachability: Shape abstraction in the presence of pointer arithmetic. In: Yi, K. (ed.) SAS 2006. LNCS, vol. 4134, Springer, Heidelberg (2006)
2. Chase, D.R., Wegman, M.N., Zadeck, F.K.: Analysis of pointers and structures. In: PLDI, pp. 296–310 (1990)
3. Chatterjee, S., Lahiri, S., Qadeer, S., Rakamaric, Z.: A reachability predicate for analyszing low-level software. In: TACAS (2007)
4. Choi, J.-D., Burke, M.G., Carini, P.R.: Efficient flow-sensitive interprocedural computation of pointer-induced aliases and side effects. In: POPL (1993)
5. Deutsch, A.: Interprocedural may-alias analysis for pointers: Beyond k -limiting. In: PLDI, pp. 230–241 (1994)
6. Distefano, D., O'Hearn, P., Yang, H.: A local shape analysis based on separation logic. In: Hermanns, H., Palsberg, J. (eds.) TACAS 2006 and ETAPS 2006. LNCS, vol. 3920, pp. 287–302. Springer, Heidelberg (2006)
7. Flanagan, C., Freund, S.N.: Type-based race detection for java. In: PLDI, pp. 219–232 (2000)
8. Gopan, D., Reps, T.W., Sagiv, S.: A framework for numeric analysis of array operations. In: POPL, pp. 338–350 (2005)
9. Gotsman, A., Berdine, J., Cook, B.: Interprocedural shape analysis with separated heap abstractions. In: Yi, K. (ed.) SAS 2006. LNCS, vol. 4134, Springer, Heidelberg (2006)
10. Gulwani, S., Tiwari, A.: Combining abstract interpreters. In: PLDI, pp. 376–386 (June 2006)
11. Gulwani, S., Tiwari, A.: Static analysis for heap-maniuplating low level software. Technical Report MSR-TR-2006-160, Microsoft Research (November 2006)
12. Hubert, T., Marché, C.: A case study of C source code verification: the Schorr-Waite algorithm. In: 3rd IEEE Intl. Conf. SEFM'05 (2005)
13. Jensen, J.L., Jørgensen, M.E., Klarlund, N., Schwartzbach, M.I.: Automatic verification of pointer programs using monadic second-order logic. In: PLDI (1997)
14. Lahiri, S.K., Qadeer, S.: Verifying properties of well-founded linked lists. In: POPL, pp. 115–126 (2006)
15. Landi, W., Ryder, B.G.: A safe approximation algorithm for interprocedural pointer aliasing. In: PLDI (June 1992)
16. Leino, K.R.M., Müller, P.: A verification methodology for model fields. In: Sestoft, P. (ed.) ESOP 2006 and ETAPS 2006. LNCS, vol. 3924, pp. 115–130. Springer, Heidelberg (2006)
17. Magill, S., Nanevsky, A., Clarke, E., Lee, P.: Inferring invariants in separation logic for list-processing programs. In: SPACE (2006)

18. McPeak, S., Necula, G.C.: Data structure specifications via local equality axioms. In: Etessami, K., Rajamani, S.K. (eds.) CAV 2005. LNCS, vol. 3576, pp. 476–490. Springer, Heidelberg (2005)
19. Reynolds, J.C.: Separation logic: A logic for shared mutable data structures. In: LICS, pp. 55–74 (2002)
20. Sagiv, S., Reps, T.W., Wilhelm, R.: Parametric shape analysis via 3-valued logic. ACM TOPLAS 24(3), 217–298 (2002)
21. Touili, T.: Regular model checking using widening techniques. Electr. Notes Theor. Comput. Sci. 50(4) (2001)

Adaptive Symmetry Reduction*

Thomas Wahl

Department of Computer Sciences, The University of Texas at Austin, USA
wahl@cs.utexas.edu

Abstract. Symmetry reduction is a technique to counter state explosion for systems of regular structure. It relies on idealistic assumptions about *indistinguishable* components, which in practice may only be *similar*. In this paper we present a generalized algebraic approach to symmetry reduction for exploring a structure without any prior knowledge about its global symmetry. The more behavior is shared among the components, the more compression takes effect. Our idea is to annotate each encountered state with information about how symmetry is violated along the path leading to it. Previous solutions only allow specific types of asymmetry, such as up to bisimilarity, or seem to incur large overhead before or during the verification run. In contrast, our method appeals through its balance between generality and simplicity. We include analytic and experimental results to document its efficiency.

1 Introduction

Symmetry reduction is a well-investigated technique to reduce the impact of state-explosion in temporal logic model checking [2,5]. It has been applied mainly to models of concurrent systems of processes, such as communication and memory consistency protocols. In an ideal scenario, symmetry reduction makes it possible to verify a model over a reduced quotient model, which is not only much smaller, but also bisimulation-equivalent to the original.

The aforementioned ideal scenario is characterized by a transition relation that is invariant under any interchange of the components. In other words, consistently renaming components in both source and target state of any transition must again yield a valid transition in the structure. This condition can be formally violated by systems that nevertheless seem to be approximately symmetric. For example, consider a perfectly symmetric system that evolves into an asymmetric one simply by customizations on some components. The number of transitions that would have to be added or removed in order to make it symmetric is small compared with the total number of transitions.

In this paper we present a new approach to verifying systems of processes with similar behavior. Intuitively, similarity can be expected if many transitions of the system remain valid under many permutations of the processes. Our approach is to annotate each state, space-efficiently, with information about whether and

---

* This work is supported in part by NSF grants CCR-009-8141, ITR-CCR-020-5483.

W. Damm and H. Hermanns (Eds.): CAV 2007, LNCS 4590, pp. 393–405, 2007.

how symmetry is violated along the path to it. More precisely, the annotation is a *partition* of the set of all component indices: if the path to the state contains a transition that distinguishes two components, their indices are put into different partition cells. Only components in the same cell can be permuted during future explorations from the state—the algorithm *adapts* to the state's history.

Suppose a given state can be reached along two paths: one with many asymmetric transitions and one with only symmetric ones. This state thus appears twice, once annotated with a fine partition, once with a coarse one. In order to analyze the state's future, we can assume that we reached it along the symmetric path and thus take full advantage of symmetry. The annotated state with the fine partition can be ignored; we say it is *subsumed* by the other one. Subsumption allows us to collapse many states during the exploration. The price we have to pay is that the adaptive algorithm, by its own means, is only suitable for reachability analysis. Throwing away a state subsumed by another leads to an implicit reduced structure that is not bisimulation-equivalent to the original. This price is worth paying since it allows us to improve the analysis of systems with respect to safety properties, a significant and frequent type of formula.

We present an exact and efficient algorithm for reachability analysis, suitable especially on an *approximately fully symmetric* Kripke structure. The property to be verified may be asymmetric, i.e. it may distinguish between components. Errors are discovered at minimum distance from the initial state, and paths to them can be recovered, provided a breadth-first search order. Following the presentation of the technical details of our method, we give analytic and practical results substantiating its usefulness.

2   Related Work

There are many publications on the use of symmetry for state space exploration and model checking, both of fundamental nature [2,5] and specific for tools [7,8]. One of the first to apply symmetry reduction strategies to partially symmetric systems is [6]. The authors present the notions of *near* and *rough* symmetry, which are defined with respect to a Kripke structure; especially for rough symmetry it is unclear how to verify it on a high-level system description. Examples are limited to versions of the *Readers-Writers* problem.

This work was generalized in [4] to *virtual symmetry*, the most general condition that allows a bisimilar symmetry quotient. A limitation of all preceding approaches is the existence of a strict precondition for their principle applicability. As with [6], it is left open whether virtual symmetry can be verified efficiently; the techniques presented in [4] seem to incur a cost proportional to the size of the unreduced Kripke structure. On the other hand, bisimilarity makes these approaches suitable for full μ-calculus model checking, whereas the adaptive technique trades "property coverage" in for "system coverage".

Symmetry detection solves the problem of suspected but formally unknown symmetry by inferring structure automorphisms from the program text [3]. This approach is principally different from ours. A structure automorphism is global in character, being defined over the transition relation. It ignores the possibility of a large part of the state space being unaffected by symmetry breaches. The adaptive approach, which can be viewed as *on-the-fly symmetry violation detection*, operates directly on the Kripke structure. As such, it can reduce local substructures with more symmetry than revealed by global automorphisms.

Closest in spirit to our work is that by P. Sistla and P. Godefroid [9], who also target arbitrary systems and properties. A *guarded annotated quotient* is obtained from a symmetric super-structure by marking transitions that were added to achieve symmetry. As an advantage, this method can handle arbitrary CTL* properties. In our work, annotations apply to states, not edges, and seem more space-efficient; in [9] there can be multiple annotations to a quotient edge. Further, the adaptive method does not require any preprocessing of the program text, such as in order to determine a symmetric super-structure.

3   An Example

Consider the variant of the *Readers-Writers problem* shown in figure 1. There are two "reader" processes (indices 1, 2) and one "writer" (3). In order to access some data item, each process must enter its critical section, denoted by local state C. The edge from (the non-critical section) N to (the trying region) T is unrestricted, as is the one from C back to N. There are two edges from T to C.

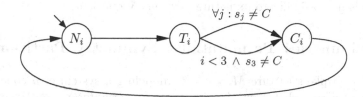

Fig. 1. Local state transition diagram of process i for an asymmetric system

The first is executable whenever no process is currently in its critical section ($\forall j : s_j \neq C$, for current state s). The second is available only to readers ($i < 3$), and the writer must be in a non-critical local state ($s_3 \neq C$). Intuitively, since readers only read, they may enter their critical section at the same time, as long as the writer is outside its own.

With each process starting out in local state N, the induced Kripke structure has 22 reachable states. The adaptive method, however, constructs a reachability tree of only 9 *abstract* states (figure 2).An abstract state of the form XYZ represents the set of concrete states obtained by permuting the local state tuple (X, Y, Z). Consider, for example, the abstract state NNT, representing (N, N, T), (N, T, N) and (T, N, N). Guard $\forall j : s_j \neq C$ of the first edge from T to C is satisfied in all three states. Executing this edge leads to the successor states (N, N, C), (N, C, N), (C, N, N), succinctly written as NNC in figure 2.

Fig. 2. Abstract reachability tree for the model induced by figure 1

Now consider the abstract state NTC. None of the six concrete states it represents satisfies the condition $\forall j : s_j \neq C$. Thus, regarding steps from T to C, we have to look at the second—asymmetric—edge, guarded by $i < 3 \wedge s_3 \neq C$. Of the six represented states, two satisfy this condition with an index $i < 3$ such that $s_i = T$, namely (T, C, N) and (C, T, N). In both cases, the edge leads to state (C, C, N). We now have to make a note that this state is reached through an asymmetric edge. The edge's guard is invariant under the transposition $(1\ 2)$, but not under any permutation displacing index 3. We express this succinctly in figure 2 as abstract state $CC \mid N$. Intuitively, permutations across the "$\mid$" are illegal; this abstract state hence represents neither (N, C, C) nor (C, N, C).

We finally remark that the induced structure is not *virtually* symmetric and hence not *nearly* or *roughly* so. To see this, consider the (valid) transition $(T, C, T) \rightarrow (C, C, T)$. Applying transposition $(2\ 3)$ to it we obtain transition $(T, T, C) \rightarrow (C, T, C)$, which is invalid, but belongs to the structure's *symmetrization* [4]. Virtual symmetry requires a way to permute the target state that makes the transition valid, which is impossible here. As a corollary, this structure is not bisimilar to its natural symmetry quotient.

4   Preliminaries: Permutations, Symmetry, Partitions

Consider a Kripke structure $M = (S, R)$ modeling a system of n concurrently executing processes. Let Sym_n be the group of *permutations* on $[1..n]$ and let $\pi \in Sym_n$ operate on a state $s \in S$ in the form $\pi(s_1, \ldots, s_n) = (s_{\pi(1)}, \ldots, s_{\pi(n)})$. M is said to be *fully symmetric* if for every $\pi \in Sym_n$,

$$(s, t) \in R \quad \text{iff} \quad (\pi(s), \pi(t)) \in R. \tag{1}$$

A symmetric structure can be reduced to a bisimilar and smaller quotient structure based on the *orbit relation*: $s \equiv t$ iff $\exists \pi : \pi(s) = t$. More details of symmetry reduction are available in the literature [2,5].

A *partition* of $[1..n]$ is a set of disjoint, non-empty subsets, called *cells*, that cover $[1..n]$. We use a notation of the form $\mid 1, 4 \mid 2, 5 \mid 3, 6 \mid$ to represent the partition into the three cells $\{1, 4\}$, $\{2, 5\}$ and $\{3, 6\}$. The coarsest partition $\mid 1, \ldots, n \mid$ consists of a single cell, the finest partition $\mid 1 \mid \ldots \mid n \mid$ consists of n singleton cells. A partition $\mathbb{P}$ induces an equivalence relation on $[1..n]$: we write $i \equiv_{\mathbb{P}} j$ exactly if i and j belong to the same cell of $\mathbb{P}$.

We say a partition $\mathbb{P}$ of $[1..n]$ *generates* all permutations π on $[1..n]$ such that for all i, $i \equiv_{\mathbb{P}} \pi(i)$. These permutations form a group, denoted by $\langle \mathbb{P} \rangle$. For example, the partition $\mid 1, 4 \mid 2, 5 \mid 3, 6 \mid$ generates a group of six permutations.

The coarsest partition $|1,\ldots,n|$ generates the entire symmetry group Sym_n. The finest partition $|1|\ldots|n|$ generates only the identity permutation.

5   Computational Model

We assume a system is modeled as a local state transition diagram. This level of abstraction is fully expressive for shared-memory systems and lets us focus on synchronization aspects. Precisely, the system is specified as a number n of processes and a graph with local states as nodes. Local transitions, called *edges*, have the form

$$A \xrightarrow{\phi,\mathbb{Q}} B. \tag{2}$$

ϕ is a two-place predicate taking a state s and an index i. State s defines the *context* in which the edge is to be executed [1]. The intended semantics is that $\phi(s,i)$ returns *true* exactly if in state s process i is allowed to transit from local state A to local state B. Predicate ϕ can be written in any efficiently decidable logic, such as propositional logic with simple arithmetic over state variables and index i. In figure 1 we have seen the predicate

$$\phi(s,i) \;=\; i < 3 \;\wedge\; s_3 \neq C. \tag{3}$$

It is asymmetric (and thus is the edge) since we can find s, i and a permutation π such that $\phi(s,i) \neq \phi(\pi(s),\pi(i))$. On the other hand, asymmetric edges are often symmetric with respect to a subgroup of Sym_n. For instance, predicate (3) is invariant under the transposition $\sigma = (1\,2)$, i.e. $\phi(s,i) = \phi(\sigma(s),\sigma(i))$ for all s, i. In common variants of the r-readers/$(n-r)$-writers problem, the asymmetric edges are immune to any products of permutations of $[1..r]$ and $[r+1..n]$. Such permutations are generated by the partition $|\,1..r\,|\,r+1..n\,|$.

Symbol $\mathbb{Q}$ in equation (2) stands for a partition generating the automorphism group of the edge, i.e. a set of permutations that preserve predicate ϕ. For the asymmetric edge in (3), we choose $\mathbb{Q} = |\,1,2\,|\,3\,|$. In approximately symmetric systems, $\mathbb{Q}$ is for most edges the coarsest partition, generating Sym_n. For the remaining edges—those that destroy the symmetry—we expect the user to provide a suitable $\mathbb{Q}$. The high-level description of the edge often suggests a group of automorphisms; see section 9 for an example. If needed, a propositional SAT-solver can aid the verification of the automorphism property.

Letting l be the number of local states, an asynchronous semantics of the induced n-process concurrent system is given by the following Kripke structure: $S := [1..l]^n$, and R is the set of transitions $(s_1,\ldots,s_n) \to (t_1,\ldots,t_n)$ with the property that there is an index $i \in [1..n]$ such that

1. there exists an edge $s_i \xrightarrow{\phi,\mathbb{Q}} t_i$ with $\phi((s_1,\ldots,s_n),i) = true$ and
2. $\forall j : j \neq i : s_j = t_j$.

Note that $\mathbb{Q}$ is irrelevant for the definition of the Kripke structure; it is instead part of the syntax of an edge. Extending the method to work with shared variables or with a synchronous execution semantics is fairly straightforward.

6 Orbits and Subsumption

The goal of this paper is an efficient exploration algorithm for the Kripke structure defined in the previous section. The algorithm accumulates states annotated with partitions that indicate how symmetry was violated in reaching this state. Thus, the formal search space of the exploration is the set $\hat{S} := [1..l]^n \times Part_n$, where $Part_n$ is the set of all partitions of $[1..n]$. The partition is used to determine which permutations can be applied to the state in order to obtain the concrete states it represents. These permutations are those that do not permute elements across cells, i.e. those generated by the partition (see end of section 4):

Definition 1. *Let π be a permutation on $[1..n]$. For an n-tuple $s = (s_1, \ldots, s_n)$, let $\pi(s)$ denote the expression $(s_{\pi(1)}, \ldots, s_{\pi(n)})$. We extend π to operate on an element $\hat{s} = (s, \mathbb{P})$ of $\hat{S}$ in the form*

$$\pi(s, \mathbb{P}) = \begin{cases} (\pi(s), \mathbb{P}) & \text{if } \pi \in \langle \mathbb{P} \rangle \\ (s, \mathbb{P}) & \text{otherwise.} \end{cases}$$

This mapping defines a bijection on $\hat{S}$. Note that π never changes the partition associated with a state; if π is not generated by $\mathbb{P}$, it does not affect $(s, \mathbb{P})$ at all.

In standard symmetry reduction, algorithms operate on representative states of orbit equivalence classes. Systems with asymmetries require a generalized notion of an orbit that defines the relationship between states in $\hat{S}$ and in S:

Definition 2. *The* orbit *of a state $\hat{s} = (s, \mathbb{P}) \in \hat{S}$ is defined as*

$$orbit(s, \mathbb{P}) = \{ t \in S : \exists \pi \in \langle \mathbb{P} \rangle : \pi(s) = t \}.$$

We say that $\hat{s}$ represents t if $t \in orbit(\hat{s})$.

Examples. For $n = 4$, consider the following states and the sizes of their orbits:

$\hat{s} = (s, \mathbb{P})$	orbit size
$(ABCD,\ \vert\, 1, 2, 3, 4\, \vert)$	$4! = 24$ (standard symmetry)
$(ABCD,\ \vert\, 1, 2\, \vert\, 3, 4\, \vert)$	$2 \times 2 = 4$
$(ABCD,\ \vert\, 1, 2\, \vert\, 3\, \vert\, 4\, \vert)$	$2 \times 1 \times 1 = 2$
$(ABCD,\ \vert\, 1\, \vert\, 2\, \vert\, 3\, \vert\, 4\, \vert)$	$1 \times 1 \times 1 \times 1 = 1$

If $\mathbb{P}$ is the coarsest partition $\vert\, 1, \ldots, n\, \vert$, then $orbit(s, \mathbb{P})$ reduces to the equivalence class that s belongs to under the standard orbit relation.

Subsumption. Orbits in standard symmetry reduction are equivalence classes and as such either disjoint or equal. In contrast, the new orbit definition is not based on an equivalence relation. Indeed, the orbits of the four example states in the table above form a strictly descending chain. It is therefore unnecessary to remember all four states if encountered during exploration: the first *subsumes* the others.

Definition 3. *State $\hat{s} \in \hat{S}$ subsumes $\hat{t} \in \hat{S}$, written $\hat{s} \triangleright \hat{t}$, if $orbit(\hat{s}) \supseteq orbit(\hat{t})$.*

Examples. For $n = 3$, consider the following states and examples of what they subsume and don't subsume ($\mathbb{Q}$ is arbitrary):

$\hat{s} = (s, \mathbb{P})$	$\hat{s}$ subsumes:	$\hat{s}$ does not subsume:
$(ABC,\ \lvert 1,2,3 \rvert)$	$(ABC,\ \mathbb{Q})$, $(BCA,\ \mathbb{Q})$	$(ABB,\ \mathbb{Q})$
$(ABC,\ \lvert 1,3 \vert 2 \rvert)$	$(ABC,\ \lvert 1 \vert 2 \vert 3 \rvert)$, $(CBA,\ \lvert 1 \vert 2 \vert 3 \rvert)$	$(BAC,\ \mathbb{Q})$
$(ABC,\ \lvert 1 \vert 2 \vert 3 \rvert)$	itself only	$(ABC,\ \lvert 1,3 \vert 2 \rvert)$

Definition 3 provides no clue about how to efficiently detect subsumption. An alternative characterization is the following. Recall that $i \equiv_{\mathbb{P}} j$ iff i and j belong to the same cell within $\mathbb{P}$.

Theorem 4. *State* $\hat{s} = (s, \mathbb{P})$ *subsumes state* $\hat{t} = (t, \mathbb{Q})$ *exactly if*

1. *$i \equiv_{\mathbb{Q}} j \Rightarrow (i \equiv_{\mathbb{P}} j \vee t_i = t_j)$ is a tautology, and*
2. *$t \in orbit(\hat{s})$.*

Remark. Condition 1 is slightly weaker than the condition $i \equiv_{\mathbb{Q}} j \Rightarrow i \equiv_{\mathbb{P}} j$, which states that $\mathbb{P}$ is coarser than $\mathbb{Q}$. As a hint why $t_i = t_j$ is needed for an equivalent characterization of subsumption, consider $\hat{s} = (AA, \lvert 1 \vert 2 \rvert)$, which has a finer partition than $\hat{t} = (AA, \lvert 1,2 \rvert)$, but subsumes $\hat{t}$.

Condition 1 can, using appropriate data structures for partitions, be decided in $\mathcal{O}(n^2)$ time. In practice, violations are often detected much faster using heuristics such as comparing the cardinalities of $\mathbb{P}$ and $\mathbb{Q}$. Condition 2 requires checking whether $\mathbb{P}$ generates a permutation π that satisfies $\pi(s) = t$. This can be decided in $\mathcal{O}(n)$ time by treating each cell $P \in \mathbb{P}$ separately: we project both s and t to the positions in P and use a counting argument to verify that the projections are the same up to permutation.

Algebraic Properties of Subsumption. Relation $\triangleright$ is a *preorder*: it is reflexive and transitive. It is, however, neither symmetric (e.g. $(AB, \lvert 1,2 \rvert) \triangleright (AB, \lvert 1 \vert 2 \rvert)$ but not vice versa) nor anti-symmetric (e.g. $(AB, \lvert 1,2 \rvert)$ and $(BA, \lvert 1,2 \rvert)$ subsume each other but differ). Thus, it is neither an equivalence nor a partial order.

We can derive an equivalence relation from a preorder by making it bidirectional: write $\hat{s} \bowtie \hat{t}$ if $\hat{s} \triangleright \hat{t} \wedge \hat{t} \triangleright \hat{s}$. How is this equivalence related to the *orbit relation* on $\hat{S}$, written $\hat{s} \equiv \hat{t}$ if there exists π such that $\pi(\hat{s}) = \hat{t}$?

Lemma 5. *For any* $\hat{s}, \hat{t} \in \hat{S}$, *$\hat{s} \equiv \hat{t}$ implies $\hat{s} \bowtie \hat{t}$.*

According to the lemma, the orbit relation achieves less compression than subsumption: the latter is coarser, i.e. it relates more states. We note that in perfectly symmetric systems, where each state is (implicitly) annotated with the coarsest partition $\lvert 1, \ldots, n \rvert$, the three relations $\triangleright$, $\bowtie$ and $\equiv$ coincide.

7   State Space Exploration Under Partial Symmetry

We are now ready to present an algorithm for state space exploration on the (partially symmetric) structure $M = (S, R)$. The goal is to compute the set of

---

Algorithm 1. State space exploration under partial symmetry

Input: initial state $s_0 \in S$
1: $Reached := Unexplored := \{(s_0, |1, \ldots, n|)\}$
2: **while** $Unexplored \neq \emptyset$ **do**
3:    let $\hat{s} = (s, \mathbb{P}) \in Unexplored$; remove $\hat{s}$ from $Unexplored$
4:    **for all** edges $e = A \xrightarrow{\phi, \mathbb{Q}} B$ **do**
5:       $\mathbb{R} := glb(\mathbb{P}, \mathbb{Q})$
6:       $U := unwind(s, \mathbb{P}, \mathbb{Q})$
7:       **for all** states $u \in U$ **do**
8:          **for all** cells $R \in \mathbb{R}$ **do**
9:             **if** $\exists i \in R : u_i = A \wedge (u, i) \models \phi$ **then**
10:                $v := (u_1, \ldots, u_{i-1}, B, u_{i+1}, \ldots, u_n)$
11:                $canonicalize(v)$
12:                $update(v, \mathbb{R})$

---

states reachable under R from some initial state $s_0 \in S$. Technically, the algorithm operates on elements of $\hat{S}$; we later present a one-to-one correspondence between the states reachable in M and the states found by algorithm 1.

In line 1, the initial state is annotated with the coarsest partition (indicating absence of symmetry violations so far) and put on the $Unexplored$ and $Reached$ lists. While available, one state $\hat{s}$ is selected from $Unexplored$ for expansion.

Successors of $\hat{s}$ are found by iterating through all edges (line 4). We now have to reconcile two partitions: $\mathbb{P}$, expressing symmetry violations on the path to s, and $\mathbb{Q}$, expressing violations to be caused by e. Routine glb in line 5 determines the partition $\mathbb{R}$ such that $\langle \mathbb{R} \rangle = \langle \mathbb{P} \rangle \cap \langle \mathbb{Q} \rangle$. $\mathbb{R}$ can be computed as the greatest lower bound (meet) of $\mathbb{P}$ and $\mathbb{Q}$ in the complete lattice of partitions, which uses "finer-than" as the partial order relation.

Edge predicate ϕ may not be invariant under permutations from $\langle \mathbb{P} \rangle$, but it is under permutations from $\langle \mathbb{Q} \rangle$ and thus from $\langle \mathbb{R} \rangle$. We account for this fact by unwinding s into a set of states to be annotated by $\mathbb{R}$ whose orbits exactly *cover* the orbit of $\hat{s} = (s, \mathbb{P})$, i.e. into a set $U \subset S$ that satisfies

$$\bigcup_{u \in U} orbit(u, \mathbb{R}) = orbit(s, \mathbb{P}). \tag{4}$$

The objective is of course to find a *small* set U with this property. In line 6, routine $unwind$ returns the set $U = \{s\} \cup \{\pi(s) : \pi \in \langle \mathbb{P} \rangle \setminus \langle \mathbb{Q} \rangle\}$, which is easily seen to satisfy (4). This step can be a bottleneck; we discuss in section 8 how to avoid it in most cases and alleviate it in the remaining ones.

Processes with indices in different cells of $\mathbb{R}$ are distinguishable; we must consider these cells separately (line 8). Edge e can be executed if there is a process i in local state A such that (u, i) satisfies ϕ. If so, we let the process proceed, resulting in a new state v (line 10). In line 11, v is *canonicalized* within R: the sequence of local states with indices in R is lexicographically sorted.

The *update* function determines whether to add a new state $\hat{v}$ to the lists $Unexplored$ and $Reached$ (algorithm 2). If some state in $Reached$ subsumes $\hat{v}$,

---

Algorithm 2. Updating *Unexplored* and *Reached*: *update*$(v, \mathbb{R})$

Input: newly computed state $\hat{v} = (v, \mathbb{R})$
 1: **if** no state in *Reached* subsumes $\hat{v}$ **then**
 2:     check whether $\hat{v}$ represents a concrete error state
 3:     remove from *Unexplored* each $\hat{w}$ such that $\hat{v} \rhd \hat{w}$
 4:     add $\hat{v}$ to *Unexplored* and to *Reached*

---

nothing needs to be done; this also covers the case $\hat{v} \in$ *Reached*. Otherwise (line 2), $\hat{v}$ is checked for errors (discussed below). Then, states that $\hat{v}$ subsumes are removed from *Unexplored*: such states are implicitly explored as part of $\hat{v}$ and are thus redundant. Finally, $\hat{v}$ is added to both lists.

States reachable from s_0 in M are related to states in *Reached* as follows.

Theorem 6. *Let $s_0 \in S$ and Reached as computed by algorithm 1. A state $s \in S$ is reachable from s_0 in M exactly if there exists $\hat{s} \in$ Reached that represents s.*

Error conditions to be checked in line 2 of algorithm 2 need not be symmetric. For example, suppose the claim is that process 3 never enters local state X. Given $\hat{v} = (v, \mathbb{R})$, we determine the unique cell $R \in \mathbb{R}$ such that $3 \in R$. An error is reported exactly if the property $\exists i \in R : v_i = X$ evaluates to *true*.

If M has an error at distance d from s_0, then algorithm 1, if organized in a breadth-first fashion, detects it at distance d from the root of the abstract reachability tree. Using back-edges from each encountered node to its predecessor, a shortest error path can be reconstructed and lifted to a concrete path as usual.

Regarding line 3 of algorithm 2, the only reason not to remove $\hat{w}$ from *Reached* (but only from *Unexplored*) is to retain the ability to trace encountered errors back to the initial state, for which those states may be needed. They are not needed for just *finding* errors or for termination detection.

8   Implementation and Efficiency

We discuss essential refinements of algorithm 1 and derive analytic results.

In approximately symmetric systems, most edges are symmetric, resulting in a search that annotates many states with the coarsest partition $| 1, \ldots, n |$. We encode this partition space-efficiently using the empty string. Further, a symmetric edge e in line 4 of algorithm 1 allows dramatic simplifications: Lines 5, 6 and 7 can be removed, as $\mathbb{R}$ equals $\mathbb{P}$ and U reduces to $\{s\}$. The test $(u, i) \models \phi$ can be factored out of the loop in line 8 (replacing i with 0), since it is independent of i (due to ϕ's symmetry). Almost the same simplifications apply if e is asymmetric but $\mathbb{Q}$ is coarser than $\mathbb{P}$ ($\langle \mathbb{Q} \rangle \supseteq \langle \mathbb{P} \rangle$), which is easy to test.

If $\mathbb{Q}$ is finer than $\mathbb{P}$, we must compute $U = \{s\} \cup \{\pi(s) : \pi \in \langle \mathbb{P} \rangle \setminus \langle \mathbb{Q} \rangle\}$. Doing this by enumerating $\langle \mathbb{P} \rangle \setminus \langle \mathbb{Q} \rangle$ is inefficient and unnecessary: state s likely contains redundancy in the form of duplicate local states (especially if there are more processes than local states). Thus, many permutations of $\langle \mathbb{P} \rangle \setminus \langle \mathbb{Q} \rangle$ result in the same state when applied to s. This redundancy can be avoided up front using *buckets*, i.e. sets of process counters for each local state, separately in each cell of $\mathbb{Q}$. Permutations outside $\langle\mathbb{Q}\rangle$ are applied to s by changing the contents of the buckets. As a result, the complexity of *unwind* is proportional to $|U|$, which is usually much smaller than $|\langle\mathbb{P}\rangle \setminus \langle\mathbb{Q}\rangle|$. The set U itself is large only when $\mathbb{Q}$ is very fine, which is not typical for approximately symmetric systems.

To make the *update* function in algorithm 2 efficient, the list *Reached* is sorted such that states with local state vectors that are permutations of each other are adjacent, for example states of the forms $(AAB, \mathbb{P}_1)$, $(AAB, \mathbb{P}_2)$, $(BAA, \mathbb{P}_3)$. Given the newly reached $\hat{v} = (v, \mathbb{R})$, we first use binary search to identify the range in which to look for candidates for subsumption as the *contiguous* range of states in *Reached* whose local state vectors are permutations of v. The search in line 1 of algorithm 2 for states subsuming $\hat{v}$ can now be limited to this range.

We present complexity bounds for the adaptive exploration technique. Consider the abstract state space $\hat{S} = S \times Part_n$, which is conceivably much bigger than S. Our algorithm, however, only explores states not subsumed by others. Comparing the adaptive technique to standard symmetry reduction and to *plain* exploration oblivious to symmetry, our informal goal is to show that

$$complexity(adaptive) \;\leq\; complexity(standard) \;<\; complexity(plain). \quad (5)$$

If the automorphism group of the structure induced by a program is non-trivial, standard symmetry reduction is guaranteed to achieve some compression[1] The meaning of "$\leq$" in (5) is that this compression is preserved by our technique.

To demonstrate this, we first quantify the effect of standard symmetry reduction on a program in our input syntax. Call two processes *friends* if they are not distinguished by any edge, i.e. for each edge $A \xrightarrow{\phi, \mathbb{Q}} B$ there is a cell $Q \in \mathbb{Q}$ containing both processes. Friendship is an equivalence relation on $[1..n]$. Each class of friends induces a group of permutations that can be extended to automorphisms of the program's Kripke structure. The orthogonal product of these groups is the largest symmetry group that can be derived from the program text.

Friends enjoy the following property:

Theorem 7. *Let F be a set of friends. Algorithm 1 reaches at most $\left(\begin{smallmatrix} |F| + l - 1 \\ |F| \end{smallmatrix}\right)$ local state tuples over the indices in F.*

The quantity in theorem 7 equals the number of representative states under standard symmetry reduction over the group $Sym\,F$ of all permutations of F. As a special case, if all n processes are friends, algorithm 1 reduces to standard symmetry reduction and introduces nearly no search overhead.

Whether the "$\leq$" in (5) is actually "$<$" or "$\ll$" depends on the way symmetry is violated and is hard to quantify analytically. We observe, however, that for the adaptive technique, the notion of *friends* can be extended to include processes not distinguished by edges that are actually *followed* during the exploration.

---

[1] We overlook the pathological case in which only symmetric states are reachable.

Unreachable asymmetric edges reduce the automorphism group, but have no effect on our algorithm. This observation is supported by our experimental results.

9   Experimental Evaluation

We tested the adaptive method in a variety of experiments. We borrow a resource controller example from the work by Sistla and Godefroid [9, p. 729ff.]. In short, process indices are partitioned into intervals of equal priority. In case of simultaneous requests, a server grants the resource to one of the highest-priority processes, thus introducing asymmetry. For a process belonging to the priority interval $[l_c..u_c]$, we annotate each asymmetric edge with the partition $| 1, \ldots, l_c-1 | l_c, \ldots, u_c | u_c+1, \ldots, n |$, separating higher, equal and lower priority.

In a first set of experiments, we compare the memory use of the adaptive technique to *plain* exploration oblivious of symmetry. Memory is measured by the (reproducible) number of reached states (memory in bytes is linear in this number, including the overhead due to the annotations). Figure 3 plots this

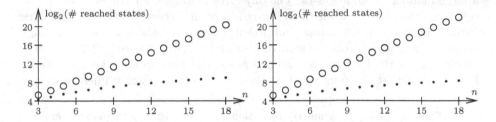

Fig. 3. Comparing the adaptive technique (small dots) to plain exploration (large circles): reached states for $n/2$ small priority classes (left) and two large classes (right)

number over various process counts n for the adaptive technique (small dots) and plain exploration (large circles) on a logarithmic scale. The graphs on the left and on the right differ in the priority scheme used. For $n = 18$, the plain algorithm reaches $1,310,716$ states on the left and $3,808,000$ on the right, whereas our algorithm reaches only 505 abstract states on the left and 316 on the right. The right scheme allows more compression due to larger priority classes; the 316 abstract states reached by our algorithm very compactly represent the $3,808,000$ concrete ones. In all cases, the adaptive algorithm took nearly zero time; for the plain algorithm the largest time measured is 7:16min.

In a second set of experiments, we compare the memory use of the adaptive technique with standard symmetry reduction, based on the induced structure's automorphism group (figure 4). For the highly fragmented scheme on the left, the standard algorithm does quite poorly (thus again the logarithmic scale): for $n = 18$, it reaches $78,729$ states, compared with 505 adaptively. The maximum symmetry group is the product of the 9 transpositions $(1\ 2)$ through $(17\ 18)$,

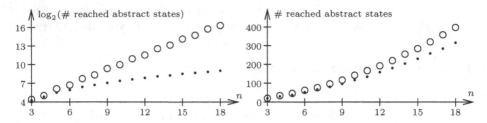

Fig. 4. Comparing the adaptive technique (small dots) to standard symmetry reduction (large circles); priority schemes as in figure 3

yielding a group size and expected compression factor of only $2^9 = 512$. This effect is much less severe for the less fragmented scheme on the right (linear scale), as is clearly revealed by the graph.

In a third set of experiments, we directly investigate how the adaptive method scales with increasing fragmentation; the idea to do this is again borrowed from [9]. The resource controller example with k priority classes is run with a large number of 80 processes. The objective is to look for states where a process holds the resource while the resource is globally recorded to be free. In a first variant, denoted "$1, 1, \ldots, rest$", all priority classes but the last contain a single process; the last contains the rest. In a second variant, denoted "$2, 2, \ldots, rest$", all classes but the last contain two processes; the last contains the rest. We see from table 1 that the number of reached states grows roughly linearly with k;

Table 1. Adaptive symmetry reduction against increasing fragmentation

k	n	"$1,1,\ldots,rest$"		"$2,2,\ldots,rest$"	
		Time	# states	Time	# states
2	80	1s	558	1s	789
3	80	2s	792	4s	1245
5	80	4s	1251	13s	2121
7	80	8s	1698	24s	2949

k	n	"$1,1,\ldots,rest$"		"$2,2,\ldots,rest$"	
		Time	# states	Time	# states
10	80	14s	2346	45s	4101
15	80	28s	3366	83s	5781
20	80	44s	4311	118s	7161
25	80	62s	5181	151s	8241

computation times are very reasonable. For fixed k, the fragmentation grows with increasing size of the initial k classes (1 vs. 2), since then the final class (hosting the majority of the processes) becomes smaller.

For $k \leq 5$, data obtained with the GQS-based method were provided in [9]. Those running times are an order of magnitude higher, although they of course depend on the machine used. Reproducible memory data for these examples (such as the number of reached states) were not given in [9].

10   Summary

We presented a new *adaptive* method for exhaustive state space exploration. It is intended for, and efficient with, *approximately fully symmetric* systems, where many transitions are shared by most processes. Verification of this feature is not required; the method is exact for any input. We introduced the notion of *subsumption*: a state subsumes another if its orbit contains that of the other one. Subsumption induces a quotient structure with an identical set of reachable states. We focused on full symmetry, since this type is the most frequent and profitable in practice. The adaptive method can be implemented as well for rotation groups; critical is the ability to represent and manipulate groups succinctly. Our implementation uses an explicit state representation. We believe the algorithm can be incorporated into the Murφ model checker [8] and extend its applicability to asymmetric systems.

The subsumption relation benefits reachability analysis by aggressively suppressing re-emerging states, even non-equivalent ones. This behavior is too crude for general model checking; how to extend the method is part of our future work.

References

1. Abdulla, P.A., Bouajjani, A., Jonsson, B., Nilsson, M.: Handling global conditions in parameterized system verification. In: Halbwachs, N., Peled, D.A. (eds.) CAV 1999. LNCS, vol. 1633, Springer, Heidelberg (1999)
2. Clarke, E.M., Enders, R., Filkorn, T., Jha, S.: Exploiting symmetry in temporal logic model checking. In: Formal Methods in System Design (FMSD) (1996)
3. Donaldson, A.F., Miller, A.: Automatic symmetry detection for model checking using computational group theory. In: Fitzgerald, J.A., Hayes, I.J., Tarlecki, A. (eds.) FM 2005. LNCS, vol. 3582, Springer, Heidelberg (2005)
4. Emerson, E.A., Havlicek, J.W., Trefler, R.J.: Virtual symmetry reduction. In: Logic in Computer Science (LICS) (2000)
5. Emerson, E.A., Sistla, A.P.: Symmetry and model checking. Formal Methods in System Design (FMSD) (1996)
6. Emerson, E.A., Trefler, R.J.: From asymmetry to full symmetry: New techniques for symmetry reduction in model checking. In: Pierre, L., Kropf, T. (eds.) CHARME 1999. LNCS, vol. 1703, Springer, Heidelberg (1999)
7. Hendriks, M., Behrmann, G., Larsen, K.G., Niebert, P., Vaandrager, F.W.: Adding symmetry reduction to Uppaal. In: Larsen, K.G., Niebert, P. (eds.) FORMATS 2003. LNCS, vol. 2791, Springer, Heidelberg (2004)
8. Ip, C.N., Dill, D.L.: Verifying systems with replicated components in *murϕ*. Formal Methods in System Design (FMSD) (1999)
9. Sistla, A.P., Godefroid, P.: Symmetry and reduced symmetry in model checking. ACM Trans. on Programming Languages and Systems (TOPLAS) (2004)

From Liveness to Promptness*

Orna Kupferman[1],**, Nir Piterman[2], and Moshe Y. Vardi[3],***

[1] Hebrew University
[2] Ecole Polytechnique Fédéral de Lausanne (EPFL)
[3] Rice University

Abstract. Liveness temporal properties state that something "good" eventually happens, e.g., every request is eventually granted. In Linear Temporal Logic (LTL), there is no a priori bound on the "wait time" for an eventuality to be fulfilled. That is, $F\theta$ asserts that θ holds eventually, but there is no bound on the time when θ will hold. This is troubling, as designers tend to interpret an eventuality $F\theta$ as an abstraction of a bounded eventuality $F^{\leq k}\theta$, for an unknown k, and satisfaction of a liveness property is often not acceptable unless we can bound its wait time. We introduce here PROMPT-LTL, an extension of LTL with the *prompt-eventually* operator F_p. A system S satisfies a PROMPT-LTL formula φ if there is some bound k on the wait time for all prompt-eventually subformulas of φ in all computations of S. We study various problems related to PROMPT-LTL, including realizability, model checking, and assume-guarantee model checking, and show that they can be solved by techniques that are quite close to the standard techniques for LTL.

1 Introduction

Since the introduction of temporal logic into computer science [11], temporal logic, in its many different flavors, has been widely accepted as an appropriate formal framework for the description of on-going behavior of reactive systems [10]. Temporal properties are traditionally classified into *safety* and *liveness* properties [2]. Intuitively, safety properties assert that nothing bad will ever happen during the execution of the system, and liveness properties assert that something good will happen eventually. Temporal properties are interpreted with respect to systems that generate infinite computations. In satisfying liveness properties, there is no bound on the "wait time", namely the time that may elapse until an eventuality is fulfilled. For example, the LTL formula $F\theta$ is satisfied at time i if θ holds at some time $j \geq i$, but $j - i$ is not a priori bounded.

In many applications, it is important to bound the wait time. This has given rise to formalisms in which the eventually operator F is replaced by a bounded-eventually operator $F^{\leq k}$. The operator is parameterized by some $k \geq 0$, and it bounds the wait time to k [4,9]. Since we assume that time is discrete, the operator $F^{\leq k}$ is simply a

---

* Part of this work was done while the authors were visiting the Isaac Newton Institute for Mathematical Science, as part of a Special Programme on Logic and Algorithms. A full version can be downloaded from the authors' web sites.
** Supported in part by BSF grant 9800096, and by a grant from Minerva.
*** Supported in part by NSF grants CCR-9988322, CCR-0124077, CCR-0311326, CCF-0613889, and ANI-0216467, by BSF grant 9800096, and by a Guggenheim Fellowship.

W. Damm and H. Hermanns (Eds.): CAV 2007, LNCS 4590, pp. 406–419, 2007.
© Springer-Verlag Berlin Heidelberg 2007

syntactic sugar for an expression in which the next operator $\mathbf{X}$ is nested. Indeed, $\mathbf{F}^{\leq k}\theta$ is just $\theta \vee \mathbf{X}(\theta \vee \mathbf{X}(\theta \vee ^{k-4} \vee \mathbf{X}\theta))$.

A drawback of the above formalism is that the bound k needs to be known in advance, which is not the case in many applications. For example, it may depend on the system, which may not yet be known, or it may change, if the system changes. In addition, the bound may be very large, causing the state-based description of the specification (e.g., an automaton for it) to be very large too. Thus, the common practice is to use liveness properties as an abstraction of such safety properties: one writes $\mathbf{F}\theta$ instead of $\mathbf{F}^{\leq k}\theta$ for an unknown or a too large k.

For some temporal logics, the abstraction is sound, in the sense that if a system S satisfies a liveness property ψ, then there is a bound k, which depends on S, such that S also satisfies the formula obtained from ψ by replacing all occurrences of $\mathbf{F}$ in ψ by $\mathbf{F}^{\leq k}$. For example, it is shown in [9] that in the case of CTL, taking k to be the number of states in S does it. Thus, if a state s satisfies $AF\theta$, then it also satisfies $AF^{\leq k}\theta$, for $k = |S|$, and similarly for $EF\theta$. Intuitively, since θ is a state formula, a wait time that is greater than $|S|$ indicates that the wait time may also be infinite (by looping in a cycle that ought to be taken during the wait time), and may also be shortened to at most $|S|$ (by skipping such cycles).

So the abstraction of safety properties by liveness properties is sound for CTL. Is it sound also for the linear temporal logic LTL? Consider the system S described in Figure 1 below. While S satisfies the LTL formula $\mathbf{FG}q$, there is no $k \geq 0$ such that S satisfies $\mathbf{F}^{\leq k}\mathbf{G}q$. To see this, note that for each $k \geq 0$, the computation that first loops in the first state for k times and only then continues to the second state, satisfies the eventuality $\mathbf{G}q$ with wait time $k + 1$.

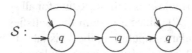

Fig. 1. S satisfies $\mathbf{FG}q$ but does not satisfy $\mathbf{F}^{\leq k}\mathbf{G}q$, for all $k \geq 0$

It follows that the abstraction of safety properties by liveness properties is not sound in the linear-time approach (which is more popular with users, cf. [7]). This is troubling, as designers tend to interpret eventualities as bounded eventualities, and satisfaction of a liveness property is often not acceptable unless we can bound its wait time.[1]

In this work we introduce and study an extension of LTL that addresses the above problem. In addition to the usual temporal operators of LTL, our logic, PROMPT-LTL, has a new temporal operator that is used for specifying eventualities with a bounded wait time. We term the operator *prompt eventually* and denote it by $\mathbf{F_p}$. Let us define the semantics of PROMPT-LTL formally. For a PROMPT-LTL formula ψ and a bound $k \geq 0$, let ψ^k be the LTL formula obtained from ψ by replacing all occurrences of $\mathbf{F_p}$ by $\mathbf{F}^{\leq k}$. Then, a system S satisfies ψ iff there is $k \geq 0$ such that S satisfies ψ^k.

---

[1] Note that the reduction of liveness to safety as described in [3] is performed by squaring the state space rather than trying to bound the wait time of eventualities. Thus, it is not related to the discussion in this paper.

Note that while the syntax of PROMPT-LTL is very similar to that of LTL, its semantics is defined with respect to an entire system, and not with respect to computations. For example, while each computation π in the system S from Figure 1 has a bound $k_\pi \geq 0$ such that $\mathbf{G}q$ is satisfied in π with wait time k_π, there is no $k \geq 0$ that bounds the wait time of all computations. It follows that, unlike linear temporal logics, we cannot characterize a PROMPT-LTL formula ψ over a set AP of atomic propositions by a set of computations $L_\psi \subseteq (2^{AP})^\omega$ such that a system S satisfies ψ iff the language of S is contained in L_ψ. On the other hand, unlike branching temporal logics, if two systems agree on their languages, then they agree also on the satisfaction of all PROMPT-LTL formulas. Thus, PROMPT-LTL intermediates between the linear and branching approaches: as in the linear approach, the specification refers to the set of computations of the system rather than its computation tree; as in the branching approach, we cannot consider these computations individually.

As further motivation to a prompt eventuality operator, consider the formula $\mathbf{F}a \rightarrow \mathbf{F}b$. A system may satisfy $\mathbf{G}\neg a \vee \mathbf{F}b$ but have no bound on the wait time to the satisfaction of the eventuality. When a user checks $\mathbf{F}a \rightarrow \mathbf{F}b$, it is quite likely that what he has in mind is $\mathbf{G}\neg a \vee \mathbf{F_p}b$. The user may not know a bound k such that $\mathbf{G}\neg a \vee \mathbf{X}^{\leq k}b$ should be checked. It is also possible that what the user has in mind is "assume $\mathbf{F}a$; assert $\mathbf{F}b$", where the bound for b ought to depend on the bound for a. Our semantics distinguishes these three different understandings of $\mathbf{F}a \rightarrow \mathbf{F}b$.

We study the basic problems of PROMPT-LTL. Consider a PROMPT-LTL formula ψ over AP. The set AP may be partitioned to sets I and O of input and output signals. Consider also a system S. We study the following problems: *realizability* (is there a strategy $f : (2^I)^* \rightarrow 2^O$ such that all the computations generated by f satisfy ψ?), *model checking* (does S satisfy ψ?), and *assume-guarantee model checking* (given an additional PROMPT-LTL formula φ, is it the case that for all systems S', if $S\|S'$ satisfies φ, then $S\|S'$ also satisfies ψ?). Since a system that satisfies a PROMPT-LTL formula may consist of a single regular computation, the satisfiability problem for prompt-LTL can be easily reduced to LTL satisfiability (simply replace all occurrences of $\mathbf{F_p}$ by $\mathbf{F}$). For the other problems, similar reductions do not work, and we have to develop a new technique in order to solve them. Let us describe our technique briefly.

Consider a prompt-LTL formula ψ over AP. Let p be an atomic proposition not in AP. Think about p as a description of one of two colors, say green (p holds) and red (p does not hold). Each computation of the system can be partitioned to blocks such that states of the same block agree on their color. We show that a system S satisfies a PROMPT-LTL formula ψ iff there is some bound $k \geq 0$ such that we can color each computation π of S so that the induced blocks are of length k, and whenever a suffix of π has to satisfy an eventuality, the eventuality is fulfilled within two blocks. Indeed, the latter condition holds iff all eventualities have wait time at most $2k$.

The key idea behind our technique is that rather than searching for a bound k for the prompt eventualities, which can be quite large, it is enough to make sure that there is a coloring in which all blocks are of a (not necessarily bounded) finite length, and then use some regularity argument in order to conclude that the size of the blocks could actually be bounded. Forcing the blocks to be of a finite length can be done by requiring the colors to alternate infinitely often. As for regularity, in the case of realizability, regularity follows from the finite-model property of tree automata. In the case of (assume-guarantee) model checking, regularity follows from the finiteness of the system.

The complexities that follow from our algorithms are encouraging: reasoning about PROMPT-LTL is not harder than reasoning about LTL: realizability is 2EXPTIME-complete, and model checking and assume-guarantee model checking are PSPACE-complete. For LTL, many heuristics have been studied and applied. Some of them are immediately applicable for PROMPT-LTL (c.f., optimal translations of formulas to automata), and some should be extended to the prompt setting (e.g., bad-cycle detection algorithms). We also study some theoretical aspects of PROMPT-LTL, such as the ability to translate PROMPT-LTL formulas to branching-temporal logics (a translation to the μ-calculus is always possible, but may involve a significant blow up), and the ability to determine whether a PROMPT-LTL formula has an equivalent LTL formula (PSPACE-complete).

2   Prompt Linear Temporal Logic

The logic PROMPT-LTL extends LTL [11] by a *prompt-eventually* operator $\mathbf{F_p}$. The syntax of PROMPT-LTL formulas (in negation normal form) is given by the grammar below, for a set AP of atomic propositions: $\varphi ::= AP \mid \neg AP \mid \varphi \vee \varphi \mid \varphi \wedge \varphi \mid \mathbf{X}\varphi \mid \mathbf{F_p}\varphi \mid \varphi \mathbf{U}\varphi \mid \varphi \mathbf{R}\varphi$. The semantics of a PROMPT-LTL formula is defined with respect to an infinite word $w = w_0, w_1, \ldots$ over the alphabet 2^{AP}, a position $i \geq 0$ in w, and a bound $k \geq 0$. We use $(w, k, i) \models \varphi$ to indicate that φ holds in location i of w with bound k. The relation $\models$ is defined by induction on the structure of φ as follows.

– For propositions, Boolean connectives, and LTL temporal operators, the definition is independent of k and coincides with the one for LTL.[2]
– $(w, i, k) \models \mathbf{F_p}\varphi$ iff there exists j such that $i \leq j \leq i + k$ and $(w, j, k) \models \varphi$.

We use $\mathbf{F}\theta$ and $\mathbf{G}\theta$ to abbreviate $true\mathbf{U}\theta$ and $false\mathbf{R}\theta$, respectively. Note that the negation of $\mathbf{F_p}$ is not expressible in PROMPT-LTL, thus the logic is not closed under negation. Given a PROMPT-LTL formula φ, let $live(\varphi)$ be the LTL formula obtained from φ by replacing every prompt-eventually operator $\mathbf{F_p}$ by a standard eventually operator $\mathbf{F}$.

A *(labeled) transition system* is $\mathcal{S} = \langle AP, S, \rho, s_0, L \rangle$, where AP is a finite set of atomic propositions, S is a finite set of states, $\rho \subseteq S \times S$ is a total transition relation, $s_0 \in S_0$ is an initial state, and $L : S \rightarrow 2^{AP}$ maps each state s to the set of propositions that hold in s. When $\rho(s, s')$, we say that s' is a *successor* of s, and s is a *predecessor* of s'. A *computation* of $\mathcal{S}$ is an infinite sequence of states $\pi = s_0, s_1, \ldots \in S^\omega$ such that for all $i \geq 0$, we have $\rho(s_i, s_{i+1})$. The computation π induces the *trace* $L(\pi) = L(s_0) \cdot L(s_1) \cdots$.

Given a system $\mathcal{S}$ and a PROMPT-LTL formula φ over AP, we say that $\mathcal{S}$ satisfies φ, denoted $\mathcal{S} \models \varphi$, if there exists some $k \geq 0$ such that for all traces w of $\mathcal{S}$, we have $(w, 0, k) \models \varphi$. We then say that $\mathcal{S}$ *satisfies* φ *with bound* k. Note that when $\mathcal{S} \not\models \varphi$, then for every $k \geq 0$, there exists a trace w such that $(w, 0, k) \not\models \varphi$.

---

[2] Recall that in LTL we have that $\pi, i \models \theta \mathbf{R}\psi$ iff for all $j \geq i$, if $\pi, j \not\models \psi$, then for some k, $i \leq k < j$, we have $\pi, k \models \theta$.

In [1], Alur et al. study an extension of LTL in which the temporal operators $\mathbf{F}$ and $\mathbf{G}$ are replaced by the operators $\mathbf{F}_{\leq x}, \mathbf{F}_{>y}, \mathbf{G}_{\leq x}$, and $\mathbf{G}_{>y}$, for variables x and y (the same variable may be used in different operators, but, to ensure decidability, the same variable cannot participate in both a lower and an upper bound). Given a system $\mathcal{S}$ and a formula in their logic, one can ask whether there is an assignment to the variables for which the system satisfies the formula, with the expected interpretation of the bounded operators.[3] Our logic can be viewed as a special case of the logic studied in [1], in which only eventualities are parameterized, and only with upper bounds. The algorithms suggested by Alur et al. are rather involved. By giving up the operators $\mathbf{F}_{>y}, \mathbf{G}_{\leq x}$, and $\mathbf{G}_{>y}$, whose usefulness is debatable, we get a much simpler model-checking algorithm, which is also similar to the classical LTL model-checking algorithm. We are also able to a solve the realizability and the assume-guarantee model checking problems.

The Alternating-Color Technique. We now describe the key idea of our technique for reasoning about PROMPT-LTL formulas. Let p be an atomic proposition not in AP. We think about p as a description of one of two colors, say green (p holds) and red (p does not hold). Each computation of the system can be partitioned to blocks such that states of the same block agree on their color. Our technique is based on the idea that bounding the wait time of prompt eventualities can be reduced to forcing all blocks to be of a bounded length, and forcing all eventualities to be fulfilled within two blocks, We now make this intuition formal.

Consider a word $w = \sigma_0, \sigma_1, \ldots \in (2^{AP})^\omega$. Let p be a proposition not in AP. A *p-coloring* of w is a word $w' = \sigma_0', \sigma_1', \ldots \in (2^{AP \cup \{p\}})^\omega$ such that w' agrees with w on the propositions in AP; i.e., for all $i \geq 0$, we have $\sigma_i' \cap AP = \sigma_i$. We refer to the assignment to p as the *color* of location i and say that i is green if $p \in \sigma_i'$ and is red if $p \notin \sigma_i'$. We say that p *changes at i* if either $i = 0$ or the colors of $i - 1$ and i are different (that is, $p \in \sigma_{i-1}'$ iff $p \notin \sigma_i'$). We then call i a *p-change point*. A subword $\sigma_i', \ldots, \sigma_{i'}'$ is a *p-block* if all positions in the subword have the same color, and i and $i' + 1$ are *p*-change points. We then say that i and $i' + 1$ are adjacent *p*-change points. For $k \geq 0$, we say that w' is *k-spaced*, *k-bounded*, and *k-tight* (with respect to p) if w' has infinitely many blocks, and all the blocks are of length at least k, at most k, and exactly k, respectively.

Consider the formula $alt_p = \mathbf{GF}p \wedge \mathbf{GF}\neg p$. It requires that the proposition p alternates infinitely often. Given a PROMPT-LTL formula φ, let $rel_p(\varphi)$ denote the formula obtained from φ by (recursively) replacing each subformula of the form $\mathbf{F_p}\psi$ by the LTL formula $(p \rightarrow (p\mathbf{U}(\neg p\mathbf{U}\psi))) \wedge (\neg p \rightarrow (\neg p\mathbf{U}(p\mathbf{U}\psi)))$. Note that the definition is recursive, thus $rel_p(\varphi)$ may be exponentially larger than φ. The number of subformulas of $rel_p(\varphi)$, however, is linear in the number of subformulas of φ, and it is this number that plays a role in the complexity analysis (equivalently, the size of the DAG-presentation of $rel_p(\varphi)$ is linear in the size of the DAG presentation of φ). For a PROMPT-LTL formula φ, we define $c(\varphi) = alt_p \wedge rel_p(\varphi)$. Thus, $c(\varphi)$ forces the computation to be partitioned into infinitely many blocks, and requires each prompt

---

[3] The work in [1] studies many more aspects of the logic, like the problem of deciding whether the formula is satisfied with *all* assignments, the problem of finding an optimal assignment, and other decidability issues.

eventuality to be satisfied in the current or next block or in the position immediately after the next block (within two blocks, for short),

Lemma 1. *Consider a* PROMPT-LTL *formula* φ, *a word* w, *and a bound* $k \geq 0$.

1. *If* $(w, 0, k) \models \varphi$, *then* $(w', 0) \models c(\varphi)$, *for every* k-*spaced* p-*coloring* w' *of* w.
2. *If* w' *is a* k-*bounded* p-*coloring of* w *such that* $(w', 0) \models c(\varphi)$, *then* $(w, 0, 2k) \models \varphi$.

The alternating-color technique sets the basis to reasoning about a PROMPT-LTL formula φ by reasoning about the LTL formula $c(\varphi)$. The formula $c(\varphi)$, however, does not require the blocks in the colored computation to be of a bounded length. Indeed, the conjunct alt_p only forces the colors to be finite, and it does not prevent, say, a p-coloring in which each block is longer than its predecessor block, and which is not k-bounded, for all $k \geq 0$. Thus, the challenge of forcing the p-coloring to be k-bounded for some k remains, and we have to address it in each of the decision procedures described in the following sections.

3   Realizability

Given an LTL formula ψ over the sets I and O of input and output signals, the *realizability problem* for ψ is to decide whether there is a *strategy* $f : (2^I)^* \rightarrow 2^O$ such that all the computations generated by f satisfy ψ [13]. Formally, a computation $w \in (2^{I \cup O})^\omega$ is generated by f if $w = (i_0 \cup o_0), (i_1 \cup o_1), (i_2 \cup o_2), \ldots$ and for all $j \geq 0$, we have $o_j = f(i_0 \cdot i_1 \cdots i_j)$. Thus, the interaction is initiated by the environment that generates i_0, and the first state in the computation is labeled $i_0 \cup f(i_0)$. Then, the environment generates i_1, and the second state in the computation is $i_1 \cup f(i_0 \cdot i_1)$, and so on. It is known that if some strategy that realizes ψ exists, then there also exists a *regular strategy* (i.e., a strategy generated by a finite-state *transducer*) that realizes ψ [6]. Formally, a transducer is $\mathcal{D} = \langle I, O, Q, \eta, q_0, L \rangle$, where I and O are the sets of input and output signals, Q is a finite set of states, $\eta : Q \times 2^I \rightarrow Q$ is a deterministic transition function, $q_0 \in Q$ is an initial state, and $L : Q \rightarrow 2^O$ maps each state to a set of output signals. The transducer $\mathcal{D}$ generates f in the sense that for every $\tau \in (2^I)^*$, we have $f(\tau) = L(\eta(\tau))$, with the usual extension of η to words over 2^I.

We first show that PROMPT-LTL realizability of a formula φ cannot be simply reduced to the realizability of $live(\varphi)$. Thus, we describe a formula φ such that $live(\varphi)$ is realizable, but for every strategy f that realizes φ and for every candidate bound $k \geq 0$, there is a computation w generated by f such that $(w, 0, k) \not\models \varphi$. Let $I = \{i\}$ and $O = \{o\}$. We define $\varphi = o \wedge (\mathbf{G}(i \rightarrow o)) \wedge ((\mathbf{X}\neg o)\mathbf{R}i) \wedge (\mathbf{F_p}\mathbf{G}o)$.

Thus, a computation satisfies φ if o holds in the present and whenever i holds, whenever i does not hold in some position, then o does not hold in this position or in an earlier one, and the computation prompt-eventually reaches a position from which o holds everywhere. It is not hard to see that $live(\varphi)$ is realizable. Indeed, the strategy that sets o to *true* everywhere except in the first time that i is *false* realizes $live(\varphi)$. On the other hand, φ is not realizable. To see this, note that the position in which the input i is set to *false* can be delayed arbitrarily by the environment, forcing a delay also in the fulfillment of the $\mathbf{G}o$ eventuality. Thus, for every candidate bound $k \geq 0$, the input sequence in which i is *false* at the $(k + 1)$-th position cannot be extended to a computation that satisfies $\mathbf{F_p}\mathbf{G}o$ with bound k.

The good news is that while realizability of φ cannot be reduced to the realizability of $live(\varphi)$, it can be reduced to the realizability of $c(\varphi)$. Intuitively, it follows from the fact that in a regular strategy, the fact that all blocks are of a finite length does imply that they are also of a bounded length. Formally, we have the following.

Theorem 1. *A* PROMPT-LTL *formula φ over input signals I and output signals O is realizable iff the LTL formula $c(\varphi)$ over input signals I and output signals $O \cup \{p\}$ is realizable.*

Since LTL realizability is 2EXPTIME-complete and every LTL formula is also a PROMPT-LTL formula, we can conclude:

Theorem 2. *The problem of prompt realizability is 2EXPTIME-complete in the size of the formula.*

As demonstrated above, the alternating-color technique is very powerful in the case of realizability. Indeed, the challenge of forcing the p-coloring to be k-bounded for some k is taken care of by the regularity of the strategy. We now proceed to the model-checking problem, where a reduction to $c(\varphi)$ is not sufficiently strong.

4   Model Checking

In this section we describe an algorithm for solving the model-checking problem for PROMPT-LTL. An alternative algorithm is described for the richer parameterized linear temporal logic in [1]. Our algorithm is much simpler, and it deviates from the standard LTL model-checking algorithm only slightly. In addition, as we show in Section 6, the idea behind our algorithm can be applied also in order to solve assume-guarantee model checking, which is not known to be the case with the algorithm in [1]. Our algorithm is based on the automata-theoretic approach to LTL model-checking, and we first need some definitions.

A *nondeterministic Büchi word automaton* (NBW for short) is $\mathcal{A} = \langle \Sigma, S, \delta, s_0, \alpha \rangle$, where Σ is a finite alphabet, S is a finite set of states, $\delta : S \times \Sigma \rightarrow 2^S$ is a transition function, $s_0 \in S$ is an initial state, and $\alpha \subseteq S$ is a *Büchi* acceptance condition. A *run* of $\mathcal{A}$ on a word $w = w_0 \cdot w_1 \cdots$ is an infinite sequence of states $s_0, s_1, \ldots$ such that s_0 is the initial state and for all $j \geq 0$, we have $s_{j+1} \in \delta(s_j, w_j)$. For a run $r = s_0, s_1, \ldots$, let $\inf(r) = \{s \in S \mid s = s_i \text{ for infinitely many } i\text{'s}\}$ be the set of all states occurring infinitely often in the run. A run is *accepting* if $\inf(r) \cap \alpha \neq \emptyset$. That is, the run visits infinitely many states from α. A word w is *accepted* by $\mathcal{A}$ if there exists some accepting run of $\mathcal{A}$ over w. The *language* of $\mathcal{A}$, is the set of words accepted by $\mathcal{A}$.

Theorem 3. [17] *For every LTL formula φ over AP there exists an NBW $\mathcal{A}_\varphi$ over the alphabet 2^{AP} such that $\mathcal{A}_\varphi$ accepts exactly all words that satisfy φ. The number of states of $\mathcal{A}_\varphi$ is at most exponential in the number of subformulas of φ.*

In order to check whether a system $\mathcal{S}$ satisfies an LTL formula φ, one takes the product of $\mathcal{S}$ with the NBW $\mathcal{A}_{\neg\varphi}$ and tests the product for non-emptiness [16]. Indeed, a path in this product witnesses a computation of S that does not satisfy φ. As discussed in Section 1, in the case of PROMPT-LTL we cannot translate formulas to languages. Moreover, we also cannot simply apply the alternating-color technique: even if we check the nonemptiness of the product of the system (an augmentation of it in which the proposition p behaves nondeterministically, thus all p-colorings are possible) with the automaton for $alt_p \wedge \neg rel_p(\varphi)$, a path in this product only implies that for some bound $k \geq 0$, the formula φ is not satisfied in S with bound k. For proving that S does not satisfy φ we have to prove something stronger, namely, that φ is not satisfied in S with bound k, for *all* bounds $k \geq 0$. For that, we do take the product of the system with the automaton for $alt_p \wedge \neg rel_p(\varphi)$, but add a twist to the nonemptiness check: we search for a path in the product in which each p-block contains at least one state that repeats. Such a state indicates that for all bounds $k \geq 0$, the p-block can be pumped to a p-block of length greater than k, implying that φ cannot be satisfied in S with bound k. We now formalize this intuition.

A *colored Büchi graph* is a tuple $G = \langle \{p\}, V, E, v_0, L, \alpha \rangle$, where p is a proposition, V is a set of vertices, $E \subseteq V \times V$ is a set of edges, $v_0 \in V$ is an initial vertex, $L : V \rightarrow 2^{\{p\}}$ describes the color of each vertex, and $\alpha \subseteq V$ is a set of accepting states. A path $\pi = v_0, v_1, v_2, \ldots$ of G is *pumpable* if all its p-blocks have at least one state that repeats. Formally, if i and i' are adjacent p-change points, then there are positions j and j' such that $i \leq j < j' < i'$ and $v_j = v_{j'}$. Also, π is *fair* if it visits α infinitely often. The *pumpable nonemptiness* problem is to decide, given G, whether is has a pumpable fair path.

Let $\bar{c}(\varphi) = alt_p \wedge \neg rel_p(\varphi)$. That is, we relativize the satisfaction of $\mathbf{F_p}$ to the new proposition p, negate the resulting formula, and require the proposition p to alternate infinitely often. Let $\mathcal{A}_{\bar{c}(\varphi)} = \langle 2^{AP \cup \{p\}}, Q, \delta, q_0, \alpha \rangle$ be the NBW for $\bar{c}(\varphi)$ per Theorem 3. Consider a system $S = \langle AP, S, \rho, s_0, L \rangle$. We now define the product of S with $\mathcal{A}_{\bar{c}(\varphi)}$ by means of a colored Büchi graph. Note that S does not refer to the proposition p, and we duplicate its state space in order to have in the product all possible p-colorings of computations in S. Thus, the product is $\mathcal{P} = \langle \{p\}, S \times \{\{p\}, \emptyset\} \times Q, M, \langle s_0, \{p\}, q_0 \rangle, L, S \times \{\{p\}, \emptyset\} \times \alpha \rangle$, where $M(\langle s, c, q \rangle, \langle s', c', q' \rangle)$ iff $\rho(s, s')$ and $q' \in \delta(q, L(s) \cup c)$, and $L(\langle s, c, q \rangle) = c$.

It is not hard to see that a path $\pi = \langle s_0, c_0, q_0 \rangle, \langle s_1, c_1, q_1 \rangle, \langle s_2, c_2, q_2 \rangle, \ldots$ in $\mathcal{P}$ corresponds to a computation $s_0, s_1, s_2, \ldots$ of S, a p-coloring $L(s_0) \cup c_0, L(s_1) \cup c_1, L(s_2) \cup c_2, \ldots$ of the trace that the computation induces, and a run $q_0, q_1, q_2, \ldots$ of $\mathcal{A}_{\bar{c}(\varphi)}$ on this p-coloring.

Theorem 4. *The system S does not satisfy φ iff the product of S and $\mathcal{A}_{\bar{c}(\varphi)}$ is pumpable nonempty.*

In Section 5, we study the problem of deciding whether a colored Büchi graph is pumpable-nonempty, and prove that it is in NLOGSPACE and can also be solved in linear time. This, together with Theorems 3 and 4, imply the upper bound in the following theorem. The lower bound follows from the known lower bound for LTL.

Theorem 5. *The model-checking problem for PROMPT-LTL is PSPACE-complete and can be solved in time exponential in the length of the formula and linear in the size of the system.*

Note that while the pumpable nonemptiness problem to which PROMPT-LTL model-checking is reduced is a variant of the nonemptiness problem to which LTL model checking is reduced, the construction of the product is almost the same. In particular, the extensive work on optimal compilation of LTL formulas to NBW (see survey in [15]), is applicable to our solution too.

Remark 6. The model-checking algorithm of the parametric linear temporal logic of [1] is based on the observation that if a PROMPT-LTL formula φ is satisfied in a system $\mathcal{S}$, then it is satisfied with bound k, for some k that is exponential in φ and polynomial in $\mathcal{S}$. One cannot hope to improve this bound. Indeed, for every $n \geq 1$, we can define a PROMPT-LTL formula ψ_n of size linear in n such that a systems satisfies ψ_n iff in all its computations, the atomic proposition q corresponds to an n-bit counter, and the value of the counter promptly eventually reaches $2^n - 1$. Clearly, ψ_n is promptly satisfied, but the minimal bound k with which ψ_n is satisfied with bound k (in some system) is exponential in n.

The algorithm in [1] can also be used in order to find the minimal bound. It is an open question whether the minimal bound can be found using our simplified algorithm.   □

5   Algorithms for Colored Büchi Graphs

In Section 4 we reduced model-checking for PROMPT-LTL to pumpable nonemptiness problems for colored Büchi graphs. In this section we solve this problems, and provide space and time bounds.

Theorem 7. *The pumpable nonemptiness problem for colored Büchi graphs is NLOGSPACE-complete and can be solved in linear time.*

Proof: Let $G = \langle \{p\}, V, E, v_0, L, \alpha \rangle$. We start with the space complexity. Essentially, as with standard Büchi nonemptiness, the pumpable nonemptiness problem can be solved by a sequence of reachability tests. In addition to reaching a vertex v in α that is reachable from itself, the algorithm should make sure that the paths from v_0 to v and from v to itself are pumpable. Thus, in each p-block, the algorithm should guess a repeated vertex (and check that it indeed repeats). Also, an easy reduction from reachability shows hardness in NLOGSPACE.

We now move to the time complexity. For standard Büchi nonemptiness, one looks for a reachable nontrivial strongly connected component that intersects α. In the colored case, we should further check that each p-block in the path can be pumped. We do this by making sure that every green p-block contains at least one vertex that belongs to a nontrivial strongly connected component in the graph of the green vertices, and similarly for the red p-blocks.

Consider the graph $G_g = \langle V_g, E_g \rangle$ obtained from G by restricting attention to green vertices. Thus, $V_g = \{v \in V \mid L(v) = \{p\}\}$ and $E_g = E \cap (V_g \times V_g)$. The graph $G_r = \langle V_r, E_r \rangle$ is defined similarly. We can find the maximal strongly connected components (MSCC) of G_g and G_r in linear time [14] (note we are interested also in MSCCs that are not reachable from v_0 in G_g and G_r). Let $S_g \subseteq V_g$ and $S_r \subseteq V_r$ denote the union of all non-trivial MSCCs in G_g and G_r, respectively.

Let $back_g(S_g)$ be the vertices that can reach some vertex in S_g, and let $e\text{-}back_g(S_g)$ be the edges that are used to reach these vertices. We tag the vertices in $back_g(S_g) \setminus S_g$ by the tag B. Formally, we define $back_0^g(S_g) = S_g$ and $back_{i+1}^g(S_g) = \{v \in V_g \mid \exists v' \in back_i^g(S_g)$ and $(v, v') \in E\}$. Then, $back_g(S_g) = S_g \cup (\bigcup_{i \geq 1} back_i^g(S_g)) \times \{B\}$. For a vertex $u \in back_g(S_g)$, let $ver(u)$ be the vertex in V that induces u; that is, the vertex obtained from u by ignoring its tag, if exists. Then, $e\text{-}back_g(S_g) = \{\langle u, u' \rangle : E(ver(u), ver(u'))$ and there is $i \geq 0$ such that $u \in back_{i+1}^g(S_g)$ and $u' \in back_i^g(S_g)\}$. In a similar way, we define $forward_g(S_g)$ to be the set of vertices that are reachable from some vertex in S_g (with vertices not in S_g tagged with F) and define $e\text{-}forward_g(S_g)$ to be the edges that are used to reach these vertices. The sets $back_r$, $e\text{-}back_r$, $forward_r$, and $e\text{-}forward_r$ are defined similarly. Another type of edges we need are edges between p-blocks. Let $E_{g \to r} = \{\langle u, u' \rangle : E(ver(u), ver(u')), u \in forward_g(S_g)$, and $u' \in back_r(S_r)\}$ be the set of edges along which the color changes from green to red, and let $E_{r \to g}$ be the set of edges along which the color changes from red to green.

Consider now the graph $G' = \langle V', E' \rangle$, where $V' = back_g(S_g) \cup forward_g(S_g) \cup back_r(S_r) \cup forward_r(S_r)$, and $E' = e\text{-}forward_g(S_g) \cup e\text{-}forward_r(S_r) \cup e\text{-}back_g(S_g) \cup e\text{-}back_r(S_r) \cup E_{g \to r} \cup E_{r \to g}$. Note that the vertices in S_g and S_r appear in G' with no tag. Other vertices (these in V_g that can reach an MSCC in S_g along green vertices and can also be reached from a different MSCC in S_g along green vertices, and similarly for V_r) may appear in G' with both tags, thus the number of vertices in G' is at most twice the number of vertices in G.

Intuitively, the graph G' contains exactly all the pumpable computations of G. Indeed, along each p-block, there must exists a vertex that belongs to an MSCC of the graph of the corresponding color. In the full version, we prove that G is pumpable nonempty iff G' has some non-trivial MSCC that is reachable from v_0 (possibly tagged with B) and contains a vertex from α.

We analyze the time it takes to construct G' and to check whether it has a non-trivial MSCC that intersects α. Clearly, the MSCC decomposition of G_g and G_r can be done in linear time. The search for $back_g$ and $forward_g$ is done by backward (resp. forward) propagation from S_g, during which the edges in $e\text{-}back_g$ and $e\text{-}forward_g$ can be marked. The case of $back_r$ and $forward_r$ is similar. This stage can be completed in linear time as well. Finally, the MSCC decomposition of G' is completed again in linear time, thus the overall running time is linear. □

We note than our algorithm is based in MSCC-decomposition. It is an open question whether a linear-time algorithm based on nested depth-first-search can be found (see discussion of these types of algorithms in [15]).

Remark 8. The algorithm described above are explicit. A symbolic PROMPT-LTL model checking algorithm follows from the translation of PROMPT-LTL to the μ-calculus described later in Theorem 14. The translation, however, involves a significant blow up. A symbolic algorithm that performs well on the colored Büchi graphs is left open. For standard Büchi graphs, algorithms can be classified as ones that are based on a nested fixed point that calculates the set of states that can reach α infinitely often [8], and ones that calculate symbolically the MSCC of the graph [5]. We believe that algorithms of the second type can be extended to colored graphs. □

6 Assume-Guarantee Model Checking

For two systems $S = \langle AP, S, \rho, s_0, L \rangle$ and $S' = \langle AP, S', \rho', s'_0, L' \rangle$, the parallel composition of S with S', denoted $S \| S'$, is the system that contains all the joint behaviors of S and S'. Formally, $S \| S' = \langle AP, S'', \rho'', s''_0, L'' \rangle$, where $S'' \subseteq S \times S'$ contains exactly all pairs that agree on their label, that is $\langle s, s' \rangle \in S''$ iff $L(s) = L'(s')$. Then, $s''_0 = \langle s_0, s'_0 \rangle$ and $\rho''(\langle s, s' \rangle, \langle t, t' \rangle)$ iff $\rho(s, t)$ and $\rho'(s', t')$. Finally, $L''(\langle s, s' \rangle) = L(s)$.

An *assume-guarantee specification* for a system S is a pair of two specifications φ_1 and φ_2. The system S satisfies the specification, denoted $\langle \varphi_1 \rangle S \langle \varphi_2 \rangle$, if it is the case that for all systems S', if $S \| S'$ satisfies φ_1, then $S \| S'$ also satisfies φ_2 [12]. In the context of LTL it is not hard to see that $\langle \varphi_1 \rangle S \langle \varphi_2 \rangle$ iff $S \models \varphi_1 \rightarrow \varphi_2$. Intuitively, since the $\|$ operator amounts to taking the intersection of the languages of S and S', it is sound to restrict attention to systems S' that correspond to single computations of S. In the case of PROMPT-LTL, we can also restrict attention to single computations, but we have to take the bounds into an account. Formally, we have the following.

Lemma 2. *Consider a system S and* PROMPT-LTL *formulas φ_1 and φ_2. The specification $\langle \varphi_1 \rangle S \langle \varphi_2 \rangle$ does not hold iff there is a bound $k_1 \geq 0$ such that for every bound $k_2 \geq 0$, there is a trace w of S such that $(w, 0, k_1) \models \varphi_1$ but $(w, 0, k_2) \not\models \varphi_2$.*

Since refuting assume-guarantee specifications refer to two bounds, we extend the alternating-color technique to refer to two sets of colors. The atomic proposition p partitions the computation to blocks that bound k_1, and a new atomic proposition q does the same for k_2. According to Lemmas 1 and 2, refuting $\langle \varphi_1 \rangle S \langle \varphi_2 \rangle$ amounts to finding a bound $k_1 \geq 0$ such that for all bounds $k_2 \geq 0$, there is a computation w of S such that w has a k_1-bounded p-coloring that satisfies $alt_p \wedge rel_p(\varphi_1)$, but w also has a k_2-spaced q-coloring that satisfies $alt_q \wedge \neg rel_q(\varphi_2)$. Indeed, such a computation satisfies φ_1 with bound k_1, and does not satisfy φ_2 with bound k_2.

We now show that the pumpable nonemptiness technique developed in Section 4 for solving the model-checking problem can be used also for solving the assume-guarantee model-checking problem, only that now the corresponding colored Büchi graphs are colored with two sets of colors, one for φ_1 and one for φ_2. Also, the definition of when a path in the graph is pumpable corresponds to the intuition above.

A *colored Büchi graph of degree two* is a tuple $G = \langle \{p, q\}, V, E, v_0, L, \alpha \rangle$. It is similar to a colored Büchi graph, only that now there are two sets of colors, described by p and q. Accordingly, $L : V \rightarrow 2^{\{p,q\}}$. Also, α is a generalized Büchi condition of index 2, thus $\alpha = \{\alpha_1, \alpha_2\}$. A path $\pi = v_0, v_1, v_2, \ldots$ of G is *pumpable* if we can pump all its q-blocks without pumping its p-blocks. Formally, if i and i' are adjacent q-change points, then there are positions j, j', and j'' such that $i \leq j < j' < j'' < i'$, $v_j = v_{j''}$ and $p \in L(v_j)$ iff $p \notin L(v_{j'})$. Also, π is *fair* if it visits both α_1 and α_2 infinitely often. The *pumpable nonemptiness* problem is to decide, given G, whether it has a pumpable fair path.

Let $c(\varphi_1) = alt_p \wedge rel_p(\varphi_1)$ and $\bar{c}(\varphi_2) = alt_q \wedge \neg rel_q(\varphi_2)$, and let $\mathcal{A}_{c(\varphi_1)} = \langle 2^{AP \cup \{p\}}, Q_1, \delta_1, q_0^1, \alpha_1 \rangle$, and $\mathcal{A}_{\bar{c}(\varphi_2)} = \langle 2^{AP \cup \{q\}}, Q_2, \delta_2, q_0^2, \alpha_2 \rangle$ be the corresponding NBWs (per Theorem 3). We define the product $\mathcal{P}$ of S with $\mathcal{A}_{c(\varphi_1)}$ and $\mathcal{A}_{\bar{c}(\varphi_2)}$ as the colored Büchi graph of degree two. Thus, $\mathcal{P} = \langle \{p, q\}, S \times 2^{\{p,q\}} \times Q_1 \times Q_2, M, \langle s_0, \{p, q\}, q_0^1, q_0^2 \rangle, L, \{S \times 2^{\{p,q\}} \times \alpha_1 \times Q_2, S \times 2^{\{p,q\}} \times Q_1 \times \alpha_2\} \rangle$, where

$M(\langle s, c, q_1, q_2 \rangle, \langle s', c', q_1', q_2' \rangle)$ iff $\rho(s, s')$, $q_1' \in \delta_1(q_1, L(s) \cup (c \cap \{p\}))$, and $q_2' \in \delta_2(q_2, L(s) \cup (c \cap \{q\}))$. Finally, $L(\langle s, c, q_1, q_2 \rangle) = c$.

Theorem 9. *The specification $\langle \varphi_1 \rangle \mathcal{S} \langle \varphi_2 \rangle$ does not hold iff the product of $\mathcal{S}$ with $\mathcal{A}_{c(\varphi_1)}$ and $\mathcal{A}_{\overline{c}(\varphi_2)}$ is pumpable nonempty,*

As detailed in the full version, solving the nonemptiness of colored Büchi graphs of degree two requires a slight modification of the algorithms in Section 5; we have to add the requirement that every q-block includes more than one p-block. The complexities stay the same, NLOGSPACE-complete and in linear time. This, together with Theorems 3 and 9, imply the upper bound in the following theorem. The lower bound follows from the known lower bound for LTL.

Theorem 10. *The assume-guarantee model-checking problem for PROMPT-LTL is PSPACE-complete and can be solved in time exponential in the length of the formulas and linear in the size of the system.*

Remark 11. For LTL, fairness constraints about the system can be specified in the formula. Thus, checking that φ_2 holds in all computations that satisfy the fairness constraint φ_1 can be reduced to model checking $\varphi_1 \rightarrow \varphi_2$. A fairness assumption can also be specified in PROMPT-LTL. Here, however, one has to allow the fairness assumption and the specification to be satisfied with different bounds. Thus, fairness should be reduced to checking $\langle \varphi_1 \rangle \mathcal{S} \langle \varphi_2 \rangle$. $\square$

For two formulas φ_1 and φ_2, we say that φ_1 *implies* φ_2 iff for every system $\mathcal{S}$, if $\mathcal{S}$ satisfies φ_1, then it also satisfies φ_2. In the case of LTL, φ_1 implies φ_2 iff the formula $\varphi_1 \rightarrow \varphi_2$ is valid. In the case of PROMPT-LTL, φ_1 *implies* φ_2 iff $\langle \varphi_1 \rangle \mathcal{U} \langle \varphi_2 \rangle$, where $\mathcal{U}$ is the universal system (a clique over 2^{AP} that contains all traces over AP). Indeed, since for every system $\mathcal{S}$ we have that $\mathcal{S} \| \mathcal{U} = \mathcal{S}$, then $\langle \varphi_1 \rangle \mathcal{U} \langle \varphi_2 \rangle$ does not hold iff there is a system $\mathcal{S}$ such that if $\mathcal{S}$ satisfies φ_1 but $\mathcal{S} \not\models \varphi_2$. Since $\mathcal{U}$ is exponential in AP, and the PSPACE complexity of assume-guarantee model checking originates from an algorithm that is polynomial in the formulas and only logarithmic in the system, we have the following (the lower bound follows from the PSPACE hardness of LTL implication).

Theorem 12. *The implication problem for PROMPT-LTL is PSPACE-complete.*

7   Expressiveness

In this section we study expressiveness aspects of PROMPT-LTL. We show that a PROMPT-LTL formula φ has an equivalent LTL formula iff φ and $live(\varphi)$ are equivalent, thus the problem of deciding whether φ can be translated to LTL is PSPACE-complete. Since the semantics of PROMPT-LTL is defined with respect to a system, a natural question is whether we can translate PROMPT-LTL formulas to branching temporal logics. We show that indeed, all PROMPT-LTL formulas can be translated to the μ-calculus.

All our results refer to finite-state systems. Thus, we say that two formulas φ and φ' are equivalent iff for all finite systems $\mathcal{S}$, we have that $\mathcal{S} \models \varphi$ iff $\mathcal{S} \models \varphi'$.

Some PROMPT-LTL formulas φ are equivalent to the LTL formula $live(\varphi)$. For example, it is not hard to see that $\mathbf{F_p}r$ is equivalent to $\mathbf{F}r$, for an atomic proposition r. On the other hand, as demonstrated in Section 1, the PROMPT-LTL formula $\mathbf{F_p G}r$ is not equivalent to the LTL formula $\mathbf{FG}r$. Is $\mathbf{F_p G}q$ equivalent to another LTL formula? A negative answer follows from the fact that for every PROMPT-LTL formula φ, there is some LTL formula equivalent to φ iff φ is equivalent to $live(\varphi)$. Since the implication $live(\varphi) \rightarrow \varphi$ can be checked in PSPACE (the other direction is always valid), we have the following. The lower bound is proven by a reduction from LTL satisfiability.

Theorem 13. *Deciding whether a* PROMPT-LTL *formula has an equivalent LTL formula is PSPACE-complete.*

It is not hard to prove that the PROMPT-LTL formula $\mathbf{F_p G}q$ is equivalent to the CTL formula $\mathbf{AFAG}q$. Indeed, a system satisfies both formulas iff there is a bound $k \geq 0$ such that all the computations may visit a state in which q does not hold only in the first k positions. One may wonder whether this argument can be generalized, leading to a simple translation of PROMPT-LTL formulas to CTL * formulas: given a PROMPT-LTL formula φ, translate it to a CTL* formula φ' by (recursively) replacing all subformulas of the form $\mathbf{F_p}\theta$ by $\mathbf{FA}\theta$ (and adding an external $\mathbf{A}$). To see that the reduction does not hold in general, consider the PROMPT-LTL formula $\varphi = \mathbf{F_p}(\mathbf{X}q \vee \mathbf{G}q)$. While the system S from Figure 1 satisfies φ (with bound 3), the system S does not satisfy the CTL* formula $\varphi' = \mathbf{AFA}(\mathbf{X}q \vee \mathbf{G}q)$. The question whether PROMPT-LTL can be expressed in CTL* is open. On the other hand, the two-color technique can be used in order to translate a PROMPT-LTL formula over P to alternating parity tree automaton over the alphabet $2^{P \cup \{p\}}$, and then to the μ-calculus over P. Formally, we have the following.

Theorem 14. *Every* PROMPT-LTL *formula has an equivalent μ-calculus formula of exponential length.*

Acknowledgment. We thank the reviewers for many helpful comments.

References

1. Alur, R., Etessami, K., Torre, S.L., Peled, D.: Parametric temporal logic for model measuring. ACM ToCL 2(3), 388–407 (2001)
2. Alpern, B., Schneider, F.B.: Defining liveness. IPL 21, 181–185 (1985)
3. Biere, A., Artho, C., Schuppan, V.: Liveness checking as safety checking. In: Proc. 7th FMICS, ENTCS, vol. 66(2) (2002)
4. Beer, I., Ben-David, S., Geist, D., Gewirtzman, R., Yoeli, M.: Methodology and system for practical formal verification of reactive hardware. In: Dill, D.L. (ed.) CAV 1994. LNCS, vol. 818, pp. 182–193. Springer, Heidelberg (1994)
5. Bloem, R., Gabow, H.N., Somenzi, F.: An algorithm for strongly connected component analysis in $n \log n$ symbolic steps. In: Johnson, S.D., Hunt, Jr., W.A. (eds.) FMCAD 2000. LNCS, vol. 1954, pp. 37–54. Springer, Heidelberg (2000)
6. Büchi, J.R., Landweber, L.HG.: Solving sequential conditions by finite-state strategies. Trans. AMS 138, 295–311 (1969)
7. Eisner, C., Fisman, D.: A Practical Introduction to PSL. Springer, Heidelberg (2006)

8. Emerson, E.A., Lei, C.-L.: Efficient model checking in fragments of the propositional μ-calculus. In: Proc. 1st LICS, pp. 267–278 (1986)
9. Emerson, E.A., Mok, A.K., Sistla, A.P., Srinivasan, J.: Quantitative temporal reasoning. In: Clarke, E., Kurshan, R.P. (eds.) CAV 1990. LNCS, vol. 531, pp. 136–145. Springer, Heidelberg (1991)
10. Manna, Z., Pnueli, A.: The Temporal Logic of Reactive and Concurrent Systems: Specification. Springer, Berlin (1992)
11. Pnueli, A.: The temporal logic of programs. In: Proc. 18th FOCS, pp. 46–57 (1977)
12. Pnueli, A.: In: Transition from global to modular temporal reasoning about programs. Logics and Models of Concurrent Systems, vol. F-13 of NATO Advanced Summer Institutes, pp. 123–144 (1985)
13. Pnueli, A., Rosner, R.: On the synthesis of a reactive module. In: Proc. 16th POPL, pp. 179–190 (1989)
14. Tarjan, R.E.: Depth first search and linear graph algorithms. SIAM Journal of Computing 1(2), 146–160 (1972)
15. Vardi, M.Y.: Automata-theoretic model checking revisited. In: Cook, B., Podelski, A. (eds.) VMCAI 2007. LNCS, vol. 4349, pp. 137–150. Springer, Heidelberg (2007)
16. Vardi, M.Y., Wolper, P.: An automata-theoretic approach to automatic program verification. In: Proc. 1st LICS, pp. 332–344 (1986)
17. Vardi, M.Y., Wolper, P.: Reasoning about infinite computations. I&C 115(1), 1–37 (1994)

Automated Assumption Generation for Compositional Verification

Anubhav Gupta[1], Kenneth L. McMillan[1], and Zhaohui Fu[2]

[1] Cadence Berkeley Labs
[2] Department of Electrical Engineering, Princeton University

Abstract. We describe a method for computing an exact minimal automaton to act as an intermediate assertion in assume-guarantee reasoning, using a sampling approach and a Boolean satisfiability solver. For a set of synthetic benchmarks intended to mimic common situations in hardware verification, this is shown to be significantly more effective than earlier approximate methods based on Angluin's L* algorithm. For many of these benchmarks, this method also outperforms BDD-based model checking and interpolation-based model checking.

1 Introduction

Compositional verification is a promising approach for alleviating the state-explosion problem in model checking. This technique decomposes the verification task for the system into simpler verification problems for the individual components of the system. Consider a system M composed of two components M_1 and M_2, and a property P that needs to be verified on M. The *assume-guarantee* style for compositional verification uses the following inference rule:

$$\frac{\langle true \rangle \; M_1 \; \langle A \rangle \qquad \langle A \rangle \; M_2 \; \langle P \rangle}{\langle true \rangle \; M_1 \parallel M_2 \; \langle P \rangle} \tag{1}$$

This rule states that P can be verified on M by identifying an assumption A such that: A holds on M_1 in all environments and M_2 satisfies P in any environment that satisfies A. In a language-theoretic framework, we model a process as a regular language, specified by a finite automaton. Process composition is intersection of languages, and a process satisfies a property P when its intersection with $\mathcal{L}(\neg P)$ is empty. The above inference rule can thus be written as:

$$\frac{\mathcal{L}(M_1) \subseteq \mathcal{L}(A) \qquad \mathcal{L}(A) \cap \mathcal{L}(M_2) \cap \mathcal{L}(\neg P) = \emptyset}{\mathcal{L}(M_1) \cap \mathcal{L}(M_2) \cap \mathcal{L}(\neg P) = \emptyset} \tag{2}$$

Let us designate the intersection of $\mathcal{L}(M_2)$ and $\mathcal{L}(\neg P)$ as M_2'. The problem of constructing an assume-guarantee argument then amounts to finding an automaton A that separates $\mathcal{L}(M_1)$ and $\mathcal{L}(M_2')$, in the sense that $\mathcal{L}(A)$ accepts all the

W. Damm and H. Hermanns (Eds.): CAV 2007, LNCS 4590, pp. 420–432, 2007.

strings in $\mathcal{L}(M_1)$, but rejects all the strings in $\mathcal{L}(M_2')$. Clearly, we would like to find an automaton A with as few states as possible, to minimize the state-explosion problem in checking the antecedents of the assume-guarantee rule.

For deterministic automata, the problem of finding a minimum-state separating automaton is NP-complete. It is reducible to the problem of finding a minimal-state implementation of an Incomplete Deterministic Finite Automaton (IDFA), shown to be NP-complete by Pfleeger [Pfl73]. To avoid this complexity, Cobleigh et al. proposed a polynomial-time approximation method [CGP03] based on a modification of Angluin's L* algorithm [Ang87, RS89] for active learning of a regular language. The primary drawback of this approach is that there is no approximation bound; in the worst case, the algorithm will return the trivial solution $\mathcal{L}(M_1)$ as the separating language, and thus provide no benefit in terms of state space reduction that could not be obtained by simply minimizing M_1. Alur et al. [AMN05] have presented a symbolic implementation of this approach, which suffers from the same drawback. In fact, in our experiments with hardware verification problems, the L*-based approach failed to produce a state reduction for any of our benchmark problems.

In this paper, we argue that it may be worthwhile to solve the minimal separating automaton problem exactly. Since the overall verification problem is PSPACE-complete when M_1 and M_2' are expressed symbolically, there is no reason to require that the sub-problem of finding an intermediate assertion be solved in polynomial time. Moreover, the goal of assume-guarantee reasoning is a verification procedure with complexity proportional to $|M_1| + |M_2'|$ rather than $|M_1| \times |M_2'|$, where $|M|$ denotes the textual size of M. If this is achieved, it may not matter that the overall complexity is exponential in $|A|$, provided A is small.

With this rationale in mind, we present an exact approach to the minimal separating automaton problem, suited to assume-guarantee reasoning for hardware verification. We apply the sampling-based algorithm used by Pena and Oliveira [PO98] for the IDFA minimization problem. This algorithm iteratively generates sample strings in $\mathcal{L}(M_1)$ and $\mathcal{L}(M_2')$, computing at each step a minimal automaton consistent with the sample set. Finding a minimal automaton consistent with a set of labeled strings is itself an NP-complete problem [Gol78], and we solve it using a Boolean Satisfiability (SAT) solver. We use the sampling approach here because the standard techniques for solving the IDFA minimization problem [KVBSV97] require explicit state representation, which is not practical for hardware verification.

For hardware applications, we must also deal with the fact that the alphabet is exponential in the number of Boolean signals connecting M_1 and M_2'. This difficulty is also observed in L*-based approaches, where the number of queries is proportional to the size of the alphabet. We handle this problem by learning an automaton over a partial alphabet and generalizing to the full alphabet using Decision Tree Learning [Mit97] methods.

Using a collection of synthetic hardware benchmarks, we show that our approach is effective in producing exact minimal intermediate assertions in cases where the approximate L* approach yields no reduction. In some cases, our method also provides a substantial reduction in overall verification time compared to direct model checking using state-of-the-art methods.

2   Preliminaries

2.1   Deterministic Finite Automaton

Definition 1. *A* Deterministic Finite Automaton (DFA) *M is a tuple* $(S, \Sigma, s_0, \delta, F)$ *where: (1) S is a finite set of states, (2) Σ is a finite alphabet, (3) $\delta : S \times \Sigma \to S$ is a transition function, (4) $s_0 \in S$ is the initial state, and (5) $F \subseteq S$ is the set of accepting states.*

Definition 2. *An* Incomplete Deterministic Finite Automaton (IDFA) *M is a tuple* $(S, \Sigma, \delta, s_0, F, R)$ *where: (1) S is a finite set of states, (2) Σ is a finite alphabet, (3) $\delta : S \times \Sigma \to (S \cup \{\bot\})$ is a partial transition function, (4) $s_0 \in S$ is the initial state, (5) $F \subseteq S$ is the set of accepting states, and (6) $R \subseteq S$ is the set of rejecting states.*

Intuitively, an IDFA is incomplete because some states may not have outgoing transitions for the complete alphabet, and some states are neither accepting nor rejecting. If there is no transition from state s on symbol a then $\delta(s, a) = \bot$. For both DFA's and IDFA's we extend the transition function δ in the usual way to apply to strings. That is, if $\pi \in \Sigma^*$ and $a \in \Sigma$ then $\delta(s, \pi a) = \delta(\delta(s, \pi), a)$ when $\delta(s, \pi) \neq \bot$ and $\delta(s, \pi a) = \bot$ otherwise.

A string s is *accepted* by a DFA M if $\delta(s_0, s) \in F$, otherwise s is *rejected* by M. A string s is *accepted* by an IDFA if $\delta(q_0, s) \in F$. A string s is *rejected* by an IDFA M if $\delta(q_0, s) \in R$.

Given two languages $L_1, L_2 \subseteq \Sigma^*$, we will say that a DFA or IDFA *separates* L_1 and L_2 when it accepts all strings in L_1 and rejects all strings in L_2. A *minimal separating automaton* (MSA) for L_1 and L_2 is an automaton with minimal number of states separating L_1 and L_2 (we will apply this notion to either DFA's or IDFA's as the context warrants).

3   The L* Approach

For comparison purposes, we first describe the L*-based approximation method for learning separating automata [CGP03]. In the L* algorithm, a *learner* infers the minimal DFA A for an unknown regular language L by posing *queries* to a *teacher*. In a *membership* query, the learner provides a string π, and the teacher replies yes if $\pi \in L$ and no otherwise. In an *equivalence* query, the learner proposes an automaton A, and the teacher replies yes if $\mathcal{L}(A) = L$ and otherwise provides a counterexample. The counterexample may be positive (*i.e.*, a string in $L \setminus \mathcal{L}(A)$) or negative (*i.e.*, a string in $\mathcal{L}(A) \setminus L$). Angluin [Ang87] gave an algorithm for the learner that guarantees to discover A in a number of queries polynomial in the size of A.

Cobleigh et al. [CGP03] modified this procedure to learn a separating automaton for two languages L_1 and L_2. Their procedure differs from the L* algorithm in the responses provided by the teacher. In the case of an equivalence query, the teacher responds yes if A is a separating automaton for L_1 and L_2. Otherwise, it provides either a positive counterexample as a string in $L_1 \setminus \mathcal{L}(A)$ or a negative counterexample as a string in $L_2 \cap \mathcal{L}(A)$. To a membership query on a string π, the teacher responds yes if $\pi \in L_1$ and no if $\pi \in L_2$. If π is in neither L_1 nor L_2, the choice is arbitrary. Since the teacher does not know the minimal separating automaton, it cannot provide the correct answer, so it simply answers no. Thus, in effect, the teacher is asking the learner to learn L_1, but is willing to accept any guess that separates L_1 and L_2. Using Angluin's algorithm for the learner, we can show that the learned separating automaton A has no more states that the minimal automaton for L_1. This can, however, be arbitrarily larger than the minimal separating automaton.

As in Angluin's original algorithm, the number of queries is polynomial in the size of A, and in particular, the number of equivalence queries is at most the number of states in A. In the assume-guarantee application, $L_1 = \mathcal{L}(M_1)$ and $L_2 = \mathcal{L}(M_2')$. For hardware verification, M_1 and M_2' are Nondeterministic Finite Automata (NFA's) represented symbolically (the nondeterminism arising from hidden inputs and from the construction of the automaton for $\neg P$). Answering a membership query is therefore NP-complete (essentially a bounded model checking problem) while answer an equivalence query is PSPACE-complete (a symbolic model checking problem). Thus, in practice the execution time of the algorithm is singly exponential in $|M_1|$ and $|M_2'|$.

4   Solving the Minimal Separating Automaton Problem

To find an exact MSA for two languages L_1 and L_2, we will follow the general approach of Pena and Oliveira [PO98] for minimizing IDFA's. This is a learning approach that uses only equivalence queries. It relies on a subroutine that can compute a minimal DFA separating two *finite* sets of strings. Although Pena and Oliveira's work is limited to finite automata, the technique can be applied to *any* languages L_1 and L_2 that have a regular separator, even if L_1 and L_2 are themselves not regular.

The overall flow of our procedure for computing the MSA for two languages is shown in Algorithm 1. We maintain two sets of sample strings, $S_1 \subseteq L_1$ and $S_2 \subseteq L_2$. The main loop begins by computing a minimal DFA A that separates S_1 and S_2 (using the SAMPLEMSA algorithm described below). The learner then performs an equivalence query on A. If A separates L_1 and L_2, the procedure terminates. Otherwise, we obtain a counterexample string π from the teacher. If $\pi \in L_1$ (and consequently, $\pi \notin \mathcal{L}(A)$) we add π to S_1, else we add π to S_2. This procedure is repeated until an equivalence query succeeds. In the figure, we test first for a negative counterexample, and then for a positive counterexample. This order is arbitrary, and in practice we choose the order randomly for each query to avoid biasing the result towards L_1 or L_2.

Algorithm 1. Computing an MSA for two languages

LANGMSA (L_1, L_2)
1: $S_1 = \{\}$; $S_2 = \{\}$;
2: **while** (1) **do**
3:     Let A be an MSA for S_1 and S_2;
4:     **if** $L_1 \subseteq \mathcal{L}(A)$ **then**
5:         **if** $\mathcal{L}(A) \cap L_2 = \emptyset$ **then**
6:             **return** true; *(A separates L_1 and L_2, property holds)*
7:         **else**
8:             Let $\pi \in L_2$ and $\pi \in \mathcal{L}(A)$; *(negative counterexample)*
9:             **if** $\pi \in L_1$ **then**
10:                 **return** false; *(L_1 and L_2 are not disjoint, property fails)*
11:             **else**
12:                 $S_1 = S_1 \cup \{\pi\}$;
13:     **else**
14:         Let $\pi \in L_1$ and $\pi \notin A$; *(positive counterexample)*
15:         **if** $\pi \in L_2$ **then**
16:             **return** false; *(L_1 and L_2 are not disjoint, property fails)*
17:         **else**
18:             $S_2 = S_2 \cup \{\pi\}$;

The teacher in this procedure can be implemented using a model checker. That is, the checks $L_1 \subseteq \mathcal{L}(A)$ and $\mathcal{L}(A) \cap L_2 = \emptyset$ are model checking problems. In our application, L_1 and L_2 are the languages of symbolically represented NFA's, and we use symbolic model checking methods [McM93] to perform the checks (note that testing containment in $\mathcal{L}(A)$ requires complementing A, but this is straightforward since A is deterministic).

Theorem 1. *Let $L_1, L_2 \subseteq \Sigma^*$, for finite Σ. If L_1 and L_2 have a regular separator, then Algorithm LANGMSA terminates and outputs a minimal separating automaton for L_1 and L_2.*

Proof. Let A' be a minimal-state separating automaton for L_1 and L_2 with k states. Since $S_1 \subseteq L_1$ and $S_2 \subseteq L_2$, it follows that A' is also a separating automaton for S_1 and S_2. Thus, A has no more than k states (since it is a minimal separating automaton for S_1 and S_2). Thus, if the procedure terminates, A is a minimal separating automaton for L_1 and L_2. Moreover, there are finitely many DFA's over finite Σ with k states. At each iteration, one such automaton is ruled out as a separator of S_1 and S_2. Thus, the algorithm must terminate. $\square$

It now remains only to find an algorithm to compute a minimal separating automaton for the finite languages S_1 and S_2. This problem has been studied extensively, and is known to be NP-complete [Gol78]. To solve it, we will borrow from the approach of Oliveira and Silva [OS98].

Definition 3. *An IDFA $M = (S, \Sigma, s_0, \delta, F, R)$ is* tree-like *when the relation $\{(s_1, s_2) \in S^2 \mid \exists a.\ \delta(s_1, a) = s_2\}$ is a directed tree rooted at s_0.*

Given any two disjoint finite sets of strings S_1 and S_2, we can construct a tree-like IDFA that accepts S_1 and rejects S_2, which we will call $\text{TREESEP}(S_1, S_2)$.

Definition 4. *Let $S_1, S_2 \subseteq \Sigma^*$ be disjoint, finite languages. The tree-like separator $\text{TREESEP}(S_1, S_2)$ for S_1 and S_2 is the tree-like DFA $(S, \Sigma, s_0, \delta, F, R)$ where S is the set of prefixes of $S_1 \cup S_2$, s_0 is the empty string, $F = S_1$, $R = S_2$, and $\delta(\pi, a) = \pi a$ if $\pi a \in S$ else $\delta(\pi, a) = \perp$.*

Oliveira and Silva [OS98] showed that every IDFA A that separates S_1 and S_2 is homomorphic to $\text{TREESEP}(S_1, S_2)$ in a sense we will define. Thus, to find a separating automaton A of k states, we have only to guess a map from the states of $\text{TREESEP}(S_1, S_2)$ to the states of A and construct A accordingly. We will call this process *folding*.

Definition 5. *Let $M = (S, \Sigma, s_0, \delta, F, R)$ and $M' = (S', \Sigma, s_0', \delta', F', R')$ be two IDFA's over alphabet Σ. The map $\phi : S \to S'$ is a folding of M onto M' when :*

- *$\phi(s_0) = s_0'$,*
- *for all $s \in S$, $a \in \Sigma$, if $\delta(s, a) \neq \perp$ then $\delta'(\phi(s), a) = \phi(\delta(s, a))$,*
- *for all $s \in F$, $\phi(s) \in F'$, and*
- *for all $s \in R$, $\phi(s) \in R'$.*

The following lemma says that every separating IDFA for S_1 and S_2 can be obtained as a folding of the tree-like automaton $\text{TREESEP}(S_1, S_2)$. The map is easily obtained by induction over the tree.

Lemma 1 (Oliveira and Silva). *Let $T = (S, \Sigma, s_0, \delta, F, R)$ be a tree-like IDFA, with accepting set S_1 and rejecting set S_2. Then IDFA A over Σ is a separating automaton for S_1 and S_2 if and only if there exists a folding ϕ from T to A.*

Now we will show how to construct a folding of the tree T by partitioning its states. If Γ is a partition of a set S, we will denote by $[s]_\Gamma$ the element of Γ containing element s of S.

Definition 6. *Let $M = (S, \Sigma, s_0, \delta, F, R)$ be an IDFA over Σ. A consistent partition of M is a partition Γ of S such that*

- *for all $s, t \in S$, $a \in \Sigma$, if $\delta(s, a) \neq \perp$ and $\delta(t, a) \neq \perp$ and $[s]_\Gamma = [t]_\Gamma$ then $[\delta(s, a)]_\Gamma = [\delta(t, a)]_\Gamma$, and*
- *for all $s \in F$ and $t \in R$, $[s]_\Gamma \neq [t]_\Gamma$.*

Definition 7. *Let $M = (S, \Sigma, s_0, \delta, F, R)$ be an IDFA and let Γ be a consistent partition of S. The quotient M/Γ is the IDFA $(\Gamma, \Sigma, s_0', \delta', A', R')$ such that*

- *$s_0' = [s_0]_\Gamma$,*
- *$\delta'(s', a) = \sqcup\{\delta(s, a) \mid [s]_\Gamma = s'\}$,*
- *$F' = \{[s]_\Gamma \mid s \in F\}$, and*
- *$R' = \{[s]_\Gamma \mid s \in R\}$.*

In the above definition, $\sqcup$ represents the least upper bound in the lattice with partial order $\preceq$; containing the bottom element $\perp$, the top element $\top$ and the elements of S; such that for all $s, t \in S$ if $s \neq t$ then $s \not\preceq t$. Consistency guarantees that the least upper bound is never $\top$.

Theorem 2. *Let T be a tree-like IDFA with accepting set S_1 and rejecting set S_2. There exists an IDFA of k states separating S_1 and S_2 exactly when T has a consistent partition Γ of cardinality k. Moreover, T/Γ separates S_1 and S_2.*

Proof. Suppose Γ is a consistent partition of $S(T)$. It follows that the function ϕ mapping s to $[s]_\Gamma$ is a folding of T onto T/Γ. Thus, by the lemma, T/Γ is separates S_1 and S_2, and moreover it has k states. Conversely, suppose A is an IDFA of k states separating S_1 and S_2. By the lemma, there is a folding ϕ from T to A. By the definition of folding, the partition induced by ϕ is consistent and has (at most) k states.   □

According to this theorem, to find a minimal separating automaton for two disjoint finite sets S_1 and S_2, we have only to construct a corresponding tree-like automaton T, and then find the minimal consistent partition Γ of $S(T)$. The minimal automaton A is then T/Γ.

We use a SAT solver to find the minimal partition, using the following encoding of the problem of existence of a consistent partition of k states. Let $n = \lceil log_2 k \rceil$. For each state $s \in S(T)$, we introduce a vector of Boolean variables $\bar{v}_s = (v_s^0 \ldots v_s^{n-1})$. This represents the number of the partition to which s is assigned (and also the corresponding state of the quotient automaton). We then construct a set of Boolean constraints that guarantee that the partition is consistent. First, for each s, we must have $\bar{v}_s < k$ (expressed over the bits of $\bar{v}_s$). Then, for every pair of states s and t that have outgoing transitions on symbol a, we have a constraint $\bar{v}_s = \bar{v}_t \Rightarrow \bar{v}_{\delta(s,a)} = \bar{v}_{\delta(t,a)}$ (that is, the partition must respect the transition relation). Finally, for every pair of states $s \in F$ and $t \in R$, we have the constraint $\bar{v}_s \neq \bar{v}_t$ (that is, a rejecting state and an accepting state cannot be put in the same partition). We call this set of constraints $\textsc{SatEnc}(T)$. A truth assignment ψ satisfies $\textsc{SatEnc}(T)$ exactly when the partition $\Gamma = \{\Gamma_0, \ldots, \Gamma_{k-1}\}$ is a consistent partition of T where $\Gamma_i = \{s \in S \mid \bar{v}_s = i\}$. Thus, from a satisfying assignment, we can extract a consistent partition.

Algorithm 2 outlines our approach for computing a minimal separating automaton for two finite languages. Note that the quotient automaton T/Γ is an IDFA. We can convert this to a DFA by completing the partial transition function δ in any way we choose (for example, by making all the missing transitions go to a rejecting state), yielding an DFA that separates S_1 and S_2.

This completes the description of our LANGMSA procedure for computing an MSA for two languages L_1 and L_2. To find an intermediate assertion for assume-guarantee reasoning, we have only to compute an MSA for $\mathcal{L}(M_1)$ and $\mathcal{L}(M_2')$, using LANGMSA.

Let us now consider the overall complexity of assume-guarantee reasoning using the LANGMSA algorithm. We will assume that M_1 and M_2' are expressed symbolically as Boolean circuits with textual size $|M_1|$ and $|M_2'|$ respectively. The

---

Algorithm 2. Computing an MSA for two finite languages, using SAT encoding

SAMPLEMSA (S_1, S_2)
 1: Let $T = \text{TREESEP}(S_1, S_2)$;
 2: Let $k = 1$;
 3: **while** (1) **do**
 4:     **if** $\text{SATENC}(T)$ is satisfiable **then**
 5:         Let ψ be a satisfying assignment of $\text{SATENC}(T)$;
 6:         Let $\Gamma = \{\{s \in S(T) \mid \bar{v}_s = i\} \mid i \in 0 \ldots k - 1\}$;
 7:         Let $A = T/\Gamma$;
 8:         Extend $\delta(A)$ to a total function;
 9:         **return** DFA A
10:     Let $k = k + 1$;

---

number of states of these DFA's is then $O(2^{|M_1|})$ and $O(2^{|M_2'|})$ respectively. Let $|A|$ be the textual size of the MSA (note this is proportional to both the number of states and the size of Σ). Each iteration of the main loop involves solving the SAT problem $\text{SATENC}(T)$ and solving two model checking problems. The SAT problem can, in the worst case, be solved by enumerating all the possible DFA's of the given size, and thus is $O(2^{|A|})$. The model checking problems are $O(|A| \times 2^{|M_1|})$ and $O(|A| \times 2^{|M_2'|})$. The number of iterations is at most $2^{|A|}$, the number of possible automata, since each iteration rules out one automaton. Thus the overall run time is $O(2^{|A|}(2^{|A|} + |A| \times (2^{|M_1|} + 2^{|M_2'|})))$. This is singly exponential in $|A|$, $|M_1|$ and $|M_2'|$, but notably we do not incur the cost of computing the product of M_1 and M_2. Fixing the size of A, we have simply $O(2^{|M_1|} + 2^{|M_2'|})$.

Unfortunately, $|A|$ is worst-case exponential in $|M_1|$, since in the worst case we have $\mathcal{L}(A) = \mathcal{L}(M_1)$. This means that the overall complexity is doubly exponential in the input size. It may seem illogical to apply a doubly exponential algorithm to a PSPACE-complete problem. However, we will observe that in practice, if there is a small intermediate assertion, this approach can be more efficient than singly exponential approaches. In the case when the alphabet is large, however, we will need some way to compactly encode the transition function.

4.1 Optimizations

We use two optimizations to the above approach that effectively reduce the size of the search space when finding a consistent partition of T. First, we exploit the fact that $\mathcal{L}(M_1)$ is prefix closed in the case of hardware verification (on the other hand $\mathcal{L}(M_2')$ may not be prefix closed, since it includes the negation of the property P). This means that if string π is in the accepting set of T, we can assume that all its prefixes are accepted as well. This allows us to mark the ancestors of any accepting state of T as accepting, thus reducing the space of consistent partitions. In addition, since M_1 is prefix closed, it follows that there is a prefix closed intermediate assertion and we can limit our search to prefix closed languages. These languages can always be accepted by an automaton with a single rejecting state. Thus, we can group all the rejecting states into a single partition, again reducing the space of possible partitions.

Our second optimization is to compute the consistent partition incrementally. We note that each new sample obtained as a counterexample from the teacher adds one new branch to the tree T. In our first attempt to obtain a partition we restrict all the pre-existing states of T to be in the same partition as in the previous iteration. Only the partitions of the new states of T can be chosen. This forces us, if possible, to maintain the old behavior of the automaton A for all the pre-existing samples and to change only the behavior for the new sample. If this problem is infeasible, the restriction is removed and the algorithm proceeds as usual. Heuristically, this tends to reduce the SAT solver run time in finding a partition, and also tends to reduce the number of samples, perhaps because the structure of the automaton remains more stable.

5   Generalization with Decision Tree Learning

As mentioned earlier, in hardware verification, the size of the alphabet Σ is exponential in the number of Boolean signals passing between M_1 and M_2. This means that in practice the samples we obtain of $\mathcal{L}(M_1)$ and $\mathcal{L}(M_2')$ can contain only a minuscule fraction of the alphabet symbols. Thus, the IDFA A that we learn will also contain transitions for just a small fraction of Σ. We therefore need some way to generalize from this IDFA to a DFA over the full alphabet in a reasonable way. This is not a very well-defined problem. In some sense we would like to apply Occam's razor, inferring the "simplest" total transition function that is consistent with the partial transition function of the IDFA. There might be many ways to do this. For example, if the transition from a given state on symbol a is undefined in the IDFA, we could map it to the next state for the nearest defined symbol, according to some distance measure.

The approach we take here is to use decision tree learning methods to try to find the simplest generalization of the partial transition function as a decision tree. Given an alphabet symbol, the decision tree branches on the values of the Boolean variables that define the alphabet, and at its leaves gives the next state of the automaton. We would like to find the simplest decision tree expressing a total transition function consistent with the partial transition function of the IDFA. Put another way, we can think of the transition function of any state as a classifier, classifying the alphabet symbols according to which state they transition to. The partial transition function can be thought of as providing "samples" of this classification and we would like to find the simplest decision tree that is consistent with these samples. Intuitively, we expect the intermediate assertion to depend on only a small set of the signals exchanged between M_1 and M_2, thus we would like to bias the procedure toward transition functions that depend on few signals. To achieve this, we use the ID3 method for learning decision trees from examples [Qui86].

This allows us (line 8 of Algorithm 2) to generalize the IDFA to a symbolically represented DFA that represents a guess as to what the full separating language should be, based on the samples of the alphabet seen thus far. If this guess is incorrect, the teacher will produce a counterexample that refutes it, and thus refines the next guess.

6 Results

We have implemented our techniques on top of Cadence SMV [McM]. The user specifies a decomposition of the system into two components. We use Cadence SMV as our BDD-based model checker to verify the assumptions, and also as our incremental BMC engine to check whether counterexamples are real. We use an internally developed SAT solver. We implemented a variant of the ID3 [Qui86] algorithm to generate decision trees. We also implemented the L*-based approach (LSTAR) proposed by Cobleigh et al. [CGP03], using the optimized version of the L* algorithm suggested by Rivest and Schapire [RS89]. All out experiments were carried on a 3GHz Intel Xeon machine with 4GB memory, running Linux. We used a timeout of 1000s for our experiments. We compared our approach against LSTAR, and the Cadence SMV implementation of standard BDD-based model checking and interpolation-based model checking.

We generated two sets of benchmarks for our experiments. For all our benchmarks, the property is true and all the circuit elements are essential for proving the property. Therefore localization-based verification techniques will not be effective. These benchmark sets are representative of the following typical scenario. A component of the system is providing a service to the rest of the system. The system is feeding data into the component and is reading data from the component. The verification task is to ensure that the data flowing through the system is not corrupted. This property can be verified by using a very simple assumption about the component. The assumption essentially states that the component does not corrupt the data. For example: consider a processor and memory communicating over a bus. In order to prove the correctness of the behavior of the processor on some instruction sequence, the only assumption that the bus needs to satisfy is that it transfers that data correctly. Any buffering or arbitration that happens on the bus is irrelevant.

Each circuit in the first benchmark set consists of a sequence of 3 shift registers: R_1, R_2 and R_3, such that R_1 feeds into R_2 and R_2 feeds into R_3. The property that we want to prove is that we see some (fixed) symbol a at the output of R_3 only if it was observed at the input of R_1. We varied the lengths and widths of the shift registers. Our results are shown in Table 1. For the circuit $S\_m\_n\_o$, m is the width of the shift registers, n is the length of R_2, and o is the length of R_1 and R_3. In our decomposition, M_1 consists of R_2, and $M2$ consists of R_1 and R_2. We compare our approach against LSTAR. These benchmarks were trivial (almost 0s runtime) for BDD-based and interpolation-based model checking. For LSTAR, we report the total running time (Time), the number of states in the assumption DFA (States), and the number of membership queries

Table 1. Comparison of LANGMSA against LSTAR on simple shift register based benchmarks

Circuit	LSTAR			LANGMSA					
	Time(s)	States	Queries	Iter	MC(s)	Max(s)	Chk(s)	States	Time(s)
S_1_6_3	338.81	65	16703	9	0.28	0.04	0.00	3	0.35
S_1_8_4	_	80	25679	9	0.37	0.04	0.00	3	0.44
S_1_10_4	_	78	24413	9	0.28	0.04	0.00	3	0.37
S_2_6_3	_	45	32444	27	1.31	0.04	0.01	3	1.29
S_2_8_4	_	43	29626	27	1.56	0.08	0.01	3	1.77
S_2_10_4	_	41	26936	27	1.83	0.09	0.01	3	2.11
S_3_6_3	_	24	35350	91	5.46	0.09	0.03	3	7.48
S_3_8_4	_	22	30997	90	10.68	0.28	0.03	3	14.36
S_3_10_4	_	21	26899	90	21.39	0.69	0.04	3	27.23

(Queries). In case of a timeout, we report the number of states, and queries made, for the last generated DFA. For our approach, we report the number of model checking calls (Iter), time spent in model checking (MC), maximum time spent in a model checking run (Max), time spent in counterexample checks (Chk), number of states in the assumption DFA (States), and the total running time (Time). A '_' symbol indicates a timeout. On this benchmark set, our approach clearly outperforms LSTAR both in the total runtime and in the size of the assumption automaton. Our approach identifies the 3 state assumption, which says that a can be seen at the output of M_1 only if a has been inputted into M_1. LSTAR only terminates on S_1_6_3, where it learns the assumption of size 65, which is the same as M_1.

For the second benchmark set, we replaced the shift registers with circular buffers. We also allowed multiple parallel circular buffers in R_2. Our results are shown in Table 2. For the circuit C_m_n_o_p, m is the width of the circular buffers, n is the number of parallel buffers in R_2, o is the length of

Table 2. Comparison of LANGMSA against BDD-based model checking and LSTAR on circular buffer based benchmarks

Circuit	BDD	LSTAR		LANGMSA					
	Time(s)	States	Queries	Iter	MC(s)	Max(s)	Chk(s)	States	Time(s)
C_1_1_6_3	23.61	78	22481	29	2.09	0.17	0.05	3	2.42
C_1_1_8_4	198.36	78	22481	27	2.84	0.21	0.05	3	3.09
C_1_1_10_5	_	78	22481	33	3.99	0.42	0.89	3	4.41
C_1_2_6_3	_	57	16433	33	8.68	3.43	0.76	3	8.96
C_1_2_8_4	_	57	16433	26	531.92	521.89	0.05	3	532.14
C_2_1_6_3	_	30	26893	128	21.27	0.52	0.10	3	23.55
C_2_1_8_4	_	30	26893	102	25.62	3.21	0.06	3	26.48
C_2_1_10_5	_	30	26893	152	63.39	5.75	0.17	3	65.79
C_3_1_6_3	_	12	33802	427	569.50	19.90	0.23	3	622.15

the buffers in R_2, and p is the length of R_1 and R_3. We report the total running time (Time) of BDD-based model checking. LSTAR and interpolation-based model checking timed-out for all these benchmarks. On this benchmark set, our approach learns the smallest separating assumption and can scale to much larger designs compared to LSTAR, interpolation-based model checking and BDD-based model checking.

7 Conclusion and Future Work

We have presented an automated approach for assume-guarantee reasoning that generates the smallest assumption DFA. Our experiments indicate that this technique can outperform existing L*-based approaches for computing an assumption automaton that is not guaranteed to be minimal. For many of our benchmarks, our approach performed better than state-of-the-art non-compositional methods as well.

There are many directions for future research: (1) Our framework only uses equivalence queries. Can membership queries be used for enhancing our technique? (2) Can the performance of our algorithm be improved by imposing additional restrictions on the assumption? For example: if we assume that the assumption language is stuttering closed, it can prune out long repeating sequences from the counterexamples. (3) Which generalization techniques (besides decision tree learning) would be effective in out framework? (4) Can we learn a parallel composition of DFAs?

References

[AMN05]   Alur, R., Etessami, K., Torre, S.L., Peled, D.: Parametric temporal logic for model measuring. ACM ToCL 2(3), 388–407 (2001)

[Ang87]   Angluin, D.: Learning regular sets from queries and counterexamples. Information and Computation 75, 87–106 (1987)

[CGP03]   Cobleigh, J., Giannakopoulou, D., Pasareanu, C.: Learning assumptions for compositional verification. In: Garavel, H., Hatcliff, J. (eds.) ETAPS 2003 and TACAS 2003. LNCS, vol. 2619, Springer, Heidelberg (2003)

[Gol78]   Gold, E.M.: Complexity of automaton identification from given data. Information and Computation 37, 302–320 (1978)

[KVBSV97] Kam, T., Villa, T., Brayton, R., Sangiovanni-Vincentelli, A.L.: Synthesis of FSMs: Functional Optimization. Kluwer Academic Publishers, Dordrecht (1997)

[McM]   McMillan, K.L.: Cadence SMV. Cadence Berkeley Labs, CA

[McM93]   McMillan, K.L.: Symbolic Model Checking. Kluwer Academic Publishers, Boston (1993)

[Mit97]   Mitchell, T.M.: Machine Learning. WCB/McGraw-Hill, New York (1997)

[OS98]   Oliveira, A.L., Marques, J.P.: Efficient search techniques for the inference of minimum size finite automata. In: Arlindo, L. (ed.) Proceedings of the Symposium on String Processing and Information Retrieval (SPIRE), pp. 81–89 (1998)

[Pfl73]   Pfleeger, C.F.: State reduction in incompletely specified finite state machines. IEEE Transactions on Computers C-22, 1099–1102 (1973)

[PO98]   Pena, J.M., Oliveira, A.L.: A new algorithm for the reduction of incompletely specified finite state machines. In: Jorge, M. (ed.) Proceedings of the IEEE/ACM International Conference on Computer-Aided Design (ICCAD), pp. 482–489. ACM Press, New York, NY, USA (1998)

[Qui86]   J.R. Quinlan.: Induction of decision trees. Machine Learning (1986)

[RS89]   Rivest, R.L., Schapire, R.E.: Inference of finite automata using homing sequences. In: Proceedings of the ACM Symposium on Theory of Computing (STOC), pp. 411–420. ACM Press, New York, NY, USA (1989)

Abstraction and Counterexample-Guided Construction of ω-Automata for Model Checking of Step-Discrete Linear Hybrid Models*

Marc Segelken

OFFIS e.V.

Abstract. For the verification of reactive hybrid systems existing approaches do not scale well w.r.t. large discrete state spaces, since their excellence mostly applies to data computations. However, especially control dominated models of industrial relevance in which computations on continuous data are comprised only of subsidiary parts of the behavior, these large discrete state spaces are not uncommon. By exploiting typical characteristics of such models, the herein presented approach addresses step-discrete linear hybrid models with large discrete state spaces by introducing an iterative abstraction refinement approach based on learning reasons of spurious counterexamples in an ω-automaton. Due to the resulting exclusion of comprehensive classes of spurious counterexamples, the algorithm exhibits relatively few iterations to prove or disprove safety properties. The implemented algorithm was successfully applied to parts of industrial models and shows promising results.

Keywords: automata construction, counterexample guidance, iterative abstraction refinement, model-checking, step-discrete hybrid systems.

1 Introduction

For the analysis of discrete control systems, formal verification has already been successfully applied in recent years on industrial-sized controllers. However, the analysis of hybrid systems still represents a challenge, particularly with regard to controller models modeled and validated with CASE tools such as Statemate, Scade, Ascet and Simulink, which are typically open-loop discrete-time models combining a large discrete state space with a nontrivial number of floating point variables.

Among other approaches, a rich set of different abstraction techniques were developed for verifying hybrid models, transforming the inherently infinite state system into a finite-state model. The more sophisticated ones are usually based on iterative refinement techniques eliminating spurious counterexamples by refining the abstracted model for subsequent iterations, and by thus making the observed counterexample impossible to occur again in future runs. A prominent representative is, e.g., [CFH+03] where path fragments in the discrete state space are excluded. Other techniques limit the continuous dynamics to simple abstractions based on rectangular inclusions or polyhedrons such

---

* This research was partially supported by the German Research Foundation (DFG) under contract SFB/TR 14 AVACS, see www.avacs.org.

W. Damm and H. Hermanns (Eds.): CAV 2007, LNCS 4590, pp. 433–448, 2007.

Table 1. Open-loop industrial versus closed-loop academic models

Industrial models	discrete states	continuous variables *total/input/state*	regulation laws
Window lifting system (Ascet,BMW)	2^{26}	27/2/5	~ 60
Flight controller (Scade,Verilog)	2^{51}	423/7/25	~ 80
Desante, casts abstracted (Scade,Hispano-Suiza)	2^{1055}	358/14/0	8
Academic models			
Cruise Control System [SFHK04]	2^4	6/0/6	~ 24
Distributed Robot Control [AHH96]	2^9	12/0/12	< 1000
Mutual Exclusion example [ADI02]	2^6	3/0/3	~ 16

as in HYTECH [HH94], PHAVER [Fre05], Checkmate [SK00] or d/dt [ADM02]. Their typical target models are hybrid systems where the continuous computations dominate while the discrete part of the system is only in charge of distinguishing between different modes such that the system can react by, e.g., applying different continuous control laws. Consequently, the existing approaches reflect these characteristics by focusing on the continuous items only, not considering the discrete fragment as a problem.

However, as Table 1 shows, industrial hybrid models might comprise considerable discrete fragments as well. A huge number of discrete states is to be seen alongside of only few different applied regulation laws. This effect is inevitably connected to the usage of discrete timers, validation- and error counters, different clocks and especially the parallel composition of interacting subcomponents including discrete ones such as state machines or communication protocols, which every bigger model naturally consists of. Such industrial models require algorithms capable of large discrete systems as well, an aspect that has been neglected by most research activities.

The approach presented in the following deals with such models by exploiting the relatively small number of different regulation laws. This is done by applying an iterative abstraction refinement that eliminates a comprehensive class of counterexamples represented by the spurious one by generalizing regulation law violations, leading to a considerable amount of refinement in each step and keeping the overall number of iterations needed to confirm or reject a safety property quite small. Since many different traces are spurious for equal reasons being the same or similar continuous computation sequences only starting in different discrete states, this is possible by excluding these continuous computation sequences in general, not only single discrete path fragments. The abstraction technique is conservative, meaning that no property gets a wrong affirmative result. The procedure is a semi-decision one, i.e. it might fail to prove a property in a bounded number of iteration steps, whereas bounded counterexamples can always be found.

As shown schematically in Figure 1, the procedure starts with a simple abstraction, a discrete automaton A_0 having the same structure as the hybrid automaton H. In each iteration, the spurious counterexample is analyzed, and minimal infeasible subsets (conflicts) of the computation on continuous items being implied by the counterexamples projection on the concrete hybrid model are determined. These subsets are sequences of applied regulation laws consisting of conjunctions of formulas guarding and describing the continuous state space transformations of transitions. By incrementally

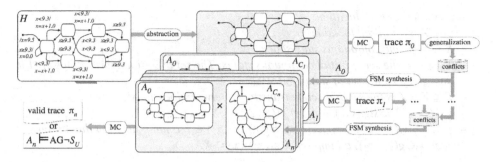

Fig. 1. Schematic overview on iterative refinement process

constructing a simple structured ω-automaton A_C with no fairness constraints that allows all runs except the ones containing any of the infeasible subsets detected so far, we get an automaton that prohibits all classes of known spurious counterexamples. With the parallel composition of $A_{C_{i+1}}$ being constructed based on the known conflicts in the ith step and A_0 being the starting point of the iteration, we get the automaton $A_{i+1} = A_{C_{i+1}} \times A_0$ to be checked in the next iteration. Thus, we directly refine only $A_{C_{i+1}}$ and create the parallel composition A_{i+1} in each step, refining the overall model A_{i+1} indirectly.

The presented technique called ω-CEGAR (Counter-example guided abstraction refinement) was developed and advanced in the industrial context of the SafeAir project [GGB+03], which motivated the specialization to the practically important step-discrete hybrid automata, i.e. classical automata controlling continuous state variables without time-continuous evolution, thus following the synchrony hypothesis. Such automata are modeled by industrially applied CASE-tools such as SCADE, STATEMATE, ASCET, SILDEX, etc., and the herein presented abstraction refinement approach has already been extended to these as well. The abstraction approach shows promising results in parts of industrial case studies.

The paper is organized as follows: In Section 2 some mathematical definitions are introduced. Section 3 describes in detail the basic approach of the abstraction refinement based on ω-automata construction, followed by Section 4 presenting an enhancement of the approach. After presenting experimental results and discussing related work in Section 5 the paper is concluded with Section 6.

2   Preliminaries

2.1   Step-Discrete Hybrid Automata

Models developed with the previously mentioned CASE tools follow the synchrony hypothesis and assume that all computations are instantaneous. Therefore we consider step-discrete hybrid systems in the following. The definitions in this section originate from [CFH+03] and were adapted to step-discrete systems accordingly.

Definition 1 (Step-discrete Hybrid Automaton). *A step-discrete hybrid automaton is a tuple* $H = (Z, z_0, X, X_0, T, g, j)$ *where*

- Z is a finite set of locations.
- $z_0 \in Z$ is an initial location.
- $X \subseteq \mathbb{R}^n$ is the continuous state space.
- $X_0 \subseteq X$ is the set of initial continuous states. The set of initial hybrid states of H is thus given by the set of states $\{z_0\} \times X_0$.
- $T \subseteq Z \times Z$ is the set of discrete transitions between locations[1].
- $g : T \to 2^X$ assigns a guard set $g((z_1, z_2)) \subseteq X$ to $(z_1, z_2) \in T$.
- $j : T \to (X \to 2^X)$ assigns to each pair $(z_1, z_2) \in T$ a jump function that assigns to each $x \in g((z_1, z_2))$ a jump set $j((z_1, z_2))(x) \subseteq X$.

We denote the set of all guard sets with $G = \{g(t) | t \in T\}$ and the set of all jump set functions with $J = \{j(t) | t \in T\}$. Note that both G and J are finite.

2.2 Semantics

The corresponding semantics is defined with the notion of transition systems:

Definition 2 (Transition System). *A* transition system *is a triple* $TS = (S, S_0, E)$ *with a (possibly infinite) state set* S, *an initial set* S_0 *and a set of transitions* $E \subseteq S \times S$. *We denote the set of all transition systems as* $\mathfrak{T}$.

Definition 3 (Path). *A* path π *of a transition system* $TS = (S, S_0, E)$ *is a (possibly finite) sequence* $(s_0, s_1, s_2, ...)$ *with* $s_0 \in S_0$, *each* $s_i \in S$ *and each pair of successive states* $(s_i, s_{i+1}) \in E$. *We denote the set of all paths of a transition system* TS *with* $\overrightarrow{TS} := \bigcup_{m \in \mathbb{N}} \{(s_0, s_1, s_2, ..., s_m) | s_0 \in S_0, s_i \in S, (s_i, s_{i+1}) \in E\}$.

During the iterative refinement itself only finite paths can occur as false negatives, since we restrict ourselves to safety properties. Thus infinite paths do not have to be considered in this paper.

Definition 4 (Semantics). *The* translational semantics *of a step-discrete hybrid automaton* H *is a transition system* $TS_H = (S, S_0, E)$ *with:*

- $S = Z \times X$ *being set of all hybrid states* (z, x) *of* H,
- $S_0 = \{z_0\} \times X_0$ *being the set of initial hybrid states and*
- $E = (Z \times X) \times (Z \times X)$ *being the set of transitions with* $((z_1, x_1), (z_2, x_2)) \in E$, *iff* $\exists (z_1, z_2) \in T : x_1 \in g((z_1, z_2)) \wedge x_2 \in j((z_1, z_2))(x_1)$.

2.3 Safety Properties

The presented procedure aims at the verification of safety properties, i.e. computes the reachability of a subset of states that are not considered safe. Let $S_U \subseteq S$ denote the unsafe states within a transition system $TS = (S, S_0, E)$. Then the model-checker has to compute whether

---

[1] For simplicity reasons, only one transition between two states is allowed. By doubling states, multiple transitions can easily be projected on such a restricted model.

- the system is safe w.r.t. S_U ($TS \models \mathbf{AG} \neg S_U$), formally $\not\exists \pi \in \overrightarrow{TS} : \pi = (s_0, \dots, s_m)$, $s_0 \in S_0, s_i \in S, s_m \in S_U$ or
- the system is unsafe w.r.t. S_U ($TS \not\models \mathbf{AG} \neg S_U$), formally $\exists \pi \in \overrightarrow{TS} : \pi = (s_0, \dots, s_m)$, $s_0 \in S_0, s_i \in S, s_m \in S_U$.

If the model-checker is able to find an answer, it is either a path π showing a simulation run leading to an unsafe state $s \in S_U$, or the confirmation of TS to be safe w.r.t. the unsafe states S_U.

2.4   Abstraction

We use abstraction to get a purely discrete model to be checked by a finite state model-checker. In general an abstraction of a transition system TS is a transition system A that allows at least as much behavior as TS:

Definition 5 (Abstraction). *A transition system $A = (\hat{S}, \hat{S}_0, \hat{E})$ is an* abstraction *of a system $TS = (S, S_0, E)$, denoted $A \geq TS$, iff there exists a relation $\alpha \subseteq S \times \hat{S}$ such that:*

- $\hat{S}_0 = \{\hat{s}_0 | \exists s_0 \in S_0 : (s_0, \hat{s}_0) \in \alpha\}$ *and*
- $\hat{E} = \{(\hat{s}_1, \hat{s}_2) | \exists s_1, s_2 \in S : (s_1, s_2) \in E \wedge \{(s_1, \hat{s}_1), (s_2, \hat{s}_2)\} \subseteq \alpha\}$

Lemma 1. *For a transition system TS and its abstraction A, formally $A \geq TS$, the following condition always holds, if $\forall s_0 \in s_0 : \exists \hat{s}_0 \in \hat{S}_0 : \alpha(s_0, \hat{s}_0)$:*

$$\forall \pi = (s_0, s_1, \dots, s_n) : \pi \in \overrightarrow{TS} \rightarrow \exists \hat{\pi} = (\hat{s}_0, \hat{s}_1, \dots, \hat{s}_n) \in \overrightarrow{A}, \forall_{0 \leq i \leq n}(s_i, \hat{s}_i) \in \alpha$$

This entails $A \models \mathbf{AG} \neg \hat{S}_U \implies TS \models \mathbf{AG} \neg S_U, \hat{S}_U = \{\hat{s} \in \hat{S} | \exists s \in S_U : (s, \hat{s}) \in \alpha\}$.

The previous lemma directly follows from the property of α. However, we cannot conclude $A \not\models \mathbf{AG} \neg \hat{S}_U \implies TS \not\models \mathbf{AG} \neg S_U$.

3   The ω-Automaton Based Iterative Abstraction Approach

3.1   Path Projection

During the analysis phase we need to retrieve the guard sets and jump set functions that are to be applied to the continuous state space if a path found in the abstract transition system is to be concretized. We achieve this by ensuring that any state $\hat{s} \in \hat{S}$ of our abstract transition system A can be projected to a discrete location $z \in Z$ of H by a function $\tilde{\alpha}^{-1} : \hat{S} \rightarrow Z$ which allows to reconstruct the transitions along with their associated guard- and jump set functions such that we can project paths of A to sequences of guard-/jump set function pairs.

Definition 6 (Guard-/Jump-set Sequence). *A guard-/jump-set sequence (abbrev. GJ-sequence) is defined by $((\gamma_0, \zeta_0), (\gamma_1, \zeta_1), \dots, (\gamma_n, \zeta_n)), \gamma_i \in G, \zeta_i \in J$. We denote the set of all finite guard-/jump-set sequences with $C = \bigcup_{n \in \mathbb{N}} (G \times J)^n$.*

Definition 7 (Projecting Paths to GJ-sequences). *From a path $\hat{\pi} = (\hat{s}_0, ..., \hat{s}_n)$ of $A = (\hat{S}, \hat{s}_0, \hat{T})$ derived from TS_H by an abstraction relation α we compute the underlying GJ-sequence $c \in C$ with $\theta : \overrightarrow{A} \to C$:*

$$c = \theta(\hat{\pi}) = ((\gamma_1, \zeta_1), ..., (\gamma_n, \zeta_n)) \text{ with}$$
$$\gamma_i = g(t_i), \zeta_i = j(t_i), t_i = \tilde{\alpha}^{-1}((\hat{s}_i, \hat{s}_{i+1})) := (\tilde{\alpha}^{-1}(\hat{s}_i), \tilde{\alpha}^{-1}(\hat{s}_{i+1}))$$

In the following we refine the iterative abstraction process in Figure 1.

3.2   Initial Abstraction

Definition 8 (Initial Abstraction α_0). *The* initial abstraction $A_0 = (\hat{Z}, \hat{z}_0, \hat{E})$ *of TS_H of H with $\hat{Z} \cong Z$, $\hat{z}_0 \cong z_0$ and $\hat{E} \cong T$ is defined by a function $\alpha_0 : S \to \hat{Z}$ such that for any state $z_k \in Z$ there exists a state $\hat{z}_k \in \hat{Z}$ with*

$$\alpha_0((z_k, x)) = \hat{z}_k$$

The structure of transition system A_0 is isomorphic to the structure of H w.r.t. discrete locations and transitions while any conditions or operations on the continuous state space are omitted. Trivially by definition of A_0, $A_0 \succeq TS_H$.

Now A_0 can be analyzed by any standard model checker such as the *vis* model-checker [RGA+96] in our case, to check if a given safety property as defined in Section 2.3 is fulfilled. If no bad state in $\hat{S}_U$ is reachable we can conclude that also in TS_H no bad state in S_U is reachable, according to Lemma 1. Otherwise if we get a path $\hat{\pi}$, we proceed with the following analysis phase.

3.3   Analyzing Counterexamples

Given a path $\hat{\pi}$ we need to analyze whether it is a valid or a spurious counterexample and in the latter case we need to refine our transition system.

For this analysis, we first convert $\hat{\pi} = (\hat{z}_0, \hat{z}_1, ..., \hat{z}_n)$ into a guard-/jump-set sequence $c = \theta(\hat{\pi}) = ((\gamma_1, \zeta_1), ..., (\gamma_n, \zeta_n))$, which describes the step-wise transformations on the initial continuous state space X_0. Following the semantical definition of TS_H in Definition 4, the alternating application of an intersection with guard set γ_i and a transformation by jump set ζ_i on the state space X_i in the ith step leads to a sequence $X_{seq} = (X_0, X_1, ..., X_n) \in 2^{X^{n+1}}$ of continuous state spaces with $X_i = \{x' | \exists x \in (X_{i-1} \cap \gamma_i) \wedge x' \in \zeta_i(x)\}$. If $X_n \neq \emptyset$ then $\exists(x_0, x_1, ..., x_n), x_i \in X_i$ and consequently there exists also a complying trace $\pi \in \overrightarrow{TS_H}$ with $\pi = ((\tilde{\alpha}^{-1}(\hat{z}_0), x_0), (\tilde{\alpha}^{-1}(\hat{z}_1), x_1), ..., (\tilde{\alpha}^{-1}(\hat{z}_n), x_n))$ representing a valid counterexample. For subsequent reuse we define the function $\mathcal{L} : C \times 2^X \to 2^X$ to compute X_n for a GJ-sequence c of length n and an initial continuous state space $\tilde{X}$ according to the previous explanation.

In practice we use the solver lp_solve [BEN04] to implement $\mathcal{L}' : C \times 2^X \to \mathbb{B}$ that computes whether $\exists(x_0, x_1, ..., x_n) \in X^{n+1}, x_0 \in X_0, x_1 \in X_1, ..., x_n \in X_n, (X_0, X_1, ..., X_n) = X_{seq}$ and the function $\tilde{\mathcal{L}}' : C \times 2^X \to \mathbb{B} \times X^{n+1}$ to include the discovered solution vector in the results as well. This is the point where we restrict ourselves to linear Hybrid Systems. However instead we could use e.g. flow-pipe approximation approaches to

---

Algorithm 1. $r: C \to 2^C \times 2^C$. Computing reduced conflict sets $C_{\hat{n}}$ and $C_{\hat{n}}$ from a conflict $c_\perp = ((\gamma_0, \zeta_0), \ldots, (\gamma_n, \zeta_n))$.

$(i, k, C_{\hat{n}}, C_{\hat{n}}) := (0, 0, \emptyset, \emptyset)$
while $C_{\hat{n}} \cup C_{\hat{n}} = \emptyset$ **do**
    while $i + k \leq n$ **do**
        if $i = 0 \wedge \mathcal{L}'(((\gamma_0, \zeta_0), \ldots, (\gamma_{i+k}, \zeta_{i+k})), X_0) = false$ **then**
            $C_{\hat{n}} := C_{\hat{n}} \cup \{((\gamma_0, \zeta_0), \ldots, (\gamma_{i+k}, \zeta_{i+k}))\}$
        if $i > 0 \wedge \mathcal{L}'(((\gamma_0, \zeta_0), \ldots, (\gamma_{i+k}, \zeta_{i+k})), X) = false$ **then**
            $C_{\hat{n}} := C_{\hat{n}} \cup \{((\gamma_i, \zeta_i), \ldots, (\gamma_{i+k}, \zeta_{i+k}))\}$
        $i := i + 1$
    end
    if $C_{\hat{n}} \cup C_{\hat{n}} = \emptyset$ **then** $k := k + 1, i := 0$
end
return $(C_{\hat{n}}, C_{\hat{n}})$ % $r_{\hat{n}}: C \to 2^C$ returns $C_{\hat{n}}$, $r_{\hat{n}}: C \to 2^C$ returns $C_{\hat{n}}$

---

address non-linear models as well, without any other impact on the herein presented approach.

If $\hat{\pi}$ was a spurious counterexample indicated by $\mathcal{L}(\theta(\hat{\pi}), X_0) = \emptyset$, we extract conflicts from it as a basis for refining A through A_C as shown in Figure 1.

Definition 9 (Conflict). *A conflict $c_\perp$ is a GJ-sequence with $\mathcal{L}(c_\perp, \tilde{X}) = \emptyset, \tilde{X} \subseteq X$. If $\tilde{X} = X$ the conflict is termed invariant, if $\tilde{X} = X_0$ the conflict is termed initial.*

To get more comprehensive classes of conflicts, the shortest guard-/jump-set sequences still being initial or invariant conflicts are isolated by a reduction function $r: C \to 2^C \times 2^C$ defined by Algorithm 1, resulting in a pair of initial and invariant conflict sets.

3.4 Consideration of Refinement Strategy

As mentioned in the introduction, we construct an automaton A_C to be combined with A_0 in order to rule out comprehensive classes of all previously detected initial and invariant conflicts, $C_{\perp \hat{n}}$ and $C_{\perp \hat{n}}$, with

$$A_C \models \neg \left(\bigvee_{c_i \in C_{\perp \hat{n}}} \lambda(c_i) \right) \wedge \neg \mathbf{F} \left(\bigvee_{c_v \in C_{\perp \hat{n}}} \lambda(c_v) \right) \tag{1}$$

with λ generating the LTL-Formula $\lambda(c) = ((\gamma_0, \zeta_0) \wedge \mathbf{X}((\gamma_1, \zeta_1) \wedge \mathbf{X}(\ldots \wedge \mathbf{X}(\gamma_n, \zeta_n))))$ for a conflict $c = ((\gamma_0, \zeta_0), (\gamma_1, \zeta_1), \ldots, (\gamma_n, \zeta_n))$, using $(\gamma_i, \zeta_i) \in G \times J$ as atomic names of characters of an alphabet $\Sigma = G \times J$.

Due to the important observation that for industrial models, guard-/jump-set sequences associated with a path $\hat{\pi}$ and even more so smallest parts of them are replicated multiple times on other paths as well, this approach is reasonable. For a hybrid system dominated by discrete transitions, we have a huge state space with only few different guard-/jump-set pairs constituting the regulation laws replicated all over the transition system, formally:

$$\{(g(t), j(t)) | t \in T\} | \ll |Z| \lesssim |T| \tag{2}$$

Table 1 shows the relationship between the amount of states[2] and guard-/jump-set pairs (regulation laws) for some examples. For the industrial models the number of pairs was determined empirically by observed occurrences in simulation runs and iterative refinements. This property of control dominated systems in practice is fundamental for the presented approach in this paper and is exploited extensively by ruling out all replications of conflicting guard-/jump-set sequences in the abstract model in one sweep.

3.5   Construction of ω-Automaton

To construct an ω-automaton A_C satisfying (1) we could apply existing LTL-to-Bchi translation algorithm such as [SB00]. However, since our formulas have a special structure, we can apply a dedicated incremental algorithm generating a very small co-1-accepting ω-automaton. As table 2 shows later, such a dedicated algorithm is much more efficient and generates significant smaller automata.

We apply the following algorithm for constructing an ω- and a regular automaton A_{C_ω} and A_{C_R} addressing invariant and initial conflicts each and compose the final ω-automaton A_C of both of them afterwards.

The ω-automaton is a Bchi automaton $\mathcal{A}_{C_\omega} = (Q_\omega, q_{\omega_0}, \Sigma, T_\omega, F_\omega) \in \mathfrak{B}$, with Q_ω being the set of states, q_{ω_0} being the initial state, $\Sigma = G \times J$ consisting of all guard-/jump set function pairs, $T_\omega \subseteq Q_\omega \times \Sigma \times Q_\omega$ being the transition relation and $F_\omega \subseteq Q_\omega$ being the set of accepting states. The regular $\mathcal{A}_{C_R} = (Q_R, q_{R_0}, \Sigma, T_R, F_R) \in \mathfrak{R}$ is a similar tuple, applying the classical acceptance condition for final words.

During construction, the automaton will have non-deterministic auxiliary transitions required to inherit transitions from other states tracking shorter words with matching prefixes. To identify such transitions a partial order $<$ on states is introduced based on a distance-to-default-state metrics. Such information can be efficiently locally computed and maintained for each state throughout construction. Based on such information we define the function $tgt : Q \times \Sigma \to Q$ to return the most distant state q reachable by a transition (p, δ, q) for a given δ.

Starting with the automaton $A_{C_\omega} = (\{q_0\}, q_0, \Sigma, \{(q_0, \delta, q_0) | \delta \in \Sigma\}, \{q_0\})$ with the default state q_0 accepting any infinite word, Algorithm 2 is used to incrementally add finite words $(\delta_0, \delta_1, \ldots, \delta_n)$ such that $A_{C_\omega} \models \neg \mathbf{F}(\delta_0 \wedge \mathbf{X}(\delta_1 \wedge \mathbf{X}(\cdots \wedge \mathbf{X}\delta_n)))$.

After all sequences have been added, auxiliary transitions are removed by a function $strip : \mathfrak{B} \to \mathfrak{B}$, keeping only the transitions $\{(p, \delta, q) \in T | q = tgt(p, \delta)\}$.

Finally, the automaton is efficiently minimized by Algorithm 3. The size of this ω-automaton is not monotonically increasing since adding conflicts might enable new minimization possibilities leading even to reduction. An extension of the algorithm not being described in detail due to space constraints exploits this observation by probing potential sequences that would have such a benefit. If confirmed as conflicts, they are added to the automaton as well, reducing its size while covering more conflicts at the same time.

---

[2] Since guard-/jump-set pairs are replicated over transitions and not states, statistics on transitions would have been more accurate, but are not accessible for technical reasons. However since the number of transitions always outnumbers the number of (reachable) states, the latter is a safe lower bound.

Algorithm 2. $Add_\omega : \mathfrak{B} \times \Sigma^* \to \mathfrak{B}$. Adding $(\delta_0, \delta_1, \ldots, \delta_n)$ to $A_{C_\omega} = (Q, q_0, \Sigma, T, F)$

$p := q_0$
for $0 \leq i \leq n$ **do**
  $q := \mathit{tgt}(p, \delta_i)$
  if $p < q \vee q \notin F$ **then**
    $p := q$
  else
    $Q := Q \cup \{q'\}$ with q' being a new state
    $H_p := \{h | \exists p' \in Q, \delta \in \Sigma : \{(p', \delta, p), (p', \delta, h)\} \subseteq T, p < h\}$
    $L_{q'} := \{l | (p, \delta_i, l) \in T, l < q'\}$
    $T := T \cup \bigcup_{h \in H_p \cup \{p\}} \{(h, \delta_i, q')\} \cup \bigcup_{l \in L_{q'}} \{(q', \delta, r) | \exists (l, \delta, r) \in T\}$
    if $i \neq n$ **then** $F := F \cup \{q'\}$
    $p := q'$
end
return (Q, q_0, Σ, T, F)

Algorithm 3. Minimization of regular- and ω-automaton (Q, q_0, Σ, T, F)

$M := \{Q \backslash F\}$
foreach $M_k \in M$ **do**
  foreach $q_i, q_j \in M_k, q_i \neq q_k$ **do**
    if $\forall p \in Q, \delta \in \Sigma : \exists (q_i, \delta, p) \in T \Leftrightarrow \exists (q_j, \delta, p) \in T$ **then**
      $T := T \cup \{(p, \delta, q_i) | \exists (p, \delta, q_j) \in T\}$
      $T := T \backslash (\{(p, \delta, q_j) \in T\} \cup \{(q_j, \delta, p) \in T\})$
      $F := F \backslash \{q_j\}$
      $Q := Q \backslash \{q_j\}$
      $M := (M \backslash \{M_k\}) \cup \{p | \exists \delta \in \Sigma : (p, \delta, q_i) \in T\}$
  end
end
return $(Q, \{q_0\}, \Sigma, T, F)$

The regular automaton for conflicts of $C_{\downarrow ri}$ is constructed with a similar algorithm $Add_R : \mathfrak{R} \times \Sigma^* \to \mathfrak{R}$ by starting from $A_{C_R} = (\{q_0, \mathit{fin}\}, q_0, \Sigma, \{(q_0, \delta, \mathit{fin}) | \delta \in \Sigma\}, \{q_0, \mathit{fin}\})$, using $T := (T \backslash \{(p, \delta_i, \mathit{fin})\}) \cup \{(p, \delta_i, q)\} \cup \{(p, \delta, \mathit{fin}) | \delta \in \Sigma \backslash \{\delta_i\} \wedge \nexists (p, \delta, r) \in T\}$ as transitions computation, making the auxiliary sets H_p and $L_{q'}$ obsolete.

Cross Product. Both automata A_{C_R} and A_{C_ω} are composed in parallel to a cross-product automaton $A_C = (Q, q_0, \Sigma, T_C, F)$ with $Q = Q_R \times Q_\omega$, $q_0 = (q_{R_0}, q_{\omega_0})$, $F = F_R \times F_\omega$ and $T_C = \{((q_{R_1}, q_{\omega_1}), \sigma, (q_{R_2}, q_{\omega_2})) | (q_{R_1}, \sigma, q_{R_2}) \in T_R, (q_{\omega_1}, \sigma, q_{\omega_2}) \in T_\omega\}$, which is the basis for the final composition of A.

Consideration of Partitioning. The partitioning $\mathfrak{P} = \{X_{q_1}, \ldots, X_{q_n}\} \subseteq 2^X$ of the continuous state space X can be envisioned as $n = |Q|$ partitions induced by the states Q of A_C. Let C_q be the set of all GJ-sequences leading to state $q = (q_R, q_\omega) \in Q$. Then each partition $X_q \in \mathfrak{P}$ is described by $\chi : Q \to X$ with

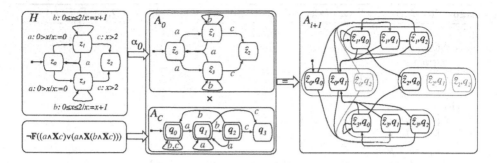

Fig. 2. Simplified example of abstraction refinement. Given an unsafe state z_2, the counterexamples $\hat{\pi} = (\hat{z}_0, \hat{z}_1, \hat{z}_2)$ and $\hat{\pi} = (\hat{z}_0, \hat{z}_1, \hat{z}_1, \hat{z}_2)$ are ruled out in A_{i+1} starting from $(\hat{z}_0, q_0)$. A_C is the conflict Büchi automaton, $A_C \models \neg\mathbf{F}((a \wedge \mathbf{X}c) \vee (a \wedge \mathbf{X}(b \wedge \mathbf{X}c)))$, with $a = (\{x|0 > x\}, x \mapsto 0), b = (\{x|0 \le x \le 2\}, x \mapsto x + 1), c = (\{x|x > 2\}, x \mapsto x)$.

$$\chi(q) = \begin{cases} \bigcup_{c \in C_q} \mathcal{L}(c, X_0) & \text{if } q_R \ne \textit{fin} \\ \bigcup_{c \in C_q} \mathcal{L}(c, X) & \text{if } q_R = \textit{fin} \end{cases}$$

Proof: Let H_C be the isomorphic mapping of A_C to a step-discrete Hybrid automaton. Then its semantics is a transition system TS_{H_C} with states $Q \times X$. It is obvious that any path in TS_{H_C} leading to a state $(q, x) \in Q \times X$ entails a GJ-sequence $c \in C_q$. Since $\mathcal{L}$ was derived from the translational semantics, by its definition $X_q = \mathcal{L}(c, X)$ describes exactly the set of reachable continuous states X_q such that $(q, x), x \in X_q$.

3.6   Refinement of A_{i+1}

For equation (1) to be valid not only for A_{C_j} but also for A_j, we compose $A_0 = (\hat{Z}, \hat{Z}_0, \hat{E})$ and A_{C_j} in parallel by using a cross-product-similar combination of both: $\dot\times : \mathfrak{T} \times \mathfrak{B} \to \mathfrak{T}$ such that $A = A_0 \dot\times A_C = (\hat{S}, \hat{S}_0, \hat{T})$ with

- $\hat{S} = \hat{Z} \times Q$
- $\hat{S}_0 = \hat{Z}_0 \times \{q_0\}$
- $\hat{T} = \{((\hat{z}_1, q_1), (\hat{z}_2, q_2))|(\hat{z}_1, \hat{z}_2) \in \hat{E} \wedge (q_1, \sigma, q_2) \in T_C \wedge \exists t \in T : t = \tilde{\alpha}^{-1}((\hat{z}_1, \hat{z}_2)) \wedge \sigma = (g(t), j(t)) \wedge q_2 \in F\}$

Algorithm 4 summarizes all previously detailed steps, and Figure 2 shows a very simple example of the abstraction refinement for one iteration.

With the previous construction approach for a state $(z, x) \in Z \times X = S$ of the infinite state space of the trace transition system TS_H of H and a state $(\hat{z}, q) \in \hat{Z} \times Q = \hat{S}$ of A_j the *general abstraction* relation α is given by

$$\alpha = \{((z, x), (\hat{z}, q)) \in (Z \times X) \times (\hat{Z} \times Q)|\tilde{\alpha}^{-1}(\hat{z}) = z \wedge x \in \chi(q)\}$$

This follows directly from the construction of A_j and the partitioning χ. It is obvious that this relation fulfills Definition 5, thus $A_j \ge TS_H$.

Algorithm 4. ω-CEGAR process, returns *true* or path $\pi = (s_0, \ldots, s_n) \in \overrightarrow{TS_H}, s_n \in S_U$

$A_{C_R} := (\{q_0, \mathit{fin}\}, q_0, \Sigma, \{(q_0, \delta, \mathit{fin}) | \delta \in \Sigma\}, \{q_0, \mathit{fin}\})$

$A_{C_\omega} := (\{q_0\}, q_0, \Sigma, \{(q_0, \delta, q_0) | \delta \in \Sigma\}, \{q_0\})$

$A := A_0$

while $A \not\models \mathbf{AG}\neg\hat{S}_U$ **do**   % Model-Checker run

    $\hat{\pi} = (\hat{z}_0, \hat{z}_1, \ldots, \hat{z}_n), \hat{z}_n \in \hat{S}_U$ % Path from Model-Checker

    $(result, (x_0, x_1, \ldots, x_n)) := \tilde{\mathcal{L}}'(\theta(\hat{\pi}), X_0)$

    if $result = false$ **then**   % spurious counterexample

        foreach $c_\perp \in r_{\mathit{fin}}(\theta(\hat{\pi}))$ **do** $A_{C_R} := Add_R(A_{C_R}, c_\perp)$ **end**

        foreach $c_\perp \in r_{\mathit{inv}}(\theta(\hat{\pi}))$ **do** $A_{C_\omega} := Add_\omega(A_{C_\omega}, c_\perp)$ **end**

        $A := (Minimize(strip(A_{C_R})) \times Minimize(strip(A_{C_\omega}))) \dot{\times} A_0$

    else return $\pi := ((\tilde{\alpha}^{-1}(\hat{z}_0), x_0), (\tilde{\alpha}^{-1}(\hat{z}_1), x_1), \ldots, (\tilde{\alpha}^{-1}(\hat{z}_n), x_n))$ % valid path

end

return *true*   % $TS_H \models \mathbf{AG}\neg S_U$

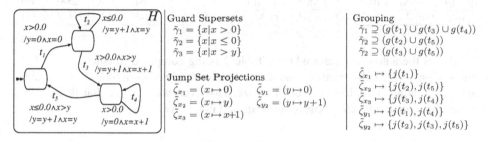

Guard Supersets	Grouping
$\tilde{\gamma}_1 = \{x \| x > 0\}$	$\tilde{\gamma}_1 \supseteq (g(t_1) \cup g(t_3) \cup g(t_4))$
$\tilde{\gamma}_2 = \{x \| x \leq 0\}$	$\tilde{\gamma}_2 \supseteq (g(t_2) \cup g(t_5))$
$\tilde{\gamma}_3 = \{x \| x > y\}$	$\tilde{\gamma}_2 \supseteq (g(t_3) \cup g(t_5))$

Jump Set Projections		
$\tilde{\zeta}_{x_1} = (x \mapsto 0)$	$\tilde{\zeta}_{y_1} = (y \mapsto 0)$	$\tilde{\zeta}_{x_1} \mapsto \{j(t_1)\}$
$\tilde{\zeta}_{x_2} = (x \mapsto y)$	$\tilde{\zeta}_{y_2} = (y \mapsto y+1)$	$\tilde{\zeta}_{x_2} \mapsto \{j(t_2), j(t_5)\}$
$\tilde{\zeta}_{x_3} = (x \mapsto x+1)$		$\tilde{\zeta}_{x_3} \mapsto \{j(t_3), j(t_4)\}$
		$\tilde{\zeta}_{y_1} \mapsto \{j(t_1), j(t_4)\}$
		$\tilde{\zeta}_{y_2} \mapsto \{j(t_2), j(t_3), j(t_5)\}$

Fig. 3. Simple example for syntactic creation of guard supersets and and jump set projections

4 Further Generalization of Conflicts

By using subsets $(\tilde{\gamma}, \tilde{\zeta}) \in \Sigma' \subseteq 2^{G \times J}$ instead of elements $(\gamma, \zeta) \in \Sigma \subseteq G \times J$, we can generalize conflicts having common reasons. Different guard sets $\gamma_1, \ldots, \gamma_m$ are subsumed by guard supersets $\tilde{\gamma}$ such that $\tilde{\gamma} \supseteq (\gamma_1 \cup \cdots \cup \gamma_m)$. Jump sets ζ are generalized by their projection $\tilde{\zeta}$ on fewer or single dimensions. Such $\tilde{\zeta}$ comprise all $\zeta_1, \ldots, \zeta_k$ having the same projection. As the example in figure 3 shows, reasonable guard supersets and jump set projections can even be computed syntactically.

With a function r extended accordingly to further generalize the conflicts with the introduction of $(\tilde{\gamma}, \tilde{\zeta})$ characters as described above, this generalization leads to dramatically reduced iteration numbers, since many similar conflicts are now comprised by one single sequence of sets of guard-/jump sets.

With the previously described construction of A_C, this automaton is no longer deterministic, since each (γ, ζ) might map to several of the sets described above. We determine it with a transformation intuitively considering A_C as a directed graph with attributed edges with a new operational semantics where each node $q_j \in Q = \{q_0, q_1, \ldots, q_n\}$ represents a boolean variable $b_j \in \mathbb{B}$ being computed by a function $b^* : \{0, \ldots, n\} \times \Sigma \times \mathbb{B}^n \to \mathbb{B}$ with

$$b^*(j, \delta, (b_0, b_1, \ldots, b_n)) = \begin{cases} 1 & \text{iff } j = 0 \\ \bigvee_{q_i \in Q:(q_i, \delta', q_j) \in T, [q_j] = j, \delta \in \delta', q_i < q_j} b_{[q_i]} & \text{iff } j > 0 \end{cases}$$

using a function $[] : Q \to \mathbb{N}$ with $[q_i] = i$. Thus we use the structure of $A_C = (Q, q_0, \Sigma, T, F)$ to create a deterministic automaton A_C^* such that $A_C^* = (Q^*, q_0^*, \Sigma, T^*, F^*)$ with $Q^* = \{(1, b_1, b_2, \ldots, b_n) | b_i \in \mathbb{B}\}$, $q_0^* = (1, 0, \ldots, 0)$, the transitions $T^* := \{((b_0, \ldots, b_n), \delta, (b_0', \ldots, b_n')) \in Q^* \times \Sigma \times Q^* | b_j' = b^*(j, \delta, (b_0, \ldots, b_n))\}$ and the accepting states $F^* := \{(1, b_1, \ldots, b_k, \ldots, b_n) \in Q^* | \forall k \in \mathbb{N}, p \in Q \setminus F : [p] = k \implies b_k = 0\}$.

Table 2. Comparison of ω-automaton construction and general LTL-to-Bchi automata construction implementation Wring 1.1.0 based on [SB00]

LTL formula	ω-construction states	ω-construction time[s]	Wring 1.1.0 states	Wring 1.1.0 time[s]
$\neg \mathbf{F}(a \wedge \mathbf{X}(b \wedge \mathbf{X}(b \wedge \mathbf{X}c)))$	8	0.1	20	0.6
$\neg \mathbf{F}(a \wedge \mathbf{X}(b \wedge \mathbf{X}c) \vee b \wedge \mathbf{X}(e \wedge \mathbf{X}(f \wedge \mathbf{X}d)))$	32	0.1	180	100.2
$\neg \mathbf{F}(a \wedge \mathbf{X}(b \wedge \mathbf{X}c) \vee b \wedge \mathbf{X}(e \wedge \mathbf{X}(f \wedge \mathbf{X}d)) \vee x \wedge \mathbf{X}c)$	64	0.1	288	551
$\neg \mathbf{F}(a \wedge \mathbf{X}(b \wedge \mathbf{X}c) \vee b \wedge \mathbf{X}(e \wedge \mathbf{X}(f \wedge \mathbf{X}d)) \vee c \wedge \mathbf{X}(f \wedge \mathbf{X}(g \wedge \mathbf{X}h)))$	256	0.1	2160	161871

This is the automaton referred to in Table 2 being compared to other LTL-to-Bchi translations, which also have non-mutual exclusive atomic propositions. A_C^* is certainly no longer minimal and of considerable size. However, we will see that this conflict generalization dramatically reduces the required iterations.

5   Experimental Results and Related Work

The ω-CEGAR approach was successfully applied to industrial examples ranging up to a hundred state bits and dozens of continuous variables. Table 3 gives an overview for two example models. The car window lifting system is a model from BMW which is modeled in ASCET. Depending on HMI interface and sensors it controls the engine lifting the car window, also maintaining its current position. The reachability of certain window positions was computed. The Flight Controller example is modeled with SCADE and controls the altitude depending on pilot command and sensor readings. The model contains three-dimensional vectors for positions and velocities, including plausibility computation. Here, various reachability analyses refering to expected reactions to pilot commands in a Normal Operations Mode (*NO*) were made. For two of these, Figure 4 (a) and (b) shows typical evolutions of quantities during the iteration process.

Figure 4 (c) shows the process for the same proof as (a), but without using sequences of sets of *GJ*-pairs as introduced in the previous section. The difference clearly reveals the benefit of such a conflict generalization.

Considering the size of the discrete state space $|Z|$ in the examples, we have remarkably few iterations until getting valid traces. Especially the case where the safety property was fulfilled and the bad state was not reachable as, e.g., in Proof 3 of the Flight Controller system deserves some attention. Here, after only 7 iterations and 13 generalized conflicts, the approach was able to prove the non-reachability. Considering the

Table 3. Experimental results using conflict generalization. Numbers refer to cone-reduced models. Table shows number of discrete locations, number of continuous dimensions (*inputs+state-based*), size of Σ / Σ', number of conflicts, iterations, final path length, size of Q representing state bits of A_C^* and total runtime including integration overhead.

Model / Proof	$|Z|$	dimensions	$|\Sigma|/|\Sigma'_{ini}|/|\Sigma'_{inv}|$	$-C_{ini}|/|C_{inv}|$	iter	$|\pi|$	$|Q|$	time
Flight Controller System								
1 $\mathbf{AG}(NO \implies p), p := (\Delta v_x = 0)$	2^{35}	$5+18$	$41/2/43$	$1/24$	21	13	33	16 min
2 $\mathbf{AG}(NO \wedge p \implies \mathbf{X}p)$	2^{35}	$5+18$	$67/2/60$	$1/36$	29	514	78	75 min
3 Proof 2 on corrected model	2^{31}	$5+18$	$26/2/22$	$1/13$	7	$\mathbf{\nexists}\pi$	12	4 min
Car Window Lifting System								
4 $\mathbf{EF}(pos_1 \leq pos_{window} \leq pos_2)$	2^{26}	$2+3$	$92/12/63$	$14/79$	59	10	41	52 min
5 $\mathbf{EF}(pos_{window} > pos_3)$	2^{26}	$2+3$	$59/11/42$	$13/35$	32	$\mathbf{\nexists}\pi$	18	19 min

diameter of 513 of that model meaning that internally, the model checker had to analyze that many steps of the model until the fix-point was reached, the result is quite remarkable and demonstrates the power of the approach when it comes to certification issues.

Related Work. Among the various approaches on abstraction refinement to model-check hybrid models, most commonalities with the herein presented approach seem to be shared by two of them. First, there is the INFINITE-STATE-CEGAR algorithm [CFH+03] which also uses a fully automated iterative refinement technique. For any spurious counterexample identified as such by a polyhedral over-approximation of successor states, the corresponding path fragment of length n in the abstract model is ruled out by replicating up to $n-1$ states and modifying concerned transitions accordingly such that any other trace not containing the spurious path fragment is still observable. However, this does not prevent false negatives in other areas of the model where the same GJ-sequence is linked to different locations. According to the previously made observation in equation (2), this omission might lead to a huge number of iterations with false negatives caused by reasons already detected. The advantage of a slowly growing abstract model size is easily turned down by the huge number of iterations required for the herein targeted model class.

By including source- and target states in the alphabet characters, $\Sigma = \{(z_1, z_2, g(t), j(t)) | t = (z_1, z_2) \in T\}$, we modify our algorithm to exclude exactly the same path fragments that would be ruled out in [CFH+03], making a direct comparison w.r.t. abstraction refinement iterations possible. Figure 4 (d) shows the different evolution of a still uncompleted iteration process. Being compared to (a), it confirms the above statements w.r.t. the given example.

Second, an analysis via predicate abstraction approach described in [ADI02] constructs an automaton with 2^k states which is composed in parallel with the abstract model to rule out spurious counterexamples. Based on a set of k predicates, it is computed in advance which transitions in the added automaton are possible. The fixed size of the automaton results from the reservation of one boolean variable per predicate, encoding its truth-value. Refinement is realized by manually adding additional predicates, making the approach only half-automatic with no counterexample guidance. The

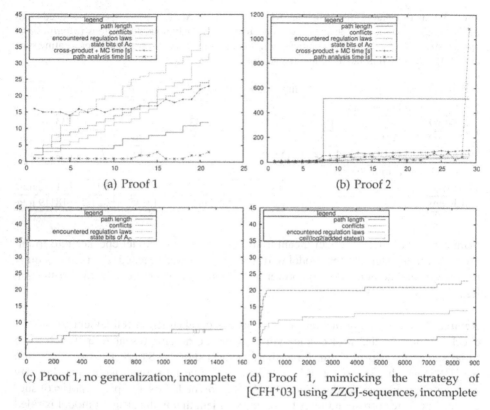

(a) Proof 1

(b) Proof 2

(c) Proof 1, no generalization, incomplete

(d) Proof 1, mimicking the strategy of [CFH+03] using ZZGJ-sequences, incomplete

Fig. 4. Evolutions of iterative refinement, x-coordinate shows iteration steps

approach exploits the model characteristics of equation (2), but besides the required manual intervention, the predicates are only state-expressions with no temporal operators, making it impossible to directly rule out spurious counterexamples based on multi-step conflicts. Disregarding problems of manual intervention and automaton construction, an extension with LTL-formula predicates would make that approach more similar to the herein presented one. However, recent research activities described in [ADI03] automate the process of finding new predicates by looking for predicates for separation of polyhedra, thus following a different strategy.

6   Conclusion

In this paper an iterative abstraction refinement approach called ω-CEGAR for verifying step-discrete hybrid models exploiting the characteristics of control dominated models being observed in industrial practice was presented. The small number of applied regulation laws leading to vast cases of recurrence of continuous state space computations throughout different discrete transition sequences is exploited by forbidding impossible continuous computation sequences globally if only a single representative is detected. The construction of an ω-automaton being composed in parallel with the coarsely abstracted original model realizes this in an efficient way. Many iterations of model-checker and path validation runs being the most costly operations can be saved. The application of the ω-CEGAR approach on parts of industrial models already shows its efficacy on the targeted class of models, especially in comparison to the INFINITE-STATE-CEGAR approach.

Acknowledgements

The author likes to thank Werner Damm, Martin Frnzle, Hardi Hungar, Hartmut Wittke, Christian Herde and Tino Teige for many valuable discussions and feedback on previous versions of this paper.

References

[ADI02]   Alur, R., Dang, T., Ivančić, F.: Reachability analysis of hybrid systems via predicate abstraction. In: Tomlin, C.J., Greenstreet, M.R. (eds.) HSCC 2002. LNCS, vol. 2289, pp. 35–48. Springer, Heidelberg (2002)

[ADI03]   Alur, R., Dang, T., Ivancic, F.: Counter-example guided predicate abstraction of hybrid systems. In: 9th International Conference on Tools and Algorithms for the Construction and Analysis of Systems (April 2003)

[ADM02]   Asarin, E., Dang, T., Maler, O.: Eugene Asarin, Thao Dang, and Oded Maler. In: Brinksma, E., Larsen, K.G. (eds.) CAV 2002. LNCS, vol. 2404, pp. 365–370. Springer, Heidelberg (2002)

[AHH96]   Alur, R., Henzinger, T.A., Ho, P.: Automatic symbolic verification of embedded systems. In: Real-Time, I.E.E.E. (ed.) IEEE Real-Time Systems Symposium, pp. 2–11 (1996)

[BEN04]   Berkelaar, K., Eikland, M., Notebaert, P.: Open source (mixed-integer) linear programming system. In: Eindhoven University of Technology (May 2004)

[CFH⁺03] Clarke, E.M., Fehnker, A., Han, Z., Krogh, B.H., Ouaknine, J., Stursberg, O., Theobald, M.: Abstraction and counterexample-guided refinement in model checking of hybrid systems. Int. J. Found. Comput. Sci. 14(4), 583–604 (2003)

[Fre05]   Frehse, G.: PHAVer: Algorithmic Verification of Hybrid Systems past HyTech. In: Morari, M., Thiele, L. (eds.) HSCC 2005. LNCS, vol. 3414, pp. 258–273. Springer, Heidelberg (2005)

[GGB⁺03] Gaudre, T., Guillermo, H., Baufreton, P., Goshen, D., Cruz, J., Dupont, F., Leviathan, R., Segelken, M., Winkelmann, K., Halbwachs, N.: A methodology and a tool set designed to develop aeronautics, automotive and safety critical embedded control-systems. In: Convergence 2003 (2003)

[HH94]   Henzinger, T.A., Ho, P.-H.: Hytech: The cornell hybrid technology tool. In: Hybrid Systems, pp. 265–293 (1994)

[RGA⁺96] Brayton, R.K., Hachtel, G.D., Sangiovanni-Vincentelli, A., Somenzi, F., Aziz, A., Cheng, S.-T., Edwards, S., Khatri, S., Kukimoto, Y., Pardo, A., Qadeer, S., Ranjan, R.K., Sarwary, S., Shiple, T.R., Swamy, G., Villa, T.: VIS: a system for verification and synthesis. In: Alur, R., Henzinger, T.A. (eds.) CAV 1996. LNCS, vol. 1102, Springer, Heidelberg (1996)

[SB00]   Somenzi, F., Bloem, R.: Efficient Büchi Automata from LTL Formulae. In: Emerson, E.A., Sistla, A.P. (eds.) CAV 2000. LNCS, vol. 1855, pp. 248–263. Springer, Heidelberg (2000)

[SFHK04]   Stursberg, O., Fehnker, A., Han, Z., Krogh, B.H.: Verification of a cruise control system using counterexample-guided search. In: Control Engineering Practice, Elsevier, Amsterdam (2004)

[SK00]   Silva, B.I., Krogh, B.H.: Formal verification of hybrid systems using checkmate: a case study. In: Proceedings of the American Control Conference, pp. 1679–1683 (2000)

Test Coverage for Continuous and Hybrid Systems

Tarik Nahhal and Thao Dang

VERIMAG, 2 avenue de Vignate
38610 Gières, France

Abstract. We propose a novel test coverage measure for continuous and
hybrid systems, which is defined using the star discrepancy notion. We
also propose a test generation method guided by this coverage measure.
This method was implemented in a prototype tool that can handle high
dimensional systems (up to 100 dimensions).

1 Introduction

Hybrid systems have been recognized as a high-level model appropriate for embedded systems, since this model can describe, within a unified framework, the
logical part and the continuous part of an embedded system. Due to the gap between the capacity of exhaustive formal verification methods and the complexity
of embedded systems, testing is still the most commonly-used validation method
in industry. Its success is probably due to the fact that testing suffers less from
the 'state explosion' problem. Indeed, the engineer can choose the 'degree of
validation' by the number of tests. In addition, this approach can be applied to
the real system itself and not only to its model. Generally, testing of a reactive
system is carried out by controlling the inputs and checking whether its behavior
is as expected. Since it is impossible to enumerate all the admissible external
inputs to the hybrid system in question, much effort has been invested in defining and implementing notions of *coverage* that guarantee, to some extent, that
the finite set of input stimuli against which the system is tested is sufficient for
validating correctness. For discrete systems, specified using programming languages or hardware design languages, some syntactic coverage measures can be
defined, like exercising every statement or transition, etc. In this work, we treat
continuous and hybrid systems that operate in a metric space (typically $\mathbb{R}^n$)
and where there is not much inspiration coming from the syntax to the coverage
issue. On the other hand, the metric nature of the state space encourages more
semantic notions of coverage, namely that all system trajectories generated by
the input test patterns form a kind of dense network in the reachable state space
without too many big unexplored 'holes'.

In this work we adopt a model-based testing approach. This approach allows
the engineer to perform validation during the design, where detecting and cor-
recting errors on a model are less expensive than on an implementation. The
main contributions of the paper can be summarized as follows. We propose a

W. Damm and H. Hermanns (Eds.): CAV 2007, LNCS 4590, pp. 449–462, 2007.
© Springer-Verlag Berlin Heidelberg 2007

test coverage measure for hybrid systems, which is defined using the star discrepancy notion from statistics. This coverage measure is used to quantify the validation 'completeness'. It is also used to guide input stimulus generation by identifying the portions of the system behaviors that are not adequately examined. We propose an algorithm for generating tests from hybrid systems models, which is based on the RRT (Rapidly-exploring Random Tree) algorithm [8] from robotic motion planning and guided by the coverage measure. The rest of the paper is organized as follows. We first describe our test coverage measure and its estimation. We then present our test generation algorithm. In Section 5 we describe an implementation of the algorithm and some experimental results. Before concluding, we discuss related work.

2   Testing Problem

As a model for hybrid systems, we use hybrid automata. Note that a continuous system can be modeled as a hybrid automaton with only one discrete state. A hybrid automaton is an automaton augmented with continuous variables that evolve according to some differential equations. Formally, a *hybrid automaton* is a tuple $\mathcal{A} = (\mathcal{X}, Q, F, \mathcal{I}, \mathcal{G}, \mathcal{R})$ where $\mathcal{X} \subseteq \mathbb{R}^n$ is the continuous state space; Q is a (finite) set of locations (or discrete states); $E \subseteq Q \times Q$ is a set of discrete transitions; $F = \{F_q \mid q \in Q\}$ is a set of continuous vector fields such that for each $q \in Q$, $F_q = (U_q, f_q)$ where $U_q \subset \mathbb{R}^p$ is a set of inputs and $f_q : \mathbb{R}^n \times U_q \to \mathbb{R}^n$; $\mathcal{I} = \{\mathcal{I}_q \subseteq \mathbb{R}^n \mid q \in Q\}$ is a set of staying conditions; $\mathcal{G} = \{\mathcal{G}_e \mid e \in E\}$ is a set of guards such that for each discrete transition $e = (q, q') \in E$, $\mathcal{G}_e \subseteq \mathcal{I}_q$; $\mathcal{R} = \{\mathcal{R}_e \mid e \in E\}$ is a set of reset maps. For each $e = (q, q') \in E$, $\mathcal{R}_e : \mathcal{G}_e \to 2^{\mathcal{I}_{q'}}$ defines how x may change when $\mathcal{A}$ switches from q to q'. A *hybrid state* is a pair (q, x) where $q \in Q$ and $x \in \mathcal{X}$ and the hybrid state space is $\mathcal{S} = Q \times \mathcal{X}$. In location q, the evolution of the continuous variables is governed by $\dot{x}(t) = f_q(x(t), u(t))$. We assume that all f_q are Lipschitz continuous[1]. The admissible input functions $u(\cdot)$ are piecewise continuous. We denote the initial state of the automaton by (q_0, x_0). A state (q, x) of $\mathcal{A}$ can change in two ways as follows. By *continuous evolution*, the continuous state x evolves according to the dynamics f_q while the discrete state q remains constant. By *discrete evolution*, x satisfies the guard condition of an outgoing transition, the system changes the location by taking this transition and possibly changing the values of x according to the associated reset map. We assume that discrete transitions are instantaneous. It is important to note that this model allows to capture non-determinism in both continuous and discrete dynamics. This non-determinism is useful for describing disturbances from the environment and imprecision in modelling and implementation. The hybrid automata we consider are assumed to be non-blocking and non-Zeno.

A system under test often operates within some environment. In our testing problem, the tester plays the role of the environment. Given a hybrid automaton

---

[1] This ensures the existence and uniqueness of solutions of the differential equations.

modeling the behavior of the system under test, the tester can have the following controls on the system: first, it can control all the continuous inputs of the system; second, it can decide whether the system should take a given transition (among the enabled ones) or continue with the same continuous dynamics. Indeed, for simplicity of explanation, we do not include the control of the tester over the non-determinism in the reset maps. We also assume that the state of the system can be *fully observed* by the tester. Since we want to implement the tester as a computer program, we could assume that the continuous input functions generated by the tester are piecewise-constant with a fixed period h (i.e. they can change their values only after a fixed period of time), and h is called the *time step*. Hence, there are two types of control actions the tester can perform: continuous and discrete. A *continuous control action* denoted by a continuous dynamics and the value of the corresponding input, such as (f_q, v_q). It specifies that the system continues with the dynamics f_q under the input $u(t) = v_q$ for exactly h time. A *discrete control action* specifies a discrete transition to be taken by the system. We denote an action of this type by the corresponding transition, such as (q, q'). For a continuous action (f_q, v_q), we define its 'associated' transition as (q, q). A sequence of control actions is called *admissible* if after replacing all the continuous actions by their associated transitions, it corresponds to a path (i.e. a sequence of consecutive transitions) in the hybrid automaton $\mathcal{A}$ augmented with a self-loop at every location.

Definition 1 (Test case). *A test case is an admissible sequence of control actions $a_1, a_2, a_3, \ldots$ which is coherent with the initial state of the system, that is if $a_1 = (f_q, v_q)$ then $q = q_0$ and if $a_1 = (q, q')$ then $q = q_0$.*

Our testing problem can thus be stated as to automatically generate a set of test cases from the system model to satisfy a coverage criterion that we formally define in the following.

Test Coverage. Test coverage is a way to evaluate testing quality. More precisely, it is a way to relate the number of tests to carry out with the fraction of the system's behaviors effectively explored. As mentioned earlier, the classic coverage notions mainly used in software testing, such as statement coverage and if-then-else branch coverage, path coverage (see for example [16,14]), are not appropriate for the trajectories of continuous and hybrid systems defined by differential equations. However, geometric properties of the hybrid state space can be exploited to define a coverage measure which, on one hand, has a close relationship with the properties to verify and, on the other hand, can be efficiently computed or estimated. In this work, we are interested in state coverage and focus on a measure that describes how 'well' the visited states represent the reachable set of the system. This measure is defined using the *star discrepancy* notion in statistics, which characterises the uniformity of the distribution of a point set within a region. We first briefly recall the star discrepancy. The star discrepancy is an important notion in equidistribution theory as well as in quasi-Monte Carlo techniques (see for example [1]). Recently, it was also used in probabilistic motion planning to enhance the sampling uniformity [3].

Star Discrepancy. Let P be a set of k points inside $\mathcal{B} = [l_1, L_1] \times \ldots \times [l_n, L_n]$. Let Γ be the set of all sub-boxes J of the form $J = \prod_{i=1}^{n} [l_i, \beta_i]$ with $\beta_i \in [l_i, L_i]$ (see Figure 1 for an illustration). The local discrepancy of the point set P with respect to the subbox J is defined as follows: $D(P, J) = |\dfrac{A(P, J)}{k} - \dfrac{\lambda(J)}{\lambda(\mathcal{B})}|$ where $A(P, J)$ is the number of points of P that are inside J, and $\lambda(J)$ is the volume of the box J. The star discrepancy of P with respect to the box $\mathcal{B}$ is defined as:

$$D^*(P, \mathcal{B}) = sup_{J \in \Gamma} D(P, J) \tag{1}$$

Note that $0 < D^*(P, \mathcal{B}) \leq 1$. Intuitively, the star discrepancy is a measure for

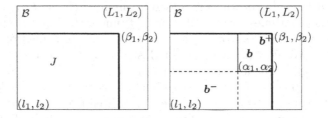

Fig. 1. Illustration of the star discrepancy notion

the irregularity of a set of points. A large value $D^*(P, \mathcal{B})$ means that the points in P are not much equidistributed over $\mathcal{B}$. When the region is a hyper-cube, the star discrepancy measures how badly the point set estimates the volume of the cube. Since a hybrid system can only evolve within the staying sets of the locations, we are interested in the coverage with respect to these sets. For simplicity we assume that all the staying sets are boxes.

Definition 2 (Hybrid System Test Coverage). *Let* $\mathcal{P} = \{(q, P_q) \mid q \in Q \wedge P_q \subset \mathcal{I}_q\}$ *be the set of states. The coverage of* $\mathcal{P}$ *is defined as:* $Cov(\mathcal{P}) = \frac{1}{\|Q\|} \sum_{q \in Q} 1 - D^*(P_q, \mathcal{I}_q)$ *where* $\|Q\|$ *is the number of locations in* Q.

If a staying set $\mathcal{I}_q$ is not a box, we can take the smallest oriented box that encloses it, and apply the star discrepancy definition in (1) to that box after an appropriate coordination change. We can see that a large value of $Cov(\mathcal{P})$ indicates a good space-covering quality. If $\mathcal{P}$ is the set of states visited by a set of test cases, our objective is to maximize $Cov(\mathcal{P})$.

3   Test Generation

Our test generation is based on a randomized exploration of the reachable state space of system. It is inspired by the Rapidly-exploring Random Tree (RRT) algorithm, which is a successful motion planning technique for finding feasible trajectories of robots in an environment with obstacles (see [8] for a survey). More precisely, we extend the RRT algorithm to hybrid systems and combine it with a guiding tool in order to achieve a good coverage of the system's behaviors we want to test. In this context, we use the coverage measure defined in the previous section. Some preliminary results for continuous systems were described in [12].

The visited states are stored in a tree $\mathcal{T}$, the root of which corresponds to the initial state. The construction of the tree is summarized in Algorithm 1. In each iteration, a hybrid state $s_{goal} = (q_{goal}, x_{goal})$ is sampled to indicate the direction towards which the tree is expected to evolve. Expanding the tree towards s_{goal} is done by making a continuous step as follows:

- First, a starting state $s_{init} = (q_{init}, x_{init})$ for the current iteration is determined. It is natural to choose s_{init} to be a state near s_{goal}. The definition of the distance between hybrid states will be given later.
- Next, the procedure CONTINUOUSSTEP tries to find the input $u_{q_{init}}$ such that, after one time step h, the current continuous dynamics at q_{init} takes the system from s_{init} towards s_{goal}, and this results in a new continuous state x_{new}. A new edge from s_{init} to $s_{new} = (q_{init}, x_{new})$, labeled with the associated input $u_{q_{init}}$, is then added to the tree.

Then, from s_{new}, we compute its successors by all possible discrete transitions. Each time we add a new edge, we label it with the associated control action. The algorithm terminates after reaching a satisfactory coverage value or after some maximal number of iterations. From the tree constructed by the algorithm we can then extract test cases. In addition, when applying such test cases to the system, the tree can be used to decide whether the system under test behaves as expected. In the classic RRT algorithms, which work in a continuous setting,

---

Algorithm 1. Test generation algotihm

$\mathcal{T}.init(s_0), j = 1$ $\triangleright s_0$: initial state
repeat
     $s_{goal} = \text{SAMPLING}(\mathcal{S})$ $\triangleright \mathcal{S}$: hybrid state space
     $s_{init} = \text{NEIGHBOR}(\mathcal{T}, s_{goal})$
     $(s_{new}, u_{q_{init}}) = \text{CONTINUOUSSTEP}(s_{init}, h)$ $\triangleright h$: time step
     $\text{DISCRETESTEPS}(\mathcal{T}, s_{new}), j{+}{+}$
until $j \geq J_{max}$

---

only x_{goal} needs to be sampled, and a commonly used sampling distribution of x_{goal} is uniform over $\mathcal{X}$. In addition, the point x_{init} is defined as a nearest neighbor of x_{goal} in some usual distance, such as the Euclidian distance. In Algorithm 1, the function SAMPLING plays the role of guiding the exploration via a biased sampling of x_{goal}, which will be discussed in detail later. The computation of discrete successors in DISCRETESTEPS, which involves testing a guard condition and applying a reset map, is straightforward. In the following, we show how to compute the functions NEIGHBOR and CONTINUOUSSTEP.

Finding a Neighbor. To define the distance between two hybrid states, we first define the average length of a path. Given a path of two transitions $e = (q, q')$ and $e' = (q', q'')$, let $\sigma(e, e') = \overline{d}(\mathcal{R}_{(q,q')}(\mathcal{G}_{(q',q'')}), \mathcal{G}_{(q',q'')})$ where $\overline{d}$ is the average distance between two sets defined as the Euclidian distance between their centroids. Given a path $\gamma = e_1, e_2, \ldots e_m$ where $e_i = (q_i, q_{i+1})$, we define its average length as: $len(\gamma) = \sum_{i=1}^{m-1} \sigma(e_i, e_{i+1})$. Note that from one location to another, there can be more than one path. Let $\Gamma(q, q')$ be the set of all paths from q to q'. Given two hybrid states $s = (q, x)$ and $s' = (q', x')$, if $q = q'$, we define the *hybrid distance* $d_H(s, s')$ from s to s' as the Euclidian distance between the continuous states x and x': $d_H(s, s') = ||x - x'||$. If $q \neq q'$,

$$
d_H(s, s') = \begin{cases} \min_{\gamma \in \Gamma(q,q')} \overline{d}(x, fG(\gamma)) + len(\gamma) + \overline{d}(x', lR(\gamma)), & \text{if } \Gamma(q, q') \neq \emptyset \\ \infty & \text{otherwise.} \end{cases}
$$

where $fG(\gamma) = \mathcal{G}_{(q_1, q_2)}$, the first guard of γ, and $lR(\gamma) = \mathcal{R}_{(q_k, q_{k+1})}(\mathcal{G}_{(q_k, q_{k+1})})$, that is the set resulting from applying the reset map of the last transition to its guard set. Intuitively, $d_H(s, s')$ is obtained by adding to the average length of γ the distance from x to the first guard and the distance from the last 'reset set' to x'. This distance can be thought of as an average length of the trajectories from s to s'. The function NEIGHBOR can thus be computed using this hybrid distance as follows: $s_{init} = argmin_{s \in V} d_H(s_{goal}, s)$ where V is the set of states stored in the tree.

Continuous Step. If the states s_{init} and s_{goal} have the same discrete location component, we want to expand to tree from x_{init} towards x_{goal} as closely as possible. Otherwise, let γ be the path from q_{init} to q_{goal} with the shortest average length, we want to steer the system from x_{init} towards the first guard of γ. In both cases, this is an optimal control problem with the objective of minimizing the distance to some target point. This problem is difficult especially for systems with non-linear continuous dynamics. Thus, we can trade some optimality for computational efficiency. When the input set is not finite, we can sample a set of input values and pick from this set an optimal input. In addition, we can prove that by an appropriate sampling of the input set, the completeness property of the RRT algorithm is preserved [2].

Coverage Estimation. To evaluate the coverage of a set of states, we need to compute the star discrepancy of a point set, which is not an easy problem (see for example [7]). Many theoretical results for one-dimensional point sets are not generalizable to higher dimensions, and among the fastest algorithms we can mention the one proposed in [7] of time complexity $\mathcal{O}(k^{1+n/2})$. In this work, we do not try to compute the star discrepancy but approximate it by estimating a lower and upper bound. These bounds as well as the information obtained from their estimation are then used to decide which parts of the state space have been 'well explored' and which parts need to be explored more. This estimation is done using a method published in [10]. Let us briefly describe this method for computing the star discrepancy $D^*(P, \mathcal{B})$ of a point set P w.r.t. a box $\mathcal{B}$.

Although in [10], the box $\mathcal{B}$ is $[0,1]^n$, we extended it to the case where $\mathcal{B}$ can be any full-dimensional box. Let $\mathcal{B} = [l_1, L_1] \times \ldots \times [l_n, L_n]$. We define a box partition of $\mathcal{B}$ as a set of boxes $\Pi = \{\boldsymbol{b}^1, \ldots, \boldsymbol{b}^m\}$ such that $\cup_{i=1}^m \boldsymbol{b}^i = \mathcal{B}$ and the interiors of the boxes $\boldsymbol{b}^i$ do not intersect. Each such box is called an *elementary box*. Given a box $\boldsymbol{b} = [\alpha_1, \beta_1] \times \ldots \times [\alpha_n, \beta_n] \in \Pi$, we define $\boldsymbol{b}^+ = [l_1, \beta_1] \times \ldots \times [l_n, \beta_n]$ and $\boldsymbol{b}^- = [l_1, \alpha_1] \times \ldots \times [l_n, \alpha_n]$ (see Figure 1 for an illustration).

For any finite box partition Π of $\mathcal{B}$, the star discrepancy $D^*(P, \mathcal{B})$ of the point set P with respect to $\mathcal{B}$ satisfies: $C(P, \Pi) \leq D^*(P, \mathcal{B}) \leq B(P, \Pi)$ where the upper and lower bounds are:

$$B(P, \Pi) = \max_{\boldsymbol{b} \in \Pi} \max\{\frac{A(P, \boldsymbol{b}^+)}{k} - \frac{\lambda(\boldsymbol{b}^-)}{\lambda(\mathcal{B})}, \frac{\lambda(\boldsymbol{b}^+)}{\lambda(\mathcal{B})} - \frac{A(P, \boldsymbol{b}^-)}{k}\} \qquad (2)$$

$$C(P, \Pi) = \max_{\boldsymbol{b} \in \Pi} \max\{|\frac{A(P, \boldsymbol{b}^-)}{k} - \frac{\lambda(\boldsymbol{b}^-)}{\lambda(\mathcal{B})}|, |\frac{A(P, \boldsymbol{b}^+)}{k} - \frac{\lambda(\boldsymbol{b}^+)}{\lambda(\mathcal{B})}|\} \qquad (3)$$

The imprecision of this approximation is the difference between the upper and lower bounds, which can be bounded by $B(P, \Pi) - C(P, \Pi) \leq W(\Pi)$ where follows:

$$W(\Pi) = \max_{\boldsymbol{b} \in \Pi}(\lambda(\boldsymbol{b}^+) - \lambda(\boldsymbol{b}^-))/\lambda(\mathcal{B}) \qquad (4)$$

Thus, one needs to find a partition Π such that this difference is small.

Coverage-Guided Sampling. We show how to use the estimation of the coverage measure to derive a guiding strategy. Recall that our goal is to achieve a good testing coverage quality, which is equivalent to a small value of the star discrepancy of the points visited at each discrete location. More concretely, in each iteration, we want to bias the goal state sampling distribution according to the current coverage of the visited states. To do so, we first sample a discrete location and then a continuous state. Let $\mathcal{P} = \{(q, P_q) \mid q \in Q \wedge P_q \subset \mathcal{I}_q\}$ be the current set of visited states. The discrete location sampling distribution depends on the current continuous state coverage of each location:

$$Pr[q_{goal} = q] = \frac{D^*(P_q, \mathcal{I}_q)}{\sum_{q' \in Q} D^*(P_{q'}, \mathcal{I}_{q'})}.$$

We now show how to sample x_{goal}, assuming that we have already sampled a discrete location $q_{goal} = q$. In the remainder of the paper, to give geometric intuitions, we often call a continuous state a point. In addition, since all the staying sets are assumed to be boxes, we denote the staying set $\mathcal{I}_q$ by the box $\mathcal{B}$ and denote the current set of visited points at location q simply by P instead of P_q. Let k be the number of points in P. Let Π be a finite box partition of $\mathcal{B}$ that is used to estimate the star discrepancy of P. The sampling process consists of two steps. In the first step, we sample an elementary box $\boldsymbol{b}_{goal}$ from the set Π; in the second step we sample a point x_{goal} in $\boldsymbol{b}_{goal}$ uniformly. The elementary box sampling distribution in the first step is biased in order to optimize the coverage. The intuition behind this guiding strategy is to favor the selection of an elementary box such that a new point x added in this box results in a smaller star discrepancy of the new point set $P \cup \{x\}$. The strategy is determined so as to reduce both the lower bound $C(P, \Pi)$ and the upper bound $B(P, \Pi)$.

Reducing the lower bound. We associate with each box $\mathcal{B} \subseteq \Pi$ a number $A^*(\boldsymbol{b})$ such that $\dfrac{\lambda(\boldsymbol{b})}{\lambda(\mathcal{B})} = \dfrac{A^*(\boldsymbol{b})}{k}$. We denote $\Delta_A(\boldsymbol{b}) = \frac{1}{k}(A(P, \boldsymbol{b}) - A^*(\boldsymbol{b}))$. Denote $c(\boldsymbol{b}) = \max\{|\Delta_A(\boldsymbol{b}^+)|, |\Delta_A(\boldsymbol{b}^-)|\}$, and the lower bound of the star discrepancy of the point set P over the bounding box $\mathcal{B}$ becomes: $C(P, \Pi) = \max_{\boldsymbol{b} \in \Pi}\{c(\boldsymbol{b})\}$. Note that in comparison with A^*, the negative (respectively positive) sign of $\Delta_A(\boldsymbol{b})$ indicates that in this box there is a lack (respectively an excess) of points; its absolute value indicates how significant the lack (or the excess) is. We now compare the values of $|\Delta_A(\boldsymbol{b}^+)|$ in two cases: the newly added point x_{new} is in $\boldsymbol{b}$ and x_{new} is not in $\boldsymbol{b}$. If $\Delta_A(\boldsymbol{b}^+)$ is positive, the value of $|\Delta_A(\boldsymbol{b}^+)|$ in the former case is smaller than or equal to that in the latter case; otherwise it is greater than or equal to. However, adding a new point in $\boldsymbol{b}$ does not affect the values of $A(P, \boldsymbol{b}^-)$ (see Figure 1). Thus, we define a function reflecting the potential influence on the lower bound as follows:

$$\xi(\boldsymbol{b}) = \frac{1 - \Delta_A(\boldsymbol{b}^+)}{1 - \Delta_A(\boldsymbol{b}^-)}, \tag{5}$$

and we favor the selection of $\boldsymbol{b}$ if the value $\xi(\boldsymbol{b})$ is large. Note that $1 - \Delta_A(\boldsymbol{b}) > 0$ for any box $\boldsymbol{b}$ inside $\mathcal{B}$. The intepetation of ξ is as follows. If $\Delta_A(\boldsymbol{b}^+)$ is negative and its absolute value is large, the 'lack' of points in $\boldsymbol{b}^+$ is significant. In this case, $\xi(\boldsymbol{b})$ is large, meaning that the selection of $\boldsymbol{b}$ is favored. On the other hand, if $\Delta_A(\boldsymbol{b}^-)$ is negative and its absolute value is large, then $\xi(\boldsymbol{b})$ is small, because it is preferable not to select $\boldsymbol{b}$ in order to increase the chance of adding new points in $\boldsymbol{b}^-$.

Reducing the upper bound. The upper bound in (2) can be rewritten as

$$B(P, \Pi) = \max_{\boldsymbol{b} \in \Pi} f_m(\boldsymbol{b}) \tag{6}$$

where $f_m(\boldsymbol{b}) = \max\{f_c(\boldsymbol{b}), f_o(\boldsymbol{b})\}$ and $f_c(\boldsymbol{b}) = \frac{1}{k}(A(P, \boldsymbol{b}^+) - A^*(\boldsymbol{b}^-))$ and $f_o(\boldsymbol{b}) = \frac{1}{k}(A^*(\boldsymbol{b}^+) - A(P, \boldsymbol{b}^-))$. Since the value of f_m is determined by comparing f_c with f_o. After straightforward calculations, the inequality $f_c(\boldsymbol{b}) - f_o(\boldsymbol{b}) \leq 0$ is equivalent to $f_c(\boldsymbol{b}) - f_o(\boldsymbol{b}) = \Delta_A(P, \boldsymbol{b}^+) + \Delta_A(P, \boldsymbol{b}^-) \leq 0$. Therefore,

$$f_m(\boldsymbol{b}) = \begin{cases} f_o(\boldsymbol{b}) & \text{if } \Delta_A(\boldsymbol{b}^+) + \Delta_A(\boldsymbol{b}^-) \leq 0, \\ f_c(\boldsymbol{b}) & \text{otherwise.} \end{cases} \tag{7}$$

Again, the value of $f_c(\boldsymbol{b})$ when the new point x_{new} is added in $\boldsymbol{b}$ is larger than that when x_{new} is not in $\boldsymbol{b}$, but the fact that x_{new} is in $\boldsymbol{b}$ does not affect $f_o(\boldsymbol{b})$. To reduce $f_o(\boldsymbol{b})$ we need to add points in $\boldsymbol{b}^-$. Hence, if $\boldsymbol{b}$ is a box in Π that maximizes f_m in (6), it is preferable not to add more points in $\boldsymbol{b}$ but in the boxes where the values of f_m are much lower than the current value of $B(P, \Pi)$ (in particular those inside b^-). Using the same reasoning for each box b locally, the smaller $|\Delta_A(P, b^+) + \Delta_A(P, b^-)|$ is, the smaller sampling probability we give to b. Indeed, as mentionned earlier, if $f_m(b) = f_c(b)$, increasing $f_c(b)$ directly increases $f_m(b)$. On the other hand, if $f_m(b) = f_o(b)$, increasing $f_c(b)$ may make it greater than $f_o(b)$ and thus increase $f_m(b)$, because small $|\Delta_A(P, b^+) + \Delta_A(P, b^-)|$ implies that $f_c(b)$ is close to $f_o(b)$.

We define two functions reflecting the global and local potential influences on the upper bound: $\beta_g(b) = B(P, \Pi) - f_m(b)$ and $\beta_l(b) = \beta_g(b)|\Delta_A(P, b^+) + \Delta_A(P, b^-)|$. We can verify that $\beta_g(b)$ and $\beta_l(b)$ are always positive. Now, combining these functions with ξ in (5) that describes the potential influence on the lower bound, we define: $\kappa(b) = \gamma_\xi \xi(b) + \gamma_g \beta_g(b) + \gamma_l \beta_l(b)$ where γ_ξ, γ_g, and γ_l are non-negative weights that can be user-defined parameters. Then, the probability of choosing the box b can be defined as follows $Pr[b_{goal} = b] = \dfrac{\kappa(b)}{\sum_{b \in \Pi} \kappa(b)}$.

4   Implementation

In addition to the tree that is used to store the explored executions, to facilitate the computation of geometric operations, such as finding a neighbor, we store the points reachable by the dynamics at each location using a data structure similar to a k-d tree. Each node of the tree has exactly two children. Each internal node is associated with the information about a partitioning plane: its axis i and position c, and the partitioning plane is thus $x_i = c$ (where x_i is the ith coordinate of x). The additional information associated with a leaf is a set of visited points. Each node thus corresponds to an elementary box resulting from a hierarchical box-partition of the state space. The box of the root of the tree is $\mathcal{B}$. The tree and the partition of a 2-dimensional example is shown in Figure 2, where the axes of the partitioning planes are specified by the horizontal and vertical bars inside the nodes.

Approximate Neighbors. Since the computation of exact nearest neighbors is expensive (even in a continuous setting), we approximate a neigbor of x as follows: find the elementary box b which contains at least one visited point and, in addition, is closest to x (note that some elementary boxes may not contain any visited points). Then, we find a point in b which is closest to x. It is easy to see that b does not necessarily contain a nearest neighbor of x. We use this approximation because, on one hand the sampling distribution reflects the boxes we want to explore, and on the other hand, it has lower complexity w.r.t. dimensions. In addition, as we will show later, this approximation preserves the completeness.

Update the discrepancy estimation. After adding a new point x, we need to update the estimation of the star discrepancy. More concretely, we need to find all the elementary boxes b such that the new point has increased the number of points in the corresponding boxes b^- and b^+. These boxes are indeed those which intersect with the box $B_x = [x_1, L_1] \times \ldots \times [x_n, L_n]$. In addition, if b is a subset of B_x, the numbers of points in both b^+ and b^- need to be incremented;

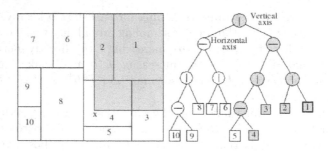

Fig. 2. Illustration of the update of the star discrepancy estimation

if b intersects with B_x but is not entirely inside B_x, only the number of points in b^+ needs to be incremented. Searching for all the elementary boxes that are affected by x can be done by traversing the tree from the root and visiting all the nodes the boxes of which intersect with B_x. In the example of Figure 2, the box B_x is the dark rectangle, and the nodes of the trees visited in this search are drawn as dark cirles.

Box splitting. When the difference between the lower and upper bounds in the star discrepancy estimation is large, some boxes need to be split as indicated by (4). Additionally, splitting is also needed for efficiency of the neighbor computation.

Completeness Property. Probabilistic completeness is an important property of the RRT algorithm. Roughly speaking, it states that if the trajectory we seach for is feasible, then the probability that the algorithm finds it approaches 1 as the number k of iterations approaches infinity [8]. Although this property is mainly of theoretical interest, it is a way to explain a good space-covering property and the success of the RRT algorithm in solving practical robotic motion planning problems. We can prove that our test generation algorithm preserves this completeness property.

Theorem 1. [Reachability completeness] *Let V^k be the set of states visited after k iterations of Algorithm 1. Given $\varepsilon > 0$ and a **reachable** state (q, x), the probability that there exists a state $(q, x') \in V^k$ such that $||x - x'|| \leq \varepsilon$ approaches 1 when k approaches infinity, i.e. $\lim_{k \to \infty} Pr[\exists (q, x') \in V^k : ||x - x'|| \leq \varepsilon] = 1$.*

Sketch of Proof. The proofs of the completeness of RRTs are often established for the algorithms where the goal point sampling distribution is uniform and all the operations are exactly computed (see for example [8]). We first identify the following condition: at each iteration k, $\forall s \in V^k : Pr[s_{init} = s] > 0$. We can prove that this condition is sufficient for the completeness proofs to remain valid, even when the sampling distribution is non-uniform and the operations are not exactly computed. The proof of this is rather technical and thus omitted (see [2]). We now give a sketch of proof that our guided sampling method and nearest neighbor approximation satisfy this condition. We first observe that, both the location and elementary box sampling distributions guarantee that all the locations and all the boxes have non-null probability of being selected. We consider only the case where the elementary box b within which we search for a neighbor of x_{goal} contains x_{goal} (the other case can be handled similarly). Let P_b be the set of visited points that are inside b. Let V_b be the Voronoi diagram of P_b restricted to b and C_p the corresponding Voronoi cell of a visited point $p \in P_b$. (Recall that the Voronoi cell of a point p is the set of all points that are closer to p than to any other point). We can prove that the volume of C_p is strictly positive. Since the goal point sampling distribution within b is uniform, $Pr[x_{goal} \in C_p] > 0$, and hence the probability that p is the approximate neighbor is also positive. It then follows that any visited point has a positive probability of being selected to be x_{init}. This implies that at each iteration, any visited state has a positive probability to be s_{init}.   ∎

5   Experimental Results

We implemented the test generation algorithm using C++ in a prototype tool, and the results reported here were obtained by running the tool on a 1.4 GHz Pentium III. First, to demonstrate the performance of our algorithm, we use a set of examples of linear systems $\dot{x} = Ax + u$ in various dimensions. In this experiment, we did not exploit the linearity of the dynamics and the tested systems were randomly generated: the matrix A is in Jordan canonical form, each diagonal value of which is randomly chosen from $[-3, 3]$ and the input set U contains 100 values randomly chosen from $[-0.5, 0.5]^n$. We fix a maximal number $K_{max} = 50000$ of visited states. In terms of coverage, the star discrepancy of the results obtained by our algorithm and the classic RRT algorithm are shown in Table 1 (left), which indicates that our algorithm has better coverage quality. These discrepancy values were computed for the final set of visited states, using a partition optimal w.r.t. to the imprecision bound in (4). Note that in each iteration of our test generation algorithm we do not compute such a partition because it is very expensive. The results obtained on a 2-dimensional system are visualized in Figure 3. Table 1 (right) shows the time efficiency of our algorithm for linear systems of dimensions up to 100.

   To illustrate the application of our algorithm to hybrid systems, we use the well-known aircraft collision avoidance problem [11]. The dynamics of each

Table 1. Discrepancy results and computation time for some linear systems

dim n	Lower bound		Upper bound	
	Algo 1	RRT	Algo 1	RRT
3	0.451	0.546	0.457	0.555
5	0.462	0.650	0.531	0.742
10	0.540	0.780	0.696	0.904

dim n	Time (min)
5	1
10	3.5
20	7.3
50	24
100	71

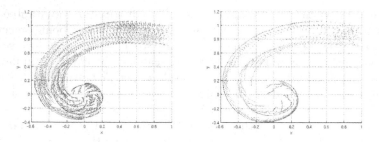

Fig. 3. Results obtained using Algorithm 1 (left) and the RRT algorithm (right)

aircraft is as follows: $\dot{x}_i = vcos(\theta_i) + d_1 sin(\theta_i) + d_2 cos(\theta_2)$, $\dot{y}_i = vsin(\theta_i) - d_1 cos(\theta_i) + d_2 sin(\theta_2)$, $\dot{\theta}_i = \omega$ where x_i, y_i describe the position and θ_i is the relative heading. The continuous inputs are d_1 and d_2 describing the external disturbances on the aircrafts and $-\delta \leq d_1, d_2 \leq \delta$. There are three discrete modes. At first, each aircraft begins in straight flight with a fixed heading (mode 1). Then, as soon as two aircrafts are within the distance between each other, they enter mode 2, at which point each makes an instantaneous heading change of 90 degrees, and begins a circular flight for π time units. After that, they switch to mode 3 and make another instantaneous heading change of 90 degrees and resume their original headings from mode 1. Thus for N aircrafts, the system has $3N + 1$ continuous variables (one for modeling a clock). For the case of $N = 2$ aircrafts, when the collision distance is 5 no colission was detected after visiting 10000 visited states, and the computation time was 0.9 min. The result for $N = 8$ aircrafts with the disturbance bound $\delta = 0.06$ is shown in Figure 4. For this example, the computation time for 50000 visited states was 10 min and a collision was found. For a similar example with $N = 10$ aicrafts, the computation time was 14 minutes and a collision was also found.

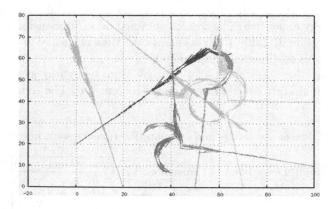

Fig. 4. Eight-aircraft collision avoidance (50000 visited states, computation time: 10 min)

6   Related Work and Conclusion

Classical model-based testing frameworks use Mealy machines or finite labeled transition systems and their applications include testing of digital circuits, communication protocols and software. Recently, these frameworks have been extended to real-time systems and hybrid systems. Here we only discuss related works in hybrid systems testing. The paper [13] proposed a framework for generating test cases from simulation of hybrid models specified using the language CHARON. A probabilistic test generation approach, similiar to ours, was presented in [5]. In this paper, the authors also proposed a coverage measure based on a discretized version of dispersion. This measure is defined over a set of grid points with a fixed size δ. The spacing s_g of a grid point g is the distance from g to the tree if it is smaller than δ, and $s_g = \delta$ otherwise. Let S be the sum of the spacings of all the grid points. This means that the value of S is the largest when the tree is empty. Then, the coverage measure is defined in terms of how much the vertices of the tree reduce the value of S. While in our work, the coverage measure is used to guide the simulation, in [5] it is used as a termination criterion. The RRT algorithms have also been used to solve other hybrid systems analysis problems such as hybrid systems control and verification [6,4]. Biasing the sampling process is guided by geometric constraints (such as avoiding sampling near the obstacles) in [15] and by the exploration history (to predict unreachable parts) in [5]. The difference which is also the novelty in our method for guiding test generation is that we use the information about the current coverage in order to improve it.

To conclude, in this paper we described a test coverage measure for continuous and hybrid systems and a test generation algorithm. The originality of our paper is a way to guide the test generation process by the coverage measure. The experimental results obtained using an implementation of the test generation algorithm show its scalability to high dimensional systems and good coverage quality. A number of directions for future research can be identified. First, we are interested in defining a measure for trace coverage. Partial observability also needs to be considered. Convergence rate of the exploration in the test generation algorithm is another interesting theoretical problem to tackle. This problem is particular hard especially in the verification context where the system is subject to uncontrollable inputs. Finally, we intend to apply the results of this research to validation of analog and mixed-signal circuits, a domain where testing is a widely used technique.

Acknowledgement. This research is supported by a fund ANR-06-SETI-018 of Agence Nationale de la Recherche.

References

1. Beck, J., Chen, W.: Irregularities of Distribution. Cambridge Univ. Press, Cambridge (1987)
2. Dang, T., Nahhal, T.: Randomized simulation of hybrid systems. In: Technical report, Verimag, IMAG (May 2006)

3. LaValle, S.M., Branicky, M.S., Lindemann, S.R.: On the relationship between classical grid search and probabilistic roadmaps. Intl. Journal of Robotics Research 23(7-8), 673–692 (2004)

4. Branicky, M.S., Curtiss, M.M., Levine, J., Morgan, S.: Sampling-based reachability algorithms for control and verification of complex systems. In: Proc. Thirteenth Yale Workshop on Adaptive and Learning Systems, New Haven, CT (2005)

5. Esposito, J.M., Kim, J., Kumar, V.: Adaptive RRTs for validating hybrid robotic control systems. In: Int. Workshop on the Algorithmic Founddations of Robotics (2004)

6. Bhatia, A., Frazzoli, E.: Incremental Search Methods for Reachability Analysis of Continuous and Hybrid Systems. In: Alur, R., Pappas, G.J. (eds.) HSCC 2004. LNCS, vol. 2993, pp. 142–156. Springer, Heidelberg (2004)

7. Dobkin, D., Eppstein, D.: Computing the discrepancy. In: Proceedings of the Ninth Annual Symposium on Computational Geometry, pp. 47–52 (1993)

8. LaValle, S.M., Kuffner, J.J.: Rapidly-exploring random trees: Progress and prospects. In: Algorithmic and Computational Robotics: New Directions, pp. 293–308. A K Peters, Wellesley, MA (2001)

9. Lee, D., Yannakakis, M.: Principles and Methods of Testing Finite State Machines - A Survey. In: Proceedings of the IEEE, vol. 84 (1996)

10. Thiémard, E.: An algorithm to compute bounds for the star discrepancy. J. Complexity 17(4), 850 (2001)

11. Mitchell, I., Tomlin, C.: Level Set Methods for Computation in Hybrid Systems. In: Lynch, N.A., Krogh, B.H. (eds.) HSCC 2000. LNCS, vol. 1790, Springer, Heidelberg (2000)

12. Nahhal, T., Dang, T.: Guided randomized simulation. In: HSCC. LNCS, Springer, Heidelberg (2007)

13. Tan, L., Kim, J., Sokolsky, O., Lee, I.: Model-based Testing and Monitoring for Hybrid Embedded Systems. In: IRI, pp. 487–492 (2004)

14. Tretmans, J.: Testing Concurrent Systems: A Formal Approach. In: Baeten, J.C.M., Mauw, S. (eds.) CONCUR 1999. LNCS, vol. 1664, Springer, Heidelberg (1999)

15. Yershova, A., Jaillet, L., Simeon, T., LaValle, S.M.: Dynamic-domain RRTs: Efficient exploration by controlling the sampling domain. In: Proc. IEEE International Conference on Robotics and Automation, IEEE Computer Society Press, Los Alamitos (2005)

16. Zhu, H., Hall, P.A.V., May, J.H.R.: Software Unit Test Coverage and Adequacy. In: ACM Computing Surveys, vol. 29(4), ACM Press, New York (1997)

Hybrid Systems:
From Verification to Falsification

Erion Plaku, Lydia E. Kavraki, and Moshe Y. Vardi

Department of Computer Science, Rice University
Houston TX 77005, USA
{plakue, kavraki, vardi}@cs.rice.edu

Abstract. We propose `HyDICE`, Hybrid DIscrete Continuous
Exploration, a multi-layered approach for hybrid-system testing that integrates continuous sampling-based robot motion planning with discrete
searching. The discrete search uses the discrete transitions of the hybrid
system and coarse-grained decompositions of the continuous state spaces
or related projections to guide the motion planner during the search for
witness trajectories. Experiments presented in this paper, using a hybrid
system inspired by robot motion planning and with nonlinear dynamics
associated with each of several thousand modes, provide an initial validation of `HyDICE` and demonstrate its promise as a hybrid-system testing
method. Comparisons to related work show computational speedups of
up to two orders of magnitude.

1 Introduction

Hybrid systems play an increasingly important role in transportation networks
[1], manufacturing processes [2], robotics [3], and medicine and biology [4, 5].
Today we find hybrid systems in sophisticated embedded controllers used in
the automotive and airplane industry, and also in medical devices that monitor
serious health conditions. Recently, it has been shown that hybrid systems are a
powerful tool for modeling biological processes and for analyzing how complex
systems, such as living organisms, survive [5].

Hybrid systems are formal models that combine discrete and continuous dynamics by associating continuous dynamics with each operating mode, while
using discrete logic to switch between operating modes. For example, a hybrid
system may model a vehicle whose underlying motion dynamics varies discretely
depending on terrain conditions. As another example, a hybrid system may
model air-traffic control, where the modes correspond to the cruising of the
planes and the discrete logic models conflict-resolution protocols.

As hybrid systems model more and more complex behaviors, and as they are
often part of devices operating in safety-critical situations, the verification of
safety properties becomes increasingly important. A hybrid system is considered
safe if unsafe states cannot be reached from initial safe states. In general, hybrid-
system verification consists of formally guaranteeing that a certain property is

W. Damm and H. Hermanns (Eds.): CAV 2007, LNCS 4590, pp. 463–476, 2007.

true for the system. A rich theory exists for this problem [6, 7, 8, 9, 10], as well as several tools, such as CHECKMATE[1], HYTECH[2], and PHAVER[3].

Unfortunately, even for safety properties, where verification is equivalent to reachability checking, decidability holds only for hybrid systems with very simple continuous dynamics (essentially some types of linear dynamics) [11]. To handle more general hybrid systems, tools have to resort to overapproximation techniques, surveyed in [12, 13]. Such techniques are semi-decidable, since when a hybrid system is unsafe it may not be possible to show that unsafe states are reachable. Other recent approaches are semi-decidable in the opposite direction: capable of finding unsafe behaviors when the system is unsafe, but unable to determine that a system is safe [14, 15]. In essence, the focus in these recent approaches shifts from *verification* to *falsification*, which often is the main focus of model checking in industrial applications [16].

In this work we study the following problem: *Can we produce a hybrid-system trajectory from a safe state to an unsafe state when such trajectories exist?* This problem is commonly known as *hybrid-system testing*. When a hybrid system is safe, it may not be possible to prove that unsafe states are unreachable. Such an approach trades completeness for the ability to discover safety violations for complex systems that current verification methods cannot handle. Under appropriate conditions and for certain classes of algorithms, as discussed later in the paper, as the running time increases, we can also increase our confidence in the safety of the system, since the testing method has not been able to produce a trajectory that violates safety properties. An efficient framework for finding trajectories to unsafe states can shed light on the operation of the hybrid system and may suggest possible interventions. Such framework is particularly useful in the early stages of hybrid-system development, when errors in design are common.

This work approaches hybrid-system testing using a robotics-inspired method. Initially, we exploit the insight that hybrid-system testing is in many respects related to robot motion planning. The motion-planning problem consists of searching a continuous space for a trajectory for a robotic system from an initial to a final state, such that kinodynamic constraints on the robot motion are respected and collision with obstacles are avoided [17, 18]. Hybrid-system testing is also a reachability analysis on the state space of the hybrid system. In particular, finding a trajectory from a safe to an unsafe state in a hybrid system entails searching a high-dimensional state space with continuous and discrete components.

The connection with motion planning becomes deeper when we consider state-of-the art motion-planning algorithms as the starting point for the methods used for searching the continuous state space of a hybrid system. Recent advances in motion planning have made it possible to efficiently find trajectories from initial to final states even for continuous systems with hundreds of dimensions whose motion is governed by nonlinear dynamics [17, 18, 19, 20, 21, 22, 23, 24].

---

[1] http://www.ece.cmu.edu/~webk/checkmate/

[2] http://embedded.eecs.berkeley.edu/research/hytech/

[3] http://www.cs.ru.nl/~goranf/

The most successful planning methods are numerical, sampling-based methods. These methods generate samples in the state space and connect them with simple trajectories. (e.g., PRM [25], RRT [19], EST [20], PDST [22], GRIP [23], DSLX-Plan [24], and others [17,18]). Motion planning methods, such as RRT, have already been used for hybrid-system testing for nonlinear hybrid systems with few modes [15,14].

Departing from traditional robot motion planning, we introduce a discrete component to our work that is responsible for managing the potentially huge complexity of the discrete transitions. The contribution of this work is the development of a multi-layered framework for hybrid-system testing that blends sampling-based motion planning with discrete searching. The motivation and many of our design decisions come from our earlier work [26,24]. In [26] we use discrete search to obtain a sequence of transitions that guides the generation of motions for a hybrid robotic system with 10–30 modes and mostly linear dynamics. In [24] we show that traditional motion-planning problems can be solved more efficiently by combining sampling-based motion planning with discrete search over an artificially imposed decomposition of the environment on which the robot moves (which in general can be regarded as a projection of its state space). The work presented in this paper combines and extends ideas developed in [26,24] to obtain an effective testing method for hybrid systems with thousands of modes and nonlinear dynamics.

The proposed method, HyDICE, imposes a coarse-grained decomposition on the continuous state space associated with each mode. The decomposition and the discrete transitions of the hybrid system are used to construct a discrete search graph. Vertices of the search graph correspond to decomposition regions, while edges connect vertices corresponding to two adjacent decomposition regions or two decomposition regions that are connected by a discrete transition. The search graph is used to find *leads*, that is sequences of decomposition regions that constitute search directions and may be useful in finding a trajectory from a safe to an unsafe state. The search inside each of the continuous decomposition regions is done by a state-of-the-art sampling-based motion-planning technique. Information gathered during exploration, such as region coverage, exploration time and progress, and other quantities, are used to refine the discrete search and improve the quality of the lead computed for the next exploration step.

In contrast to previous work [15,14], the multi-layered approach developed in this paper is well-suited for systems with many modes and transitions and offers considerable computational improvements over existing methods as demonstrated in this paper. Initial validation of HyDICE is provided by testing hybrid systems inspired by motion-planning problems that have thousands of modes and transitions and nonlinear dynamics associated with each mode. As indicated by the experiments, the tight integration of discrete search and exploration enables HyDICE to be up to two orders of magnitude faster than other related methods.

The rest of the paper is as follows. The hybrid-testing problem and the hybrid system used in the experiments are described in Section 2. Details of HyDICE are provided in Section 3. Experiments and results are presented in Section 4. We conclude in Section 5 with a discussion.

2 Problem Description

2.1 Hybrid Automata and Hybrid-Testing Problem

In this work, hybrid systems are modeled by hybrid automata [6]. A hybrid automaton is a tuple $H = (S, E, G, J, f, U, I, F)$, where $S = Q \times X$; Q is a discrete and finite set; each $X_q \in X$, $X_q \subseteq R^{\dim(X_q)}$, represents the continuous space associated with $q \in Q$; $E \subseteq Q \times Q$ indicates discrete transitions; each $G_{(q_i,q_j)} \in G$, $G_{(q_i,q_j)} \subseteq X_{q_i}$, and each $J_{(q_i,q_j)} \in J$, $J_{(q_i,q_j)} : X_{q_i} \rightarrow X_{q_j}$, represent the guard set and reset function associated with $(q_i, q_j) \in E$, respectively. The continuous dynamics of the system in each $q \in Q$ is governed by a set of differential equations $f_q : X_q \times U_q \rightarrow \mathrm{Tg}X_q$, where $f_q \in f$, $U_q \subseteq R^{\dim(U_q)}$ denotes the set of possible input controls, and $\mathrm{Tg}X_q$ denotes the tangent space of X_q. Each $X_q \in X$ usually includes derivatives of different orders, e.g., velocity and acceleration of a car, and thus f_q is typically nonlinear. The function f_q has the form $f_q(x, u_q(x))$, where the input $u_q(x) \in U_q$ associated with each $x \in X_q$ could represent continuous controls, nondeterminism, uncertainties, disturbances from the environment, or actions of other systems. In order to model these factors, the assignment $u_q(x) \in U_q$ could be non-deterministic or selected according to some probability distribution associated with U_q.

A hybrid system trajectory consists of one or more continuous trajectories interleaved with discrete transitions. Starting at some state $(q_0, x_0) \in I$, where $I \in S$ denotes the set of initial states, the system evolves according to f_{q_0} until it reaches $G_{(q_0,q_1)}$, for some $q_1 \in Q$. Then a discrete transition to q_1 occurs and the continuous state is reset by $J_{(q_0,q_1)}(x_0)$. The system evolution continues in such manner until the end of execution time.

A hybrid system is considered unsafe if a witness trajectory is produced that takes the hybrid system from some initial safe state $s_{\mathrm{safe}} \in I$ to some $s_{\mathrm{unsafe}} \in F$, where $F \subseteq S$ denotes a set of unsafe states.

2.2 A Hybrid System Inspired by Motion Planning Problems

The hybrid system used throughout this paper consists of an autonomous robotic car, whose underlying dynamics change discretely depending on terrain conditions. The choice of this specific system is to provide a concrete, scalable benchmark in which the competitiveness of our approach can be tested.

A given environment is divided into a number of terrains $\{R_1, \ldots, R_N\}$, where each R_i corresponds to an operating mode $q_i \in Q$. The motion of the robotic car inside each terrain is specified by a set of ordinary differential equations. A discrete transition (q_i, q_j) occurs when the robotic car enters a part of R_i designated as the guard set $G_{(q_i,q_j)}$. The discrete transition indicates necessary changes in the way the robotic car should be controlled to adapt to changes in terrain conditions. After entering R_j, the continuous state of the robotic car is reset as specified by $J_{(q_i, q_j)}$ and the underlying dynamics of the car is specified according to the motion equations associated with $q_j \in Q$. The robotic car is said to have entered some unsafe state, for example, if it is in a particular terrain R_j and the speed is above a certain predefined threshold. The robotic car could behave as a kinematic (first-order) car (KCar), smooth (second-order) car (SCar), smooth Reeds-Shepp car (RSCar), smooth unicycle (SUni), or smooth differential drive (SDDrive). Detailed descriptions of these models can be found in [17,18].

Kinematic Car (KCar): A continuous state x is of the form $x = [p, \theta]$, where $p \in \mathbb{R}^2$ and $\theta \in (-\pi, \pi]$ denote the position and orientation of the robotic car. The motion equations are $\dot{p}_0 = u_0(x) \cos(\theta); \dot{p}_1 = u_1(x) \sin(\theta); \dot{\theta} = u_0(x) \tan(u_1(x))/L$, where $u_0(x) \in [-1, 1]$ and $u_1(x) \in [-1, 1]$ are the speed and steering wheel controls and L is the distance between the front and rear axles.

Smooth Car (SCar): The kinematic car model can be extended to a second-order model by expressing the velocity v and steering angle ϕ as differential equations of the acceleration $u_0(x)$ and the rotational velocity of the steering wheel $u_1(x)$ controls, as follows: $x = [p, \theta, v, \phi]$ and $\dot{p}_0 = v \cos(\theta); \dot{p}_1 = v \sin(\theta); \dot{\theta} = v \tan(\phi)/L; \dot{v} = u_0(x); \dot{\phi} = u_1(x)$.

Smooth Reeds-Shepp Car (RSCar): A smooth Reeds-Shepp car is similar to a smooth car, but the acceleration control $u_0(x)$ is only allowed to be from the set $\{-\max, 0, \max\}$, where $\max \in \mathbb{R}$ is some predefined parameter.

Smooth Unicycle (SUni): The continuous state x is $x = [p, \theta, v, \omega]$, where p, θ, v are as in the smooth car model and ω indicates the rotational velocity. The motion equations are $\dot{p}_0 = v \cos(\theta); \dot{p}_1 = v \sin(\theta); \dot{\theta} = \omega; \dot{v} = u_0(x); \dot{\omega} = u_1(x)$.

Smooth Differential Drive (SDDrive): The motion equations are $\dot{p}_0 = 0.5r(\omega_\ell + \omega_r) \cos(\theta); \dot{p}_1 = 0.5r(\omega_\ell + \omega_r) \sin(\theta); \dot{\theta} = r(\omega_r - \omega_\ell)/L; \dot{\omega}_\ell = u_0(x); \dot{\omega}_r = u_1(x)$, where $x = [p, \theta, \omega_\ell, \omega_r]$ is the continuous state; ω_ℓ and ω_r are the rotational velocities of the left and right wheels, respectively; r is the wheel radius; and L is the length of the axis connecting the centers of the two wheels.

The controls $u_0(x)$ and $u_1(x)$ could be thought of as playing the role of the automatic driver. The objective of hybrid-system testing is then to test the safety of the automatic driver, i.e., the driver is unsafe if a witness trajectory is produced that indicates that it is possible for the robotic car to enter an unsafe state. Due to length limitations of this paper, we only provide high-level descriptions of the automatic drivers.[4] These driver models consist of simple if-then-else statements depending on the state values and motion equations. In the first model, RandomDriver, $u_0(x)$ and $u_1(x)$ are selected pseudo-uniformly at random from some $[-\max_0, \max_0]$ and $[-\max_1, \max_1]$, respectively. In a second model, StudentDriver, the driver follows an approach similar to stop-and-go. When the speed is close to zero, StudentDriver selects $u_0(x)$ and $u_1(x)$ as in the RandomDriver model. Otherwise, StudentDriver selects controls that reduce the speed. The third model, HighwayDriver attempts to maintain the speed

---

[4] See http://www.cs.rice.edu/CS/Robotics/CAV2007data/ for more details.

within acceptable low and upper bounds and avoid sharp turns. When the speed is too low, `HighwayDriver` selects controls that increase the speed. When the speed is too high, `HighwayDriver` selects controls that slow down the robotic car. When the speed is between the low and upper bounds, `HighwayDriver` selects controls that do not change the speed too much.

3 Methods

As discussed in the introduction, `HyDICE` constructs a discrete search graph based on the discrete transitions and a decomposition of the continuous state spaces. Observe that any witness trajectory from $s_{safe} \in I$ to $s_{unsafe} \in F$ passes through a sequence of decomposition regions. Although the converse does not hold, a sequence of connected decomposition regions, starting and ending in two regions containing states in I and F, respectively, *may* contain a witness trajectory. Such sequences of connected regions, referred to as *leads*, provide search directions which are used by the sampling-based motion-planning method as guides for the exploration of the state space of a given hybrid system.

Algorithm 1. Pseudocode for `HyDICE`

Input: $H = (S, Inv, E, G, J, f, U, I, F)$: hybrid system; $t_{max} \in \mathbb{R}$: upper bound on overall computation time; $t_e \in \mathbb{R}$: short time allocated to each exploration step
Output: A witness trajectory or **FAILURE** if no witness trajectory is found

1: StartClock1
2: $T = (V_T, E_T); V_T \leftarrow \{s_{safe}\}; E_T \leftarrow \emptyset$
3: $D \leftarrow$ CoarseGrainedDecomposition(H)
4: $G_D = (V_D, E_D) \leftarrow$ DiscreteSearchGraph(D)
5: InitExplorationEstimates(G_D)
6: **while** ElapsedTime1 $< t_{max}$ **do**
7:     $\sigma \leftarrow$ DiscreteLead(G_D)
8:     StartClock2
9:     **while** ElapsedTime2 $< t_e$ **do**
10:       $s \leftarrow$ SelectState(T, σ)
11:       $s_{new} \leftarrow$ PropagateForward(H, T, s, σ)
12:       $V_T \leftarrow V_T \cup \{s_{new}\}; E_T \leftarrow E_T \cup \{(s, s_{new})\}$
13:       **if** $s_{new} \in F$ **then return** WitnessTrajectory(T, s_{new})
14:     UpdateExplorationEstimates(G_D, σ)
15: **return FAILURE**

The search for a witness trajectory proceeds iteratively. Throughout the search, `HyDICE` maintains an exploration tree $T = (V_T, E_T)$, which initially contains only s_{safe}, i.e., $V_T = \{s_{safe}\}$ and $E_T = \emptyset$. The vertices V_T are states of S, while an edge $(s', s'') \in E_T$ indicates that a hybrid-system trajectory connects $s' \in S$ to $s'' \in S$. At each iteration, `HyDICE` uses the discrete search graph to compute a lead and then sampling-based motion planning to extend the branches of T in the direction specified by the lead. The branches of T are extended by adding new vertices and edges to V_T and E_T, respectively. A witness trajectory is found when a state $s_{\text{unsafe}} \in F$ is added to $\mathcal{T}$. Otherwise, the search continues until an upper bound on computation time is exceeded. Pseudocode is provided in Algorithm 1. The discrete search and the sampling-based motion planning are described in Sections 3.1 and 3.2, respectively.

3.1 Discrete Search

Coarse-grained Decomposition. HyDICE constructs a coarse-grained decomposition $D = \{D_{q_1}, \ldots, D_{q_N}\}$, where $D_{q_i} = \{D_{q_i,1}, \ldots, D_{q_i,n_i}\}$ denotes the decomposition of X_{q_i} into $n_i \in \mathbb{N}$ different regions (line 3 of Algorithm 1). HyDICE does not impose any strict requirements on the decomposition. D_{q_i} is usually computed as a set of nonoverlapping regions in some low-dimensional projection of X_{q_i}. For the hybrid system used in this work, HyDICE projects each X_{q_i} onto $\mathbb{R}^2$ and constructs a cell-based decomposition. Other types of projections and decompositions are possible [17, 18].

Discrete Search Graph. D is used to create a search graph $G_D = (V_D, E_D)$. A vertex $v_{q_i,j}$ is added to V_D for each $D_{q_i,j}$. An edge $(v_{q_i,j}, v_{q_i,k})$ is added to E_D for each two adjacent regions $D_{q_i,j}$ and $D_{q_i,k}$. Furthermore, an edge $(v_{q_i,j}, v_{q_\ell,k})$ is added to E_D for each two regions $D_{q_i,j}$ and $D_{q_\ell,k}$ such that there is a discrete transition from some state (q_i, x_1), $x_1 \in D_{q_i,j}$, to some state (q_ℓ, x_2), $x_2 \in D_{q_\ell,k}$. There are also two special vertices v_{safe} and v_{unsafe} added to V_D. An edge $(v_{\text{safe}}, v_{q_i,j})$ is added to E_D for each $D_{q_i,j}$ such that $D_{q_i,j} \cap I \neq \emptyset$. Similarly, an edge $(v_{q_i,j}, v_{\text{unsafe}})$ is added to E_D for each $D_{q_i,j}$ such that $D_{q_i,j} \cap F \neq \emptyset$. This operation is found in line 4 of Algorithm 1.

Importance of Leads. A central issue is which lead to choose from the combinatorially large number of possibilities. This issue is addressed by associating a weight $w_{(v_{q_i,j}, v_{q_\ell,k})}$ with each $(v_{q_i,j}, v_{q_\ell,k}) \in E_D$, which estimates the importance of including $(v_{q_i,j}, v_{q_\ell,k}) \in E_D$ as an edge in the lead. Preference is given to leads associated with higher edge weights. For the moment assume that there is no distinction between edges corresponding to discrete transitions and edges connecting adjacent regions in the decomposition. At the end we discuss the possibility of using different weighting schemes depending on the edge type.

Initially, the weights are set to a fixed value (line 5) and updated (line 14) after each exploration step. The weight $w_{(v_{q_i,j}, v_{q_\ell,k})}$ depends on the *coverage* of $D_{q_i,j}$ and $D_{q_\ell,k}$ by $\mathcal{T}$. The coverage $c(\mathcal{T}, D_{q_i,j})$ is computed by imposing an implicit uniform grid on $D_{q_i,j}$ and measuring the fraction of cells that contain at least one state from $\mathcal{T}$. Let $c_{\text{prev}}(\mathcal{T}, D_{q_i,j})$ denote $c(\mathcal{T}, D_{q_i,j})$ at the beginning of the current exploration step (before line 9) and let $c_{\text{after}}(\mathcal{T}, D_{q_i,j})$ denote $c(\mathcal{T}, D_{q_i,j})$ at the end of the exploration step (after line 13). Thus $\Delta c(\mathcal{T}, D_{q_i,j}) = c_{\text{after}}(\mathcal{T}, D_{q_i,j}) - c_{\text{prev}}(\mathcal{T}, D_{q_i,j})$ indicates the change in the coverage of $D_{q_i,j}$ by $\mathcal{T}$ as a result of the current exploration step. $c(\mathcal{T}, D_{q_\ell,k})$, $c_{\text{prev}}(\mathcal{T}, D_{q_\ell,k})$, $c_{\text{after}}(\mathcal{T}, D_{q_\ell,k})$, and $\Delta c(\mathcal{T}, D_{q_\ell,k})$ are defined similarly. Let t denote the computation time devoted to the exploration of $D_{q_i,j}$ and $D_{q_\ell,k}$ during the current exploration step and let $t_{\text{acc}}(D_{q_i,j}, D_{q_\ell,k})$ denote the accumulated exploration time devoted to $D_{q_i,j}$ and $D_{q_\ell,k}$. Then, the weight $w_{(v_{q_i,j}, v_{q_\ell,k})}$ is defined as

$$w_{(v_{q_i,j},v_{q_\ell,k})} = (1 - \epsilon)(\Delta c(\mathcal{T}, D_{q_i,j}) + \Delta c(\mathcal{T}, D_{q_\ell,k}))/(2t) + \epsilon/t_{\mathrm{acc}}(D_{q_i,j}, D_{q_\ell,k}),$$

where $0 < \epsilon < 1$ is a normalization constant. Large values of $w_{(v_{q_i,j},v_{q_\ell,k})}$ indicate promising leads, since such values are obtained when $\mathcal{T}$ in a short amount of time reaches previously uncovered parts of $D_{q_i,j}$ and $D_{q_\ell,k}$. $t_{\mathrm{acc}}(i,j)$ is used to increase the weight of those regions that have been explored less frequently.

As described so far the same procedure determines $w_{(v_{q_i,j},v_{q_\ell,k})}$, regardless of whether the edge from $D_{q_i,j}$ to $D_{q_\ell,k}$ corresponds to a discrete transition or adjacency in the decomposition. Intuitively, edges corresponding to discrete transitions may be more important, as they guide the sampling-based motion planner to extend branches of $\mathcal{T}$ from one continuous state space to another. For this reason, each $w_{(v_{q_i,j},v_{q_\ell,k})}$ corresponding to a discrete transition is multiplied by some constant $w > 1$. Depending on the problem, it may also be beneficial to estimate the weights corresponding to discrete transitions differently.

Computation of Leads. Leads associated with higher edge weights are selected more frequently. At the same time, each lead has a non-zero probability of being selected. In this way, HyDICE aims to obtain a balance between greedy and methodical search. The computation of leads is essentially a graph-search problem and there is extensive literature on the subject [27]. The approach undertaken in this work is to use combinations of different strategies, such as randomized depth-first search where the weights associated with each edge in E_D are used to select the successor vertices in the search process, Dijkstra's algorithm, and other graph-search methods [27]. For considerably larger problems, approaches from model checking, such as bounded model checking [28] or directed model checking [29], could also be used (see also discussion in Section 5).

DISCRETELEAD(G_D) (line 7) returns more frequently the most probable lead and the lead associated with the highest sum of edge weights and less frequently leads computed by randomized depth-first search. The most probable lead is computed using Dijkstra's algorithm and setting the weight function used in the graph search to $-\log(w_{(v_{q_i,j},v_{q_\ell,k})}/w_{\mathrm{total}})$ for $(v_{q_i,j}, v_{q_\ell,k}) \in E_D$, where $w_{\mathrm{total}} = \sum_{(v',v'')\in E_D} w_{(v',v'')}$. The lead with the highest sum of edge weights is computed using Dijkstra's algorithm and setting the weight function to $w_{\max} - w_{(v_{q_i,j},v_{q_\ell,k})}$ for $(v_{q_i,j}, v_{q_\ell,k}) \in E_D$, where $w_{\max}$ denotes the maximum weight.

3.2   Sampling-Based Motion Planning

The objective of the exploration step (lines 9–13) is to use the lead σ to extend $\mathcal{T}$ toward F. The exploration step proceeds iteratively by selecting a state s from $\mathcal{T}$ and propagating forward from s to a new state s_{new}.

Conceptually, forward propagation provides the necessary mechanism for sampling-based motion planning to extend the branches of $\mathcal{T}$ and explore the state space. The forward propagation from s entails simulating the evolution of H starting at s and for a duration of t units of time, where t is selected pseudo-uniformly at random from $[\min_t, \max_t] \subset (0, \infty)$. The simulation can be computed by numerically integrating the motion equations for a short period of time and following the appropriate discrete transitions when guard conditions are met. The simulation terminates if at any point an unsafe state is reached (see [14] for more details). The new state s_{new} obtained at the end of the simulation and the edge (s, s_{new}) are added to the vertices and edges of $\mathcal{T}$, respectively.

SELECTSTATE$(\mathcal{T}, \sigma)$ (line 10) selects more frequently states s from $\mathcal{T}$, which, when propagated forward, bring $\mathcal{T}$ closer to F. Let $D_{q_{i_1},j_1}, \ldots, D_{q_{i_n},j_n}$ be the coarse-grained decomposition regions associated with the sequence of vertices $v_{\text{safe}}, v_{q_{i_1},j_1}, \ldots, v_{q_{i_n},j_n}, v_{\text{unsafe}}$ in σ. Since σ is a sequence of edges from v_{safe} to v_{unsafe}, the order $1 \le k \le n$ in which $v_{q_{i_k},j_k}$ appears in σ provides an indication of how close $D_{q_{i_k},j_k}$ is to F. Since the objective of the exploration step is to extend branches of $\mathcal{T}$ closer to F, HyDICE gives preference to regions $D_{q_{i_k},j_k}$ that are closer to F, i.e., k is close to n. To balance this greedy approach, HyDICE also takes into account the overall exploration time $t_{\text{acc}}(D_{q_{i_k},j_k})$ spent in each $D_{q_{i_k},j_k}$ and the coverage $c(\mathcal{T}, D_{q_{i_k},j_k})$. If $D_{q_{i_k},j_k}$ contains states from $\mathcal{T}$, let $w_k = \alpha k/n + \beta/c(\mathcal{T}, D_{q_{i_k},j_k}) + \gamma/t_{\text{acc}}(D_{q_{i_k},j_k})$, where α, β, and γ are normalization constants. Otherwise, let $w_k = 0$. SELECTSTATE$(\mathcal{T}, \sigma)$ selects a region $D_{q_{i_k},j_k}$ with probability $w_k / \sum_{h=1}^{m} w_h$. Each state s from $\mathcal{T}$ that is contained in $D_{q_{i_k},j_k}$ is selected with probability $1/\text{nsel}(s)$, where $\text{nsel}(s)$ is the number of times s has been previously selected. Preference is thus given to states that have been selected less frequently, since such states, when propagated forward, can cause $\mathcal{T}$ to extend in previously unexplored directions.

PROPAGATEFORWARD$(H, \mathcal{T}, s, \sigma)$ attempts to extend s toward $D_{q_{i_{k+1}},j_{k+1}}$ and thus bring $\mathcal{T}$ closer to F. Since the evolution of H can be nondeterministic, PROPAGATEFORWARD$(H, \mathcal{T}, s, \sigma)$ tries several times to propagate forward from s. Let s_{new_i} be the state obtained after simulating the evolution of H from s for a duration of t_i units of time, where t_i is selected pseudo-uniformly at random from $[\min_t, \max_t]$. PROPAGATEFORWARD$(H, \mathcal{T}, s, \sigma)$ computes s_{new} as the state s_{new_i} that is the closest to $D_{q_{i_{k+1}},j_{k+1}}$. A witness trajectory is found if $s_{\text{new}} \in F$. The witness trajectory is computed by reconstructing the evolution of the hybrid system from s_{safe} to s_{new} following the appropriate edges of $\mathcal{T}$ (line 13).

4   Experiments and Results

Experiments are performed using the hybrid robotic system described in Section 2.2. The hybrid robotic system is made increasingly complex by increasing the number of modes. This paper presents experiments with up to 10000 modes.

An important part of experiments is the comparison with previous related work. The closest work we can compare to is the application of RRT to hybrid systems [14, 15]. We also provide experiments that indicate the impact of the discrete search on the computational efficiency of HyDICE.

A problem instance is obtained by fixing the number N of operating modes of the hybrid robotic car. The continuous dynamics associated with each mode q_i (or terrain R_i) is selected pseudo-uniformly at random from KCar, SCar, RSCar, SUni, and SDDrive. The set of discrete transitions E is created as follows. Initially, discrete transitions are added between each pair R_i, R_j of neighboring terrains. A disjoint-set strategy, similar to maze creation, is then used to remove certain discrete transitions. Furthermore, each remaining discrete transition is kept with probability p. We experimented with different values of p and found that it has minimal impact on the comparisons between HyDICE and RRT. Experiments reported in this paper use $p = 0.1$. For each problem instance, we create 30 safety properties. Each safety property is created by selecting pseudo-uniformly at random one terrain as safe and another one as unsafe. As discussed in Section 2.2, the hybrid robotic car is said to have entered some unsafe state, if it is in an unsafe terrain and its speed is above a certain predefined threshold. In all the experiments, the systems were unsafe. For safe systems, since the hybrid-system testing problem is generally undecidable, all the tools used in the experiments would timeout.

Results. For each problem instance, experiments are run using each of the driver models. Results are summarized in Table 1. We report the average computational time in seconds required by RRT, HyDICE*, and HyDICE to test 30 safety properties. HyDICE* refers to the version of HyDICE that does not use the discrete-search component, i.e., HyDICE* is the sampling-based motion planner of HyDICE with some minor modifications.[5] Comparisons include HyDICE* to investigate the importance of the discrete search on HyDICE. An entry marked with X indicates that the testing method timed out. The upper bound on time was set to 3000s for each safety property testing. The time allocated to each exploration step by HyDICE (t_e in Algorithm 1) was set to 1s. The Rice PBC Cluster and Rice Cray XD1 Cluster ADA were used for code development. Experiments were run on ADA, where each processor runs at 2.2GHz and has up to 8GB of RAM.

Table 1. Summary of experimental comparisons. Time is in seconds

	RandomDriver			StudentDriver			HighwayDriver		
$\|Q\|$	RRT	HyDICE*	HyDICE	RRT	HyDICE*	HyDICE	RRT	HyDICE*	HyDICE
100	22.30	4.34	2.68	74.01	6.74	2.20	21.29	4.92	2.82
225	117.79	14.02	6.24	336.85	32.44	5.24	230.88	21.64	6.30
525	295.88	75.60	6.87	792.45	65.40	15.52	668.67	106.56	16.31
900	504.93	175.96	13.74	X	120.48	17.06	2596.50	182.54	36.96
1600	2159.24	289.94	32.52	X	464.56	34.14	X	374.44	37.26
2500	X	910.86	60.18	X	699.66	62.30	X	929.36	71.44
10000	X	X	439.88	X	X	457.60	X	X	445.52

Table 1 shows that HyDICE is consistently more efficient than RRT. When the RandomDriver model is used, HyDICE is 8.32, 18.87, 43.06, and 66.39 times faster than RRT, as the number of modes is increased to 100, 225, 525, and 1600, respectively. Furthermore, RRT times out when $|Q| = 2500$, while HyDICE requires only 60.18s. Similarly, when the StudentDriver model is used, the computational

---

[5] HyDICE* can be obtained from the implementation of HyDICE by computing the lead σ as $v_{\text{safe}}, \gamma, v_{\text{unsafe}}$, where γ is a random permutation of $V_D - \{v_{\text{safe}}, v_{\text{unsafe}}\}$, where, as described in Section 3, $G_D = (V_D, E_D)$ is the search graph.

speedups obtained by HyDICE vary from 33.64 to 51.05 on instances where RRT does not time out. Under the StudentDriver model, RRT times out on instances with $|Q| = 900$, while HyDICE requires only 17.06s. The StudentDriver model is particularly computationally challenging for RRT since the stop-and-go approach it uses makes it difficult for RRT to extend the exploration tree. On the other hand, since HyDICE relies on a discrete search component it successfully extends the exploration tree and quickly reaches unsafe states. Similar observations are made for the HighwayDriver model as well.

Table 1 indicates that HyDICE is up to two orders of magnitude computationally faster than RRT. Table 1 also shows that HyDICE scales up reasonably well with respect to $|Q|$. In fact, RRT timed out in all cases when $|Q| \geq 2500$, while HyDICE is shown to handle problems even with $|Q| = 10000$ quite efficiently.

The second set of experiments provides insight on the observed computational efficiency of HyDICE. In particular, we investigate the importance of the discrete search on HyDICE. Table 1 shows that although HyDICE* is still faster than RRT, it is considerably slower than HyDICE. (For a discussion on issues related to the computational efficiency of RRT and sampling-based motion planners similar to HyDICE* see [17, 18, 21, 24].) For example, when $|Q| = 2500$, HyDICE* is 11–15 times slower than HyDICE. Furthermore, HyDICE* times out on instances with $|Q| = 10000$, while HyDICE handles such instances efficiently. These results highlight the importance of the discrete search and agree with observations made in [24]. The interplay between lead computations and sampling-based exploration has the desired effect of quickly improving the quality of future leads and explorations and bringing the search closer to obtaining a solution. By guiding the exploration, the discrete search significantly improves the computational efficiency of HyDICE.

5   Discussion

We have presented HyDICE, a multi-layered approach for hybrid-system testing that blends sampling-based motion planning with discrete searching. The discrete search, responsible for managing the potentially huge complexity of discrete transitions, also uses coarse-grained decompositions of the continuous state spaces or related projections to guide the motion planner during the search for witness trajectories. The motion planner feeds back to the discrete search information gathered during the exploration, which is then used to further refine the discrete search and guide the motion planner toward increasingly promising search directions. This tight integration of discrete search and motion planning in the framework of HyDICE offers considerable computational advantages over related work. Experiments presented in this paper, using a hybrid robotic car, different driving models, and nonlinear dynamics associated with each of the several thousand modes, provide initial validation of HyDICE and demonstrate its promise as a hybrid-system testing method. Comparisons to related work show computational speedups of up to two orders of magnitude.

Although HyDICE was shown to handle a system with thousands of modes and nonlinear dynamics, the scalability issue is relevant and remains open to further research. As the number of modes becomes significantly large, the simple graph-search strategies used in this work becomes a computational bottleneck and need to be replaced with state-of-the-art techniques developed in the verification community which can handle discrete systems with billions of modes [30].

Additionally, the search graph is based on a decomposition of the continuous state spaces or related projections and the ability to determine whether or not two decomposition regions are connected by a discrete transition. Depending on the hybrid system, guard sets, and reset functions it may be challenging to determine if such discrete transition exists. In such cases, a viable approach would be to resort to approximations of guard sets and reset functions, which also requires investigating the overall impact of approximations on HyDICE.

One important theoretical issue that is subject of ongoing research relates to guarantees HyDICE can offer for general hybrid-system testing. Although completeness cannot be guaranteed, since the problem is generally undecidable, our belief is that HyDICE offers a weaker form of completeness, referred to as *probabilistic completeness*. Guaranteeing probabilistic completeness means that, for unsafe systems, the probability of finding a witness trajectory goes to one as the running time approaches infinity [17]. Probabilistic completeness allows us to increase the confidence in the safety of the system as the running time increases. The work in [31] has already proven probabilistic completeness in a continuous setting for certain classes of motion-planning methods, such as the one used by HyDICE. The theoretical framework developed in [31] is also promising for showing probabilistic completeness in a hybrid-system setting and we are currently investigating such an approach.

We also intend in future work to experiment with HyDICE in other settings and apply it to increasingly realistic and complex hybrid systems.

Acknowledgment

This work has been supported in part by NSF CNS 0615328 (EP, LEK, MYV), NSF 0308237 (EP, LEK), a Sloan Fellowship (LEK), and NSF CCF 0613889 (MYV). Experiments were obtained on equipment supported by NSF CNS 0454333 and NSF CNS 0421109 in partnership with Rice University, AMD, and Cray.

References

1. Glover, W., Lygeros, J.: A stochastic hybrid model for air traffic control simulation. In: Alur, R., Pappas, G.J. (eds.) HSCC 2004. LNCS, vol. 2993, pp. 372–386. Springer, Heidelberg (2004)
2. Pepyne, D., Cassandras, C.: Optimal control of hybrid systems in manufacturing. Proceedings of IEEE 88(7), 1108–1123 (2000)
3. Johansson, R., Rantzer, A. (eds.): Nonlinear and Hybrid Systems in Automotive Control. Springer, London, UK (2003)

4. Dounias, G., Linkens, D.A.: Adaptive systems and hybrid computational intelligence in medicine. Artificial Intelligence in Medicine 32(3), 151–155 (2004)
5. Piazza, C., Antoniotti, M., Mysore, V., Policriti, A., Winkler, F., Mishra, B.: Algorithmic algebraic model checking I: Challenges from systems biology. In: Etessami, K., Rajamani, S.K. (eds.) CAV 2005. LNCS, vol. 3576, pp. 5–19. Springer, Heidelberg (2005)
6. Alur, R., Courcoubetis, C., Henzinger, T., Ho, P.H.: Hybrid automata: an algorithmic approach to the specification and verification of hybrid systems. In: Grossman, R.L., Ravn, A.P., Rischel, H., Nerode, A. (eds.) Hybrid Systems. LNCS, vol. 736, pp. 209–229. Springer, Heidelberg (1993)
7. Henzinger, T., Kopke, P., Puri, A., Varaiya, P.: What's decidable about hybrid automata? In: STOC, pp. 373–382. ACM Press, New York (1995)
8. Henzinger, T.: The theory of hybrid automata. In: Proc. 11th IEEE Symp. on Logic in Computer Science, DIMACS, pp. 278–292. IEEE Computer Society Press, Los Alamitos (1996)
9. Lafferriere, G., Pappas, G., Yovine, S.: A new class of decidable hybrid systems. In: Vaandrager, F.W., van Schuppen, J.H. (eds.) HSCC 1999. LNCS, vol. 1569, pp. 137–151. Springer, Heidelberg (1999)
10. Puri, A.: Theory of Hybrid Systems and Discrete Event Systems. PhD thesis, University of California, Berkeley (1995)
11. Tomlin, C.J., Mitchell, I., Bayen, A., Oishi, M.: Computational techniques for the verification and control of hybrid systems. In: Proc. of IEEE, vol. 91(7), pp. 986–1001 (2003)
12. Chutinan, C., Krogh, B.H.: Computational techniques for hybrid system verification. IEEE Transactions on Automatic Control 48(1), 64–75 (2003)
13. Silva, B., Stursberg, O., Krogh, B., Engell, S.: An assessment of the current status of algorithmic approaches to the verification of hybrid systems. In: IEEE Conf. on Decision and Control. vol. 3, pp. 2867–2874 (2001)
14. Esposito, J.M., Kim, J., Kumar, V.: Adaptive RRTs for validating hybrid robotic control systems. In: WAFR, Zeist, Netherlands, PP. 107–132 (2004)
15. Kim, J., Esposito, J.M., Kumar, V.: An RRT-based algorithm for testing and validating multi-robot controllers. In: RSS, Boston, MA, 249–256 (2005)
16. Copty, F., Fix, L., Fraer, R., Giunchiglia, E., Kamhi, G., Tacchella, A., Vardi, M.: Benefits of bounded model checking at an industrial setting. In: Berry, G., Comon, H., Finkel, A. (eds.) CAV 2001. LNCS, vol. 2102, pp. 436–453. Springer, Heidelberg (2001)
17. Choset, H., Lynch, K.M., Hutchinson, S., Kantor, G., Burgard, W., Kavraki, L.E., Thrun, S.: Principles of Robot Motion: Theory, Algorithms, and Implementations. MIT Press, Cambridge, MA (2005)
18. LaValle, S.M.: Planning Algorithms. Cambridge University Press, Cambridge (2006)
19. LaValle, S.M., Kuffner, J.J.: Rapidly-exploring random trees: Progress and prospects. In: Donald, B.R., Lynch, K., Rus, D. (eds.) WAFR, pp. 293–308 (2000)
20. Hsu, D., Kindel, R., Latombe, J.C., Rock, S.: Randomized kinodynamic motion planning with moving obstacles. IJRR 21(3), 233–255 (2002)
21. Plaku, E., Bekris, K.E., Chen, B.Y., Ladd, A.M., Kavraki, L.E.: Sampling-based roadmap of trees for parallel motion planning. IEEE Trans. on Robotics 21(4), 597–608 (2005)
22. Ladd, A.M., Kavraki, L.E.: Motion planning in the presence of drift, underactuation and discrete system changes. In: RSS, Boston, MA, pp. 233–241 (2005)

23. Bekris, K.E., Kavraki, L.E.: Greedy but safe replanning under kinodynamic constraints. In: IEEE ICRA, Rome, Italy (2007)
24. Plaku, E., Vardi, M.Y., Kavraki, L.E.: Discrete search leading continuous exploration for kinodynamic motion planning. In: RSS, Atlanta, GA (2007)
25. Kavraki, L.E., Švestka, P., Latombe, J.C., Overmars, M.H.: Probabilistic roadmaps for path planning in high-dimensional configuration spaces. IEEE Transactions on Robotics and Automation 12(4), 566–580 (1996)
26. Plaku, E., Kavraki, L.E., Vardi, M.Y.: A motion planner for a hybrid robotic system with kinodynamic constraints. In: IEEE ICRA, Rome, Italy (2007)
27. Zhang, W.: State-space Search: Algorithms, Complexity, Extensions, and Applications. Springer, New York (2006)
28. Biere, A., Cimatti, A., Clarke, E., Fujita, M., Zhu, Y.: Symbolic model checking using SAT procedures instead of BDDs. In: Proc. 36th Design Automation Conference, pp. 317–320. IEEE Computer Society Press, Los Alamitos (1999)
29. Edelkamp, S., Jabbar, S.: Large-scale directed model checking ltl. In: Valmari, A. (ed.) Model Checking Software. LNCS, vol. 3925, pp. 1–18. Springer, Heidelberg (2006)
30. Burch, J., Clarke, E., McMillan, K., Dill, D., Hwang, L.: Symbolic model checking: 10^{20} states and beyond. Information and Computation 98(2), 142–170 (1992)
31. Ladd, A.M.: Motion Planning for Physical Simulation. PhD thesis, Rice University, Houston, TX (2006)

Comparison Under Abstraction
for Verifying Linearizability

Daphna Amit[1,*], Noam Rinetzky[1,**], Thomas Reps[2,***], Mooly Sagiv[1],
and Eran Yahav[3]

[1] Tel Aviv University
{amitdaph,maon,msagiv}@tau.ac.il
[2] University of Wisconsin
reps@cs.wisc.edu
[3] IBM T.J. Watson Research Center
eyahav@us.ibm.com

Abstract. *Linearizability* is one of the main correctness criteria for implementations of concurrent data structures. A data structure is *linearizable* if its operations appear to execute atomically. Verifying linearizability of concurrent unbounded linked data structures is a challenging problem because it requires correlating executions that manipulate (unbounded-size) memory states. We present a static analysis for verifying linearizability of concurrent unbounded linked data structures. The novel aspect of our approach is the ability to prove that two (unbounded-size) memory layouts of two programs are isomorphic in the presence of abstraction. A prototype implementation of the analysis verified the linearizability of several published concurrent data structures implemented by singly-linked lists.

1 Introduction

Linearizability [1] is one of the main correctness criteria for implementations of concurrent data structures (a.k.a. *concurrent objects*). Intuitively, linearizability provides the illusion that any operation performed on a concurrent object takes effect instantaneously at some point between its invocation and its response. One of the benefits of linearizability is that it simplifies reasoning about concurrent programs. If a concurrent object is linearizable, then it is possible to reason about its behavior in a concurrent program by reasoning about its behavior in a (simpler) sequential setting.

Informally, a concurrent object o is linearizable if each concurrent execution of operations on o is equivalent to some permitted sequential execution, in which the global order between non-overlapping operations is preserved. The equivalence

* Supported by a grant from the Israeli Academy of Science.
** Supported in part by the German-Israeli Foundation for Scientific Research and Development (G.I.F.), and in part by a grant from the Israeli Academy of Science.
*** Supported by ONR under grant N00014-01-1-0796 and by NSF under grants CCF-0540955 and CCF-0524051.

W. Damm and H. Hermanns (Eds.): CAV 2007, LNCS 4590, pp. 477–490, 2007.

is based on comparing the arguments and results of operations (responses). The permitted behavior of the concurrent object is defined in terms of a specification of the desired behavior of the object in a sequential setting.

Linearizability is a widely-used concept, and there are numerous non-automatic proofs of linearizability for concurrent objects (See Sec. 6). Proving linearizability is challenging because it requires correlating any concurrent execution with a corresponding permitted sequential execution. Proving linearizability for concurrent objects that are implemented by dynamically allocated linked data-structures is particularly challenging, because it requires correlating executions that may manipulate memory states of unbounded size.

In this paper, we present a novel technique for *automatically* verifying the linearizability of concurrent objects implemented by linked data structures. Technically, we verify that a concurrent object is linearizable by simultaneously analyzing the concurrent implementation with an *executable sequential specification* (i.e., a sequential implementation). The two implementations manipulate two disjoint instances of the data structure. The analysis maintains a partial isomorphism between the memory layouts of the two instances. The abstraction is precise enough to maintain isomorphism when the difference between the memory layouts is of bounded size. Note that the memory states themselves can be of unbounded size.

Implementation. We have implemented a prototype of our approach, and used it to automatically verify the linearizability of several concurrent algorithms, including the queue algorithms of [2] and the stack algorithm of [3]. As far as we know, our approach is the first *fully automatic proof* of linearizability for these algorithms.

Limitations. Our analysis has several limitations: (i) Every concurrent operation has a (specified) *fixed linearization point*, a statement at which the operation appears to take effect. (This restriction can be relaxed to several statements, possibly with conditions.) (ii) We verify linearizability for a fixed but arbitrary number of threads. (iii) We assume a garbage collected environment. Sec. 4 discusses the role of these limitations. We note that the analysis is always sound, even if the specification of linearization points is wrong (see [4]).

Main Results. The contributions of this paper can be summarized as follows:
- We present the first fully automatic algorithm for verifying linearizability of concurrent objects implemented by unbounded linked data structures.
- We introduce a novel heap abstraction that allows an isomorphism between mutable linked data structures to be maintained under abstraction.
- We implemented our analysis and used it to verify linearizability of several unbounded linked data structures.

Due to space reasons, we concentrate on providing an extended overview of our work by applying it to verify the linearizability of a concurrent-stack algorithm due to Treiber [3]. Formal details can be found in [4].

```
[10] #define EMPTY -1
[11] typedef int data_type;
[12] typedef struct node_t {
[13]    data_type d;
[14]    struct node_t *n
[15] } Node;
[16] typedef struct stack_t {
[17]    struct node_t *Top;
[18] } Stack;
```
(a) Stack and Node type definitions

```
[40] void client(Stack *st) {
[41]    do {
[42]       if (?)
[43]          push(st, rand());
[44]       else
[45]          pop(st);
[46]    } while (1);
[47] }
```
(c) The most general client of Stack

```
[20] void push(Stack *S, data_type v){
[21]    Node *x = alloc(sizeof(Node));
[22]    x->d = v;
[23]    do {
[24]       Node *t = S->Top;
[25]       x->n = t;
[26]    } while (!CAS(&S->Top,t,x));   // @1
[27] }

[30] data_type pop(Stack *S){
[31]    do {
[32]       Node *t = S->Top;           // @2
[33]       if (t == NULL)
[34]          return EMPTY;
[35]       Node *s = t->n;
[36]    } while (!CAS(&S->Top,t,s));   // @3
[37]    data_type r = t->d;
[38]    return r;
[39] }
```
(b) Concurrent stack procedures

Fig. 1. A concurrent stack: (a) its type, (b) implementation, and (c) most general client

2   Verification Challenge

Fig. 1(a) and (b) show C-like pseudo code for a concurrent stack that maintains its data items in a singly-linked list of nodes, held by the stack's Top-field. Stacks can be (directly) manipulated only by the shown procedures push and pop, which have their standard meaning.

The procedures push and pop attempt to update the stack, but avoid the update and retry the operation when they observe that another thread changed Top concurrently. Technically, this is done by repeatedly executing the following code: At the beginning of every iteration, they read a local copy of the Top-field into a local variable t. At the end of every iteration, they attempt to update the stack's Top-field using the Compare-and-Swap (CAS) synchronization primitive. CAS(&S->Top,t,x) atomically compares the value of S->Top with the value of t and, if the two match, the CAS succeeds: it stores the value of x in S->Top, and evaluates to 1. Otherwise, the CAS fails: the value of S->Top remains unchanged and the CAS evaluates to 0. If the CAS fails, i.e., Top was modified concurrently, push and pop restart their respective loops.

Specification. The linearization point of push is the CAS statement in line [26] (marked with @1). This linearization point is conditional: Only a successful CAS is considered to be a linearization point. Procedure pop has two (conditional) linearization points: Reading the local copy of Top in line [32] (marked with @2) is a linearization point, if it finds that Top has a *NULL*-value. The CAS in line [36] (marked with @3) is a linearization point, if it succeeds.

Goal. We verify that the stack algorithm is linearizable with the specified linearization points for 2 threads, using its own code as a sequential specification.

3   Our Approach

We use abstract interpretation of a non-standard concrete semantics, the *correlating semantics*, abstracted by a novel *delta heap abstraction* to conservatively verify that every execution of any program that manipulates a stack using 2 threads is linearizable. Technically, we simulate the executions of all such programs using a single program that has two threads running the stack's most-general-client and using a shared stack. (The stack's most general client, shown in Fig. 1(c), is a procedure that invokes an arbitrary nondeterministic sequence of operations on the stack.)

3.1   The Correlating Semantics

The correlating semantics "checks at runtime" that an execution is linearizable. It simultaneously manipulates two memory states: the *candidate* state and the *reference* state. The *candidate* state is manipulated according to the interleaved execution. Whenever a thread reaches a linearization point in a given procedure, e.g., executes a successful CAS while pushing data value 4, the correlating semantics invokes the same procedure with the same arguments, e.g., invokes push with 4 as its value argument, on the reference state. The interleaved execution is not allowed to proceed until the execution over the reference state terminates. The reference response (return value) is saved, and compared to the response of the *corresponding* candidate operation when it terminates. This allows to directly test the linearizability of the interleaved execution by constructing a (serial) *witness* execution for every interleaved execution. In the example, we need to show that corresponding pops return identical results.

Example 1. Fig. 2(a) shows a part of a candidate execution and the corresponding fragment of the reference execution (the witness) as constructed by the correlating semantics. Fig. 2(b) shows some of the correlated states that occur in the example execution. Every correlated state consists of two states: the candidate state (shown with a clear background), and the reference state (shown with a shaded background).

The execution fragment begins in the correlated state σ_a. The candidate (resp. reference) state contains a list with two nodes, pointed to by the Top-*field* of the candidate (resp. reference) stack. To avoid clutter, we *do not draw the Stack object* itself. In the reference state we add an r-superscript to the names of fields and variables. (We subscript variable names with the id of the thread they belong to.) For now, please ignore the edges crossing the boundary between the states.

In the example execution, thread B pushes 7 into the stack, concurrently with A pushing 4. The execution begins with thread B allocating a node and linking it to the list. At this point, σ_b, thread A's invocation starts. Although B's invocation precedes A's invocation, thread A reaches a linearization point before B. Thus, after thread A executes a successful CAS on state σ_c, resulting in state σ_d, the correlating semantics freezes the execution in the candidate state and starts A executing push(4) uninterruptedly in the reference state. When

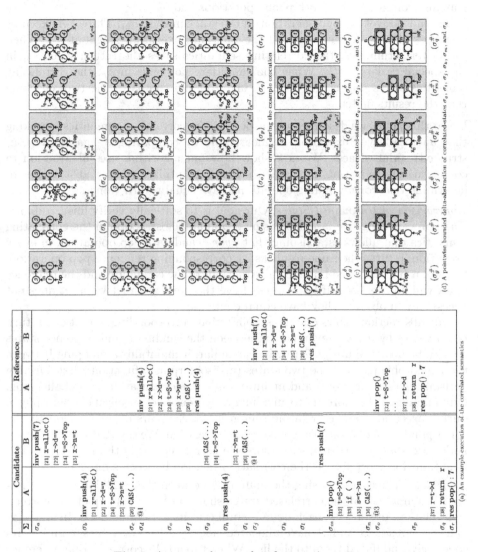

Fig. 2. An example correlated execution trace

the reference execution terminates, in σ_g, the candidate execution resumes. In this state, thread B has in $\mathtt{t}_B$ an old copy of the value of the stack's Top. Thus, its CAS fails. B retries: it reads the candidate's Top again and executes another (this time successful) CAS in state σ_i. Again, the correlating semantics freezes the candidate execution, and makes B execute push(7) on the reference state starting from σ_j. In σ_m, both push operations end.

Thread A invokes a pop operation on the stack in state σ_m. Thread A executes a successful CAS on state σ_n, and the reference execution starts at σ_o. When the latter terminates, the correlating semantics saves the return value, 7, in the special variable ret^r_A. When the candidate pop ends in σ_r, the correlating semantics stores the return value, 7, in ret_A, and compares the two, checking that the results match.

Up to this point, we described one aspect of the correlating semantics: checking that an interleaved execution is linearizable by comparing it against a (constructed) serial witness. We now show how our algorithm uses abstraction to conservatively represent unbounded states and utilizes (delta) abstraction to determine that corresponding operations have equal return values.

Comparison of Unbounded States. Our goal is to statically verify linearizability. The main challenge we face is devising a bounded abstraction of the correlating semantics that allows establishing that *every* candidate pop operation, in every execution, returns the same result as its corresponding reference pop operation. Clearly, using separated bounded abstractions of the candidate and the reference stack will not do: Even if both stacks have the same abstract value, it does not necessarily imply that they have equal contents.

Our abstraction allows one to establish that corresponding operations return equal values by using the similarity between the candidate and reference states (as can be observed in Fig. 2(b)). In particular, it maintains a mapping between the isomorphic parts of the two states (an isomorphism function). Establishing an isomorphism function—and maintaining it under mutations—is challenging. Our approach, therefore, is to incrementally construct a specific isomorphism during execution: The correlating semantics tracks pairs of nodes allocated by corresponding operations using a *correlation* relation. We say that two correlated nodes are *similar* if their n-successors are correlated (or both are *NULL*). The maintained isomorphism is the correlation relation between similar nodes.

Example 2. The edges crossing the boundary between the candidate and the reference component of the correlated states shown in Fig. 2(b) depict the correlation relation. In state σ_a, each node is similar to its correlated node. In states σ_b and σ_c, threads B and A have allocated nodes with data values 7 and 4, respectively, and linked them to the list. When thread A's corresponding reference operation allocates a reference node, it becomes correlated in σ_e with the candidate node that A allocated. When the reference node is linked to the list, in σ_f, the two become similar. (The node allocated by B undergoes an analogous sequence of events in σ_k and σ_l).

Comparing Return Values. The analysis needs to verify that returned values of corresponding pops match. Actually, it establishes a stronger property: the returned values of corresponding pops come from correlated nodes, i.e., nodes that were allocated by corresponding pushs. Note that a node's data value, once initialized, is immutable. To simplify the presentation, and the analysis, we consider correlated nodes to also have equal data values. Our analysis tracks the nodes from which the return values are read (if this is the case) and verifies that these nodes are correlated. Sec. 4 discusses the comparison of actual data values.

Example 3. Thread A executes a pop and gets the reference return value by reading the data field of the node pointed to by t_A^r, in σ_p. The corresponding candidate pop gets the return value by reading the data field of the node pointed to by t_A, resulting in σ_q, with 7 being r_A's value. Our analysis verifies that these nodes are indeed correlated. Furthermore, consider an incorrect implementation of (concurrent) push in which the loop is removed and the CAS in line [26] is replaced by the standard pointer-update statement S->Top=x. Running our example execution with this implementation, we find that thread B manages to update Top in state σ_g (instead of failing to do so with a CAS). As a result, the candidate Top is redirected to the node that B allocated, and the current node at the top of the *candidate* stack (pushed by A) is lost. However, the node that A pushed onto the reference stack is still (eventually) in the reference stack. As a result, when it is popped from the stack, it will not be correlated with the node popped from the candidate stack. Our analysis will find this out and emit a warning.

3.2   Delta Heap Abstraction

Our abstraction summarizes an unbounded number of nodes while maintaining a partial-isomorphism between the reference state and the candidate state. The main idea is to abstract *together* the isomorphic parts of the states (comprised of pairs of correlated nodes) and to explicitly record the differences that distinguish between the states. Technically, this is performed in two abstraction steps: In the first step, we apply *delta abstraction*, which *merges* the representations of the candidate and reference states by fusing correlated nodes, losing their actual addresses. In the second step, we bound the resulting *delta memory state* into an *abstract delta memory state* using *canonical abstraction* [5], losing the exact layout of the isomorphic subgraphs while maintaining a bounded amount of information on their distinguishing differences. This abstraction works well in cases where the differences are bounded, and loses precision otherwise.

Delta Abstraction. We abstract a correlated memory state into a *delta state* by *sharing* the representation of the correlated parts. Pictorially, the delta abstraction superimposes the reference state over the candidate state. Each *pair of correlated nodes* is fused into a *duo-object*. The abstraction preserves the layout of the reference memory state by maintaining a double set of fields, candidate-fields and reference-fields, in every duo-object. Recall that a pair of correlated nodes is similar if their n-successors are correlated (or both are *NULL*). In the delta representation, the candidate-field and the reference-field of a duo-object representing similar nodes are equal. Thus, we refer to a duo-object representing a pair of similar nodes as a *uniform duo-object*.

Example 4. Fig. 2(c) depicts the delta states pertaining to some of the correlated states shown in Fig. 2(b). The delta state σ_m^δ represents σ_m. Each node in σ_m is correlated, and similar to its correlated node. A duo-object is depicted as a rectangle around a pair of correlated nodes. All the duo-objects in σ_m^δ are uniform. (This is visually indicated by the $\sim$ sign inside the rectangle.) The n-edge of every uniform duo-object implicitly represents the (equal) value of its n^r-edge. This is indicated graphically, by drawing the n-edge in the middle of the uniform duo-object. For example, the n-edge leaving the uniform duo-object with value 1, implicitly records the n^r-edge from the reference node with value 1 to the reference node with value 3. Note that the candidate Top and the reference Top, that point to correlated nodes in σ_m, point to the same duo-object in σ_m^δ.

The delta state σ_k^δ represents σ_k. The duo-object with data-value 7 in σ_k^δ is nonuniform; it represents the pair of nodes allocated by thread B before it links the reference node to the list. (Nonuniform duo-objects are graphically depicted without a $\sim$ sign inside the rectangle.) Note that the n-edge of this nonuniform duo-object is drawn on its *left*-side. The lack of a n^r-edge on the right-side indicates that the n^r-field is *NULL*.

The delta state σ_i^δ represents σ_i. The non-correlated node with data-value 7 is represented as a "regular" node.

Bounded Delta Abstraction. We abstract a delta state into a bounded-size *abstract delta state*. The main idea is to represent only a bounded number of objects in the delta state as separate (non-summary) objects in the abstract delta state, and summarize all the rest. More specifically, each uniform duo-object, nonuniform duo-object, and node which is pointed to by a variable or by a Top-field, is represented by a unique *abstract uniform duo-object*, *abstract nonuniform duo-object*, and *abstract node*, respectively. We represent all other uniform duo-objects, nonuniform duo-objects, and nodes, by one *uniform summary duo-object*, one *nonuniform summary duo-object*, and one *summary node*, respectively. We conservatively record the values of pointer fields, and abstract away values of data fields. (Note, however, that by our simplifying assumption, every duo-object represents nodes with equal data values.)

Example 5. Fig. 2(d) depicts the abstract delta states pertaining to the delta states shown in Fig. 2(c). The abstract state $\sigma_i^\sharp$ represents σ_i^δ. The duo-objects with data values 1 and 3 in σ_i^δ are represented by the summary duo-object, depicted with a double frame. The duo-object u with data value 4 in σ_i^δ is represented by its own abstract duo-object in $\sigma_i^\sharp$ (and not by the summary duo-object) because u is pointed to by (both) Top-fields. The non-correlated node w with data-value 7 in σ_i^δ is pointed to by x_B. It is represented by its own abstract node pointed to by x_B. The n-field between the candidate node w and the duo-object u in σ_i^δ is represented in the abstract state by the solid n-labeled edge. The absence of an n-labeled edge between abstract nodes or abstract duo-objects represents the absence of pointer fields. Finally, the dotted edges represent loss of information in the abstraction, i.e., pointer fields which may or may not exist. Note that the summary duo-object in $\sigma_i^\sharp$ is uniform. This information is key to our analysis: it records the fact that the candidate and reference states have (potentially unbounded-sized) isomorphic subgraphs.

The abstract delta state $\sigma_k^\sharp$ represents σ_k^δ. The nonuniform duo-object v in σ_k^δ is represented by an abstract nonuniform duo-object in $\sigma_k^\sharp$. Note that the abstraction maintains the information that the duo-object pointed to by v's candidate n-field, is also pointed to by the reference Top. This allows to establish that once thread B links the reference node to the list, the abstract nonuniform duo-object v is turned into a uniform duo-object.

Recap. The delta representation of the memory states, enabled by the novel use of similarity and duo-objects, essentially records isomorphism of subgraphs in a *local* way. Also, it helps *simplify* other elements of the abstraction: the essence of our bounded abstraction is to keep distinct (i.e., not to represent by a summary node or a summary duo-object) nodes and pairs of correlated nodes which are pointed-to by variables or by a Top-field. Furthermore, by representing the reference edges of similar nodes by the candidate edges and the similarity information recorded in (uniform) duo-objects, the bounded abstraction can maintain only a single set of edges for these nodes. Specifically, if there is a bounded number of differences between the memories, the bounded abstraction is, essentially, abstracting a singly-linked list of duo-objects, with a bounded number of additional edges. In addition, to represent precisely the differences between the states using this abstraction, these differences have to be bounded, i.e., every non-similar or uncorrelated node has to be pointed to by a variable or by a Top-field.

Example 6. The information maintained by the abstract delta state suffices to establish the linearizability of the stack algorithm. Consider key points in our example trace:

- When thread B performs a CAS on σ_g, its abstraction $\sigma_g^\sharp$ carries enough information to show that it fails, and when B tries to reperform the CAS on σ_i, its abstraction $\sigma_i^\sharp$ can establish that the CAS definitely succeeds.
- When linking the reference node to the list in state σ_e and later in σ_k, the abstracted states can show that newly correlated nodes become similar.
- $\sigma_m^\sharp$, the abstraction of σ_m, which occurs when no thread manipulates the stack, indicates that the candidate and the reference stacks are isomorphic.
- Finally, $\sigma_q^\sharp$, the abstraction of σ_q, indicates that the return value of the reference pop was read from a node correlated to the one from which r_A's value was read (indicated by ret_A^r pointing into the correlated node). This allows our analysis to verify that the return values of both pops agree.

Our analysis is able to verify the linearizability of the stack. Note that the abstraction does not record any particular properties of the list, e.g., reachability from variables, cyclicly, sharing, etc. Thus, the summary duo-object might represent a cyclic list, a shared list, or even multiple unreachable lists of duo-objects. Nevertheless, we know that the uniform summary duo-object represents an (unbounded-size) isomorphic part of the candidate and reference states.

4 Discussion

In this section, we shortly discuss some key issues in our analysis.

Soundness. The soundness of the analysis requires that every operation of the executable sequential specification is fault-free and always terminates. This ensures that triggering a reference operation never prevents the analysis from further exploring its candidate execution path. Our analysis conservatively verifies the first requirement in situ. The second requirement can be proved using termination analysis, e.g., [6]. Once the above requirements are established, the soundness of the abstract interpretation follows from the soundness of [5]'s framework for program analysis, in which our analysis is encoded. We note that for many of our benchmarks, showing termination is rather immediate because the procedures perform a loop until a CAS statement succeeds; in a serial setting, a CAS always succeeds.

Correlating Function. We used the same correlation function in all of our benchmarks: nodes allocated by corresponding operations are correlated. (In all our benchmarks, every operation allocates at most one object. More complicated algorithms might require more sophistication.) We note that *our analysis is sound with any correlation function.*

Comparison of Return Values. We simplified the example by not tracking actual data values. We now show how return values can be tracked by the analysis. The flow of data values *within corresponding operations* can be tracked from the pushed value parameter to the data fields of the allocated nodes (recall that corresponding operations are invoked with the same parameters). We then can record data-similarity, in addition to successor-similarity, and verify that data-fields remain immutable. This allows to automatically detect that return values (read from correlated nodes) are equal. Such an analysis can be carried out using, e.g., the methods of [7].

Precision. As far as we know, we present the first shape analysis capable of maintaining isomorphism between (unbounded-size) memory states. We attribute the success of the analysis to the fact that in the programs we analyze the memory layouts we compare only "differ a little". The analysis tolerates local perturbations (introduced, e.g., by interleaved operations) by maintaining a precise account of the difference (*delta*) between the memory states. In particular, during our analysis, it is always the case that every abstract object is pointed to by a variable or a field of the concurrent object, except, possibly, uniform duo-objects. Thus, we do not actually expect to summarize nonuniform duo-objects or regular nodes. In case the analysis fails to verify the linearizability of the concurrent implementation, its precision may be improved by refining the abstraction.

Operational Specification. We can verify the concurrent implementation against a *simple* sequential specification instead of its own code. For example, in the *operational specification* of push and pop, we can remove the loop and replace the CAS statement with a (more natural) pointer-update statement. Verifying a code against a specification, and not against itself, can improve performance.

For example, we were not able to verify a sorted-set example using its own code as a specification (due to state explosion), but we were able to verify it using a simpler specification. Also, it should be much easier to prove fault-freedom and termination for a simplified specification.

Parametric Shape Abstraction. We match the shape abstraction to the way the operations of the concurrent objects traverse the heap: When the traversal is limited to a bounded number of links from the fields of the concurrent object, e.g., stacks and queues, we base the abstraction on the values of variables. When the traversal is potentially unbounded, e.g., a sorted set, we also record sharing and reachability.

Automation. In the stack example, we used a very simple abstraction. In other cases, we had to refine the abstraction. For example, when analyzing the nonblocking-queue [2], we found it necessary to also record explicitly the successor of the tail. Currently, we refine the abstraction manually. However, it is possible to automate this process using the methods of [8]. We define the abstract transformers by only specifying the concrete (delta) semantics. The abstract effect of statements on the additional information, e.g., reachability, is derived automatically using the methods of [9]. The latter can also be used to derive the delta operational semantics from the correlating operational semantics.

Limitations. We now shortly discuss the reasons for the imposed limitations.

Fixed Linearization Points. Specifying the linearization points of a procedure using its own statements simplifies the triggering of reference operations when linearization points are reached. In addition, it ensures that there is only one (prefix of a) sequential execution corresponding to every (prefix of a) concurrent execution. This allows us to represent only one reference data structure. Extending our approach to handle more complex specification of linearization points, e.g., when the linearization point occurs in the body of another method, is a matter of future investigation.

Bounded Number of Threads. The current analysis verifies linearizability for a fixed (but arbitrary) number k of threads. However, our goal is not to develop a *parametric* analysis, but to lift our analysis to analyze an unbounded number of threads using the techniques of Yahav [10].

No Explicit Memory Deallocation. We do not handle the problem of using (dangling) references to reclaimed memory locations, and assume that memory is automatically reclaimed (garbage collected). Dangling references can cause subtle linearizability errors because of the ABA problem.[1] Our model is simplified by forbidding explicit memory deallocation. This simplifying assumption guar-

---

[1] The ABA problem occurs when a thread reads a value v from a shared location (e.g., Top) and then other threads change the location to a different value, say u, and then back to v again. Later, when the original thread checks the location, e.g., using read or CAS, the comparison succeeds, and the thread erroneously proceeds under the assumption that the location has not changed since the thread read it earlier [11].

Table 1. Experimental results. Time is measured in seconds. Experiments performed on a machine with a 3.8 Ghz Xeon processor and 4 Gb memory running version 4 of the RedHat Linux operating system with Java 5.0, using a 1.5 Gb heap.

Client type	(a) General client			(b) Producers / Consumers		
Data Structure	Threads	Time	# States	Threads	Time	# States
Stack [3]	3	555	64,618	2/2	1,432	82,497
Nonblocking queue [2]	2	1,874	116,902	1/1	15	2,518
Nonblocking queue [15]	2	340	34,611	1/1	12	1,440
Two-lock queue [2]	4	1,296	115,456	3/3	4,596	178,180
Pessimistic set [16]	2	14,153	229,380	1/1	2,981	51,755

antees that the *ABA* problem does not occur, and hence need not be treated in the model. We believe that our approach can be extended to support explicit memory deallocation, as done, e.g., in [12]. In our analysis, we do not model the garbage collector, and never reclaim garbage.

5   Implementation and Experimental Results

We have implemented a prototype of our analysis using the TVLA/3VMC [13,10] framework. Tab. 1 summarizes the verified data structures, the running times, and the number of configurations. Our system does not support automatic partial-order reductions (see, e.g., [14]). For efficiency, we manually combined sequences of thread-local statements into atomic blocks.

The stack benchmark is our running example. We analyze two variants of the well-known nonblocking queue algorithm of Michael and Scott: the original algorithm [2], and a slightly optimized version [15]. The two-lock queue [2] uses two locks: one for the head-pointer and one for the tail-pointer. The limited concurrency makes it our most scalable benchmark. The pessimistic set [16] is implemented as a sorted linked list. It uses *fine-grained locking*: Every node has its own lock. Locks are acquired and released in a "hand-over-hand" order; the next lock in the sequence is acquired before the previous one is released.

We performed our experiments in two settings: (a) every thread executes the most general client and (b) every thread is either a *producer*, repeatedly adding elements into the data structure, or a *consumer*, repeatedly removing elements. (The second setting is suitable when verifying linearizability for applications which can be shown to use the concurrent object in this restricted way.) Our analysis verified that the data structures shown in Tab. 1 are linearizable, for the number of threads listed (e.g., for the stack, we were able to verify linearizability for 4 threads: 2 producer threads and 2 consumer threads, and for 3 threads running general clients).

We also performed some *mutation experiments*, in which we slightly mutated the data-structure code, e.g., replacing the stack's CAS with standard pointer-field assignment, and specified the wrong linearization point. In all of these cases, our analysis reported that the data structure may not be linearizable. (See [4].)

6   Related Work

This section reviews some closely related work. For additional discussion, see [4].

Conjoined Exploration. Our approach for conjoining an interleaved execution with a sequential execution is inspired by Flanagan's algorithm for verifying commit-atomicity of concurrent objects in bounded-state systems [17]. His algorithm explicitly represents the candidate and the reference memory state. It verifies that at *quiescent points* of the run, i.e., points that do not lie between the invocation and the response of any thread, the two memory states completely match. Our algorithm, on the other hand, utilizes abstraction to conservatively represent an unbounded number of states (of unbounded size) and utilizes (delta) abstraction to determine that corresponding operations have equal return values.

Automatic Verification. Wang and Stoller [18] present a static analysis that verifies linearizability (for an unbounded number of threads) using a two-step approach: first show that the concurrent implementation executed sequentially satisfies the sequential specification, and then show that procedures are atomic. Their analysis establishes atomicity based primarily on the way synchronization primitives are used, e.g., compare-and-swap, and on a specific coding style. (It also uses a preliminary analysis to determine thread-unique references.) If a program does not follow their conventions, it has to be rewritten. (The linearizability of the original program is manually proven using the linearizability of the modified program.) It was used to derive manually the linearizability of several algorithms including the nonblocking queue of [2], which had to be rewritten. We automatically verify linearizability for a bounded number of threads. Yahav and Sagiv [12] automatically verify certain safety properties listed in [2] of the nonblocking queue and the two-lock queue given there. These properties do not imply linearizability. We provide a direct proof of linearizability.

Semi-Automatic Verification. In [15,19,20], the *PVS* theorem prover is used for a semi-automatic verification of linearizability.

Manual Verification. Vafeiadis *et. al.* [16] manually verify linearizability of list algorithms using rely-guarantee reasoning. Herlihy and Wing [1] present a methodology for verifying linearizability by defining a function that maps every state of the concurrent object to the set of all possible *abstract values* representing it. (The state can be instrumented with properties of the execution trace). Both techniques do not require fixed linearization points.

Acknowledgments. We are grateful for the comments of A. Gotsman, T. Lev-Ami, A. Loginov, R. Manevich, M. Parkinson, V. Vafeiadis, and M. Vechev.

References

1. Herlihy, M.P., Wing, J.M.: Linearizability: a correctness condition for concurrent objects. Trans. on Prog. Lang. and Syst. 12(3) (1990)
2. Michael, M., Scott, M.: Simple, fast, and practical non-blocking and blocking concurrent queue algorithms. In: PODC (1996)

3. Treiber, R.K.: Systems programming: Coping with parallelism. Technical Report RJ 5118, IBM Almaden Research Center (1986)
4. Amit, D.: Comparison under abstraction for verifying linearizability. Master's thesis, Tel Aviv University (2007) Available at
   http://www.cs.tau.ac.il/~amitdaph
5. Sagiv, M., Reps, T., Wilhelm, R.: Parametric shape analysis via 3-valued logic. Trans. on Prog. Lang. and Syst. (2002)
6. Berdine, J., Cook, B., Distefano, D., O'Hearn, P.: Automatic termination proofs for programs with shape-shifting heaps. In: Ball, T., Jones, R.B. (eds.) CAV 2006. LNCS, vol. 4144, Springer, Heidelberg (2006)
7. Gopan, D., DiMaio, F., Dor, N., Reps, T.W., Sagiv, S.: Numeric domains with summarized dimensions. In: Jensen, K., Podelski, A. (eds.) TACAS 2004. LNCS, vol. 2988, Springer, Heidelberg (2004)
8. Loginov, A., Reps, T.W., Sagiv, M.: Abstraction refinement via inductive learning. In: Etessami, K., Rajamani, S.K. (eds.) CAV 2005. LNCS, vol. 3576, Springer, Heidelberg (2005)
9. Reps, T., Sagiv, M., Loginov, A.: Finite Differencing of Logical Formulas for Static Analysis. In: Degano, P. (ed.) ESOP 2003 and ETAPS 2003. LNCS, vol. 2618, Springer, Heidelberg (2003)
10. Yahav, E.: Verifying safety properties of concurrent Java programs using 3-valued logic. In: POPL (2001)
11. Michael, M.M.: Hazard pointers: Safe memory reclamation for lock-free objects. IEEE Trans. Parallel Distrib. Syst. 15(6) (2004)
12. Yahav, E., Sagiv, M.: Automatically verifying concurrent queue algorithms. In: Electronic Notes in Theoretical Computer Science, vol. 89, Elsevier, Amsterdam (2003)
13. Lev-Ami, T., Sagiv, M.: TVLA: A framework for Kleene based static analysis. In: Palsberg, J. (ed.) SAS 2000. LNCS, vol. 1824, Springer, Heidelberg (2000)
14. Clarke, E.M., Grumberg, J., Peled, O.: Model checking. MIT Press, Cambridge, MA, USA (1999)
15. Doherty, S., Groves, L., Luchangco, V., Moir, M.: Formal verification of a practical lock-free queue algorithm. In: Núñez, M., Maamar, Z., Pelayo, F.L., Pousttchi, K., Rubio, F. (eds.) FORTE 2004. LNCS, vol. 3236, Springer, Heidelberg (2004)
16. Vafeiadis, V., Herlihy, M., Hoare, T., Shapiro, M.: Proving correctness of highly-concurrent linearisable objects. In: PPoPP (2006)
17. Flanagan, C.: Verifying commit-atomicity using model-checking. In: Graf, S., Mounier, L. (eds.) Model Checking Software. LNCS, vol. 2989, Springer, Heidelberg (2004)
18. Wang, L., Stoller, S.D.: Static analysis of atomicity for programs with non-blocking synchronization. In: PPOPP (2005)
19. Colvin, R., Groves, L., Luchangco, V., Moir, M.: Formal verification of a lazy concurrent list-based set algorithm. In: Ball, T., Jones, R.B. (eds.) CAV 2006. LNCS, vol. 4144, Springer, Heidelberg (2006)
20. Gao, H., Hesselink, W.H.: A formal reduction for lock-free parallel algorithms. In: Alur, R., Peled, D.A. (eds.) CAV 2004. LNCS, vol. 3114, Springer, Heidelberg (2004)

Leaping Loops in the Presence of Abstraction

Thomas Ball[1], Orna Kupferman[2], and Mooly Sagiv[3]

[1] Microsoft Research
tball@microsoft.com
[2] Hebrew University
orna@cs.huji.ac.il
[3] Tel-Aviv University
msagiv@post.tau.ac.il

Abstract. Finite abstraction helps program analysis cope with the huge state space of programs. We wish to use abstraction in the process of error detection. Such a detection involves reachability analysis of the program. Reachability in an abstraction that under-approximates the program implies reachability in the concrete system. Under-approximation techniques, however, lose precision in the presence of loops, and cannot detect their termination. This causes reachability analysis that is done with respect to an abstraction to miss states of the program that are reachable via loops. Current solutions to this loop-termination challenge are based on fair termination and involve the use of well-founded sets and ranking functions.

In many cases, the concrete system has a huge, but still finite set of states. Our contribution is to show how, in such cases, it is possible to analyze termination of loops without refinement and without well-founded sets and ranking functions. Instead, our method is based on conditions on the structure of the graph that corresponds to the concrete system — conditions that can be checked with respect to the abstraction. We describe our method, demonstrate its usefulness and show how its application can be automated by means of a theorem prover.

1 Introduction

Finite abstraction (such as predicate or Boolean abstraction [7,2]) helps program analysis cope with the huge state space of programs. Finite abstraction is helpful for proving properties of programs but less helpful for proving the presence of errors. The reason, as we demonstrate below, is that reachability analysis that is done with respect to an abstraction misses states of the program that are reachable via loops.

Consider the procedure simple appearing in Figure 1. The procedure is indeed simple and it increments the value of a variable x in a deterministic manner. It is not hard to see that the value of x eventually exceeds the value $3n$ and that the single execution of the procedure eventually reaches the failing assertion. Most counterexample-driven refinement methods, however, will generate a predicate for each loop iteration, quickly overwhelming the ability of their analysis engines to cope with the resulting state space explosion.

W. Damm and H. Hermanns (Eds.): CAV 2007, LNCS 4590, pp. 491–503, 2007.
© Springer-Verlag Berlin Heidelberg 2007

```
procedure simple (int n)
  int x:=0;
  while (x < n) do x:=x+1;
  while (x < 2n) do x:=x+2;
  while (x < 3n) do x:=x+3;
  assert false
```

Fig. 1. The procedure `simple`

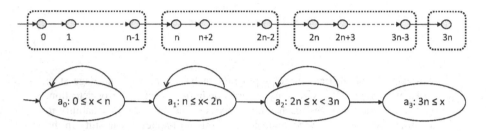

Fig. 2. The concrete state space of the procedure `simple` and its abstraction

To see the problem in more detail, consider Figure 2, where we describe the state space of the procedure `simple`[1] and its abstraction according to the predicates $\{0 \leq x < n, n \leq x < 2n, 2n \leq x < 3n, 3n \leq x\}$. Since the abstraction over-approximates the transitions in the concrete system, and over-approximating transitions are not closed under transitivity, we cannot conclude, based on the abstraction, that a concrete state corresponding to a_3 is reachable from the a concrete state corresponding to a_0. Formally, the abstraction is a modal transition system (MTS) [11] in which all the transitions are *may* transitions. According to the three-valued semantics for modal transition systems [9], the property "exists a path in which $3n \leq x$" has truth value "unknown" and the abstraction should be refined. Since the three-valued abstraction gives a definite true value for reachability properties only if they hold along *must* transitions, the only refinement that would work bisimulates the concrete system. Augmenting MTSs with hyper-must transitions [12,14] does not help in this setting either (and is orthogonal to the contribution we describe here).

Proving reachability along loops is a long-standing challenging problem in program abstraction. Recently, significant progress has been made by automatically proving termination [13,5,6,4]. The main idea is to synthesize ranking functions proving well foundedness. However, these techniques require the generation of rank functions and/or are not suitable for proving that there exists a trace leading to a certain configuration in non-deterministic systems, which is a goal of our work.

In many cases (in particular, in all realistic implementations of software with variables over unbounded domains), the concrete system has a huge, but still finite set of states. Our contribution is to show how, in such cases, it is possible to analyze

---

[1] The concrete values in Figure 2 correspond to the case $n = 0 \bmod 6$. Otherwise, the maximal value in a_1 may not be $2n - 2$, and similarly for a_2 and $3n - 3$.

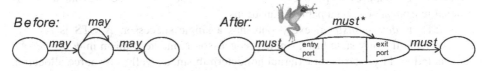

Fig. 3. Applying our method

reachability in the concrete system without refinement of loops and without well-founded sets and ranking. Instead, our method is based on conditions on the structure of the graph that corresponds to the concrete system — conditions that can be checked automatically with respect to the abstraction.

Figure 3 illustrates the idea of our method, which is to replace the may transitions to and from an abstract state a by *must* transitions to an *entry port* for a and from an *exit port* for a, and to replace the intermediate may transition by a sequence of must transitions from the entry port to the exit port. Essentially, this is done by checking conditions that guarantee that the transitions of the concrete system embody a connected acyclic graph that has the entry port as its source and has the exit port as its sink. Finiteness of the set of concrete states associated with the abstract state then guarantees the finiteness of this graph. The checks we do, as well as the declaration of the entry and the exit ports, are automatic, refer to the abstract system, and are independent of the size of the concrete system. While our conditions are sufficient but not necessary, they are expected to hold in many cases.

An approach similar to ours is taken in [10], where loop leaping is also performed without well-founded sets. Like our approach, the algorithm in [10] is based on symbolic reasoning about the concrete states associated with the loop. The conditions that the algorithm in [10] imposes, however, are different, and the algorithm is much more complicated. Essentially, loop detection along an abstract path $a_1, \ldots, a_n$ is reduced in [10] to the satisfiability of a propositional formula that specifies the existence of locations a_i and a_j along the path such that a_i is reachable from a_j and a_j is reachable from a_i. The size of the formula is quadratic in size of the concrete state space. Our conditions, on the other hand, are independent of the size of the concrete state space, and are much simpler. As we argue in the paper, the conditions we give are likely to be satisfied in many common settings.

2 Preliminaries

Programs and Concrete Transition Systems. Consider a program P. Let X be the set of variables appearing in the program and variables that encode the program counter (pc), and let D be the domain of all variables (for technical simplicity, we assume that all variables are over the same domain). We model P by a concrete transition system in which each state is labeled by a valuation in $D^{|X|}$.

A *concrete transition system* (CTS) is a tuple $C = \langle S_C, I_C, \longrightarrow_C \rangle$, where S_C is a (possibly infinite) set of states, $I_C \subseteq S_C$ is a set of initial states, $\longrightarrow_C \subseteq S_C \times S_C$ is a total transition relation. Given a concrete state $c \in S_C$, let $s(c)$ denote the successor states of c; that is, $s(c) = \{c' \in S_C \mid c \longrightarrow_C c'\}$, and let $p(c)$ denote the predecessor states of c; that is, $p(c) = \{c' \in S_C \mid c' \longrightarrow_C c\}$. Let $c \longrightarrow_C^* c'$ denote that state c' is reachable from state c via a path of transitions.

A CTS is *deterministic* if every state has a single successor. A CTS is *reverse-deterministic* if every state has a single predecessor. Nondeterminism in concrete systems is induced by internal or external nondeterminism, as well as resource allocation and built-in abstractions in the programs they model.

Predicate Abstraction. Let $\Phi = \{\phi_1, \phi_2, \ldots, \phi_n\}$ be a set of predicates (formulas of first-order logic) over the program variables X. Given a program state c and formula ϕ, let $c \models \phi$ denote that formula ϕ is true in state c (c is a model of ϕ). For a set $a \subseteq \Phi$ and an assignment $c \in D^{|X|}$, we say that c *satisfies* a iff $c \models \bigwedge_{\phi_i \in a} \phi_i$.

In predicate abstraction, we merge a set of concrete states into a single abstract state, which is defined by means of a subset of the predicates. Thus, an abstract state is given by a set of predicates $a \subseteq \Phi$.[2] We sometimes represent a by a formula, namely the conjunction of predicates in a. For example, if $a = \{(x \geq y), (0 \leq x < n)\}$ then we also represent a by the formula $(x \geq y) \wedge (0 \leq x < n)$. We define the set of concrete states corresponding to a, denoted $\gamma(a)$, as all the states c that satisfy a; that is, $\gamma(a) = \{c \mid c \models a\}$.

May and Must Transitions. Given a concrete transition system and its (predicate) abstraction via a set of predicates Φ, its *modal transition system* (MTS) contains three kinds of abstract transitions between abstract states a and a' ($a, a' \subseteq \Phi$, and we assume that Φ is clear from the context):

- $may(a, a')$ if there is $c \in \gamma(a)$ and a $c' \in \gamma(a')$, such that $c \longrightarrow_C c'$.
- $must^+(a, a')$ only if for every $c \in \gamma(a)$, there is $c' \in \gamma(a')$ such that $c \longrightarrow_C c'$.
- $must^-(a, a')$ only if for every $c' \in \gamma(a')$, there is $c \in \gamma(a)$ such that $c \longrightarrow_C c'$.

Must transitions are closed under transitivity, and can therefore be used to prove reachability in the concrete system. Formally, if there is a sequence of $must^+$-transitions from a to a' (denoted by $must^{+*}(a, a')$) then for all $c \in \gamma(a)$, there is $c' \in \gamma(a')$ such that $c \longrightarrow_C^* c'$. Dually, if there is a sequence of $must^-$-transitions from a to a' (denoted by $must^{-*}(a, a')$) then for all $c' \in \gamma(a')$, there is $c \in \gamma(a)$ such that $c \longrightarrow_C^* c'$. On the other hand, may transitions are not transitive. Indeed, it may be the case that $may(a, a'), may(a', a'')$, and still for all $c \in a$ and $c'' \in a''$, we have $c \not\longrightarrow_C^* c''$.

Let us go back to the procedure simple and its abstraction in Figure 2. Since every concrete state in a_3 has a predecessor in a_2, we have that $must^-(a_2, a_3)$. On the other hand, all the other transitions in the abstraction are may transitions. As such, we cannot use the abstraction in order to conclude that the failing statement is reachable from the initial state. We want to detect such reachability, and we want to do it without well-founded orders and without refining the abstraction further!

---

[2] In the full generality of predicate abstraction, an abstract state is represented by a set of sets of predicates (that is a, disjunction of conjunction of predicates). All our results hold for the more general setting.

Weakest Preconditions and Strongest Postconditions. In many applications of predicate abstraction, Φ includes a predicate for the program counter. Accordingly, each abstract state is associated with a location of the program, and thus it is also associated with a statement. For a statement s and a predicate e over X, the *weakest precondition* $\mathrm{WP}(s, e)$ and the *strongest postcondition* $\mathrm{SP}(s, e)$ are defined as follows [8]:

- The execution of s from every state that satisfies $\mathrm{WP}(s, e)$ results in a state that satisfies e, and $\mathrm{WP}(s, e)$ is the weakest predicate for which the above holds.
- The execution of s from a state that satisfies e results in a state that satisfies $\mathrm{SP}(s, e)$, and $\mathrm{SP}(s, e)$ is the strongest predicate for which the above holds.

For example, in the procedure `simple`, we have $\mathrm{WP}(x := x + 2, n \leq x < 2n) = n \leq x + 2 < 2n$, $\mathrm{SP}(x := x + 2, n \leq x < 2n) = n + 2 \leq x < 2n + 2$.

Must transitions can be computed automatically using weakest preconditions and strongest postconditions. Indeed, statement s induces the transition $must^+(a, a')$ iff $a \Rightarrow \mathrm{WP}(s, a')$, and induces the transition $must^-(a, a')$ iff $a' \Rightarrow \mathrm{SP}(s, a)$.

We sometimes use also the Pre predicate. For a statement s and a predicate e over X, the execution of s from a state that satisfies $\mathrm{Pre}(s, e)$ may result in a state that satisfies e. Formally, $\mathrm{Pre}(s, e) = \neg \mathrm{WP}(s, \neg e)$.

3 Leaping Loops

Unfortunately, an abstraction of loops usually results in may transitions. As discussed above, may transitions are not closed under transitivity, thus abstraction methods cannot cope with reachability of programs with loops. In this section we describe our method for coping with loops.

An *entry port* of an abstract state a is a predicate e_a such that $\gamma(e_a) \subseteq \gamma(a)$ and for all $c_e \in \gamma(e_a)$, either c_e is initial or $p(c_e) \setminus \gamma(a) \neq \emptyset$. That is, every concrete state c_e represented by entry port e_a is inside a and either c_e is initial or some predecessor of c_e lies outside a.

Dually, an *exit port* of an abstract state a is a predicate x_a such that $\gamma(x_a) \subseteq \gamma(a)$ and for all $c_x \in \gamma(x_a)$, we have that $s(c_x) \setminus \gamma(a) \neq \emptyset$. That is, every concrete state c_x represented by exit port x_a is in a and some successor of c_x lies outside a.

In Section 4.1, we describe how entry and exit ports can be calculated automatically be means of weakest preconditions and strongest postconditions. We now use entry and exit ports in order to reason about loops.

Theorem 1. *Consider an abstract state a. Let e_a and x_a be entry and exit ports of a such that all the following conditions hold:*

1. *$\gamma(a)$ is finite;*
2. *for all $c \in \gamma(a \wedge \neg x_a)$, we have that $\mid s(c) \cap \gamma(a) \mid \leq 1$. That is, every concrete state in $\gamma(a \wedge \neg x_a)$ has at most one successor in $\gamma(a)$.*
3. *$must^-(a \wedge \neg x_a, a \wedge \neg e_a)$. That is, every concrete state in $\gamma(a \wedge \neg e_a)$ has a predecessor in $\gamma(a \wedge \neg x_a)$.*

Then, $must^{-*}(e_a, x_a)$. That is, for all $c' \in \gamma(x_a)$, there is $c \in \gamma(e_a)$ such that $c \longrightarrow_C^* c'$.

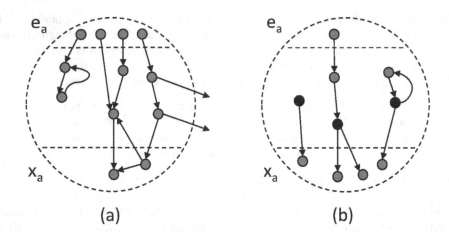

Fig. 4. Inside an abstract state

Note that Conditions 1-3 imply that e_a cannot be empty (unless x_a is empty, in which case the theorem holds trivially).

The proof of Theorem 1 is based on constructing a DAG in which all states are reachable from the source. The finiteness of $\gamma(a)$ then implies that source vertices of the DAG are contained in $\gamma(e_a)$. Note that the DAG induces a well-founded order on the states of $\gamma(a)$. The well-founded order, however, is hidden in the proof and the user does not have to provide it. The detailed proof is given in the full version. Here we give some intuition and an example to its application. Figure 4(a) illustrates the intuition underlying Theorem 1. The large dashed circle represents the abstract state a with entry port e_a and exit port x_a. The grey nodes represent concrete states that are consistent with the theorem. Every grey node that is not in the exit port has at most one successor in a (but may have arbitrarily many successors outside a). Every grey node in $\gamma(a \wedge \neg e_a)$ has a predecessor in $a \wedge \neg x_a$ (and may have more than one predecessor). Note that the conditions permit cycles in the concrete state space, as shown on the left of the figure.

The black nodes in Figure 4(b) illustrate configurations in the concrete state space that are not permitted by the theorem. We see that the conditions of the theorem rule out unreachable cycles, as well as non-determinism inside a. Finally, it is not permitted to have a state in $\gamma(a \wedge \neg e_a)$ that does not have predecessor in $\gamma(a \wedge \neg x_a)$.

Example 1. Consider the procedure simple from Figure 1 and its abstraction in Figure 2. The application of our method on the abstraction is described in Figure 5. The abstract state $a_0 : 0 \leq x < n$ has entry port $x = 0$ and exit port $x = n - 1$. The conditions of Theorem 1 hold for a_0 with these ports: first, as n is finite, so is $\gamma(a_0)$. Second, since the procedure is deterministic, each concrete state has a single successor. Finally, each concrete state except for $x = 0$ has a predecessor in a_0. We can therefore conclude that $must^{-*}(x = 0, x = n - 1)$. In a similar way, the conditions of the theorem hold for a_1 with entry port $x = n$ and exit port $2n - 2 \leq x < 2n$, and for a_2 with entry port $2n \leq x \leq 2n + 1$ and exit port $3n - 3 \leq x < 3n$. From this, we can conclude that $must^{-*}(x = n, 2n - 2 \leq x < 2n)$ and $must^{-*}(2n \leq x \leq 2n + 1, 3n - 3 \leq x < 3n)$.

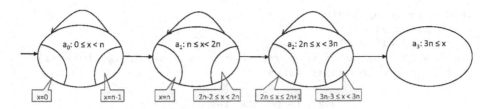

Fig. 5. Entry and exit ports in the abstraction of the procedure simple

Since, in addition, $must^-(x = n - 1, x = n)$, $must^-(2n - 2 \leq x < 2n, 2n \leq x \leq 2n+1)$, and $must^-(3n-3 \leq x < 3n, 3n \leq x)$, we can conclude, from the transitivity of $must^-$, that $must^{-*}(x = 0, 3n \leq x)$.

We now state a similar theorem for a forward traversal. The proof is dual to the proof of Theorem 1.

Theorem 2. *Consider an abstract state a. Let e_a and x_a be entry and exit ports of a such that all the following conditions hold:*

1. *$\gamma(a)$ is finite.*
2. *for all $c \in \gamma(a \wedge \neg e_a)$, we have that $\mid p(c) \cap \gamma(a) \mid \leq 1$. That is, every concrete state in $\gamma(a \wedge \neg e_a)$ has at most one predecessor in $\gamma(a)$.*
3. *$must^+(a \wedge \neg x_a, a \wedge \neg e_a)$. That is, every concrete state in $\gamma(a \wedge \neg x_a)$ has a successor in $\gamma(a \wedge \neg e_a)$.*

Then, $must^{+*}(e_a, x_a)$. That is, for all $c \in \gamma(e_a)$, there is $c' \in \gamma(x_a)$ such that $c \longrightarrow_C^* c'$.

Below we discuss the conditions required for the application of Theorems 1 and 2 and describe more involved examples.

The $\gamma(a)$ finiteness assumption. Precondition (1) of Theorems 1 and 2 is that $\gamma(a)$ is finite. To see that the finiteness requirement is crucial, consider an abstract state over the whole numbers $a = (x \geq 0 \wedge y \geq 0)$, and assume that the statement executed in a is `while true do if y=0 then x:=x-1`. Let $e_a = (x \geq 0 \wedge y > 0)$ and $x_a = (x = y = 0)$. Note that e_a and x_a satisfy the conditions required from entry and exit ports: $\gamma(e_a) \subseteq \gamma(a)$, and $\gamma(e_a)$ may have predecessors not in $\gamma(a)$. Also, $\gamma(x_a) \subseteq \gamma(a)$, and the successor of the single concrete state in $\gamma(x_a)$ is not in $\gamma(a)$. Conditions (2) and (3) of Theorem 1 are satisfied: Each state in $\gamma(a)$ has a single successor, and all states in $\gamma(a \wedge \neg e_a) = \{\langle x, y \rangle : x \geq 0 \wedge y = 0\}$, have a predecessor in $\gamma(a \wedge \neg x_a)$. Still, we do not have $must^{-*}(e_a, x_a)$. Indeed, all states in $\gamma(e_a)$ satisfy $y \neq 0$ and therefore they have a self loop.

Note that while $\gamma(a)$ has to be finite, it is unbounded. Thus, for applications like detecting errors representing extreme out of bound resources, e.g., stack overflow, our method is applicable. Types like integers or reals have infinite domains. In practice, however, we run software on machines, where all types have finite representations. Thus, if for example, x is an integer and the abstract state $a : (x \geq 0)$ has an infinite

```
procedure less_simple (int n)
    int x:=0; y:=0;
    x:=1; {y:=1|skip};
    while (x < n) do if x >= y+2 then y:=x else {x:=x+1|y:=x+1};
    if x >= y then assert false
```

Fig. 6. The procedure less_simple

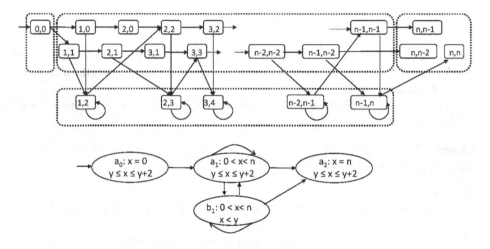

Fig. 7. An abstraction of the procedure less_simple

$\gamma(a)$, we can view a as defined by the predicate $(0 \leq x \leq \text{max\_int})$, which is finite. Different machines have different policies for variables that go above their maximal or beyond their minimal values. It is possible to adjust the abstract system to account for these policies ("wrap around", error messages, etc.).

Another source of infiniteness are variables that the abstraction ignores. Consider for example a concrete state space over two integer variables, x and y. The abstract state $a : (1 \leq x \leq n)$ constrains x to have one of $|n|$ values but leaves y unconstrained, making $\gamma(a)$ infinite. Since, however, the behavior inside a is independent of y, its infiniteness is irrelevant to termination of a loop that traverses the values of x. This point, of coping with an abstraction that hides part of the variables is studied in [3]. Using *partitioned-must* transitions that are studied there, it is possible to apply Theorems 1 and 2 in settings in which there are finitely many equivalence classes in a partition of $\gamma(a)$ according to the value of x.

The determinization assumption. Consider the procedure less_simple described in Figure 6. A statement $s_1|s_2$ denotes a nondeterministic choice between statements s_1 and s_2. Thus, for example, in x:=x+1|y:=x+1, the procedure may either increment the value of x by 1 or assign $x + 1$ to y. As in the procedure simple, the value of the variable x is incremented, but now the procedure may also assign values to the variable y, and the increments to x, as well as the failure assertion, depend on the relation between x and y.

The behavior of the variables x and y is described in Figure 7. The figure also contains an abstraction of the procedure according to the predicates $\{(x = 0), (0 < x < n), (x \geq n), (y \leq x \leq y + 2), (x < y)\}$. We restrict the figure to states that are reachable along may transitions. Since the transition from a_1 to a_2 in the abstraction is a may transition, we cannot conclude that failure states are reachable from the initial state.

Let us focus on the abstract state a_1, where $0 < x < n$ and $y \leq x \leq y + 2$. The predicate $(y \leq x = 1 \leq y + 2)$ is an entry port for a_1. Note that the state $x = y = 2$ is not in the entry port and still has a predecessor not in $\gamma(a_1)$, but an entry port need not be maximal. As an exit port, we take the predicate $(y \leq x = n - 1 \leq y + 2)$. Note that the transitions from some of the concrete states in a_1 (all these for which $y \leq x \leq y+1$) are nondeterministic. One of the nondeterministic choices, however, takes us out of a_1. Indeed, an attempt to use Theorem 1 without refining the predicate $0 < x < n$ to $y \leq x \leq y + 2$, $x < y$, and $x > y + 2$ fails. Note also that all the concrete states in $\gamma(a_1 \wedge \neg e_{a_1})$ have predecessors in $\gamma(a_1 \wedge \neg x_{a_1})$. Thus, $must^-(a_1 \wedge \neg x_{a_1}, a_1 \wedge \neg e_{a_1})$. The fact that some states (these in which $x = y$) have two predecessors, one of which is in b_1, does not violate the conditions of Theorem 1. By the theorem, all concrete states in the exit port are reachable from states in the entry port. Since, in addition, the error states $(x = n) \wedge (n - 2 \leq x \leq n - 1)$ are reachable from the exit port, and all states in the entry port are reachable from $x = y = 0$, we can conclude that some error states in `less_simple` are reachable from the initial state.

Nested loops. Proving termination is harder in the presence of nested loops. Our method, however, is applicable also to programs with nested loops. Consider the procedure `nested` in the right. Reasoning about the procedure with well-founded orders requires working with pairs in $\mathbb{N} \times \mathbb{N}$. Using our method, we can have a single abstract state $a : (0 \leq x, y \leq n)$, define the entry and exit ports to be $e_a = (x = y = 0)$ and $x_a = (x = y = n)$, respectively, and verify that the following conditions, of Theorem 2, hold: (1) $\gamma(a)$ is finite, (2) every concrete state in $\gamma(a \wedge \neg e_a)$ has at most one predecessor in $\gamma(a)$, and (3) every concrete state in $\gamma(a \wedge \neg x_a)$ has a successor in $\gamma(a \wedge \neg e_a)$.

Now, we can conclude that $must^{+^*}(x = y = 0, x = y = n)$. Note that Theorems 1 and 2 can also be applied to more complicated variants of `nested` in which, for example,

```
procedure nested (int n)
    int y, x:=0;
    while x < n do
        x++; y:=0; while y < n do y++
    if y=n then assert false
```

the increment to y depends on x. Complicated dependencies, however, may violate Condition (3) of the theorem, and the state a has to be refined in order for the condition to hold.

In general, our method is independent of the cause to the loop in the abstract state and can be applied to various cases like nested loops, recursive calls, and mutual recursive calls.

4   In Practice

In this section we discuss the implementation of our method and ways to use a theorem prover in order to automate it. We assume that the abstraction was obtained by predicate abstraction and that each abstract state is associated with a statement executed in all its corresponding concrete states.

We consider the following application: the user provides two abstract states a and a' and asks whether a' is *weakly reachable* from a'; that is, are there concrete states $c_0, c_1, \ldots, c_n$ such that $c_0 \in \gamma(a), c_n \in \gamma(a')$, and for all $0 \leq i < n$, we have $c_i \longrightarrow_C c_{i+1}$. As discussed in Section 1, we have to check whether $must^{+*}(a, a')$ or $must^{-*}(a, a')$[3].

We start by considering a simpler mission, where the user also provides a path $a_1, a_2, \ldots, a_n$ in the abstract system such that $a = a_1$ and $a' = a_n$. Our method enters the picture in cases there is $1 < i < n$ such that a_i is associated with a loop, $may(a_{i-1}, a_i)$ or $may(a_i, a_{i+1})$. Then, as illustrated in Figure 3, we find entry and exit ports for a_i and check whether the conditions in Theorem 1 (or 2) are satisfied.

Below we describe how to automate both parts. We start with the detection of entry and exit ports.

4.1   Automatic Calculation of Ports Along a Path

For two abstract states a and a', and a statement s executed in a, we say that $e_{a'}$ is an *entry port for a' from a* if $\gamma(e_{a'}) \subseteq \gamma(a')$ and for all $c \in e_{a'}$, we have $p(c) \cap \gamma(a) \neq \emptyset$. Thus, $e_{a'}$ is an entry port and all its states have predecessors in a. Likewise, we say that x_a is an *exit port for a to a'* if $\gamma(x_a) \subseteq \gamma(a)$ and for all $c \in x_a$, we have $s(c) \cap \gamma(a') \neq \emptyset$. Thus, x_a is an exit port and all its states have successors in a'.

Lemma 1. *Consider two abstract states a and a'. Let s be the statement executed in a.*

- $e_{a'}$ *is an entry port for a' from a iff $e_{a'} \Rightarrow a' \land \mathrm{SP}(s, a)$.*
- x_a *is an exit port for a to a' iff $x_a \Rightarrow a \land \mathrm{Pre}(s, a')$.*

The proof of Lemma 1 can be found in the full version. The lemma suggests that when we glue a_{i-1} to a_i, we proceed with entry port $a_i \land \mathrm{SP}(s, a_{i-1})$ for a_i. Then, when we glue state a_i to a_{i+1}, we proceed with exit port $a_i \land \mathrm{WP}(s, a_{i+1})$ for a_i.

Example 2. In Example 1, we described an application of our method to the procedure simple. The entry and exit ports used in the example (see Figure 5) have been generated automatically using the characterization in Lemma 1. Consider, for example, the states $a_0 : (0 \leq x < n)$ and $a_1 : (n \leq x < 2n)$. Recall that the statement s executed in a_0 is while x < n do x:=x+1. The exit port of a_0 is then $a_0 \land \mathrm{WP}(s, a_1) = (x = n - 1)$ and the entry port of a_1 is $a_1 \land \mathrm{SP}(s, a_0) = (x = n)$.

The ports induced by the Lemma are the maximal ones. Note, however, that the conditions in Theorem 1 and 2 are monotonic with respect to the entry port (the bigger it is, the more likely it is for the conditions to hold), Condition (2) is monotonic and Condition (3) is anti-monotonic with respect to the exit port. Thus, one can always take the maximal entry port (the way we have defined it also guarantees that it is possible

---

[3] As noted in [1], if there are abstract states b and b' such that $must^{-*}(a, b)$, $may(b, b')$, and $must^{+*}(b', a')$, we can still conclude that a' is weakly reachable from a. This "one flip trick" is valid also in the reasoning we describe here. For the sake of simplicity, we restrict attention to the closure of either $must^+$ or $must^-$ transitions.

to "glue" it to a_{i-1}), start also with a maximal exit port, and search for a subset of the maximal exit port in case Condition (3) does not hold but $must^-(a, a \wedge \neg e_a)$ holds. The search for the subset can use a theorem prover and the characterization of $must^-$ transitions by means of weakest preconditions. Reasoning is dual for Theorem 2.

4.2 Checking the Conditions

Once entry and exit ports are established, we proceed to check the conditions in Theorems 1 or 2. In many cases, the program is known to be deterministic, thus the determinism check in Theorem 1 is redundant. Theorem 1, however, is applicable also when the program is nondeterministic, or not known to be deterministic, and we have to check a weaker condition, namely for all $c \in \gamma(a \wedge \neg x_a)$, we have that $| s(c) \cap \gamma(a) | \leq 1$. In order to automate the check, we use the statement s that is executed in a, and the fact that the successors of a state satisfy $\mathrm{WP}(s, a)$, which can be decomposed for nondeterministic statements. Formally, we have the following.

Lemma 2. *Let $s_1|s_2$ be a nondeterministic statement executed in a, for deterministic statements s_1 and s_2. If there exists $c \in \gamma(a)$ such that $| s(c) \cap \gamma(a) | > 1$, then the formula $a \wedge \neg x_a \wedge \mathrm{WP}(s_1, a) \wedge \mathrm{WP}(s_2, a)$ is satisfiable.*

Lemma 2 refers to nondeterminism of degree two, and to a statement in which the nondeterminism is external [4].

Similarly, to check the reverse-nondeterminism condition in Theorem 2, we have to find $c \in \gamma(a \wedge \neg e_a)$ such that c is reachable from two states in $\gamma(a)$. If the nondeterministic statement executed in a is $s_1|s_2$ and then there exists $c \in \gamma(a)$ such that $| p(c) \cap \gamma(a) | > 1$, then the formula $a \wedge \neg e_a \wedge \mathrm{SP}(s_1, a) \wedge \mathrm{SP}(s_2, a)$ is satisfiable.

Checking the local reachability conditions in Theorems 1 and 2 can be done using the characterization of $must^-$ and $must^+$ transitions. Specifically, $must^-(a \wedge \neg x_a, a \wedge \neg e_a)$ iff $a \wedge \neg e_a \Rightarrow \mathrm{SP}(s, a \wedge \neg x_a)$ and $must^+(a \wedge \neg x_a, a \wedge \neg e_a)$ iff $a \wedge \neg x_a \Rightarrow \mathrm{WP}(s, a \wedge \neg e_a)$.

Remark 1. An advantage of forward reasoning (Theorem 2) is that the check for $must^+$ transitions involves weakest preconditions, which are often easier to compute than strongest postconditions, which are required for checking $must^-$ transitions. Indeed, for an assignment statement x:=v, we have that $\mathrm{WP}(x := v, e) = e[x/v]$ (that is, e with all occurrences of x replaced by v, whereas $\mathrm{SP}(x := v, e) = \exists x'.(e[x/x'] \wedge x = v)$. On the other hand, an advantage of backwards reasoning (Theorem 1) is the fact that checking that a program is deterministic is often easier than checking that it is reverse deterministic, especially in cases the program is known to be deterministic.

4.3 Proceeding Without a Suggested Path

So far, we assumed that weak reachability from a to a' is checked along a path suggested by the user. When the user does not provide such a path, one possible way to proceed is

---

[4] In order for the second direction of the lemma to hold, one has to check that executing s_1 and s_2 from c results in different states. If this is not the case, then the nondeterminism in a is only syntactic, and one can apply Theorem 1 by disabling one of the nondeterministic choices (see Section 5).

```
procedure jump_beyond_n (int n)
  int x:=0
  while (x < n) do case
                  x = 1 mod 2: x:=x-1|x:=x-3;
                  x = 0 mod 4: x:=x+5;
                  x = 2 mod 4: x:=x+1;
  assert false
```

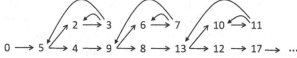

Fig. 8. The procedure jump_beyond_n

to check all simple paths from a to a'. Since these are paths in the abstract MTS and the cost of each check depends only on the size of the MTS, this is feasible. Alternatively, we can check the path obtained by proceeding in a BFS from a along the MTS. Thus, the path along which we check reachability is $a_0, a_1, \ldots, a_n$, where $a_0 = a$ and a_i is the union of states that are reachable in the MTS from a_{i-1}. We stop at a_n that contains a'. We now try to prove that $must^{-*}(a_0, a_n)$, which implies that a' is weakly reachable from a. We start with $i = n$ and when we come across an iteration i such that $must^-(a_{i-1}, a_i)$ does not hold, we check whether a_{i+1} involves a loop and Theorem 1 is applicable. If this is not the case, we refine a_{i+1}.

5   Making the Method More General

The application of Theorem 1 requires the concrete system to be deterministic with respect to $\gamma(a)$. That is, every concrete state in $\gamma(a)$ should have at most one successor in $\gamma(a)$. As demonstrated in Section 3, one way to cope with nondeterminism is to refine a so that, while being nondeterministic, the program is deterministic with respect to $\gamma(a)$. In this section we discuss how generalize our method to handle cases in which the program is nondeterministic and there is no way to refine a efficiently and make it deterministic with respect to a. As an example, consider the procedure jump_beyond_n appearing in Figure 8. The figure also depicts the concrete state space. Abstracting it to three abstract states according to the predicates $x = 0, 0 < x < n$, and $x \geq n$ results in the problematic setting of Figure 3, where we cannot conclude that the error state $x \geq n$ is reachable from the initial state $x = 0$. The procedure has a nondeterministic choice (when $x = 1$ mod 1, it can be decreased by either 1 or 3) and there is no way to refine the abstract state $0 < x < n$ so that the conditions of Theorem 1 hold.

Our technique is to generate programs with fewer behaviors, with a hope that we preserve weak reachability and satisfy the conditions of the theorem. The programs we try first are deterministic programs obtained from the original program by disabling some of its nondeterministic choices. In our example, we try to apply Theorem 1 with respect to the two procedures obtained from jump_beyond_n by replacing the statement x:=x-1|x:=x-3 by x:=x-1 or x:=x-3. As can be seen in the description of the concrete state space, for this example, this would work – going always with x:=x-1 increments x to go beyond n. Thus, in order to apply Theorem 1, we have to disable the x:=x-3 branch and refine the abstract state to $2 \leq x < n$ (the state $x = 1$ is unreachable).

Disabling nondeterministic branches works when reachability can be achieved by always taking the same transition. As we discuss below, this is not always possible. A more general approach is to determinize the program by adding predicates that "schedule" the different branches. Thus, a nondeterministic choice $s_1|s_2| \cdots |s_k$ is replaced by case $b_1 : s_1; \ldots ; b_k : s_k$, for mutually exclusive predicates $b_1, \ldots, b_k$. The predicates $b_1, \ldots, b_k$ can be automatically generated (for example, proceed in a round-robin fashion among all branches) or can be obtained from the user.

Remark 2. Reachability in a CTS can be checked along simple paths. On the other hand, since each state in an MTS corresponds to several concrete states, weak reachability may have to traverse the same abstract state several times. The traversal need not be *stationary*, in the sense that different nondeterministic choices may be taken in order to reach an exit port.

References

1. Ball, T.: A theory of predicate-complete test coverage and generation. In: 3rd International Symposium on Formal Methods for Components and Objects (2004)
2. Ball, T., Bounimova, E., Cook, B., Levin, V., Lichtenberg, J., McGarvey, C., Ondrusek, B., Rajamani, S.K., Ustuner, A.: Thorough static analysis of device drivers. In: EuroSys (2006)
3. Ball, T., Kupferman, O.: Better under-approximation of programs by hiding of variables. In: Proc. 7th VMCAI (2006)
4. Berdine, J., Chawdhary, A., Cook, B., Distefano, D., O'Hearn, P.: Variance analyses from invariance analyses. In: Proc. 34th POPL (2007)
5. Bradley, A.R., Manna, Z., Sipma, H.: Linear Ranking with Reachability. In: Etessami, K., Rajamani, S.K. (eds.) CAV 2005. LNCS, vol. 3576, pp. 491–504. Springer, Heidelberg (2005)
6. Cook, B., Podelski, A., Rybalchenko, A.: Termination proofs for systems code. In: Proc. ACM PLDI, pp. 415–426. ACM Press, New York (2006)
7. Cousot, P., Cousot, R.: Abstract interpretation: a unified lattice model for the static analysis of programs by construction or approximation of fixpoints. In: Proc. 4th POPL, pp. 238–252. ACM Press, New York (1977)
8. Dijkstra, E.W.: A Discipline of Programming. Prentice-Hall, Englewood Cliffs (1976)
9. Godefroid, P., Jagadeesan, R.: Automatic abstraction using generalized model checking. In: Brinksma, E., Larsen, K.G. (eds.) CAV 2002. LNCS, vol. 2404, pp. 137–150. Springer, Heidelberg (2002)
10. Kroening, D., Weissenbacher, G.: Counterexamples with loops for predicate abstraction. In: Ball, T., Jones, R.B. (eds.) CAV 2006. LNCS, vol. 4144, pp. 152–165. Springer, Heidelberg (2006)
11. Larsen, K.G., Thomsen, G.B.: A modal process logic. In: Proc. 3th LICS (1988)
12. Larsen, K.G., XinXin, L.: Equation solving using modal transition systems. In: Proc. 5th LICS, pp. 108–117 (1990)
13. Podelski, A., Rybalchenko, A.: Transition invariants. In: Proc. 19th LICS, pp. 32–41 (2004)
14. Shoham, S., Grumberg, O.: Monotonic abstraction-refinement for CTL. In: Jensen, K., Podelski, A. (eds.) TACAS 2004. LNCS, vol. 2988, pp. 546–560. Springer, Heidelberg (2004)

Configurable Software Verification: Concretizing the Convergence of Model Checking and Program Analysis*

Dirk Beyer[1], Thomas A. Henzinger[2], and Grégory Théoduloz[2]

[1] Simon Fraser University, B.C., Canada
[2] EPFL, Switzerland

Abstract. In automatic software verification, we have observed a theoretical convergence of model checking and program analysis. In practice, however, model checkers are still mostly concerned with precision, e.g., the removal of spurious counterexamples; for this purpose they build and refine reachability trees. Lattice-based program analyzers, on the other hand, are primarily concerned with efficiency. We designed an algorithm and built a tool that can be configured to perform not only a purely tree-based or a purely lattice-based analysis, but offers many intermediate settings that have not been evaluated before. The algorithm and tool take one or more abstract interpreters, such as a predicate abstraction and a shape analysis, and configure their execution and interaction using several parameters. Our experiments show that such customization may lead to dramatic improvements in the precision-efficiency spectrum.

1 Introduction

Automatic program verification requires a choice between precision and efficiency. The more precise a method, the fewer false positives it will produce, but also the more expensive it is, and thus applicable to fewer programs. Historically, this trade-off was reflected in two major approaches to static verification: program analysis and model checking. While in principle, each of the two approaches can be (and has been) viewed as a subcase of the other [18, 19, 7], such theoretical relationships have had little impact on the practice of verification. Program analyzers, by and large, still target the efficient computation of few simple facts about large programs; model checkers, by contrast, focus still on the removal of false alarms through ever more refined analyses of relatively small programs. Emphasizing efficiency, static program analyzers are usually path-insensitive, because the most efficient abstract domains lose precision at the join points of program paths. Emphasizing precision, software model checkers, on the other hand, usually never join abstract domain elements (such as predicates), but explore an abstract reachability tree that keeps different program paths separate.

In order to experiment with the trade-offs, and in order to be able to set the dial between the two extreme points, we have extended the software model checker BLAST [11] to permit customized program analyses. Traditionally, customization has

---

* This research was supported in part by the grant SFU/PRG 06-3, and by the Swiss National Science Foundation.

W. Damm and H. Hermanns (Eds.): CAV 2007, LNCS 4590, pp. 504–518, 2007.

meant to choose a particular abstract interpreter (abstract domain and transfer functions, perhaps a widening operator) [13, 8, 14, 20], or a combination of abstract interpreters [10, 6, 4, 12]. Here, we go a step further in that we also configure the execution engine of the chosen abstract interpreters. At one extreme (typical for program analyzers), the execution engine propagates abstract domain elements along the edges of the control-flow graph of a program until a fixpoint is reached [5]. At the other extreme (typical for model checkers), the execution engine unrolls the control-flow graph into a reachability tree and decorates the tree nodes with abstract domain elements, until each node is 'covered' by some other node that has already been explored [11]. In order to customize the execution of a program analysis, we define and implement a meta engine that needs to be configured by providing, in addition to one or more abstract interpreters, a *merge* operator and a *termination* check.

The merge operator indicates when two nodes of a reachability tree are merged, and when they are explored separately: in classical program analysis, two nodes are merged if they refer to the same control location of the program; in classical model checking, no nodes are merged. The termination check indicates when the exploration of a path in the reachability tree is stopped at a node: in classical program analysis, when the corresponding abstract state does not represent new (unexplored) concrete states (i.e., a fixpoint has been reached); in classical model checking, when the corresponding abstract state represents a subset of the concrete states represented by another node. Our motivation is practical, not theoretical: while it is theoretically possible to redefine the abstract interpreter to capture different merge operators and termination checks within a single execution engine, we wish to reuse abstract interpreters as building blocks, while still experimenting with different merge operators and termination checks. This is particularly useful when several abstract interpreters are combined. In this case, our meta engine can be configured by defining a *composite merge operator* from the component merge operators; a *composite termination check* from the component termination checks; but also a *composite transfer function* from the component transfer functions.

Combining the advantages of different execution engines for different abstract interpreters can yield dramatic results, as was shown by *predicated lattices* [9]. That work combined predicate abstraction with a data-flow domain: the data-flow analysis becomes more precise by distinguishing different paths through predicates; at the same time, the efficiency of a lattice-based analysis is preserved for facts that are difficult to track by predicates. However, the configuration of predicated lattices is just one possibility, combining abstract reachability trees for the predicate domain with a join-based analysis for the data-flow domain. Another example is *lazy shape analysis* [2], where we combined predicate abstraction and shape analysis. Again, we 'hard-wired' one particular such combination: no merging of nodes; termination by checking coverage between individual nodes; cartesian product of transfer functions. Our new, configurable implementation permits the systematic experimentation with many variations, and the results are presented in this paper. We show that different configurations can lead to large, example-dependent differences in precision and performance. In particular, it is often useful to use non-cartesian transfer functions, where information flows between multiple abstract interpreters, e.g., from the predicate state to the shape state (or lattice state), and vice versa. By choosing suitable abstract interpreters and configuring the meta engine, we can also compare the effectiveness and efficiency of symbolic versus explicit representations of values, and the use of different pointer alias analyses in software model checking.

In recent years we have observed a convergence of historically distinct program verification techniques. It is indeed difficult to say whether our configurable verifier is a model checker (as it is based on BLAST) or a program analyzer (as it is configured by choosing a set of abstract interpreters and some parameters for executing and combining them). We believe that the distinction is no longer practically meaningful (it has not been theoretically meaningful for some time), and that this signals a new phase in automatic software verification tools.

2   Formalism and Algorithm

We restrict the presentation to a simple imperative programming language, where all operations are either assignments or assume operations, and all variables range over integers.[1] A *program* is represented by a *control-flow automaton* (CFA), which consists of a set L of control locations (models the program counter pc), an initial location pc_0 (models the program entry), and a set $G \subseteq L \times Ops \times L$ of control-flow edges (models the operation that is executed when control flows from one location to another). The *concrete state* of a program is a variable assignment c that assigns to each variable from $X \cup \{pc\}$ a value. The set of all concrete states of a program is denoted by C. Each edge $g \in G$ defines a (labeled) transition relation $\overset{g}{\to} \subseteq C \times \{g\} \times C$. The complete transition relation $\to$ is the union over all edges: $\to \ = \ \bigcup_{g \in G} \overset{g}{\to}$. A concrete state c_n is *reachable* from a region r, denoted by $c_n \in Reach(r)$, if there exists a sequence of concrete states $\langle c_0, c_1, \ldots, c_n \rangle$ such that $c_0 \in r$ and for all $1 \leq i \leq n$, we have $c_{i-1} \to c_i$.

2.1   Configurable Program Analysis

A *configurable program analysis* $\mathbb{D} = (D, \leadsto, \mathsf{merge}, \mathsf{stop})$ consists of an abstract domain D, a transfer relation $\leadsto$, a merge operator merge, and a termination check stop, which are explained in the following. These four components *configure* our algorithm and influence the precision and cost of a program analysis.

1. The *abstract domain* $D = (C, \mathcal{E}, \llbracket \cdot \rrbracket)$ is defined by a set C of concrete states, a semi-lattice $\mathcal{E}$, and a concretization function $\llbracket \cdot \rrbracket$. The semi-lattice $\mathcal{E} = (E, \top, \bot, \sqsubseteq, \sqcup)$ consists of a (possibly infinite) set E of elements, a top element $\top \in E$, a bottom element $\bot \in E$, a preorder $\sqsubseteq \subseteq E \times E$, and a total function $\sqcup : E \times E \to E$ (the join operator). The lattice elements from E are the abstract states. The concretization function $\llbracket \cdot \rrbracket : E \to 2^C$ assigns to each abstract state its meaning, i.e., the set of concrete states that it represents. The abstract domain determines the objective of the analysis.

2. The *transfer relation* $\leadsto \subseteq E \times G \times E$ assigns to each abstract state e possible new abstract states e' that are abstract successors of e, and each transfer is labeled with a control-flow edge g. We write $e \overset{g}{\leadsto} e'$ if $(e, g, e') \in \leadsto$, and $e \leadsto e'$ if there exists a g with

---

[1] In our implementation based on BLAST, we allow C programs as inputs, and transform them into the intermediate language CIL [16]. Interprocedural analysis is supported.

$e\overset{g}{\leadsto}e'$. For soundness and progress of the program analysis, the abstract domain and the corresponding transfer relation have to fulfill the following requirements:

(a) $[\![\top]\!] = C$ and $[\![\bot]\!] = \emptyset$;
(b) $\forall e, e' \in E: [\![e \sqcup e']\!] \supseteq [\![e]\!] \cup [\![e']\!]$
    (the join operator is precise or over-approximates);
(c) $\forall e \in E: \exists e' \in E: e \leadsto e'$ (the transfer relation is total);
(d) $\forall e \in E, g \in G : \bigcup_{e \overset{g}{\leadsto} e'} [\![e']\!] \supseteq \bigcup_{c \in [\![e]\!]} \{c' \mid c \overset{g}{\to} c'\}$
    (the transfer relation over-approximates operations).

3. The *merge operator* merge $: E \times E \to E$ combines the information of two abstract states. To guarantee soundness of our analysis, we require that $e' \sqsubseteq \text{merge}(e, e')$ (the result can only be more abstract than the second parameter). Dependent on the element e, the result of merge can be anything between e' and $\top$, i.e., the operator weakens the second parameter depending on the first parameter. Furthermore, if $\mathbb{D}$ is a composite analysis, the merge operator can join some of the components dependent on others. Note that the operator merge is not commutative, and is not the same as the join operator $\sqcup$ of the lattice, but merge can be based on $\sqcup$. Later we will use the following merge operators: $\text{merge}^{sep}(e, e') = e'$ and $\text{merge}^{join}(e, e') = e \sqcup e'$.

4. The *termination check* stop $: E \times 2^E \to \mathbb{B}$ checks if the abstract state that is given as first parameter is covered by the set of abstract states given as second parameter. We require for soundness of the termination check that $\text{stop}(e, R) = true$ implies $[\![e]\!] \subseteq \bigcup_{e' \in R}[\![e']\!]$. The termination check can, for example, go through the elements of the set R that is given as second parameter and search for a single element that subsumes ($\sqsubseteq$) the first parameter, or —if D is a powerset domain[2]— can join the elements of R to check if R subsumes the first parameter. Note that the termination check stop is not the same as the preorder $\sqsubseteq$ of the lattice, but stop can be based on $\sqsubseteq$. Later we will use the following termination checks (the second requires a powerset domain):

$$\text{stop}^{sep}(e, R) = (\exists e' \in R : e \sqsubseteq e') \text{ and } \text{stop}^{join}(e, R) = (e \sqsubseteq \bigsqcup_{e' \in R} e').$$

Note that the abstract domain on its own does not determine the precision of the analysis; each of the four configurable components (abstract domain, transfer relation, merge operator, and termination check) independently influences both precision and cost.

Among the program analyses that we use later in the experiments are the following:

Location Analysis. A configurable program analysis $\mathbb{L} = (D_\mathbb{L}, \leadsto_\mathbb{L}, \text{merge}_\mathbb{L}, \text{stop}_\mathbb{L})$ that tracks the reachability of CFA locations has the following components: the domain $D_\mathbb{L}$ is based on the flat lattice for the set L of CFA locations; the transfer relation $\leadsto_\mathbb{L}$ with $l \overset{g}{\leadsto}_\mathbb{L} l'$ if there exists an edge $g = (l, op, l') \in G$, and $l \overset{g}{\leadsto}_\mathbb{L} \bot$ otherwise (the syntactical successor in the CFA without considering the semantics of the operation op); the merge operator $\text{merge}_\mathbb{L} = \text{merge}^{sep}$; and the termination check $\text{stop}_\mathbb{L} = \text{stop}^{sep}$.

Predicate Abstraction. A program analysis for cartesian predicate abstraction was defined by Ball et al. [1]. Their framework can be expressed as a configurable program

---

[2] A *powerset domain* is an abstract domain such that $[\![e_1 \sqcup e_2]\!] = [\![e_1]\!] \cup [\![e_2]\!]$.

Algorithm 1. $CPA(\mathbb{D}, e_0)$

Input: a configurable program analysis $\mathbb{D} = (D, \rightsquigarrow, \mathsf{merge}, \mathsf{stop})$,
         an initial abstract state $e_0 \in E$, let E denote the set of elements of the semi-lattice of D
Output: a set of reachable abstract states
Variables: a set reached of elements of E, a set waitlist of elements of E
   waitlist $:= \{e_0\}$
   reached $:= \{e_0\}$
   while waitlist $\neq \emptyset$ **do**
     pop e from waitlist
     for each e' with $e \rightsquigarrow e'$ **do**
       for each $e'' \in$ reached **do**
         // Combine with existing abstract state.
         $e_{new} :=$ merge(e', e'')
         if $e_{new} \neq e''$ **then**
           waitlist $:= \big($waitlist $\cup \{e_{new}\}\big) \setminus \{e''\}$
           reached $:= \big($reached $\cup \{e_{new}\}\big) \setminus \{e''\}$
      if $\neg$ stop$(e',$ reached$)$ **then**
        waitlist $:=$ waitlist $\cup \{e'\}$
        reached $:=$ reached $\cup \{e'\}$
   return reached

---

analysis $\mathbb{P}$ by using their abstract domain and transfer relation, and choosing the merge operator $\mathsf{merge}_{\mathbb{P}} = \mathsf{merge}^{sep}$ and the termination check $\mathsf{stop}_{\mathbb{P}} = \mathsf{stop}^{sep}$.

Shape Analysis. Shape analysis is a static analysis that uses finite structures (shape graphs) to represent instances of heap-stored data structures. We can express the framework of Sagiv et al. [17] as a configurable program analysis $\mathbb{S}$ by using their abstract (powerset) domain and transfer relation, and choosing the merge operator $\mathsf{merge}_{\mathbb{S}} = \mathsf{merge}^{join}$ and the termination check $\mathsf{stop}_{\mathbb{S}} = \mathsf{stop}^{join}$.

2.2 Execution Algorithm

The reachability algorithm CPA computes, for a given configurable program analysis and an initial abstract state, a set of reachable abstract states, i.e., an over-approximation of the set of reachable concrete states. The configurable program analysis is given by the abstract domain D, the transfer relation $\rightsquigarrow$ of the input program, the merge operator merge, and the termination check stop. The algorithm keeps updating two sets of abstract states, a set reached to store all abstract states that are found to be reachable, and a set waitlist to store all abstract states that are not yet processed (frontier). The state exploration starts with the initial abstract state e_0. For a current abstract state e, the algorithm considers each successor e', obtained from the transfer relation. Now, using the given operator merge, the abstract successor state is combined with an existing abstract state from reached. If the operator merge has added information to the new abstract state, such that the old abstract state is subsumed, then the old abstract state is replaced by the new one.[3] If after the merge step the resulting new abstract state is not covered by the set reached, then it is added to the set reached and to the set waitlist.[4]

Theorem 1 (Soundness). *For a given configurable program analysis $\mathbb{D}$ and an initial abstract state e_0, Algorithm CPA computes a set of abstract states that over-approximates the set of reachable concrete states:* $\bigcup\limits_{e \in CPA(\mathbb{D}, e_0)} [\![e]\!] \supseteq Reach([\![e_0]\!])$.

We now show how model checking and data-flow analysis are instances of configurable program analysis.

Data-Flow Analysis. Data-flow analysis is the problem of assigning to each control-flow location a lattice element that over-approximates the set of possible concrete states at that program location. The least solution (smallest over-approximation) can be found by computing the least fixpoint, by iteratively applying the transfer relation to abstract states and joining the resulting abstract state with the abstract state that was assigned to the location in a previous iteration. The decision whether the fixpoint is reached is usually based on a working list of data-flow facts that were newly added. In our configurable program analysis, the data-flow setting can be realized by choosing the merge operator merge^{join} and the termination check stop^{join}.

Note that a configurable program analysis can model improvements (in precision or efficiency) for an existing data-flow analysis without redesigning the abstract domain of the existing data-flow analysis. For example, a new data-flow analysis that uses a subset of the powerset domain 2^D, instead of D itself, can be represented by a configurable program analysis reusing the domain D and its operators, but using an appropriate new merge operator that is different from merge^{join}. Moreover, static analyzers such as ASTRÉE [3] use delayed joins, or path partitioning [15], to improve the precision and efficiency of the analysis. We can model these techniques within our framework by changing only the merge operator.

Model Checking. A typical model-checking algorithm explores the abstract reachable state space of the program by unfolding the CFA, which results in an *abstract reachability tree*. For a given abstract state, the abstract successor state is computed and added as successor node to the tree. Branches in the CFA have their corresponding branches in the abstract reachability tree, but since two paths never meet, a join operator is never applied. This tree data structure supports the required path analysis in CEGAR frameworks, as well as reporting a counterexample if a bug is found. The decision whether the fixpoint is reached is usually implemented by a coverage check, i.e., the algorithm checks each time a new node is added to the tree if the abstract state of that node is already subsumed by some other node. BLAST's model-checking algorithm can be in-

---

[3] Implementation remark: The operator merge can be implemented in a way that it operates directly on the reached set. If the set reached is stored in a sorted data structure, there is no need to iterate over the full set of reachable abstract states, but only over the abstract states that need to be combined.

[4] Implementation remark: The termination check can be done additionally before the merge process. This speeds up cases where the termination check is cheaper than the merge.

stantiated as a configurable program analysis by choosing the merge operator merge^{sep} and the termination check stop^{sep}.

Combinations of Model Checking and Program Analysis. Due to the fact that the model-checking algorithm never uses a join operator, the analysis is automatically path-sensitive. In contrast, path-sensitivity in data-flow analysis requires the use of a more precise data-flow lattice that distinguishes abstract states on different paths. On the other hand, due to the join operations, the data-flow analysis can reach the fixpoint much faster in many cases. Different abstract interpreters exhibit significant differences in precision and cost, depending on the choice for the merge operator and termination check. Therefore, we need a mechanism to combine the best choices of the operators for different abstract interpreters when composing the resulting program analyses.

2.3 Composite Program Analyses

A configurable program analysis can be composed of several configurable program analyses. A *composite program analysis* $\mathcal{C} = (\mathbb{D}_1, \mathbb{D}_2, \leadsto_\times, \mathsf{merge}_\times, \mathsf{stop}_\times)^5$ consists of two configurable program analyses $\mathbb{D}_1$ and $\mathbb{D}_2$, a composite transfer relation $\leadsto_\times$, a composite merge operator $\mathsf{merge}_\times$, and a composite termination check $\mathsf{stop}_\times$. The three composites $\leadsto_\times$, $\mathsf{merge}_\times$, and $\mathsf{stop}_\times$ are expressions over the components of $\mathbb{D}_1$ and $\mathbb{D}_2$ ($\leadsto_i, \mathsf{merge}_i, \mathsf{stop}_i, [\![\cdot]\!]_i, E_i, \top_i, \bot_i, \sqsubseteq_i, \sqcup_i$), as well as the operators $\downarrow$ and $\preceq$ (defined below). The composite operators can manipulate lattice elements only through those components, never directly (e.g., if $\mathbb{D}_1$ is already a result of a composition, then we cannot access the tuple elements of abstract states from E_1, nor redefine merge_1). The only way of using additional information is through the operators $\downarrow$ and $\preceq$. The *strengthening* operator $\downarrow : E_1 \times E_2 \to E_1$ computes a stronger element from the lattice set E_1 by using the information of a lattice element from E_2; it has to meet the requirement $\downarrow(e, e') \sqsubseteq e$. The strengthening operator can be used to define a composite transfer relation $\leadsto_\times$ that is stronger than a pure product relation. For example, if we combine predicate abstraction and shape analysis, the strengthening operator $\downarrow_{S,P}$ can 'sharpen' the field predicates of the shape graphs by considering the predicate region. Furthermore, we allow the definitions of composite operators to use the *compare* relation $\preceq \subseteq E_1 \times E_2$, to compare elements of different lattices.

For a given composite program analysis $\mathcal{C} = (\mathbb{D}_1, \mathbb{D}_2, \leadsto_\times, \mathsf{merge}_\times, \mathsf{stop}_\times)$, we can construct a configurable program analysis $\mathbb{D}_\times = (D_\times, \leadsto_\times, \mathsf{merge}_\times, \mathsf{stop}_\times)$, where the product domain $D_\times$ is defined as the direct product of D_1 and D_2: $D_\times = D_1 \times D_2 = (C, \mathcal{E}_\times, [\![\cdot]\!]_\times)$. The product lattice is $\mathcal{E}_\times = \mathcal{E}_1 \times \mathcal{E}_2 = (E_1 \times E_2, (\top_1, \top_2), (\bot_1, \bot_2), \sqsubseteq_\times, \sqcup_\times)$ with $(e_1, e_2) \sqsubseteq_\times (e_1', e_2')$ iff $e_1 \sqsubseteq_1 e_1'$ and $e_2 \sqsubseteq_2 e_2'$, and $(e_1, e_2) \sqcup_\times (e_1', e_2') = (e_1 \sqcup_1 e_1', e_2 \sqcup_2 e_2')$. The product concretization function $[\![\cdot]\!]_\times$ is such that $[\![(d_1, d_2)]\!]_\times = [\![d_1]\!]_1 \cap [\![d_2]\!]_2$. The literature agrees that this direct product itself is often not sharp enough [6,4]. Even improvements over the direct product (e.g., the reduced product [6] or the logical product [10]) do not solve the problem completely. However, in a configurable program analysis, we can specify the desired degree of 'sharpness' in the composite operators $\leadsto_\times$, $\mathsf{merge}_\times$, and $\mathsf{stop}_\times$. For a given product domain, the definition of

---

[5] We extend this notation to any finite number of $\mathbb{D}_i$.

the three composite operators determines the precision of the resulting configurable program analysis. In previous approaches, a redefinition of basic operations was necessary, but using configurable program analysis, we can reuse the existing abstract interpreters.

Example: BLAST's Domain. The program analysis that is implemented in the tool BLAST can be expressed as a configurable program analysis $\mathbb{D}$ that derives from the composite program analysis $\mathcal{C} = (\mathbb{L}, \mathbb{P}, \leadsto_\times, \text{merge}_\times, \text{stop}_\times)$, where the components are the configurable program analysis $\mathbb{L}$ for locations and the configurable program analysis $\mathbb{P}$ for predicate abstraction. We construct the composite transfer relation $\leadsto_\times$ such that $(l, r) \overset{g}{\leadsto}_\times (l', r')$ iff $l \overset{g}{\leadsto}_\mathbb{L} l'$ and $r \overset{g}{\leadsto}_\mathbb{P} r'$. We choose the composite merge operator $\text{merge}_\times = \text{merge}^{sep}$ and the composite termination check $\text{stop}_\times = \text{stop}^{sep}$.

Example: BLAST's Domain + Shape Analysis. The combination of predicate abstraction and shape analysis [2] can now be expressed as the composite program analysis $\mathcal{C} = (\mathbb{L}, \mathbb{P}, \mathbb{S}, \leadsto_\times, \text{merge}_\times, \text{stop}_\times)$ with the three components: location analysis $\mathbb{L}$, predicate abstraction $\mathbb{P}$, and shape analysis $\mathbb{S}$. In our previous work [2] we used a configuration that corresponds to the composite merge operator $\text{merge}_\times = \text{merge}^{sep}$ and the composite termination check $\text{stop}_\times = \text{stop}^{sep}$. Our new tool allows us now to define the three composite operators $\leadsto_\times$, $\text{merge}_\times$, and $\text{stop}_\times$ in many different ways, and we report the results of our experiments in Sect. 3.

Example: BLAST's Domain + Pointer Analysis. Fischer et al. used a particular combination (called *predicated lattices*) of predicate abstraction and a data-flow analysis for pointers [9], which we can express as the composite program analysis $\mathcal{C} = (\mathbb{L}, \mathbb{P}, \mathbb{A}, \leadsto_\times, \text{merge}_\times, \text{stop}_\times)$, where $\mathbb{A}$ is a configurable pointer analysis. The transfer relation $\leadsto_\times$ is such that $(l, r, d) \overset{g}{\leadsto}_\times (l', r', d')$ iff $l \overset{g}{\leadsto}_\mathbb{L} l'$ and $r \overset{g}{\leadsto}_\mathbb{P} r'$ and $d \overset{g}{\leadsto}_\mathbb{A} d'$. We can configure the algorithm of Fischer et al. by choosing the composite termination check $\text{stop}_\times = \text{stop}^{sep}$ and the composite merge operator that joins the third elements if the first two agree:

$$\text{merge}_\times((l, r, d), (l', r', d')) = \begin{cases} (l', r', \text{merge}_\mathbb{A}(d, d')) & \text{if } l = l' \text{ and } r = r' \\ (l', r', d') & \text{otherwise} \end{cases}$$

with $\text{merge}_\mathbb{A}(d, d') = d \sqcup_\mathbb{A} d'$.

Remark: Location Domain. Traditional data-flow analyses do not consider the location domain as a separate abstract domain; they assume that the locations are always explicitly analyzed. In contrast, we leave this completely up to the interpreter. We find it interesting to consider the program counter as just another program variable, and define a location domain that makes the program counter explicit when composed with other domains. This releases the other abstract domains from defining the location handling, and only the parameters for the composite program analysis need to be set. This keeps different concerns separate. Usually, only the program counter variable is modeled explicitly, and all other variables are represented symbolically (e.g., by predicates or shapes). We have the freedom to treat *any* program variable explicitly, not only the program counter; this may be useful for loop indices. Conversely, we can treat the program counter symbolically, and let other variables 'span' the abstract reachability tree.

3   Experiments

We evaluated our new approach on several combinations of abstract interpreters, under several different configurations. We implemented the configurable program analysis as an extension of the model checker BLAST, in order to be able to reuse many components that are necessary for an analysis tool but out of our focus in this work. BLAST supports recursive function calls, as well as pointers and recursive data structures on the heap. For representing the shape-analysis domain we use parts of the TVLA implementation [13]. For pointer-alias analysis, we use the implementation that comes with CIL [16]. We use the configuration of Fischer et al. [9] to compare with predicated lattices.

3.1   Configuring Model Checking + Shape Analysis

For our first set of experiments, we consider the combination of predicate abstraction and shape analysis. To demonstrate the impact of various configurations on performance and precision, we ran our algorithm on the set of example C programs from [2], extended by some programs to explore scalability. These examples can be divided into three categories: (1) examples that require only unary and binary (shape) predicates to be proved safe (list_i, simple, and simple_backw), (2) examples that require in addition nullary predicates (alternating and list_flag), and (3) an example that requires that information from the nullary predicates is used to compute the new value of unary and binary predicates (list_flag2). The verification times are given in Table 1 for the six different configurations (A-F). When BLAST fails to prove the program safe for a given configuration, a false alarm (FP) is reported.

A: Predicated Lattice (merge-pred-join, stop-sep). In our first configuration we use the traditional model-checking approach (no join) for the predicate abstraction, and the predicated-join approach for the shape analysis. This corresponds to the following composite operators:

1. $(l, r, s) \overset{g}{\leadsto}_\times (l', r', s')$ iff $l \overset{g}{\leadsto}_{\mathbb{L}} l'$ and $r \overset{g}{\leadsto}_{\mathbb{P}} r'$ and $s \overset{g}{\leadsto}_{\mathbb{S}} s'$

2. $\mathsf{merge}_\times ((l, r, s), (l', r', s')) = \begin{cases} (l', r', \mathsf{merge}_{\mathbb{S}}(s, s')) & \text{if } l = l' \text{ and } r = r' \\ (l', r', s') & \text{otherwise} \end{cases}$

3. $\mathsf{stop}_\times ((l, r, d), R) = \mathsf{stop}^{sep}((l, r, d), R)$

The transfer relation is cartesian, i.e., the successors of the different components are computed independently (cf. [2]). The merge operator joins the shape graphs of abstract regions that agree on both the location and the predicate region. The predicate regions are never joined. Termination is checked using the coverage against a single abstract state. This configuration corresponds to Fischer et al.'s *predicated lattice* [9].

Example. To illustrate the difference between the various configurations, we use the C program in Fig. 1(a). This program constructs a lists that contains the data values 1 or 2, depending on the value of the variable flag, and ends with a single 3. We illustrate the example using the following abstractions. In the predicate abstraction, we keep track of the nullary predicate *flag*. In the shape analysis, we consider shape graphs for the list

```
 1 typedef struct node {
 2   int h;   struct node *n;
 3 } *List;
 4 void foo(int flag) {
 5   List a = (List) malloc(...);
 6   if (a == NULL) exit(1);
 7   List p = a;
 8   while (random()) {
 9     if (flag)   p->h = 1;
10     else        p->h = 2;
11     p->n = (List) malloc(...);
12     if (p->n == NULL) exit(1);
13     p = p->n;   }
14   p->h = 3;
15 }
```

(a) Example C program   (b) Example shape graphs

Fig. 1. Example program and two list representations

pointed to by program variable a, and field predicates for the assertions $h = 1$, $h = 2$, and $h = 3$. (These abstractions are automatically discovered by BLAST's refinement procedure [2], but this is not the subject of this paper). Figure 1(b) shows some shape graphs that are encountered during the analysis. The nodes of a shape graph correspond to memory cells. Summary nodes (double circles) represent $0, 1$, or more nodes. Shape graphs are defined by the valuation of predicates over nodes in a three-valued logic. Predicates are either unary (e.g., the points-to predicate a or the field predicates $h = 1$, $h = 2$, and $h = 3$) or binary (e.g., the *next* predicate n).

To understand how this composite program analysis works on this example, we consider abstract states for which the location component has the value 15 (program exit point). Because of the merge operator, abstract states that agree on both the location and the predicates are joined. Consequently, shape graphs corresponding to lists with different lengths are collected in a single abstract state. At the end of the analysis, we therefore find at most one abstract state per location and predicate valuation, e.g., $(15, flag, \{g_1, g_{2,1}, g_{3,1}, g_{4,1}\})$ and $(15, \neg flag, \{g_1, g_{2,2}, g_{3,2}, g_{4,2}\})$.

Experimental Results. Precision: Shape analysis is based on a powerset domain, and therefore the join has no negative effect on the precision of the analysis. *Performance:* The idea behind the join in data-flow analysis is to keep the number of abstract states small for efficiency and progress reasons, and in a typical data-flow analysis the join operations are efficient. However, since an abstract state contains a set of shape graphs in our analysis, the effect is the opposite: the join operations add extra work, because larger sets of shape graphs need to be manipulated. In addition, when the algorithm computes successors of a joined set, the work that may have been done already for some subset is repeated. This results in unnecessarily many, highly expensive operations.

B: As Precise as Model Checking (merge-sep, stop-sep). Now we want to avoid that the merge operator causes join overhead in the analysis when computing abstract successor states. This is easy to achieve in our composite program analysis: we replace the composite merge operator $merge_\times$ by the merge operator $merge^{sep}$. The new composite program analysis joins neither predicate regions nor shape regions, and corresponds to *lazy shape analysis* [2].

Example. Since this composite program analysis is not joining elements, there is no reached abstract state with a set of shape graphs of size larger than 1 (unlike in the previous configuration A). Instead, we maintain distinct abstract states. In particular, at the exit location, the set of reached abstract states contains the following abstract states: $(15, flag, \{g_1\})$, $(15, flag, \{g_{2,1}\})$, $(15, flag, \{g_{3,1}\})$, $(15, flag, \{g_{4,1}\})$, $(15, \neg flag, \{g_1\})$, $(15, \neg flag, \{g_{2,1}\})$, $(15, \neg flag, \{g_{3,1}\})$, and $(15, \neg flag, \{g_{4,1}\})$. This set of abstract states represents exactly the same set of concrete states as the result of the previous analysis (configuration A).

Experimental Results. All examples in our experiments have smaller run times using this configuration, and the precision in the experiments does not change, compared to configuration A. *Precision:* Shape analysis is based on a powerset domain, and therefore, joins are precise. The precision of the predicated lattice is the same as the precision of this variant without joins. *Performance:* Although the number of explored abstract states is slightly higher, this configuration improves the performance of the analysis. The size of lattice elements (i.e., the average number of shape graphs in an abstract state) is considerably smaller than in the predicated-lattice configuration (A). Therefore, we achieve a better performance, because operations (in particular the successor computations) on small sets of shape graphs are much more efficient than on large sets.

C: More Precision by Improved Transfer Relation (merge-sep, stop-sep, transfer-new). From the first to the second configuration, we could improve the performance of the analysis. Now, we show how the precision of the analysis can be improved. We replace the cartesian transfer relation [2] by a new version that does not compute successors completely independently for the different sub-domains:

$$(l, r, s) \overset{g}{\rightsquigarrow}_\times (l', r', s') \text{ iff } l \overset{g}{\rightsquigarrow}_{\mathbb{L}} l' \text{ and } r \overset{g}{\rightsquigarrow}_{\mathbb{P}} r' \text{ and } s \overset{g}{\rightsquigarrow}_{\mathbb{S}} s'' \text{ and } s' = \downarrow_{\mathbb{S},\mathbb{P}}(s'', r')$$

The strengthening operator improves the precision of the transfer relation by using the predicate region to sharpen the shape information.

Example. In the example, the strengthening operator has no effect, because the nullary predicate *flag* has no relation with any predicates used in the shape graph. The strengthening operator would prove useful if, for example, the shape graphs had in addition a unary field predicate $h = x$ (indicating that the field h of a node has the same value as the program variable x), and the predicate abstraction had the nullary predicate $x = 3$. Consider the operation at line 14 (p->h = 3). The successor of the shape graph before applying the strengthening operator can only update the unary field predicate $h = x$ to value $1/2$, while the unary field predicate $h = 3$ can be set to value 1 for the node pointed to by p. Supposing $x = 3$ holds in the predicate region of the abstract successor, the strengthening operator updates the field predicate $h = x$ to value 1 as well.

Experimental Results. This configuration results in an improvement in precision over published results for a 'hard-wired' configuration [2], at almost no cost. *Precision:* Because of the strengthening operator, the abstract successors are more precise than using the cartesian transfer relation. Therefore, the whole analysis is more precise.

Performance: The cost of the strengthening operator is small compared to the cost of the shape-successor computation. Therefore, the performance is not severely impacted when compared to a cartesian transfer relation.

D: As Precise as Model Checking with Improved Termination Check (merge-sep, stop-join). Now we try to achieve another improvement over configuration B: we replace the termination check with one that checks the abstract state against the join of the reached abstract states that agree on locations and predicates:

$$\mathsf{stop}_\times((l, r, s), R) \ = \ (s \sqsubseteq_\mathsf{S} \bigsqcup_\mathsf{S}\{s' \mid (l, r, s') \in R\})$$

The previous termination check was going through the set of already reached abstract states, checking against every abstract state for coverage. Alternatively, abstract states that agree on the predicate abstraction can be summarized by one single abstract state that is used for the termination check. This is sound because the shape-analysis domain is a powerset domain.

Example. To illustrate the use of the new termination check in the example, consider a set of reached abstract states that contains at some intermediate step the following abstract states: $(15, flag, \{g_1\})$, $(15, flag, \{g_{2,1}\})$, $(15, \neg flag, \{g_1\})$, and $(15, \neg flag, \{g_{2,2}\})$. If we want to apply the termination check to the abstract state $(15, flag, \{g_1, g_{2,1}\})$ and the given set of reached abstract states, we check whether the set $\{g_1, g_{2,1}\}$ of shape graphs is a subset of the join of all shape graphs already found for this location and valuation of predicates (that is, the set $\{g_1, g_{2,1}\}$). The check would not be positive at this point using termination check stop^{sep}.

Experimental Results. The overall performance impact is slightly negative. *Precision:* This configuration does not change the precision for our examples. *Performance:* We expected improved performance by (1) avoiding many single coverage checks because of the summary abstract state, and (2) fewer successor computations, because we may recognize earlier that the fixpoint is reached. However, the performance impact in our examples is negligible, because a very small portion of the time is spent on termination checks, and the gain is more than negated by the overhead due to the joins.

E: Join at Meet-Points as in Data-Flow Analysis (merge-join, stop-join). To compare with a classical data-flow analysis, we choose a configuration such that the data-flow elements are joined where the control flow meets, independently of the predicate region. We use the following merge operator, which joins with *all* previously computed shape graphs for the program location of the abstract state:

$$\mathsf{merge}_\times((l, r, d), (l', r', d')) = \begin{cases} (l', r', \mathsf{merge}_\mathsf{S}(d, d')) & \text{if } l = l' \\ (l', r', d') & \text{otherwise} \end{cases}$$

Example. The composite program analysis encounters, for example, the abstract state $(15, flag, \{g_1, g_{2,1}, g_{2,2}, g_{3,1}, g_{3,2}, \ldots\})$, which contains shape graphs for lists that contain either 1s or 2s despite the fact that *flag* has the value *true*. Therefore, we note a loss of precision compared to the predicated-lattice approach (configuration A), be-

Table 1. Time for the different configurations[8] (false alarm: FP)

Program	A pred-join stop-sep	B merge-sep stop-sep	C merge-sep stop-sep transfer-new	D merge-sep stop-join	E merge-join stop-join	F merge-join stop-join join preds
simple	0.53 s	0.32 s	0.40 s	0.34 s	0.51 s	0.50 s
simple_backw	0.43 s	0.28 s	0.26 s	0.31 s	0.44 s	0.45 s
list_1	0.42 s	0.37 s	0.41 s	0.32 s	0.41 s	0.41 s
list_2	5.24 s	0.85 s	1.25 s	0.86 s	5.34 s	5.36 s
list_3	138.97 s	1.79 s	2.62 s	2.10 s	132.08 s	132.07 s
list_4	> 600 s	9.67 s	15.44 s	11.87 s	> 600 s	> 600 s
alternating	0.86 s	0.61 s	0.96 s	0.60 s	FP	FP
list_flag	0.69 s	0.49 s	0.79 s	0.46 s	FP	FP
list_flag2	FP	FP	0.81 s	FP	FP	FP

Table 2. Time for examples run with a predicated lattice

Program	CFA nodes	LOC	A: orig. (join)	B: more precision (no join)
s3_clnt	272	2 547	0.680 s	0.830 s
s3_srvr	322	2 542	0.560 s	0.590 s
cdaudio	968	18 225	33.50 s	> 600 s
diskperf	549	14 286	248.330 s	> 600 s

cause the less precise merge operator looses the correlation between the value of the nullary predicate *flag* and the shape graphs.

Experimental Results. The analysis is not able to prove several of the examples that were successfully verified with previous configurations. *Precision:* The shape-analysis component has lost the path-sensitivity: the resulting shape graphs are similar to what a classical fixpoint algorithm for data-flow analysis would yield. Therefore, the analysis is less precise. *Performance:* The run time is similar to configuration A.

F: Predicate Abstraction with Join (merge-join for preds). We now evaluate a composite program analysis that is similar to a classical data-flow analysis, i.e., both predicates and shapes are joined for the abstract states that agree on the program location. We consider the following merge operator:

$$\mathsf{merge}_\times((l, r, s), (l', r', s')) = \begin{cases} (l', \mathsf{merge}_\mathbb{P}(r, r'), \mathsf{merge}_\mathbb{S}(d, d')) & \text{if } l = l' \\ (l', r', d') & \text{otherwise} \end{cases}$$

where $\mathsf{merge}_\mathbb{P}(r, r') = r \sqcup_\mathbb{P} r'$ is the weakest conjunction of predicates that implies $r \vee r'$. This composite program analysis corresponds exactly to a data-flow analysis on the direct product of the two lattices: the set of reached abstract states contains only one abstract state per location, because the merge operator joins abstract states of the same location.

Example. At location 15, we have one abstract state: $(15, \mathit{true}, \{g_1, g_{2,1}, g_{2,2}, \dots\})$.

Experimental Results. This configuration can prove the same example programs as configuration E, and the run times are also similar to configuration E.

Precision: This composite program analysis is the least precise in our set of configurations, because the merge operator joins both the predicates and the shape graphs independently, for a given location. While join is suitable for many data-flow analyses, predicate abstraction becomes very imprecise when predicate regions are joined, because then it is not possible to express disjunctions of predicates by the means of separate abstract states for the same location. *Performance:* Compared to configuration E, the number of abstract states is smaller (only one per location), but the shape graphs have the same size. Therefore, this configuration is less precise, although not more efficient.

Summary. For our set of examples, the experiments have shown that configuration C is the best choice, and we provided justifications for the results. However, we cannot conclude that configuration C is the preferred configuration for *any* combination of abstract interpreters, and we provide evidence for this in the next subsection.

3.2 Configuring Model Checking + Pointer Analysis

In the experimental setting of this subsection we show that for a certain kind of abstract interpreter the join is not only better, but that algorithms without join show prohibitive performance, or do not terminate. We consider the combination of BLAST's predicate domain and a pointer-analysis domain, as described at the end of Sect. 2. In Table 2 we report the performance results for two different algorithms: configuration A for a "predicated lattice," as described by Fischer et al. [9], and configuration B for an algorithm without join, using the merge operator $merge^{sep}$. The experiments give evidence that the number of abstract states explodes and blows up the computational overhead, but the gained precision is not even necessary for proving our example programs correct.

4   Conclusion

When the goal is as difficult as automatic software verification, it is imperative to bring to bear insights and optimizations no matter if they originated in model checking, program analysis, or automated theorem proving (which is heavily used in BLAST, to compute transfer functions and to perform termination checks). We have therefore modified BLAST from a tree-based software model checker to a tool that can be configured using different lattice-based abstract interpreters, composite transfer functions, merge operators, and termination checks. Specifically configured extensions of BLAST with lattice-based analysis had been implemented before, e.g., in predicated lattices [9] and in lazy shape analysis [2]. As a side-effect, we can now express the algorithmic settings of these papers in a simple and systematic way, and moreover, we have found different configurations that perform even better.

References

1. Ball, T., Podelski, A., Rajamani, S.K.: Boolean and cartesian abstractions for model checking C programs. In: Margaria, T., Yi, W. (eds.) ETAPS 2001 and TACAS 2001. LNCS, vol. 2031, pp. 268–283. Springer, Heidelberg (2001)
2. Beyer, D., Henzinger, T.A., Théoduloz, G.: Lazy shape analysis. In: Ball, T., Jones, R.B. (eds.) CAV 2006. LNCS, vol. 4144, pp. 532–546. Springer, Heidelberg (2006)

---

[8] A: predicated join; B: no join (model checking); C: no join and more precise transfer relation; D: no join, termination check with join; E: normal join of shapes (data-flow analysis); F: join for predicate abstraction. All experiments were run on a 3 GHz Intel Xeon processor.

3. Blanchet, B., Cousot, P., Cousot, R., Feret, J., Mauborgne, L., Miné, A., Monniaux, D., Rival, X.: Design and implementation of a special-purpose static program analyzer for safety-critical real-time embedded software. In: Mogensen, T.Æ., Schmidt, D.A., Sudborough, I.H. (eds.) The Essence of Computation. LNCS, vol. 2566, pp. 85–108. Springer, Heidelberg (2002)

4. Codish, M., Mulkers, A., Bruynooghe, M., de la Banda, M., Hermenegildo, M.: Improving abstract interpretations by combining domains. In: Proc. PEPM, pp. 194–205. ACM Press, New York (1993)

5. Cousot, P., Cousot, R.: Abstract interpretation: A unified lattice model for the static analysis of programs by construction or approximation of fixpoints. In: Proc. POPL, pp. 238–252. ACM Press, New York (1977)

6. Cousot, P., Cousot, R.: Systematic design of program analysis frameworks. In: Proc. POPL, pp. 269–282. ACM Press, New York (1979)

7. Cousot, P., Cousot, R.: Compositional and inductive semantic definitions in fixpoint, equational, constraint, closure-condition, rule-based and game-theoretic form. In: Wolper, P. (ed.) CAV 1995. LNCS, vol. 939, pp. 293–308. Springer, Heidelberg (1995)

8. Dwyer, M.B., Clarke, L.A.: A flexible architecture for building data-flow analyzers. In: Proc. ICSE, pp. 554–564. IEEE Computer Society Press, Los Alamitos (1996)

9. Fischer, J., Jhala, R., Majumdar, R.: Joining data flow with predicates. In: Proc. ESEC/FSE, pp. 227–236. ACM Press, New York (2005)

10. Gulwani, S., Tiwari, A.: Combining abstract interpreters. In: Proc. PLDI, pp. 376–386. ACM Press, New York (2006)

11. Henzinger, T.A., Jhala, R., Majumdar, R., Sutre, G.: Lazy abstraction. In: Proc. POPL, pp. 58–70. ACM Press, New York (2002)

12. Lerner, S., Grove, D., Chambers, C.: Composing data-flow analyses and transformations. In: Proc. POPL, pp. 270–282. ACM Press, New York (2002)

13. Lev-Ami, T., Sagiv, M.: TVLA: A system for implementing static analyses. In: Palsberg, J. (ed.) SAS 2000. LNCS, vol. 1824, pp. 280–301. Springer, Heidelberg (2000)

14. Martin, F.: PAG: An efficient program analyzer generator. STTT 2, 46–67 (1998)

15. Mauborgne, L., Rival, X.: Trace partitioning in abstract interpretation based static analyzers. In: Sagiv, M. (ed.) ESOP 2005. LNCS, vol. 3444, pp. 5–20. Springer, Heidelberg (2005)

16. Necula, G., McPeak, S., Rahul, S., Weimer, W.: CIL: Intermediate language and tools for analysis and transformation of C programs. In: Horspool, R.N. (ed.) CC 2002 and ETAPS 2002. LNCS, vol. 2304, pp. 213–228. Springer, Heidelberg (2002)

17. Sagiv, M., Reps, T.W., Wilhelm, R.: Parametric shape analysis via 3-valued logic. ACM TOPLAS 24, 217–298 (2002)

18. Schmidt, D.A.: Data-flow analysis is model checking of abstract interpretations. In: Proc. POPL, pp. 38–48. ACM Press, New York (1998)

19. Steffen, B.: Data-flow analysis as model checking. In: Proc. TACS, pp. 346–365 (1991)

20. Tjiangan, S.W.K., Hennessy, J.: SHARLIT: A tool for building optimizers. In: Proc. PLDI, pp. 82–93. ACM Press, New York (1992)

A Decision Procedure for Bit-Vectors and Arrays

Vijay Ganesh and David L. Dill

Computer Systems Laboratory
Stanford University
{vganesh, dill}@cs.stanford.edu

Abstract. STP is a decision procedure for the satisfiability of quantifier-free formulas in the theory of bit-vectors and arrays that has been optimized for large problems encountered in software analysis applications. The basic architecture of the procedure consists of word-level pre-processing algorithms followed by translation to SAT. The primary bottlenecks in software verification and bug finding applications are large arrays and linear bit-vector arithmetic. New algorithms based on the abstraction-refinement paradigm are presented for reasoning about large arrays. A solver for bit-vector linear arithmetic is presented that eliminates variables and parts of variables to enable other transformations, and reduce the size of the problem that is eventually received by the SAT solver.

These and other algorithms have been implemented in STP, which has been heavily tested over thousands of examples obtained from several real-world applications. Experimental results indicate that the above mix of algorithms along with the overall architecture is far more effective, for a variety of applications, than a direct translation of the original formula to SAT or other comparable decision procedures.

1 Introduction

Decision procedures for fragments of first-order logic are increasingly being used in modern hardware verification and theorem proving tools. These decision procedures usually support integer and real arithmetic, uninterpreted functions, bit-vectors, and arrays. Examples of such decision procedures include Yices, SVC, CVC Lite,UCLID [9,3,2,13]. Although theorem-proving and hardware verification have been the primary users of decision procedures, increasingly they are being used in large-scale program analysis, bug finding and test generation tools [7,16]. These tools often symbolically analyze code and generate constraints for the decision procedure to solve, and use the results to guide analysis or generate new test cases.

Software analysis tools create demands on decision procedures that are different from those imposed by hardware applications. These applications often generate very large array constraints, especially when tools choose to model system memory as one or more arrays. Also, software analysis tools need to be able to reason about bit-vectors, and especially mod-2^n arithmetic, which is an important source of incorrect system behavior. The constraint problems are large and extremely challenging to solve.

This paper reports on STP, a decision procedure for quantifier-free first order logic with bit-vector and array datatypes [17]. The design of STP is has been driven primarily by the demands of software analysis research projects. STP is being used in several

W. Damm and H. Hermanns (Eds.): CAV 2007, LNCS 4590, pp. 519–531, 2007.

software analysis, bug finding and hardware verification applications. Notable applications include the EXE project [7] at Stanford, which generates test cases for C programs using symbolic execution, and uses STP to solve the constraints. Other projects include the Replayer project [16] and Minesweeper [5] at Carnegie Mellon University which produce constraints from symbolic execution of machine code, and the CATCHCONV project [14] at Berkeley which tries to catch errors due to type conversion in C programs. The CATCHCONV project produced the largest example solved by STP so far. It is a 412 Mbyte formula, with 2.12 million 32 bit bit-vector variables, array write terms which are tens of thousands of levels deep, a large number of array reads with non-constant indices (corresponding to aliased reads in memory), many linear constraints, and liberal use of bit-vector functions and predicates, and STP solves it in approx. 2 minutes on a 3.2GHz Linux box.

There is a nice overview of bit-vector decision procedures in [6], which we do not repeat here. STP's architecture is different from most decision procedures that support both bit-vectors and arrays [18,2,9], which are based on backtracking and a framework for combining specialized theories such as Nelson-Oppen [15]. Instead, STP consists of a series of word-level transformations and optimizations that eventually convert the original problem to a conjunctive-normal form (CNF) formula for input to a high-speed solver for the satisfiability problem for propositional logic formulas (SAT) [10]. Thus, STP fully exploits the speed of modern SAT solvers while also taking advantage of theory-specific optimizations for bit-vectors and arrays. In this respect, STP is most similar to UCLID [13].

The goal of this paper is to describe the factors that enable STP to handle the large constraints from software applications. In some cases, simple optimizations or a careful decision about the ordering of transformations can make a huge difference in the capacity of the tool. In other cases, more sophisticated optimizations are required. Two are discussed in detail: An on-the-fly solver for mod-2^n linear arithmetic, and abstraction-refinement heuristics for array expressions. The rest of the paper discusses the architecture of STP, the basic engineering principles, and then goes into more detail about the optimizations for bit-vector arithmetic and arrays. Performance on large examples is discussed, and there is a comparative evaluation with Yices [9], that is well-known for its efficiency.

2   STP Overview

STP's input language has most of the functions and predicates implemented in a programming language such as C or a machine instruction set, except that it has no floating point datatypes or operations. The current set of operations supported include $TRUE$, $FALSE$, propositional variables, arbitrary Boolean connectives, bitwise Boolean operators, extraction, concatenation, left and right shifts, addition, multiplication, unary minus, (signed) division and modulo, array read and write functions, and relational operators. The semantics parallel the semantics of the SMTLIB bit-vector language [1] or the C programming language, except that in STP bit-vectors can have any positive length. Also, all arithmetic and bitwise Boolean operations require that the inputs be of the same length. STP can be used as a stand-alone program, and can parse input files in a special human readable syntax and also the SMTLIB QF_UFBV32 syntax [1]. It can also be used as a library, and has a special C-language API that makes it relatively easy to integrate with other applications.

STP converts a decision problem in its logic to propositional CNF, which is solved with a high-performance off-the-shelf CNF SAT solver, MiniSat [10] (MiniSat has a nice API, and it is concise, clean, efficient, reliable, and relatively unencumbered by licensing conditions). However, the process of converting to CNF includes many word-level transformations and optimizations that reduce the difficulty of the eventual SAT problem. Problems are frequently solved during the transformation stages of STP, so that SAT does not need to be called.

STP's architecture differs significantly from many other decision procedures based on case splitting and backtracking, including tools like SVC, and CVC Lite [3,2], and other solvers based on the Davis-Putnam-Logemann-Loveland (DPLL(T)) architecture [11]. Conceptually, those solvers recursively assert atomic formulas and their negations to a theory-specific decision procedures to check for consistency with formulas that are already asserted, backtracking if the current combination of assertions is inconsistent. In recent versions of this style of decision procedure, the choice of formulas to assert is made by a conventional DPLL SAT solver, which treats the formulas as propositional variables until they are asserted and the decision procedures invoked.

Architectures based on assertion and backtracking invoke theory-specific decision-procedures in the "inner loop" of the SAT solver. However, modern SAT solvers are very fast largely because of the incredible efficiency of their inner loops, and so it is difficult with these architectures to take the best advantage of fast SAT solvers.

STP on the other hand does all theory-specific processing *before* invoking the SAT solver. The SAT solver works on a purely propositional formula, and its internals are not modified, including the highly optimized inner loop. Optimizing transformations are employed before the SAT solver when they can solve a problem more efficiently than the SAT solver, or when they reduce the difficulty of the problem that is eventually presented to the SAT solver.

DPLL(T) solvers often use Nelson-Oppen combination [15], or variants thereof, to link together multiple theory-specific decision procedures. Nelson-Oppen combination needs the individual theories to be disjoint, stably-infinite and requires the exchange of equality relationships deduced in each individual theory, leading to inflexibility and implementation complexity. In return, Nelson-Oppen ensures that the combination of theories is complete. STP is complete because the entire formula is converted by a set of satisfiability preserving steps to CNF, the satisfiability of which is decided by the SAT solver. So there is no need to worry about meeting the conditions of Nelson-Oppen combination. Furthermore, the extra overhead of communication between theories in the Nelson-Oppen style decision procedures can become a bottleneck for the very large inputs that we have seen, and this overhead is avoided in STP.

The STP approach is not always going to be superior to a good backtracking solver. A good input to STP is a conjunction of many formulas that enable local algebraic transformations. On the other hand, formulas with top-level disjunctions may be very difficult. Fortunately, the software applications used by STP tend to generate large conjunctions, and hence STP's approach has worked well in practice.

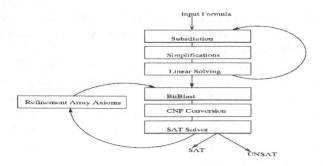

Fig. 1. STP Architecture

In more detail, STP's architecture is depicted in Figure 1. Processing consists of three phases of word-level transformations; followed by conversion to a purely Boolean formula and Boolean simplifications (this process is called "Bit Blasting"); and finally conversion to propositional CNF and solving by a SAT solver. The primary focus of this paper is on word level optimizations for arithmetic, arrays and refinement for arrays.

Expressions are represented as directed acyclic graphs (DAGs), from the time they are created by the parser or through the C-interface, until they are converted to CNF. In the DAG representation, isomorphic subtrees are represented by a single node, which may be pointed to by many parent nodes. This representation has advantages and disadvantages, but the overwhelming advantage is compactness.

It is possible to identify some design principles that have worked well during the development of STP. The overarching principle is to procrastinate when faced with hard problems. That principle is applied in many ways. Transformations that are risky because they can significantly expand the size of the expression DAG are postponed until other, less risky, transformations are performed, in the hope that the less risky transformation will reduce the size and number of expressions requiring more risky transformations. This approach is particularly helpful for array expressions.

Counter-example-guided abstraction/refinement is now a standard paradigm in formal tools, which can be applied in a variety of ways. It is another application of the procrastination principle. For example, the UCLID tool abstracts and refines the precision of integer variables.

A major novelty of STP's implementation is the particular implementation of the refinement loop in Figure 1. In STP, abstraction is implemented (i.e. an *abstract formula* is obtained) by omitting conjunctive constraints from a *concrete formula*, where the concrete formula must be equisatisfiable with the original formula. (Logical formulas ϕ and ψ are equisatisfiable iff ϕ is satisfiable exactly when ψ is satisfiable.)

When testing an abstract formula for satisfiability, there can be three results. First, STP can determine that the abstracted formula is unsatisfiable. In this case, it is clear that the original formula is unsatisfiable, and hence STP can return "unsatisfiable" without additional refinement, potentially saving a massive amount of work.

A second possible outcome is that STP finds a satisfying assignment to the abstract formula. In this case, STP converts the satisfying assignment to a (purported) concrete model, [1] and also assigns zero to any variables that appear in the original formula but not the abstract formula, and evaluates the original formula with respect to the purported model. If the result of the evaluations is $TRUE$, the purported model is truly a model of the original formula (i.e. the original formula is indeed satisfiable) and STP returns the model without further refinement iterations.

The third possible outcome is that STP finds a purported model, but evaluating the original formula with respect to that model returns $FALSE$. In that case, STP refines the abstracted formula by heuristically choosing additional conjuncts, at least one of which must be false in the purported model and conjoining those formulas with the abstracted formula to create a new, less abstract formula. In practice, the abstract formula is not modified; instead, the new formulas are bit-blasted, converted to CNF, and added as clauses to the CNF formula derived from the previous abstract formula, and the resulting CNF formula solved by the SAT solver. This process is iterated until a correct result is found, which must occur because, in the worst case, the abstract formula will be made fully concrete by conjoining every formula that was omitted by abstraction. When all formulas are included, the result is guaranteed to be correct because of the equisatisfiability requirement above.

3 Arrays

As was mentioned above, arrays are used heavily in software analysis applications, and reasoning about arrays has been a major bottleneck in many examples. STP's input language supports one-dimensional (non-extensional) arrays [17] that are indexed by bit-vectors and contain bit-vectors. The operations on arrays are $read(A, i)$, which returns the value at location $A[i]$ where A is an array and i is an index expression of the correct type, and $write(A, i, v)$, which returns a new array with the same value as A at all indices except possibly i, where it has the value v. The value of a $read$ is a bit-vector, which can appear as an operand to any operation or predicate that operates on bit-vectors. The value of an array variable or an array write has an array type, and may only appear as the first operand of a $read$ or $write$, or as the then or else operand of an if-then-else. In particular, values of an array type cannot appear in an equality or any other predicate.

In the unoptimized mode, STP reduces all formulas to an equisatisfiable form that contains no array $read$s or $write$s, using three transformations. (In the following, the expression $ite(c_1, e_1, e_2)$ is shorthand for *if c_1 then e_1 else e_2 endif*.) These transformations are all standard.

The **Ite-lifting** transformation converts $read(ite(c, write(A, i, v), e), j)$ to $ite(c, read(write(A, i, v), j), e)$. (There is a similar transformation when the $write$ is in the "else" part of the ite.) The **read-over-write** transformation eliminates all write terms by transforming $read(write(A, i, v), j)$ to $ite(i = j, v, read(A, j))$. Finally, the **read elimination** transformation eliminates $read$ terms by introducing a fresh bit-vector variable for each such expression, and adding more predicates to ensure consistency. Specifically, whenever a term $read(A, i)$ appears, it is replaced by a fresh variable v, and new

---

[1] A model is an assignment of constant values to all of the variables in a formula such that the formula is *satisfied*.

predicates are conjoined to the formula $i = j \Rightarrow v = w$ for all variables w introduced in place of read terms $read(A, j)$, having the same array term as first operand. As an example of this transformation, the simple formula $(read(A, 0) = 0) \wedge (read(A, i) = 1)$ would be transformed to $v_1 = 0 \wedge v_2 = 1 \wedge (i = 0 \Rightarrow v_1 = v_2)$. The formula of the form $(i = 0 \Rightarrow v_1 = v_2)$ is called an *array read axiom*.

3.1 Optimizing Array Reads

Read elimination, as described above, expands each formula by up to $n(n-1)/2$ nodes, where n is the number of syntactically distinct index expressions. Unfortunately, software analysis applications can produce thousands of reads with variable indices, resulting in a lethal blow-up when this transformation is applied. While this blow-up seems unavoidable in the worst case, appropriate procrastination leads to practical solutions for many very large problems. Two optimizations which have been very effective are *array substitution* and abstraction-refinement for reads, which we call *read refinement*.

The array substitution optimization reduces the number of array variables by substituting out all constraints of the form $read(A, c) = e_1$, where c is a constant and e_1 does not contain another array read. Programs often index into arrays or memory using constant indexes, so this is a case that occurs often in practice.

The optimization has two passes. The first pass builds a substitution table with the left-hand-side of each such equation $(read(A, c))$ as the key and the right-hand-side (e_1) as the value, and then deletes the equation from the input query. The second pass over the expression replaces each occurrence of a key by the corresponding table entry. Note that for soundness, if a second equation is encountered whose left-hand-side is already in the table, the second equation is not deleted and the table is not changed. For example, if STP saw $read(A, c) = e_1$ then $read(A, C) = e_2$, the second formula would not be deleted and would later be simplified to $e_1 = e_2$.

The second optimization, *read refinement*, delays the translation of array *reads* with non-constant indexes in the hope of avoiding read elimination blowup. Its main trick is to solve a less-expensive approximation of the formula, check the result in the original formula, and try again with a more accurate approximation if the result is incorrect.

Read formulas are abstracted by performing read elimination, *i.e.*, replacing reads with new variables, but not adding the array read axioms. This abstracted formula is processed by the remaining stages of STP. As discussed in the overview, if the result is unsatisfiable, that result is correct and can be returned immediately from STP. If not, the abstract model found by STP is converted to a concrete model and the original formula is evaluated with respect to that model. If the result is $TRUE$, the answer is correct and STP returns that model. Otherwise, some of the array read axioms from read elimination are added to the formula and STP is asked to satisfy the modified formula. This iteration repeats until a correct result is found, which is guaranteed to happen (if memory and time are not exhausted) because all of the finitely many array read axioms will eventually be added in the worst case.

The choice of which array read axioms to add during refinement is a heuristic that is important to the success of the method. A policy that seems to work well is to find a non-constant array index term for which at least one axiom is violated, then add all of the violated axioms involving that term. Adding at least one false axiom during refinement guarantees that STP will not find the same false model more than once. Adding all the axioms for a particular term seems empirically to be a good compromise between adding just one formula, which results in too many iterations, and adding all formulas, which eliminates all abstraction after the first failure.

For example, suppose STP is given the formula $(read(A, 0) = 0) \wedge (read(A, i) = 1)$. STP would first apply the substitution optimization by deleting $read(A, 0) = 0$ from the formula, and inserting the pair $(read(A, 0), 0)$ in the substitution table. Then, it would replace $read(A, i)$ by a new variable v_i, thus generating the under-constrained formula $v_i = 1$. Suppose STP finds the solution $i = 1$ and $v_i = 1$.

STP then translates the solution to the variables of the original formula to get $(read(A, 0) = 0) \wedge read(A, 1) = 1$. This solution is satisfiable in the original formula as well, so STP terminates since it has found a true satisfying assignment.

However, suppose that STP finds the solution $i = 0$ and $v_i = 1$. Under this solution, the original formula eventually evaluates to $read(A, 0) = 0 \wedge read(A, 0) = 1$, which after substitution gives $0 = 1$. Hence, the solution to the under-constrained formula is not a solution to the original formula.

In this case, STP adds the array read axiom $i = 0 \Rightarrow read(A, i) = read(A, 0)$. When this formula is checked, the result must be correct because the new formula includes the complete set of array read axioms.

3.2 Optimizing Array Writes

Efficiently dealing with array writes is crucial to STP's utility in software applications, some of which produce deeply nested write terms when there are many successive assignments to indices of the same array. The **read-over-write** transformation creates a performance bottleneck by destroying sharing of subterms, creating an unacceptable blow-up in DAG size. Consider the simple formula: $read(write(A, i, v), j) = read(write(A, i, v), k)$, in which the *write* term is shared.

The **read-over-write** transformation translates this to $ite(i = j, v, read(A, j)) = ite(i = k, v, read(A, k))$. When applied recursively to the deeply nested *write* terms, it essentially creates a new copy of the entire DAG of write terms for every distinct read index, which exhausts memory in large examples.

Once again, the procrastination principle applies. The **read-over-write** transformation is delayed until after other simplification and solving transformations are performed, except in special cases like $read(write(A, i, v), i + 1)$, where the read and write indices simplify to terms that are always equal or not equal. In practice, the simple transformations convert many index terms to constants. The **read-over-write** transformation is applied in a subsequent phase. When that happens, the formula is smaller and contains more constants. This simple optimization is enormously effective, enabling STP to solve many very large problems with nested writes that it is otherwise unable to do.

Abstraction and refinement can also be used on write expressions, when the previous optimization leaves large numbers of *read*s and *write*s, leading to major speed-ups on some large formulas. For this optimization, array read-over-write terms are replaced by new variables to yield a conjunction of formulas that is equisatisfiable to the original set. The example above is transformed to:

$$v_1 = v_2$$
$$v_1 = ite(i = j, v, read(A, j))$$
$$v_2 = ite(i = k, v, read(A, k))$$

where the last two formulas are called *array write axioms*. For the abstraction, the array write axioms are omitted, and the abstracted formula $v_1 = v_2$ is processed by the remaining phases of STP. As with array reads, the refinement loop iterates only if STP finds a model of the abstracted formula that is also not a model of the original formula. Write axioms are added to the abstracted formula, and the refinement loop iterates with the additional axioms until a definite result is produced. Although, this technique leads to improvement in certain cases, the primary problem with it is that the number of iterations of the refinement loop is sometimes very large.

4   Linear Solver and Variable Elimination

One of the essential features of STP for software analysis applications is its efficient handling of linear twos-complement arithmetic. The heart of this is an *on-the-fly* solver. The main goal of the solver is to eliminate as many bits of as many variables as possible, to reduce the size of the transformed problem for the SAT solver. In addition, it enables many other simplifications, and can solve purely linear problems outright, so that the SAT solver does not need to be used.

The solver solves for one equation for one variable at a time. That variable can then be eliminated by substitution in the rest of the formula, whether the variable occurs in linear equations or other formulas. In some cases, it cannot solve an entire variable, so it solves for some of the low-order bits of the variable. After bit-blasting, these bits will not appear as variables in the problem presented to the SAT solver. Non-linear or word-level terms (extracts, concats etc.) appearing in linear equations are treated as bit-vector variables.

The algorithm has worst-case time running time of $O(k^2 n)$ multiplications, where k is the number of equations and n is the number of variables in the input system of linear bit-vector equations.[2] If the input is unsatisfiable the solver terminates with *FALSE*. If the input is satisfiable it terminates with a set of equations in *solved form*, which symbolically represent all possible satisfying assignments to the input equations. So, in the special case where the formula is a system of linear equations, the solver leads to a sound and complete polynomial-time decision procedure. Furthermore, the equations are reduced to a closed form that captures all of the possible solutions.

Definition 1. Solved Form: *A list of equations is in solved form if the following invariants hold over the equations in the list.*

---

[2] As observed in [4], the theory of linear mod 2^n arithmetic (equations only) in tandem with concatenate and extract operations is NP-complete. Although STP has concatenate and extraction operations, terms with those operations are treated as independent variables in the linear solving process, which is polynomial.

A hard NP-complete input problem constructed out of linear operations, concatenate and extract operations will not be solved completely by linear solving, and will result in work for the SAT solver.

1) Each equation in the list is of the form $x[i : 0] = t$ or $x = t$, where x is a variable and t is a linear combination of the variables or constant times a variable (or extractions thereof) occuring in the equations of the list, except x

2) Variables on the left hand side of the equations occuring earlier in the list may not occur on the right hand side of subsequent equations. Also, there may not be two equations with the same left hand side in the list

3) If extractions of variables occur in the list, then they must always be of the form $x[i : 0]$, i.e. the lower extraction index must be 0, and all extractions must be of the same length

4) If an extraction of a variable $x[i : 0] = t$ occurs in the list, then an entry is made in the list for $x = x^1 @ t$, where x^1 is a new variable refering to the top bits of x and $@$ is the concatenation symbol

The algorithm is illustrated on the following system:

$$3x + 4y + 2z = 0$$
$$2x + 2y + 2 = 0$$
$$4y + 2x + 2z = 0$$

where all constants, variables and functions are 3 bits long.

The solver proceeds by first choosing an equation and always checks if the chosen equation is *solvable*. It uses the following theorem from basic number theory to determine if an equation is solvable: $\sum_{i=1}^{n} a_i x_i = c_i \bmod 2^b$ is solvable for the unknowns x_i if and only if the greatest common divisor of $\{a_1, \ldots, a_n, 2^b\}$ divides c_i.

In the example above, the solver chooses $3x + 4y + 2z = 0$ which is solvable since the $gcd(3, 4, 2, 2^3)$ does indeed divide 0. It is also a basic result from number theory that a number a has a multiplicative inverse mod m iff $gcd(a, m) = 1$, and that this inverse can be computed by the extended greatest-common divisor algorithm [8] or a method from [4]. So, if there is a variable with an odd coefficient, the solver isolates it on the left-hand-side and multiplies through by the inverse of the coefficient. In the example, the multiplicative inverse of 3 mod 8 is also 3, so $3x + 4y + 2z = 0$ can be solved to yield $x = 4y + 6z$.

Substituting $4y + 6z$ for x in the remaining two equations yields the system

$$2y + 4z + 2 = 0$$
$$4y + 6z = 0$$

where all coefficients are even. Note that even coefficients do not have multiplicative inverses in arithmetic mod 2^b, and, hence we cannot isolate a variable. However, it is possible to solve for *some bits* of the remaining variables.

The solver transforms the whole system of solvable equations into a system which has at least one summand with an odd coefficient. To do this, the solver chooses an equation which has a summand whose coefficient has the minimum number of factors of 2. In the example, this would the equation $2y + 4z + 2 = 0$, and the summand would be $2y$. The whole system is divided by 2, and the high-order bit of each variable is dropped, to obtain a reduced set of equations

$$y[1:0] + 2z[1:0] + 1 = 0$$
$$2y[1:0] + 3z[1:0] = 0$$

where all constants, variables and operations are 2 bits. Next, $y[1:0]$ is solved for to obtain $y[1:0] = 2z[1:0] + 3$. Substituting for $y[1:0]$ in the system yields a new system of equations $3z[1:0] + 2 = 0$. This equation can be solved for $z[1:0]$ to obtain $z[1:0] = 2$. It follows that original system of equations is satisfiable. It is important to note here that the bits $y[2:1]$ and $z[2:1]$ are unconstrained. The solved form in this case is $x = 4y + 6z \wedge y[1:0] = 2z[1:0] + 3 \wedge z[1:0] = 2$ (Note that in the last two equations all variables, constants and functions are 2 bits long).

Algorithms for deciding the satisfiability of a system of equations and congruences in modular or residue arithmetic have been well-known for a long time. However, most of these algorithms do not provide a solved form that captures all possible solutions. Some of the ideas presented here were devised by Clark Barrett and implemented in the SVC decision procedure [12,4], but the SVC algorithm has exponential worst-case time complexity while STP's linear solver is polynomial in the worst-case.

The closest related work is probably in a paper by Huang and Cheng [12], which reduces a set of equations to a solved form by Guassian elimination. On the other hand, STP implements an online solving and substitution algorithm that gives a closed form solution. Such algorithms are easier to integrate into complex decision procedures.

5   Experimental Results

This section presents empirical results on large examples from software analysis tools, and on randomly generated sets of linear equations. The effects of abstraction and linear solving in STP are examined. It is difficult to compare STP with other decision procedures, because no publicly available decision procedures except CVCL (from the authors research group) can deal with terms involving both bit-vectors and arrays indexed by bit-vectors. CVCL is hopelessly inefficient compared with STP, which was written to replace it. Terms in Yices can include bit-vectors and uninterpreted functions over bit-vectors. Uninterpreted functions are equivalent to arrays with no *write* operations, so it is possible to compare the performance of STP and Yices on examples with linear arithmetic and one realistic example with a read-only array.

In Table 1, STP is compared with all optimizations on (All ON), Array Optimizations on (Arr-ON,Lin-OFF), linear-solving on (Arr-OFF,Lin-ON), and all optimizations off (ALL OFF) on the BigArray examples (these examples are heavy on linear arithmetic and array reads). Table 2 summarizes STP's performance, with and without array write abstraction, on the big array examples with deeply nested writes. Table 3 compares STP with Yices on a very small version of a BigArray example, and some randomly generated linear system of equations. All experiments were run on a 3.2GHz/2GB RAM Intel machine running Linux.

Table 1 includes some of the hardest of the BigArray examples which are usually tens of megabytes of text, typically hundreds of thousands of 32 bit bit-vector variables, lots of array reads, and large number of linear constraints derived from [14,16]. The primary reason for timeouts is an out-of-memory exception. Table 1 shows that all optimizations

Table 1. STP performance in different modes over BigArray Examples. Names are followed by the nodesize. Approximate node size is in millions of nodes. 1M is one million nodes. Shared nodes are counted exactly once. NR stands for No Result. All timings are in seconds. MO stands for out of memory error. These examples were generated using the CATCHCONV tool.

Example Name (Node Size)	Result	All ON	Arr-ON,Lin-OFF	Arr-OFF,Lin-ON	All OFF
testcase15 (0.9M)	sat	66	192	64	MO
testcase16 (0.9M)	sat	67	233	66	MO
thumbnailout-spin1 (3.2M)	sat	115	111	113	MO
thumbnailout-spin1-2 (4.3M)	NR	MO	MO	MO	MO
thumbnailout-noarg (2.7M)	sat	840	MO	840	MO

Table 2. STP performance in different modes over BigArray Examples with deep nested writes. Names are followed by the nodesize. 1M is one million nodes (1K is thousand nodes). Shared nodes are counted exactly once. NR stands for No Result. All timings are in seconds. MO stands for out of memory error.These examples were generated using the CATCHCONV and Minesweeper tools.

Example Name (Node Size)	Result	WRITE Abstraction	NO WRITE Abstraction
grep0084 (69K)	sat	109	506
grep0095 (69K)	sat	115	84
grep0106 (69K)	sat	270	> 600
grep0117 (70K)	sat	218	> 600
grep0777 (73K)	NR	MO	MO
610dd9dc (15K)	sat	188	101
testcase20 (1.2M)	sat	67	MO

are required for solving the hardest real-world problems. As expected, STP's linear solver is very helpful in solving these examples.

Table 2 includes examples with deeply nested array writes and modest amounts of linear constraints derived from various applications. The "grep" examples were generated using the Minesweeper tool while trying to find bugs in unix grep program. The 610dd9c formula is generated by a Minesweeper analysis of a program that is used in "botnet" attack. The formula testcase20 was generated by CATCHCONV. As expected, STP with write abstraction-refinement ON can yield a very large improvement over STP with write abstraction-refinement switched OFF, although it is not always faster.

Yices and STP were also compared on small, randomly-generated systems of linear equations with coefficients ranging from 1 to 2^{16}, from 4 to 256 variables of 32 bits each, and 4 to 256 equations. Yices consistently timed out at 200 seconds on examples with 32 or more variables, and was significantly slower than STP on the smaller examples. The hardest problem for STP in this set of benchmarks was a test case with 32 equations and 256 variables of 32 bits, which STP solved in 90 seconds. There are two cases for illustration in Table 3. Yices times out on even a 50 variable 50 equation example, and when it does finish it is much slower than STP.

There is one large, real example with read-only arrays, linear arithmetic and bit-vectors which is suitable for comparison with Yices. On this example, Yices is nearly

Table 3. STP vs. Yices. Timeout per example: 600sec. The last example was generated using the Replayer tool.

Example	STP	Yices
25 var/25 equations(unsat)	0.8s	42s
50 var/50 equations(sat)	13s	TimeOut
cookie checksum example(sat)	2.6s	218s

one hundred times slower than STP. Unfortunately, we could not compare Yices with STP on examples with array writes since Yices does not support array writes with bit-vector indexing. More meaningful comparisons will have to wait till competing decision procedures includes bit-vector operations and a theory of arrays indexed by bit-vectors. All tests in this section are available at http://verify.stanford.edu/stp.html

6 Conclusion

Software applications such as program analysis, bug finding, and symbolic simulation of software tend to impose different conditions on decision procedures than hardware applications. In particular, arrays become a bottleneck. Also, the constraints tend to be very large with lots of linear bit-vector arithmetic in them. Abstraction-refinement algorithms is often helpful for handling large array terms. Also, the approach of doing phased word-level transformations, starting with the least expensive and risky transformations, followed by translation to SAT seems like a good design for decision procedures for the applications considered. Finally, linear solving, when implemented carefully, is effective in variable elimination.

Acknowledgements

We are indebted to the following users for their feedback and for great examples: David Molnar from Berkeley; Cristian Cadar, Dawson Engler and Aaron Bradley from Stanford; Jim Newsome, David Brumley, Ivan Jaeger and Dawn Song from CMU;

This research was supported by Department of Homeland Security (DHS) grant FA8750-05-2-0142 and by National Science Foundation grant CNS-0524155. Any opinions, findings, and conclusions or recommendations expressed in this material are those of the author and do not necessarily reflect the view of the Department of Homeland Security or the National Science Foundation.

References

1. SMTLIB website: http://www.csl.sri.com/users/demoura/smt-comp/
2. Barrett, C., Berezin, S.: CVC Lite: A new implementation of the cooperating validity checker. In: Alur, R., Peled, D.A. (eds.) CAV 2004. LNCS, vol. 3114, Springer, Heidelberg (2004)

3. Barrett, C., Dill, D., Levitt, J.: Validity checking for combinations of theories with equality (Palo Alto, California, November 6–8). In: Srivas, M., Camilleri, A. (eds.) FMCAD 1996. LNCS, vol. 1166, pp. 187–201. Springer, Heidelberg (1996)
4. Barrett, C.W., Dill, D.L., Levitt, J.R.: A decision procedure for bit-vector arithmetic. In: Proceedings of the 35th Design Automation Conference, San Francisco, CA (June 1998)
5. Brumley, D., Hartwig, C., Liang, Z., Newsome, J., Song, D., Yin, H.: Towards automatically identifying trigger-based behavior in malware using symbolic execution and binary analysis. Technical Report CMU-CS-07-105, Carnegie Mellon University School of Computer Science (January 2007)
6. Bryant, R.E., Kroening, D., Ouaknine, J., Seshia, S.A., Strichman, O., Brady, B.: Deciding bit-vector arithmetic with abstraction. In: 13th Intl. Conference on Tools and Algorithms for the Construction of Systems (TACAS) (2007)
7. Cadar, C., Ganesh, V., Pawlowski, P., Dill, D., Engler, D.: EXE: Automatically generating inputs of death. In: Proceedings of the 13th ACM Conference on Computer and Communications Security, ACM Press, New York (October-November 2006)
8. Cormen, T.H., Leiserson, C.E., Rivest, R.L.: Introduction to Algorithms (chapter 11), pp. 820–825. MIT Press, Cambridge (1998)
9. Dutertre, B., de Moura, L.: A Fast Linear-Arithmetic Solver for DPLL(T). In: Ball, T., Jones, R.B. (eds.) CAV 2006. LNCS, vol. 4144, pp. 81–94. Springer, Heidelberg (2006)
10. Een, N., Sorensson, N.: An extensible sat-solver. In: Proc. Sixth International Conference on Theory and Applications of Satisfiability Testing, May 2003, pp. 78–92 (May 2003)
11. Ganzinger, H., Hagen, G., Nieuwenhuis, R., Oliveras, A., Tinelli, C.: Dpll(t): Fast decision procedures (2004)
12. Huang, C., Cheng, K.: Assertion checking by combined word-level atpg and modular arithmetic constraint-solving techniques. In: Design Automation Conference (DAC), pp. 118–123 (2001)
13. Lahiri, S.K., Seshia, S.A.: The uclid decision procedure. In: Alur, R., Peled, D.A. (eds.) CAV 2004. LNCS, vol. 3114, pp. 475–478. Springer, Heidelberg (2004)
14. Molnar, D., Wagner, D., Seshia, S.A.: Catchconv: A tool for catching conversion errors. Personal Communications (2007)
15. Nelson, G., Oppen, D.C.: Simplification by cooperating decision procedures. ACM Transactions on Programming Languages and Systems 1(2), 245–257 (1979)
16. Newsome, J., Brumley, D., Franklin, J., Song, D.: Replayer: Automatic protocol replay by binary analysis. In: The Proceedings of the 13th ACM Conference on Computer and and Communications Security (CCS), ACM Press, New York (2006)
17. Stump, A., Barrett, C., Dill, D., Levitt, J.: A Decision Procedure for an Extensional Theory of Arrays. In: 16th IEEE Symposium on Logic in Computer Science, pp. 29–37. IEEE Computer Society Press, Los Alamitos (2001)
18. Stump, A., Barrett, C.W., Dill, D.L.: Cvc: A cooperating validity checker. In: Brinksma, E., Larsen, K.G. (eds.) CAV 2002. LNCS, vol. 2404, pp. 500–504. Springer, Heidelberg (2002)

Boolean Abstraction for Temporal Logic Satisfiability*

Alessandro Cimatti[1], Marco Roveri[1], Viktor Schuppan[1], and Stefano Tonetta[2]

[1] FBK-irst, IT-38050 Trento, Italy
{cimatti,roveri,schuppan}@itc.it
[2] University of Lugano, Faculty of Informatics, CH-6904 Lugano, Switzerland
tonettas@lu.unisi.ch

Abstract. Increasing interest towards property based design calls for effective satisfiability procedures for expressive temporal logics, e.g. the IEEE standard Property Specification Language (PSL).

In this paper, we propose a new approach to the satisfiability of PSL formulae; we follow recent approaches to decision procedures for Satisfiability Modulo Theory, typically applied to fragments of First Order Logic. The underlying intuition is to combine two interacting search mechanisms: on one side, we search for assignments that satisfy the Boolean abstraction of the problem; on the other, we invoke a solver for temporal satisfiability on the conjunction of temporal formulae corresponding to the assignment. Within this framework, we explore two directions. First, given the fixed polarity of each constraint in the theory solver, aggressive simplifications can be applied. Second, we analyze the idea of conflict reconstruction: whenever a satisfying assignment at the level of the Boolean abstraction results in a temporally unsatisfiable problem, we identify inconsistent subsets that can be used to rule out possibly many other assignments. We propose two methods to extract conflict sets on conjunctions of temporal formulae (one based on BDD-based Model Checking, and one based on SAT-based Simple Bounded Model Checking). We analyze the limits and the merits of the approach with a thorough experimental evaluation.

1 Introduction

The role of properties in the design flow is becoming increasingly important. Properties can be used to describe design intent, document designs, and enable for earlier validation steps (e.g. in requirements analysis, realizability, and even in synthesis). Satisfiability engines for temporal logic formulae can be important backbones of property-based design. They can be used to show that a set of requirements is consistent, or entails some required properties, or is compatible with some desirable behaviors [27].

Given the degree of sophistication of model checking technologies, it would be tempting to reduce temporal logic satisfiability to model checking algorithms. However, model checking and requirements analysis are inherently different, and substantial problems from the user's perspective are open. For example, providing diagnostic information in case of inconsistency of a specification can not be solved by searching for

---

* This work has been partly supported by ORCHID, a project sponsored by the Provincia Autonoma di Trento, and by the European Commission under contract 507219 (PROSYD).

W. Damm and H. Hermanns (Eds.): CAV 2007, LNCS 4590, pp. 532–546, 2007.

a counterexample trace: the user is working at the level of requirements, and thus the inconsistency should be identified at the same level, e.g. as a subset of inconsistent requirements. Furthermore, this approach may have some limitations: in fact, techniques and tools for temporal logic model checking are focusing on complexity in the model, and even reductions on the temporal logic formula [30] are oriented to dominating the complexity in the model.

In this paper we propose a novel approach to the satisfiability of temporal logic. The intuition is to combine two forms of search: Boolean enumeration and temporal reasoning. Boolean enumeration is carried out on the propositional abstraction of the specification, where temporal atoms are abstracted into Boolean atoms; once a satisfying assignment is available, temporal reasoning is invoked on the corresponding set of temporal formulae. If a model is found, then the problem is satisfiable, otherwise reasoning theory is used to reconstruct a conflict, and the iteration is restarted.

This approach is mutuated by recent work on Satisfiability Modulo Theories (SMT) [8]. To the best of our knowledge, this is the first time the SMT paradigm, typically used for decidable fragments of First Order Logics, is applied to temporal satisfiability. This choice provides a clear conceptual framework, and suggests several important directions. First, don't cares in the Boolean abstraction of the problem pinpoint temporal formulae that are irrelevant for satisfiability, and can be safely ignored, thus reducing the effort to be carried out in temporal reasoning. Second, fixed polarity constraints are given in input to the theory solver: this enables more aggressive simplifications of the input problem (e.g. pure literal rule). Third, the theory solvers for temporal logic should be extended to provide unsatisfiable cores (or simply unsat cores): these are explanations for unsatisfiability, i.e. inconsistent subsets of the problem in input. This information can be used to rule out all those assignments that satisfy the Boolean abstraction of the problem, but are associated with a superset of an unsatisfiable core. We extend two satisfiability checking algorithms, one based on BDD-based language emptiness [12], and one on SAT-based Simple Bounded Model Checking (SBMC) [20], to return unsat cores. This is in general an interesting aspect, since it enables to provide explanations for unsatisfiability, and ultimately to generalize the idea of unsatisfiable core to the case of temporal logic.

We instantiate our approach on the Property Specification Language (PSL) [1], for its high expressiveness (it captures all ω-regular languages), and its practical interest. We remark however that the approach is general, and independent of the specific temporal logic at hand. The approach has been implemented within the NuSMV model checker [9]. A notable feature at the implementation level is that we use Binary Decision Diagrams as the top level enumeration mechanism. This is in contrast to the current trends in SMT, where DPLL-based enumeration is becoming a de facto standard. A DPLL-based enumeration could have been adopted here, and will be in fact investigated in the future. The BDD-based approach is justified by the fact that for the problems at hand the Boolean splitting is dominated by the temporal one, and as such, BDD-based reasoning turns out not to be a bottleneck. The approach has been experimentally evaluated on a large set of benchmarks, both for BDD-based and SAT-based techniques, and the results are very promising.

This paper is structured as follows. In Section 2, we shortly present the temporal logic PSL. In Section 3, we discuss previous approaches to temporal logic satisfiability. In Section 4, we overview the proposed approach. In Section 5, we discuss the idea of pure literal simplification, and the algorithms for the extraction of unsat cores. In Section 6, we experimentally evaluate our approach. Finally, in Section 7, we draw some conclusions and outline directions for future work.

2   The Property Specification Language PSL

In this paper, we use PSL [1] as our temporal logic. PSL is a very rich language. Here we consider a subset, which is mostly used in practice, and provides ω-regular expressiveness [3]. The subset combines Linear Temporal Logic [28] (LTL) and Sequential Extended Regular Expressions (SERE) [1]. (SEREs extend classical regular expressions with language intersection, thus allowing for a greater succinctness at a cost of a possible exponential blow-up in the conversion to automata. Moreover, the atoms of SEREs are Boolean expressions enabling efficient determinization of automata.)

In the definition of the PSL syntax, for technical reasons, we introduce the "suffix conjunction" connective as a dual of the suffix implication. Moreover, we consider only the strong version of the temporal operators (the weak operators can be rewritten in terms of the strong ones [1]) and the strong version of the SEREs (though our approach can be easily extended to deal also with the weak semantics).

Definition 1 (PSL **syntax**). *Assume a set $\mathscr{A}$ of atomic propositions. We define the PSL formulae, as follows:*

- *if $p \in \mathscr{A}$, p is a PSL formula;*
- *if ϕ_1 and ϕ_2 are PSL formulae, then $\neg\phi_1$, $\phi_1 \wedge \phi_2$, $\phi_1 \vee \phi_2$ are PSL formulae;*
- *if ϕ_1 and ϕ_2 are PSL formulae, then $\mathbf{X}\phi_1$, $\phi_1 \mathbf{U} \phi_2$, $\phi_1 \mathbf{R} \phi_2$ are PSL formulae;*
- *if r is a SERE and ϕ is a PSL formulae, then $r \Diamond\!\!\to \phi$ and $r \mapsto \phi$ are PSL formulae;*
- *if r is a SERE, then r is a PSL formula.*

The $\mathbf{X}$ ("next-time"), the $\mathbf{U}$ ("until"), and the $\mathbf{R}$ ("releases") operators are called *temporal operators*. We call the $\Diamond\!\!\to$ ("suffix conjunction"), and the $\mapsto$ ("suffix implication"), *suffix operators*. Notice that, the r not occurring in the left side of a suffix operator is the *strong* version of a SERE ($r!$ in the PSL notation). In the following, we will consider such r as an abbreviation for $r \Diamond\!\!\to True$ [4]. We also use $\mathbf{G}\phi$ as an abbreviation for $\neg(True \ \mathbf{U} \ \neg\phi)$. LTL can be seen as a subset of PSL in which the suffix operators and the SEREs are suppressed.

We refer the reader to [1] for a formal definition of the semantics of PSL, and in particular of the entailment relation $w \models \phi$ for any infinite word w over a given alphabet Σ ($\Sigma = 2^{\mathscr{A}}$) and PSL formula ϕ. Notice that we can build Boolean expressions by means of atomic formulae and Boolean connectives. The language of a PSL formula ϕ over the alphabet Σ is defined as the set $\mathscr{L}(\phi) := \{w \in \Sigma^{\omega} \mid w \models \phi\}$. The satisfiability problem is to check if $\mathscr{L}(\phi) \neq \emptyset$ for a given PSL formula ϕ.

3 Previous Approaches to PSL Satisfiability

Satisfiability of temporal logics [15] has been widely studied. The seminal work of [32] established the PSPACE-completeness of the satisfiability problem for LTL. Since then, many techniques have been proposed to solve the problem. The first decision procedures are based on tableau systems [34,24,23]. The tableau rules exploit the connection between the syntax of formulae and the tableau structures. The expansion is terminated by some criteria based either on the recurrence of nodes or on maximal strongly connected components. Temporal resolution has been devoted some attention [16] and has been used as a basis for works based on theorem proving, as well as inspiration for SNF-based LTL bounded model checking. Satisfiability of LTL can also be reduced to check language emptiness of Nondeterministic Büchi automata (NBA) [33] or to check the existence of a winning strategy for focus games [22].

In particular, if we reduce the satisfiability problem to checking the emptiness of the language of an NBA, we can exploit model checking engines: it is possible to check the satisfiability of formula ϕ by model checking the validity of the negation of ϕ on a completely nondeterministic Kripke Structure. This way we can exploit symbolic techniques both for the translation of the formula into Büchi automata and for the emptiness checking [12]. Alternatively, it is possible to use SAT based bounded model checking techniques as in [5].

The satisfiability problem has been extended also to other temporal logics. In particular, [2] studied the satisfiability of richer languages that combine LTL with regular expressions, such as ForSpec [2] and PSL [1]. The satisfiability of subsets of ITL [18] has also been studied in [26].

We now concentrate on recent approaches to dealing with satisfiability of PSL, namely [19,7,10,29,11]. The first step in the so-called monolithic approaches is to convert the PSL problem in a monolithic alternating Büchi automaton (ABA); during the conversion, semantic simplification steps (such as the elimination of unreachable states, and restricted forms of minimization by observational equivalence) are applied. The ABA is then converted into a symbolically represented NBA. In [7], this is done by means of a symbolic encoding of Miyano and Hayashi [25], and can be applied both to BDD-based and SAT-based approaches. In [19], an encoding of the ABA that is specialized for bounded model checking is proposed.

The conversion proposed in [10] is based on the so called Suffix Operator Normal Form (SONF). The idea is to partition the translation, by first converting a PSL formula ϕ into an equi-satisfiable formula in SONF, structured as $\bigwedge_i \phi_i \wedge \bigwedge_j \mathbf{G}(p_I^j \rightarrow$ $(r_j \leftrightarrow\!\!\!* \ p_F^j))$, where ϕ_i are LTL formulae, r_j are SEREs, p_I^j and p_F^j are propositional atoms, and $\leftrightarrow\!\!\!*$ is either $\mapsto$ or $\diamondsuit\!\!\rightarrow$. Formulae of the form $\mathbf{G}(p_I^j \rightarrow (r_j \leftrightarrow\!\!\!* \ p_F^j))$ are called Suffix Operator Subformulae (SOS's). The translation first converts the formula in NNF, and then "lifts out" the occurrences of suffix operators, by introducing fresh variables (intuitively, the p^j in the formula above), together with the corresponding SOS. For lack of space, we omit the details regarding the conversion of SOS into NBA; we only mention that the translation is specialized to exploit the structure of SOS (see [10] for details).

The translation presented in [29] introduces a new variable for every subformula. A difference is that the testers of [29] set the new variable to true *if and only if* the

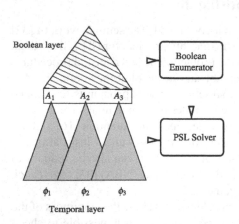

Boolean layer

A_1 A_2 A_3

Boolean Enumerator

PSL Solver

ϕ_1 ϕ_2 ϕ_3

Temporal layer

Fig. 1. Satisfiability modulo theory schema for PSL

```
1: function PSLSAT(Φ)
2:     φ̄ ← ABSTRACT(φ)
3:     INIT(ImpIter, φ̄)
4:     while (HASNEXT(ImpIter)) do
5:         μ ← GETNEXT(ImpIter)
6:         Φ_μ ← CONCRETIZE(μ)
7:         (res, reason) ← ISPSLSAT(Φ_μ)
8:         if (res = "sat") then
9:             return "sat"
10:        else
11:            PRUNE(ImpIter, reason)
12:        end if
13:    end while
14:    return "unsat"
15: end function
```

Fig. 2. The PSL satisfiability algorithm

subformula is satisfied, while in SONF the subformula is triggered by an implication, and is, as such, more amenable to the exploitation of don't cares.

In [10], a substantial experimental evaluation is carried out on PSL satisfiability. The SONF based approach results in dramatic improvements in PSL automata compilation time. However, on those problems where the ABA construction succeed to build an automaton within the time limit, the search time is typically in favor of the monolithic approach. This is mainly due to the fact that in certain examples the semantic simplifications are extremely effective. In [11], additional improvements over [10] are obtained by applying cheap syntactic simplification rules, that result in additional savings not only in search but also in construction time.

4   Boolean Abstraction for Temporal Satisfiability

Consider the temporal satisfiability problem $\Phi \doteq (\phi_1 \leftrightarrow (\phi_2 \vee \phi_3))$. If it is possible to show that the set $\{\phi_1, \phi_3\}$ is temporally satisfied by a word w, then ϕ_2 is irrelevant: intuitively, the truth value of ϕ_2 over w can not affect the truth of Φ. However, all the automata-based approaches presented in the previous section are going to compile the formula *statically*: this means, for instance, that they will generate and search an automaton taking into account each ϕ_i. Information could be potentially disregarded because of the Boolean structure of the formula is in fact taken into account.

In this paper we propose a new approach that tries to overcome this problem. The idea, depicted in Fig. 1, is to decouple the search for a temporal model in two interacting, hierarchically connected phases: in the first, we look for a propositionally satisfying assignment (an implicant) to the Boolean abstraction of the problem; in the second, we check whether the set of temporal formulae corresponding to the implicant is temporally satisfiable.

We see a temporal property Φ as a Boolean combination $BoolComb(\phi_1, \ldots, \phi_n)$, where ϕ_i are distinct temporal formulae. The Boolean abstraction of Φ is

$\overline{\phi} \doteq BoolComb(A_1, \ldots, A_n)$, where the A_i are distinct Boolean variables (called the Boolean abstraction of ϕ_i); in the example above, $\overline{\phi}$ is $(A_1 \leftrightarrow (A_2 \lor A_3))$. We define an assignment μ for $\overline{\phi}$ as a mapping from each A_i to $\{True, False, X\}$. We call μ_t the atoms assigned to $True$, μ_f the atoms assigned to $False$, and μ_x the atoms assigned to X (for don't care). We say that μ propositionally satisfies $\overline{\phi}$ iff the formula obtained by replacing each occurrence of $A_i \in \mu_t$ with $True$, and each $A_i \in \mu_f$ with $False$, evaluates to $True$. A temporal model for Φ can be seen as an assignment μ satisfying $\overline{\phi}$, plus a temporal model for the conjunction of the required temporal formulae.

Theorem 1. *Φ is satisfiable iff there exists a truth assignment μ for $\overline{\phi}$ such that Φ_μ is satisfiable, where*

$$\Phi_\mu \doteq \bigwedge_{i.A_i \in \mu_t} \phi_i \land \bigwedge_{j.A_j \in \mu_f} \neg\phi_j$$

This theorem suggests an algorithm to check the satisfiability of a PSL formula Φ, and in general of any temporal formula. The (disjunctive) Boolean structure of Φ, expressible as a disjunction of Φ_μ, can be used to obtain several (hopefully) smaller automata, that can then be analyzed individually, with standard language emptiness checks (or other techniques).

Figure 2 reports the algorithm. The function PSLSAT( ) takes in input a PSL property Φ and returns "sat" iff Φ is satisfiable, otherwise it returns "unsat". ABSTRACT( ) builds the Boolean abstraction for Φ. *ImpIter* enables enumeration of the implicants (satisfying assignments) of $\overline{\phi}$. HASNEXT( ) returns $True$ iff there is at least one (yet unexplored) implicant left. GETNEXT( ) returns the next such implicant. If there is none, then the PSL formula is unsatisfiable and "unsat" is returned (line 14). Otherwise, we iterate for each implicant (lines 4–13). From μ the function CONCRETIZE(μ) builds the formula Φ_μ corresponding to the implicant μ. ISPSLSAT( ) is a function that takes a PSL property and returns "sat" if the property is unsatisfiable, otherwise it possibly returns a reason for the unsatisfiability. This function can simply be any of the functions reported in Sect. 3. If the Φ_μ is temporally satisfiable, then we are done and the top level function returns "sat". Otherwise, at line **??**, the result is analyzed by PRUNE( ), removing all remaining prime implicants that can be inferred to be unsatisfiable from the obtained *reason*. In our implementation *reason* is a set of implicants corresponding to a set of unsatisfiable cores of Φ_μ. Note that the unsatisfiability of Φ_μ establishes Φ_μ itself as an unsatisfiable core.

Relations to Satisfiability Modulo Theories. The high level schema presented above is largely inspired by the standard approaches to decision procedures for Satisfiability Modulo Theories (SMT), implemented in a number of systems and for a number of theories. In SMT, the enumeration of satisfying assignments is often carried out by a DPLL-based solver, that incrementally constructs an assignment for the Boolean abstraction of the formula. A typical technique is *early pruning*, where the theory solvers are called on the concretization of the assignment while this is being constructed. The advantage of early pruning is that it can prune a partial assignment as soon as its concretization becomes theory-unsatisfiable.

Some SMT solvers do attempt to extract don't care information on the Boolean abstraction; the combination with early pruning, however, appears to be nontrivial. Here we take a different perspective: we do not rely on early pruning, and try to exploit the presence of don't cares as much as possible, by enumerating prime implicants. This enables us to limit the number of theory constraints (PSL properties) sent to the theory solver. We base our Boolean enumeration on a BDD package, that provides primitives for on-the-fly extraction of one prime implicant. This choice is mostly motivated by the fact that the complexity of the temporal reasoning often dominates the problem, and thus BDD-based enumeration of prime implicants is not a bottleneck; in the future we also plan to experiment with DPLL-based enumeration. Another interesting feature is that "essential literals", i.e. literals that are common to all prime implicants, can be extracted at a reasonable cost. Notice that the set of essential literals includes all literals that can be obtained by standard SAT-based unit propagation and potentially more.

A key issue with SMT is the ability to avoid the same mistake in theory reasoning: more precisely, we don't want to try a prime implicant, if its intersection with a previously disproved one concretizes to an inconsistent set of temporal formulae. This problem is addressed by requiring that theory solvers should return a conflict set, i.e. an inconsistent subset of the problem it was given in input. In DPLL-based SMT, theory solvers are able to express conflicts in form of *conflict clauses*, that can be easily integrated with the conflict analysis and back-jumping mechanism. In the next section, we discuss how to address this problem in the setting of temporal satisfiability.

5 A Theory Solver for Temporal Logic

We now discuss how to design a theory solver. First, we exploit the fact that the input problem is a conjunction of temporal constraints with fixed polarity. This opens up to many optimizations. A particularly interesting simplification, given the fixed polarity of the constraints, is based on the notion of pure literal for PSL (Sect. 5.1). Then, we propose two new methods for the extraction of unsatisfiable cores (conflict sets) from the standard PSL satisfiability algorithms, one based on the use of BDD techniques (Sect. 5.2), and the second based on the use of SAT techniques (Sect. 5.3).

5.1 Pure Literal Simplification for PSL

First, we extend the notion of positive/negative occurrence of a proposition (the notion of positive/negative occurrence of a proposition in a Boolean expression is assumed to be known), and then we extend the notion to PSL formulae.

Definition 2. *If an occurrence of p in a Boolean expression b is positive [resp., negative] and b occurs in a SERE r, then that occurrence of p is positive [resp., negative] in r too.*

Let ϕ be a PSL formula and p a proposition. We define if an occurrence of p in ϕ is positive [resp., negative] recursively on the syntax of PSL formulae:

- *p is a positive occurrence of p in p*
- *every positive [resp., negative] occurrence of p in ϕ is a negative [resp., positive] occurrence in ¬ϕ*

– *every positive [resp., negative] occurrence of p in ϕ is a positive [resp., negative] occurrence in $X\phi$, $\psi \wedge \phi$, $\phi \wedge \psi$, $\psi U \phi$, $\phi U \psi$, $\phi R \psi$, $\psi R \phi$, $r \mapsto \phi$, and $r \diamond\!\!\!\rightarrow \phi$*
– *every positive [resp., negative] occurrence of p in r is a positive [resp., negative] occurrence in $r \diamond\!\!\!\rightarrow \phi$*
– *every positive [resp., negative] occurrence of p in r is a negative [resp., positive] occurrence in $r \mapsto \phi$*

We now define when a proposition is pure. Intuitively, if the proposition is pure, we can substitute every occurrence with either true or false, depending on the polarity, without affecting the satisfiability.

Definition 3. *Let ϕ be a PSL formula and p a proposition. p is pure positive [pure negative, resp.] in ϕ iff all the occurrences of p are positive [negative, resp.].*

Theorem 2. *If p is pure positive [pure negative, resp.] in ϕ, then ϕ is satisfiable iff $\phi[\top/p]$ [resp., $\phi[\bot/p]$] is satisfiable.*

5.2 BDD-Based Inconsistency Analysis

The first inconsistency analysis technique exploits a BDD-based computation of the fair states, i.e. those states that are the starting point of an accepting path. The standard symbolic procedure to check language emptiness (LE) [12] builds an automaton for the input formula Φ, computes the set of fair states and intersects it with the initial states: the resulting set (denoted with $[[\Phi]]$) contains all states that are the starting point of some path that accepts Φ.

Let $\phi_0, \ldots, \phi_n$ be temporal formulae with a top-level temporal operator over a set of atomic propositions AP. For each temporal formula ϕ_i, we introduce an activation variable. Let $A_0, \ldots, A_n$ be atomic propositions not in AP. We define a formula Ψ as

$$\Psi = \bigwedge_i A_i \rightarrow \phi_i(x)$$

The set $[[\Psi]]$ resulting from applying LE to Ψ is conditioned by the activation variables: it contains tuples of state variables from the automata of the ϕ_i together with the activation variables A_i. In order to obtain the sets of temporal formulae ϕ_i which are inconsistent, we look at those tuples of activation variables that do not have any corresponding state in $[[\Psi]]$.

Formally, suppose that M_Ψ is an automaton represented with a set V of state variables and that M_Ψ encodes the formula Ψ so that a set $[[\Psi]]$ of states is defined in such a way that:

1. all states in $[[\Psi]]$ are the starting point of some path accepting Ψ;
2. all words satisfying Ψ are accepted by some path starting from $[[\Psi]]$.

Suppose that V contains a variable v_{A_i} for every activation variable A_i such that a state s assigns v_{A_i} to true iff all paths starting from s accept the propositional formula A_i. Let $V_A = \{v_{A_0} \ldots v_{A_n}\}$ and $V' = V_\Psi \setminus V_A$. [1]

---

[1] Note that the LTL compilation of [12] and the PSL compilation discussed in Section 3 satisfy all these assumptions.

Theorem 3. *Let UC be a subset of* $\{0,\ldots,k\}$. *Then, there exists a state s in* $[[\Psi]]$ *such that* $s \models \bigwedge_{i\in UC} v_{A_i}$ *iff* $\bigwedge_{i\in UC} \phi_i$ *is satisfiable.*

Corollary 1.
$$\exists V'([[\Psi]]) = \{s \in 2^{V_A} \mid \bigwedge_{i.s\models v_{A_i}} \phi_i \text{ is sat}\}$$
$$\neg\exists V'([[\Psi]]) = \{s \in 2^{V_A} \mid \bigwedge_{i.s\models v_{A_i}} \phi_i \text{ is unsat}\}$$

Thus, the set $\neg\exists V'([[\Psi]])$ encodes all the possible subset of the implicant $\phi_0,\ldots,\phi_n$ that are inconsistent. When using SAT-based enumeration of implicants, we should not add all the clauses corresponding to the above set as blocking clauses. Instead, techniques to minimize the configurations should be employed. In our BDD-based setting, the information can be directly fed back to the main search (by a simple conjunction within the prime implicants enumeration routine) in order to prevent the next iterations of Boolean enumeration from producing PSL-unsatisfiable configurations.

5.3 SAT-Based Inconsistency Analysis

Standard incremental SAT-based bounded model checkers with completeness, such as [19], can be used off-the-shelf to determine language emptiness for LTL formulae. These approaches can be extended to extract an unsatisfiable core from a conjunction of temporal constraints.

Intuitively, the extraction relies on the ability of a Boolean SAT solver such as Mini-Sat [14] to check satisfiability of a Boolean formula f under a set of assumed literals $\{l_i\}$, i.e., $(\bigwedge_i l_i) \wedge f$. If that turns out to be unsatisfiable, the SAT solver returns a subset $UC \subseteq \{l_i\}$ such that $UC \wedge f$ is still unsatisfiable. Given a prime implicant Φ_μ we prefix the formulae ϕ_i with activation variables A_i as in the previous section. We then supply the literals corresponding to the value *True* for the activation variables at the initial time step as assumptions to the SAT solver. When a subset of these literals is reported to cause a conflict, it is straightforward to obtain the corresponding unsatisfiable core of Φ_μ. This SAT approach, differently from the BDD-based approach, computes only a single rather than the set of all unsatisfiable cores for Φ_μ. In the following we formalize that intuition.

SAT-based bounded model checking [5] represents a finite path π of length k over a set of variables V as the valuations of a set of variables $V[0,k]$, where $V[0,k]$ contains one variable $v[i]$ for each $v \in V$ and $0 \le i \le k$.

Given a set of variables V, a linear temporal logic formula ϕ, and a natural number k, a SAT-based bounded model checker following the approach [6] in Fig. 3 generates the following Boolean formulae:[2]

1. a *witness formula* $|[V,\phi,k]|$ over (a superset of) $V[0,k]$. The set of satisfying assignments of $|[V,\phi,k]|$ corresponds exactly to the set of paths $\pi[0,k]$ such that π represents a lasso-shaped path that satisfies ϕ.

---

[2] Model checking typically involves both, a model and a temporal logic formula. As we are only concerned with satisfiability of linear temporal logic formulae, we disregard the model part. To simplify the presentation we also disregard that (1) the witness formula typically allows to detect finite violating prefixes of safety properties [21] and (2) guaranteeing termination requires additional constraints [31,6]. Our implementation handles both.

```
 1: function LE_SAT(Φ_μ)
 2:     k ← 0
 3:     while (True) do
 4:         (res, UC) ← SAT_ASSUME(⟨⟨V ∪ V_A, ψ, k⟩⟩, {v_A[0] | v_A ∈ V_A})
 5:         if (res = Unsat) then   return (Unsat, {φ_i | v_{A_i}[0] ∈ UC})
 6:         res ← SAT((⋀_{v_A ∈ V_A} v_A[0]) ∧ |[V ∪ V_A, ψ, k]|)
 7:         if (res = Sat) then   return Sat
 8:         k ← k + 1
 9:     end while
10: end function
```

Fig. 3. SAT-based language emptiness with unsatisfiable cores

2. a *completeness formula* $\langle\langle V, \phi, k \rangle\rangle$ over (a superset of) $V[0,k]$. If $\langle\langle V, \phi, k \rangle\rangle$ is unsatisfiable, then ϕ is unsatisfiable.

Let Φ_μ be a prime implicant with atoms $\{\phi_0, \ldots, \phi_n\}$ and activation variables $\{A_0, \ldots, A_n\}$, and let ψ be Φ_μ prefixed with activation variables as in the previous section. Then we have

Lemma 1. $(\bigwedge_i v_{A_i}[0]) \wedge |[V \cup V_A, \psi, k]|$ *is satisfiable iff there is a lasso-shaped witness* $\pi[0, l-1] \circ \pi[l, k]^\omega$ *of* Φ_μ.

Lemma 2. *Let* $UC \subseteq \{0, \ldots, n\}$. *If* $\langle\langle V \cup V_A, \psi, k \rangle\rangle$ *is unsatisfiable under assumptions* $\{v_{A_i}[0] \mid i \in UC\}$ *then* $\bigwedge_{i \in UC} \phi_i$ *is unsatisfiable.*

Theorem 4. *The algorithm in Fig. 3 returns Sat iff* Φ_μ *is satisfiable. If it returns* (Unsat, UC), *then UC is an unsatisfiable core of* Φ_μ.

6   Experiments

The algorithms described in previous sections have been implemented within the NuSMV model checker [9]. To show the effectiveness of the proposed approach, we carried out an experimental evaluation, based on the benchmarks proposed in [10,11], in [17], and also on some benchmarks collected from the web. The benchmarks from [10,11] are random properties obtained by applying to randomly generated SEREs typical patterns extracted from industrial case studies [13]. The benchmarks are either randomly generated Boolean combinations of such typical properties, or implications/bi-implications between large conjunctions of such typical properties. The latter cases model refinement and equivalence among specifications, as is often seen in requirements engineering. The benchmarks from [17] are properties coming from a requirements engineering domain, and model whether a given property is implied by a big conjunction of other properties.

We evaluate the Boolean abstraction approach using BDD-based theory solving, and SAT-based SBMC theory solving, both based on the SONF algorithm for PSL satisfiability presented in [11]. The same approach was also chosen as a base line for the evaluation of performance improvements. (We also considered the possibility to include in

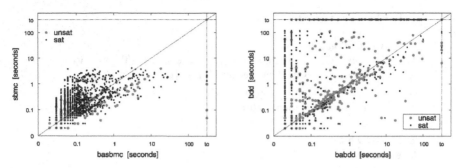

Fig. 4. Solving time of approaches with and without Boolean abstraction

our comparison other tools, e.g. [22,26], at least for pure LTL problems. However, some preliminary experiments on moderate-sized problems clearly indicated that the satisfiability based on model checking is vastly superior, at least in terms of the currently available implementations.) In the experiments, we evaluate the impact of Boolean abstraction, pure literal simplification, and feedback.

All experiments were run on a 3 GHz Intel CPU equipped with 4 GB of memory running Linux; for each run, we used a timeout of 120 seconds and a memory limit of 768 MB. For all methods, we used the settings that turned out to provide better results in [10,11]. For BDD-based methods, dynamic variable reordering was used, and forward reachability simplification was enabled on the tableau automata. For SAT-based methods, we used MiniSAT [14], and we enabled the completeness check based on the simple path constraint. The complete test suite and an extended version of this paper can be found at http://sra.itc.it/people/roveri/cav07-bapsl/.

In the following we use method descriptors consisting of up to five parts to describe an approach. (1) If ba is present, Boolean abstraction is used. (2) sbmc or bdd indicates whether SAT- or BDD-based solvers are used. (3) Presence of fb indicates that feedback is used. Finally, (4) pt and (5) ppi stand for pure literal simplification applied at the top and prime-implicant levels, respectively. As an example, babddptppi stands for BDD-based solver with Boolean abstraction and with the pure literal simplification applied both to the the top-level formula and to each prime implicant, but without using feedback. bdd and sbmc mark the respective base line approaches.

In Fig. 4, we report the scatter plots comparing the Boolean abstraction approaches (no pure literal simplification and no feedback) against the corresponding base line without Boolean abstraction. The plots show that the Boolean enumeration approach may lead to advantages in the case of SAT, and is vastly superior in the case of BDDs.

In Fig. 5, we compare Boolean abstraction with and without pure literal simplification. The plots show that the pure literal simplification dramatically reduces search time, both when applied at the prime implicant (row 1) and at the top level (row 2). Row 3 demonstrates that the application on the prime implicant level can gain an additional advantage even after the application on the top level. For our set of examples, the reverse is not true, see row 4. Rather, there seems to be a small penalty induced by the overhead of pure literal simplification at the top. In all cases the impact with BDD-based solvers turns out to be much stronger than with SAT-based solvers.

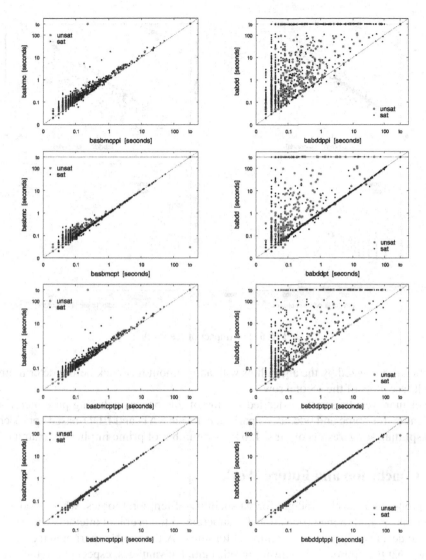

Fig. 5. Solving time of approaches with Boolean abstraction and combinations of pure literal simplification at the top- and/or prime implicant levels

We now analyze the impact of feedback. In Fig. 6, upper row, we compare basbmc and babdd with the corresponding configurations with feedback activated. The plots show that enabling conflict extraction sometimes pays off, but most often it degrades the overall performance. However, the degraded performance can be explained with the fact that the current implementation of the feedback is rather naïve, and uses the theory solvers as off-the-shelf. Interestingly enough, the generation of conflicts sets can dramatically reduce the search space, by avoiding to reconsider implicants that proved to be inconsistent in previous calls. This is clear if we plot the number of prime

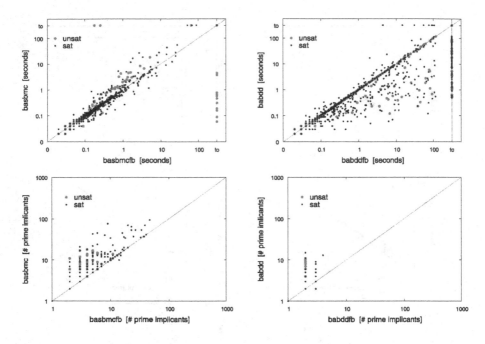

Fig. 6. The impact of feedback

implicants analyzed by the algorithms with and without feedback before determining a result (see plots of the second row).

For more results see the extended version of this paper, including pure literal simplification for sbmc and bdd, a comparison between SAT- and BDD-based approaches, and splitting some results of Figs. 4, 6 by the number of prime implicants examined.

7   Conclusion and Future Work

We proposed a novel paradigm for satisfiability of temporal logics, where model enumeration applied to the propositional abstraction of the problem interacts with a solver able to decide conjunctions of temporal formulae. A thorough experimental evaluation shows that the approach may result in substantial advantages, especially in the case of BDD-based reasoning, and the advantage mostly leverages on a generalization of the pure literal simplification rule to PSL. We also defined ways for computing unsatisfiable cores from the temporal solvers, and showed that their use may indeed reduce the search space, currently at the price of a penalty in performance.

In the future, a short term activity is to optimize the computation of conflict sets. In the longer term, the adoption of an SMT framework for temporal satisfiability suggests different research directions. First, we will investigate how to enable early pruning by means of incremental theory reasoning. Second, we will work on ways to combine BDD-based and SAT-based techniques: in fact, a comparison of the two technologies (see the extended version of this paper), clearly highlights their complementarity. This includes not only identifying conditions that will suggest which one to use for which implicant, but also trying to let each method benefit from results obtained with the other. Finally, we will consider to exploit the temporal hierarchy to identify sufficient conditions for temporal satisfiability.

References

1. Accellera. Property specification language reference manual, version 1.1
2. Armoni, R., Fix, L., Flaisher, A., Gerth, R., Ginsburg, B., Kanza, T., Landver, A., Mador-Haim, S., Singerman, E., Tiemeyer, A., Vardi, M.Y., Zbar, Y.: The ForSpec Temporal Logic: A New Temporal Property-Specification Language. In: Katoen, J.-P., Stevens, P. (eds.) ETAPS 2002 and TACAS 2002. LNCS, vol. 2280, Springer, Heidelberg (2002)
3. Beer, I., Ben-David, S., Eisner, C., Fisman, D., Gringauze, A., Rodeh, Y.: The temporal logic Sugar. In: Berry, G., Comon, H., Finkel, A. (eds.) CAV 2001. LNCS, vol. 2102, Springer, Heidelberg (2001)
4. Ben-David, S., Bloem, R., Fisman, D., Griesmayer, A., Pill, I., Ruah, S.: Automata Construction Algorithms Optimized for PSL, 2005. In: PROSYD deliverable D 3.2/4 (2005)
5. Biere, A., Cimatti, A., Clarke, E., Zhu, Y.: Symbolic model checking without BDDs. In: Cleaveland, W.R. (ed.) ETAPS 1999 and TACAS 1999. LNCS, vol. 1579, Springer, Heidelberg (1999)
6. Biere, A., Heljanko, K., Junttila, T., Latvala, T., Schuppan, V.: Linear encodings of bounded LTL model checking. Logical Methods in Computer Science 2 (2006)
7. Bloem, R., Cimatti, A., Pill, I., Roveri, M., Semprini, S.: Symbolic Implementation of Alternating Automata. In: Ibarra, O.H., Yen, H.-C. (eds.) CIAA 2006. LNCS, vol. 4094, Springer, Heidelberg (2006)
8. Bozzano, M., Bruttomesso, R., Cimatti, A., Junttila, T., van Rossum, P., Schulz, S., Sebastiani, R.: MathSAT: Tight integration of SAT and mathematical decision procedures. Journal of Automated Reasoning 35(1–3), 265–293 (2005)
9. Cimatti, A., Clarke, E.M., Giunchiglia, F., Roveri, M.: NUSMV: a new Symbolic Model Verifier. In: Halbwachs, N., Peled, D.A. (eds.) CAV 1999. LNCS, vol. 1633, Springer, Heidelberg (1999)
10. Cimatti, A., Roveri, M., Semprini, S., Tonetta, S.: From PSL to NBA: a modular symbolic encoding. In: FMCAD (2006)
11. Cimatti, A., Roveri, M., Tonetta, S.: Syntactic optimizations for PSL verification. In: TACAS (2007)
12. Clarke, E., Grumberg, O., Hamaguchi, K.: Another look at LTL model checking. Formal Methods in System Design 10(1), 47–71 (1997)
13. Ben David, S., Orni, A.: Property-by-Example guide: a handbook of PSL/Sugar examples. In: PROSYD deliverable D 1.1/3 (2005)
14. Eén, N., Sörensson, N.: An extensible SAT-solver. In: SAT (2003)
15. Emerson, A.: Temporal and modal logic. In: van Leeuwen, J. (ed.) Handbook of TCS, Volume B: Formal Models and Sematics, pp. 995–1072 (1990)
16. Fisher, M., Dixon, C., Peim, M.: Clausal temporal resolution. ACM Trans. Comput. Logic 2(1), 12–56 (2001)
17. Fuxman, A., Liu, L., Pistore, M., Roveri, M., Mylopoulos, J.: Specifying and analyzing early requirements in Tropos: Some experimental results. In: RE (2003)
18. Halpern, J.Y., Manna, Z., Moszkowski, B.C.: A hardware semantics based on temporal intervals. In: Díaz, J. (ed.) Automata, Languages and Programming. LNCS, vol. 154, Springer, Heidelberg (1983)

19. Heljanko, K., Junttila, T., Keinänen, M., Lange, M., Latvala, T.: Bounded model checking for weak alternating büchi automata. In: Ball, T., Jones, R.B. (eds.) CAV 2006. LNCS, vol. 4144, Springer, Heidelberg (2006)

20. Heljanko, K., Junttila, T., Latvala, T.: Incremental and complete bounded model checking for full PLTL. In: Etessami, K., Rajamani, S.K. (eds.) CAV 2005. LNCS, vol. 3576, Springer, Heidelberg (2005)

21. Kupferman, O., Vardi, M.: Model checking of safety properties. Formal Methods in System Design 19(3), 291–314 (2001)

22. Lange, M., Stirling, C.: Focus Games for Satisfiability and Completeness of Temporal Logic. In: LICS (2001)

23. Lichtenstein, O., Pnueli, A.: Propositional Temporal Logics: Decidability and Completeness. Logic Journal of the IGPL 8(1) (2000)

24. Manna, Z., Pnueli, A.: The Temporal Logic of Reactive and Concurrent Systems. Springer, Heidelberg (1992)

25. Miyano, S., Hayashi, T.: Alternating finite automata on ω-words. Theoretical Computer Science 32, 321–330 (1984)

26. Moszkowski, B.C.: A Hierarchical Completeness Proof for Propositional Interval Temporal Logic with Finite Time. Journal of Applied Non-Classical Logics 14(1-2), 55–104 (2004)

27. Pill, I., Semprini, S., Cavada, R., Roveri, M., Bloem, R., Cimatti, A.: Formal analysis of hardware requirements. In: DAC (2006)

28. Pnueli, A.: The temporal logic of programs. In: FOCS (1977)

29. Pnueli, A., Zaks, A.: PSL Model Checking and Run-Time Verification Via Testers. In: Misra, J., Nipkow, T., Sekerinski, E. (eds.) FM 2006. LNCS, vol. 4085, pp. 573–586. Springer, Heidelberg (2006)

30. Sebastiani, R., Tonetta, S.: "More Deterministic" vs. "Smaller" Büchi Automata for Efficient LTL Model Checking. In: Geist, D., Tronci, E. (eds.) CHARME 2003. LNCS, vol. 2860, Springer, Heidelberg (2003)

31. Sheeran, M., Singh, S., Stålmarck, G.: Checking safety properties using induction and a SAT-solver. In: Johnson, S.D., Hunt Jr., W.A. (eds.) FMCAD 2000. LNCS, vol. 1954, Springer, Heidelberg (2000)

32. Sistla, A., Clarke, E.: The complexity of propositional linear temporal logics. J. ACM 32(3), 733–749 (1985)

33. Vardi, M., Wolper, P.: Reasoning about infinite computations. Information and Computation 115, 1–37 (1994)

34. Wolper, P.: Temporal Logic Can Be More Expressive. Information and Control 56(1/2), 72–99 (1983)

A Lazy and Layered SMT($\mathcal{BV}$) Solver
for Hard Industrial Verification Problems*

Roberto Bruttomesso[1], Alessandro Cimatti[1], Anders Franzén[1,2], Alberto Griggio[2],
Ziyad Hanna[3], Alexander Nadel[3], Amit Palti[3], and Roberto Sebastiani[2]

[1] FBK-irst, Povo, Trento, Italy
{bruttomesso,cimatti,franzen}@itc.it
[2] DIT, Università di Trento, Italy
{griggio,rseba}@dit.unitn.it
[3] Logic and Validation Technologies, Intel Architecture Group of Haifa, Israel
{ziyad.hanna,alexander.nadel,amit.palti}@intel.com

Abstract. Rarely verification problems originate from bit-level descriptions. Yet, most of the verification technologies are based on *bit blasting*, i.e., reduction to boolean reasoning.

In this paper we advocate reasoning at higher level of abstraction, within the theory of bit vectors ($\mathcal{BV}$), where structural information (e.g. equalities, arithmetic functions) is not blasted into bits. Our approach relies on the *lazy* Satisfiability Modulo Theories (SMT) paradigm. We developed a satisfiability procedure for reasoning about bit vectors that carefully leverages on the power of boolean SAT solver to deal with components that are more naturally "boolean", and activates bit-vector reasoning whenever possible. The procedure has two distinguishing features. First, it relies on the on-line integration of a SAT solver with an incremental and backtrackable solver for $\mathcal{BV}$ that enables dynamical optimization of the reasoning about bit vectors; for instance, this is an improvement over static encoding methods which may generate smaller slices of bit-vector variables. Second, the solver for $\mathcal{BV}$ is *layered* (i.e., it privileges cheaper forms of reasoning), and it is based on a flexible use of term rewriting techniques.

We evaluate our approach on a set of realistic industrial benchmarks, and demonstrate substantial improvements with respect to state-of-the-art boolean satisfiability solvers, as well as other decision procedures for SMT($\mathcal{BV}$).

1 Introduction

Historically, algorithmic verification has been based on efficient reasoning engines, such as Binary Decision Diagrams [7], and more recently on SAT procedures [15], reasoning at the *boolean level*. However, the source of verification problems has increasingly moved from the boolean level to higher levels: most designers work at least at Register Transfer Level (or even higher levels). Thus, the mapping to verification

* This work has been partly supported by ORCHID, a project sponsored by Provincia Autonoma di Trento, and by a grant from Intel Corporation. The last author would also like to thank the EU project S3MS "Security of Software and Services for Mobile System" contract n. 27004 for supporting part of his research.

engines is typically based on some form of synthesis to the boolean level. With this process, hereafter referred to as *bit blasting*, boolean representations are generated for structured constructs (e.g., arithmetic operators), and even simple assignments result in fairly large formulae (e.g., conjunctions of equivalences between the bits in the words).

This impacts verification in several ways. For instance, high-level structural information is not readily available for a solver to exploit (and arithmetic is typically not handled efficiently by boolean reasoners). Furthermore, the hardness of the verification exhibits a dependence of the width of the data path.

The importance of avoiding (or controlling) the use of bit blasting has been strongly advocated by [18], where the theory of bit vectors is identified as a suitable representation formalism for practical industrial problems from many application domains, and the development of effective solvers for SMT($\mathcal{BV}$) is highlighted as an important goal for the research community.

In this paper we take on this challenge and propose a new, scalable approach to SMT($\mathcal{BV}$) based on the *lazy* SMT paradigm. We have developed a satisfiability procedure for reasoning in the theory of bit vectors, that leverages the power of boolean SAT solver to deal with components that are more naturally "boolean", and activates reasoning on bit vectors whenever possible.

The procedure has two distinguishing features. First, it is based on the *lazy* SMT paradigm, that is, it relies on the *on-line* integration of a SAT solver with an *incremental and backtrackable* solver for $\mathcal{BV}$ ($\mathcal{BV}$-solver), that allows us to dynamically optimize the reasoning about bit vectors. For instance, this has the advantage that word chunks are kept as large as possible, since the splitting is carried out according to the control path currently activated; this addresses one of the drawbacks of static encoding methods [4,2], which may result in an unnecessary slicing of bit vector variables.

Second, the $\mathcal{BV}$-solver makes aggressive use of *layering*, i.e., subsolvers for cheaper theories are invoked first, and more expensive ones are called only when required, and on simplified subproblems. The cheapest levels are implemented by means of flexible use of *term rewriting* techiques.

Our approach also relies on a preprocessor, aiming at simplifying the problem before the search, and on a novel boolean enumeration algorithm for circuits that generates *partial* satisfying assignments.

We evaluate our approach experimentally on a set of realistic industrial benchmarks. We analyze the impact of the proposed optimizations, showing that they all contribute to gaining efficiency. We then compare our solver with several state of the art approaches, including MiniSat 2.0, the winners of the last SMT competition on bit vectors, and BAT [13]. The results indicate that our approach, despite the preliminary status of the implementation, has a great potential: on the hardest instances it is often able to largely outperform the other approaches.

This paper is structured as follows. In §2 we describe the problem of Satisfiability Modulo the theory of bit vectors, and in §3 we describe the previous approaches. In §4 we overview our approach. In §5 we discuss the details of the preprocessing, and in §6 we present the $\mathcal{BV}$-solver. In §7 we experimentally evaluate our approach. Finally, in §8 we draw some conclusions and outline directions for future research.

2   SMT($\mathcal{BV}$): Satisfiability Modulo the Theory of Bit Vectors

A bit vector of a given width n is an array of bits and hence it may assume (decimal) values in the range $[0, 2^n - 1]$, accordingly to the binary value expressed by its individual bits. From now on we will implicitly assume bit vector variables to have a fixed width, whose maximal value N is determined a priori. In the remainder of the paper we shall use the notation $\mathbf{x}^n$ to represent a bit vector variable of width n or simply $\mathbf{x}$ when the width is not important or it can be deduced from the context. Constants will be denoted either with their decimal or binary value (in the latter case a subscript "b" is added).

The easiest possible theory of bit vectors (here denoted as $\mathcal{BV}(\varepsilon)$) includes only bit vector variables, constants, and the equality ($=$) as predicate symbol. Notice that, since we are dealing with fixed-width bit vectors, any interpretation of the theory must satisfy implicit finite domain constraints; for instance it is not possible to satisfy formulae of the kind $\bigwedge_{i=1}^{2^n+1} \bigwedge_{j=i+1}^{2^n+1} \mathbf{x_i}^n \neq \mathbf{x_j}^n$, because only 2^n different values may be represented with n bits.

More interesting theories may be obtained with the addition of other operators to $\mathcal{BV}(\varepsilon)$. The most common ones can be divided into three main sets:

core operators. $\{[i : j], :: \}$, named selection (or extraction) and concatenation respectively; i is the most significant bit in the selection ($i \geq j$). The result of a selection is a bit vector of size $i - j + 1$ whose k-th bit is equivalent to the $k + j$-th bit of the selected term, for $k \in [0, i - j + 1]$. Concatenation returns a bit vector resulting from the justapposition of the bits of its arguments;

arithmetic operators. (and relations) $\{+, -, *, < \}$, i.e., plus, minus, multiplication by constant, and less than. The intended semantic is the one of arithmetic modulo 2^n, n being the width of the arguments of the operators;

bitwise operators. { **AND** , **OR** , **NOT** } that apply basic logical functions to correspondent bits of the arguments.

In [9] it is shown a polynomial algorithm to solve $\mathcal{BV}(\varepsilon)$ augmented with core operators ($\mathcal{BV}(\mathbf{C})$). As soon as other operators are added to the theory, either arithmetic ($\mathcal{BV}(\mathbf{CA})$) or bitwise ($\mathcal{BV}(\mathbf{CB})$) or both ($\mathcal{BV}(\mathbf{CAB})$ or $\mathcal{BV}$), the problem of deciding a conjunction of atoms becomes NP-Hard [3]. In the following, a bit vector *term* is defined to be either a constant, a variable, or the application of an operator to a term. A bit vector *atom* is an application of a relation ($=$, $<$) to two terms.

Given a decidable first-order theory $\mathcal{T}$, we call the *decision problem* on $\mathcal{T}$ (DEC($\mathcal{T}$)) the problem of deciding the satisfiability in $\mathcal{T}$ of sets/conjunctions of ground atomic formulas ($\mathcal{T}$-*atoms*) and their negations in the language of $\mathcal{T}$. We call a $\mathcal{T}$-*solver* any tool able to decide DEC($\mathcal{T}$). *Satisfiability Modulo (the) Theory* $\mathcal{T}$ (SMT($\mathcal{T}$)) is the problem of deciding the satisfiability of *boolean combinations* of propositional atoms and theory atoms. (Consequently, DEC($\mathcal{BV}$) and SMT($\mathcal{BV}$) represent respectively the decision and the SMT problem in $\mathcal{BV}$.) We call an SMT($\mathcal{T}$) *solver* any tool able to decide SMT($\mathcal{T}$). Notice that, unlike with DEC($\mathcal{T}$), SMT($\mathcal{T}$) involves handling also boolean connectives.

3   An Analysis of Previous Approaches

In this section we overview and analyze the main approaches for the verification of an RTL circuit design.

Eager encoding into SAT (bit blasting). The traditional approach (*bit blasting*) is that of encoding the problem into a boolean formula, which is then fed to a boolean solver: words are encoded into arrays of boolean atoms, and $\mathcal{BV}$ operators are decomposed into their gate-level representation, each gate being a boolean connective. Pre- and post-processing steps can further enhance the performance (see, e.g., [11,13,12,10]). Notice that the winners of SMT-COMP'06 for SMT($\mathcal{BV}$) were all based on bit blasting.

A variant of this approach is followed in [17,2]: abstract representations of an RTL circuit are generated by abstracting away information on the data path, and the resulting encoding is then fed into a propositional SAT solver. The approach in [2] is subject to loss of information, and iterative refinement may be required.

Eager encodings into DEC($\mathcal{BV}$). The approaches proposed in [9,14,3] encode the problem into a set of atomic formulas in (fragments of) $\mathcal{BV}$, which is fed to a $\mathcal{BV}$-solver. Novel and optimized $\mathcal{BV}$-solvers have been introduced there: particular attention is paid in optimizing the partitioning of bit vectors due to core operators [14] and in handling modulo-arithmetic operators [3].

Eager encodings into DEC($\mathcal{LA}(\mathbb{Z})$). The approaches proposed in [19,6] encode the problem into a set of literals in the theory of linear arithmetic on the integers ($\mathcal{LA}(\mathbb{Z})$) which is then fed to a $\mathcal{LA}(\mathbb{Z})$-solver: bit-vector variables $\mathbf{x_i}^n$ are encoded as integer variables $x_i \in [0, 2^n - 1]$, RTL constructs [19]) are encoded, into $\mathcal{LA}(\mathbb{Z})$ constraints.

Eager encoding into SMT($\mathcal{LA}(\mathbb{Z})$). The approach we proposed in [4] encodes the problem into an SMT($\mathcal{LA}(\mathbb{Z})$) formula, which is fed to an SMT($\mathcal{LA}(\mathbb{Z})$)-solver. The design is partitioned into *control-path* and *data-path* components: control lines are encoded as boolean atoms, and control constructs into boolean combinations of control variables and predicates over data-path variables; data-path bit-vector variables and linearizable data-path constructs are encoded similarly to the DEC($\mathcal{LA}(\mathbb{Z})$) approach; non-linearizable data-path constructs are encoded by bit-blasting, or by means of uninterpreted functions. Some other constraints are introduced to represent the interface between the control and data-path lines.

Generalizing a standard terminology of the SMT community, we call the approaches above, *eager approaches*, because the encodings into SAT, DEC($\mathcal{BV}$), DEC($\mathcal{LA}(\mathbb{Z})$) and SMT($\mathcal{LA}(\mathbb{Z})$) respectively are performed eagerly at the beginning of the process, before starting any form of search.

We now discuss the above approaches. The key issue of the approaches based on bit-blasting is that they encode bits into boolean *atoms*, and consequently words into arrays of boolean atoms and gates into *boolean connectives*. On the one hand, this allows for a straightforward encoding of all constructs of the $\mathcal{BV}$ language; moreover, as all the search is demanded to an external SAT solver, it allows for selecting the SAT solver off-the-shelf; more importantly, these approaches allows for exploiting the full power of modern boolean solvers in handling the search due to the control logic. On the other hand, a predominant part of the computational effort is wasted in performing useless boolean search on the bitwise encoding of data-path variables and arithmetical operations (e.g., up to a 2^{32} factor in the amount of boolean search for a 32-bit integer value). In particular, notice that boolean solvers are typically "bad at mathematics", in the sense that reasoning on the boolean encoding of arithmetical operations causes a blowup of the computational effort. To this extent, we say that the bit-blasting approaches are "*control-path oriented*", in the sense that they are well-suited for problems where the control-path component dominates, but may suffer when the data-path component dominates, in particular when lots of arithmetic is involved.

The key issue of the encoding-into-DEC($\mathcal{T}$) approaches is that they encode words into *terms* in some first order theory $\mathcal{T}$ (typically some fragment of either $\mathcal{BV}$ or $\mathcal{LA}(\mathbb{Z})$), and consequently gates and RTL operators into *function symbols* of $\mathcal{T}$. On the one hand, these approaches allows and ad-hoc $\mathcal{T}$-solver for handling each word as a single term in $\mathcal{T}$, preventing the bit-blasting of the world itself and the consequent potential blowup in boolean search; moreover, arithmetic operators can be handled directly and efficiently by an ad-hoc solver. On the other hand, the fact that control bits and gates are encoded into terms and function symbols respectively prevents from exploiting the full power of modern boolean solvers in handling the search due to the control logic. To this extent, we say that the encoding-into-DEC($\mathcal{T}$) approaches are "*data-path oriented*", in the sense that they are well-suited for problems where the data-path part dominates, in particular when lots of arithmetic is involved, but may suffer when the control-path part dominates.

The key issue of the encoding-into-SMT($\mathcal{LA}(\mathbb{Z})$) approach is that control bits and gates are encoded into boolean atoms and connectives respectively, whilst words and RTL operators are encoded into terms, function and predicate symbols in $\mathcal{LA}(\mathbb{Z})$ respectively. Remarkably, some bits may have both a control-path and a data-path role, and have a double encoding. On the one hand, this approach allows for exploiting the power of the boolean solver embedded in the SMT($\mathcal{LA}(\mathbb{Z})$) solver in handling the search due to the control logic, preventing the blowup in boolean search due to the bit-blasting of data-path words.

On the other hand, it suffers from other important weaknesses: first, some constructs (e.g., bitwise operators) cannot be encoded into $\mathcal{LA}(\mathbb{Z})$, and must bit-blasted anyway; second, the $\mathcal{LA}(\mathbb{Z})$ constraints resulting from the encoding of core $\mathcal{BV}$ operations, like selection and concatenation, turns out to be very expensive to handle by $\mathcal{LA}(\mathbb{Z})$-solvers; third, many $\mathcal{LA}(\mathbb{Z})$ constraints resulting from the encoding of some $\mathcal{BV}$ constructs prevent and efficient propagation of integer values and boolean values, corresponding to unit-propagation in the equivalent bit-blasted encoding. (These problems are shared also by the encoding-to-DEC($\mathcal{LA}(\mathbb{Z})$) approach.) Overall, from our experience the approach turned out to be less efficient than expected, mostly due to too many and too expensive calls to $\mathcal{LA}(\mathbb{Z})$-solvers.

We see our encoding-into-SMT($\mathcal{LA}(\mathbb{Z})$) approach of [4] as a first and very preliminary attempt to merge control-path-oriented and data-path-oriented approaches. In next sections we push this idea forward, within the lazy SMT($\mathcal{BV}$) framework.

4   A Lazy Approach to SMT($\mathcal{BV}$)

Our novel SMT($\mathcal{BV}$) solver is based on the layered lazy approach to SMT($\mathcal{T}$) (see, e.g., [5]). A *preprocessor* takes as input a representation of (the negation of) an RTL verification problem, and produces a simpler and equivalently-satisfiable SMT($\mathcal{BV}$) CNF formula φ. The search is based on the *boolean abstraction* of φ, that is a boolean formula φ^p obtained by substituting every distinct $\mathcal{BV}$-atom in φ with a fresh propositional atom. φ is also called the *refinement* of φ^p. The boolean abstraction φ^p of φ is then fed to a *modified DPLL engine*, which enumerates a complete list $\mu_1^p, ..., \mu_n^p$ of partial truth assignments which satisfy φ^p. Every time a new assignment μ_i^p is generated, the set μ_i of $\mathcal{BV}$ literals corresponding to μ_i^p is fed to a $\mathcal{BV}$-solver. If μ is found $\mathcal{BV}$-consistent, then φ is $\mathcal{BV}$-consistent and the whole procedure stops. Otherwise, the $\mathcal{BV}$-solver returns the subset $\eta \subseteq \mu$ which caused the inconsistency of μ (called a *theory conflict set*). The boolean abstraction η^p of η is then used by the DPLL engine to prune the future boolean search (by backjumping and learning [15]). If at the end of the boolean search none of the μ_i's is found $\mathcal{BV}$-consistent, then φ is $\mathcal{BV}$-inconsistent and the whole procedure stops.

In order to increase the efficiency of the $\mathcal{BV}$ reasoning, the $\mathcal{BV}$-solver is organized into three *layers* of increasing expressivity and complexity, s.t. the more expensive layers come into play only when strictly needed [5]. In particular, the DPLL engine invokes the $\mathcal{BV}$-solver also on assignments under construction (*"early pruning"*), which can be pruned if they are found unsatisfiable in $\mathcal{BV}$. As these checks are not necessary for the correctness and completeness of the procedure, in early-pruning calls only the cheaper layers of the $\mathcal{BV}$-solver are invoked. (We omit the description of other SMT optimizations we adopted, which can be found in [5].)

The preprocessor and the $\mathcal{BV}$-Solver are described in details in §5 and §6 respectively.

Notice that, unlike the eager approaches described in §3, our approach is *lazy*, in the sense that the encoding is performed by the $\mathcal{BV}$-solver, *on demand* and *ad hoc* for every branch in the search. Thus, only a strict subset of the $\mathcal{BV}$ atoms are assigned by DPLL and passed to the $\mathcal{BV}$-solver, corresponding to only the sub-circuits that are given an active role by the control variables assigned in the branch. This reduces the computational effort required to the $\mathcal{BV}$-solver, in particular when expensive arithmetical constructs come into play, and addresses one of the major source of inefficiency we encountered with the SMT($\mathcal{LA}(\mathbb{Z})$) approach [4]. Another advantage is that bit-vector chunks are kept as large as possible, since the splitting is carried out according to the control path currently activated; this addresses one of the drawbacks of eager encoding methods [14,2,4], which may result in an unnecessary slicing of bit-vector variables.

5 Preprocessing

The schema of the preprocessor is outlined in the left part of Figure 1. It consists mainly on a sequence of six processing steps.

1. Bool to word-1 encoding. The first step addresses the fact that in an RTL circuit there is not always a clear separation between the *data paths* and the *control paths*; in particular, there is no distinction between control lines and word variables of width one. This distinction is crucial when our SMT approach is used, because the former and the latter ones must be encoded respectively as propositional *atoms* and as *terms* in the theory [4].

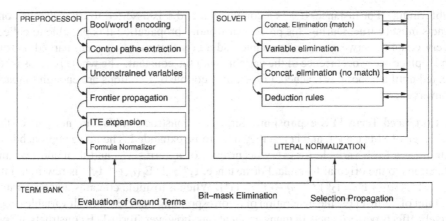

Fig. 1. The architecture of the preprocessor and of the second layer of the solver

The encoder tags all the nodes of the circuit either as `bool` ("control") or as `word` ("data"): outputs from predicates ($=$, $<$) and words of width one are tagged `bool`; the result of concatenations or arithmetic operators is instead tagged as `word`. The tagging information is then propagated back and forth to the remaining parts of the circuit. (Bitwise operators with `bool` inputs are converted into boolean operators.) When tag clashes occurs (e.g., a node tagged `bool` is in input to a concatenation), they are resolved with the introduction of a one of two *tag-casting operators*: `bool`($\mathbf{w}^1$), which casts a word $\mathbf{w}^1$ into a bool, and `word1`(b) that translates a bool b into a word of size 1. `bool`($\mathbf{w}^1$) is translated into $\mathbf{w}^1 = \mathbf{1}^1$, while `word1`(b) is replaced by a fresh variable $\mathbf{w}^1$, and the axioms $(b \rightarrow \mathbf{w}^1 = \mathbf{1}^1) \land (\neg b \rightarrow \mathbf{w}^1 = \mathbf{0}^1)$ are added to the global formula.

2. Control-paths extraction. When `word1`(.) constructs occur in matching positions in an equality, then the equality is split into a conjunction of equalities, and the equalities between word1 variables are transformed into equivalences between booleans. For instance, $(\mathbf{t_1}^7 :: \text{word1}(p) :: \mathbf{t_2}^8) = (\mathbf{t_3}^7 :: \text{word1}(q) :: \mathbf{t_4}^8)$ is rewritten into the equivalent form $(\mathbf{t_1}^7 = \mathbf{t_3}^7) \land (p \leftrightarrow q) \land (\mathbf{t_2}^8 = \mathbf{t_4}^8)$.

3. Propagation of unconstrained variables. Industrial benchmarks often contain unconstrained variables (i.e., input variables that occur only once in the formula) used to abstract more complex subparts. An unconstrained variable may assume an arbitrary value, and hence we can rewrite the original formula ϕ into an *equisatisfiable* formula ϕ' using the following rules ($\mathbf{v}$, $\mathbf{v_1}$, and $\mathbf{v_2}$ are unconstrained variables, $\mathbf{f}$ is a fresh variable, p is a fresh propositional variable):

$$\mathbf{v}^n + \mathbf{t}^n \rightarrow \mathbf{f}^n \qquad \mathbf{v_1}^n :: \mathbf{v_2}^m \rightarrow \mathbf{f}^{n+m} \qquad\qquad \mathbf{v}^n = \mathbf{t}^n \rightarrow p$$
$$\mathbf{t}^n + \mathbf{v}^n \rightarrow \mathbf{f}^n \qquad\qquad \mathbf{NOT}\ \mathbf{v}^n \rightarrow \mathbf{f}^n \qquad\qquad \mathbf{v}^n < \mathbf{t}^n, t \not\equiv \mathbf{0}^n \rightarrow p$$
$$\mathbf{v}^n - \mathbf{t}^n \rightarrow \mathbf{f}^n \qquad \mathbf{v_1}^n\ \mathbf{AND}\ \mathbf{v_2}^n \rightarrow \mathbf{f}^n \qquad \mathbf{t}^n < \mathbf{v}^n, t \not\equiv \mathbf{2^n} - \mathbf{1}^n \rightarrow p$$
$$\mathbf{t}^n - \mathbf{v}^n \rightarrow \mathbf{f}^n \qquad \mathbf{v_1}^n\ \mathbf{OR}\ \mathbf{v_2}^n \rightarrow \mathbf{f}^n$$

4. Frontier Propagation and Variable Inlining. When a boolean formula ϕ is asserted to a truth value, the truth value information may be propagated backward to its subformulae. For instance, if ϕ is a conjunction and ϕ is asserted to true, also its conjuncts must be true. During this process of frontier propagation it is possible to collect every equality between a word variable and a constant that has been marked as true and replace every occurrence of the variable with the constant. The whole process is repeated until a fixpoint is reached. (Typically a couple of iterations are enough to reach convergence.)

5. Enhanced Term-ITE expansion. Term-ITE constructs (ITE_t) are not part of the language of $\text{SMT}(\mathcal{BV})$, and hence they have to be expanded. The naive approach is to introduce a fresh variable for every occurrence of a Term-ITE, and then add two implications to the original formula. For instance, $\mathbf{t_1}^n = \text{ITE}_t(q, \mathbf{t_2}^n, \mathbf{t_3}^n)$ is rewritten into $\mathbf{t_1}^n = \mathbf{f}^n \wedge (q \rightarrow \mathbf{f}^n = \mathbf{t_2}^n) \wedge (\neg q \rightarrow \mathbf{f}^n = \mathbf{t_3}^n)$. When a formula contains a considerable amount of Term-ITEs, the generation of a corresponding number of fresh variables negatively affects performance. In many applications, however, Term-ITE constructs are organized in complex clusters with the structure of a directed acyclic graph. Any maximal cluster in the formula can be transfomed into a correspondent Boolean-ITE (ITE_b) cluster by pushing the external predicate toward the leaves of the DAG. For instance, $\mathbf{t_1}^n = \text{ITE}_t(q_1, \text{ITE}_t(q_2, \mathbf{t_2}^n, \mathbf{t_3}^n), \mathbf{t_4}^n)$ can be rewritten into $\text{ITE}_b(q_1, \text{ITE}_b(q_2, \mathbf{t_1}^n = \mathbf{t_2}^n, \mathbf{t_1}^n = \mathbf{t_3}^n), \mathbf{t_1}^n = \mathbf{t_4}^n)$ saving the introduction of two fresh variables.

6. Normalization. In the language of $\mathcal{BV}$ the problem of transforming a generic bit vector expression into a canonical form is an NP-Hard problem in itself. Weaker, but effective, polynomial transformations on bit vector terms are performed, for instance elimination of concatenation with perfect match: $\mathbf{t_1}^m :: \mathbf{t_2}^n = \mathbf{t_3}^m :: \mathbf{t_4}^n$ is reduced to the conjunction of $\mathbf{t_1}^m = \mathbf{t_3}^m$ and $\mathbf{t_2}^n = \mathbf{t_4}^n$.

During the whole six-step process above, a set of cheap and "local" linear transformations are applied in order to simplify $\mathcal{BV}$ terms.

Evaluation of Ground terms. Whenever a term is composed solely of constants it is replaced by the constant of the appropriate value; similarly for boolean formulas. For example, $0100_b :: 0001_b + 00001001_b$ is evaluated into 01001010_b.

Bit-masks elimination. When a constant occurs in a binary bitwise operation, it is rewritten into concatenations of maximal sequences of 0's and 1's. For example, the constant 00011101_b is split as $000_b :: 111_b :: 0_b :: 1_b$. Then, similar splitting is applied to the other term, and then the operator is evaluated. For instance, $\mathbf{t}^8 \text{ AND } 00011101_b$ is rewritten into $000_b :: \mathbf{t}[4:2] :: 0_b :: \mathbf{t}[0:0]$.

Selection propagation. Selection operators are propagated through concatenation and bitwise operators. After this process, only selection on variables, ITE's or arithmetic operators can be left.

These transformations are implemented within the "term bank", a layer that allows for the dynamic creation of new terms, implementing perfect sharing; both the preprocessor and the solver, described in next section, rely on the term bank, and benefit from the transformations above.

6   An Incremental and Layered $\mathcal{BV}$-Solver for SMT($\mathcal{BV}$)

In this section we describe the $\mathcal{BV}$-solver, that decides the consistency of a set of bit vector literals, and in case of inconsistency, it produces a conflict set. The $\mathcal{BV}$-solver is intended to be called on-line, while the boolean search is constructing a boolean model, in order to apply early pruning. For this reason, it is implemented to be *incremental* and *backtrackable*, i.e., it is possible to add and remove constraints without restarting from scratch.

The theory solver is *layered* [5], i.e. it analyzes the problem at hand trying to detect inconsistency in layers of theories of increasing power, so that cheaper layers are called first. The *first layer* is a solver for the logic of Equality of Uninterpreted Functions ($\mathcal{EUF}$). Here all bit vector operators (functions and predicates) are treated as uninterpreted, the finiteness of the domain and codomain of variables and functions is not taken into account; all constants are however treated as distinct. The $\mathcal{EUF}$ solver [16] is incremental, backtrackable, produces conflict sets, and has the capability to deduce unassigned theory literals, which will be propagated to the boolean enumerator. In this layer, conflicts of the type $\mathbf{x} < \mathbf{y} :: \mathbf{z}$, $\neg(\mathbf{x} < \mathbf{w})$, $\mathbf{w} = \mathbf{y} :: \mathbf{z}$ can be detected.

The *second layer* is an incomplete solver, based on a set of inference rules for bit-vector constraints, that can be applied in an incremental and backtrackable manner. The main idea driving the design of this solver is that a complete solver is very seldom necessary. Thus, a solver based on a small number of inference rules, that can be efficiently implemented, may suffice to decide most formulas.

The *third layer* is a complete solver for conjunctions of bit vector constraints, that ultimately relies on the encoding into $\mathcal{LA}(\mathbf{Z})$ proposed in [6]. In early pruning, the first two, cheaper layers are active; the third, more expensive layer is activated only in complete calls, when a definite answer is necessary, i.e. when a satisfying boolean assignment is being analyzed.

In the rest of this section, we focus on the second layer, which is the most novel component of the solver. The architecture of the second layer is depicted in the right part of Figure 1. The control is organized into a sequence of four main stages, described below. Each of the stages transforms a set of currently active facts, by means of a syntactic inference engine, in an incremental and backtrackable manner.

Similarly to the preprocessor, the solver relies on the term bank, so that whenever a new term is created, the local simplification rules described in §5 are automatically applied. In addition, whenever a new literal is created, a set of normalization rules is used to obtain simpler literals. The rules include a subset of the normalizations applied in the preprocessor which are described in §5; in addition, negated equalities of the form $\neg(\mathbf{t}^1 = \mathbf{1}^1)$ are turned into the positive correspondent $\mathbf{t}^1 = \mathbf{0}^1$. Early termination is enforced upon detection of inconsistency: whenever a literal is reduced to false, the computation is immediately stopped. The stages are the following:

Concatenation Elimination (match). The rule for the elimination of concatenation with perfect match (see Section 5) is applied to all the literals that are amenable for reduction. We notice that the rule does not introduce any selection operator.

Variable Elimination. Whenever a fact of the form $\mathbf{v} = \mathbf{t}$ is active, and $\mathbf{v}$ does not occur in $\mathbf{t}$, then it is removed from the active facts, and every occurrence of $\mathbf{v}$ in the

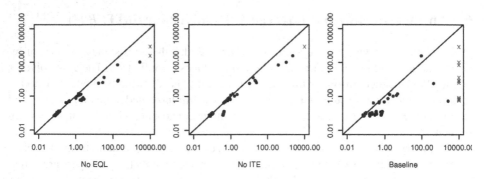

Fig. 2. Comparison between different optimizations. Execution times measured as 0 seconds have been adjusted to 0.01 seconds.

other active facts is replaced by **t**. During substitution, new terms may be generated in the term bank, so that the corresponding local rules are applied, together with the literal normalization rules.

Concatenation Elimination (no match). All top-level concatenations are simplified, regardless of the match of the sizes. In particular, each active fact having the form $t_1{}^m :: t_2{}^n = t_3{}^{m+n}$ is replaced by $t_1{}^m = t_3[m+n:n]$ and $t_2{}^n = t_3[n-1:0]$. We notice that at this stage concatenations may be replaced by selections, requiring thus the creation of new terms, which in turn fire local rules and literal normalization rules.

Deduction Rules. The final step is the application of the following simplification rules, until fix point is reached (here "**c**" denotes a constant).

$$\frac{t_1 = t_2 \quad t_2 = t_3}{t_1 = t_3}\ Tr1 \quad \frac{t_1 < t_2 \quad t_2 < t_3}{t_1 < t_3}\ Tr2 \quad \frac{c < t_1 \quad t_1 < t_2}{c+1 < t_2}\ Tr3 \quad \frac{A \quad \neg A}{\bot}\ Exc.$$

Some remarks are in order. First, the issue of incrementality and backtrackability poses nontrivial constraints on the implementation of the stages; in particular, variable elimination is not applied destructively, and it is, in the current implementation, the most expensive stage. It is likely that additional efficiency may be achieved by means of optimizations of the underlying data structures. Second, new rules can be plugged in with relatively little effort, possibly in a way that is dependent on the application domain; additional efficiency could be achieved by scoring their activity on the fly, with a mechanism similar to the VSIDS heuristic for SAT.

Finally, a very relevant issue is the generation of informative (i.e., small) conflict sets. Currently, if an inconsistency is detected, the leaves of the proof tree can be taken as a conflict set. However, the conflict sets generated may contain irrelevant literals, depending on the order in which inference rules are applied. Currently, we start from the assumptions of the proof and obtain a smaller conflict sets by means of deletion filtering [8]: one constraint is dropped from the conflict set, and then consistency is checked again. If the set is still inconsistent, the dropped constraint was irrelevant. This is repeated until a fix point is reached, and the remaining set of literals can be used as a conflict set. A method based on proof storing and analysis could be used to improve

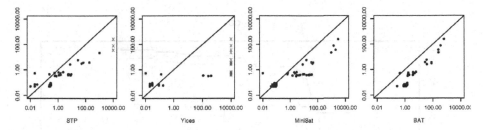

Fig. 3. Scatter plots between MathSAT and the other solvers. Execution times measured as 0 seconds have been adjusted to 0.01 seconds.

the quality of the conflict set; however, an efficient implementation may be nontrivial to achieve, and it is left as the object of future research.

7 Experimental Evaluation

The approach described in previous sections was implemented within the MathSAT system, and was experimentally evaluated on industrial verification problems. In this section we first describe the experimental set up, and report the evaluation in two parts. First we show the impact of the different optimizations. Second, we compare our solver against alternative approaches.

Experimental Set Up. We evaluated our approach in a set of industrial benchmarks provided by Intel. Unfortunately, we can not disclose the benchmarks or any details on the original application domain.

For the benefit of the reader, in order to give a feeling of their structural properties we report in a technical report available at [1] for each of the benchmarks the number of: constants, words of size 1, words of size > 1, equalities, core operators, arithmetic operators, bitwise operators, ITEs, boolean connectives. We also report the size of the boolean abstraction of the SMT($\mathcal{BV}$) encoding, and the size of the bitblasted formula.

The experiments were run on an Intel Xeon 3GHz processor running Linux. For each run, the time limit was set to 1 hour and the memory limit was set to 1500 MB.

Evaluation of the Optimizations. In this section we compare the impact of eq-layering and enhanced ITE expansion on the overall performance of the solver. We compare the best configuration (the one with all optimizations enabled), against configurations that have a single option disabled at a time, and against the baseline configuration, where no optimization is active. Results are shown in figure 2. The results clearly show that each of the optimizations contributes to improving the performance; we also see that without them the solver is virtually unable to solve any of the interesting instances.

Comparison with Other Solvers. We compared our approach against the following systems.

- MiniSat 2.0, considered as the best system based on bit blasting; We are using the SatELite-like simplifying version as it performed better on these instances.

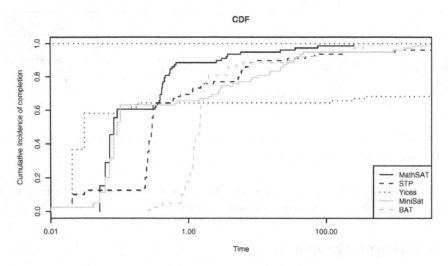

Fig. 4. Cumulative distribution functions (survival plots) comparing the solvers in log scale. Execution times measured as 0 seconds have been adjusted to 0.01 seconds.

- STP, as one of the winners of the bit-vector division of the latest SMT-COMP competition; STP extends bit blasting with a normalization/preprocessing step, built on top of an incremental SAT engine. We are using a recent version provided by the authors of STP.
- Yices 1.0.3, as the other winner of the latest SMT-COMP in the bit-vector division. To the best of our knowledge, the solver for bit vector reasoning in Yices is based on bit blasting [10].
- BAT 0.2 is a recently-released system that specializes in structured, modular problems with memories. It combines a clever encoding of memory term rewriting techniques and reduction to SAT.

The problems were given in input to STP and Yices in SMT format. As for MiniSat, we generated a DIMACS file both before and after the preprocessing, and we used the one that resulted in better performance, i.e., the one before preprocessing; surprisingly, our preprocessor degraded the performance of MiniSat significantly.

Scatter plots of the execution times can be seen in figure 3. As can be seen from the figure, MathSAT clearly outperforms other solvers on the majority of instances. The notable exception is BAT which is comparable on the two hardest, although slightly slower (see Table 1 for the precise time taken).

From the cumulative distribution functions in figure 4 the percentiles can be read. On the easiest instances Yices is fast, but there are 25 instances it cannot solve within the time limit. MathSAT, on the other hand, is clearly superior approximately above the 60th percentile.

We now focus on the "hardest" instances, i.e. those instances where at least two systems used an execution time greater than 60 seconds. In particular, we extended

Table 1. Execution times for the hardest instances. All times are rounded to the nearest second.

Instance	MathSAT		STP		Yices		MiniSat		BAT	
Intel-35	3	3	72	50	>18000	>18000	42	19	81	80
Intel-37	4	3	84	68	>18000	>18000	47	17	80	80
Intel-39	4	4	133	189	>18000	>18000	35	38	28	28
Intel-76	256	76	>18000	>18000	>18000	>18000	1393	8658	344	348
Intel-77	29	22	2687	1781	>18000	>18000	948	559	245	248
Intel-78	580	252	8451	9699	>18000	>18000	2973	2199	611	611
Intel-79	62	36	>18000	9968	>18000	>18000	1929	8065	240	242

the execution time limit to 5 hours. In addition, we experimented with two different translations from the source file format. (For each solver in figures 3 and 4 the translation corresponding to the best performance has been used.) The results are reported in Table 1: for each system, we report the result for both encodings. We see that Math-SAT outperforms the other solvers, regardless of translation. We also notice that the translation schema may induce substantial differences in performance, in particular for STP and MiniSat: with the second translation, STP solves one more instance within the extended time limit, whereas MiniSat performs considerably worse on two instances. Yices is not able to solve any of these benchmarks within the time with either translation, while the performance of BAT is remarkably stable.

8 Conclusions and Future Work

The work described in this paper is motivated by the fact that many verification problems, especially in industrial settings, are naturally described at a level of abstraction that is higher than boolean – the additional structure is typically used to describe data paths.

We have developed a new decision procedure for Satisfiability Modulo the Theory of fixed-width bit vectors. The procedure is tailored towards hard industrial problems, and has two distinguishing features. First, it is lazy in that it invokes a solver on the theory of bit vectors *on the fly* during the search. Second, it is layered, i.e. it tries to apply incomplete but cheap forms of reasoning (e.g. equality and uninterpreted functions, term rewriting), and deal with complete solvers only when required. As a result structural information is used to significantly speed up the search, without incurring in a substantial penalty with reasoning about purely boolean parts. In an empirical evaluation performed on industrial problems, our solver outperforms state-of-the-art competitor systems by an order of magnitude on many instances.

In the future, we plan to work on the following problems. First, the current implementation can be heavily optimized; in particular the generation of conflict sets is currently an issue. Second, we plan to investigate the application of advanced theorem proving techniques. We would also like to experiment with abstraction refinement techniques, and to integrate the solver within a CEGAR loop based on the NuSMV model checker.

References

1. http://mathsat.itc.it/cav07-bitvectors/
2. Andraus, Z.S., Sakallah, K.A.: Automatic abstraction and verification of verilog models. In: Proc. D.A.C. (ed.) Proc. DAC '04, ACM Press, New York (2004)
3. Barrett, C.W., Dill, D.L., Levitt, J.R.: A Decision Procedure for Bit-Vector Arithmetic. In: Design Automation Conference, pp. 522–527 (1998)
4. Bozzano, M., Bruttomesso, R., Cimatti, A., Franzén, A., Hanna, Z., Khasidashvili, Z., Palti, A., Sebastiani, R.: Encoding RTL Constructs for MathSAT: a Preliminary Report. In: Proc. PDPAR'05. ENTCS, vol. 144 (2), Elsevier, Amsterdam (2006)
5. Bozzano, M., Bruttomesso, R., Cimatti, A., Junttila, T., van Rossum, P., Schulz, S., Sebastiani, R.: MathSAT: A Tight Integration of SAT and Mathematical Decision Procedure. Journal of Automated Reasoning 35(1-3) (2005)
6. Brinkmann, R., Drechsler, R.: RTL-datapath verification using integer linear programming. In: Proc. ASP-DAC 2002, pp. 741–746. IEEE Computer Society Press, Los Alamitos (2002)
7. Bryant, R.E.: Graph-Based Algorithms for Boolean Function Manipulation. IEEE Transactions on Computers C35(8), 677–691 (1986)
8. Chinneck, J.W., Dravnieks, E.W.: Locating Minimal Infeasible Constraint Sets in Linear Programs. ORSA Journal on Computing 3(2), 157–168 (1991)
9. Cyrluk, D., Möller, O., Rue H., .: An Efficient Decision Procedure for the Theory of Fixed-Sized Bit-Vectors. In: Grumberg, O. (ed.) CAV 1997. LNCS, vol. 1254, Springer, Heidelberg (1997)
10. Dutertre, B., de Moura, L.: System Description: Yices 1.0. In: Proc. SMT-COMP'06 (2006)
11. Ganesh, V., Berezin, S., Dill, D.L.: A Decision Procedure for Fixed-width Bit-vectors. Technical report, Stanford University (2005), http://theory.stanford.edu/~vganesh/
12. Johannsen, P., Drechsler, R.: Speeding Up Verification of RTL Designs by Computing One-to-one Abstractions with Reduced Signal Widths. In: VLSI-SOC (2001)
13. Manolios, P., Srinivasan, S.K., Vroon, D.: Automatic Memory Reductions for RTL-Level Verification. In: Proc. ICCAD 2006, ACM Press, New York (2006)
14. Möller, M.O., Ruess, H.: Solving bit-vector equations. In: Gopalakrishnan, G.C., Windley, P. (eds.) FMCAD 1998. LNCS, vol. 1522, Springer, Heidelberg (1998)
15. Moskewicz, M.W., Madigan, C.F., Zhang, Y.Z.L., Malik, S.: Chaff: Engineering an efficient SAT solver. In: Design Automation Conference (2001)
16. Nieuwenhuis, R., Oliveras, A.: Congruence closure with integer offsets. In: Vardi, M.Y., Voronkov, A. (eds.) LPAR 2003. LNCS, vol. 2850, Springer, Heidelberg (2003)
17. Seshia, S.A., Lahiri, S.K., Bryant, R.E.: A Hybrid SAT-Based Decision Procedure for Separation Logic with Uninterpreted Functions. In: Proc. DAC'03 (2003)
18. Singerman, E.: Challenges in making decision procedures applicable to industry. In: Proc. PDPAR'05. ENTCS, vol. 144 (2), Elsevier, Amsterdam (2006)
19. Zeng, Z., Kalla, P., Ciesielski, M.: LPSAT: a unified approach to RTL satisfiability. In: Proc. DATE '01, IEEE Computer Society Press, Los Alamitos (2001)

Author Index

Lecture Notes in Computer Science

For information about Vols. 1–4471

please contact your bookseller or Springer